THE DIGEST OF
SOCIAL
EXPERIMENTS

THIRD EDITION

S0-BRQ-210

David Greenberg

AND

Mark Shroder

Also of interest from the Urban Institute Press:

Social Experimentation and Public Policymaking,
by David Greenberg, Donna Linksz, and Marvin Mandell

Choosing a Better Life? Evaluating the
Moving to Opportunity Social Experiment,
edited by John Goering and Judith D. Feins

THE DIGEST OF
SOCIAL
EXPERIMENTS

THIRD EDITION

Montante Family Library
D'Youville College

THE URBAN INSTITUTE PRESS
Washington, D.C.

THE URBAN INSTITUTE PRESS
2100 M Street, NW
Washington, DC 20037

Editorial Advisory Board

Jeffrey Butts

Kathleen Courrier

William Gorham

Jack Hadley

Demetra S. Nightingale

George E. Peterson

Robert D. Reischauer

John Rogers

Raymond J. Struyk

Copyright © 2004. The Urban Institute. All rights reserved. Except for short quotes, no part of this book may be reproduced or utilized in any form or by any means, electronic or mechanical, including photocopying, recording, or by information storage or retrieval system, without written permission from The Urban Institute Press.

Library of Congress Cataloging-in-Publication Data

Greenberg, David H.
   The digest of social experiments / David Greenberg and Mark Shroder.— 3rd ed.
       p. cm.
   ISBN 0-87766-722-5 (alk. paper)
  1. United States—Social policy. 2. Evaluation research (Social action programs)—United States. 3. Public welfare administration—United States. 4. Human services—United States. I. Shroder, Mark. II. Title.
   HN59.2.G74 2004
   361.6'1'0973—dc22

                                                      2004002066

ISBN 0-87766-722-5 (paper, alk. paper)

Printed in the United States of America

10 09 08 07 06 05 04   1 2 3 4 5

BOARD OF TRUSTEES

Joel L. Fleishman, Chairman
Robert M. Solow, Vice Chairman
Dick Thornburgh, Vice Chairman
Robert D. Reischauer, President
Stephanie K. Bell-Rose
Michael Beschloss
John M. Deutch
Richard B. Fisher
Richard C. Green Jr.
Fernando A. Guerra, MD
Robert S. McNamara
Charles L. Mee Jr.
Louis A. Simpson
Judy Woodruff

LIFE TRUSTEES

Joan T. Bok
Warren E. Buffett
James E. Burke
Joseph A. Califano Jr.
Marcia L. Carsey
Carol Thompson Cole
William T. Coleman Jr.
Anthony Downs
George J. W. Goodman
William Gorham
Aileen C. Hernandez
Carla A. Hills
Vernon E. Jordan Jr.
Bayless A. Manning
Stanley Marcus
David O. Maxwell
Arjay Miller
J. Irwin Miller
Robert C. Miller
Sol Price
Lois D. Rice
William D. Ruckelshaus
Herbert E. Scarf
Charles L. Schultze
William W. Scranton
Mortimer B. Zuckerman

THE URBAN INSTITUTE is a nonprofit, nonpartisan policy research and educational organization established in Washington, D.C., in 1968. Its staff investigates the social, economic, and governance problems confronting the nation and evaluates the public and private means to alleviate them. The Institute disseminates its research findings through publications, its web site, the media, seminars, and forums.

Through work that ranges from broad conceptual studies to administrative and technical assistance, Institute researchers contribute to the stock of knowledge available to guide decisionmaking in the public interest.

Conclusions or opinions expressed in Institute publications are those of the authors and do not necessarily reflect the views of officers or trustees of the Institute, advisory groups, or any organizations that provide financial support to the Institute.

Contents

PART

2

EXPERIMENTS IN THE UNITED STATES

PART
3

EXPERIMENTS OUTSIDE THE UNITED STATES

PART

4

TRENDS

Acknowledgments

ASSISTANCE. Our assistants in this third edition of the *Digest* were, in alphabetical order, Jonathan Duckart, Barbara Hintzman Hartman, John Mulaa, Ryan Mutter, Jennifer Shand, and Jane Weisbaum. In the previous edition, our sole assistant was Matthew Onstott. We take this opportunity to express our appreciation for their able and conscientious work.

FUNDING. Four funding sources made the third edition of this book possible:

- the graduate school of the University of Maryland–Baltimore County;
- the W.E. Upjohn Institute for Employment Research;
- the UMBC Policy Sciences Department; and
- the Office of Policy Development and Research of the U.S. Department of Housing and Urban Development.

PERMISSION. We thank the American Economic Association for permission to reprint our article, "The Social Experiment Market," from the *Journal of Economic Perspectives*, volume 13, number 3, summer 1999, pages 157–72.

OMISSIONS AND OTHER ERRORS. We ask those with knowledge of omitted social experiments, or of other errors or omissions, to inform the corresponding author, Mark Shroder, U.S. Department of Housing and Urban Development, Office of Policy Development and Research, 451 7th St. SW, Washington DC 20410-6000. E-mail—Mark_D._Shroder@HUD.gov.

EDITING. We wish to acknowledge the very considerable labors of Fiona Blackshaw of the Urban Institute Press on this edition.

DISCLAIMERS. The authors take full responsibility for all errors and omissions. Opinions expressed in this book should not be attributed to any other agency, organization, or individual. Specifically, the authors' opinions are not necessarily shared by policymakers in the U.S. Department of Housing and Urban Development.

PART 1

INTRODUCTION

1

An Overview of Social Experimentation and the *Digest*

This book testifies to the breadth and depth of a distinctive modern form of social research activity—the randomized social experiment. Such experiments have been conducted since the late 1960s to evaluate proposed changes in program or policy. Some experiments have been large and highly publicized—among them the Seattle-Denver Income Maintenance Experiment, the RAND Health Insurance Study, and the more recent experimental evaluations of state-run welfare-to-work programs and of programs run under the Jobs Training Partnership Act of 1982; others have been small and obscure. Some have "pilot tested" major innovations in social policy; others have been used to assess incremental changes in existing programs. A few have provided the basis for evaluating the overall efficacy of major existing programs. Most have been used to evaluate policies targeted at disadvantaged population groups.

This *Digest* contains brief summaries of 240 known completed social experiments. In addition, for purposes of contrast, we also provide summaries of 11 completed quasi experiments. Each summary, typically two or three pages long and presented in a standardized format, outlines the cost and time frame of the demonstration, the treatments tested, outcomes of interest, sample sizes and target population, research components, major findings, important methodological limitations and design issues encountered, and other relevant topics. The experiments summarized are those for which findings were available by April 2003. In addition, very brief outlines of 21 experiments and one quasi experiment still in progress at that time are also provided.

This introduction provides background information for readers regarding social experiments. Rather than attempting to comprehensively discuss social experimentation—a topic that would require an entire book of its own[1]—we touch upon a number of areas pertinent to interpreting the *Digest*'s summaries. We begin by providing our definition of social experiments. This is important because we used it in determining the evaluations to include in this volume. This is followed by discussions of the concepts of internal and external validity of experimental findings and the categories into which experiments tend to fall. We then briefly describe quasi experiments, noting their strengths and weaknesses. Next, we examine the reasons for conducting social experiments, provide an overview of ethical issues, and describe nonexperimental methodologies that have been proposed as substitutes. Some common threats to the external validity of social experiments are then reviewed, as well as "optional" features often found in experiments. A discussion of the uses of social experiments in the policy process follows. We then present a brief history of social experiments. The final section of this introduction explains the uses and organization of this volume, so that readers can make optimal use of the summaries.

WHAT IS A SOCIAL EXPERIMENT?

The summaries in this *Digest* focus on field studies of social programs in which individuals, households, or (in rare instances) firms or organizations were randomly assigned to two or more alternative treatments. The primary research objective of the experiments was to measure the effects, which are often called "impacts," of the alternative treatments on market behavior (such as the receipt of earnings) and corresponding government fiscal outcomes (such as the receipt of transfer benefits). Thus, a social experiment has at least the following features:

- *Random assignment:* Creation of at least two groups of human subjects who differ from one another by chance alone.
- *Policy intervention:* A set of actions ensuring that different incentives, opportunities, or constraints confront the members of each of the randomly assigned groups in their daily lives.

- *Follow-up data collection:* Measurement of market and fiscal outcomes for members of each group.
- *Evaluation:* Application of statistical inference and informed professional judgment about the degree to which the policy interventions have caused differences in outcomes between the groups.

Random assignment involves neither choice nor discretion. Whereas human subjects may or may not have the right to choose to participate in the experiment, they do not have the right to decide which group within the experiment they will join. Similarly, those administering the policy intervention may restrict eligibility for participation in the experiment, but once a person is admitted, program staff cannot determine the group in which that subject is enrolled, except by using randomization.

Social experiments test policy interventions: They are attempts to influence the endowments of, and the incentives and disincentives facing, human subjects. Thus, in most social experiments, one of the randomly assigned groups, the control group, represents the status quo and is only eligible for benefits and services under the existing policy regime. The remaining group or groups, the treatment group(s), are subjected to the policy innovation or innovations being tested. Comparisons of the control group with the treatment group(s) indicate the impacts of the tested innovations.

Social experiments are designed to determine whether (or how much) the policies being tested would affect the market behavior of individuals (e.g., their employment and earnings; consumption of food, energy, housing, and health care services; receipt of government benefits). Taken together, the second and third features of our definition exclude random-assignment experiments in medicine, psychology, economics, criminology, and education that are not designed to measure changes in subjects' transactions in their daily environment in response to policy innovations. For example, we exclude randomized clinical trials of prescription drugs intended to affect health status; we also exclude randomization of students to competing school curricula intended to improve scores on standardized tests.

Although outcome data may be collected by a variety of means, readers of this volume's summaries will notice that over time social experimenters have relied increasingly on administrative data rather than surveys. Once collected, outcomes among the groups of randomly assigned individuals are compared. Outcome differences between the groups provide estimates of the impacts of the tested policy interventions. However, the data do not speak for themselves. Analysts must decide what data transformations are appropriate; what, if any, nonexperimental factors should be considered; what statistical techniques to use; and what results do and do not make sense.

Internal and External Validity

If implemented properly, the results of social experiments generally are *internally valid*, that is, they provide unbiased impact estimates for targeted people subject to different treatments at the particular time and place they were administered. However, evaluation, including that based on random assignment designs, requires considerable care and is often expensive. A number of the experiments summarized here were done "on the cheap" and hurriedly. Many of these experiments tended to be poorly designed and implemented, and as a result, some of them either produced findings that lacked internal validity or did not produce findings at all.

Even when carefully implemented, the extent to which social experiments possess *external validity*—applicability to other individuals, places, and times—may be controversial and is always problematic. For example, differences in timing imply that social attitudes, government institutions, the business cycle, the relative demand for unskilled and skilled labor, the rate of inflation, and other factors may vary from what they were when the

experiment was conducted. Different locations may result in dissimilarities in age, sex, racial, or ethnic mixes; social attitudes; state and local government institutions; industrial structure; and many other factors.

Categories of Social Experiments

Several of this volume's social experiments—notably the four income maintenance experiments, the Housing Allowance Demand Experiment, and the RAND Health Insurance Study—were designed to estimate "response surfaces"—that is, their designs allowed two or more continuous parameters of the program being tested to vary within wide ranges. For example, tax rates and guarantee levels in the income maintenance experiments varied greatly across treatment groups. Estimates of responses to program parameters can, at least in principle, be used to project the effects of any program that has the basic features of the one tested, even if the specific values of the program parameters differ.

In contrast to response-surface experiments, most social experiments permit only "black box" assessments of whether the tested intervention "works." That is, they provide different randomly selected groups of individuals with different "packages" of services and incentives (for example, job training, child care assistance, and job search assistance) and then determine whether outcomes (for example, postprogram earnings) differ among the groups. Only limited information is typically provided on the degree to which these impacts can be attributed to specific components of the service packages or on the effects of changes in program design. Findings from the response-surface technique are in some ways more flexible for projecting the effects of future policy, but it may not be possible in practice to carry out intervention(s) in the form of variations in the values of two or more continuous variables.

A second important distinction is between experiments that are mandatory and those that are voluntary. An experiment is mandatory if the individual cannot enjoy certain benefits without participating. Many unemployment insurance and welfare experiments in this volume have been mandatory. The Minnesota Income Tax Compliance Experiment, in which certain taxpayers were randomly selected for a higher probability of audit, was mandatory in a broader sense, because the individuals had not applied for any specific benefits.

Individuals must in some way apply to enter a voluntary experiment. Experimental evaluations of training programs and electric-rate experiments have usually been voluntary. As demonstrated later, the fact that individuals chose to enter an experiment may complicate the evaluation of the outcomes.

Government agencies often consider themselves legally and ethically justified in conducting mandatory experiments if the alternative treatments are within the agency's ordinary administrative discretion. For example, randomly selecting certain taxpayers for audits is a necessary function of a tax office. Voluntary experiments generally require some type of informed consent by the subject.

A third distinction between experiments concerns the sort of policy intervention they test. There are three possibilities: they can test new programs; they can test incremental changes to existing programs; and they can be used to evaluate existing programs, although they are relatively rarely used for this last purpose.

WHAT IS A QUASI EXPERIMENT?

In addition to summarizing randomized social experiments, this book also contains outlines of quasi-experimental demonstrations. Scholars and evaluation professionals have attached several conflicting meanings to the term *quasi experiment;* to keep the scope of this book manageable, we have limited the term to policy demonstrations in which potential *sites* are randomized to treatment or control group status, and individuals or households at that site are clustered together for analysis.[2] An example illustrates.

Suppose that six sites are considered for a demonstration, and some 1,500 individuals will be subjects of the experiment at these sites. On some prior basis, the evaluators determine beforehand that site A is most like site B, site C most similar to site D, and site E is best matched with site F. By flipping a coin (or using a more sophisticated random process), the evaluators determine whether the innovative treatment will occur at site A and the control at site B or vice versa; at site C versus site D; and so on. For concreteness, let the treatment sites be A, D, and F, and the control sites be B, C, and E. The intention is to compare the ADF outcomes with the BCE outcomes and, if they are significantly different, to attribute that difference to the policy intervention.

Significant theoretical and practical reasons may exist for choosing site randomization over randomizing individuals within a site. For example, an innovation may be intended to change "the culture of the welfare office" or "the culture of public housing projects"; for this cultural change to occur, the innovation must affect all similarly situated individuals who are members of the culture. Feedback and information processes, which may be crucial (and are treated at greater length later in this introduction), might only function if an innovation is adopted on a sitewide basis. The responses on "the other side of the market" from employers or landlords may also be important, and randomization within sites might attenuate these responses. For any number of reasons, it also may be simply impractical to administer different treatments within the same site.

The most serious problem with the site randomization concept is that there may be too few sites for effective randomization to occur. Although the sites have been assigned to treatment and control status by chance, the people within the sites have not been randomized. People do not randomly choose whether to live at site *A* or at site *B;* they choose purposefully, and their choices create both observed and unobserved differences between sites subject to the different treatments.[3] Economic and social conditions in the two sets of sites will vary at the outset of the demonstration, and these conditions may change in the course of the demonstration for reasons unrelated to the demonstration itself. In short, both observed and unobserved differences will occur in the initial conditions as well as in the changes in those conditions.

If, at the close of the quasi experiment, *ADF* outcomes are significantly different from *BCE* outcomes, the evaluators and the readers of the evaluation must decide whether the difference in outcome is due to the difference in treatment or to one or more of the sources of unobserved difference noted earlier.[4] They may find this decision very difficult (see Hollister and Hill 1995). If there were 1,500 randomized sites, rather than 6, the problem of unobserved random differences across sites would have no practical importance, but experimentation on such a vast scale is unlikely to be attempted.

REASONS FOR CONDUCTING SOCIAL EXPERIMENTS

The motives for undertaking a social experiment invariably differ from one experiment to the next (for a detailed analysis, see Greenberg, Linksz, and Mandell 2003). We begin with the most cynical motive—that the social experiment is conducted to replace difficult political decisions with symbolic action. This charge, which was leveled against the

income maintenance experiments, will always have surface appeal; for many, legislative and administrative actions have greater symbolism than content. Indeed, some groups often gain a political advantage by delaying a decision, and evaluations with any pretension to scientific standards do take time.

Despite the superficial attractiveness of this argument, we believe such a motive can be easily dismissed. A demonstration may serve as a symbol of a policymaker's sympathies, but no political logic requires a rigorous objective assessment of that demonstration. The usual purpose of delaying tactics is to make the issue go away. If that were the goal, an objective evaluation based on random assignment would act like a bomb with a very slow fuse, detonating years later, perhaps with embarrassing consequences for the policymaker's career.

Policymakers seem well aware of this. Egregiously pork barrel or purely symbolic "demonstrations," or transparently political "programs" often seem deliberately designed to make future evaluations of any sort impossible. To the cynics, we suggest that policymakers have many other useful pretexts for delay that present fewer risks.[5]

We turn now to less cynical explanations. First, an experiment may be intended for a specific policy decision. Feldman (1989, 80) has contended that if research were intended to influence a specific policy decision, both the timing of the decision and the alternatives to be considered would have to be known in advance. Otherwise, the research would probably not be available when the decision is made or would not be pertinent to the decision. Indeed, these conditions are seldom met in practice.

A less demanding explanation of why social experiments are initiated is that policymakers plan to use the information gained whenever it becomes available. Therefore, if a social experiment demonstrates convincingly that an idea really works, it will help to generate the political support required to place it on the policy agenda.

A final possibility is that the experiment is intended to create an inventory of information for future policymaking (Feldman 1989, 92–96). The implied intention is for the experiment to contribute to a stock of knowledge, reducing uncertainty should a relevant issue reach the policy agenda.

All but the cynical explanation for social experiments suggest that such demonstrations are intended to generate information relevant to the policy process. Almost without exception, social experiments test the power of particular policies to solve or mitigate serious social problems—long-term welfare receipt; rising health care costs; inadequate or unaffordable shelter for low-income families; long-term unemployment; the clouded future for former offenders, substance addicts, and at-risk youth. Experiments are funded when disagreement over appropriate policy interventions is caused, at least in part, by uncertainty over their potential consequences. If policymakers knew the outcomes, there would be little justification for sponsoring experiments. It is useful to keep this apparently banal idea in mind when considering whether social experiments are ethical and whether they are the best form of research for assessing policy choices.

ARE EXPERIMENTS ETHICAL?

Policy interventions are intended to change people's lives; it strikes many people as wrong, or at least strange, to change them randomly.

A social experiment is ethical if the treatment received by each group of human subjects is ethical. The experiment is unethical if one or more of the treatments are unethical. The loudest critics of certain experiments have alleged either that the innovation being tested was unethical or that the status quo—the existing laws and regulations governing some aspect of society—was unethical. Random assignment itself is ethically neutral.

In practice, there is usually some restriction on the availability of benefits or services tested (because of budgetary limitation, for instance). If

such restrictions exist, then the fact that assignment between treatment and control groups is random is a matter of ethical indifference. A first-come, first-served approach may be more convenient for the program staff but has precisely the same moral value. Shutting the door on people who apply after 4:00 PM Tuesday is just as arbitrary as shutting the door on people who were born on an odd-numbered day, or for whom the last two digits of their Social Security number add up to 12, or for whom a computer generates a random number ending in an even digit.

If we knew in advance that all members of a population would benefit or suffer from the application of a policy toward them, would an experiment on some fraction of them be unethical? Perhaps. Under the principle of horizontal equity, similarly situated individuals should be similarly treated, and singling out some members of a class for arbitrary rewards or punishments not applied to others is, in general, unjust.

When the effects of a policy are unknown, however, the same generalization cannot apply. Many treatments summarized in this book were expected (or at least were intended) to make the individuals subject to them better off but failed to do so; sometimes they made at least some of them worse off. Individuals who were assigned to control groups and, hence, were randomly denied access to those treatments often seem to have lost nothing important. The state of honest ignorance required to justify disparate treatment existed at the time the experiment began.

In other instances, we may believe a priori that members of a target population will be better off, on average, as a result of an innovation (e.g., the income maintenance experiments). However, we may also believe that people outside the target population will be worse off (e.g., taxpayers). We do not know a priori whether the benefits are larger than the costs.[6] Not knowing the trade-off, some policymakers will refuse to institute the innovation until the benefits and costs are better measured, and this is the ethical justification for the experiment.

ALTERNATIVES TO SOCIAL EXPERIMENTATION

Given honest ignorance, it does not follow that random assignment is always the optimal form of evaluation. Social experiments can be quite costly, because they require extensive follow-up data on both treatment and control groups, and some types of policy interventions are better evaluated using nonexperimental methods. We now examine those methods and consider their advantages and disadvantages relative to experimentation.

The most obvious feasible alternative to random assignment is to compare persons who participate in a particular program with persons who do not participate; the participants then constitute the treatment group and the nonparticipants the comparison group. The least sophisticated version of this approach consists of selecting the comparison group from among people who initially applied for program benefits, but for one reason or another did not actually participate. A more sophisticated version involves drawing a comparison group from among people sampled in national micro-data sets (for example, the Current Population Survey [CPS]) by statistically matching these people on the basis of their personal characteristics with members of the treatment group to make the two groups as comparable as possible.

Other approaches are feasible when a program is carried out in some geographic locations, but not in others. A treatment group, for example, might comprise individuals who live at the sites that have the program, and a comparison group might consist of similar individuals living at other sites. Alternatively, one might compare outcomes in the same set of sites before and after an innovation has been introduced.

An obvious problem with the geographic and chronological comparison groups is that economic and social circumstances differ from place to place and change over time; it is very difficult to control

for these factors in a manner that allows the effects of the innovation to be isolated. The superiority of a randomly assigned control group over the "non-participant" comparison group alternatives may be less obvious.

There is essentially one reason for social experimentation: random assignment is the only known means of eliminating *selection bias*. If an individual can choose whether a policy intervention will or will not apply to himself, then people who choose treatment A will differ from those who choose treatment B in both observable and unobservable ways. The same is true if program administrators make the choice for individuals, rather than having the individuals choose for themselves. Selection factors will also bias comparisons across sites that have and have not implemented an innovation, if, as is usually the case, the decision as to whether to adopt the innovation was made locally.[7] For example, the sites may differ in terms of local economic conditions and in population characteristics.

If individuals in treatment and comparison groups differ only in observable ways, then the analyst can, in principle, adjust for them when researching outcomes.[8] However, absent random assignment, individuals in treatment groups are also likely to differ from those in comparison groups in unobservable ways. The unobserved factors that influence which group they enter are also likely to influence outcomes.

For example, it has been well known since the 1970s that workers who volunteer for training have often experienced a sharp drop in their recent earnings. They cannot properly be compared with workers who have the same observable characteristics but no such dip. Earnings fluctuation may also be permanent or transitory; workers with the same observable dips as training participants will not be comparable if their dips have dissimilar causes.

In one common scenario, workers who have suffered short-term setbacks realize that their careers will recover without additional training, whereas others recognize their old careers have hit a dead end. The latter then try to enter a new path through training, sometimes unsuccessfully. In comparing workers who have temporary dips and do not enter training with those who have had lasting setbacks and do enter training, we may find that the trained have lower earnings than the untrained. We may then falsely attribute the lower earnings to poor training programs.

In this example, selection bias is negative—it makes the program being evaluated look worse than it is. Selection bias can be either positive or negative, and usually neither policymakers nor analysts know with certainty which is the case. Findings from numerous studies have suggested that selection bias, in whatever direction, can be very large relative to the actual effect of an intervention (Bell et al. 1995; Fraker and Maynard 1987; Friedlander and Robins 1995; LaLonde 1986; LaLonde and Maynard 1987). These studies used the presumably unbiased estimates of program impacts from experiments to assess impact estimates obtained by matching treatment groups with carefully drawn nonexperimental comparison groups. The selection bias associated with the nonexperimental estimates was often larger than the true program impact. Selection bias proved large enough to affect the statistical significance in most cases, the direction of the impact (positive or negative) in far too many cases, and any benefit–cost analysis in nearly all cases.

Bias of unknown sign and unknown but possibly critical magnitude must reduce the usefulness of nonexperimental forms of evaluation. Attempts have been made to develop techniques using nonexperimental data that would have the same degree of internal validity as experimental data (see, for example, Dehejia and Wahba 1995, 2002; Heckman and Hotz 1989; Heckman, Ichimura, and Todd 1997; Heckman et al. 1995, 1998). So far, unfortunately, there is little evidence that these techniques can consistently do so.

For example, Bell et al. (1995) have argued that selection by program staff might generate a comparison group with correctable bias if the criteria for selection are documented and consistently exercised. In principle, the analyst could then control for the observed selection factors. However,

the one test of this hypothesis reported in their monograph fails. This might have been because the selection process was not, in fact, fully documented and consistent; this could occur, for example, if program staff selects people who are more likable, attractive, persistent, or literate than those screened out or if the staff selection process effectively allows potential participants to screen themselves in or out.

Most experts in social program evaluation would probably agree with Burtless (1995) and Hollister and Hill (1995) that no alternative method can produce impact estimates that have as much internal validity as a social experiment with random assignment can. This is, however, a reluctant majority. Social experiments are subject to important limitations of their own. Most of these shortcomings concern threats to the external validity of social experiments. The next section lists the most important of these limitations.[9] These shortcomings are not unique to randomized evaluations; they also apply to most forms of nonexperimental evaluation.

THREATS TO EXTERNAL VALIDITY OF IMPACT ESTIMATES

Whether evaluated by random assignment or by nonexperimental methods, innovations to social programs are often tested on a small-scale demonstration or pilot basis.[10] Manski and Garfinkel (1992) and Garfinkel, Manski, and Michalopoulos (1992) have suggested that an important component of some policy innovations intended for widespread adaptation is that they cause changes in community attitudes and norms; these, in turn, result in feedback effects that influence the innovation's success. These authors further suggested that program success depends on information diffusion to potential participants. They argued that feedback effects and information diffusion will not occur unless the innovation is adopted on a large scale, and that these effects will be missed by small-scale tests.[11]

Potentially important marketwide effects may also not occur in small-scale tests. For example, training programs could affect the level of wages in a community. They might also affect the number of employers in a community, if enough workers receive the training to induce firms to move into the area. Little is usually known about the importance of such effects. One can only speculate whether small-scale tests of social policies are seriously biased by their absence.

In arguments that are also applicable to non-experimental evaluations of small-scale demonstrations, Heckman (1992), Heckman and Smith (1995), and Manski (1995) have contended that participants in small-scale experiments may not be representative of individuals who would participate in ongoing, full-scale programs. This could occur because of a lack of information diffusion, the reluctance of some individuals to subject themselves to random assignment, resource constraints in full-scale programs that result in program administrators restricting participants to people meeting certain criteria, and numerous other reasons.[12]

One approach for eliminating biases caused by testing innovations on a small scale is to incorporate them on a sitewide basis in some locations and use other sites (perhaps statistically matched) that have not adopted the innovation for comparison purposes. For example, the effect of housing subsidy on rents in a housing market can only be learned through "saturation" of the community—that is, by providing the subsidy to all eligible households (see Lowry 1983). A saturation design, however, does not allow feedback, information diffusion, and market effects to be measured separately from other types of program impacts. Moreover, as previously discussed, such a design will produce biased impact estimates if the treatment and comparison sites differ in ways that are inadequately controlled for in the evaluation.

Social experiments are always limited to relatively few geographic areas. This is also true of many nonexperimental evaluations, especially those that rely on saturation designs. Because these sites are rarely selected randomly,[13] the external validity of the evaluations can be questioned (see Heckman 1992; Heckman and Smith 1995; Hotz 1992). Difficulties in obtaining a representative sample of program sites are especially acute in cases where local administrators' cooperation is essential. However, the degree to which site selectivity translates into bias in the results of an impact analysis has not been proved empirically.[14]

Another potential shortcoming of social experiments concerns entry effects (Manski and Garfinkel 1992; Moffitt 1996). For example, if only unemployed people or people with incomes below certain thresholds are eligible for a training program being evaluated experimentally, and the services provided by this program are perceived as beneficial, some ineligibles may leave their jobs or otherwise reduce their incomes to qualify. In welfare-to-work programs that are mandatory for transfer recipients, and perceived by them as burdensome, some individuals who might otherwise have entered the welfare rolls may decide not to do so to avoid participating. Measuring entry effects in a random-assignment context requires that ineligibles be included in the evaluation sample, but because of cost considerations, this is seldom done.[15]

A few experiments stand out as exceptions to this rule. In the Self-Sufficiency Project evaluation, a random assignment experiment recently conducted in Canada (Michalopoulos et al. 2002), only people who had been on welfare for at least one year qualified for the substantial increase in transfer payments made available through the tested program. By design, the experimental sample included transfer recipients who had been on welfare for less than one year—to see if some of them would extend their stay on the rolls to qualify for the new benefit schedule (Berlin et al. 1998). Similarly, the income maintenance experiments included households whose earnings at intake were too high to qualify for program benefits—to see if some of these households would reduce their earnings to qualify.

The behavior of participants in a pilot test of program or policy could be influenced by knowledge that they are part of the pilot test, a so-called "Hawthorne effect." For example, if members of a research sample know that their behavior will be measured in terms of certain outcomes, such as earnings or educational attainment, some of them might attempt to succeed in terms of these outcomes. There is virtually no information about whether Hawthorne effects bias findings from social experiments. It seems possible that members of both the treatment and control groups could respond similarly to being part of a social experiment. If so, such effects will cancel out in measuring impacts, and there would be no bias. Alternatively, some control group members could be discouraged by the fact that they were allocated to the control group, rather than the treatment group, and alter their behavior for that reason.

In both experimental and nonexperimental evaluations, members of the control or comparison group may, in practice, receive many of the same services as those received by members of the treatment group. For example, in the case of training programs, training of many types may already be available through community colleges and adult schools, and members of control or comparison groups can often obtain financing for these activities through existing nondemonstration sources. Consequently, estimates of program effects on participants do not measure impacts of the receipt of service against the nonreceipt of services. Rather, such estimates represent the *incremental* effect of the program services over the control services.

The existence of alternative services in the community and the measurement of incremental effects are not necessarily detrimental to an evaluation, depending on the evaluation's goal. Often the goal is to determine the effect of an innovation relative to the actual environment, rather than relative to the complete absence of alternative services. Nonetheless, in interpreting impact estimates from social experiments and other evaluations, one should keep in mind that these estimates usually pertain to incremental effects, rather than to a control environment in which no services are available. Naturally, this limits the extent to which findings may be generalized from one environment to another. In addition, what Heckman and Smith (1995) call "substitution bias" is possible. Substitution bias can occur if a new program being tested experimentally absorbs resources that would otherwise be available to members of the control group or, instead, if as result of serving some members of a target group, the new program frees up resources available under other programs that can now be used to better serve member of the control group.

The summaries in this *Digest* give the reader some sense of the ambiguities that even the best experiments can create. We have also included some outright failures, where the demonstration never answered and, in hindsight, never could have answered the policy questions asked. Social experimentation is a specialized research tool, suitable for some inquiries and not for others—a chisel that cannot substitute for a screwdriver, but is the best instrument yet developed for many purposes.

ARE EXPERIMENTS UNDULY EXPENSIVE?

Social experiments have also been criticized for their cost (Levitan 1992).[16] Experimental costs fall into three basic categories:

- Implementing the innovative treatments;[17]
- Collecting data on the different groups; and
- Analyzing the data.

It is worth noting that most of these costs are typically incurred regardless of whether a program is evaluated through random assignment or using nonexperimental methods. The major difference in costs is that the random assignment process must be carefully implemented and monitored, but this is usually not very costly. In addition, the data needed for a nonexperimental evaluation (but not a random assignment evaluation) is occasionally already being collected for other purposes. If so, a nonexperimental evaluation can be considerably less expensive than one that relies on random assignment. However, it is fairly rare when the data needed for an evaluation do not have to be specifically collected for that purpose; and when this does occur, it is usually in the case of an evaluation of an ongoing program, rather than a test of a new policy initiative. Most social experiments have been used to evaluate new policy initiatives.

There are two perspectives on the costs of a social experiment. The first compares costs with benefits: Will the experiment be likely to generate information sufficiently valuable to the political or institutional process to justify the costs? There are three facets to this question: it must be answered *prospectively,* before the information exists; it involves the value of information provided by social scientists in a democracy; and it must be explicitly answered affirmatively by decisionmakers before the experiment can take place.

A somewhat different perspective looks at the experiment's opportunity cost, weighing the net benefits of the experiment against the net benefits of the most probable alternative use of the resources. If the funds are federal, the most probable alternative use is another project at the same agency or agencies.[18] Perhaps, for example, the funds would be better spent on

■ Implementing a nationally representative in-depth survey, of, say, 50,000 households (at an annual cost in the United States of around $20 million, with the exact cost depending on design choices);

■ Demonstrating the feasibility of implementing a program change, rather than (or at least prior to) attempting to measure its impact (at an evaluation cost of between $20,000 and $20 million, depending on scale and number of sites); or

■ Improving program management information systems (costs vary too much to provide a range).

From either perspective, sponsoring a social experiment requires complex resource allocation decisions. A variety of different decisionmakers (including politicians, political appointees, civil servants, and foundation directors), representing a wide spectrum of political views, authorized the social experiments conducted to date. Some were professional social scientists who could readily evaluate the technical merit of a proposed experiment on the basis of their own training and experience; the rest usually had as much access to expert opinion as they wished. It is striking that many very different individuals decided that this type of investigation is worth its costs. Nevertheless, controversy over the use of experimental techniques continues.

WHAT "OPTIONAL FEATURES" CAN EXPERIMENTS HAVE?

All social experiments are intended to provide impact estimates of the tested policy or policies. These estimates have already been discussed at some length. In addition to impact analyses, social experiments also commonly, but far from universally, feature two other types of analyses.

One of these, "process analysis," goes by sundry other names and has a number of purposes. For example, an experiment's sponsor may desire third-party verification that the treatments were administered as planned. The sponsor may wish to know how many people received the treatment and the nature and intensity of the services received. The sponsor may want to know the character of the environment in which the services were delivered and whether subjects understood the incentives provided to them by the experiment. The process analysis may also attempt to convey participants' and the program staff's subjective reactions to the experiment, or may speculate about whether certain identifiable subgroups would be likely to experience a greater or lesser impact than the sample as a whole.

An experiment without a process analysis is not necessarily useless. One may test the performance of a machine without any knowledge of the internal components. The lack of attention to "how it all really works" need not invalidate the findings, but analysts may have greater difficulty interpreting the data and may be more prone to err in attempting to do so. Lack of attention to nonexperimental factors can lead to a "type-two" statistical error—the finding of no policy impact when in fact an impact exists. For one thing, a process analysis may reveal that an innovation was never really implemented,[19] and therefore data analysis is (probably) pointless; or that the assignments were not really random, so that internal validity is questionable.

A more subtle contribution of process analysis is in discovering relevant subgroups. These may only become clear to people who spend time in the field observing and interviewing. If two groups in an experiment really do differ only randomly, then a simple test comparing the mean outcome in one group with the mean outcome in the other yields an unbiased estimate of policy impact. Analysis by subgroup, however, may show that the treatment has significant impact for subjects of one type but not another. For the same reason, process analysis may turn up nonexperimental variables that should be controlled for in a regression analysis.

A second common, but far from universal, feature of social experiments is a benefit–cost analysis. Even policies with positive benefits for the target population are unjustified, if the cost to the rest of society is too high. A benefit–cost analysis aggregates benefits of the tested policy over time, both to participants and to society at large, and compares them to costs. Such analyses have greater value for some demonstrations than others. There is no need to compare benefits with costs, for example, if there are no demonstrable benefits.

Benefit–cost analyses encounter numerous difficult problems: what value to place on the loss of leisure to participants in training and welfare-to-work programs; how much future benefits and costs should be discounted; how to extrapolate experimental impacts beyond the period over which data were collected. These are all areas of significant controversy. The value to nonparticipants of changes in the behavior of program participants may be especially difficult to quantify. There is little evidence, for example, on the dollar value that nonparticipants place on seeing welfare recipients go to work; or on low-income people enjoying increased consumption of health care, food, or housing; or on reductions in criminal offenses.

HOW MIGHT SOCIAL EXPERIMENTS BE USED?

Frequently, it is anticipated that results from a given social experiment will lead to a yes or no decision on the policy being tested. However, the relationship between experimental findings and policy decisions often does not appear to be so direct. Findings from social experiments are used in many ways, some of them unanticipated.

For example, it is unlikely that findings from the income maintenance experiments had any major role in the failure to adopt the policy tested, the negative income tax (Greenberg, Linksz, and Mandell 2003, chapter 6).[20] However, the experiments did demonstrate that certain innovations used in administering the transfer programs (monthly reporting and retrospective accounting) could be successfully implemented. Partly as a result, these innovations were adopted nationally in existing welfare programs.

Findings from the income maintenance experiments also altered the commonly held pre-experimental view that extending cash assistance to intact families would enhance their marital stability. The experiments suggested that this did not occur. In addition, the income maintenance experiments provided useful information about the effects of transfer programs on hours of work by different types of adults. These findings were in turn used to guide decisions about other transfer programs, such as Food Stamps and Aid to Families with Dependent Children.

There are at least three different dimensions on which using findings from an experiment (or any other types of evaluation) might be mapped (Greenberg, Linksz, and Mandell 2003). First, findings may either influence specific policy decisions or address unresolved scientific or intellectual issues. In our previous example, the finding that monthly reporting and retrospective accounting were operationally feasible affected the everyday administration of welfare programs, a policy effect. Both the unexpected findings on marital stability and the expected findings on the relative inelasticity of male labor supply had broader intellectual impacts.

Second, findings used may be more or less central to social policy. On one end of the continuum, research findings may influence core policy decisions or general intellectual orientations; at the other end are cases in which research findings influence relatively narrow elements of policy and its implementation—elaborative or peripheral uses. The income maintenance experiments demonstrated that male heads of household did not cut back much on hours of work when an income guarantee was available; this finding was a major intellectual contribution. The same experiments showed that retrospective accounting was feasible; this finding was elaborative or peripheral (which is not the same as unimportant).

A final dimension of utilization distinguishes between predecision and postdecision utilization (see Majone 1989, chapter 2). An old joke informs us that some people use statistics the way a drunk uses a lamppost—not for illumination but for support. If the positions of policymakers are established, at least in part, on the basis of research findings, we can say the research was used for illumination (the use is predecision). Postdecision utilization refers to the use of research findings to advocate already established positions. Findings on retrospective accounting seem to have changed the minds of key administrators; findings on male labor supply seem to have changed nobody's mind, but were used to support previously determined positions (see Greenberg, Linksz, and Mandell 2003, chapter 6, for further discussion).

WHAT IS THE HISTORY OF SOCIAL EXPERIMENTS?

The idea of a control group was firmly established by 19th century pioneers of medical and biological research. For example, in one classic experiment, Louis Pasteur divided a flock of sheep into two groups. In one group he injected attenuated material from other animals that had died of anthrax, so that they could develop immunity; the second group did not receive this injection. Both groups were then injected with anthrax-infected matter. None of the treatment sheep became sick, but all the control sheep died.

If Pasteur's results had been less dramatic, critics would surely have claimed that for some reason the control group was more anthrax-vulnerable than the treatment group. Over time, the charge that controls were "inadequate" became commonplace, without any rigorous idea of adequacy being developed, since no treatment group was ever *identical* to the control group.

The concept of randomization, like many other fundamental statistical tools, was conceived by Ronald Fisher.[21] The concept appeared initially in a 1925 book by Fisher, *Statistical Methods for Research Workers,* and then was fully elaborated in his 1935 book, *The Design of Experiments.* Fisher pointed out that no two groups could ever be identical because every organism, test tube, soil sample, and so forth would vary slightly from every other. Therefore, the researcher's task was to design the difference between groups in such a manner that the mechanism for allocating cases to one group or another could not be related to the issue being studied. Allocation by pure chance (a coin flip, a table of random numbers) did exactly that.

Social experimentation, however, did not come about until much later. It is usually traced to the New Jersey Income Maintenance Experiment, which was initiated in 1968. The idea of conducting an income maintenance experiment is attributed to Heather Ross, who in 1966 was a Massachusetts Institute of Technology graduate student in economics.[22] In that year, Ross was beginning work on her dissertation as a fellow at the Brookings Institution in Washington, D.C. Ross was frustrated that inferences about the responses of low-income people to transfer payments could not be readily drawn from existing data. She was also concerned by the use of unsubstantiated anecdotes about welfare recipients by politicians. She wished to collect data that could be used to determine what poor people would actually do if they were provided money. Would they work less? Would they quit work altogether? How would they spend the additional money? To answer such questions, she proposed to conduct a random assignment experiment.

To fund this project, Ross wrote a proposal in 1967 to the U.S. Office of Economic Opportunity, which had a staff of social scientists. Ultimately, as Ross puts it, she ended up with a "$5 million thesis," which at the time was an extraordinary sum of money for a single social science research project.

Her proposal germinated in the New Jersey Experiment. Its importance as a landmark in social science research is hard to overstate.[23] Although the technique of randomly assigning individuals for purposes of clinical health trials and educational innovations had been used for years, the New Jersey Experiment was the first prominent study to use this technique to test social programs. Other social experiments, including additional income maintenance experiments, followed fairly quickly.

WHAT IS THE FUTURE FOR SOCIAL EXPERIMENTS?

Numerous experiments are still in progress, and therefore are only briefly summarized in this *Digest*. We expect many more to be initiated in the future. Intractable social problems, unfortunately, show no sign of vanishing; substantial uncertainty clouds debate over proposed solutions; and the selection problem remains.

However, certain types of social experiments will probably not be conducted in our lifetime, even when technically feasible. One such area is community development, where the appropriate unit of analysis is neither the individual nor the household, but the neighborhood or city.

An example illustrates. Suppose it is hypothesized that a $5 million investment of a particular type will generate more than $5 million in benefits in an average community of 10,000 people. However, the benefits are expected to be sufficiently modest—say $5.3 million—that 250 treatment communities and 250 control communities would be required in order to have an 80 percent probability of detecting the benefits with 95 percent confidence. Therefore, testing the hypothesis requires distributing a total of $1.25 billion to 250 randomly selected communities throughout the country. Such a test would allow one community to enjoy a benefit denied another, not because of some formula in law, and not because of the personal and political influence of their representatives in Congress, but because of the impersonal operation of a lottery. The aggregate appropriation and the number of communities not funded would make the program difficult to ignore or to gloss over. It seems highly unlikely that any Congress would countenance this experiment or anything like it.

Other policy controversies do not seem technically amenable to the experimental evaluation. A topical example might be the sensitivity of taxpayer savings and investment behavior to the tax rate on capital gains. Suppose one group of taxpayers were randomly assigned to a capital gains tax rate lower than the rate for other taxpayers, in order to evaluate the effects of rate reduction on the national economy. Members of the treatment group could obtain arbitrage profits by getting other taxpayers to sell property to them at below-market prices, permitting the sellers to avoid (evade) much of the capital gains tax that would otherwise be levied on them. (The arbitrage profit would be split with the sellers through a side payment.) Obviously, this would bias the estimated impact of the experiment.

The general point is that the feasibility of the experiment may depend on the ingenuity and deviousness of the target population. On the other hand, the people who design and implement the experiment may also have ingenuity, expertise, resources, and perhaps a little deviousness of their own. In the previous example, the detection of tax arbitrage activity is a constant pursuit of the tax authorities; we merely doubt that they would be willing to devote the substantial resources that an adequate capital gains tax experiment would require.

USES AND ORGANIZATION OF THIS BOOK

This volume is intended to serve as an archive, a reference, an "armory," and a textbook supplement:

- *Archive.* Social experiments deliver credible evidence on the responsiveness of human behavior to policy, but the findings from most social experiments have been only narrowly disseminated. We want to increase awareness of and access to this material, much of which may eventually become inaccessible in its current form.

- *Reference.* We hope to provide a one-stop guide to all experimental findings on particular interventions, which can be used as a first step in developing literature reviews, options papers, and the like.

- *"Armory."* The idea and practice of social policy experiments remain controversial. We expect that this book will supply all sides of the debate with weapons and ammunition.

- *Textbook supplement.* We hope that these experiments can give students in a variety of courses—public policy and administration, economics, social work, education, vocational rehabilitation, sociology, statistics, political science, metropolitan planning, and other fields—an appreciation for the interaction of theory, policy, statistics, and daily life.

To develop the list of social experiments summarized in this volume, we began with the 37 compiled by Greenberg and Robins (1986). We learned of a few additional older social experiments from a lengthy bibliography by Boruch, McSweeny, and Soderstron (1978). About a dozen experiments in the early childhood intervention literature came from a literature review by Benasich, Brooks-Gunn, and Clewell (1992). Names of additional experiments were obtained in response to numerous written, telephone, and e-mail requests to academics, government employees, and employees of prominent social science research firms. Others were listed in abstracts of research reports provided on the web by the Economic Research Network (ERN). Still other experiments were acquired from various reports disseminated by research firms and the government and from journal articles. Finally, we used "snowballing" techniques: when interviewing people associated with experiments with which we were familiar, we asked if they knew of any others. We may have overlooked some smaller social experiments, but we do not believe we have missed many large ones.

The first two editions of the *Digest* listed only four social experiments conducted outside the United States. For this edition, we have made a special effort to locate such experiments. We have added 29 completed experiments, six completed quasi experiments, and three ongoing experiments to the four in the previous edition. We missed 18 of these in assembling the previous edition, while the remainder were initiated after work on that edition was completed. Although we are still more likely to miss experiments conducted outside, than those conducted within, the United States, it seems apparent that the United States accounts for the vast majority of social experiments.

Twenty-five of the experiments listed as "ongoing" in the second edition of the *Digest* were not completed and, consequently, are not included in the third edition.[24] In 23 of these planned experiments, either the planned treatment was not implemented or (much more often) it was implemented but not formally evaluated. In the remaining two cases, formal evaluations were conducted, but the random assignment design was dropped. All but two of the 25 planned experiments were targeted at public assistance recipients. Almost all of those targeted at public assistance recipients were terminated in response to passage of the Personal Responsibility and Work Opportunity Reconciliation Act in 1996. In most instances, states had been required to conduct experimental tests of welfare reform provisions that they wanted to implement in exchange for receiving federal waivers; but the need for these waivers was removed by the 1996 legislation.

The information contained in the experiment summaries came from two major sources. First, we reviewed at least one research report on each experiment. Second, information not available from the research reports was obtained from telephone interviews and e-mail exchanges with staff members of the organizations that conducted the evaluations and the government agencies that sponsored them. Often one interaction of this sort was sufficient, but sometimes several were necessary.

Most items appearing in the summaries for each social experiment are self-explanatory, but a few require a brief comment.

COST: Of all the information about social experiments that we attempted to collect, cost data were the most difficult, for a number of reasons. Sometimes the information once existed, but the necessary records could no longer be located. When an experiment was administered by an existing government agency, it was often difficult to separate the incremental cost of administering the experimental treatment from other costs incurred by the agency. Sometimes the total cost was available, but administrative costs could not be separated from the evaluation costs. In other cases, the experiment was part of a larger research project, and costs were not separately allocated to the experimental and nonexperimental parts of the research. In the summaries, we usually attempt to indicate what the cost figures we report cover. Costs shown are contemporaneous with the demonstration; we do not adjust them for inflation and seldom convert foreign currency to dollars.

NUMBER OF TREATMENT GROUPS: The number of treatment groups always includes the group or groups used for control purposes.

MAJOR FINDINGS: Information on findings reported in the summaries was typically obtained from the final reports we reviewed. For a few experiments, alternative sets of findings have been produced by a methodological approach different from that used in the final report. We usually ignored such findings. Some experiments have a large volume of results. To keep the summaries brief and the reported numbers manageable, we have concentrated on those findings that pertain as directly as possible to the major experimental outcomes of interest.

DESIGN ISSUES: Numerous issues arise in selecting treatment and control groups, administering experimental treatments, collecting data on outcomes, analyzing these data, and so forth. Decisions concerning these issues can have a major influence on findings from social experiments, sometimes rendering the findings invalid. For each experiment, we attempt to alert readers to the most important design issues. The number of design issues we list for a particular experiment is unimportant. Some design issues are much more important than others. Although we have uncovered some of the design issues we mention on our own, in many instances we simply repeat information we found in the evaluation reports. Careful evaluators are especially likely to list important caveats.

TREATMENT ADMINISTRATOR: The treatment administrator is the organization responsible for rendering the treatment. Treatments tested in early social experiments were often administered by separate offices set up by the evaluator expressly for that purpose; since 1975, the treatments tested in most social experiments have been administered through existing agencies.

ENABLING LEGISLATION: Federal and state legislation have often mandated that social programs, especially those tried on a pilot basis, are evaluated. Some experiments that we reviewed began as a result of legislative mandates for evaluation.

POLICY EFFECTS: In a number of instances an experiment's findings appear to have directly influenced the direction of policy, and we say so. As with all other elements of the summary, we admit the possibility of errors of omission and commission in these conclusions.

INFORMATION SOURCES: Each summary indicates at least one source for more detailed written information (usually a final report) on the experiment described. In some cases, the report has been published in a journal or book, but more typically it can only be obtained from the research firm that conducted the evaluation or the government agency that sponsored it. In a few instances, the report is not written in English.

We have sorted the experiments by their target populations: welfare recipients, unemployed, and so on. Within each target population, experiments appear in approximately chronological order. Thus, brief summaries of ongoing experiments appear after the longer summaries of completed experiments.

Following the summaries of the experiments, an article entitled "The Social Experiment Market" appears. This article, which was originally published in the *Journal of Economic Perspectives* in 1999, is largely based on information extracted from the summaries of social experiments included in the second edition of the *Digest*. The article describes the characteristics of social experiments and trends in social experimentation. We reprint the article here because it appears that few of these characteristics and trends have changed in major ways since the second edition was published in 1997, even though a large number of social experiments have been initiated since then. The important changes that have occurred since 1997 are discussed in a brief postscript to the article.

The volume contains two indexes. The first lists individuals and organizations that were either associated with particular experiments or acted or commented on these experiments. The second index references the policy interventions tested by the experiments summarized in this book.

Notes

1. Two recent books that do this are Boruch (1997) and Orr (1999). In addition, in a series of essays, Hausman and Wise (1985) also discuss specific social experiments and issues that have arisen in conducting them.
2. If the behavior of a larger randomized unit (e.g., a local government, a business) is itself the subject of analysis we consider the demonstration an experiment. If the aggregated behavior of individuals associated with that larger unit is the subject of analysis we consider the demonstration a quasi experiment. Our rule is that experiments analyze and randomize at the same level of analysis, while quasi experiments analyze at a lower level than they randomize.
3. Moreover, people may move from site *A* to site *B,* and vice versa, during the demonstration; and these moves may or may not be related to differences in the treatment. If people move because of differences in the treatment, then the validity of the evaluation will probably be compromised.
4. Observed differences across sites typically cause less serious problems than unobserved differences because they often can be controlled for statistically.
5. In the specific case of the income maintenance experiments, the fact of an ongoing income maintenance

experiment was not used to delay action. On the contrary, premature, and eventually contradicted, data from the experiment were used in an attempt to push forward an income maintenance proposal by the Nixon administration that was similar to the one tested.

6. In poverty programs, some would argue that the social welfare evaluation is more complex: perhaps current benefits do long-range harm to recipients, whereas the reduction of poverty may raise the well-being of nonpoor taxpayers. These concerns are valid, but are tangential to this issue.

7. As previously discussed, quasi experiments involve using random processes to assign sites to treatment or control status. However, quasi experiments of this sort are relatively rare. One reason is that program administrators at local sites are generally very reluctant to relinquish their prerogative to decide whether to adopt particular innovations.

8. In practice, even observable differences may interact nonlinearly with treatment, and the analyst may fail to adjust for them correctly.

9. Burtless (1995) assessed most of the problems associated with conducting social experiments and vigorously defended the usefulness of the technique.

10. There is no inherent reason why social experiments must always be small-scale. For example, in some experiments, all members of the target population within a particular geographic area, but a small group of randomly selected controls, are eligible to receive program services.

11. Whereas the lack of feedback and information diffusion can threaten external validity, the presence of such effects might threaten internal validity. One possibility is that widespread media coverage of an innovative treatment might mislead control group members about what rules affect them. For example, our summary of the New Jersey Family Development Plan notes a controversy among analysts about whether subjects' confusion might have affected findings in that demonstration. A relevant question is how the concept of "confusion" is to be measured.

12. Note that the main problem is whether small-scale demonstration results generalize to large populations. Randomization per se is a relatively unimportant element here. If the pilot program has limited slots, the target population is necessarily self-selected in applying and not applying, regardless of whether the allocation mechanism is random or nonrandom.

13. Note that this refers to selecting sites randomly from the population of potential sites, not to a saturation design in which sites are assigned randomly to program and control status.

14. The standard argument is that only sites operating superior programs will acquiesce to an evaluation. However,

there may be only minimal correlation between local operators' self-appraisals and the results of a rigorous third-party evaluation. Indeed, even when sites are self-selected, estimated impacts are typically modest, suggesting that any site selection bias is not large enough to lead to an unwarranted expansion of a program in response to inflated impact estimates. Nevertheless, biases of unknown magnitude may arise from management differences among self-selected sites.

15. In nonexperimental evaluations, it is sometimes possible to estimate entry effects by using a site saturation design (Johnson, Klepinger, and Dong 1994; Marcotte 1992; Schiller and Brasher 1993; Wolf 1990).

16. We report some information about costs in the summaries of the individual experiments.

17. Costs associated with administering innovative treatments are typically counted as part of total experimental costs when the experiment is administered through special offices set up expressly for the purpose, but are rarely counted if the experiment is administered through an existing government agency.

18. The cost of the experiment will typically be a fraction of the rounding error in the appropriation for any major program of the agency, but this does not justify suboptimal use of the agency's research budget.

19. The more one knows about bureaucracy, the less surprising this news would be.

20. The most potentially damaging findings came from the Seattle-Denver Income Maintenance Experiment, which seemed to indicate that a negative income tax program would cause family splitting. When these findings first became available, the Carter administration was attempting to promote a negative-income-tax-like program in Congress. The only member of Congress known to have reacted strongly to the findings was Senator Daniel Patrick Moynihan of New York, who said: "We were wrong about a guaranteed income! Seemingly it is calamitous" (quoted in Demkovich 1978). Although Moynihan was an influential authority on welfare, for many other reasons the administration's legislation never got out of committee in the U.S. House of Representatives and thus never reached the Senate. It is not clear that even Moynihan's opposition was primarily motivated by marital stability findings; the driving force may have been fiscal relief for New York State. See Greenberg, Linksz, and Mandell (2003, chapter 6) for greater detail.

21. Randomization also seems to have been conceived independently of Fisher, and slightly earlier, by W. A. McCall (1923).

22. The information in this paragraph is based on a telephone interview with Heather Ross and has been con-

firmed by several other people who were involved in social experimentation in its early stages.

23. For classic early statements of the rationale, see Orcutt and Orcutt (1968) and Rivlin (1971, 86–119).

24. These terminated experiments are as follows: Mississippi New Direction, Families Achieving Independence in Montana, North Dakota Early Intervention Project, Hawaii Pursuit of New Opportunities (PONO), Massachusetts Welfare Reform 95, Oklahoma Learnfare, Illinois Get a Job, Illinois Six Month Paternity Establishment, Illinois Family Responsibility Initiative, Illinois Targeted Work Initiative, Illinois Work Pays Initiative, Ohio Community of Opportunity, Wyoming New Opportunities/New Responsibilities, Nebraska Welfare Reform Demonstration Project, Wisconsin AFDC Special Resource Account (SRA), Wisconsin Vehicle Asset Limit (VAL), Wisconsin AFDC Benefit Cap, Wisconsin Parental and Family Responsibility Demonstration, Georgia Personal Accountability and Responsibility (PAR), South Dakota–Strengthening of South Dakota Families, Expanded Medical Care in Nursing Homes for Acute Episodes, West Virginia Joint Opportunities for Independence (appears in the second edition as the West Virginia Opportunities for Independence), Missouri Families Mutual Responsibility, Family Service Centers for Head Start Families, and Arizona EMPOWER.

References

Bell, Stephen, Larry L. Orr, John D. Blomquist, and Glen G. Cain. 1995. *Program Applicants as a Comparison Group in Evaluating Training Programs.* Kalamazoo, MI: W. E. Upjohn Institute for Employment Research.

Benasich, April Ann, Jeanne Brooks-Gunn, and Beatriz Chu Clewell. 1992. "How Do Mothers Benefit from Early Intervention Programs?" *Journal of Applied Developmental Psychology* 13: 311–62.

Berlin, Gordon, Wendy Bancroft, David Card, Winston Lin, and Philip K. Robins. 1998. *Do Work Incentives Have Unintended Consequences? Measuring 'Entry Effects' in the Self-Sufficiency Project.* Ottawa: Social Research Demonstration Corporation.

Boruch, Robert F. 1997. *Randomized Experiments for Planning and Evaluation: A Practical Guide.* Thousand Oaks, CA: Sage Publications.

Boruch, Robert F., A. John McSweeny, and E. Jon Soderstron. 1978. "Randomized Field Experiments for Program Planning, Development, and Evaluation: An Illustrative Bibliography." *Evaluation Quarterly* 2 (November): 655–95.

Burtless, Gary. 1995. "The Case for Randomized Field Trials in Economic and Policy Research." *Journal of Economic Perspectives* 9(2, Spring): 63–84.

Dehejia, Rajeev H., and Sadek Wahba. 1995. "Causal Effects in Nonexperimental Studies: Re-Evaluating the Evaluation of Training Programs." Howard University. Photocopy, November.

———. 2002. "Propensity Score-Matching Methods for Nonexperimental Causal Studies." *The Review of Economics and Statistics* (February): 151–61.

Demkovich, Linda E. 1978. "Good News and Bad News for Welfare Reform." *National Journal* (December 30): 2061.

Feldman, Martha. 1989. *Order without Design: Information Production and Policy Making.* Stanford: Stanford University Press.

Fisher, Ronald. 1925. *Statistical Methods for Research Workers.* London: Oliver and Boyd.

———. 1935. *The Design of Experiments.* London: Oliver and Boyd.

Fraker, Thomas, and Rebecca Maynard. 1987. "Evaluating Comparison Group Designs with Employment-Related Programs." *Journal of Human Resources* 22(2, Spring): 194–227.

Friedlander, Daniel, and Philip K. Robins. 1995. "Evaluating Program Evaluations: New Evidence on Commonly Used Nonexperimental Methods." *American Economic Review* 85(4, September): 923–37.

Garfinkel, Irwin, Charles F. Manski, and Charles Michalopoulos. 1992. "Micro Experiments and Macro Effects." In *Evaluating Welfare and Training Programs,* edited by Charles F. Manski and Irwin Garfinkel (253–73). Cambridge: Harvard University Press.

Greenberg, David H., and Philip K. Robins. 1986. "The Changing Role of Social Experiments in Policy Analysis." *Journal of Policy Analysis and Management* 5(Winter): 340–62.

Greenberg, David, Donna Linksz, and Marvin Mandell. 2003. *Social Experimentation and Public Policymaking.* Washington, DC: Urban Institute Press.

Hausman, Jerry, and David Wise, eds. 1985. *Social Experimentation.* Chicago: University of Chicago Press for National Bureau of Economic Research.

Heckman, James J. 1992. "Randomization and Social Policy Evaluation." In *Evaluating Welfare and Training Programs,* edited by Charles F. Manski and Irwin Garfinkel (201–30). Cambridge: Harvard University Press.

Heckman, James J., and V. Joseph Hotz. 1989. "Choosing among Alternative Nonexperimental Methods for Estimating the Impact of Social Programs." *Journal of the American Statistical Association* 84(408, December): 862–74.

Heckman, James J., and Jeffrey A. Smith. 1995. "Assessing the Case for Social Experiments." *Journal of Economic Perspectives* 9(2, Spring): 85–110.

Heckman, James J., Hidehiko Ichimura, and Petra Todd. 1997. "Matching As an Econometric Evaluation Estimator: Evidence from Evaluating a Job Training Programme." *Review of Economic Studies Limited* 64: 605–54.

Heckman, James J., Hidehiko Ichimura, Jeffrey Smith, and Petra Todd. 1995. "Nonparametric Characterization of Selection Bias Using Experimental Data: A Study of Adult Males in JTPA." University of Chicago. Photocopy.

———. 1998. "Characterizing Selection Bias Using Experimental Data." *Econometrica* 66(5, September): 1017–98.

Hollister, Robinson G., and Jennifer Hill. 1995. "Problems in the Evaluation of Community-Wide Initiatives." In *New Approaches to Evaluating Community Initiatives: Concepts, Methods, and Contexts,* edited by James P. Connell, Anne C. Kubisch, Lisbeth B. Schorr, and Carol H. Weiss (127–72). Washington, DC: Aspen Institute.

Hotz, V. Joseph. 1992. "Designing an Evaluation of the Job Training Partnership Act." In *Evaluating Welfare and Training Programs,* edited by Charles F. Manski and Irwin Garfinkel (76–114). Cambridge: Harvard University Press.

Johnson, Terry R., Daniel H. Klepinger, and Fred B. Dong. 1994. "Caseload Impacts of Welfare Reform." *Contemporary Economics Policy* 12(January): 89–101.

LaLonde, Robert J. 1986. "Evaluating the Econometric Evaluations of Employment and Training Programs with Experimental Data." *American Economic Review* 76(4, September): 604–20.

LaLonde, Robert J., and Rebecca Maynard. 1987. "How Precise Are Evaluations of Employment and Training Programs? Evidence from a Field Experiment." *Evaluation Review* 11(4, August): 428–51.

Levitan, Sar A. 1992. *Evaluation of Federal Social Programs: An Uncertain Impact.* Washington, DC: George Washington University, Center for Social Policy Studies.

Lowry, Ira S., ed. 1983. *Experimenting with Housing Allowances: Final Report of the Housing Allowance Supply Experiment.* Cambridge, MA: Oelgenschlager, Gunn, and Hain.

Majone, Giandomenico. 1989. *Evidence, Argument, and Persuasion in the Policy Process.* New Haven: Yale University Press.

Manski, Charles F. 1995. "Learning about Social Programs from Experiments with Random Assignment of Treatments." Institute for Research on Poverty Discussion Paper 1061–95. Madison: University of Wisconsin.

Manski, Charles F., and Irwin Garfinkel. 1992. "Introduction." In *Evaluating Welfare and Training Programs,* edited by Charles F. Manski and Irwin Garfinkel (1–22). Cambridge: Harvard University Press.

Marcotte, John. 1992. "Effect of Washington State FIP on the Caseload Size." Washington, DC: The Urban Institute. Photocopy.

McCall, W. A. 1923. *How to Experiment in Education.* New York: Macmillan.

Michalopoulos, Charles, Doug Tattrie, Cynthia Miller, Philip K. Robins, Pamela Morris, David Gyarmati, Cindy Redcross, Kelly Foley, and Reuben Ford. 2002. *Making Work Pay: Final Report on the Self-Sufficiency Project for Long-Term Welfare Recipients.* Ottawa: Social Research and Demonstration Corporation.

Moffitt, Robert A. 1996. "The Effect of Employment and Training Programs on Entry and Exit from the Welfare Caseload." *Journal of Policy Analysis and Management* 15(1, Winter): 32–50.

Orcutt, Guy H., and Alice G. Orcutt. 1968. "Incentive and Disincentive Experimentation for Income Maintenance Policy Purposes." *American Economic Review* 58(September): 754–73.

Orr, Larry L. 1999. *Social Experiments: Evaluating Public Programs with Experimental Methods.* Thousand Oaks, CA: Sage Publications.

Rivlin, Alice M. 1971. *Systematic Thinking for Social Action.* Washington, DC: Brookings Institution.

Schiller, B. R., and C. Nielsen Brasher. 1993. "Effects of Workfare Saturation of AFDC Caseloads." *Contemporary Policy Issues* 11(April): 39–49.

Wolf, Douglas A. 1990. "Caseload Growth in the Evaluation Sites: Is There a FIP Effect?" Washington, DC: The Urban Institute. Photocopy.

PART 2

EXPERIMENTS IN
THE UNITED STATES

1

Public Assistance Recipients
AFDC and TANF

FORD ADMINISTRATION

AFDC Job Counselors

SUMMARY: This demonstration, conducted from 1976 to 1979, tested the effects of employment counseling and placement resistance on a large sample of "inactive" WIN clients. Subjects were followed for 90 days.

COST: Research only, $164,400 (1977).

TIME FRAME: Demonstration period, September 1976–January 1979; data collected, September 1976–January 1979; final report, December 1979.

TREATMENT TESTED:

1. Controls received certain minimal services (counseling without job referral in Oakland County, no counseling in Wayne County) from WIN.
2. Experimentals received an orientation in the Private Employment Agency (PEA) placement program, and, in general, one PEA received information on each subject's education, skills, and interests. The PEA would ask the subject to come in for an interview, and if the PEA felt it could match the subject with appropriate jobs, would refer her to employers. PEA fees were paid by the state for successful placements, based on starting salaries, with lower fees where the job duration was less than 90 days.

OUTCOMES OF INTEREST: (1) Employment; (2) Duration of employment; (3) Wages; and (4) AFDC payment reductions.

SAMPLE SIZE: Experimentals, 2,593; controls, 1,691.

TARGET POPULATION: "Inactive" WIN clients: clients not actively receiving employment services from WIN because they were regarded as relatively less employable.

NUMBER OF TREATMENT GROUPS: Two (with one control group).

NUMBER AND LOCATION OF SITES: Two—Wayne County (including Detroit) and Oakland County (including Pontiac), Michigan. Inner-city Detroit had a high unemployment rate and a predominantly black AFDC population. Oakland County is suburban with a predominantly white AFDC population.

RESEARCH COMPONENTS:
- Process analysis: Conducted with an emphasis on explaining the low placement rate.
- Impact analysis: Conducted with probit.
- Benefit–cost analysis: Cost-effectiveness only.

MAJOR FINDINGS:
1. Placement rates for experimentals were very low, in part because most experimentals never came to the PEA for an interview. In fact, over half never came to the initial orientation.

    Employment outcomes (PEA placement rates in parentheses):

	Oakland County (%)		Wayne County (%)	
	Experimentals	Controls	Experimentals	Controls
Full-time jobs	19.4 (3.5)	19.0	5.3 (2.0)	3.2
Part-time jobs	8.9 (0.2)	9.5	3.5 (0.0)	2.3
All jobs	27.4 (3.7)	27.4	8.6 (2.0)	5.5

2. The finding of no significant treatment impact in Oakland County is confirmed by a probit analysis. In Wayne County, the probability of employment, adjusted for personal characteristics, increased by a statistically significant 2.8 percent.
3. Costs per placement were $1,222 in Oakland County and $2,310 in Wayne County, but the PEA fees were only $341 and $385, respectively. The remainder of the costs were associated with the public administration side, and would have been lower per placement if the placement rate had been higher. In Oakland County, there was no significant difference in cost-effectiveness between the experimental and control treatments. In Wayne County, the experimental treatment was significantly less cost-effective because of its high costs.

TIME TRENDS IN FINDINGS: None reported.

REPLICABILITY: Replicable.

GENERALIZABILITY: The experiment is tested on a large urban population, characteristic of much of the national AFDC population. The findings could not be generalized to a similar program where there were sanctions for nonparticipation.

FUNDING SOURCE: U.S. Department of Health and Human Services, Family Support Administration. Key personnel: Ken Manihan.

TREATMENT ADMINISTRATOR: Michigan Department of Social Services. Key personnel: Robert Cecil.

EVALUATOR: Mathematica Policy Research. Key personnel: George J. Carcagno and James C. Ohls.

ENABLING LEGISLATION: None.

POLICY EFFECTS: According to Robert Cecil, the use of private employment agencies has been incorporated as an option, subject to local administrative discretion, for appropriate AFDC clients in Michigan, but is seldom chosen.

INFORMATION SOURCE: George J. Carcagno, Robert Cecil, and James C. Ohls, "Using Private Employment Agencies to Place Welfare Clients in Jobs," *Journal of Human Resources,* Winter 1982: 132–43.

PUBLIC-USE ACCESS TO DATA: We have no information about a public-use file for this demonstration.

Colorado Monthly Reporting Experiment and Pretest

SUMMARY: This demonstration, conducted from 1976 to 1979, tested the effects of monthly income reporting on a large sample of AFDC recipients. Subjects were followed for two years.

COST: $3.5 million (1977); $1.5 million for research.

TIME FRAME: Demonstration period, 1976–79; data collected, same years; final report, 1980.

TREATMENTS TESTED:

1. For controls subject to the existing AFDC system, there was a six-month eligibility determination and the expectation that they would inform caseworkers of changes in their circumstances, but there was no systematic device to report and monitor such changes.
2. Experimentals were required to submit monthly reports on income and household composition, and monthly grants were adjusted on the basis of the report for the prior month. Failure to meet reporting deadlines or incomplete/inconsistent reporting would lead to delays in payment or, ultimately, to discontinuation.

OUTCOMES OF INTEREST: (1) Reductions in overall payments; (2) Impact of reporting on recipients; (3) Increases in administrative costs; and (4) Responsiveness of grants to changes in family circumstances.

SAMPLE SIZE: Experimentals, 1,825; controls, 1,841.

TARGET POPULATION: AFDC-regular (AFDC-R) and AFDC-unemployed-parent (AFDC-U) recipients.

NUMBER OF TREATMENT GROUPS: Two (with one control group).

NUMBER AND LOCATION OF SITES: One—Denver, Colorado.

RESEARCH COMPONENTS:

- Process analysis: Conducted. Concerns centered on the ability of recipients to complete forms and on the effects on caseworkers. The difference between the findings of the early and the later reports is partly attributable to a change in the treatment of controls by the agency, which moved to regular in-person redeterminations for the whole nonexperimental caseload four months after the experiment began. The policy change coincided with an increase in discontinuance rates among controls and a decline in savings from monthly reporting. Other changes at that time (increasing automation of paperwork for the nonexperimental caseload, reductions in caseload per worker for controls but not experimentals) probably had a similar direction of impact on the experiment.
- Impact analysis: Conducted. Comparison of means. Subsequent regression study of characteristics of discontinued households.
- Benefit–cost analysis: Budgetary analysis only.

MAJOR FINDINGS:

1. Early findings were a 4.3 percent reduction in AFDC-R payments and a 5.6 percent reduction in AFDC-U payments. The primary cause was a higher rate of discontinuation, somewhat offset by higher rates of reapproval. Ninety-six percent of report forms were returned, but 44 percent of all treatment recipients had to wait at least an additional seven days for payment at least once during the first year owing to reporting errors, mainly of income. Grant changes other than discontinuations happened much more frequently in the treatment groups: increases were five times more frequent, and decreases were 2.2 times more frequent. An approximate 4 percent increase in administrative costs was found (from a nonexperimental demonstration in Boulder), or about one-twelfth the calculated savings in payments. Eligibility staff believed the experimental process was fairer than the prior one, and, overall, improved their work and working conditions.

2. Later findings contradicted the earlier ones. Payment reductions over two years were about 1.8 percent, and in the second year were −0.7 percent. Investigators attributed the difference between the first- and second-year results to improved administration of the control group by the Denver office during the second period, using regular in-person reviews of case circumstances. Monthly savings of 15 percent were reported for the one-quarter of AFDC-R households that ever reported earnings and were zero for the three-quarters of the caseload who never did. Changes in the administration of controls made administrative costs difficult to estimate.

TIME TRENDS IN FINDINGS: In the 1979 project report, the effects of the system were markedly higher for new AFDC applicants than for prior recipients. This was confirmed in the 1982 report: Two-year estimates overstated the long-run impact on payments because the major impact was on new recipients, not on longer-run cases.

DESIGN ISSUES: Problems in the administration of the experiment occurred:

1. Some households received payments as experimentals in the first assistance spell, as controls in a subsequent spell, and vice versa.
2. Several assigned experimental cases were channeled into the control group because agency workers believed they were short-term cases.
3. Payment dates differed between the two systems, so a pay date difference could account for some of any observed impact.
4. Experimental cases were supposed to receive transition payments to cover the three weeks between their initial prospective payment and their first retrospective payment, but these checks were not always issued.
5. An evident potential problem in the experiment was the self-selection of the Denver social services agency.

REPLICABILITY: Replicable.

GENERALIZABILITY: Impact would probably vary inversely with the degree of aggressiveness already present in caseload management techniques used in the different states and counties.

FUNDING SOURCE: U.S. Department of Health and Human Services, Office of the Assistant Secretary for Planning and Evaluation. Key personnel: John Bayne.

TREATMENT ADMINISTRATOR: Colorado Department of Social Services. Key personnel: Jacob Shockley and Joseph Thompson.

EVALUATOR: Mathematica Policy Research. Key personnel: Robert G. Williams, Alan M. Hershey, and John A. Burghardt.

ENABLING LEGISLATION: Waivers of Colorado State Plan.

POLICY EFFECTS: Alan Hershey has stated that monthly reporting was incorporated into all AFDC and Food Stamp programs in the country, based on the early findings.

INFORMATION SOURCES: Robert G. Williams, David L. Horner, Alan M. Hershey, and Nancy L. Graham, *First Year Research Results, Colorado Monthly Reporting Experiment and Pretest,* Mathematica Policy Research, 1979; John A. Burghardt, *Impact of a Monthly Retrospective Reporting Requirement on AFDC-Benefit Payments: Evidence from the Second Year of the Colorado Monthly Reporting Experiment,* Mathematica Policy Research, 1982.

PUBLIC-USE ACCESS TO DATA: We have no information about a public-use file for this demonstration.

WIN Job-Finding Clubs

SUMMARY: This demonstration, conducted from 1976 to 1978, tested the effects of mandatory supervised group job search training and assistance on a medium-sized sample of Work Incentive Program registrants. Subjects were followed for one year.

COST: Administrative costs of the program at the three sites where a counselor was assigned full-time to the Job Club treatment were $167 per placement, excluding office rent and furniture. Multiplying by the number of placements (300) at all five sites yields $50,100 (1977), excluding counselor-training and research costs. However, the participants would have received some treatment in any case, and Elise Bruml, in an internal DOL memorandum, estimated $87 per experimental, which would mean $42,369 (1977). The cost of research only was roughly $300,000 (1977).

TIME FRAME: Demonstration period, September 1976–March 1978; data collected, essentially the same period; final report, 1978.

TREATMENTS TESTED:
1. Controls received whatever regular WIN (Work Incentive) program Intensive Manpower Service regime was in use at that site, such as counseling, training, subsidized job placement, and referrals to agency listings. The Wichita regime included group counseling and role-playing. Because the control regime was not standardized across sites, it is safest to assume five different control groups. The more conservative assumption does not materially affect the findings.
2. Experimentals received daily group job search training and supervised job search until a job was obtained. Further detail is given in the Carbondale Job-Finding Club summary (p. 294).

Both controls and experimentals received $1.50 plus carfare per session attended.

OUTCOME OF INTEREST: Employment.

SAMPLE SIZE: Experimentals, 487; controls, 490.

TARGET POPULATION: Registrants for the WIN (Work Incentive) program. Exclusions from this population varied by site. Wichita, Tacoma, and New Brunswick only enrolled "job-ready clients"; New York excluded "non-English speakers, illiterates, and clients already designated to receive training or counseling"; Milwaukee made no exclusions.

NUMBER OF TREATMENT GROUPS: Ten (one experimental and one control group at each site).

NUMBER AND LOCATION OF SITES: Five—New York City (Harlem), New York; New Brunswick, New Jersey; Milwaukee, Wisconsin; Wichita, Kansas; and Tacoma, Washington.

RESEARCH COMPONENTS:
- Process analysis: After training, the counselors were observed by the experimenters for the first few sessions of their initial Job Club groups to ensure general adherence to the experimental program. Experimentals also received all services from a single counselor; controls might receive them from several.
- Impact analysis: Conducted as a difference in means.
- Benefit–cost analysis: Not conducted.

MAJOR FINDINGS:
1. Percent employed (over 20 hours/week) after three months:

City	Experimentals	Controls
New York	56	35
New Brunswick	63	30
Tacoma	72	39
Wichita	60	39
Milwaukee	54	12
Mean starting wage (per week)	$137	$137

2. Effects were statistically significant for all groupings (by sex, age, education, ethnic group) except Hispanics.
3. Job Club effects were much stronger for mandatory participants (participation was a condition of continued receipt of AFDC) than for voluntary participants (83 percent of the sample were mandatories). This might have to do with the mandatory aspect or with the fact that volunteers generally had children less than six years old, whereas mandatories had older children.
4. Twenty-one percent of all jobs obtained by controls were temporary, compared with 16 percent

of experimentals' jobs; 25 percent of controls' jobs were subsidized, compared with 16 percent of experimentals'.

5. AFDC payments to experimentals six months after enrollment were reduced by 48 percent; payments to controls were down by 15 percent.

TIME TRENDS IN FINDINGS: Follow-up questionnaires had a fairly poor response rate. Six-month differences from those who did respond do not show a drop-off in the experimental effect.

DESIGN ISSUES:

1. Job Club counselors were selected for training by their local WIN agency, probably not randomly. Their performance, at least initially, was more closely observed than that of their peers; thus a differential Hawthorne effect is a possibility.
2. At the same time, this observation was clearly necessary to standardize the treatment. Implementing the "Job Club model" on a larger scale would require extensive training and supervision.

REPLICABILITY: Replicable.

GENERALIZABILITY: This study would seem to generalize the earlier experiments for an important and relatively homogeneous group.

FUNDING SOURCE: U.S. Department of Labor, Employment and Training Administration. Key personnel: Unknown.

TREATMENT ADMINISTRATOR: WIN agencies of five states, all of whom were receiving training from the Anna Mental Health Center. Key personnel: Personnel at different agencies.

EVALUATOR: Anna Mental Health Center. Key personnel: Nathan H. Azrin.

ENABLING LEGISLATION: None.

POLICY EFFECTS: Job Club became a requirement of the WIN program, and of some subsequent welfare-to-work programs.

INFORMATION SOURCES: Nathan H. Azrin, Robert A. Philip, P. Thienes-Hontos, and V. A. Besalel, "Comparative Evaluation of the Job Club Program with Welfare Recipients," *Journal of Vocational Behavior,* 1980: 133–45; ibid., "Follow-up on Welfare Benefits Received by Job Club Clients," *Journal of Vocational Behavior,* 1981: 253–54.

PUBLIC-USE ACCESS TO DATA: We have no information about a public-use file for this demonstration.

CARTER ADMINISTRATION

Massachusetts Work Experience Program

SUMMARY: This demonstration, conducted from 1978 to 1979, tested the effects of a mandatory work experience program, assisted job search, and a lower tax rate on earnings on a medium-sized sample of unemployed fathers receiving Aid to Families with Dependent Children (AFDC). Subjects were followed for one year.

COST: $760,000 (if CETA-salaried staff not included, $570,000), 1978; research only, $300,000.

TIME FRAME: Demonstration period, January 1978–March 1979; data collected, same period; final report, October 1980.

TREATMENTS TESTED:

1. Controls received no treatment "other than any normal WIN actions."
2. Experimental group 1 received a waiver of the 100-hours-per-month-maximum-labor limitation for AFDC–Unemployed Fathers program recipients. Instead, they were subject to the "30 and ⅓" rule for six months. Under the latter, the first $30 earned does not count against the wel-

fare benefit received, and earnings above $30 are subject to a 67 percent tax rate.

3. Experimental group 2 received the above treatment and, in addition, were assigned to unpaid work for public or nonprofit agencies three days a week. Failure to report to work could result in sanctions amounting to partial loss of AFDC benefits. The other two days a week were for participation in the agency-assisted job search. Unpaid workers received $30 per month incentive pay and lunch and travel reimbursement. If unable to find regular work within 13 weeks, they were assigned to a second work site.

OUTCOMES OF INTEREST: (1) Employment and (2) AFDC savings.

SAMPLE SIZE: Group 1, 150; group 2, 140; and group 3, 725.

TARGET POPULATION: Unemployed fathers receiving AFDC were screened for the following criteria: (1) not already in a special WIN treatment program, (2) unemployed for at least six months, (3) referred unsuccessfully to regular or CETA jobs, (4) "unsuitable for referral to another WIN component," and (5) found on interview to be physically and emotionally able to work.

NUMBER OF TREATMENT GROUPS: Three (with one control group).

NUMBER AND LOCATION OF SITES: Massachusetts, statewide.

RESEARCH COMPONENTS:

▪ Process analysis: Extensive. Interviews conducted with WIN staff on selection and work-site assignment process, with work supervisors and experimental subjects.

▪ Impact analysis: Conducted with logit regressions.

▪ Benefit–cost analysis: Conducted.

MAJOR FINDINGS:

Percentage finding unsubsidized employment over the five quarters: controls, 28.7 percent; experimental 1, 30.7 percent; and experimental

2, 34.2 percent. These results were not statistically significant.

AFDC payments, average over five quarters: controls, $839; experimental 1, $864; and experimental 2, $925. (The authors pointed out that controls also received lower payments on average before the experiment began.)

Received no AFDC for at least one quarter: controls, 42.3 percent; experimental 1, 35.2 percent; and experimental 2, 38.3 percent.

TIME TRENDS IN FINDINGS: Nonattenders at work sites in experimental group 2 reported finding employment faster than attenders in early quarters; the reverse was true in later quarters. It is possible that for some nonattenders the program either was incompatible with employment not reported to Public Welfare workers or provided additional incentive to find work.

DESIGN ISSUES:

1. The Work Experience program was the subject of intense public controversy for months before its implementation. A court injunction was in force from March 14 to April 10, 1978, during which all work performed under it had to be voluntary. Also the ultimately unsuccessful court challenge made the intake process much more selective. Both unemployables and very employables were screened out, and it would be difficult to compare the resulting sample with a population of interest.

2. The screening process was highly discretionary; people assigned to the sample varied from 15 percent to 61 percent of the underlying pool, from one region of the state to another.

3. Cutbacks in CETA staff led to many potential subjects never being called in for an interview. This had different effects across the state and introduced an additional regional bias.

4. Sanctions were weak and were seldom used. Two-thirds of experimental group 2 never went to assigned work sites, many of them because they were never told to. Some WIN

teams in the state made no effort to enforce the sanctions, and the WIN staff in one region seems to have encouraged clients not to cooperate with the program.

5. Additional assistance in job search was minimal. The change in rules from the 100 hour rule to the 30 and ⅓ hour rule was only effectively communicated to the WIN teams rather late in the experiment, which means it was never communicated to many of the subjects in experimental group 2.

REPLICABILITY: The treatment described in official documents is replicable.

GENERALIZABILITY: Workfare experiments in other states might have similar implementation problems, but the effects here are so severe that the findings probably cannot be generalized.

FUNDING SOURCE: U.S. Department of Labor, Manpower Administration. Key personnel: Howard Rosen.

TREATMENT ADMINISTRATORS: Massachusetts Department of Employment Security (MDES) and Massachusetts Department of Public Welfare (MDPW). Key personnel: Richard Sullivan and Richard Dill for MDES; Richard McKinnon for MDPW.

EVALUATOR: Brandeis University, Center for Employment and Income Studies. Key personnel: Barry Friedman.

ENABLING LEGISLATION: None.

INFORMATION SOURCE: Barry Friedman, Barbara Davenport, Robert Evans, Andrew Hahn, Leonard Hausman, and Cecile Papirno, "An Evaluation of the Massachusetts Work Experience Program," U.S. Department of Health and Human Services, Social Security Administration, Publication No. 13-11730, October 1980.

PUBLIC-USE ACCESS TO DATA: We have no information about a public-use file for this demonstration.

Louisville Immediate Job Search Assistance Experiment

SUMMARY: This demonstration, conducted from 1978 to 1980, tested the efforts of immediate employment-assistance services and a counselor-directed job search program on a large sample of new female WIN registrants. Subjects were followed for one year.

COST: One of the WIN Labs experiments, which collectively, including the nonexperimental projects, cost $2.5 million.

TIME FRAME: Demonstration period, November 1978–January 1980; data collected, November 1978–summer 1980; final report, June 1981.

TREATMENTS TESTED:
1. Controls received "the regular services offered to WIN clients under normal procedures." Service delivery delays of 2 to 10 weeks under these procedures were common while approvals for welfare and other social services were pending.
2. Experimentals received services immediately on registering with WIN, making them immediately eligible for reimbursement of child care, transportation, and lunch expenses and providing an incentive payment for going to counseling sessions and job interviews.

The most important counseling technique was a counselor-directed, individual job search for four hours a day; participation in this was voluntary (it did not affect the AFDC grant). Those who found employment continued to be eligible for child care services for up to 90 days, even if they still had not been found eligible for welfare.

At the initiation of the experiment, staff were randomly assigned between controls and experimentals. Subsequent personnel changes could not be kept random, but were not deliberately biased.

OUTCOMES OF INTEREST: (1) Employment; (2) Earnings; and (3) AFDC payments.

SAMPLE SIZE: Experimentals, 811; controls, 808.

TARGET POPULATION: New female WIN registrants (AFDC recipients and applicants). Clients already committed to a job, school, or training could refuse to participate.

NUMBER OF TREATMENT GROUPS: Two (with one control group).

NUMBER AND LOCATION OF SITES: One— Louisville, Kentucky.

RESEARCH COMPONENTS:
- Process analysis: Analysis of factors influencing willingness to participate in counseling programs.
- Impact analysis: Comparison of means, linear regression, and logit.
- Benefit–cost analysis: Data needed for such an analysis are reported.

MAJOR FINDINGS:
(Data are regression-adjusted.)
1. Percentage employed:

Quarter of follow-up	Experimentals	Controls
First (includes month registered)	35.9	30.0
Second	39.1	33.6
Third	37.4	32.9
Fourth	34.7	28.8
Fifth	35.9	30.6

Note: All differences are statistically significant.

2. Average earnings:

Quarter of follow-up	Experimentals ($)	Controls ($)
First	218.93	163.59
Second	327.63	261.10
Third	381.20	346.23
Fourth	388.72	340.39
Fifth	408.14	338.48
Total	1,724.62	1,449.88

Note: Differences are statistically significant in the first, second, fifth, and last rows. Numbers may not add to totals because of rounding.

3. Average AFDC payments:

Quarter of follow-up	Experimentals ($)	Controls ($)
First	443.02	448.73
Second	452.84	469.65
Third	402.07	418.41
Fourth	372.92	385.13
Fifth	351.05	376.37
Sixth	337.47	356.75
Total	2,359.37	2,455.03

Note: Differences are statistically significant in the second, fifth, and last rows. Numbers may not add to totals because of rounding.

4. Sample is too small to reliably test the relative success of the experimental treatment on subgroups of the target population.
5. Estimated incremental administrative costs were about $77–$115 per experimental. The experimental treatment may be marginally cost-effective in terms of AFDC payment reductions. Earnings impacts are two to three times the administrative cost, so the experiment would pass a social benefit–cost test.

TIME TRENDS IN FINDINGS: Displayed above.

DESIGN ISSUES:
1. Although participation in job search counseling was voluntary, the WIN staff involved in the experiment were under considerable pressure to get experimentals to enroll in it, and this may have affected the way they communicated the fact of its being voluntary: "Any inferences about likely participation rates should recognize that participation is likely to be influenced by the type and intensity of encouragement received by the potential participants" (Goldman 1981). About half of the experimentals were either considered unemployable at intake and therefore were not offered the intensive counseling service or did not participate when offered it.
2. Site self-selection bias is possible. Most state WIN programs were not anxious to participate in the experiments.

REPLICABILITY: Treatments are documented.

GENERALIZABILITY: Generalization might be affected by the relative generosity of welfare benefits in other states and the relative employability of those states' WIN populations.

FUNDING SOURCE: U.S. Department of Labor. Key personnel: Howard Rosen, Merwin Hans, and Gordon Berlin.

TREATMENT ADMINISTRATOR: Kentucky Department of Human Resources. Key personnel: Geralynne Clements.

EVALUATOR: Manpower Demonstration Research Corporation. Key personnel: Barbara S. Goldman.

ENABLING LEGISLATION: None.

INFORMATION SOURCE: Barbara S. Goldman, *Impacts of the Immediate Job Search Assistance Experiment,* Manpower Demonstration Research Corporation, June 1981.

PUBLIC-USE ACCESS TO DATA: Public-use access does not exist.

WIN Services to Volunteers

SUMMARY: These two demonstrations, conducted from 1978 to 1979, tested the efforts of a special recruitment effort and enriched employment-assistance services in a large sample of female recipients of Aid to Families with Dependent Children (AFDC) whose children were five years old or younger. Subjects were followed for one year.

COST: See Louisville Immediate Job Search Assistance Experiment on page 32.

TIME FRAME: Demonstration period, October 1978–March 1979; data collected, October 1978–December 1980; final report, June 1981.

TREATMENTS TESTED: There were two experiments, A and B.
A. Effect of Recruitment
    A random sample of AFDC recipients with children age five or younger and not already voluntarily enrolled (volunteers) in WIN.

1. Controls were not subject to a special recruitment effort.
2. Experimentals received letters inviting them to recruitment meetings in their neighborhoods, at which WIN services were described. They were paid $5 if they attended. To register for the services, they still had to go to the WIN office.
B. Effect of Special Services
    A random sample of walk-in volunteers who were not in either group A1 or A2.
1. Controls received regular WIN services.
2. Experimentals received special enriched services: (1) Orientations were not focused on AFDC sanctions for nonparticipation; (2) information sessions included day care choices; (3) training was available at a larger number of educational institutions; (4) on-the-job training wages were 75 percent (rather than 50 percent) subsidized; and (5) the social services and employment services staff were better integrated to improve service delivery.

OUTCOMES OF INTEREST: (1) Number of volunteers; (2) Employment; (3) Earnings; and (4) AFDC payments.

SAMPLE SIZE: A1, 1,003; A2, 1,003; B1, 114; B2, 110.

TARGET POPULATION: Female AFDC recipients with children five years old or younger.

NUMBER OF TREATMENT GROUPS: Four (with two control groups).

NUMBER AND LOCATION OF SITES: One—Denver, Colorado.

RESEARCH COMPONENTS:
- Process analysis: Interviews with volunteers and nonvolunteers were conducted.
- Impact analysis: Conducted as a difference in means.
- Benefit–cost analysis: Cost-effectiveness analysis (budgetary point of view).

MAJOR FINDINGS:
In experiment B, the finding is a statistically significant, upward impact on AFDC payments to

experimentals. As the pre-enrollment experimentals' earnings in this fairly small sample were significantly higher than those of the controls, the most likely reason is that a much higher percentage of experimentals were provided with institutional training than was the case with controls. The training reduced experimental earnings in subsequent quarters by reducing the time available for work. After registration, there are no significant differences in earnings.

Experiment A	Experimentals	Controls
Volunteer WIN registrants	160	20
Incremental cost per recruit	$27.27	NA

Note: Employment, earnings, and AFDC payment differences are all statistically insignificant. NA = not applicable.

TIME TRENDS IN FINDINGS: In experiment B, significant reductions in AFDC payments to experimentals occurred in the third, fourth, and fifth quarters after registration.

DESIGN ISSUES: The sample in B was too small and many of the enhancements in services were too subtle to expect statistically significant differences to emerge.

REPLICABILITY: Experiment A is replicable; experiment B is a rather diffuse experiment, and aspects of it might not be replicable.

GENERALIZABILITY: The most frequent reason for registering with WIN was to get help in finding a job. The Denver labor market at this time had very low unemployment, and, therefore, subjects may have felt little need for WIN services.

FUNDING SOURCE: See Louisville Immediate Job Search Assistance Experiment.

TREATMENT ADMINISTRATOR: Colorado Department of Social Services.

EVALUATOR: Center for Social Research and Development, University of Denver. Key personnel: Ellen L. Slaughter and Edward C. Baumheier.

ENABLING LEGISLATION: None.

INFORMATION SOURCE: Ellen L. Slaughter, Paulette Turshak, Gale G. Whiteneck, and Edward C. Baumheier, *Final Report on WIN Services to Volunteers: Denver WIN Research Laboratory Project,* Manpower Demonstration Research Corporation, June 1981.

PUBLIC-USE ACCESS TO DATA: Public-use access does not exist.

Madison and Racine Quality Employment Experiment

INFORMATION SOURCE: Joan M. Leiman, *The WIN Labs: A Federal/Local Partnership in Social Research,* Manpower Demonstration Research Corporation, July 1982.

SUMMARY FROM ABOVE SOURCE: This experiment sought to place women from the Madison and Racine, Wisconsin, WIN programs into better-paying, nontraditional jobs. The centerpiece of the strategy was an employer subsidy, with up to a 100 percent reimbursement for on-the-job training through the first third of a contract (maximum length 50 weeks), declining first to 75 percent and then to 50 percent over the remaining term, provided the wage offered was over $4 an hour. The program also offered a peer support group for women adjusting to on-the-job problems. New registrants were randomly assigned to either the treatment or the control group.

> Wisconsin's main problem was the small size of the registrant pool, compounded by the fact that it was very slow to get the marketing and job development efforts underway. The result was a substantial shortfall in the number of women finding employment through the experimental program, so substantial that three-quarters of the way through the project, it was clear that there would be very little probability of seeing any impact from the demonstration. There was also little possibility of increasing the numbers, given the small registrant pool. . . . A decision was therefore made in the fall of 1979 to

phase down the demonstration before its scheduled end, and also to discontinue the Madison/Racine complex as a Lab (Leiman 1982).

PUBLIC-USE ACCESS TO DATA: Public-use access does not exist.

Denver Postplacement Services Project

SUMMARY: This demonstration, conducted from 1980 to 1982, tested the effects of postplacement case management on a medium-sized sample of AFDC recipients who had recently found employment. Subjects were followed for six months.

COST: See Louisville Immediate Job Search Assistance Experiment on page 32.

TIME FRAME: Demonstration period, April 1980–May 1982; data collected, same period; final report, December 1982.

TREATMENTS TESTED: Experimentals were telephoned seven times over a six-month period, whether still receiving AFDC or not. Counselors inquired about job-related problems and offered to help. If a job was lost, help was offered in finding a new one. Controls were not telephoned. They were still eligible for WIN services (principally, child care subsidies for 90 days).

OUTCOMES OF INTEREST: (1) Employment; (2) Earnings; (3) AFDC recipiency; and (4) AFDC payments.

SAMPLE SIZE: Experimentals, 270; controls, 281.

TARGET POPULATION: WIN-mandatory AFDC recipients who had recently found full-time, permanent employment.

NUMBER OF TREATMENT GROUPS: Two (with one control group).

NUMBER AND LOCATION OF SITES: One—Denver, Colorado.

RESEARCH COMPONENTS:
▪ Process analysis: Conducted principally through client interviews. The project report authors found that the average experimental had 8.3 contacts with WIN staff and that the average control had 6.6, in both cases mostly connected with the mandatory WIN job search after loss of the initial job. Concerning WIN staff intervention, participants mostly reported that "they talked with [us] about how to solve" a problem. Experimentals were more likely to receive child care subsidies, whereas controls were more likely to either leave children with older siblings or leave them unattended. Controls were more likely to leave their jobs because of child care conflicts, but experimentals were more likely to leave their jobs because of conflicts with supervisors and coworkers.
▪ Impact analysis: Comparison of means.
▪ Benefit–cost analysis: Cost-effectiveness only.

MAJOR FINDINGS:
1. No impact on job retention beyond one month.
2. Experimental/control differences in earnings, AFDC payments, and recipiency status were statistically insignificant.
3. Costs per experimental were $320 higher than costs per control, and thus the project was not cost-effective.

TIME TRENDS IN FINDINGS: Experimental/control job retention rates are significantly different (at the 10 percent level) in the first month, and insignificantly different thereafter.

DESIGN ISSUES: None apparent.

REPLICABILITY: Replicable.

GENERALIZABILITY: There is no obvious reason why this approach should work elsewhere when it did not work in Denver.

FUNDING SOURCE: See Louisville Immediate Job Search Assistance Experiment.

TREATMENT ADMINISTRATOR: Denver Department of Social Services.

EVALUATOR: Center for Social Research and Development, University of Denver. Key personnel: Ellen L. Slaughter and Edward C. Baumheier.

ENABLING LEGISLATION: None.

INFORMATION SOURCE: Ellen L. Slaughter, Gale G. Whiteneck, and Edward C. Baumheier, *Postplacement Services to WIN Clients: Final Report of a Denver WIN Laboratory Project,* Manpower Demonstration Research Corporation, December 1982.

PUBLIC-USE ACCESS TO DATA: Public-use access does not exist.

Louisville Group Job Search Experiment

SUMMARY: This demonstration, conducted from 1980 to 1981, tested the effects of immediate employment-assistance services and incentive payments on a medium-sized sample of female WIN registrants. Subjects were followed for one year.

COST: See Louisville Immediate Job Search Assistance Experiment on page 32.

TIME FRAME: Demonstration period, October 1980–May 1981; data collected through December 1981; final report, November 1983.

TREATMENTS TESTED: Experimentals received essentially the Job Club treatment, incentive payments of $1.50 per day, and transportation and child care payments. These services were available immediately on registration. Controls received "the usual WIN services"; these might have included intensive counseling, on-the-job training, or classroom instruction, but the great majority of controls actually received no services. Controls who were given services received them after the usual administrative delays, sometimes up to 10 weeks.

OUTCOMES OF INTEREST: (1) Employment; (2) Earnings; and (3) AFDC payments.

SAMPLE SIZE: Experimentals, 376; controls, 374.

TARGET POPULATION: Female WIN registrants who were not already employed or in training or school, who did not have medical or personal problems preventing them from working, and who volunteered to participate.

NUMBER OF TREATMENT GROUPS: Two (with one control group).

NUMBER AND LOCATION OF SITES: One— Louisville, Kentucky.

RESEARCH COMPONENTS:
- Process analysis: Conducted through observations and interviews. Job search techniques taught were fewer than in the Azrin model (see Carbondale Job-Finding Club on page 294 and Job Club Behavioral Supervision Test on page 298)—apparently the only one taught was cold calls from the Yellow Pages.
- Impact analysis: Comparison of means, ordinary least squares (OLS) regression, and logit.
- Benefit–cost analysis: Cost-effectiveness only.

MAJOR FINDINGS:
Over two quarters of follow-up:

	Experimentals	Controls	Difference significant?
Percentage ever employed	49	34	Yes, at 1%
Total average earnings	$550	$406	Yes, at 5%
AFDC payments	$1,680	$1,710	No

Employment impacts were largest for WIN volunteers; they were generally insignificant for WIN mandatories. Impacts were much larger for those who had not been recently employed than for those who had. The incremental cost was $195 per experimental. This is not cost-effective in budgetary terms, because the AFDC savings are insignificant. However, the Louisville experiment was clearly overstaffed compared with Azrin's, which had similar employment results.

An important finding is that "job-readiness" ratings, a major WIN criterion, were inherently subjective; consequently, job readiness could be affected by changing personal circumstances and group experience. In fact, 32 percent of non-job-ready experimentals found jobs.

TIME TRENDS IN FINDINGS: Earnings and employment in the second quarter increased over earnings and employment in the first quarter.

DESIGN ISSUES:

1. Findings for the early sample (covering the first six months of intake) were discarded because of dissatisfaction with the initial implementation of the treatment. Treatment procedures were revised, and findings are for the later sample only.
2. Because the program was voluntary, AFDC savings from one possible source in the Azrin WIN Job Club experiment could not have occurred. Azrin believed that some recipients had employment that they concealed from welfare officials; since holding a job and going to daylong, supervised workshops and job search simultaneously would be difficult, he speculated that savings even from nonparticipants were possible if the Job Club were mandatory. Even without concealed employment, mandatory attendance would be a disincentive to recipiency. The MDRC report, on the other hand, emphasizes the importance of group reinforcement and solidarity in the frustrating telephone job search, and questions whether a mandatory program would have these elements.
3. Job retention is not reported.

REPLICABILITY: This experiment is a replication.

GENERALIZABILITY: The project report authors argued that the impact estimates were not very different from Azrin's WIN Job Club impact estimates, when adjusted for differences in sample characteristics and job markets.

FUNDING SOURCE: See Louisville Immediate Job Search Assistance Experiment.

TREATMENT ADMINISTRATOR: Kentucky Department of Human Resources. Key personnel: Geralynne Clements and Ruth Harvey.

EVALUATOR: Manpower Demonstration Research Corporation. Key personnel: Barbara S. Goldman.

ENABLING LEGISLATION: None.

INFORMATION SOURCES: Joanna Gould-Stuart, *Welfare Women in a Group Job Search Program: Their Experiences in the Louisville WIN Research Laboratory Project,* Manpower Demonstration Research Corporation, April 1982; Carl Wolfhagen with Barbara S. Goldman, *Job Search Strategies: Lessons from the Louisville WIN Laboratory,* Manpower Demonstration Research Corporation, November 1983.

PUBLIC-USE ACCESS TO DATA: Public-use access does not exist.

Dayton Wage-Subsidy Voucher Experiment

SUMMARY: This demonstration, conducted from 1980 to 1981, tested the effects of a tax credit voucher for employers or a direct cash subsidy to employers on a medium-sized sample of welfare recipients. Subjects were followed for one year.

COST: It is not possible to separate the cost of the experiment from the cost of the Employment Opportunities Pilot Project (EOPP), a large-scale demonstration of employment and training initiatives under the Carter administration that was aborted by the Reagan administration in May 1981. Burtless has stated that his best guess of the incremental cost of the experiment, beyond that of the EOPP, would be well under $500,000 (1980), largely for the research design. A second experiment also planned under the EOPP was never started, again because the new administration canceled it.

TIME FRAME: Demonstration period, December 1980–May 1981; data collected, same period.

TREATMENTS TESTED:

1. Tax credit voucher. These experimentals received a Job-Club-type treatment. They were

also given vouchers, which employers could use to obtain credits on their tax returns, and training and written materials on using this subsidy to good advantage in their job search. The credit was good for 50 percent of wages paid in the first year of employment, with the total credit not to exceed $3,000, and 25 percent of wages in the second year of employment, with total credit not to exceed $1,500.
2. Direct cash subsidy. These experimentals received the same treatment as the first group, except that the subsidy was to be paid quarterly directly by the program operator, without regard to the employer's tax liability.
3. Controls. Controls received the Job Club treatment, but no voucher. They received instead a one-day course in using job bank listings at the local employment service (a placebo treatment). They were not told that they were eligible for wage subsidies (although by law they were).

OUTCOMES OF INTEREST: (1) Placement in an unsubsidized job and (2) Initial wage.

SAMPLE SIZE: Tax credit group, 247; direct cash group, 299; controls, 262.

TARGET POPULATION: There were two: (1) Recipients of general assistance, typically single, or if a member of a couple, childless ("many were only temporarily destitute"); and (2) AFDC recipients, whose participation was not mandatory. However, many of those referred were WIN mandatories who had been unsuccessful in other WIN activities.

NUMBER OF TREATMENT GROUPS: Three (with one control group).

NUMBER AND LOCATION OF SITES: One—Montgomery County, Ohio, which includes Dayton.

RESEARCH COMPONENTS:
▪ Process analysis: Not conducted because the experiment was canceled. Data are available only on those who had completed an eight-week

cycle (two weeks of Job Club and six weeks of job search, for experimentals) as of that date.
▪ Impact analysis: Conducted as a difference in means.
▪ Benefit–cost analysis: Not conducted.

MAJOR FINDINGS:
1. Job placement rates were as follows: Controls, 20.6 percent; tax credit group, 13.0 percent; direct cash group, 12.7 percent. The advantage of the controls over the experimentals is statistically significant.
2. Of 70 voucher-holders who found employment, only 19 worked for firms that requested certification for wage subsidies.
3. Average initial wages in all three groups were nearly identical.
4. Job-finding rates of AFDC and general assistance groups were almost equal. "When economically disadvantaged workers are clearly identified to potential employers as disadvantaged (by a subsidy offer), their chances of employment are harmed."

TIME TRENDS IN FINDINGS: No data available beyond eight weeks.

DESIGN ISSUES:
1. The experiment was conducted during a period of high and growing unemployment in the local area.
2. It is likely that marginally employable welfare recipients are not in a good position to explain and market their own wage subsidies. It is possible that job developers could improve on the results found here, but it is not clear that this improvement would be sufficient to justify the subsidy itself.
3. The absence of process analysis means that no documentation exists on any extraneous influences that might contaminate the findings.

REPLICABILITY: Replicable.

GENERALIZABILITY: The experiment took place in a depressed region, and its abrupt termination leaves open some questions about its administration. However, other experiments with wage subsidies (for example, the Wage-Subsidy Variation Experiment and the Florida TRADE Welfare for Work experiment) have results that are consistent with those reported here.

FUNDING SOURCE: U.S. Department of Labor, Office of the Assistant Secretary for Policy, Evaluation and Research (ASPER). Key personnel: Gary Burtless, Larry L. Orr, and John Cheston.

TREATMENT ADMINISTRATOR: The CETA agency in Montgomery County, Ohio. Key personnel: Not available.

EVALUATORS: Mathematica Policy Research and U.S. Department of Labor, ASPER. Key personnel: The experiment was designed by John A. Burghardt, Gary Burtless, John Cheston, Larry Orr, and Harold Watts. It was canceled by the Reagan administration at an early stage; Gary Burtless analyzed the limited data available, which had been collected by John Cheston.

ENABLING LEGISLATION: CETA (Comprehensive Employment and Training Act) Reauthorization Act of 1978.

INFORMATION SOURCE: Gary Burtless, "Are Targeted Wage Subsidies Harmful? Evidence from a Wage Voucher Experiment," *Industrial and Labor Relations Review,* October 1985: 105–14.

PUBLIC-USE ACCESS TO DATA: We have no information about a public-use file for this demonstration.

FIRST REAGAN ADMINISTRATION

Monthly Reporting in the AFDC Program

SUMMARY: This demonstration, conducted from 1981 to 1982, tested the effects of required monthly reporting of household information on a large sample of AFDC recipients. Subjects were followed for one year.

COST: Operations, $5.5 million; research, $3 million (1982).

TIME FRAME: Demonstration period in Illinois, October 1981–September 1982, in Massachusetts, August 1981–July 1982; data collected, same period; final report, September 1985.

TREATMENTS TESTED: Experimentals had to return a monthly report as a condition of continued receipt of AFDC. The report covered income received in the previous month and household composition. Payments for the following month (e.g., March) were determined by the report for the previous month (January). Thus, the accounting principle was retrospective. (Prospective accounting attempts to match grants to anticipated household needs.) Face-to-face redetermination of eligibility with a caseworker was conducted annually in Massachusetts; Illinois had no redetermination requirement.

Illinois controls faced retrospective accounting for income, prospective accounting for other factors, and semiannual face-to-face redeterminations. Monthly reports were required only for households with earnings.

Massachusetts had two controls. The conventionals faced retrospective accounting, semi-annual redeterminations, and no regular reporting requirement. The voluntaries received a form each month that they had to return only if income or household composition had changed; accounting was prospective, and redeterminations were semiannual.

OUTCOMES OF INTEREST: (1) AFDC payments; (2) Caseloads; (3) Error rate; and (4) Administrative costs.

SAMPLE SIZE: Illinois: experimentals, 7,000; controls, 3,600. Massachusetts: experimentals, 2,500; voluntary controls, 2,300; conventional controls, 5,100.

TARGET POPULATION: AFDC-recipient households.

NUMBER OF TREATMENT GROUPS: Five (with three control groups). A uniform experimental treatment was tested against controls that varied by state. Illinois had one control group, Massachusetts had two.

NUMBER AND LOCATION OF SITES: Two—Chicago, Illinois; and Boston, Massachusetts.

RESEARCH COMPONENTS:

■ Process analysis: Conducted in both states, but more intensively in Illinois. Illinois encountered substantial problems with the automated data processing system that had been developed to support monthly reporting. These problems led to erroneous payments, inappropriate case closings, and a suspension of the policy of closing cases for failure to file reports. The fairness of the experimental treatment was studied with regard to terminations and the reporting burden. The investigators concluded that terminations for noncooperation occurred with roughly equal frequency in Illinois under both the experimental and control systems; the burden of reporting was minor for most experimentals in Illinois (seven minutes once they were used to it).

■ Impact analysis: Conducted as a difference in means.

■ Benefit–cost analysis: Effects on government budgets discussed.

MAJOR FINDINGS

1. Effect on total payments over 12 months, experimentals versus conventionals: Illinois, +4.3 percent; Massachusetts, −1.9 percent. The Illinois figure is statistically significant; but for the second six months, when computer problems had been resolved, the measured impact was +0.6 percent, which was not statistically significant. The Massachusetts figure is not statistically significant.

2. Effect on caseload size over 12 months, experimentals versus conventionals: Illinois, +3.0 percent, Massachusetts, −2.7 percent. Both figures are statistically significant, but neither is important. The Illinois figure for the second six months is +0.5 percent (not statistically signifi-

cant). The Massachusetts reduction is concentrated around the fourth month of the experiment: "The policy of termination for failure to file was not implemented in Massachusetts until the fourth month of the demonstration. . . . A few months later, the caseloads under monthly reporting and the conventional system were approximately equal."

3. Effects on average AFDC payment size over 12 months, experimentals versus conventionals: Illinois +1.2 percent (statistically significant, but 1.0 percent and not significant the second six months); Massachusetts +0.8 percent (statistically significant). Monthly reporting led to more frequent grant adjustments; total increases exceeded total reductions.

4. Effects of voluntary change reporting in Massachusetts over 12 months for controls versus conventionals are not statistically significant.

5. Effects on error rate in Illinois over 12 months for experimentals versus conventionals are not statistically significant.

6. Effects on administrative cost, experimentals versus conventionals: Net savings in Illinois of about $1 per case per month; net increase in Massachusetts of about $4.80 per case per month.

7. Net government expenditure effects for experimentals versus conventionals are not statistically significant in either state.

8. Net government expenditure effects, voluntary controls versus conventional controls: Net increase of about $4.15 per case per month.

TIME TRENDS IN FINDINGS: Noted in "Major Findings."

DESIGN ISSUES: Illinois effects affected by computer problems noted above.

REPLICABILITY: Replicable.

GENERALIZABILITY: Sample sizes are very large. The substantial experimental effects in the Denver, Colorado, experiment were shown to be the consequence of the particular control treatment in that state at the time the experiment began. The effects of monthly reporting in large, urban, AFDC populations were shown in these experiments to be minor when compared with more-active welfare regimes. Although the effects on rural or medium-city populations are not tested, there is no obvious reason why they should be different.

FUNDING SOURCE: U.S. Department of Health and Human Services, Office of the Assistant Secretary for Planning and Evaluation. Key personnel: John Baine.

TREATMENT ADMINISTRATOR: Welfare Departments in Illinois and Massachusetts. Key personnel: Massachusetts officials no longer with the department; in Illinois, Stephen Spence.

EVALUATOR: Abt Associates. Key personnel: William L. Hamilton and Nancy R. Burstein.

ENABLING LEGISLATION: None.

POLICY EFFECTS: This study's finding that monthly reporting makes little difference was revealed after Congress had passed changes in the law making reporting mandatory. Subsequent welfare reforms have overturned this legislation.

INFORMATION SOURCE: William L. Hamilton, *Monthly Reporting in the AFDC Program: Executive Summary of Demonstration Results,* Abt Associates, September 1985.

PUBLIC-USE ACCESS TO DATA: Public-use access does not exist.

Washington State Intensive Applicant Employment Services Evaluation

SUMMARY: This quasi-experimental demonstration, conducted from 1982 to 1983, tested the effects of offering immediate services to AFDC applicants and extending work search requirements on a large sample of AFDC applicants. Subjects were followed for up to 10 months.

COST: Not available.

TIME FRAME: Demonstration period, April 1982–April 1983; data collected, same period; final report, June 1983.

TREATMENTS TESTED: The program provided counseling, job search assistance, day care, and transportation services to applicants for public assistance. At the same time, work search requirements were extended to include applicants as well as current AFDC recipients. Further, applicants with children ages 3–5 were required to participate in work search activities. The control group did not receive any services until they were actually recipients of public assistance. They were exempt from work search requirements until that time, and they were exempt if they had children under 6 years of age.

OUTCOMES OF INTEREST: (1) Application for, and participation in, AFDC; (2) Employment; (3) Earnings; and (4) Program costs.

SAMPLE SIZE: Experimentals, 1,802; controls, 1,621.

TARGET POPULATION: AFDC applicants with children ages 3 or older.

NUMBER OF TREATMENT GROUPS: Two (with one control group).

NUMBER AND LOCATION OF SITES: Each of the Washington State Department of Social and Health Services' Community Service Offices (CSOs) was paired with another that was as similar as possible in terms of a number of variables (population, size, cost of living). A table of random numbers was used to determine which member of each pair became a experimental CSO and which became a control CSO. There were 20 experimental CSOs, 18 of which had a matched-comparison CSO.

RESEARCH COMPONENTS:
- Process analysis: Analysis of population data was used to examine project operations and applicant participation.

- Impact analysis: Comparison of means.
- Benefit–cost analysis: A cost-effectiveness analysis was conducted.

MAJOR FINDINGS:

1. The program appeared to serve as a disincentive to applying for AFDC. The rate of growth in AFDC applications was three times lower in experimental areas than in control areas. The program also reduced the proportion of applicants who received AFDC grants. The difference was most pronounced in the first months after application, but persisted until at least the 10th month.
2. Average grants for nonexempt applicants were reduced by $142.10 per application annually. As a result, annual AFDC grant expenditures were $2.6 million lower than without the program.
3. Rates of employment and average earnings per applicant, as measured from unemployment compensation accounts, were not affected by the program.
4. After subtracting program costs, net annual program savings were $1.7 million. This is a return of $2.77 for each dollar spent.

TIME TRENDS IN FINDINGS: The program's effect on the proportion of applicants who received AFDC was greatest in the first month following application and was dissipating by the 10th month.

DESIGN ISSUES: The project report presented no information regarding the statistical significance of the findings or the use of statistical techniques that might have compensated for any initial differences between matched sites. This makes interpretation of the findings difficult.

REPLICABILITY: Replicable.

GENERALIZABILITY: Designed to generalize to the entire state of Washington. There are no obvious limitations on generalizability to this population.

FUNDING SOURCE: Washington State Department of Social and Health Services (DSHS), Division of Administration and Personnel, Office of Research and Data Analysis.

TREATMENT ADMINISTRATOR: Washington State DSHS.

EVALUATOR: Fred P. Fiedler, DSHS, Office of Research and Data Analysis.

ENABLING LEGISLATION: None.

INFORMATION SOURCE: Fred P. Fiedler, *Intensive Applicant Employment Services Evaluation,* Washington State Department of Social and Health Services, Division of Administration and Personnel, Olympia, July 1983.

PUBLIC-USE ACCESS TO DATA: Not available.

West Virginia Community Work Experience Demonstration

SUMMARY: This demonstration, conducted from 1983 to 1986, tested the effects of mandatory work experience on a large sample of AFDC recipients. Subjects were followed for two years.

COST: This was one of 10 State Welfare-to-Work Initiatives, which had a combined research cost of $7.9 million. Operating cost was $277 per experimental, or about $513,000 total.

TIME FRAME: Demonstration period, July 1983– April 1984; data collected through January 1986; final report, September 1986.

TREATMENTS TESTED: Experimentals participated in mandatory Workfare in return for AFDC benefits, with no time limit on the obligation. Controls were excluded from the Workfare program.

OUTCOMES OF INTEREST: (1) Level of participation; (2) Earnings; and (3) AFDC recipiency and payments.

SAMPLE SIZE: Experimentals, 1,853; controls, 1,841.

TARGET POPULATION: All female WIN-mandatory AFDC recipients and both new registrants and prior registrants. As elsewhere, this excludes parents of children under age six. Also excluded were recipients already enrolled in full-time school or training, people who were already employed, and WIN volunteers.

NUMBER OF TREATMENT GROUPS: Two (with one control group).

NUMBER AND LOCATION OF SITES: Twenty-one counties in West Virginia.

RESEARCH COMPONENTS:
- Process analysis: Conducted. Major emphasis on clients' attitudes toward jobs and supervisors' attitudes toward clients.
- Impact analysis: Conducted with ordinary least squares (OLS) regressions.
- Benefit–cost analysis: Conducted.

MAJOR FINDINGS:
1. Negligible effect on earnings.
2. Small reductions in transfer payments.
3. Net social benefit of the program was positive, because the cost of running it is small and the output of experimentals was large. (In fact, the productivity of experimentals was rated slightly higher than that of regular employees.)

TIME TRENDS IN FINDINGS: Participation rates were higher in the first six months.

DESIGN ISSUES:
1. The possible differential bias from experimentals migrating out of state to avoid the Workfare obligation while controls remain in-state is not addressed.
2. The difficulty (or lack thereof) of job finding or creation or both is not addressed in the report.
3. West Virginia had a high unemployment rate, which may affect the findings and might imply a displacement effect.
4. Sanctions for refusal to participate in Workfare were rare.
5. Valuation of program output may be problematic.

REPLICABILITY: Replicable.

GENERALIZABILITY: The West Virginia AFDC population is not representative of the U.S. AFDC population as a whole, nor was its level of unemployment. Also, the state's fiscal distress results in a large number of readily identified community needs for which Workfare is not only appropriate but also the only affordable source of labor that can meet them.

FUNDING SOURCES: The Ford Foundation, the U.S. Department of Health and Human Services, West Virginia State Department of Human Services, and the Claude Worthington Benedum Foundation.

TREATMENT ADMINISTRATOR: West Virginia Department of Human Services.

EVALUATOR: Manpower Demonstration Research Corporation. Key personnel: Joseph Ball and Daniel Friedlander.

ENABLING LEGISLATION: Omnibus Budget Reconciliation Act of 1981.

INFORMATION SOURCES: Daniel Friedlander, Marjorie Erickson, Gayle Hamilton, and Virginia Knox, *West Virginia: Final Report on the Community Work Experience Demonstrations*, Manpower Demonstration Research Corporation, September 1986; Joseph Ball with Gayle Hamilton, Gregory Hoerz, Barbara S. Goldman, and Judith M. Gueron, *West Virginia: Interim Findings on the Community Work Experience Demonstrations*, Manpower Demonstration Research Corporation, November 1984.

PUBLIC-USE ACCESS TO DATA: Public-use access does not exist.

West Virginia Community Work Experience Program (CWEP)

SUMMARY: This quasi-experimental demonstration, conducted from 1983 through 1986, tested the effects of saturation community work experience on a large sample of AFDC-U recipients (unemployed heads of two-parent families). Subjects were followed for two years.

COST: Operating cost figures are not available. This was one of 10 State Welfare-to-Work Initiatives, which had a combined research cost of $7.9 million.

TIME FRAME: Intake period, March 1983–April 1984; data collected, January 1986; final report, September 1986.

TREATMENTS TESTED: The effects of creating and filling as many Community Work Experience Program (CWEP) positions as possible (the saturation areas) versus limiting CWEP participation to 40 percent of the caseload (the comparison areas). The CWEP program consists of mandatory "workfare" in return for AFDC benefits.

OUTCOMES OF INTEREST: (1) Participation levels; (2) Employment; (3) Earnings; and (4) Welfare receipt.

SAMPLE SIZE: AFDC-U registrants in saturation areas, 2,798; AFDC-U registrants in comparison areas, 2,832.

TARGET POPULATION: All new and existing AFDC-U applicants; 93 percent of this sample was male.

NUMBER OF TREATMENT GROUPS: Two, those in saturation areas and those in comparison areas.

NUMBER AND LOCATION OF SITES: Eight—Four pairs of sites were matched, then randomly assigned to either the saturation condition or the comparison condition. The saturation sites were Huntington, Martinsburg, Parkersburg, and Princeton. The comparison sites were Clarksburg, Fairmont, Fayetteville, and Grafton.

RESEARCH COMPONENTS:
- Process analysis: Researchers reviewed with caseworkers the situation of each nonparticipating AFDC-U recipient in the saturation areas to determine why these men were not participating.
- Impact analysis: Conducted using OLS regressions, two-tailed.
- Benefit–cost analysis: Conducted.

MAJOR FINDINGS:
1. AFDC-U caseload participation rates for the saturation areas as a whole peaked at 69 percent in June 1983. This is the percentage of registrants in the caseload each month who held CWEP jobs during that month. As planned, participation rates for the comparison areas peaked at 40 percent in July 1983. The Parkersburg area achieved the highest caseload participation rate—81 percent in August 1983. In all study areas, rates began to decline in the fall of 1983 as the size of caseloads increased. During most months for which rates were calculated, the difference between rates for saturation and comparison sites was about 30 percentage points.
2. Employment rates for the saturation areas remained roughly the same throughout the follow-up, with no statistically significant differences in any quarter. Earnings decreased slightly for the saturation members, averaging $2,582 from quarters two through six, compared with $2,785 for the comparison members. Whereas significant differences were found in two quarters, these total figures are not statistically significant.
3. AFDC-Us in the saturation areas received, on average, significantly less welfare benefits than did those in the comparison areas. In the saturation areas, 89.5 percent had received at least some payments in quarters two through seven versus 91 percent in the comparison areas. Average total AFDC payments received in the saturation areas were $1,915.87 versus $2,144.76 in the comparison areas.

TIME TRENDS IN FINDINGS: Participation rates declined, as noted above.

DESIGN ISSUES:
1. Despite careful matching of the saturation and comparison sites, they differed on certain key factors. Although the analysis used techniques

to statistically adjust for differences in the demographic and economic characteristics of the areas, the observed differences in outcomes may still partly reflect differences in the characteristics of the areas.

2. The quality of employment and earnings data probably differed in the saturation and comparison areas. For example, the UI earnings records that were relied upon in the evaluation do not contain information on individuals working out of state. All four saturation sites bordered on other states, whereas only two comparison sites were on borders.

REPLICABILITY: Replicable.

GENERALIZABILITY: Designed to generalize to the entire state. The West Virginia AFDC population likely faces greater barriers to employment than the population in most parts of the nation. Unemployment rates in the study areas were very high (up to 30 percent) during this demonstration.

FUNDING SOURCES: West Virginia Department of Human Services, the Ford Foundation, and the Claude Worthington Benedum Foundation.

TREATMENT ADMINISTRATOR: West Virginia Department of Human Services.

EVALUATOR: Manpower Demonstration Research Corporation (MDRC). Principal investigator: Joseph Ball. Other key personnel: Daniel Friedlander, Marjorie Erickson, Gayle Hamilton, and Virginia Knox.

ENABLING LEGISLATION: Omnibus Budget Reconciliation Act of 1981.

INFORMATION SOURCE: Daniel Friedlander, Marjorie Erickson, Gayle Hamilton, and Virginia Knox, *West Virginia: Final Report on the Community Work Experience Demonstration,* Manpower Demonstration Research Corporation, September 1986.

PUBLIC-USE ACCESS TO DATA: Not available.

Baltimore Options Program (Maryland Employment Initiatives)

SUMMARY: This demonstration, conducted from 1982 to 1985, tested the effects of education, training, job search, and work experience on a large sample of AFDC recipients. Subjects were followed for two years.

COST: $1,000 per experimental for the program costs, or $1.4 million total. This was one of 10 State Welfare-to-Work Initiatives, which had a combined research cost of $7.9 million.

TIME FRAME: Demonstration period, November 1982–December 1983; data collected, November 1982–March 1985; final report, December 1985.

TREATMENTS TESTED:

1. The experimental treatment consisted of a packet of options to enhance the employability of the subject, depending on her own perceived needs. The options included training programs, general equivalency diploma (GED) tutoring, job search (both group and individual), and work experience with on-the-job training funded in part by diversion of the AFDC grant.
2. Controls received regular WIN services. In fact, few of them received any formal services.

OUTCOMES OF INTEREST: (1) Employment; (2) Earnings; and (3) Welfare receipt.

SAMPLE SIZE: Experimentals, 1,362; controls, 1,395.

TARGET POPULATION: New WIN mandatories (mostly AFDC recipients with no children under 6 years old) and new applicants for AFDC who were in WIN-mandatory categories.

NUMBER OF TREATMENT GROUPS: Two (with one control group).

NUMBER AND LOCATION OF SITES: One—Baltimore County, Maryland.

RESEARCH COMPONENTS:

▪ Process analysis: Conducted. Operation of the program components is extensively reported.

▪ Impact analysis: Used ordinary least squares (OLS) regressions.

▪ Benefit–cost analysis: Conducted from taxpayer, recipient, and social perspectives.

MAJOR FINDINGS:

1. Average earnings per control for the three-year follow-up were $6,595, compared with $7,638 per experimental. The 16 percent difference is statistically significant.

2. The experimental treatment produced persistent increases in earnings for sample members who lacked recent work experience (over half the sample).

3. The earnings gains of experimentals were not accompanied by aggregate reductions in welfare incidence or grant expenditures.

4. From a budgetary perspective, the experimental treatment cost more than it saved in AFDC payments.

TIME TRENDS IN FINDINGS: Employment impacts declined slightly over time; earnings impacts increased slightly. Insignificance of treatment for welfare receipt was lasting.

DESIGN ISSUES:

1. The Baltimore Job Training Partnership Act agency "is nationally recognized and locally influential . . . and had lobbied vigorously to run the new Options program" (Friedlander et al. 1985). Thus, there is a possible site self-selection bias.

2. The authors suggested several reasons for the paradox of higher earnings without lower benefits. First, Baltimore was somewhat more generous than other areas in counting work-related expenses. Second, some of the differential occurred among individuals who would have moved off welfare in any case. Third, information about earnings was often not communicated to the income maintenance workers either by the Options staff or by the recipients.

REPLICABILITY: Package of options is replicable.

GENERALIZABILITY: There is no obvious limitation on the generalizability of the demonstration.

FUNDING SOURCES: U.S. Department of Health and Human Services and Ford Foundation. Key personnel: Howard Rolston for HHS, and Gordon Berlin and Prudence Brown for Ford.

TREATMENT ADMINISTRATOR: Maryland Department of Human Resources. Key personnel: Alvin Truesdale.

EVALUATOR: Manpower Demonstration Research Corporation. Key personnel: Daniel Friedlander.

ENABLING LEGISLATION: Omnibus Budget Reconciliation Act (OBRA) of 1981.

POLICY EFFECTS: Reports on the State Welfare-to-Work Initiatives were frequently cited in Congress during the framing of the Family Support Act (FSA) of 1988.

INFORMATION SOURCES: Daniel Friedlander, Gregory Hoerz, David A. Long, and Janet Quint, *Maryland: Final Report on the Employment Initiatives Evaluation,* Manpower Demonstration Research Corporation, December 1985.

Daniel Friedlander, *Maryland: Supplemental Report on the Baltimore Options Program,* Manpower Demonstration Research Corporation, October 1987.

Janet Quint with Joseph Ball, Barbara S. Goldman, Judith M. Gueron, and Gayle Hamilton, *Interim Findings from the Maryland Employment Initiatives Program,* Manpower Demonstration Research Corporation, February 1984.

Maryland Department of Human Resources, *Final Evaluation of Maryland's Grant Diversion/ OJT Demonstration Program,* Office of Welfare Employment Policy, August 28, 1987.

PUBLIC-USE ACCESS TO DATA: Public-use file exists; contact MDRC about *Welfare Employment Studies* 1 through 4.

San Diego Job Search and Work Experience Demonstration

SUMMARY: This demonstration, conducted from 1982 to 1985, tested the effects of mandatory job placement assistance and work experience on a large sample of AFDC recipients. Subjects were followed for two years.

COST: This was one of 10 State Welfare-to-Work Initiatives, which had a combined research cost of $7.9 million. For the second treatment, administrative costs of $636–$727 per experimental; for the first treatment, $562–$587 per experimental, or about $2.8 million total (1983).

TIME FRAME: Demonstration period, October 1982–August 1983; data collected through March 1985; final report, February 1986.

TREATMENTS TESTED: Random assignment occurred at the time of application for AFDC. Impacts per applicant therefore include those who were found ineligible for AFDC (and were therefore ineligible for programs).

1. Experimental group 1 received job placement assistance on day of AFDC application, followed by three weeks of Job Club.
2. Experimental group 2 received the same treatment as group 1, but if still unemployed at the end of 3 weeks, required to hold an unpaid work experience job at a public or nonprofit agency for up to 13 weeks. The hours of unpaid work were set by the family's welfare grant divided by the minimum wage.
3. Controls received minimal WIN services.

OUTCOMES OF INTEREST: (1) Employment; (2) Earnings; and (3) AFDC recipiency and payments.

SAMPLE SIZE: AFDC-R: group 1, 856; group 2, 1,502; controls, 873. AFDC-U: group 1, 831; group 2, 1,376; group 3, 813.

TARGET POPULATION: AFDC-R and AFDC-U applicants who were WIN-mandatory. Refugees, people with language barriers, and applicants with children under age 6 were excluded.

NUMBER OF TREATMENT GROUPS: Three (with one control group).

NUMBER AND LOCATION OF SITES: San Diego County, California, countywide.

RESEARCH COMPONENTS:
- Process analysis: Conducted.
- Impact analysis: Conducted with ordinary least squares (OLS) regressions.
- Benefit–cost analysis: Conducted.

MAJOR FINDINGS:
1. Work experience supervisors found the productivity of their assigned subjects roughly comparable to those of regular entry-level employees.
2. Sanctions were applied to 4–8 percent of experimentals, but to 1 percent or less of controls.

Findings for AFDC-Regular

1. Both experimental groups had significantly higher rates of employment (61 percent to 55 percent) over six quarters than the controls, but the group 1 (no Workfare) differential faded to insignificance after the third quarter.
2. The Workfare group had $700 more in earnings per subject over six quarters than the control; the non-Workfare group had $251 more in earnings, but this was not significant.
3. Neither treatment had much effect on AFDC recipiency.
4. Over six quarters, the AFDC payments per Workfare experimental were $288 less than those per control; payments to Job-Club-only experimentals were $203 less than those per control, but this difference was not significant.
5. Program gains were largest among those in the sample who had no previous employment experience.

Findings for AFDC-U

1. "For both program models, there were statistically significant and substantial reductions in welfare payments, but no significant impacts on the employment and earnings of AFDC-U

applicants." The Workfare subjects received on average $530 less in AFDC payments over six quarters than did controls; the job-search-only subjects received $470 less.

2. "Sanctioning rates were higher for experimentals than for controls, and those sanctioned faced larger grant reductions than did AFDC's (regulars)."

3. "In general, mandating [Workfare] for AFDC-U's did not improve program outcomes compared to those found for the Job Search program." The benefit–cost analysis findings are that there were consistent, large net gains to taxpayers and government budgets for both programs and for both applicant groups. AFDC-R applicants also benefited financially from the Workfare treatment; the job-search-only treatment did not always have positive benefits. AFDC-U applicants were made worse off by the treatments, because they reduced their benefits without increasing their earnings.

TIME TRENDS IN FINDINGS: AFDC-R welfare savings from the Workfare treatment declined over time. AFDC-U welfare savings from the two treatments seem to decline gradually over time.

DESIGN ISSUES:

1. Site self-selection. Workfare was not politically acceptable everywhere.

2. The San Diego job market tightened over the course of the experiment. This affected the applicant mix. The study attempts to compare earlier cohorts with later cohorts to examine this.

3. The work experience programs seem to have been unusually well run, without any sense of make-work or strong client resentment detected in the process analysis. It is not clear that other counties could replicate that success.

REPLICABILITY: Replicable, but see above.

GENERALIZABILITY: Generalization to the full AFDC population tested in the Saturation Work Initiative Model (SWIM) experiment.

FUNDING SOURCES: U.S. Department of Health and Human Services, Ford Foundation, and the State of California. Key personnel: Howard Rolston for HHS, Gordon Berlin and Prudence Brown for Ford, and Virginia Hamilton for California.

TREATMENT ADMINISTRATOR: State Employment Service Agency and the County Welfare Department. Key personnel: Ray Koenig and Joan Zinser.

EVALUATOR: Manpower Demonstration Research Corporation. Key personnel: Barbara S. Goldman.

ENABLING LEGISLATION: Omnibus Budget Reconciliation Act (OBRA) of 1981.

POLICY EFFECTS: Reports on the State Welfare-to-Work Initiatives were frequently cited in Congress during the framing of the Family Support Act (FSA) of 1988. This demonstration also led to the SWIM experiment.

INFORMATION SOURCE: Barbara S. Goldman, Daniel Friedlander, and David A. Long, *California: Final Report on the San Diego Job Search and Work Experience Demonstration,* Manpower Demonstration Research Corporation, February 1986.

PUBLIC-USE ACCESS TO DATA: Public-use access does not exist.

Washington Community Work Experience Program

SUMMARY: This demonstration, conducted from 1982 to 1983, tested the effects of work experience and job search assistance on a small sample of AFDC recipients. Subjects were followed for one year.

COST: Administrative cost, $85,565 (1982).

TIME FRAME: Demonstration period, October 1982–May 1983; data collected through August 1983; final report, June 1984.

TREATMENTS TESTED:

1. Community Work Experience Program (CWEP): Workfare placement with public or nonprofit agencies for four months. Child care and transportation reimbursement were provided. "Persons assigned to CWEP who refused to work were counseled by the CWEP coordinator and if a reasonable settlement was not achieved, these persons could be sanctioned. The sanction discontinued the client's portion of support from her grant for three months" (Nelson 1984).
2. Employment and training (E&T): A Job-Club-based model, with three or four days of group job preparation, followed by five or six days in a phone lab, followed by individual job search.
3. Controls: No treatment. Presumably eligible for some WIN services.

OUTCOMES OF INTEREST: (1) Employment and (2) AFDC case closures and savings.

SAMPLE SIZE: CWEP, 64; E&T, 66; controls, 42.

TARGET POPULATION: WIN-mandatory AFDC recipients. Exclusions for those deemed more or less unemployable.

NUMBER OF TREATMENT GROUPS: Three (with one control group).

NUMBER AND LOCATION OF SITES: Two—Spokane County and Pierce County (which includes Tacoma), Washington.

RESEARCH COMPONENTS:
- Process analysis: Not conducted.
- Impact analysis: Comparison of means. No tests of statistical significance.
- Benefit–cost analysis: Budgetary perspective only.

MAJOR FINDINGS:

1. Thirty percent of CWEP clients found unsubsidized employment after participating in it, as did 39 percent of E&T clients; 14 percent of controls "were employed at some time during the one-year study period."

2. The author found evidence that CWEP was more useful than E&T to clients with less than a high school education.
3. Program expenditures exceeded AFDC payment reductions during the study year.

TIME TRENDS IN FINDINGS: Only one year of data.

DESIGN ISSUES:

1. The sample sizes, which are substantially smaller than planned in the research design, are too small for useful analysis. Sample sizes were kept low by failure of the welfare staff to refer clients to WIN (which is run by Employment Security, a separate agency) and by discretionary removal of 63 clients from the experimental samples, either by the program staff or the evaluators. The discretionary removal of 37 percent of the sample appears to open the door to selection bias by either the clients themselves or others. Much of this was caused by reliance on client follow-up interviews as the primary data source on outcomes.
2. No follow-up interviews were conducted with controls, so the data sources used for experimentals and controls do not match. In fact, it is not clear what data source was used for controls.

REPLICABILITY: Replicable.

GENERALIZABILITY: None. Sample is too small.

FUNDING SOURCES: U.S. Department of Health and Human Services, Social Security Administration.

TREATMENT ADMINISTRATOR: Washington Department of Social and Health Services. Key personnel: Gladys McCorkhill and Judith Merchant.

EVALUATOR: Washington Department of Social and Health Services, Office of Research and Data Analysis. Key personnel: Hal Nelson.

ENABLING LEGISLATION: Omnibus Budget Reconciliation Act (OBRA) of 1981.

INFORMATION SOURCE: Hal Nelson, *Evaluation of the Community Work Experience Program,* Washington Department of Social and Health Services,

Division of Administration and Personnel, Office of Research and Data Analysis, Program Research and Evaluation Section, Report #06-23, June 1984.

PUBLIC-USE ACCESS TO DATA: We have no information about a public-use file for this demonstration.

Arkansas Work Program

SUMMARY: This demonstration, conducted from 1983 to 1985, tested the effects of mandatory job search and work experience on a medium-sized sample of AFDC recipients. Subjects were followed for one year.

COST: This was one of 10 State Welfare-to-Work Initiatives, which had a combined research cost of $7.9 million. Administrative cost of $158 per experimental, or about $92,000 total.

TIME FRAME: Demonstration period, June 1983–March 1984; data collected through January 1985; final report, September 1985.

TREATMENTS TESTED:
1. Experimentals received a fixed sequence of services, beginning with group job search (Job Club model), followed by individual job search, followed by work experience (i.e., Workfare). Few people ever participated in work experience, which was limited to 12 weeks and 20 to 30 hours per week. The most job-ready individuals could skip the Job Club.
2. Controls received virtually no services.

OUTCOMES OF INTEREST: (1) Levels of program participation; (2) Employment; (3) Earnings; (4) Welfare receipt; and (5) Welfare payments.

SAMPLE SIZE: Experimentals, 583; controls, 570.

TARGET POPULATION: AFDC applicants and WIN-mandatory recipients. This included recipients with children between ages 3 and 6, but in practice those with severe employment barriers were excluded from the research sample.

NUMBER OF TREATMENT GROUPS: Two (with one control group).

NUMBER AND LOCATION OF SITES: Two—Pulaski County (Little Rock) and Jefferson County (Pine Bluff), Arkansas.

RESEARCH COMPONENTS:
- Process analysis: Conducted with emphasis on program participation.
- Impact analysis: Conducted with ordinary least squares (OLS) regressions.
- Benefit–cost analysis: Conducted from taxpayer, recipient, and social perspectives.

MAJOR FINDINGS:
1. Thirty-eight percent of the experimentals actually participated in at least one part of the program; 5 percent were sanctioned.
2. Employment rates increased by about 5 percentage points.
3. Earnings also improved.
4. There were substantial reductions in the incidence of welfare and in the amounts of welfare received. For example, in the third and last follow-up quarter, welfare payments were reduced by about 15 percent.
5. The program resulted in modest positive net benefits from the social, budgetary, and taxpayer perspectives. There were net losses from the recipient perspective. Budgetary expenditures in running the program were small (about $250 per participant).

TIME TRENDS IN FINDINGS: Short follow-up.

DESIGN ISSUES:
1. A high priority was placed on treating the most job-ready clients first. With less "creaming," the apparent effectiveness of the program might be lower.
2. It is not clear that the Workfare program can be expanded to treat the entire population.
3. As with most employment programs, private-sector displacement bias is a possibility.
4. Local staff were given considerable discretion to give participation exemptions and to decide

which recipients were suitable for which components.

5. Staff turnover in Jefferson County probably reduced the treatment impact, because the Job Club component was less well run.

REPLICABILITY: Replicable.

GENERALIZABILITY: This experiment can be compared to the Job Club experiments, which generally found larger effects. The level of unemployment was high in both counties: 7.7 percent in Pulaski and 10.5 percent in Jefferson.

FUNDING SOURCES: U.S. Department of Health and Human Services, Ford Foundation, the State of Arkansas, and Winthrop Rockefeller Foundation. Key personnel: Howard Rolston for HHS, and Gordon Berlin and Prudence Brown for Ford.

TREATMENT ADMINISTRATOR: Arkansas Department of Human Services. Key personnel: Jerry Evans.

EVALUATOR: Manpower Demonstration Research Corporation. Key personnel: Daniel Friedlander.

ENABLING LEGISLATION: Omnibus Budget Reconciliation Act (OBRA) of 1981. A special federal waiver was obtained to mandate WIN status for some parents of children between the ages of 3 and 6.

POLICY EFFECTS: Reports on the State Welfare-to-Work Initiatives were frequently cited in Congress during the framing of the Family Support Act (FSA) of 1988.

INFORMATION SOURCE: Daniel Friedlander, Gregory Hoerz, Janet Quint, and James Riccio, *Final Report on the WORK Program in Two Counties,* Manpower Demonstration Research Corporation, September 1985.

PUBLIC-USE ACCESS TO DATA: Public-use file exists; contact MDRC about *Welfare Employment Studies* 1 through 4.

Maine Training Opportunities in the Private Sector (TOPS)

SUMMARY: This demonstration, conducted from 1983 to 1987, tested the effects of vocational training and work experience on a medium-sized sample of unemployed single AFDC recipients. Subjects were followed for two years.

COST: This was one of 10 State Welfare-to-Work Initiatives, which had a combined research cost of $7.9 million. Operating cost was about $2,600 per experimental, or $770,000 total.

TIME FRAME: Demonstration period, October 1983–June 1985; data collected, October 1983–September 1987; final report, April 1988.

TREATMENTS TESTED: Experimentals received the following prescribed treatment sequence: Prevocational training lasted two to five weeks, stressing personal growth and job-seeking and job-holding skills. Work experience consisted of 20 hours per week of unpaid work in public or nonprofit sectors for up to 12 weeks. Those who demonstrated motivation and skills acquisition were eligible for on-the-job training (OJT) positions, preferably in the private sector. The training period was limited to a maximum of six months, and the employer subsidy was set at 50 percent of wages; the subsidy was funded by grant diversion. Controls could receive other WIN services from the treatment administrator.

OUTCOMES OF INTEREST: (1) Earnings; (2) Employment; and (3) AFDC payments.

SAMPLE SIZE: Experimentals, 297; controls, 147.

TARGET POPULATION: The experiment was open only to AFDC recipients who applied. Applicants who met the program criteria were then randomly assigned an experimental or a control status. Applicants had to meet the following criteria: (1) single heads of households, (2) AFDC recipients for at least six months, (3) not currently employed, and (4) able to read at the level of the materials used in prevocational training. In addition, the intake staff used their discretion to screen out women who had (a) child care, transportation, health, or other problems that could interfere with participation, (b) low motivation, or (c) unrealistic ambitions. About 3 out of 10 applicants were considered inappropriate and were screened out prior to random assignment.

NUMBER OF TREATMENT GROUPS: Two (with one control group).

NUMBER AND LOCATION OF SITES: Statewide.

RESEARCH COMPONENTS:
- Process analysis: Conducted.
- Impact analysis: Conducted as a difference in regression-adjusted means.
- Benefit–cost analysis: Conducted.

MAJOR FINDINGS:
1. TOPS had sustained positive impacts on earnings over the entire follow-up period (second through 11th quarters). Experimentals had earnings of $7,344 on average, controls had $5,599 average earnings, and the difference is statistically significant. However, differences in employment, AFDC recipiency, and AFDC payments were in general insignificant.
2. The project report authors speculated that the discrepancy between the earnings increase and the nonreduction in AFDC payments may be the result of three factors: (1) relatively generous allowances for work-related expenses; (2) substantial numbers of participants were already working—thus, at some point their earnings exceeded the AFDC break-even level and further earnings would not result in further benefit reductions; and (3) experimentals were trained in how to become "your own best advocate" within the welfare system.
3. Because there were no AFDC payment reductions, there was no positive budgetary impact. However, TOPS raised the income of experimentals about $3,000 each at a cost of about $1,100. "TOPS can be viewed as a much more efficient means of transferring income to

this group than simply raising their AFDC benefits."

TIME TRENDS IN FINDINGS: The earnings effect grew stronger over time.

DESIGN ISSUES: A high degree of selectivity in the initial screening of the research sample makes it difficult to generalize the results.

REPLICABILITY: Replicable.

GENERALIZABILITY: The Maine AFDC population is unrepresentative of the U.S. AFDC population as a whole. It is mostly white, and historically many recipients worked, often full-time. A well-run OJT program funded by grant diversion in a state with low unemployment could be an effective but very limited part of the overall welfare strategy in other states as well.

FUNDING SOURCES: U.S. Department of Health and Human Services and Ford Foundation. Key personnel: Howard Rolston for HHS, and Gordon Berlin and Prudence Brown for Ford.

TREATMENT ADMINISTRATOR: Maine Department of Human Services. Key personnel: Tomie McLean.

EVALUATOR: Manpower Demonstration Research Corporation. Key personnel: Patricia Auspos.

ENABLING LEGISLATION: Omnibus Budget Reconciliation Act (OBRA) of 1981.

POLICY EFFECTS: Reports on the State Welfare-to-Work Initiatives were frequently cited in Congress during the framing of the Family Support Act (FSA) of 1988.

INFORMATION SOURCE: Patricia Auspos, George Cave, and David A. Long, *Maine: Final Report on the Training Opportunities in the Private Sector Program,* Manpower Demonstration Research Corporation, April 1988.

PUBLIC-USE ACCESS TO DATA: Public-use access does not exist.

Virginia Employment Services Program (ESP)

SUMMARY: This demonstration, conducted from 1983 to 1985, tested the effects of mandatory job search and work experience on a large sample of AFDC recipients. Subjects were followed for one year.

COST: This was one of 10 State Welfare-to-Work Initiatives, which had a combined research cost of $7.9 million. Administrative cost of $388 per experimental, or about $920,000 total (1984).

TIME FRAME: Demonstration period, August 1983–September 1984; data collected through August 1985; final report, August 1986.

TREATMENTS TESTED:

1. Job search/work experience. Participants were required to provide proof of three contacts with potential employers. If these contacts were unsuccessful, participants were then offered job search assistance, either individual or group, and community work experience, but in practice these were not mandatory. Group job search did not include a telephone bank for supervised employer contacts.
2. All Employment Services Program (ESP) services. In addition to the above treatment, it was intended that these experimentals would have available greater education or training options. In fact, there were no additional resources for education or training for this group, so there was no separate treatment.
3. Controls were not subject to either treatment.

OUTCOMES OF INTEREST: (1) Participation in services; (2) Employment; (3) Earnings; and (4) AFDC recipiency and payments.

SAMPLE SIZE: Job search/work experience, 1,061; all ESP services, 1,077; controls, 1,046.

TARGET POPULATION: WIN-mandatory female clients who did not fall into the following excluded categories: parents of children under 6, those already in education or training programs, WIN volunteers, and those already assigned to nonexperimental treatment.

NUMBER OF TREATMENT GROUPS: Three (with one control group).

NUMBER AND LOCATION OF SITES: Eleven Virginia counties—Campbell, Carroll, Chesapeake, Fairfax, Galax, Grayson, Hampton, Henry, Martinsville, Newport News, and Pittsylvania.

RESEARCH COMPONENTS:
- Process analysis: Conducted. Emphasis on what treatments were actually received.
- Impact analysis: Conducted with ordinary least squares (OLS) regressions.
- Benefit–cost analysis: Conducted.

MAJOR FINDINGS:

Because treatments in the two experimental groups did not in fact differ, findings reported concentrate on differences between experimentals and controls.

Outcome	Experimentals	Controls
Ever employed, second to fourth quarters after random assignment	43.8%	40.5%
Average total earnings, those quarters	$1,119	$1,038
Received any AFDC payment, those quarters	86.0%	86.1%
Total payments received, including quarter of assignment	$1,923	$2,007

Note: Differences are significant in the first and fourth rows.

Differences were larger in urban than in rural areas, although sample sizes in rural areas would make it difficult to find an impact. The project report authors found increasing, long-term employment gains among applicants and short-term, temporary welfare savings among recipients.

From the subjects' perspective, the treatment resulted in income gains. From the perspective of government budgets, the treatment produced net positive benefits within five years for applicants; costs and benefits were roughly equal for recipients.

TIME TRENDS IN FINDINGS: Employment gains from the treatment among applicants were concentrated in later periods.

DESIGN ISSUES:
1. An element of site self-selection may bias the findings.
2. Treatments varied across sites, and it is impossible to determine whether this caused the impacts to vary as well.
3. The project report authors noted that Virginia is a relatively low-benefit state and that employable individuals would be less attracted to AFDC than would be the case in higher-benefit states.
4. Virginia also has a highly decentralized welfare system. Treatment-standardization problems encountered in this experiment would be characteristic of policy-implementation problems in decentralized systems.
5. It is not clear why this treatment should be producing long-term rather than short-term employment gains. Benefit–cost analysis based on projections to 5 years from 18 months of data may not be robust.

REPLICABILITY: Replicable.

GENERALIZABILITY: Doubtful; see "Design Issues."

FUNDING SOURCES: U.S. Department of Health and Human Services and Ford Foundation. Key personnel: Howard Rolston for HHS, and Gordon Berlin and Prudence Brown for Ford.

TREATMENT ADMINISTRATOR: Virginia Department of Social Services. Key personnel: Local agency heads listed in report.

EVALUATOR: Manpower Demonstration Research Corporation. Key personnel: James Riccio.

ENABLING LEGISLATION: Omnibus Budget Reconciliation Act (OBRA) of 1981.

POLICY EFFECTS: Reports on the State Welfare-to-Work Initiatives were frequently cited in Congress during the framing of the Family Support Act (FSA) of 1988.

INFORMATION SOURCE: James Riccio, George Cave, Stephen Freedman, and Marilyn Price, *Virginia: Final Report on the Virginia Employment Services Program,* Manpower Demonstration Research Corporation, August 1986.

PUBLIC-USE ACCESS TO DATA: Public-use file exists; contact Manpower Demonstration Research Corporation about *Welfare Employment Studies* 1 through 4.

Florida Trade Welfare for Work

SUMMARY: This demonstration, conducted from 1984 to 1986, tested the effects of subsidized work experience and on-the-job training on a large sample of AFDC recipients. Subjects were followed for one year.

COST: $734,363; research only, $163,191.

TIME FRAME: Demonstration period, July 1984–July 1986; data collected through September 1986; final report, February 1987.

TREATMENTS TESTED: The WIN regime in Florida consisted of a two-week job search in which clients looked for jobs on their own and were expected to complete at least six job applications (clients would be subject to sanctioning if they failed to do so). Those who did not find employment within two weeks were required to attend job clubs. Those who did not find employment within the Job Club time limits were randomly assigned to one of three groups:
1. WIN controls were placed in "extended job search," during which they were expected to fill out six employment applications a month and to address deficiencies in their employability. (In practice, sanctions in all three treatments appear to have been rare.) The usual expenditure subsidies for travel, work clothes, and child care were available. Subsidies could continue for up to three months after employment.

2. JTPA controls were referred to the local Job Training Partnership Act agency. If found "appropriate" for on-the-job training (OJT), they could be placed with a private employer, who would receive a 50 percent subsidy on their wages (always the legal minimum) for a period not to exceed six months. If not found suitable, they were referred back to WIN.

3. TRADE experimentals were also referred to JTPA. If found "appropriate" for OJT, they could be placed with a private employer who received both the 50 percent JTPA subsidy and an additional $1.10 an hour subsidy from diversion of AFDC grants. Thus, an hour's work, at the minimum wage, would cost the employer 58 cents.

OUTCOMES OF INTEREST: (1) Unsubsidized employment; (2) Increase in JTPA placements of AFDC recipients; and (3) AFDC payments.

SAMPLE SIZE: TRADE experimentals, 2,617; JTPA controls, 1,024; WIN controls, 934.

TARGET POPULATION: WIN-mandatory and WIN-voluntary female clients. Usual exemptions for children under 6, illness, or disability.

NUMBER OF TREATMENT GROUPS: Three (with two control groups).

NUMBER AND LOCATION OF SITES: Seventeen of the state's 24 JTPA agencies, covering most of the population of Florida.

RESEARCH COMPONENTS:
- Process analysis: Conducted. Based on staff interviews and a survey questionnaire to subjects and employers.
- Impact analysis: Conducted as a difference in means.
- Benefit–cost analysis: Cost-effectiveness analysis.

MAJOR FINDINGS:
1. The evaluators found statistically significant differences between TRADE and JTPA subjects on the one hand, and WIN controls on the other, in months on AFDC, employment, and earnings. They found no differences between TRADE experimentals and JTPA controls. These findings are all based on extremely small samples (see "Design Issues").

2. Only 9 percent of the TRADE experimentals were actually placed in OJT, compared with 7.5 percent of the JTPAs and 5.8 percent of the WIN controls. One-third of the TRADE placements were without the special $1.10 subsidy. The program goal was OJT placement of one-half of all experimentals.

3. Cost-effectiveness analysis suggests savings from the program, but the analysts themselves say the data are not adequate to support any firm conclusions.

TIME TRENDS IN FINDINGS: Not applicable.

DESIGN ISSUES:
1. Twenty-seven percent of experimentals, 25 percent of JTPA controls, and 23 percent of WIN controls appeared in the Job Training Partnership Act (JTPA) information system. The implication for the first two groups is that the majority of "clients were never referred to the SDAs [JTPA agencies], were referred but did not go, or were referred but were not registered." The WIN controls should not have appeared in the system. The implication of their appearance there is that "participants went to the SDAs on their own, or were inappropriately referred to them." Breakdown of WIN supervision and/or the random assignment system appears very likely, especially since some WIN personnel with TRADE responsibilities reported that they had received no training or direction in the program.

2. The Department of Health and Rehabilitative Services (DHRS) information system on the subjects of the experiment could not be used "due to the lack of accurate and available data in the system on key indicators."

3. For some reason, which the report does not explain, the evaluators obtained the unemployment insurance and AFDC payment records of only a random sample of subjects, not the entire research sample. "Sufficient information

was available for only 125 TRADE group participants, 99 JTPA group participants, and 126 WIN group participants." The data used came from the routine quality control audit performed on a random sample of the welfare population.

4. The report is quite vague on what difference was supposed to exist between the treatment of JTPA controls by the SDAs and the treatment of TRADE experimentals. The SDA staffs refused to attempt to place people in OJT who were "inappropriate" because they lacked skills, training, or education. But the lack of these attributes was presumably the rationale for the deep wage subsidy. The leading cause for the lack of placements, however, was that the experimentals never showed up at the SDA offices.

5. The report seems to have been hastily assembled.

REPLICABILITY: Not replicable because of the lack of clarity cited in "Design Issues," number 4.

GENERALIZABILITY: Interagency coordination failure severely limits the generalizability of the findings. Other wage subsidy experiments, however, also have found very low employer responsiveness.

FUNDING SOURCE: U.S. Department of Health and Human Services, Office of Family Assistance.

TREATMENT ADMINISTRATORS: Florida DHRS and local JTPA agencies. Key personnel: Jim Clark.

EVALUATOR: The experiment was designed by Manpower Demonstration Research Corporation, which is not associated with the evaluation. The latter was performed by the Florida DHRS, Office of the Inspector General, Office of Evaluation and Management Review. Key personnel: Dawn Case.

ENABLING LEGISLATION: Florida Public Assistance Productivity Act.

INFORMATION SOURCE: Florida Department of Health and Rehabilitative Services, Office of the

Inspector General, Office of Evaluation and Management Review, *Evaluation of the TRADE Welfare for Work Program,* February 1987.

PUBLIC-USE ACCESS TO DATA: Public-use access does not exist.

New Jersey Grant Diversion Project

SUMMARY: This demonstration, conducted from 1984 to 1987, tested the effects of subsidized on-the-job training on a large sample of AFDC recipients. Subjects were followed for one year.

COST: This was one of 10 State Welfare-to-Work Initiatives, which had a combined research cost of $7.9 million. Administrative cost of $921 per experimental, or about $910,000 total.

TIME FRAME: Demonstration period, October 1984–June 1987; data collected through August 1987; final report, November 1988.

TREATMENT TESTED: Experimentals were allowed to volunteer for on-the-job training (OJT) with private-sector employers. Fifty percent of wages were subsidized through diversion of the AFDC grant. Controls were not offered this opportunity, but remained eligible for other WIN services.

OUTCOMES OF INTEREST: (1) Employment; (2) Earnings; and (3) AFDC receipt and payments.

SAMPLE SIZE: Experimentals, 988; controls, 955. Much of the analysis, however, is based on a subsample of 508 experimentals and 488 controls, the "early sample."

TARGET POPULATION: Job-ready, WIN-eligible AFDC recipients.

NUMBER OF TREATMENT GROUPS: Two (with one control group).

NUMBER AND LOCATION OF SITES: Nine—Atlantic, Burlington, Camden, Essex, Hudson, Mercer,

Middlesex, Monmouth, and Passaic counties, which include all the major New Jersey cities.

RESEARCH COMPONENTS:
- Process analysis: Conducted.
- Impact analysis: Conducted with OLS regressions.
- Benefit–cost analysis: Conducted.

MAJOR FINDINGS:

1. "Nearly 43 percent of all experimentals worked at some point in an OJT position." The low rate of placement (200 a year) was attributed to various factors, one of them the high turnover rate among job developers. About half of the placements completed the prescribed subsidy period (averaging 10 weeks), and nearly all of those who completed the subsidy period were retained by the employer without subsidy.

2. The treatment led to substantial employment gains in the first two quarters for experimentals versus controls. The impact essentially vanished by the fourth quarter.

3. The treatment "produced a statistically significant earnings gain of $634 during the first year after random assignment. Average earnings for experimentals were 22 percent higher than average earnings for controls." In combination with the first finding, this suggests that "experimentals worked in jobs that either paid more or provided more hours of employment than the jobs in which controls were employed."

4. "Experimentals spent fewer months on AFDC and received $265 less in welfare payments than controls during the first year after random assignment." The difference is statistically significant.

5. Benefit–cost analysis: "Over a five-year period, enrollees . . . are likely to benefit by an estimated $971 to $1,554 per person. . . . From the perspective of government budgets, the program can be expected to pay for itself within about two and one-half years. Net savings of between $601 and $1,284 are likely over a five-year period" (Freedman et al. 1988).

TIME TRENDS IN FINDINGS: Experimental/control differences in employment were insignificant in the early sample. In quarters five through seven, however, experimentals averaged $468 more in earnings than did controls and $238 less in AFDC payments. This latter difference was declining.

DESIGN ISSUES: The early sample was less disadvantaged than the remaining cohorts, because of improvements in the overall unemployment picture in the state and because Hudson and Middlesex counties, which joined the experiment later than the other seven, had higher numbers of very disadvantaged recipients.

REPLICABILITY: Replicable in principle, but the treatment is complex.

GENERALIZABILITY: A well-run OJT program funded by grant diversion in a state with low unemployment could be an effective but very limited part of the overall welfare strategy in other states as well. WIN registration in the nine counties averaged about 80,000 per month. About 20 OJT placements per month were made.

FUNDING SOURCES: U.S. Department of Health and Human Services and Ford Foundation. Key personnel: Howard Rolston for HHS, and Gordon Berlin and Prudence Brown for Ford.

TREATMENT ADMINISTRATORS: New Jersey Department of Human Services (DHS) and the New Jersey Department of Labor (DOL). Key personnel: Sybil Stokes and Rowena Bopp for DHS, and Sally Hall for state DOL.

EVALUATOR: Manpower Demonstration Research Corporation. Key personnel: Stephen Freedman.

ENABLING LEGISLATION: Omnibus Budget Reconciliation Act (OBRA) of 1981.

POLICY EFFECTS: Reports on the State Welfare-to-Work Initiatives were frequently cited in Congress during the framing of the Family Support Act (FSA) of 1988.

INFORMATION SOURCE: Stephen Freedman, Jan Bryant, and George Cave, *New Jersey: Final*

Report of the Grant Diversion Project, Manpower Demonstration Research Corporation, November 1988.

PUBLIC-USE ACCESS TO DATA: Public-use access does not exist.

SECOND REAGAN ADMINISTRATION

Cook County Job Search and Work Experience

SUMMARY: This demonstration, conducted from 1985 to 1987, tested the effects of mandatory training and work experience on a large sample of AFDC recipients. Subjects were followed for two years.

COST: This was one of 10 State Welfare-to-Work Initiatives, which had a combined research cost of $7.9 million. Estimated incremental operating cost per experimental: Group 1, $157; group 2, $127 (about $636,000 and $515,000 total, respectively).

TIME FRAME: Demonstration period, February 1985–September 1985; data collected, February 1985–March 1987; final report, November 1987.

TREATMENTS TESTED:
1. Experimental group 1 was assigned first to WIN orientation and independent job search (IJS), under which they were expected to contact 20 potential employers a month on their own; progress was monitored in biweekly two-hour group meetings. If unsuccessful in finding work, members were assigned thereafter to any of the other program components: the IWEP (Illinois Work Experience Program, i.e., Workfare), pre-employment (educational- or vocational-skills training programs), or modified job search (a holding status). However, the program staff did not emphasize alternatives other than the IWEP. Program staff were evaluated largely on

the basis of the grant reductions they achieved, and tended to sanction recipients automatically for failure to satisfy program requirements.
2. Experimental group 2 was assigned in the same manner as group 1, except for exclusion from the IWEP.
3. Controls were required to attend orientation (they could be sanctioned for failure to attend), but were eligible thereafter only for support services if they were independently involved in educational or training activities.

OUTCOMES OF INTEREST: (1) Employment; (2) Earnings; and (3) AFDC payments.

SAMPLE SIZE: Group 1, 4,050; group 2, 4,057; controls, 3,805.

TARGET POPULATION: WIN-eligible AFDC recipients (but not AFDC-U recipients).

NUMBER OF TREATMENT GROUPS: Three (with one control group).

NUMBER AND LOCATION OF SITES: One—Cook County, Illinois.

RESEARCH COMPONENTS:
- Process analysis: Conducted.
- Impact analysis: Comparison of means and ordinary least squares (OLS) regressions.
- Benefit–cost analysis: Conducted.

MAJOR FINDINGS:
1. Experimental/control differences in employment and earnings were not statistically significant.
2. Average AFDC payments, six quarters: Group 1, $4,416; group 2, $4,346; controls, $4,486. Differences of $70 and $140, respectively, are statistically significant. According to the project report, "The welfare savings were achieved mainly through closing welfare grants, rather than from reductions in the dollar amounts of grants that remained open. There does not appear to be any clear additional effect from the IWEP component over and above the effect of IJS."

3. "The reduction in AFDC and Medicaid expenditures, combined with the very low cost of the program, led to a net savings for the government. However, the welfare recipients assigned to the program did not benefit financially . . . since the losses in AFDC and Medicaid equaled or exceeded any earnings gains that might have occurred."

4. Among controls, 7.6 percent were sanctioned for failing to attend the WIN orientation. Among experimentals, 11.7 percent had been sanctioned within nine months after intake, either for failing to attend the WIN orientation or for failing to satisfy subsequent program requirements.

5. The project report authors could only speculate about the source of the AFDC savings, since they occurred in the absence of any earnings increase. Staff were more familiar with experimentals' activities and therefore initiated more grant reduction actions because they learned of new employment more quickly. Also, the IJS program required regular attendance at various tasks and may have served as a deterrent to continued recipiency for experimentals with unreported earnings. Controls with unreported earnings had no such deterrent.

TIME TRENDS IN FINDINGS: Group 1 (Workfare) experimentals had higher AFDC payments, a tendency that seemed to grow over time.

DESIGN ISSUES:

1. A sufficiently strong deterrent effect from the treatments might have sent experimentals across state lines, causing a possible attrition bias not addressed here.

2. The higher motivation of the administrative staff to generate AFDC payment savings in this experiment compared with the other experiments is worth noting. It might explain why this experiment detected such savings, whereas many of the others did not.

REPLICABILITY: Replicable.

GENERALIZABILITY: The demonstration took place in two-thirds of the WIN offices of Cook County,

which includes Chicago. This represents a large urban population.

FUNDING SOURCES: Ford Foundation and Illinois Department of Public Aid. Key personnel: Gordon Berlin for Ford.

TREATMENT ADMINISTRATOR: Illinois Department of Public Aid. Key personnel: Randale Valenti.

EVALUATOR: Manpower Demonstration Research Corporation. Key personnel: Daniel Friedlander.

ENABLING LEGISLATION: Omnibus Budget Reconciliation Act (OBRA) of 1981.

POLICY EFFECTS: Illinois subsequently changed the focus of its WIN program from the techniques employed in this experiment to a greater encouragement of education and training and less frequent application of sanctions.

INFORMATION SOURCE: Daniel Friedlander, Stephen Freedman, Gayle Hamilton, and Janet Quint, *Illinois: Final Report on Job Search and Work Experience in Cook County*, Manpower Development Research Corporation, November 1987.

PUBLIC-USE ACCESS TO DATA: Public-use access does not exist.

Saturation Work Initiative Model (SWIM)

SUMMARY: This demonstration, conducted from 1985 to 1988, tested the effects of mandatory job search assistance and work experience on a large sample of AFDC recipients. Subjects were followed for two years.

COST: This was one of 10 State Welfare-to-Work Initiatives, which had a combined research cost of $7.9 million.

TIME FRAME: Demonstration period, July 1985–September 1987; data collected, July 1985–March 1988; final report, November 1989.

TREATMENTS TESTED:

1. Experimentals received a fixed program sequence. They were initially assigned to a two-week job search workshop. Those who had not found jobs at the end of two weeks were assigned to three months of unpaid work experience and biweekly job club sessions. Those still unemployed after completing the work experience assignment were assessed and possibly referred to community education and training programs, which were not part of the experiment proper.
2. Controls received no services from the experimental program.

OUTCOMES OF INTEREST: (1) Employment; (2) Earnings; and (3) Welfare receipt.

SAMPLE SIZE: Experimentals, 1,604; controls, 1,607.

TARGET POPULATION: WIN eligibles (single heads of AFDC households with children age 6 or older, principal earners of two-parent AFDC-U households), both registrants and new applicants.

NUMBER OF TREATMENT GROUPS: Two (with one control group).

NUMBER AND LOCATION OF SITES: One—San Diego, California.

RESEARCH COMPONENTS:
- Process analysis: Conducted.
- Impact analysis: Conducted with ordinary least squares (OLS) regressions.
- Benefit–cost analysis: Conducted.

MAJOR FINDINGS:

1. "For AFDC (regular) registrants, SWIM led to sustained gains in employment and earnings and sustained reductions in welfare receipt and payments. During the 2 years following random assignment, experimentals had average earnings of $4,932 and controls had average earnings of $3,923, for a program effect of $1,009, a 26 percent increase over the control group mean. Over these 2 years, 63 percent of experimentals were employed at some point compared to 51 percent of controls, a 12 percentage point improvement. The data suggest that most of the earnings gains resulted from increased employment among experimentals rather than greater earnings during employment. For AFDC recipients—the more disadvantaged part of the sample—the employment and earnings impacts were strong and sustained; for AFDC applicants, initial employment and earnings gains declined substantially by the end of the follow-up period."
2. "During the follow-up period, experimentals received $8,590 in welfare payments, $1,097 less than the control group mean payments of $9,687, a savings of 11 percent. By the end of the follow-up period, 48 percent of experimentals were receiving welfare payments compared to 55 percent of controls, a 7 percentage point reduction in welfare use. Both applicants and recipients experienced sustained welfare grant reductions."
3. The experimental treatment appeared to raise earnings and lower welfare payments for AFDC-U recipients. However, sample sizes were small.
4. "Net program costs were $919 per AFDC experimental and $817 per AFDC-U experimental. . . . Over the five-year period (which includes projections) SWIM produced substantial net savings for governmental budgets, amounting to more than $1,500 per experimental among both AFDC and AFDC-U registrants" (Hamilton and Friedlander 1989).
5. From the perspective of all subjects, the treatment had little effect on net income over the five-year period, suggesting that earnings increases and welfare reductions were roughly offsetting. However, some subgroups had net gains and others net losses.

TIME TRENDS IN FINDINGS: Experimental/control differences among recipients did not seem to diminish over time, although these differences did diminish over time among applicants.

DESIGN ISSUES:

1. San Diego County volunteered to perform this program. It was a natural outgrowth of existing rigorous welfare employment programs, which enjoy widespread political support. There is possible site self-selection bias.
2. Program operated in a tight labor market.

REPLICABILITY: Replicable.

GENERALIZABILITY: See "Design Issues."

FUNDING SOURCES: U.S. Department of Health and Human Services, Ford Foundation, and the State of California. Key personnel: Howard Rolston for HHS, Gordon Berlin and Prudence Brown for Ford, and Steve Munro for California.

TREATMENT ADMINISTRATOR: Welfare Department of San Diego County. Key personnel: John Robbins.

EVALUATOR: Manpower Demonstration Research Corporation. Key personnel: Gayle Hamilton.

ENABLING LEGISLATION: Omnibus Budget Reconciliation Act (OBRA) of 1981.

POLICY EFFECTS: Reports on the State Welfare-to-Work Initiatives were frequently cited in Congress during the framing of the Family Support Act (FSA) of 1988.

INFORMATION SOURCES: Gayle Hamilton, *Interim Report on the Saturation Work Initiative Model in San Diego,* Manpower Demonstration Research Corporation, August 1988; Gayle Hamilton and Daniel Friedlander, *Final Report on the Saturation Work Initiative Model,* Manpower Demonstration Research Corporation, November 1989.

PUBLIC-USE ACCESS TO DATA: Public-use file exists; contact MDRC about *Welfare Employment Studies* 1 through 4.

Pennsylvania Saturation Work Program (PSWP)

SUMMARY: This demonstration, conducted from 1985 to 1987, tested the effects of intensive employment services on a large sample of welfare recipients. Subjects were followed for two years.

COST: Evaluation costs, $2.1 million.

TIME FRAME: Demonstration period, July 1985–September 1987; final report, October 1989.

TREATMENTS TESTED: The PSWP was a mandatory program with sanctions for noncompliance. Services included individual case management, workshops, training and education, community work experience (CWEP), job clubs, and assistance with work plan development. The control group continued to receive existing County Assistance Office (CAO) services.

OUTCOMES OF INTEREST: (1) Employment; (2) Earnings; and (3) Welfare receipt.

SAMPLE SIZE: Experimentals, 4,024; controls, 3,318.

TARGET POPULATION: Work-mandatory AFDC and AFDC-U claimants.

NUMBER OF TREATMENT GROUPS: Two (with one control group).

NUMBER AND LOCATION OF SITES: Six—district CAO offices in Philadelphia, Pennsylvania.

RESEARCH COMPONENTS:

▪ Process analysis: Conducted. Frequent on-site visits and data examination were used to ensure that services were constant across sites and throughout the study. A three-month pilot program was conducted in one of the sites prior to beginning services at all sites.

Impact analysis: Conducted using comparison of means.

Benefit–cost analysis: Not conducted.

MAJOR FINDINGS:

1. AFDC experimental participants had significantly higher average earnings than control group participants in the first four quarters following random assignment. "Over the full two-year follow-up period, the treatment group had $340 more in average earnings, which is also a significant difference."

2. AFDC "not-job-ready" experimental participants (the priority caseload for this project) showed the most significant gains over the control group in employment and earnings.

3. No significant differences in welfare receipt between the AFDC-U experimental and control groups were produced. For the AFDC-R (i.e., AFDC-regular) participants, significantly fewer experimental group members received welfare assistance for all quarters of follow-up. This was true for both job-ready and not-job-ready AFDC-R recipients.

TIME TRENDS IN FINDINGS: The rate of employment and average earnings increased steadily over the evaluation period for both experimental and control group members (for both AFDC-R and AFDC-U).

For AFDC-R, experimental group employment and earnings were significantly higher than those of the control group for the first year following random assignment, but differences dissipated in the second year.

For both experimental and control groups, there was a steady decline in the percentage of persons receiving welfare benefits over the two-year period, though there were no significant differences between experimental and control group members.

DESIGN ISSUES:

1. During the early part of the project, more emphasis was given to education and training than was intended. Later, these services were made concurrent with job search activities.

2. Job-ready participants were to move immediately into an independent job search for 90 days, but it was discovered that many were receiving intensive services prior to the end of their 90-day independent search. A memorandum was sent to case workers to bring the implementation of these services in line with original plans. The evaluators felt that more monitoring was needed, but caseloads were too large.

3. A longer follow-up period was considered but did not materialize owing to loss of staff and a lack of funding.

4. The evaluators suspected that some case managers were "creaming" their caseloads; that is, they were putting more effort into helping those clients who they felt had the best chances of success. It is unclear whether this may have biased impacts or affected generalizability.

REPLICABILITY: Replicable.

GENERALIZABILITY: Designed to generalize to the city of Philadelphia. Site selection was based on the physical plant of the various districts, district performance, and demographic characteristics (six of Philadelphia's 19 districts were chosen). Researchers felt the six sites "generally reflected the city's welfare population." Unemployment rates for Philadelphia at this time were comparable to the state and national averages.

FUNDING SOURCE: U.S. Department of Health and Human Services, Office of Family Assistance. Key personnel: Liza Barnes.

TREATMENT ADMINISTRATORS: Pennsylvania Department of Public Welfare, Office of Policy, Evaluation, and Development; Sam McClea, director; Bureau of Policy, Evaluation, and Research; Frederick Richmond, director. Project director: Kathleen Nazar.

EVALUATOR: Pennsylvania Department of Public Welfare. Key personnel: Suzanne Hogarth and Roger Martin.

ENABLING LEGISLATION: State of Pennsylvania Act 1982-75.

POLICY EFFECTS: The evaluators noted that the state administration (Department of Public Welfare, Division of Income Maintenance) used the study results in implementing statewide changes in service delivery.

INFORMATION SOURCES: Suzanne Hogarth and Roger Martin, *Pennsylvania Saturation Work Program: Process Evaluation,* 1988; Suzanne Hogarth, Roger Martin, and Kathleen Nazar, *Pennsylvania Saturation Work Program: Impact Evaluation,* 1989. Both publications available through Pennsylvania Department of Public Welfare.

PUBLIC-USE ACCESS TO DATA: Available at Pennsylvania Department of Public Welfare.

Illinois On-Line Cross-Match Demonstration

SUMMARY: This demonstration, conducted in 1986, tested the effects of immediate access to client information by caseworkers on a large sample of AFDC recipients and applicants. Subjects were followed for six months.

COST: Administrative cost, $148,000; research only, $69,290.

TIME FRAME: Demonstration period, May 1986–October 1986; data collected through December 1986; final report, September 1987.

TREATMENTS TESTED: At the initial determination of eligibility for AFDC and at subsequent face-to-face redetermination meetings, a caseworker could immediately call up on a computer screen certain information on experimentals: marriage and death information, state payroll and retirement pension data, and, in some cases, school records. Caseworkers were required to perform these cross-match inquiries for experimentals (odd last-digit identification numbers), and the system would not accept inquiries for controls (even last-digit identifications). School district information was available for Chicago and Rockford. The tested treatment was an incremental increase in the information already immediately accessible to the caseworker, the most important of which was wage records from the Illinois Department of Employment Security. Under the existing system (the control treatment), the additional information on marriages, deaths, and so forth would be periodically updated and circulated to caseworkers in hard copy.

OUTCOMES OF INTEREST: (1) AFDC applications denied and (2) Savings in payments.

SAMPLE SIZE: New applicants: experimentals, 5,305; controls, 5,489. Ongoing cases: experimentals, 20,429; controls, 20,323.

TARGET POPULATION: AFDC applicants and recipients.

NUMBER OF TREATMENT GROUPS: Two (with one control group).

NUMBER AND LOCATION OF SITES: Seven—four welfare offices in Cook County and three in other counties.

RESEARCH COMPONENTS:
  Process analysis: Conducted through interviews and computer records to determine whether caseworkers actually used the system and whether they perceived it as useful. Workers who were using a fully automated system and who had access to school district records found it useful, and some of them succeeded in evading the system block on even numbers to use it on controls (thereby contaminating the control sample). Computer records showed that this happened in one office only; project report authors noted that although this produced a downward bias in the measured effect of the treatment in that office, it is itself evidence of

perceived treatment effectiveness. Many workers did not understand the data format for state payments, marriages, and deaths.

- Impact analysis: Comparison of means, ordinary least squares (OLS) regression.
- Benefit–cost analysis: Cost-effectiveness analysis.

MAJOR FINDINGS:

	Experimentals	Controls
New applications denied	39.5%	40.5%
For applicants:		
Mean AFDC payments	$625.08	$609.34
Mean food stamps paid	238.24	231.49
For ongoing cases:		
Mean AFDC payments	1,571.02	1,574.22
Mean food stamps paid	774.63*	782.20

* Difference is statistically significant at 90 percent confidence level.

1. Three Cook County offices had access to school records and had a fully automated information system. In these offices, denials of new applications increased from 23.9 percent to 26.4 percent (statistically significant at the 90 percent level). The difference in benefits paid was not statistically significant.
2. Although some downward bias was present, owing to the contamination discussed above under "Process analysis" (in "Research Components"), the project report authors did not believe it was large enough to change the analysis significantly.
3. Under most reasonable assumptions about benefits and costs, benefits of the system exceeded costs when school records were available, but the authors did not claim that the benefits were very precisely measured.

TIME TRENDS IN FINDINGS: There were no time trends, but there were curious discrepancies in treatment impacts across offices, which the authors discussed but could not explain.

DESIGN ISSUES:
1. The inclusion of offices that were not fully automated (and where, accordingly, use of the additional data was more difficult) added little to the value of the experiment. Apparently it was not anticipated before the experiment that only the school records would be of much use to caseworkers.
2. The contamination of the control sample, previously noted, was not the only result of a vulnerable computer system. In particular, the authors had trouble designating the new applicant sample, for reasons discussed in the evaluation report.

REPLICABILITY: Replicable.

GENERALIZABILITY: The sample size is very large, but most results were not statistically significant. That would seem to imply that the savings are very small; on the other hand, the system costs seem to be small as well.

FUNDING SOURCE: U.S. Department of Health and Human Services, Office of Family Assistance. Key personnel: Penny Pendell.

TREATMENT ADMINISTRATOR: Illinois Department of Public Aid. Key personnel: Alan Whitaker.

EVALUATOR: Mathematica Policy Research. Key personnel: John A. Burghardt.

ENABLING LEGISLATION: None.

POLICY EFFECTS: Alan Whitaker has stated that the disappointing findings on the effects of the online cross-match treatment led the state not to extend further the scope of data collection for on-line use by caseworkers.

INFORMATION SOURCE: Nancy Holden, John A. Burghardt, and James C. Ohls, *Final Report for the Evaluation of the Illinois On-Line Cross-Match Demonstration,* Mathematica Policy Research, September 11, 1987.

PUBLIC-USE ACCESS TO DATA: We have no information about a public-use file for this demonstration.

New York State Comprehensive Employment Opportunity Support Centers (CEOSC) Program

SUMMARY: This demonstration, conducted from 1987 to 1993, tested the effects of training, job search assistance and supportive services on a medium-sized sample of single AFDC parents of preschool children. Subjects were followed for up to four years.

COST: Evaluation costs, approximately $500,000.

TIME FRAME: Demonstration period, 1987–93; data collected, same period; final report, 1994.

TREATMENTS TESTED: This voluntary program tested assessment, education, skills training, job search assistance, child care, counseling, case management, and other supportive services. The control group received nothing from the demonstration.

OUTCOMES OF INTEREST: (1) Employment; (2) Earnings; (3) Welfare dependency; and (4) Welfare payments.

SAMPLE SIZE: Experimentals, 261; controls, 268.

TARGET POPULATION: Single AFDC parents of preschool children. This population is overwhelmingly female (98.7 percent).

NUMBER OF TREATMENT GROUPS: Two (with one control group).

NUMBER AND LOCATION OF SITES: One—Albany, New York.

RESEARCH COMPONENTS:
- Process analysis: An implementation study was conducted over the first year of program operations.
- Impact analysis: Comparison of means and regression analysis.
- Benefit–cost analysis: Not conducted.

MAJOR FINDINGS:
1. The experimental group's rate of public assistance receipt was significantly lower than that of the control group, though only in the final (14th) quarter of follow-up (58.1 percent versus 69.3 percent). In no quarter was there a significant impact on the monthly amount of public assistance received.
2. No significant impacts were found on the receipt, nor the benefit amount, of food stamps.
3. Employment rates were significantly lower for the experimental group in the fifth and sixth quarters, compared with the control group, but were somewhat higher than those of the control group after the 12th quarter. Employment earnings were significantly higher for the experimental group from the 12th quarter on.
4. Impacts were greater for an "early cohort" that had entered the sample earlier in the life of the program. This includes significant impacts on receipt of food stamps and public assistance.

TIME TRENDS IN FINDINGS: Impacts on earnings for the Albany site took longer to appear than in other welfare-to-work programs. Participants in the experimental group tended to remain outside the labor force during training, and participation in the program was sporadic. Once this group did enter the labor market, they appeared to find more stable, higher-paying employment on average than did control group members.

DESIGN ISSUES: Program enrollment during the period of intake for the research sample was lower than expected. Further, only a small percentage (approximately 29 percent) of the experimental group ever received training through the program beyond a two-week preemployment workshop.

REPLICABILITY: Replicable. The evaluation report contains various sample forms, surveys, and guidelines for implementation.

GENERALIZABILITY: Participation rates were quite low. The program was voluntary, with random assignment after volunteering. Findings on welfare dependency are similar to those found in other welfare-to-work demonstrations. Findings on income developed over a longer period of time than in other programs, though direction of impacts was the same.

FUNDING SOURCE: New York State Department of Social Services. Key personnel: George Falco, director of research.

TREATMENT ADMINISTRATOR: New York State Department of Social Services oversaw both sites. The Albany program was administered by the Albany County Department of Social Services. The New York City site was administered by Federation Employment and Guidance Service, a private nonprofit organization.

EVALUATOR: Abt Associates. Key personnel: Alan Werner.

ENABLING LEGISLATION: None.

INFORMATION SOURCE: Alan Werner, Gregory Mills, Michael Walker, and Nandinee Kutty, *The Evaluation of New York State Comprehensive Employment Opportunity Support Centers Program: Impact Study,* Abt Associates, January 1994.

PUBLIC-USE ACCESS TO DATA: Not available.

Teenage Parent Demonstration

SUMMARY: This demonstration, conducted between 1987 and 1991, tested the effects of case management and employment and training services on a large sample of teenage mothers receiving welfare. Subjects were followed for up to seven years.

COST: First phase, $6.3 million for the 30-month follow-up; second phase, $2.3 million for the 6 ½ year follow-up.

TIME FRAME: Demonstration period, 1987–91; data collected, same period and for 30-month and 6 ½ year follow-ups.

TREATMENTS TESTED: Individual case management. Participants were required to attend an initial series of personal skills workshops, followed by full-time (30 hours per week) participation in education, training, and/or employment services. Sanctions for nonparticipation consisted of a reduction in the monthly AFDC grant. Child care and transportation assistance were available.

OUTCOMES OF INTEREST: (1) Employment; (2) Earnings; (3) Welfare receipt; (4) School attendance; (5) Subsequent childbearing; and (6) Child outcomes.

SAMPLE SIZE: Experimentals, 2,647; controls, 2,650.

TARGET POPULATION: Teenage mothers with only one child, receiving AFDC for the first time.

NUMBER OF TREATMENT GROUPS: Two (with one control group).

NUMBER AND LOCATION OF SITES: Three—Chicago, Illinois; and Newark and Camden, New Jersey.

RESEARCH COMPONENTS:

- Process analysis: Focus on participation rates and service delivery at the three sites. Forty to 50 percent of the New Jersey participants and 30 percent of those in Chicago were sanctioned (benefits were reduced until they complied with program requirements).
- Impact analysis: Conducted predominantly with multivariate models.
- Benefit–cost analysis: Not conducted.

MAJOR FINDINGS:

Early Results

1. Participation in employment and, especially, education activities was significantly higher for the experimental group (79 percent) than for the control group (66 percent). By the end of the two-year follow-up period, a significantly higher percentage of experimental group members, compared with control group members, had spent some time in school. These differences were largest in Camden (46 percent versus 26 percent). In Chicago and Camden, significantly more experimental group members obtained a diploma or equivalent.

2. The demonstration produced consistent but modest impacts on employment outcomes. For both Camden and Chicago, there were positive significant experimental–control differences in the percentage ever employed (Camden, 6.5 percent, Chicago, 7 percent) and in the percentage of total demonstration period employed (Camden, 2.4 percent, Chicago, 3.5 percent). There were no significant differences for the Newark site on employment outcomes.

3. Average monthly earnings were significantly higher for the experimental group at the Chicago site only ($24.40 higher than controls). In the New Jersey sites, the experimental groups had average monthly earnings of roughly $21 over the control groups, but this was not statistically significant.

4. Welfare receipt was reduced by 7–8 percent in all three sites. Particularly in New Jersey, these reductions resulted from a combination of higher earnings and higher sanctions for noncompliance. Only the Chicago program produced a sustained significant reduction in the probability of receiving AFDC.

Follow-up Results

1. Early program impacts generally disappeared once the demonstration ended and the program services and sanctions for noncompliance were discontinued (see "Time Trends in Findings").

2. All programs significantly increased school participation. Programs in Camden and Chicago also significantly increased participation in vocational training in the first phase.

3. In Newark, experimentals were significantly less likely to be living with a husband or partner (12 percent, compared with 18 percent of controls).

4. There were little or no significant differences between experimental and control groups in children's cognitive and social-emotional well-being or physical health.

TIME TRENDS IN FINDINGS: The first phase of the demonstration showed that the programs increased rates of school enrollment, job training, and employment over the 30-month evaluation period. Modest employment increases were accompanied by earning gains that reduced rates of welfare dependence. However, impacts on employment and welfare receipt did not last once the demonstration ended. Roughly 70 percent of the mothers in the experimental and control groups were still receiving welfare at the time of the 6 ½ year follow-up. Overall, there were no long-term impacts on subsequent births, employment, earnings, educational attainment, or child development.

DESIGN ISSUES:

1. The evaluator reported that this project was very well designed and was implemented with few difficulties. The problems that existed related to how quickly the three sites implemented the project and to how faithfully they monitored it. One site was fairly slow to implement and another site was inconsistent in monitoring the project.

2. Sample sizes for outcomes based on resurvey and retest data are substantially smaller than those based on records data. This was purposeful and not owing to attrition and nonresponse (response to the surveys was roughly 85 percent). Evaluators attempted to survey and retest only 75 percent of the Chicago sample.

REPLICABILITY: Replicable.

GENERALIZABILITY: Findings appear reasonably generalizable to urban teenage parents.

FUNDING SOURCE: U.S. Department of Health and Human Services, Administration for Children and Families. Key personnel: Reuben Snipper, Nancye Campell, and Judith Reich.

TREATMENT ADMINISTRATORS: In Chicago, Project Advance. Key personnel: Melba McCarty. In Newark, Teen Progress. Key personnel: Yvonne Johnson. In Camden, Teen Progress. Key personnel: Frank Ambrose.

EVALUATOR: Mathematica Policy Research. Key personnel: Ellen Kisker.

ENABLING LEGISLATION: None.

INFORMATION SOURCES: Rebecca Maynard, Walter Nicholson, and Anu Rangarajan, *Breaking the Cycle of Poverty: The Effectiveness of Mandatory Services for Welfare-Dependent Teenage Parents,* Mathematica Policy Research, December, 1993; Ellen Eliason Kisker, Anu Rangarajan, and Kimberly Boller, *Moving into Adulthood: Were the Impacts of Mandatory Programs for Welfare-Dependent Teenage Parents Sustained after the Programs Ended?* Mathematica Policy Research, February 1998.

PUBLIC-USE ACCESS TO DATA: Available through U.S. Department of Health and Human Services. Contact Reuben Snipper, Office of the Assistant Secretary for Planning and Evaluation.

Wisconsin Welfare Employment Experiment—Rock County

SUMMARY: This demonstration, conducted from 1987 to 1990, tested the effects of job support services and workfare on a medium-sized sample of AFDC recipients. Subjects were followed for three years. The Rock County experiment was part of a statewide demonstration but was the only site to use random assignment in its design.

COST: Evaluation costs, approximately $20,000–$30,000 for Rock County alone; approximately $200,000 for all counties. Funding was terminated prior to completion of the final report.

TIME FRAME: Demonstration period, 1987–90; data collected, same period; final report, September 1993.

TREATMENTS TESTED: The Work Experience and Job Training Program (WEJT) featured an extensive array of services including remedial education, job search, subsidized employment, job training, and day care. Those clients not finding work after completing their training were required to participate in a mandatory Community Work

Experience Program (CWEP), a Workfare program. The control group received existing services (mainly job search activities).

OUTCOMES OF INTEREST: (1) Employment; (2) Earnings; and (3) Welfare receipt.

SAMPLE SIZE: Rock County only: experimentals, 538; controls, 487.

TARGET POPULATION: AFDC recipients.

NUMBER OF TREATMENT GROUPS: Two (with one control group).

NUMBER AND LOCATION OF SITES: One—Rock County, Wisconsin.

RESEARCH COMPONENTS:
- Process analysis: Several chapters of the final report are dedicated to the process of implementing the WEJT/CWEP program. Descriptions of the programs, participation patterns, and the roles of service providers are included.
- Impact analysis: Comparison of means.
- Benefit–cost analysis: Not conducted.

MAJOR FINDINGS:
1. By the fourth quarter of 1990 (three years after program implementation), 59 percent of the experimental group and 69 percent of the control group were off AFDC. Although this finding was not statistically significant, it reflects a lack of success of the experimental treatment.
2. Likewise, experimental group participants did not show improved earnings compared with the control group. For two-parent families, experimentals had average fourth-quarter earnings of $2,126, compared with $2,354 for the control group. For single-parent families, the experimental group showed average quarterly earnings of $1,288, compared with $1,364 for the controls.

TIME TRENDS IN FINDINGS: None reported.

DESIGN ISSUES: According to one evaluator, there was an "adversarial relationship" between the evaluators and the Wisconsin State Department of

Health and Social Services. Considerable time and money were spent trying to get data from "recalcitrant bureaucrats" who did not want to supply it. The legislature, which had mandated the study, was used to enforce cooperation. The administrators did not agree with the findings and halted the evaluation. The evaluators then completed the data analysis and final report on their own.

REPLICABILITY: Replicable.

GENERALIZABILITY: The findings in Rock County are consistent with nonexperimental data collected by the Wisconsin Department of Health and Social Services evaluation staff in 1988.

FUNDING SOURCES: Wisconsin Department of Health and Social Services and U.S. Department of Health and Human Services.

TREATMENT ADMINISTRATOR: Wisconsin Department of Health and Social Services. Key personnel: Richard Larang.

EVALUATOR: Employment and Training Institute, University of Wisconsin–Milwaukee. Key personnel: John Pawasarat and Lois M. Quinn.

ENABLING LEGISLATION: Wisconsin Act 413.

INFORMATION SOURCE: John Pawasarat and Lois M. Quinn, *Wisconsin Welfare Employment Experiments: An Evaluation of the WEJT and CWEP Programs,* Employment and Training Institute, University of Wisconsin–Milwaukee, September 1993.

PUBLIC-USE ACCESS TO DATA: Not available.

Child Assistance Program (CAP)

SUMMARY: This demonstration, conducted from 1988 to 1995, tested the effects of financial incentives and intensive case management on a large sample of AFDC recipients. Subjects were followed for five years.

COST: Evaluation costs, approximately $1.9 million for initial evaluation and $1.2 million for the extension.

TIME FRAME: Demonstration period, October 1988–March 1994; data collected through 1995.

TREATMENTS TESTED: The Child Assistance Program (CAP) was a voluntary alternative to AFDC. Participation was limited to single-parent AFDC cases in which at least one child was covered by a child support order. The treatment consisted of economic incentives (including an earned income disregard of 90 percent up to the poverty level and 33 percent beyond that; no $50 pass-through for child support; no resource limit; and cashed-out Food Stamp benefits) and intensive case management.

Controls did not receive these incentives or services.

OUTCOMES OF INTEREST: (1) Establishment of child support orders; (2) Employment; and (3) Earnings.

SAMPLE SIZE: Total, 4,287. Roughly half assigned to each group.

TARGET POPULATION: AFDC recipients.

NUMBER OF TREATMENT GROUPS: Two (with one control group).

NUMBER AND LOCATION OF SITES: Only three sites used random assignment and are included in this analysis—Monroe, Niagara, and Suffolk counties, New York. There were also four saturation sites.

RESEARCH COMPONENTS:

- Process analysis: Identified operational, organizational, and environmental factors associated with the implementation. These included participation rates, random assignment procedures, recruitment, and agency coordination.
- Impact analysis: Three experimental sites only were estimated using regression analysis.
- Benefit–cost analysis: Conducted.

MAJOR FINDINGS:

1. At the two-year follow-up, there were statistically significant increases in the earnings of the experimental group. Average earnings over the two years were 27 percent higher for the exper-

imental group (including those who did not participate) than for the control group. An earnings impact of roughly this magnitude or greater is also estimated for the full five-year follow-up.

2. There was a significant increase in the establishment of child support orders. Most recipients began the experiment lacking orders for at least one child. On average, over the five years, clients were 21 percent more likely to gain new orders if they were in the experimental group. There was also an indication of increased child support payments, but this effect was not statistically significant.

3. At the two-year follow-up, there were no significant program impacts on the receipt of public assistance. At the five-year follow-up, there was a significant reduction in combined Food Stamp/AFDC payments (approximately 4 percent) and in Medicaid, but the reduction of cash assistance, by itself, was not statistically significant.

4. After combining benefit payments and administrative costs for the five years as a whole, there was a sizable savings in government outlays. Increased administrative costs resulting from CAP were more than offset by reductions in Food Stamp and cash assistance benefits and an increase in child support collections.

TIME TRENDS IN FINDINGS: Program impacts were sustained or increased over the full five-year period.

DESIGN ISSUES:

1. Client (self-report) surveys at one and two years were used to obtain employment and earnings data, because the New York system made access to employer data difficult. This could introduce error owing to faulty memory or other biases. Regulations were changed during the project, and employer data were available for the three-, four-, and five-year follow-ups.

2. Program enrollment relied heavily on recruitment efforts of staff. Staff needed to convince clients of the program's advantages. Program enrollment over the five-year period was

roughly 16 percent of the AFDC caseload, although it varied by county. CAP had a clear priority in the Departments of Social Services of Monroe and Niagara counties. Enrollments were higher in these counties than in Suffolk.

REPLICABILITY: Replicable.

GENERALIZABILITY: Designed to generalize to the entire state. The project was voluntary, and AFDC clients needed to meet certain requirements (obtain child support orders, earn $350 per month) before being deemed eligible. Because of this feature, most AFDC recipients would never enroll in the program, though evaluators predicted that more than the 16 percent enrollment that occurred in this demonstration would enroll in a nonexperimental program.

The full experimental sample was reasonably representative of the single-parent AFDC caseload nationwide. It was actually more comparable to the U.S. caseload than that of upstate New York. The full sample contained higher percentages of black and Hispanic clients, never-married clients, and clients with a child under age 3 than the upstate New York average.

FUNDING SOURCE: New York State Department of Social Services. Key personnel: Mike Warner and Susan Mitchell-Herzfeld.

TREATMENT ADMINISTRATOR: New York State Department of Social Services and the corresponding county departments in the experimental sites. Key personnel: Mike Warner and Susan Mitchell-Herzfeld.

EVALUATOR: Abt Associates. Key personnel: William Hamilton and Nancy Burstein.

ENABLING LEGISLATION: Omnibus Budget Reconciliation Act of 1987, section 9122, and provisions of section 1115 of the Social Security Act and section 17(b)(1) of the Food Stamp Act.

POLICY EFFECTS: On June 6, 1994, the U.S. Department of Health and Human Services authorized continued operation and expansion (to additional sites) of the Child Assistance Program from

April 1, 1994, through March 31, 1999. The program continued to operate in the seven original counties and in seven additional counties. Although 10 percent of the new caseload was assigned to a control group, there were no immediate plans to continue gathering experimental data. The five-year follow-up, which ended in March 1995, marks the completion of the experimental evaluation.

INFORMATION SOURCES: William L. Hamilton, Nancy R. Burstein, Margaret Hargreaves, David A. Moss, and Michael Walker, *The New York State Child Assistance Program: Program Impacts, Costs, and Benefits,* Abt Associates, July 1993; William L. Hamilton, Nancy R. Burstein, August J. Baker, Alison Earle, Stefanie Gluckman, Laura Peck, and Alan White, *The New York State Child Assistance Program: Five-Year Impacts, Costs, and Benefits,* Abt Associates, October 1996.

PUBLIC-USE ACCESS TO DATA: Upon completion of the analysis, Abt Associates turned over the data set to the State of New York, Department of Social Services.

Greater Avenues for Independence (GAIN)

SUMMARY: This demonstration, conducted from 1988 to 1990, tested the effects of basic education, job search, and skills training on a large sample of AFDC recipients. Subjects were followed for up to four and one-half years.

COST: Manpower Demonstration Research Corporation's (MDRC's) multiyear contract with California encompassed much more than the six-county demonstration, and evaluators were thus unable to separate the costs. Average net program cost per experimental was $3,422 and per control, $1,472.

TIME FRAME: Demonstration period, March 1988–June 1990; final report, September 1994.

TREATMENTS TESTED: Experimentals were subject to the Greater Avenues for Independence (GAIN)

participation mandate, which combined basic education, job search activities, assessments, skills training, and work experience. The control group was precluded from receiving those services from the program but could seek other services in the community on their own.

OUTCOMES OF INTEREST: (1) Participation in employment-related activities; (2) Earnings; (3) Welfare receipt; and (4) Employment.

SAMPLE SIZE: Experimentals, 24,528; controls, 8,223.

TARGET POPULATION: AFDC recipients. Four of the six counties had resources to include all mandatory registrants; two focused on long-term recipients.

NUMBER OF TREATMENT GROUPS: Two (with one control group).

NUMBER AND LOCATION OF SITES: Six—Alameda, Butte, Los Angeles, Riverside, San Diego, and Tulare counties in California.

RESEARCH COMPONENTS:

■ Process analysis: Implementation among the six counties was analyzed, with special attention paid to communication, participation, use of sanctions, and services delivered.

■ Impact analysis: Impact estimates were regression-adjusted.

■ Benefit–cost analysis: Conducted.

MAJOR FINDINGS: Effects varied by county.

1. Over the full four and one-half years, GAIN significantly increased the earnings for AFDC-FG (single parents) compared with those of the control group. There was a total difference of $2,527 per participant (24 percent). This is an all-county average, with each county weighted equally.

2. AFDC total benefit payments were, on average, $1,365 (7 percent) lower for the AFDC-FG experimental group than for the controls.

3. Earnings gains and AFDC-FG benefit reductions were greatest for Riverside County (+44 percent and −15 percent, respectively). Earnings gains and AFDC-U reductions for

Riverside County were +15 percent and −14.3 percent, respectively. Riverside's staff placed much more emphasis on moving registrants into the labor market quickly than did staff in any other county. Riverside staff attempted to communicate a strong message to all registrants that employment was the central goal of the program. In addition, the county's management established job placement standards as one means of assessing staff performance.

4. Employment and welfare savings impacts for the AFDC-U (two-parent families) group were less striking than for the AFDC-FG group, though they were statistically significant. The all-county average earnings for experimental group members was 12 percent higher than those of their control group counterparts.

TIME TRENDS IN FINDINGS: The earnings impacts grew progressively stronger over time, whereas the impacts on AFDC receipt tended to level off over time.

DESIGN ISSUES:

1. For group assignment, registrants were required to appear for orientation and appraisal. One-third of mandatory registrants did not appear and thus were not part of the research sample. By the six-month follow-up, two-thirds of these no-shows had either left welfare or were officially excused.
2. Four of the six counties were able to enroll the full mandatory caseload. Funding levels did not permit full enrollment in Alameda and Los Angeles, where they chose to focus exclusively on long-term recipients. Different intake policies and differences in the general makeup of each county's local population yielded research samples that varied markedly in demographic composition.

REPLICABILITY: A replication study of the Riverside County approach was conducted in Los Angeles County—see LA Jobs-First GAIN Evaluation, p. 127.

GENERALIZABILITY: Designed to generalize to the entire state of California. The program was mandatory under pre-JOBS rules. Thus, single parents with children under the age of 6 were exempt. The six counties represent diverse geographical regions of the state, vary widely in local economic conditions and population characteristics, and constitute a mix of urban and rural areas. GAIN, as California's version of the JOBS program, existed statewide. Although participants in the six experimental counties were not strictly representative of the statewide population, over one-half of the entire state AFDC caseload lived in those counties.

FUNDING SOURCE: California Department of Social Services (CDSS).

TREATMENT ADMINISTRATOR: CDSS. Key personnel: Eloise Anderson, Michael Genest, and Bruce Wagstaff, as well as the county welfare directors in the six experimental counties.

EVALUATOR: MDRC. Key personnel: James Riccio (principal investigator), Daniel Friedlander, and Stephen Freedman.

ENABLING LEGISLATION: None.

INFORMATION SOURCE: James Riccio, Daniel Friedlander, and Stephen Freedman, *GAIN: Benefits, Costs and Three Year Impacts of a Welfare to Work Program,* Manpower Demonstration Research Corporation, 1994.

PUBLIC-USE ACCESS TO DATA: Available through MDRC.

Washington State Family Independence Program (FIP)

SUMMARY: This quasi-experimental demonstration, conducted between 1988 and 1993, tested the effects of financial incentives (bonuses) intended to encourage training and work on a large sample of AFDC recipients. Subjects were followed for three years.

COST: $4.75 million over five years.

TIME FRAME: Demonstration period, July 1988–June 1993; data collected, same period.

TREATMENTS TESTED: The Family Independence Program (FIP) provided financial incentives to AFDC recipients to encourage education, training, and work; changed the structure of the income support system (e.g., "cashed-out" food stamps); expanded the availability of child care and supportive services; and provided transitional child care and Medicaid for one year. The comparison counties received traditional AFDC benefits, which were initially provided under the Washington Employment Opportunity Program (WEOP) and subsequently under JOBS in 1990. JOBS services were similar to those of FIP.

OUTCOMES OF INTEREST: (1) Participation in education and training; (2) Employment; and (3) Welfare receipt.

SAMPLE SIZE: Experimentals, 17,495; controls, 15,809.

TARGET POPULATION: New and recertifying AFDC recipients.

NUMBER OF TREATMENT GROUPS: Two (with one control group).

NUMBER AND LOCATION OF SITES: Ten—five experimental sites and five control sites throughout the state of Washington. Site selection involved first obtaining five matched pairs of sites. A coin toss was then used to assign one site in each matched pair to experimental status and the other to control status. Experimental sites were Everett/Skyhomish Valley; Spokane North; Burien/West Seattle; Columbia River Gorge; and Moses Lake/Othello.

RESEARCH COMPONENTS:

   Process analysis: Addressed how the FIP offices and the AFDC offices differed in their treatment of recipients, how FIP components differed from AFDC, how both programs changed over time, and how service delivery differed among local programs.

   Impact analysis: Regression analysis using a differences-in-differences approach.

   Benefit–cost analysis: Conducted.

MAJOR FINDINGS:

1. Relative to the AFDC program (the control group), FIP had little or no effect on the level of participation in education and training activities for adults in one-parent cases and men in two-parent cases. FIP women in two-parent cases were significantly less likely to participate in these activities than their AFDC counterparts in four of the eight follow-up quarters.

2. Relative to the AFDC program, FIP had little or no effect on the probability of employment or average earnings for adults in one-parent cases or women in two-parent cases. It significantly reduced both the probability of employment and average earnings for men in two-parent cases in all follow-up quarters.

3. The net FIP effects on participation in welfare were relatively large and highly significant for both the one- and two-parent caseloads. Participants tended to stay on welfare longer under FIP, and those who did leave returned to welfare more quickly than those who exited under AFDC. Average welfare grants were also higher under FIP than under AFDC. Participation in welfare was up to 12 percentage points higher for adults in one-parent cases and 18 percentage points higher for adults in two-parent cases over the entire follow-up period.

TIME TRENDS IN FINDINGS: None reported.

DESIGN ISSUES:

1. Cost-neutrality issues and rapidly growing caseloads interfered with the implementation of some FIP components. Individualized case management and increased availability of training services were only minimally implemented, and some components (e.g., wage subsidies, emphasis on child support enforcement) were not implemented at all.

2. Client surveys indicated that a "substantial minority" of FIP participants did not fully understand the program or its benefits. Consequently, they could not be expected to change their behavior in response to those benefits.

3. Some FIP inducements intended to encourage welfare recipients to move toward self-sufficiency, in the absence of strong staff involvement or any requirements, may have instead encouraged welfare participation under FIP.

4. In October 1990, the state implemented JOBS to replace the Work Incentive program. This change progressively reduced the FIP-AFDC program differences over time.

5. For a time, the standards for two-parent families for qualifying for AFDC were greatly liberalized at FIP sites. This caused the two-parent analysis sample at FIP sites to systematically differ from the two-parent analysis sample at control sites and may have distorted comparisons between the two samples. A similar problem does not exist for comparisons between one-parent families.

REPLICABILITY: Replicable.

GENERALIZABILITY: Designed to generalize to the entire state of Washington. Welfare offices were stratified by urban/rural and east/west to ensure geographic representativeness within Washington State. Experimental and control site cohorts were very similar.

FUNDING SOURCE: Washington State Legislative Budget Committee. Key personnel: Denise Gaither and Kristen West.

TREATMENT ADMINISTRATOR: Employment Security Department and Department of Social and Health Services of the State of Washington.

EVALUATOR: The Urban Institute. Key personnel: D. Lee Bawden.

ENABLING LEGISLATION: This demonstration was federally mandated as part of the waiver of section 1115 of the Social Security Act.

INFORMATION SOURCE: Sharon K. Long, Demetra Smith Nightingale, and Douglas A. Wissoker, *The Evaluation of the Washington State Family Independence Program: Final Report,* The Urban Institute, December 1993.

PUBLIC-USE ACCESS TO DATA: Available through The Urban Institute; contact Sharon Long.

G. H. W. BUSH ADMINISTRATION

Child Day Care Recycling Fund Experiment— North Carolina

SUMMARY: This demonstration, conducted from 1989 to 1990, tested the effects of immediate, guaranteed, subsidized day care on a medium-sized sample of AFDC recipients. Subjects were followed for one year.

COST: Approximately $126,000 for planning and evaluation.

TIME FRAME: Demonstration period, February 1989–March 1990; data collected, same period.

TREATMENTS TESTED: Relatively immediate (within two weeks of a request being made), subsidized, employment-contingent child care. The control group was subject to the usual terms and conditions for receiving child care, which often meant a six- to 10-month waiting period after employment.

OUTCOMES OF INTEREST: (1) Welfare expenditures and (2) Welfare dependence.

SAMPLE SIZE: Experimentals, 300; controls, 302.

TARGET POPULATION: Eligible AFDC families with the youngest child between the ages of one and five. In addition, target families were not already receiving state-supported child care and had an adult (18 or older) case head who was not a full-time student.

NUMBER OF TREATMENT GROUPS: Two (with one control group).

NUMBER AND LOCATION OF SITES: One—Mecklenberg County, North Carolina.

RESEARCH COMPONENTS:

- Process analysis: Looked at participant characteristics and patterns of behavior, as well as service delivery by the treatment administrator.

■ Impact analysis: The evaluation design included the experimental component presented here, as well as a time-series analysis and a pre- and postintervention survey. Impact assessments for the experimental component consisted of a comparison of means and logistic regression analysis.

■ Benefit–cost analysis: Not conducted.

MAJOR FINDINGS:

1. The simple support offer of guaranteed subsidized child care assistance to support full-time employment, in isolation, had no statistically significant effect on employment outcomes or welfare expenditures (AFDC, Food Stamp, and Medicaid). The mean welfare expenditure for the experimental group was $6,205 per participant compared with $6,260 for the control group.

2. Roughly one-half of the participants in the experimental group made some response to the offer of child care. This was significantly higher than the number of control group members who made a request for child care during the project period. Only 16.67 percent actually received state subsidized child care under the auspices of the special offer.

TIME TRENDS IN FINDINGS: None reported.

DESIGN ISSUES:

1. The project's short duration of one year makes it difficult to detect changes in the primary outcome of aggregate savings for AFDC, Food Stamp Program, and Medicaid expenditures. It is likely that study participants who accepted employment during this period would tend to take lower-paying jobs. In many cases, Food Stamp and Medicaid benefits would continue.

2. The passive offer of child care, by mail, may have been a poor mechanism to reach members of this population effectively. Many experimental group members may not have been fully aware of the offer or its intent.

REPLICABILITY: Replicable.

GENERALIZABILITY: The experimental sample had characteristics and barriers to employment that were similar to those of AFDC recipients in general. The type of jobs available in Mecklenberg County (largely low-paying and without health insurance) may differ across North Carolina and other states, thus affecting employment and employability.

FUNDING SOURCES: State of North Carolina Department of Human Resources. Key personnel: Quentin Uppercue. There was a federal matching grant from the U.S. Department of Health and Human Services. Key personnel: M.I. (Penny) Pendell. Additional support came from the University of North Carolina at Chapel Hill Office of Research Services.

TREATMENT ADMINISTRATOR: State of North Carolina Department of Human Resources and the county-administered Department of Social Services in collaboration with Child Care Resources. Key personnel: Marjorie Warlick.

EVALUATOR: University of North Carolina at Chapel Hill School of Social Work. Key personnel: Gary Bowen, principal investigator; and Peter Neenan, project director.

ENABLING LEGISLATION: Pursuant to section 1115 of the Social Security Act.

INFORMATION SOURCES: Gary L. Bowen and Peter A. Neenan, *Child Day Care Recycling Fund Experiment,* University of North Carolina at Chapel Hill School of Social Work, October 1990; Gary L. Bowen and Peter A. Neenan, "Does Subsidized Child-Care Availability Promote Welfare Independence of Mothers on AFDC? An Experimental Analysis," *Research on Social Work* 3(1993): 363–84.

PUBLIC-USE ACCESS TO DATA: Available through University of North Carolina, School of Social Work.

Community Group Participation and Housing Supplementation Demonstration (Bethel Self-Sufficiency Program)

SUMMARY: This demonstration, conducted from 1989 to 1994, tested the effects of providing education, employment, and training (E&T) services through a community-based organization. The subjects were followed for up to five years.

COST: Evaluation costs, $515,000 over six years.

TIME FRAME: Demonstration period, July 1989–June 1994; data collected, same period.

TREATMENTS TESTED: A community-based organization, Bethel New Life (BNL), was used to provide E&T services under the Bethel Self-Sufficiency Program (BSSP). A small group of employed BSSP participants also had the opportunity to buy a new home using "sweat equity" as a down payment. The control group received E&T services through the local Illinois Department of Public Aid (IDPA) office. Both groups continued to receive AFDC, Food Stamp, and Medicaid services through IDPA.

OUTCOMES OF INTEREST: (1) Earnings; (2) Employment; and (3) Welfare receipt.

SAMPLE SIZE: Experimentals, 497; controls, 497.

TARGET POPULATION: AFDC recipients.

NUMBER OF TREATMENT GROUPS: Two (with one control group).

NUMBER AND LOCATION OF SITES: One—West Garfield Park neighborhood of Chicago, Illinois.

RESEARCH COMPONENTS:
- Process analysis: Service delivery and participant characteristics were monitored.
- Impact analysis: Conducted using comparison of regression-adjusted means.
- Benefit–cost analysis: Conducted.

MAJOR FINDINGS:
1. Rates of E&T assignments were higher for the experimental group clients. Eighty-one percent were assigned to at least one E&T activity sometime during the observation period as compared with 59 percent of the control group clients. More experimental group clients (53 percent) were assigned to literacy, basic education, and high school–level programs than the control group (23 percent). Rates of assignment to other activities were similar for both groups.
2. The evaluation found no significant differences between experimental and control groups in earnings or welfare receipt.
3. One impact that showed statistical significance was that of quarterly employment rates—the percentage of clients with any quarterly earnings. The average rate was 22 percent for the experimental group and 26 percent for the control group. However, there was no significant difference between average quarterly amounts earned.
4. The cost–benefit analysis indicated that the experimental yielded slightly higher net costs from a government and private provider perspective and slightly lower net benefits from a participant perspective.

TIME TRENDS IN FINDINGS: None reported.

DESIGN ISSUES:
1. Services provided by Bethel New Life, the organization working with the experimental group, were inconsistent. In the early stages, BNL was understaffed and focused primarily on providing intake and orientation services to new participants. During fall 1991, the program was fully staffed and offered a broad range of services to clients. In January 1992, they lost their director and also experienced funding problems, thus limiting services again. In addition, high staff turnover interfered with case management services.

2. The IDPA program, Project Chance, underwent staffing and fiscal crises. Therefore, control group participants also received inconsistent services.

3. The housing component of the demonstration was not implemented as planned. There was high turnover in the housing division of Bethel New Life and conflicts with the U.S. Department of Housing and Urban Development over mortgage assistance grants. By the end of the study period, only nine participants had enrolled in the program and none had yet received a house.

REPLICABILITY: Replicable.

GENERALIZABILITY: Designed to generalize to West Garfield Park and similar neighborhoods in Chicago. Demonstration participant characteristics closely matched the AFDC profile found in West Garfield Park. The sample comprised almost entirely (99 percent) African-American women. On average, they were in their 20s and 30s, with one or two children. More than two-thirds had never married, one-third reported no previous employment experience, and almost half had not finished high school.

FUNDING SOURCE: Illinois Department of Public Aid. Key personnel: Linda Brumleve and David Gruenenfelder.

TREATMENT ADMINISTRATOR: Illinois Department of Public Aid in conjunction with Bethel New Life. Key personnel: Mary Nelson.

EVALUATOR: Abt Associates. Key personnel: Gregory Mills, Bonnie Randall, Margaret Hargreaves, and Robert Kornfeld.

ENABLING LEGISLATION: None.

INFORMATION SOURCE: Margaret Hargreaves, Robert Kornfeld, and Gregory Mills, *Community Group Participation and Housing Supplementation Demonstration: Final Report*, Abt Associates, June 1995.

PUBLIC-USE ACCESS TO DATA: Not available.

Illinois Career Advancement Project

SUMMARY: This demonstration, part of the Self-Sufficiency Demonstration, was conducted between 1989 and 1993. It tested the effects of financial assistance for educational programs on a large sample of former AFDC recipients. It was not successfully implemented as planned, ending one year early due to minimal participation. Subjects were followed for up to three years.

COST: Evaluation costs, $195,000.

TIME FRAME: Demonstration period, July 1989–October 1993; data collected, same period.

TREATMENTS TESTED: Financial assistance for participation in educational programs in the form of child care and transportation expenses and reimbursement for books and class fees for educational programs. Tuition was not provided.

Controls did not receive such support through the demonstration.

OUTCOMES OF INTEREST: (1) Earnings; (2) Returns to cash welfare; and (3) Job status.

SAMPLE SIZE: Experimentals, 1,445; controls, 1,396. Sample used in the analysis: 1,771 total (869 experimentals and 902 controls).

TARGET POPULATION: Former AFDC recipients who left cash assistance rolls because of employment.

NUMBER OF TREATMENT GROUPS: Two (with one control group).

NUMBER AND LOCATION OF SITES: Throughout the state of Illinois.

RESEARCH COMPONENTS:
- Process analysis: Project implementation, participant characteristics, and participation were analyzed through surveys of program leaders and participants.
- Impact analysis: Comparison of means.
- Benefit–cost analysis: Conducted.

MAJOR FINDINGS: Analysis was limited to those who were assigned during the first nine quarters.

1. No significant differences were found between the experimental and control groups regarding earnings, the rate at which they returned to welfare, job status, or time on cash assistance.

2. When the experimental group was split into those who did and those who did not participate in Career Advancement, the average earnings of those who did participate were found to be consistently lower by several hundred dollars.

3. The benefit–cost analysis revealed negative net present values from each of three perspectives (participant, nonparticipant, and society as a whole). Net costs were $188 for both participants and nonparticipants and $375 per person from the societal perspective.

TIME TRENDS IN FINDINGS: None.

DESIGN ISSUES:

1. Very low participation (less than 9 percent of the experimental group) by those who were eligible. Little was done by the program to enhance participation beyond informing subjects of their eligibility by letter. Tuition costs and issues surrounding child care (time and emotional demands) also contributed to the low rate of participation.

2. The project was to run for five years but was terminated early, mostly owing to insufficient participation.

3. The treatment was indirect, with a tenuous link to the ultimate effects. At best, positive impacts on employment would be produced only after schooling was completed. A longer follow-up would be necessary to capture these effects.

4. The evaluators felt the time frame was too restrictive for people to make use of the program. Applicants had a time limit within which to respond to the offer and another time limit within which to use the program.

REPLICABILITY: Any replication would need to include additional effort to ensure higher participation rates.

GENERALIZABILITY: Participation rates were too low for any meaningful generalization.

FUNDING SOURCES: Illinois Department of Public Aid (IDPA) and the White House Interagency Low-Income Opportunity Advisory Board. Key personnel: Linda Brandt-Levy.

TREATMENT ADMINISTRATOR: IDPA.

EVALUATOR: Institute of Applied Research, St. Louis, Missouri. Key personnel: L. Anthony Loman and Gary Siegel.

ENABLING LEGISLATION: None.

INFORMATION SOURCE: Institute of Applied Research, *Career Advancement: Year Four Evaluation,* June 1994.

PUBLIC-USE ACCESS TO DATA: Not currently available. The data could be available in the future from the Institute of Applied Research; contact L. Anthony Loman or Gary Siegel.

Cash Incentives in a Self-Sufficiency Program—Montgomery County, Maryland

SUMMARY: This demonstration, conducted from 1989 to 1991, tested the effects of cash incentive payments on a medium-sized sample of AFDC recipients. Subjects were followed for up to two and one-half years.

COST: Evaluation costs, approximately $25,000.

TIME FRAME: Demonstration period, July 1989–June 1991; data collected through end of 1991; final report, November 1992.

TREATMENTS TESTED: Maryland's Project Independence, the state's welfare reform initiative, was a program of educational and training activities. The experimental treatment in Montgomery County was cash incentive payments for participation in the program's activities. The control group did not receive these cash incentive payments.

OUTCOMES OF INTEREST: (1) Program completion; (2) Employment; (3) Earnings; and (4) Welfare receipt.

SAMPLE SIZE: Experimentals, 379; controls, 393.

TARGET POPULATION: AFDC recipients who participate (mandatorily or voluntarily) in education and training activities.

NUMBER OF TREATMENT GROUPS: Two (with one control group).

NUMBER AND LOCATION OF SITES: One—Montgomery County, Maryland.

RESEARCH COMPONENTS:
- Process analysis: Special attention was paid to service delivery components and procedures.
- Impact analysis: Conducted with comparison of means.
- Benefit–cost analysis: Not conducted.

MAJOR FINDINGS:
1. The program performance of the clients in the experimental group in completing education and skills training courses was slightly higher than the performance of those in the control group, but the difference was not statistically significant.
2. Differences in employment rates, average wages, and receipt of welfare benefits between the two groups were not statistically significant, although they tended to favor the experimental group (higher rates of employment and wages; lower receipt of welfare benefits).
3. The experimental group had a significantly higher overall completion rate of the job-readiness training component (the first phase of the program) than did the control group. There was no difference between groups per enrollment attempt, but the experimental group was more likely to make multiple attempts at completion.
4. Forty percent of the subjects (both groups) did not receive any education and training services beyond the initial job-readiness training.

TIME TRENDS IN FINDINGS: None.

DESIGN ISSUES:
1. The project was designed to last for three years but was discontinued after two years owing to lack of significant effects of the treatment.
2. Over the first year of the project, orientation procedures changed several times. First, clients were enrolled individually, then in mixed groups (experimental and control), and finally in separate orientation groups. This last change necessitated altering the random assignment procedure. Groups of clients (rather than individuals) who were scheduled for eligibility determination and redetermination in a given month were assigned to the experimental or control group. The change in procedure was associated with shifts in the relative prior earnings between groups but actually served to make them more comparable rather than more disparate.
3. The procedure for administering the cash incentives also changed mid-project. In the first nine months, individual counselors determined awards beyond the initial job-readiness training. As of May 1990, the system for incentive awards was standardized.

REPLICABILITY: Replicable.

GENERALIZABILITY: Designed to generalize to the entire state of Maryland. For roughly 75 percent of the sample, participation in employment and training activities was mandatory. Also, roughly 75 percent of the sample were members of Maryland's Project Independence target groups (young custodial parents who were without a diploma or work experience and were long-term AFDC recipients).

FUNDING SOURCE: Maryland Department of Social Services.

TREATMENT ADMINISTRATOR: Montgomery County Department of Social Services. Key personnel: Carol Pearson.

EVALUATOR: Jeffrey J. Koshel, independent consultant.

ENABLING LEGISLATION: None.

INFORMATION SOURCE: Jeffrey J. Koshel, Brian Sumerwell, and Carol Bazell, *Final Evaluation Report: Cash Incentives in a Self-Sufficiency Program,* Montgomery County, Maryland, Department of Social Services, November 1992.

PUBLIC-USE ACCESS TO DATA: Not available.

New Chance

SUMMARY: This demonstration, conducted from 1989 to 1992, tested the effects of a comprehensive program emphasizing both human capital and personal development services on a large sample of young mothers on welfare who were high school dropouts and on their children. Subjects were followed for three and one-half years.

COST: Evaluation costs, approximately $6.5 million.

TIME FRAME: Demonstration period, 1989–92; data collected, same period; final report, January 1997.

TREATMENTS TESTED: New Chance was a voluntary program that included an orientation; adult education (basic education and GED preparation); personal and child development (Life Skills and Opportunities curricula, health education and health care services, family planning, parenting education, and pediatric health services); employment preparation (occupational skills training, internships, and job placement assistance); case management; and child care. Control group members were denied access to New Chance but could participate in other services in the community.

OUTCOMES OF INTEREST: (1) Education; (2) Employment; (3) Earnings; (4) Welfare receipt; (5) Fertility; (6) Psychological well-being; and (7) Child development.

SAMPLE SIZE: Experimentals, 1,401; controls, 678.

TARGET POPULATION: Families headed by young mothers age 16–22 who had first given birth as teenagers, who were receiving AFDC, and were high school dropouts.

NUMBER OF TREATMENT GROUPS: Two (with one control group).

NUMBER AND LOCATION OF SITES: Sixteen sites in 10 states—Chula Vista, Inglewood, and San Jose, California; Denver, Colorado; Jacksonville, Florida; Chicago Heights, Illinois; Lexington, Kentucky; Detroit, Michigan; Minneapolis, Minnesota; Bronx and Harlem, New York; Portland and Salem, Oregon; and Allentown, Philadelphia, and Pittsburgh, Pennsylvania.

RESEARCH COMPONENTS:
- Process analysis: Describes the New Chance population, the treatment implementation, and patterns of program participation. Interviews were conducted with program coordinators and other key personnel.
- Impact analysis: Regression adjustment of experimental–control differences.
- Benefit–cost analysis: Not conducted.

MAJOR FINDINGS:
1. Because of absenteeism and early departures from the program, members of the experimental group received a much lower dose of services than had been anticipated. Also, the level of service receipt among control group members was much higher than anticipated. Thus, there was not a large differential between the quantity of services received by the experimental and control groups, especially with regard to education- and employment-related services.
2. Both experimentals and controls improved their status over time (e.g., they were more likely to be employed and less likely to be on welfare), but for the most part, experimentals did not improve more than controls.
3. Experimental group members were significantly more likely to have earned a high school diploma or GED than were control group members (53 percent versus 45 percent). They

were also more likely to have earned college credits (15 percent versus 13 percent).

4. No significant differences were found between groups on measures of employment or earnings for the full 42-month follow-up period.

5. New Chance did not reduce the rates of pregnancies or childbearing or affect participants' health status.

6. The program had unexpected negative effects on participants' emotional well-being (the experimental group scored significantly higher on measures of depression and stress) and on their perceptions of their children's behavior (as measured by behavioral rating scores).

TIME TRENDS IN FINDINGS: None.

DESIGN ISSUES: Implementation of some program components (e.g., career exploration and pre-employment skills instruction) was hindered by sites' lack of experience with these kinds of services. Further, since later activities (skills training, internships, job placement) were mostly delivered off-site, they were difficult to implement and less uniform across sites.

REPLICABILITY: Replicable, although sites varied considerably in how they administered program services.

GENERALIZABILITY: Designed to generalize to young mothers on welfare who are high school dropouts, New Chance was a voluntary program. Sample characteristics at random assignment include: average age, 18.8; 71 percent nonwhite; average age of youngest child, 1.2 years; 94 percent of sample did not have a high school diploma or equivalent; 3.1 percent were employed at baseline; and 95 percent received AFDC.

FUNDING SOURCES: U.S. Department of Labor and a broad consortium of private foundations and corporations.

TREATMENT ADMINISTRATOR: Manpower Demonstration Research Corporation was responsible for the overall treatment. Direct administration was the responsibility of the individual sites.

EVALUATOR: Manpower Demonstration Research Corporation. Key personnel: Robert C. Granger.

ENABLING LEGISLATION: None.

INFORMATION SOURCE: Janet C. Quint, Hans Bos, and Denise F. Polit, *New Chance: Final Findings on a Comprehensive Program for Disadvantaged Young Mothers and Their Children,* Manpower Demonstration Research Corporation, May 1997.

PUBLIC-USE ACCESS TO DATA: Available through Manpower Demonstration Research Corporation.

Ohio Transitions to Independence Demonstration—JOBS

SUMMARY: This demonstration, conducted from 1989 to 1992, tested the effects of employment and training participation on a large sample of welfare recipients. Subjects were followed for up to three years. The JOBS demonstration was one component of a larger evaluation, which also included the Work Choice demonstration, p. 84.

COST: Evaluation costs, approximately $3 million (includes Work Choice).

TIME FRAME: Demonstration period, January 1989–December 1992; data collected, same period; final report, December 1994.

TREATMENTS TESTED: Mandatory employment and training services, which included basic and post-secondary education, community work experience, and job search assistance.

OUTCOMES OF INTEREST: (1) Employment; (2) Earnings; and (3) Welfare receipt.

SAMPLE SIZE: Experimentals, 24,120 (a random subsample was used for analysis); controls, 4,371.

TARGET POPULATION: All recipients of ADC (Ohio's AFDC program).

NUMBER OF TREATMENT GROUPS: Two (with one control group).

NUMBER AND LOCATION OF SITES: Fifteen—Brown, Champaign, Clermont, Franklin, Lake, Lawrence, Montgomery, Perry, Pickaway, Richland, Seneca, Stark, Summit, Trumbull, and Wyandot counties.

RESEARCH COMPONENTS:
- Process analysis: Implementation, participation rates, and assignment patterns analyzed.
- Impact analysis: Conducted using regression-adjusted means.
- Benefit–cost analysis: Conducted.

MAJOR FINDINGS:
1. JOBS produced significantly higher rates of employment for all experimental group cohorts compared with the control group (e.g., for third-year follow-up: experimental group, 45.5 percent; control group, 42.2 percent).
2. JOBS produced no significant differences between experimental and control groups for earnings or ADC receipt. However, subgroup analysis does indicate significant earnings impacts among clients with 12 or more years of education. This supports past research suggesting that mandatory employment and training programs tend to boost earnings more for moderately disadvantaged clients than for the most or least disadvantaged.

TIME TRENDS IN FINDINGS: No trends were evident, though the report suggests that the nature of the program assignments implies that long-run impacts could take longer to emerge than the follow-up period covered in the evaluation.

DESIGN ISSUES:
1. The state found itself having to provide a wide new array of employment and training services with extremely limited resources to a broad clientele. Implementation of JOBS coincided with a recession. The resulting effects were lengthy waits for assessment and assignment, low rates of participation, and insufficient program staff to support key case management functions (e.g., monitoring and sanctioning).
2. A tradition of autonomous county governments contributed to the slow pace of JOBS implementation. Counties often had to develop their own approaches to many tasks.
3. Two different state systems made data file construction difficult. Further, the system was changed midway through the demonstration.

REPLICABILITY: Replicable.

GENERALIZABILITY: Designed to generalize to the entire state. The sample counties' populations resembled the state's as a whole, and Ohio's ADC caseload characteristics and benefits closely resemble those of the nation as a whole. Random assignment at the point of eligibility determination provides an approximation of a fully implemented program. Impacts for the JOBS program are not as favorable as those found in other states (e.g., California and Florida).

FUNDING SOURCES: Ohio Department of Human Services. Key personnel: Jackie Martin. The U.S. Department of Health and Human Services matched state funds.

TREATMENT ADMINISTRATOR: Ohio Department of Human Services. Key personnel: Ellen Seusy and Jackie Martin. The County Departments of Human Services in the sample counties had substantial autonomy and responsibility for administering these programs.

EVALUATOR: Abt Associates. Key personnel: David Fein, Erik Beecroft, and John Blomquist.

ENABLING LEGISLATION: None.

INFORMATION SOURCE: David Fein, Erik Beecroft, and John Blomquist, *The Ohio Transitions to Independence Demonstration: Final Impacts for JOBS and Work Choice,* Abt Associates, December 1994.

PUBLIC-USE ACCESS TO DATA: A data tape from the demonstration is in the custody of the Ohio Department of Human Services. Jackie Martin, in a telephone communication (March 1997), stated that the Department had not made any decisions about public access.

Ohio Transitions to Independence Demonstration— Work Choice

SUMMARY: This demonstration, conducted from 1989 to 1990, tested the effects of voluntary employment and training services and extended transitional Medicaid and child care payments on a large sample of single-parent welfare recipients with children under age 6. These subjects were followed for up to 18 months. This was one component of a larger evaluation, which included the JOBS demonstration, p. 82.

COST: Evaluation costs, approximately $3 million (for both Work Choice and JOBS demonstrations).

TIME FRAME: Demonstration period, January 1989– December 1990; data collected, same period; final report, December 1994.

TREATMENTS TESTED: Work Choice tested the same services as JOBS (employment and training services, basic and postsecondary education, community work experience, and job search assistance) plus extended transitional Medicaid and child care payments upon leaving ADC (Ohio's AFDC program) for work.

OUTCOMES OF INTEREST: (1) Employment; (2) Earnings; and (3) Welfare receipt.

SAMPLE SIZE: Experimentals, 4,265; controls, 1,344.

TARGET POPULATION: Single-parent ADC clients with children age 1 to 5.

NUMBER OF TREATMENT GROUPS: Two (with one control group).

NUMBER AND LOCATION OF SITES: One— Montgomery Country, Ohio (including city of Dayton).

RESEARCH COMPONENTS:
- Process analysis: Implementation, participation rates, and assignment patterns analyzed.
- Impact analysis: Conducted using regression-adjusted means.
- Benefit–cost analysis: Conducted.

MAJOR FINDINGS:
1. The vast majority of Work Choice assignments were to education and training activities, mostly basic and postsecondary programs (34 percent of entrants volunteering for activities received basic education, 33 percent received postsecondary programs). By the end of follow-up, only 14 percent had volunteered for employment and training activities, half as many as in the JOBS program.
2. Work Choice had small, though significant, positive impacts on net employment and earnings. Employment rates were about 3 percentage points higher for members of the experimental group than for members of the control group, and their average earnings were about $177 higher over the 18-month period.
3. Only 4 percent of experimental group members and 3 percent of control group members used extended Medicaid sometime during the 18-month follow-up period when they left ADC. Although this 1 percentage point difference is statistically significant, it is far from clear that the extended benefits were an incentive for welfare-to-work transitions.

TIME TRENDS IN FINDINGS: No trends were evident, though the report suggests that the nature of the program assignments implies that long-run impacts could take longer to emerge than the follow-up period covered in the evaluation.

DESIGN ISSUES:
1. The state found itself having to provide a wide new array of employment and training services with extremely limited resources to a broad clientele. Implementation coincided with a recession. The resulting effects were lengthy waits for assessment and assignment, low rates of participation, and insufficient program staff to support key case management functions (e.g., monitoring and sanctioning).

2. A tradition of autonomous county governments contributed to the slow pace of implementation. Counties often had to develop their own approaches to many tasks.
3. The Work Choice demonstration ended earlier than planned when, in April 1990, the state began offering eligibility for extended Medicaid and child care benefits to members of the control group. This led to a maximum follow-up of only 18 months.
4. Two different state systems made data file construction difficult. Further, the system was changed midway through the demonstration.

REPLICABILITY: Replicable.

GENERALIZABILITY: Designed to generalize to the entire state. The sample county's population resembled the state's as a whole, and Ohio's ADC caseload characteristics and benefits closely resemble those of the nation as a whole. Random assignment at the point of eligibility determination provides an approximation of a fully implemented program.

FUNDING SOURCES: Ohio Department of Human Services. Key personnel: Jackie Martin. The U.S. Department of Health and Human Services matched state funds.

TREATMENT ADMINISTRATOR: Ohio Department of Human Services. Key personnel: Ellen Seusy and Jackie Martin. The County Departments of Human Services in the sample counties had substantial autonomy and responsibility for administering these programs.

EVALUATOR: Abt Associates. Key personnel: David Fein, Erik Beecroft, and John Blomquist.

ENABLING LEGISLATION: None.

INFORMATION SOURCE: David Fein, Erik Beecroft, and John Blomquist, *The Ohio Transitions to Independence Demonstration: Final Impacts for JOBS and Work Choice,* Abt Associates, December 1994.

PUBLIC-USE ACCESS TO DATA: A data tape from the demonstration is in the custody of the Ohio Department of Human Services. Jackie Martin, in a telephone communication (March 1997), stated that the Department had not made any decisions about public access.

Opportunity Knocks Program

SUMMARY: This demonstration, conducted from 1989 through 1992, tested the effects of intensive case management on a small sample of low-income single-parent families. Subjects were followed for two years.

COST: Evaluation costs, approximately $20,000–$22,000.

TIME FRAME: Demonstration period, July 1989–November 1991 with a one-year extension; data collected, same period; final report, April 1995.

TREATMENTS TESTED: Intensive case management, which included vocational assessment, education, training, and job search assistance. Funds were also made available for transportation, child care, and other employment-related expenses. The control group received minimal counseling and referral services, as well as job training and housing assistance.

OUTCOMES OF INTEREST: (1) Employment; (2) Earnings; and (3) Welfare receipt.

SAMPLE SIZE: Experimentals, 82; controls, 81.

TARGET POPULATION: Single-parent families receiving AFDC, applying for or residing in Section 8 housing, or at or below 125 percent of the poverty level.

NUMBER OF TREATMENT GROUPS: Two (with one control group).

NUMBER AND LOCATION OF SITES: One—DuPage County, Illinois.

RESEARCH COMPONENTS:

▪ Process analysis: Conducted to describe the process of partnership development, service delivery, and program environment.

▪ Impact analysis: Conducted using comparison of means.

▪ Benefit–cost analysis: Not conducted.

MAJOR FINDINGS:

1. After a negative impact on employment during the first quarter after enrollment, the program produced steadily increasing employment effects for the experimental group. The difference between the experimental group and the control group became statistically significant in the sixth quarter and remained significant through the eighth quarter. The total impact of the program in the second year after enrollment was also significant, culminating in an almost 12 percent difference between the groups (employment rate: experimental group, 47 percent; control group, 35.2 percent).

2. The earning impacts closely resembled those found for employment. The earnings differential steadily increased to produce a significant impact of $415 per quarter per participant in the second year (experimental group, $1,251 per quarter; control group, $836).

3. The average experimental group family, despite significant earnings gains, remained below the poverty level.

TIME TRENDS IN FINDINGS: Employment and earnings impacts were negative (experimental group was employed at a lower rate and earned less) in the first and second quarters, respectively. Positive impacts became significant and increased over time in the fifth and sixth quarters, respectively.

DESIGN ISSUES:

1. Because of problems recruiting sufficient AFDC families to the program, the target population needed to be expanded. As a result, nearly 25 percent of the sample was not receiving AFDC when they enrolled.

2. Owing to difficulties surrounding the confidentiality of the public aid records and the technical complexity of conducting a database search, the use of a cash welfare benefit measure was not included in the analysis.

3. Lack of training and ambiguous or nonexistent definitions of data elements led to coding errors and to the omission of information.

4. After a brief intake, "no one was really involved" in the application procedure to contact participants and encourage their participation. Many participants were lost at this point. Nearly 45 percent of the experimental group never showed up, did not follow through, or were unable to participate. This group of nonparticipants was included in the analysis.

REPLICABILITY: Replicable. Documentation of the procedures is available to ensure consistency of service, though more training for case managers would be necessary to improve the implementation of these procedures.

GENERALIZABILITY: The small sample size and the design and implementation issues discourage attempts at generalizability.

FUNDING SOURCES: DuPage County and U.S. Department of Health and Human Services (HHS), Administration for Children and Families, Office of Community Services.

TREATMENT ADMINISTRATOR: DuPage County Department of Human Resources, Division of Human Services. Key personnel: Jack Tenison, director, and Betsey Eben, program manager.

EVALUATOR: Center for Governmental Studies, Northern Illinois University. Key personnel: Catherine Harned, senior research associate, and Sean Fahey, research associate.

ENABLING LEGISLATION: Demonstration Partnership Program, under section 408 of the Human Services Reauthorization Act of 1986, as amended.

INFORMATION SOURCE: U.S. Department of Health and Human Services, *Summary of Final*

Evaluation Findings from FY 1991: Demonstration Partnership Program Projects. Monograph Series 100-91: Case Management/Family Development, 1995.

PUBLIC-USE ACCESS TO DATA: Available through HHS Office of Community Services.

Wisconsin Earned Income Disregard Demonstration

SUMMARY: This demonstration, conducted from 1989 to 1992, tested the effects of a more generous income disregard on a large sample of AFDC recipients. Subjects were followed for four years.

COST: The evaluations of both the Earned Income Disregard and the Medical Assistance Extension demonstrations were conducted together. Total evaluation costs, $368,953.

TIME FRAME: Demonstration period, February 1989–March 1992; data collected, same period.

TREATMENTS TESTED: An increase in the earned income disregard to $30 and one-sixth of earned income for 12 months. The control group disregard was the existing $30 and one-third of earned income for four months and $30 for the remaining eight months. The disregard is used to calculate AFDC grant amounts.

OUTCOMES OF INTEREST: (1) Welfare participation and benefit receipt; (2) Employment; (3) Family income; and (4) Program costs.

SAMPLE SIZE: Exact figures were unavailable, although the sample was the entire statewide caseload. Ninety percent of this caseload was in the experimental group; 10 percent was in the control group.

TARGET POPULATION: AFDC recipients.

NUMBER OF TREATMENT GROUPS: Two (with one control group).

NUMBER AND LOCATION OF SITES: Throughout the state of Wisconsin.

RESEARCH COMPONENTS:
- Process analysis: The evaluators met regularly with the state team to discuss the demonstration's progress.
- Impact analysis: Comparison of means.
- Benefit–cost analysis: Not conducted.

MAJOR FINDINGS: There was no significant difference between groups on welfare participation, AFDC grant level, overall program costs, or family income.

TIME TRENDS IN FINDINGS: None.

DESIGN ISSUES: Two separate evaluation teams worked on this project. Design and data collection were completed by one team. A second group of evaluators was brought in to conduct data analysis when, according to one evaluator of the second team, the state was not pleased with early results. There seems to have been little communication between the two teams. Process analysis was minimal and program goals were unclear to those involved in the analysis.

REPLICABILITY: Replicable.

GENERALIZABILITY: Designed to generalize to the entire state of Wisconsin.

FUNDING SOURCE: Wisconsin Department of Health and Social Services (DHSS). Key personnel: Richard Zynde.

TREATMENT ADMINISTRATOR: Wisconsin DHSS.

EVALUATOR: Deloitte and Touche LLP. Key personnel: Steve Blank.

ENABLING LEGISLATION: None.

INFORMATION SOURCE: Wisconsin Department of Health and Social Services, *Evaluation of Earned Income Disregard and MA Extension Waivers,* March 1995.

PUBLIC-USE ACCESS TO DATA: Available from Wisconsin DHSS.

Wisconsin Medical Assistance Extension Demonstration

SUMMARY: This demonstration, conducted from 1989 to 1990, tested the effect of extending transitional Medical Assistance benefits on a large sample of ex-AFDC recipients. Subjects were followed for 14 months.

COST: The evaluations of both the Earned Income Disregard and the Medical Assistance Extension demonstrations were conducted together. Total evaluation costs, $368,953.

TIME FRAME: Demonstration period, February 1989–April 1990. The demonstration period was designed to be longer but was cut short when the state adopted the 12-month extension for all eligible individuals.

TREATMENTS TESTED: An extension of Medical Assistance (MA) for 12 months after termination of AFDC eligibility owing to earned income or excess hours of employment. The control group received the existing 4/9 policy (cases were reviewed after 4 months and possibly approved for an additional 9 months).

OUTCOMES OF INTEREST: (1) Welfare participation and benefit receipt; (2) Employment; (3) Family income; and (4) Program costs.

SAMPLE SIZE: Experimentals, 135,334; controls, 18,493.

TARGET POPULATION: Individuals leaving the AFDC rolls owing to employment.

NUMBER OF TREATMENT GROUPS: Two (with one control group).

NUMBER AND LOCATION OF SITES: Wisconsin, statewide.

RESEARCH COMPONENTS:
- Process analysis: The evaluators met regularly with the state team to discuss the demonstration's progress.
- Impact analysis: Comparison of means.
- Benefit–cost analysis: Not conducted.

MAJOR FINDINGS:
1. There was no significant difference between groups in welfare participation, overall costs, or family income. This indicates that the treatment did not result in an incentive for cases to leave the AFDC program.
2. There was a lower rate of recidivism (returning to the AFDC rolls after leaving) for the experimental group compared with the control group. In the experimental group, 73.2 percent of cases that closed during the project period never reopened. For control group cases, this figure was 69.8 percent, for a difference of 3.4 percent.

TIME TRENDS IN FINDINGS: None.

DESIGN ISSUES:
1. Two separate evaluation teams worked on this project. Design and data collection were completed by one team. A second group of evaluators was brought in to conduct data analysis when, according to one evaluator, the state was not pleased with early results. There seems to have been little communication between the two teams. Process analysis was minimal, and program goals were unclear to those involved in the analysis.
2. There was a limited comparison period because the 12-month MA extension was implemented as the standard program statewide in April 1990, thereby making the treatment available to the entire target population.

REPLICABILITY: Replicable.

GENERALIZABILITY: Designed to generalize to the entire state of Wisconsin.

FUNDING SOURCE: Wisconsin Department of Health and Social Services (DHSS). Key personnel: Richard Zynde.

TREATMENT ADMINISTRATOR: Wisconsin DHSS.

EVALUATOR: Deloitte and Touche LLP. Key personnel: Steve Blank.

ENABLING LEGISLATION: None.

INFORMATION SOURCE: Wisconsin Department of Health and Social Services, *Evaluation of Earned Income Disregard and MA Extension Waivers,* March 1995.

PUBLIC-USE ACCESS TO DATA: Available from Wisconsin DHSS.

Ohio Learning, Earning, and Parenting Program (LEAP)

SUMMARY: This demonstration, conducted from 1989 to 1995, tested the effects of applying bonuses and sanctions to the benefit checks of a large sample of custodial or pregnant teens on welfare in order to encourage school attendance. Subjects were followed for four years.

COST: Total administrative cost, approximately $4,800,000 or $1,388 per program group teen, who participated on average for 22.3 months. The incentives did not add to the cost, because on average, teens received slightly more sanctions than bonuses.

TIME FRAME: Demonstration period, August 1989–September 1991; data collection, August 1990–September 1995; final report, July 1997.

TREATMENTS TESTED:
1. The experimentals faced a financial incentive tied to school attendance and sanctions for noncompliance. The benefit increase was $62 for school enrollment with an additional $62 for regular monthly attendance. The sanction was an equal amount and was assessed for unacceptable absences or non-enrollment. Temporary exemptions were allowed for medical, child care, and transportation reasons. Experimentals also received case management

and child care and transportation services. Cleveland had an enhanced version of LEAP, with school-based services such as child care, intensive case management, special GED classes, and other services.
2. The control group was not eligible for any component of LEAP except its child care services on an as-available basis. They had access to state-run programs that offered parenting classes, but little else.

OUTCOMES OF INTEREST: (1) School enrollment; (2) Attendance; (3) Graduation; (4) GED receipt; (5) Welfare receipt; (6) Employment; and (7) Earnings.

SAMPLE SIZE: Four-year follow-up: Experimentals, 3,479; controls, 672. Some analyses use a smaller three-year subsample.

TARGET POPULATION: Pregnant or custodial teen parents under 20 years of age who were receiving welfare.

NUMBER OF TREATMENT GROUPS: Two (with one control group).

NUMBER AND LOCATION OF SITES: Twelve counties statewide—Cuyahoga (Cleveland), Franklin, Hamilton, Jefferson, Lawrence, Lorain, Lucas, Montgomery, Muskingum, Stark, Summit, and Trumbull.

RESEARCH COMPONENTS:
- Process analysis: Administrative data review, site visits, and surveys were used to evaluate implementation. The program operated as designed after some initial start-up problems.
- Impact analysis: OLS regression.
- Benefit–cost analysis: Conducted. Calculated additional administrative costs versus LEAP-induced savings in AFDC, Food Stamps, and Medicaid expenditures.

MAJOR FINDINGS (see table, p. 90):
1. Program succeeded in reaching 93 percent of eligible teens.

Major Findings

Measure	Experimentals	Controls	Impact
Full sample			
In the 12 months after random assignment			
Number of months enrolled in high school	4.8	4.2	0.6**
Number of months enrolled in a GED program	1.3	0.8	0.5***
In the 3 years after random assignment			
Ever completed grade 11 (%)	50.0	45.4	4.6*
Ever completed high school (%)	22.9	23.5	−0.6
Ever received a GED (%)	11.1	8.4	2.7
Ever employed			
Year 2 (%)	43.8	40.6	3.1*
Year 3 (%)	51.3	49.8	1.4
Year 4 (%)	61.0	59.6	1.4
Total earnings, years 1–4 ($)	4,405	4,293	112
Amount of AFDC received, years 3 and 4 ($)	5,185	5,459	−275**
Sample members enrolled in high school or in a GED program at random assignment			
In the 12 months after random assignment			
Number of months enrolled in high school	7.3	6.6	0.7*
Number of months enrolled in a GED program	0.9	0.7	0.3
In the 3 years after random assignment			
Ever completed grade 11 (%)	60.6	58.1	2.5
Ever completed high school (%)	35.6	34.2	1.4
Ever received a GED (%)	10.0	4.4	5.6**
Ever employed			
Year 2 (%)	46.4	39.7	6.7***
Year 3 (%)	55.7	54.7	1.0
Year 4 (%)	65.1	60.5	4.6*
Total earnings, years 1–4 ($)	4,862	4,319	544
Amount of AFDC received, years 3 and 4 ($)	5,181	5,497	−316**
Sample members not enrolled in high school or in a GED program at random assignment			
In the 12 months after random assignment			
Number of months enrolled in high school	1.5	1.0	0.5*
Number of months enrolled in a GED program	1.7	0.9	0.8***
In the 3 years after random assignment			
Ever completed grade 11 (%)	35.8	28.0	7.8*
Ever completed high school (%)	6.7	7.8	−1.1
Ever received a GED (%)	12.0	14.3	−2.3
Ever employed			
Year 2 (%)	41.0	42.2	−1.2
Year 3 (%)	46.3	44.0	2.4
Year 4 (%)	56.3	58.7	−2.6
Total earnings, years 1–4 ($)	3,930	4,271	−341
Amount of AFDC received, years 3 & 4 ($)	5,172	5,395	−223

* = finding significant at the $p < .10$ level; ** = finding significant at the $p < .05$ level; *** = finding significant at the $p < .01$ level.

2. LEAP significantly increased school enrollment and attendance. Initial school status was an important predictor of program success; those who were enrolled when the program started had better outcomes.
3. Ohio Department of Human Services and taxpayers' benefits outweighed costs. LEAP teens experienced a net loss of $1,110 over the four years. This was calculated as the difference in gains in earnings and tax credits, and losses owing to reductions in AFDC, Food Stamps, and Medicaid eligibility.
4. Enhanced program in Cleveland had some impact on high school graduation rates for those teens initially enrolled.

TIME TRENDS IN FINDINGS: No consistent time trend.

DESIGN ISSUES:
1. The research sample entered the program before LEAP was fully implemented. This may have resulted in conservative results being reported.
2. Teens identified problems at school as reason for nonattendance. The LEAP program was not designed to address those problems.

REPLICABILITY: Replicable. LEAP has been used as model for other state programs.

GENERALIZABILITY: Designed to be generalizable to the rest of the country. However, the problem of identifying eligible teens, which created implementation difficulties in this program, could seriously hamper less technologically advanced systems.

FUNDING SOURCES: Ohio Department of Human Services. Key personnel: Mary Harris and Loretta Adams, project officers. Additional funding from the Ford Foundation, the Cleveland Foundation, BP America, the Treu-Mart Fund, the George Gund Foundation, the Procter & Gamble Fund, and the U.S. Department of Health and Human Services.

TREATMENT ADMINISTRATOR: Ohio Department of Human Services county offices.

EVALUATOR: Manpower Demonstration Research Corporation. Key personnel: Johannes M. Bos, Veronica Fellerath, and David Long.

ENABLING LEGISLATION: None.

INFORMATION SOURCES: Johannes Bos and Veronica Fellerath, *LEAP: Final Report on Ohio's Welfare Initiative to Improve School Attendance Among Teenage Parents,* Manpower Demonstration Research Corporation, August 1997.

David Long, Robert Wood, and Hilary Kopp, *LEAP: The Educational Effects of LEAP and Enhanced Services in Cleveland,* Manpower Demonstration Research Corporation, October 1994.

Dan Bloom, Veronica Fellerath, David Long, and Robert Wood, *LEAP: Interim Findings on a Welfare Initiative to Improve School Attendance Among Teenage Parents,* Manpower Demonstration Research Corporation, May 1993.

PUBLIC-USE ACCESS TO DATA: Not currently available. Contact Ohio Department of Human Services.

Alabama Avenues to Self-Sufficiency through Employment and Training Services (ASSETS)

SUMMARY: This quasi-experimental demonstration, conducted from July 1990 to June 1994, tested the effects of broadening the population subject to participation requirements in employment and training activities (E&T) and child support enforcement efforts (CSE); and combining Food Stamps with AFDC in one cash grant for a large sample of AFDC and Food Stamp recipients. Participants were followed for up to three years.

COST: Evaluation cost, $1,844,620 over four years.

TIME FRAME: Demonstration period and data collection, July 1990–June 1994; final report, January 1997.

TREATMENTS TESTED:

1. In experimental counties, Food Stamps (renamed Nutritional Assistance, or NA) were combined with AFDC in one cash grant. Families that would have been eligible for NA only were subject to the same participation requirements as AFDC families in both E&T and CSE. A single case manager administered all income assistance programs, determined Medicaid eligibility, and provided recipients access to E&T services. Eligibility rules, program definitions, and administrative procedures were simplified. Eligibility was extended to two-parent families with children who met certain program criteria. Sanctions for noncompliance involved loss of the portion of benefits normally paid out for the noncompliant household member.

2. In comparison counties, AFDC families had similar E&T and CSE requirements but Food Stamp families did not. Programs were administered separately. Two comparison counties did not offer E&T to Food Stamp–only participants.

OUTCOMES OF INTEREST: (1) Welfare status and benefits; (2) Employment; (3) Earnings; (4) CSE status and benefits; and (5) Food consumption.

SAMPLE SIZE: All ASSETS households and recipients active in the three demonstration counties at any time from the month of implementation to June 30, 1993. See table below.

TARGET POPULATION: AFDC and Food Stamp Program recipients in Alabama.

NUMBER OF TREATMENT GROUPS: Two (with one comparison group).

NUMBER AND LOCATION OF SITES: Six—Limestone, Clarke, and Madison counties (ASSETS group), and Chilton, Butler, and Tuscaloosa counties (comparison group). Counties were matched on certain characteristics and then the experimental and comparison counties were randomly assigned.

RESEARCH COMPONENTS:

▪ Process analysis: Conducted. The planning, development, and operation were documented.

▪ Impact analysis: Conducted in two parts. The Food Stamp Cash-Out Study measured impact on household expenditure patterns and food retailer revenues. The Welfare Dependency and Household Income Study used sample cohorts, observation periods, and client subgroups. OLS regression in both studies controlled for differences at sample entry.

▪ Benefit–cost analysis: Conducted.

MAJOR FINDINGS:

1. After adjusting for household size and composition, cash-out of food stamps resulted in 18 percent lower food expenditures for ASSETS households than for comparisons.

2. Adults were two to four times more likely to be referred to E&T programs under ASSETS than under the traditional program. This figure was even higher for those entering after full implementation.

3. There was no statistically significant increase in adults' employment or earnings over three years after entering the demonstration. The finding is the same for both those who participated in E&T and those who did not. The proportion of active welfare clients working was lower under ASSETS than in the comparison counties.

Sample Sizes

Program county	Households	Individuals	Comparison county	Households	Individuals
Limestone	4,573	12,636	Chilton	469	9,779
Clarke	3,485	10,616	Butler	2,886	8,701
Madison	21,546	49,955	Tuscaloosa	13,330	35,250

4. ASSETS increased the involvement in the CSE program of NA-only families with children. However, the only increases in support payments were in Limestone County, in all three years, and in Madison County, in the first year.

5. ASSETS increased welfare payments in Clarke and Madison counties and decreased payments in Limestone County.

6. Looking at welfare activity, defined as application for and length of time receiving benefits (AFDC and NA programs overall and individually), ASSETS reduced overall welfare activity in Limestone and Madison counties and had no effect on activity in Clarke. ASSETS generally increased AFDC activity in all three counties. Impacts on NA activity were mixed, with no significant impact in Clarke and fluctuations in Limestone and Madison.

7. The treatment reduced the administrative costs for income assistance programs, AFDC, Food Stamp, Medicaid, and E&T by 20 to 40 percent ($3.58–$7.83 per case per month) but increased them for the CSE program by 20 to 50 percent ($0.63–$1.48 per case per month).

8. ASSETS households did not spend significantly more on food outside the home than the comparisons.

9. ASSETS households spent significantly more than the comparisons on transportation (39 percent) and shelter (9 percent). Expenditures for other nonfood items were similar for both groups.

10. Eighty percent of both groups reported having enough to eat, while 5–6 percent reported having run out of food, benefits, or money in the month prior to their interview.

11. No change in rents or food prices was detected. Checks were preferred by almost 60 percent of ASSETS participants; only 15 percent preferred the coupons.

12. Food retailers reported decreased sales and profits as a result of the cash-out, but sales were not analyzed directly.

13. The treatment was not cost-effective. Clients' monthly incomes were lower, but government costs were higher under ASSETS because of higher net welfare payments. Governments (state and federal) spent $5.10 to $11.82 more per household per month under the program. The only benefit from the governments' standpoint was a $3 per month per household savings in administrative costs.

TIME TRENDS IN FINDINGS: None reported.

DESIGN ISSUES:

1. The program began operations at different times in each of the three ASSETS counties and various aspects of the program were implemented at different points throughout the first 18 months. The problem was addressed by reporting two sets of data, with differing lengths of analysis for groups depending on date of entry into the program.

2. A delay in the implementation of the new administrative computer system caused a delay in recipients receiving E&T services. Therefore the evaluation presents impact and benefit–cost results for the entire demonstration period and for the period of "full implementation" (September 1992 through June 1994).

3. The approach assumes that the factors chosen to match counties are correlated with welfare behavior and that they will remain relatively stable in both the experimental and comparison counties during the demonstration. The research design for the analysis of impacts does not permit technical adjustments that can control statistically for county differences due to changing factors.

4. The use of matching with random assignment by county leaves room for substantial error. The evaluators adjusted for preexisting differences, however, by collecting data from both the experimental and comparison counties from two years prior to the demonstration.

5. Intact two-parent families became eligible for cash grants in non-ASSETS counties through the AFDC-Unemployed Parent extension at a

later point in the program. This change resulted in the invalidation of an unknown number of observations.

REPLICABILITY: The program, modified slightly and minus the food stamp cash-out component, is currently in use throughout the state. The report noted that the low sanction rate implementation differed from the original design.

GENERALIZABILITY: Designed to be generalizable to Alabama. But the design chose the most closely matched counties in the state and these may not be completely representative of the remaining counties. For example, some of the smaller counties could not offer some of the services included in this demonstration. Two other studies, in San Diego and Alabama (pp. 161 and 162), found smaller differences in the food expenditures of households whose benefits were converted from coupons to cash.

FUNDING SOURCES: The U.S. Department of Agriculture funded the food stamp cash-out study. The second study was funded by the USDA, the U.S. Department of Health and Human Services, and the Alabama Department of Human Resources.

TREATMENT ADMINISTRATOR: Alabama Department of Human Resources. Key personnel: Gudrun Hanson and Judy Bernier.

EVALUATOR: Abt Associates. Key personnel: Alan Werner, project director.

ENABLING LEGISLATION: None.

POLICY EFFECTS: Because of findings from this and other demonstrations, USDA decided not to contemplate any further cash-out programs.

INFORMATION SOURCES: Alan Werner, David Rodda, Elsie Pan, and Lisa Plimpton, *Evaluation of the Alabama Avenues to Self-Sufficiency through Employment and Training Services (ASSETS) Demonstration.* Abt Associates Inc., January 1997.

Alan Werner and David Rodda, *Evaluation of the Alabama Avenues to Self-Sufficiency through Employment and Training Services (ASSETS) Demonstration: Interim Impact Report,* Abt Associates Inc., September 1994.

Elizabeth Davis and Alan Werner, *Food Stamp Cash-Out Study,* Abt Associates Inc., May 1993.

PUBLIC-USE ACCESS TO DATA: Available through the Alabama Department of Human Resources, 50 Ripley St., Montgomery, AL 36130, (334) 242-1773.

AFDC JOBS Participants: Paths toward Self-Sufficiency

SUMMARY: This demonstration, conducted between 1990 and 1992, tested the effects of in-home case management on a medium-sized sample of AFDC recipients. Subjects were followed for one year.

COST: Unavailable. The Demonstration Partnership Program grants were generally between $350,000 and $500,000, with roughly 10 percent going toward evaluation.

TIME FRAME: Demonstration period, October 1990–December 1992; data collected, same period; final report, December 1993.

TREATMENTS TESTED: In-home case management coupled with core support services. These included educational/job training assistance, basic living skills workshop, counseling, housing assistance, child care assistance, transportation, and health care assistance. Services were roughly the same for both the intensive and nonintensive groups, although the nature of the clients was different. The control group received existing AFDC services.

OUTCOMES OF INTEREST: (1) Earnings; (2) AFDC receipt; (3) Educational or employment status; and (4) Other measures of self-sufficiency.

SAMPLE SIZE: Initial sample: intensive group, 121; nonintensive group, 92; control group, 123.

Sample retained and used in analysis: intensive, 42; nonintensive, 70; control, 85.

TARGET POPULATION: AFDC recipients in the Lincoln, Nebraska, JOBS program, at or below 125 percent of the poverty level.

NUMBER OF TREATMENT GROUPS: Three—intensive group (phase I, not randomly assigned); nonintensive group; and control group (phase II, randomly assigned).

NUMBER AND LOCATION OF SITES: One—Lincoln, Nebraska.

RESEARCH COMPONENTS:

- Process analysis: Special attention was paid to program retention and service delivery.
- Impact analysis: Pre-/postproject comparison, comparison of means.
- Benefit–cost analysis: SRI Gallup conducted a benefit–cost analysis in a separate report issued six months into the intervention. A benefit–cost analysis was not done as part of the final report.

MAJOR FINDINGS: Note that random assignment occurred only in phase II. Direct comparisons should only be made between the nonintensive group and the control group. The project report, however, combines the two project groups in the analysis of some outcome measures.

1. For all groups, salary increased significantly and AFDC payments decreased significantly from pretest to posttest. Project group numbers were larger than those of the control group though not statistically significant. (Average change in salary: intensive, $150.74; nonintensive, $200.01; control, $156.59. Average decrease in AFDC payments: intensive, $71.33; nonintensive, $76.47; control, $53.80.)
2. A significantly higher percentage of project (intensive and nonintensive) participants continued their education compared with the control group.
3. Project groups had significantly greater gains on the Goal Attainment Scale (GAS), a measure of basic living skills, than did the control group.

TIME TRENDS IN FINDINGS: None mentioned.

DESIGN ISSUES:

1. Because of the referral process, initial participants faced severe barriers to self-sufficiency. This group was therefore not assigned randomly to experimental and control groups, but received intensive case management. They differed significantly from the other two groups on a number of variables.
2. The rate of attrition was higher than expected, especially for the intensive group. After mandatory referral from the Nebraska Department of Social Services, participants were allowed to voluntarily continue with case management. Many participants were lost at this point.
3. Staff turnover was problematic. A number of staff left the project when the agency received other longer-term grants. This may have reduced the project's effectiveness.

REPLICABILITY: The report states that replication of this project would be easy owing to the detailed explanation of the interventions used. The project's model has been replicated with other agency projects.

GENERALIZABILITY: Findings from the phase I (intensive) group are not generalizable since no similar control group was used. Random assignment of the nonintensive group does allow for comparison and generalizations, though the sample was quite small. Both experimental groups tended to have greater barriers to self-sufficiency than the AFDC population in general.

FUNDING SOURCE: U.S. Department of Health and Human Services (HHS), Administration for Children and Families, Office of Community Services. Key personnel: Anna Guidery.

TREATMENT ADMINISTRATOR: Lincoln Action Program. Key personnel: Beatty Brasch, director, and Anne Caruso.

EVALUATOR: Gary Hoeltke (deceased), SRI Gallup.

ENABLING LEGISLATION: Demonstration Partnership Program, under section 408 of the Human Services Reauthorization Act of 1986, as amended.

INFORMATION SOURCE: U.S. Department of Health and Human Services, *Demonstration Partnership Program Projects: Summary of Final Evaluation Findings from 1990.* Case Management Family Intervention Models, 1993.

PUBLIC-USE ACCESS TO DATA: Available through the DHHS Office of Community Services.

Project Independence—Florida

SUMMARY: This demonstration, conducted from 1990 to 1993, tested the effects of education, training, and enhanced support services on a large sample of AFDC recipients. Subjects were followed for three years.

COST: Evaluation costs, $3.6 million over five years.

TIME FRAME: Demonstration period, July 1990–September 1993; data collected, same period; final report, April 1995.

TREATMENTS TESTED: The experimental group was eligible to receive Project Independence services and was subject to a participation mandate. Services included independent job search, job club, assessment, basic education, and training. The control group was not eligible for these services and was not subject to a participation mandate. They were given a list of alternative employment and training services in the community.

OUTCOMES OF INTEREST: (1) Employment; (2) Earnings; and (3) AFDC receipt.

SAMPLE SIZE: Experimentals, 13,513; controls, 4,724.

TARGET POPULATION: Single-parent heads of household who were required to participate in the program (recipients of AFDC).

NUMBER OF TREATMENT GROUPS: Two (with one control group).

NUMBER AND LOCATION OF SITES: Nine—Bay, Broward, Dade, Duval, Hillsborough, Lee, Orange, Pinellas, and Volusia counties.

RESEARCH COMPONENTS:
- Process analysis: The evaluators paid special attention to the changes in service delivery and resources that occurred over the evaluation period.
- Impact analysis: Conducted using comparisons of regression-adjusted means.
- Benefit–cost analysis: Conducted.

MAJOR FINDINGS:
1. Project Independence resulted in a modest decrease in experimental group members' AFDC and food stamp receipts. Experimental group members received, on average, a total of $265 less than the control group members. This decrease persisted over the two-year follow-up period.
2. A modest earnings gain was achieved by the experimental group members in the first year but declined greatly in the second year. Average two-year earnings increased by $227 per participant, or 4 percent.
3. Larger and more persistent program effects were found for the experimental group members who were referred to Project Independence before program resources were strained by growing caseloads. This group had average earnings gains of $439 more than the control group.
4. Impacts were found mainly for individuals with no preschool-age children. Among those with preschool-age children, only those from the early group showed evidence of achieving short-term earnings gains.

TIME TRENDS IN FINDINGS: Experimental group members designated "not-job-ready" showed delayed earnings impacts in the second year follow-up. "Job-ready" members showed greater first-year impacts.

DESIGN ISSUES:
1. Caseloads and unemployment rose during the experiment. Budget-induced hiring freezes pre-

vented the project from increasing staffing capacity. Restrictions on the availability of child care also occurred during this time period. For these reasons, the researchers present data for two subgroups—the "early" group, who were exposed to Project Independence when its operations more closely matched the model originally intended, and the "late" group, who were exposed to the project during a period of restricted resources.

2. Randomization took place when people were applying for AFDC or were being assessed for eligibility for continued AFDC receipt. Most previous evaluations randomized after orientation.

3. Eighty-eight percent of the research sample were first-time applicants or were reapplying after having been off the rolls. This suggests that they have been "somewhat less disadvantaged."

4. Some control group members were exposed to Project Independence by attending an orientation or participating in its employment-related activities. A 20 percent exposure was estimated.

5. The criteria for "job-readiness" was changed during the evaluation period to allow more participants to enter education and training services.

REPLICABILITY: Replicable.

GENERALIZABILITY: Designed to generalize to the entire state of Florida. The nine sample counties closely mirror Florida as a whole on a number of salient characteristics (e.g., poverty and unemployment rates). The nine counties had a smaller percentage of their population living in rural areas and a larger percentage of Hispanics than the state as a whole. Impacts, at least on the early cohort, are similar to those found in evaluations of similar projects nationwide.

FUNDING SOURCES: Florida Department of Health and Rehabilitative Services (HRS), the Ford Foundation, and the U.S. Department of Health and Human Services.

TREATMENT ADMINISTRATOR: HRS and its subcontractors (notably, the Department of Labor

and Employment Security [LES]). Key personnel at HRS: Don Winstead and Judy Moon.

EVALUATOR: Manpower Demonstration Research Corporation (MDRC). Key personnel: James Kemple, Daniel Friedlander, and Veronica Fellerath.

ENABLING LEGISLATION: Florida Employment Opportunity Act of 1987, and Family Support Act of 1988.

POLICY EFFECTS: This study's findings were cited at a May 1994 hearing before the Subcommittee on Human Resources of the House of Representatives Committee on Ways and Means. The evaluator reported that the findings were also influential in the congressional welfare reform debates of 1996.

INFORMATION SOURCE: James J. Kemple, Daniel Friedlander, and Veronica Fellerath, *Florida's Project Independence: Benefits, Costs, and Two-Year Impacts of Florida's JOBS Program,* Manpower Demonstration Research Corporation, April 1995.

PUBLIC-USE ACCESS TO DATA: MDRC's contract with HRS did not include public-use files. They are not currently available, but should be available through MDRC at a later date.

Wisconsin Learnfare

SUMMARY: This demonstration, conducted from 1990 to 1995, tested the effects of sanctions for inadequate enrollment or school attendance on a large sample of teenage AFDC recipients and their families. Participants were followed for two to three years.

COST: Administrative costs, $51,883,150; evaluation costs, $1,038,237.

TIME FRAME: Demonstration period, September 1990–June 1995; data collected, March 1993–January 1996; final report, April 1997.

TREATMENTS TESTED:

1. The experimental group faced sanctions, ranging from $60 to $190, for failure to enroll in

or attend school with minimum acceptable frequency. Case managers were assigned to help identify and correct the causes of attendance problems. Support services such as child care, transportation, and referral to alternative education programs were provided.
2. Controls were not subject to the program requirements or services. They did remain eligible for similar services provided through other programs.

OUTCOMES OF INTEREST: (1) Enrollment; (2) Attendance; (3) Unexcused absences; (4) School completion; and (5) Welfare benefits.

SAMPLE SIZE: Experimentals, 1,620; controls, 1,585.

TARGET POPULATION: 13- to 19-year-old AFDC recipients who were either dependents or parents and who had not yet graduated from high school or an equivalency program.

NUMBER OF TREATMENT GROUPS: Two (with one control group).

NUMBER AND LOCATION OF SITES: Ten—Brown, Douglas, Eau Claire, Kenosha, La Crosse, Marathon, Marinette, Milwaukee, Portage, and Racine counties.

RESEARCH COMPONENTS:
■ Process analysis: Reviews were conducted of program administration, case management, and sanction delays in Milwaukee County. No major barriers to implementation were found.
■ Impact analysis: Conducted via OLS regression and logit analysis.
■ Benefit–cost analysis: None.

MAJOR FINDINGS:
1. Semesters one and two found some beneficial effects, although not always statistically significant, of the program in the areas of enrollment, attendance, and unexcused absences for dropouts, teen parents, older teens, and teens outside Milwaukee County. These effects disappeared by semester three.
2. The only effect in the fourth semester was a negative effect on the enrollment of students who had been enrolled when the program began.
3. The program had no significant effect on the graduation rate or AFDC benefit receipt for the full sample, or any of the subgroups, with the exception of Milwaukee County, in the first semester only.
4. For the full sample, Learnfare had no significant effect on school participation in any of the semesters.
5. Reasons for sanction delays were identified and resulted in some oversight and data processing improvements.

TIME TRENDS IN FINDINGS: Positive impacts for some groups were found for attendance, enrollment, and unexcused absences but virtually disappeared by the third semester. The percentage of individuals sanctioned increased over the length of the study.

DESIGN ISSUES:
1. Some programs did not take attendance, and that limited both implementation and analysis. However, this was approximately equal between the control and experimental groups.
2. The apparent increase in most groups' average length of enrollment from the first to the second semester is due to the fact that many individuals entered the program after the start of the school year.
3. Many Learnfare teens were not subject to its requirements for at least one month at some point during the program because of closing and reopening of their AFDC case. The proportion ranged from 17.9 percent in the first semester to 65.2 percent in the fourth semester.
4. Eligibility for AFDC was not always correctly determined, resulting in both the inclusion of ineligible in and the exclusion of eligible parties from the program.
5. The AFDC case records system was overhauled during the program. Use of both the old and new systems to obtain data resulted in fragmented implementation. Incorrect codes were

found in the system, data differed between systems, and some data were lost.

6. Problems occurred with the collection of school data. School districts in Wisconsin have the authority to set their own attendance policies. Nonuniform policies created administrative and legal difficulties in terms of timely retrieval, confidentiality, and consistency in reporting.

7. The use of attendance data to impose sanctions caused major problems, resulting in lawsuits that frequently overturned sanction determinations. Litigants alleged lack of due process and adequate opportunity to show good cause for exemption from the program.

REPLICABILITY: Replicable. The process analysis identified issues that other states should consider when trying to implement a similar program.

GENERALIZABILITY: The sample was to be representative of Wisconsin's young AFDC population, but some subgroups were overrepresented. A disproportionate number of 13-year-olds were exposed to Learnfare for administrative reasons, and the sample was taken from only 10 of 72 counties. As both factors can affect program impacts, analysis was performed on a weighted basis.

FUNDING SOURCE: Wisconsin Department of Workforce Development.

TREATMENT ADMINISTRATOR: Department of Health and Social Services until July 1996, at which time it was transferred to the Department of Workforce Development.

EVALUATOR: State of Wisconsin Legislative Audit Bureau. Key personnel: Judith Frye, Karen McKim, and Emma Caspar.

POLICY EFFECTS: This evaluation informed state policy decisions when Wisconsin replaced AFDC with Wisconsin Works (W-2) in 1996. Little of the Learnfare program was retained.

INFORMATION SOURCE: Judith Frye and Emma Caspar, *An Evaluation of The Learnfare Program Final Report,* State of Wisconsin Legislative Audit Bureau, April 1997.

PUBLIC-USE ACCESS TO DATA: Data can be obtained by contacting the Bureau at 131 W. Wilson St., Suite 402, Madison, WI 53703, (608) 266-2818 or at http://dpls.dacc.wisc.edu/learnfare.

Partnership for Hope

SUMMARY: This demonstration, conducted from 1990 to 1992, tested the effects of a case management approach (integrating family support services, mentoring, and job preparation training) on a small sample of unemployed individuals qualifying for public assistance and considered at risk for child abuse. Subjects were followed for two years.

COST: Evaluation costs, $3.6 million over five years.

TIME FRAME: Demonstration period, October 1990–December 1992; data collected, same period.

TREATMENTS TESTED: Subjects in the experimental group received intensive case management and counseling. They were reviewed by an interagency team that suggested a subsequent plan of action for training or education and were assigned to volunteer mentors. This mentored support was to continue until the client achieved and maintained a condition of economic self-sufficiency. Controls did not receive any part of the intervention.

OUTCOMES OF INTEREST: (1) Family functioning; (2) Marital adjustment; (3) Self-esteem; (4) Parenting skills; (5) Self-efficacy; (6) Job search knowledge and skills; (7) Career objectives and immediate goals; (8) Completion of education/training; (9) Level of public assistance; (10) Contact with public service agencies; (11) Income; and (12) Job performance evaluation.

SAMPLE SIZE: Total, 109. Numbers allocated to experimental and control groups not available.

TARGET POPULATION: Individuals who qualified for public assistance at the time of their referral and had at least one child at home. All subjects met loose criteria for being at risk of being involved in child abuse. Clients also could not have any handicap or condition (e.g., drug addiction) that would preclude participation in job training.

NUMBER OF TREATMENT GROUPS: Two (with one control group).

NUMBER AND LOCATION OF SITES: One—Whatcom County, Washington.

RESEARCH COMPONENTS:
- Process analysis: Interviews were conducted with caseworkers and partner-agency staff.
- Impact analysis: Comparison at means.
- Benefit–cost analysis: None conducted.

MAJOR FINDINGS:
1. Ten experimentals were employed at the end of the program, compared with 11 controls. Experimentals received significantly higher levels of public assistance than controls. There was no significant difference between experimentals and controls in measures of income.
2. Experimental subjects exhibited significantly higher levels of self-efficacy than controls. On job search knowledge and skills, career objectives and immediate goals, and completion of education/training, there was no meaningful difference between experimentals and controls.

TIME TRENDS IN FINDINGS: None reported.

DESIGN ISSUES:
1. The sample was small to begin with, but only approximately half of the original subjects submitted the final questionnaires. Out of 109 total subjects, 29 experimentals and 29 controls returned the questionnaires, reflecting a high program dropout rate, as well as a small number of individuals who finished the program but failed to return the questionnaires. "Unsuccessful attempts were made to recover information from drop outs."
2. "The personal self-sufficiency measures were not as sensitive nor as valid as was hoped for."

REPLICABILITY: Replicable.

GENERALIZABILITY: Poor, because of small sample size, high attrition rate, and problems with outcome measures.

FUNDING SOURCE: U.S. Department of Health and Human Services.

TREATMENT ADMINISTRATOR: Whatcom County Opportunity Council, Bellingham, Washington.

EVALUATOR: Richard Bulcroft, Ph.D., Sociology Department, Western Washington University.

ENABLING LEGISLATION: Demonstration Partnership Program under section 408 of the Human Services Reauthorization Act of 1986 as amended.

INFORMATION SOURCE: "Partnership for Hope, Whatcom County Opportunity Council, Bellingham, Washington," *Summary of Final Evaluation Findings from FY 1990. Demonstration Partnership Project. Monograph Series 100-90: Case Management Family Intervention Models,* U.S. Department of Health and Human Services, Administration for Children and Families, Office of Community Services, December 1994, pp. 100-4-72–110-4-83.

PUBLIC-USE ACCESS TO DATA: We have no information about a public-use file for this demonstration.

National Evaluation of Welfare-to-Work Strategies (NEWWS)

(Formerly known as Job Opportunities and Basic Skills Training [JOBS] Program Evaluation)

SUMMARY: This demonstration, conducted from 1991 to 1999, tested the effects of employment-focused strategies and education-focused strategies on a large sample of welfare recipients. Subjects were followed for five years.

COST: Research costs, approximately $31.7 million over more than 10 years.

TIME FRAME: Enrollment period, June 1991–December 1994; data collected through December 1999.

TREATMENTS TESTED: Eleven programs, broadly defined as either employment-focused or education-focused, were tested in seven sites across the United States (see table below). Participation in all programs was mandatory, although enforcement of this requirement varied among the tested programs.

In Atlanta, Grand Rapids, and Riverside, two programs operated simultaneously: (1) Labor Force Attachment (LFA)—an employment-focused program in which members were assigned to job clubs and encouraged to find work quickly; and (2) Human Capital Development (HCD)—a mandatory, education-focused program in which most members were assigned to the class deemed most appropriate: GED preparation, adult basic skills, or English as a Second Language (ESL). In Columbus, two case management strategies were tested: (1) In the traditional program, each recipient worked with two different staff members—one for income maintenance issues and one for employment and training issues. (2) In the integrated program, recipients worked with only one staff member, who handled both aspects of their cases. In both programs, participation in JOBS was mandatory. In the Portland (employment-focused) program, some enrollees were first assigned to a short-term education program to attain GED certification. Program group members were encouraged to seek well-paying jobs. In all programs, control group members received income maintenance but could not receive program services.

OUTCOMES OF INTEREST: (1) Employment; (2) Earnings; (3) Welfare receipt; (4) Cost-effectiveness; and (5) Child well-being.

SAMPLE SIZE: Full sample, 44,569.

TARGET POPULATION: Single-parent welfare recipients.

NUMBER OF TREATMENT GROUPS: Three groups each (with one control group) in Atlanta, Grand Rapids, Riverside, and Columbus; two groups each (with one control group) in Detroit, Oklahoma City, and Portland.

NUMBER AND LOCATION OF SITES: Seven—Atlanta, Georgia; Grand Rapids, Michigan; Riverside, California; Columbus, Ohio; Detroit, Michigan; Oklahoma City, Oklahoma; and Portland, Oregon.

RESEARCH COMPONENTS:
- Process analysis: Administrative records and follow-up surveys administered over five years.
- Impact analysis: Conducted using multivariate OLS regression.
- Benefit–cost analysis: Conducted from government and sample member perspectives.

Treatments Tested

| | | EMPLOYMENT-FOCUSED | | EDUCATION-FOCUSED | |
| | | Job Search First | Varied First Activity | Education or Training First | |
	Number of groups (including control)	High enforcement	Low enforcement	High enforcement	Low enforcement
Atlanta	3	X		X	
Grand Rapids	3	X		X	
Riverside	3	X		X	
Portland	2		X		
Columbus	3			X integrated X traditional	
Detroit	2				X
Oklahoma City	2				X

MAJOR FINDINGS:

1. Most control group members (ranging from 79 percent in Oklahoma City to 88 percent in Grand Rapids) worked at some point in the five-year follow-up period. Thus, there was little program effect on the percentage of experimental group members who "ever" worked.

2. Nearly all of the 11 programs increased employment and earnings. However, experimental group members without a high school diploma had larger overall impacts from the employment-focused programs than from the education-focused programs.

3. None of the programs made welfare recipients substantially better off financially. Individuals replaced welfare and Food Stamp dollars with dollars from earnings and earned income tax credits, but the total income of experimental group families did not increase above the low levels of the control group.

4. Portland's program had the largest and most consistent effect. Compared with the control group, experimental group members had a 21 percent increase in employment duration and, on average, earned $5000 more over the five-year period.

5. There were no significant program effects on employment in the two "low enforcement" sites (Detroit and Oklahoma City).

6. All programs reduced welfare expenditure relative to control levels, but the HCD approach did not produce added economic benefits relative to the LFA approach, and the HCD approach was 40 to 90 percent more expensive.

7. In Columbus, the impact on earnings was larger for the integrated group members than for the traditional group members. However, the impact was not statistically significant among those who had a high school diploma.

8. There were few program effects on measures of child well-being. The effects, when found, did not differ by HCD versus LFA strategy.

TIME TRENDS IN FINDINGS: Employment-focused programs produced effects immediately; education-focused programs did not produce effects until the second year following random assignment. Effects for most programs diminished during the last two years and were statistically insignificant by the end of year five.

DESIGN ISSUES: In a few programs, a small portion of the control group members received services under the tested interventions during years four and five.

REPLICABILITY: Replicable.

GENERALIZABILITY: Given the diversity of sites, large samples, and consistency with results of other studies, the cross-site findings on earnings, welfare receipt, and income appear generally applicable to the population of welfare families.

FUNDING SOURCE: U.S. Department of Health and Human Services (HHS) with support from U.S. Department of Education.

TREATMENT ADMINISTRATOR: Local welfare agencies.

EVALUATOR: Manpower Demonstration Research Corporation. Child Trends conducted the Child Outcomes Study.

ENABLING LEGISLATION: Mandated by the Family Support Act of 1988.

INFORMATION SOURCES: Gayle Hamilton, Stephen Freedman, Lisa Gennetian, Charles Michalopoulos, Johanna Walter, Diana Adams-Ciardullo, and Anna Gassman-Pines, *National Evaluation of Welfare-to-Work Strategies: How Effective Are Different Welfare-to-Work Approaches? Five-Year Adult and Child Impacts for Eleven Programs,* Manpower Demonstration Research Corporation, November 2001; Stephen Freedman, *National Evaluation of Welfare-to-Work Strategies: Four-Year Impacts of Ten Programs on Employment Stability and Earnings Growth,* Manpower Demonstration Research Corporation, December 2000.

PUBLIC-USE ACCESS TO DATA: Available from the National Center for Health Statistics. http://aspe.hhs.gov/hps/NEWWS.

Link-Up

SUMMARY: This demonstration, conducted between 1992 and 1994, tested the effects of waiving the 100-hour rule for a large group of AFDC-U recipients. Subjects were followed for two years.

COST: Evaluation costs, approximately $300,000.

TIME FRAME: Demonstration period, January 1992–December 1994.

TREATMENTS TESTED: The treatment was a waiver of the 100-hour rule in the eligibility criteria for Aid to Families with Dependent Children with unemployed parents (AFDC-U). Primary wage earners in the experimental group maintained eligibility for AFDC-U benefits while working 100 hours or more per month. Members in the control group became ineligible for these benefits if the primary wage earner worked 100 hours or more per month, regardless of earnings.

OUTCOMES OF INTEREST: (1) Employment; (2) Earnings; and (3) Welfare receipt.

SAMPLE SIZE: The original sample (cases entering the experiment from 1992–94) was 11,310. The first-year cohort in the final analysis was 5,948: experimentals, 4,470; controls, 1,478.

TARGET POPULATION: Recipients of AFDC-U, that is, two-parent households where both parents are unemployed.

NUMBER OF TREATMENT GROUPS: Two (with one control group).

NUMBER AND LOCATION OF SITES: Eight counties in the San Joaquin Valley, California—Fresno, Kern, Kings, Madera, Mariposa, Merced, Stanislaus, and Tulare.

RESEARCH COMPONENTS:
- Process analysis: Focused on random assignment procedures and differences among experimental sites.
- Impact analysis: Conducted using regression adjusted means.
- Benefit–cost analysis: Conducted.

MAJOR FINDINGS: An earlier report analyzed data for the entire sample of 11,310. The findings presented below are for those cases that entered the experiment during the first year (1992). This allows for a longer and more uniform follow-up period of two years.
1. Waiving the 100-hour rule had no effect on employment and earnings of the primary or secondary wage earners in AFDC-U families.
2. Except for Fresno, the treatment had little effect on time-on-aid or AFDC-U payments. In all counties but Fresno, the percentage of experimentals receiving AFDC-U payments was significantly higher than the percentage of controls only in quarters seven and eight. There were no significant differences in average total amounts of benefits received.
3. In Fresno County, experimentals stayed on aid longer than controls (16.27 months versus 13.91 months, respectively) on average, and had higher average total AFDC-U payments ($12,061 versus $10,448).

TIME TRENDS IN FINDINGS: As mentioned above, for all counties except Fresno, there was a significant experimental–control difference in AFDC-U receipt only in the last two quarters.

DESIGN ISSUES:
1. In Fresno, the 100-hour rule had been waived for all AFDC-U recipients since 1987. To establish a control group, every other new and eligible applicant was assigned to the control group. Thus, there was an overrepresentation of new AFDC-U applicants in the control group. These cases differed in terms of aid history (and perhaps in other salient ways). This is a potentially serious threat to validity and is why the Fresno results were analyzed separately.
2. The 100-hour rule might significantly reduce AFDC-U applications; this entry effect would not be measured by the experiment.

REPLICABILITY: Replicable.

GENERALIZABILITY: All sample counties were within the San Joaquin Valley area of California, but generalizability to some other parts of the state is reasonable.

FUNDING SOURCE: California State Department of Social Services.

TREATMENT ADMINISTRATOR: California Department of Social Services.

EVALUATOR: University of California–Los Angeles (UCLA), Center for Child and Family Policy Research. Principal investigator: Yeheskel Hasenfeld.

ENABLING LEGISLATION: None.

INFORMATION SOURCES: Yeheskel Hasenfeld, Alisa Lewin, and Michael Mitchell, *Link-Up Evaluation of the 100-Hour Rule Waiver for AFDC-U: Impact Analysis Revisited,* UCLA, Center for Child and Family Policy Research, School of Public Policy and Social Research, August 1996; Yeheskel Hasenfeld, Alisa Lewin, and Michael Mitchell, *Link-Up: Evaluation of the 100-Hour Rule Waiver for AFDC-U—Impact and Cost–Benefit Analysis,* UCLA, Center for Child and Family Policy Studies, 1995.

PUBLIC-USE ACCESS TO DATA: Available through California State Department of Social Services.

Maryland Primary Prevention Initiative (PPI)

SUMMARY: This demonstration, conducted from July 1992 to January 1997, tested the effects of sanctions and incentives for preventive health care and school attendance behaviors on a large sample of AFDC recipients. Participants were followed for five years.

COST: Evaluation only, $3.7 million.

TIME FRAME: Demonstration period, July 1992–January 1997; data collected, same period.

TREATMENTS TESTED: The program required school attendance at the 80 percent level for children of experimentals, annual medical checkup for school-

age children, and regular preventive health care and immunizations for their preschool-age children. A $25 sanction per child per month was applied on the AFDC grant for noncompliance. AFDC eligibility redetermination was required every six months, at which time PPI compliance had to be shown. Controls were eligible for all benefits that experimentals were, but were not subject to sanction for noncompliance with any of the PPI requirements.

OUTCOMES OF INTEREST: (1) School attendance; (2) Preventive health behavior; and (3) Prenatal care.

SAMPLE SIZE: Experimentals, 11,345; controls, 6,081.

TARGET POPULATION: Statewide AFDC recipients with preschool- and school-age children.

NUMBER OF TREATMENT GROUPS: Two (with one control group).

NUMBER AND LOCATION OF SITES: Six—one office each in Prince George's, Wicomico, and Allegany counties, and three in Baltimore City.

RESEARCH COMPONENTS:
- Process analysis: Conducted.
- Impact analysis: Conducted (comparison of means).
- Benefit–cost analysis: Conducted.

MAJOR FINDINGS:
1. No findings of statistically significant increases in school attendance, prenatal care, or preventive health behavior. "PPI did not contribute to clinically relevant increases in preventive health care visits or vaccination coverage for children 3–24 months" (Minkovitz et al. 1999).
2. Although the program had a compliance rate of 94 percent, the evaluators conclude that the $25 per month sanction did not affect client behavior.

TIME TRENDS IN FINDINGS: None reported.

DESIGN ISSUES:

1. Obtaining verification of compliance from health care providers was left up to the clients, which may have led to inaccurate measurement of compliance.
2. Feedback effects could have diluted the measured impact because the controls were the only welfare recipients in the state not subject to the PPI provisions.
3. Levels of sanctioning varied geographically, which raises questions of consistency in program implementation.
4. Recipients, when surveyed, were unaware of the program requirements.
5. Limits to obtaining health care information included failure to obtain parental consent; failure to obtain provider participation; and provider inability to supply the needed information.
6. Electronic deposit of grants may have resulted in less awareness on the part of recipients that they had been sanctioned. Survey findings suggest that most clients could not accurately identify the status of their own cases.
7. Uncertainty of the continuation of the program owing to political and cost neutrality issues may have contributed to staff turnover.

REPLICABILITY: Replicable.

GENERALIZABILITY: A significant concern is the high attrition rate stemming from failure to obtain parental consent to access records; other design issues also may reduce confidence in larger applicability. Evaluation of the Georgia Preschool Immunization Program (p. 110), a similar intervention, found significant positive impacts in a much smaller sample. The evaluators of this demonstration and the Georgia experiment do not agree on which results are more generalizable. Implementation of the intervention was clearly superior in Georgia, the focus on immunization was narrower, and responsibility for children's health was almost entirely with the public sector (the County Health Department) rather than mixed between public and private health care providers, as in Maryland.

FUNDING SOURCES: Maryland Department of Human Resources. Key personnel: Jeff Rew, Ellen Spero, Joyce Munns, and John Fowler. Additional funding from the U.S. Department of Health and Human Services, Maryland Department of Health and Mental Hygiene, and the Centers for Disease Control.

TREATMENT ADMINISTRATOR: Maryland Department of Human Resources. Key personnel: Jeff Rew, Ellen Spero, Joyce Munns, and John Fowler.

EVALUATOR: Impact study—Schaefer Center for Public Policy, University of Baltimore and Johns Hopkins University School of Hygiene and Public Health, Department of Maternal and Child Health. Key personnel: Larry Thomas and Bernard Guyer, MD. Process analysis—Maryland Institute for Policy Analysis and Research. Benefit–cost analysis—JHU Institute for Policy Studies. Key personnel: Burt Barnow.

ENABLING LEGISLATION: None.

INFORMATION SOURCES: Howard A. Moyes, "Reforming Welfare: Maryland's Primary Prevention Initiative," Council of State Governments: State Innovations Briefs, November 1995, 1–3; C. Minkovitz, E. Holt, N. Hughart, W. Hous, L. Thomas, E. Dini, and B. Guyer, "The Effect of Parental Monetary Sanctions on the Vaccination Status of Young Children: An Evaluation of Welfare Reform in Maryland," *Archives of Pediatric and Adolescent Medicine,* 1999, 153: 1242–47.

PUBLIC-USE ACCESS TO DATA: None.

To Strengthen Michigan Families (TSMF)

SUMMARY: This demonstration, conducted from 1992 to 1996, tested the effects of a social contract requirement, financial incentives, and broadened AFDC eligibility on a large group of AFDC and State Family Assistance (SFA) recipients. Subjects were followed for up to four years.

COST: Evaluation costs, $1,418,354.

TIME FRAME: Demonstration period, October 1992–September 1996; data collected, same period.

TREATMENTS TESTED: Families were grouped by time of entry: "Ongoing" families were active on welfare at the time To Strengthen Michigan Families (TSMF) was implemented; "middle" families were first certified between October 1, 1992, and September 30, 1994; "last" families were certified between October 1, 1994, and September 30, 1995.

The initial TSMF program, beginning in October 1, 1992, consisted of a social contract requirement under which adult AFDC and SFA recipients had to agree to engage in employment, education and training services, or community services for a minimum of 20 hours per week. There was also an expansion of the amount that adult AFDC recipients could earn without grant reduction after four months of employment; expansion of AFDC eligibility for two-parent families by eliminating the work history requirement and the 100-hour rule; and a permanent disregard of children's earnings and savings when determining AFDC eligibility and benefits.

Controls had no social contract requirement and a generally less generous earnings disregard. They were still affected by work history and 100-hour rules, and dependents' earnings and savings affected eligibility and benefits calculations after six months of employment.

In October 1994, several changes were made to the original TSMF program with no change to the control regime: A work search requirement (Work First) was added; those adult experimentals exempt from participating in Michigan Opportunities and Skills Training (MOST) were required to comply with the Social Contract, with full-family sanctions potentially invoked for noncompliance; immunization of preschool children was required; and business expenses and the value of one family vehicle were disregarded in determining eligibility.

OUTCOMES OF INTEREST: (1) Employment; (2) Earnings; (3) Welfare participation; (4) Benefit receipt; and (5) Child well-being.

SAMPLE SIZE: Experimentals, 9,883; controls, 9,621.

TARGET POPULATION: Families receiving AFDC or State Family Assistance.

NUMBER OF TREATMENT GROUPS: Two (with one control group).

NUMBER AND LOCATION OF SITES: Four—local welfare offices in Kalamazoo, Madison Heights, McNichols/Goddard, and Schaefer/Six Mile.

RESEARCH COMPONENTS:
- Process analysis: Administrative records, in-person interviews with Michigan Department of Social Services (MDSS) staff, and local staff surveys.
- Impact analysis: Conducted using ordinary least squares (OLS) regression and logistic regression.
- Benefit–cost analysis: Not conducted.

MAJOR FINDINGS:
1. TSMF increased the average quarterly employment rate for "ongoing" families by 1.3 percentage points and increased average annual earnings by a statistically significant $223.
2. TSMF reduced overall welfare participation rates and benefit receipt among "ongoing" families.
3. The program reduced welfare participation for "middle" families, but there were no statistically significant increases in employment or earnings.
4. "Last" families experienced the largest program impact, with a statistically significant 5.6 percent increase in the employment rate.
5. There were no statistically significant impacts on measures of child well-being.
6. The study found that funding constraints, imposed by the "cost-neutral" budget methodology (i.e., no net increase in federal funding) presented a barrier to TSMF's ability to change the culture of the local welfare offices. For

example, resources were not available for local staff training.

TIME TRENDS IN FINDINGS: The increases in earnings and employment rates for "ongoing" families disappear by the fourth follow-up year.

DESIGN ISSUES: The potential impact of the TSMF earnings disregard policy varies with the length of employment and the level of income. In some instances, the preexisting policy that governed the control group was more generous than TSMF policy.

REPLICABILITY: Replicable.

GENERALIZABILITY: Baseline characteristics of research sample are generally consistent with comparable Michigan and national populations.

FUNDING SOURCE: Michigan Department of Social Services.

TREATMENT ADMINISTRATOR: Administration for Legislation, Budget and Analysis. Key personnel: Nancy Duncan, director.

EVALUATOR: Abt Associates. Key personnel: Alan Werner and Robert Kornfeld.

ENABLING LEGISLATION: None.

INFORMATION SOURCES: Margaret B. Hargreaves, Alan Werner, and Pamela Joshi, *The Evaluation of To Strengthen Michigan Families: Process Report,* Abt Associates, February 1995; Alan Werner and Robert Kornfeld, *The Evaluation of To Strengthen Michigan Families: Final Impact Report,* Abt Associates, September 1997.

PUBLIC-USE ACCESS TO DATA: Not available.

Utah Single-Parent Employment Demo Program (SPED)

SUMMARY: This demonstration, conducted from January 1993 to June 1996, tested the effects of active diversion, mandatory participation in work-related activities, repeal of the 100-hour rule, and other work incentives on a large sample of AFDC applicants. Subjects were followed for three years.

COST: $500,000.

TIME FRAME: Demonstration period, January 1993–June 1996; data collected, same period; final report, July 1997.

TREATMENTS TESTED: Experimental-group AFDC applicants had to fill out a self-sufficiency plan with a counselor before ever addressing eligibility. One of two paths was chosen by the applicant:

1. Voluntary diversion from AFDC. The recipient received a one-time payment, not to exceed three months, of cash assistance; the payment would be prorated if she applied for assistance again within that time. Those diverted were also eligible for transitional medical and child care services. Child support payments went to the family rather than the state.

2. Mandated participation in self-sufficiency activities, based on individualized plans with no exemptions. Children over 16 not in school had to participate in school completion and employment activities. Families with earnings got priority attention for child support enforcement.

Families in group 2 received an extra $40 a month. A sanction of $100 could be imposed for nonparticipation after extensive review and conciliation, possibly leading to case closure for continued noncompliance. The first $100 plus 50 percent of the remainder of earned income was not counted when determining assistance and was not subject to a time limit. Food Stamp benefits could be redeemed in cash or coupons. Extended transitional benefits were allowed. Medicaid was available for 24 months after leaving welfare and child care indefinitely (based on a sliding scale).

Program rules were simplified for support programs such as AFDC and Food Stamps. The 100-hour rule was dropped for two-parent families, but they had to participate in a self-sufficiency activity for 40 hours a week.

Controls participated in Utah's RISE (Realizing Independence through Successful Employment) program. This federal JOBS program mandated participation for only certain target groups.

OUTCOMES OF INTEREST: (1) Diversion; (2) Earnings; (3) Employment; (4) AFDC benefits; and (5) Total income.

SAMPLE SIZE: No total available. In 1993 experimental cases reached a high of 1,315 in December, when controls were at 1,271. Numbers varied by month. Specific breakdowns were not given in years two and three.

TARGET POPULATION: Single-parent AFDC families or two-parent AFDC families with one disabled parent. (Both experimentals and controls needing, but excluded from, mental health support were allowed to enter a life skills program until openings became available.)

NUMBER OF TREATMENT GROUPS: Two (with one control group).

NUMBER AND LOCATION OF SITES: One—Kearns AFDC benefits office.

RESEARCH COMPONENTS:

- Process analysis: Used administrative data on participation.

- Impact analysis: Comparison of means. No tests for statistical significance are presented.

- Benefit–cost analysis: Government budget only.

MAJOR FINDINGS:

1. Over three years, between 16.8 and 28.3 percent of new applicants assigned to the experimental group were diverted. No corresponding report on control families that left within three months of application is presented.

2. The authors present experimental–control differences in average earnings over 36 months. The experimental mean is always greater, and the difference rises from $15 in the first month to $68 in the last month. However, this com-

parison is not a valid experimental measure. The authors look only at active welfare cases, not at the whole sample. In the experimental group, they neglect the diverted households, they include two-parent AFDC households with more than 100 hours of earned income (who would be ineligible for welfare in the controls), and they ignore attrition in both groups.

3. Differences in employment rates between active cases in the experimental and control groups are presented; the experimental group mean is about 10 to 15 percentage points above the control group. This comparison is also not a valid experimental measure.

4. Total family income is greater among active experimental cases than among controls, partly because of higher earnings and partly because of higher federal SSI payments; the experimental-group case managers took more time helping families apply for SSI than their control counterparts. Because it only involves active welfare cases, this finding is also not a valid experimental measure.

5. Welfare benefit payments were on average lower for active experimental cases than for control cases.

TIME TRENDS IN FINDINGS: Experimental–control differences in the active cases tend to rise over time.

DESIGN ISSUES: The evaluation was severely flawed by the failure to use any data other than the welfare department's own administrative data. This meant that the only earnings information available to the evaluators was self-reported by active welfare cases. As a result, the evaluators were limited to non-experimental comparisons of only those cases that were active on welfare, rather than performing experimental comparisons of all sample members.

REPLICABILITY: Program intervention was very well documented.

GENERALIZABILITY: Given the design issues noted above, no reliance can be placed on the findings.

FUNDING SOURCE: Utah Department of Human Services.

TREATMENT ADMINISTRATOR: Utah Department of Human Services and related agencies. Key personnel: Bill Biggs.

EVALUATOR: University of Utah, Graduate School of Social Work, Social Research Institute. Key personnel: Fred Janzen, Mary Jane Taylor, and Shirley Weathers.

INFORMATION SOURCE: Fred Janzen, Mary Jane Taylor, and Shirley Weathers, *An Evaluation of Utah's Single Parent Employment Demonstration Program,* Social Research Institute, July 1997.

PUBLIC-USE ACCESS TO DATA: We have no information about a public-use file for this demonstration.

California Work Pays Demonstration Program (CWPDP)

SUMMARY: This demonstration, conducted from January 1993 to June 1996, tested the effects of raising the earnings incentives and reducing the cash grant on a large sample of one- and two-parent AFDC families. Subjects were followed for up to five years.

COST: Evaluation costs, roughly $4–$5 million.

TIME FRAME: Demonstration period, January 1993–June 1996; data collected, October 1992–mid 1998; final report, October 1998.

TREATMENTS TESTED: The treatment involved changing two provisions of the AFDC program. The "$30 and one-third" provision applied to all AFDC families and allowed welfare recipients to keep the first $30 and one-third of the remaining wages before welfare grant determinations were made. However, it expired after the recipient had been in the program for four months, and thereafter dollar-for-dollar reductions in grant occurred for every dollar of earnings. Under the 100-hour

rule, which applied only to two-parent families, the total work hours per month for the primary wage earner could not exceed 100 hours without loss of eligibility.

Experimentals received a waiver of the time limit on the $30 and one-third income disregard, and a waiver of the 100-hour rule. However, the cash grants of experimentals were reduced by 8.5 percent from October 1992 to September 1993.

Controls were subject to the general AFDC rules, with expiring disregards, ineligibility after 100 hours, and higher benefits.

OUTCOMES OF INTEREST: (1) Employment; (2) Earnings; and (3) Welfare benefits.

SAMPLE SIZE: One-parent (AFDC-FG) families: experimentals, 6,278; controls, 3,276. Two-parent (AFDC-U) families: experimentals, 3,471; controls, 1,695.

TARGET POPULATION: One- and two-parent families receiving AFDC.

NUMBER OF TREATMENT GROUPS: Two (with one control group).

NUMBER AND LOCATION OF SITES: Three—Alameda, Los Angeles, and San Bernardino counties.

RESEARCH COMPONENTS:
- Process analysis: Conducted, but we have not been able to obtain details of methods used.
- Impact analysis: Logit, OLS, comparison of group means, adjusting for county differences.
- Benefit–cost analysis: Not conducted.

MAJOR FINDINGS:

Two-Parent Families (AFDC-U)

1. Experimentals were more likely to be employed than controls in most calendar quarters, with a stable difference of 3–4 percent over time.
2. The program group had increased earnings in all three demonstration counties. Strong and significant differences (61% and 70% in years one and two) occurred in San Bernardino County in some follow-up quarters. In Alameda

County, the experimental group earned significantly more than the control group if they had been receiving AFDC less than five years. The earnings of Los Angeles' experimentals were significantly larger than those of the controls in years two, three, and four.

3. Overall, no significant difference in time on AFDC was found for the AFDC-U population as a whole.

4. Overall, there was more movement from AFDC-U to AFDC-FG (one-parent families) for the control groups; however, the effect is not consistent over time.

5. The program significantly increased the likelihood of leaving AFDC in all counties for individuals with less than 12 years of school. Individuals with a more recent work history were significantly more likely to leave AFDC in all counties.

6. The replacement cohort (i.e., new AFDC recipients who were placed in the program) exhibited similar patterns as the original cohort.

One-Parent Families (AFDC-FG)

1. No significant difference existed in any measure of work activity between the experimental and control groups.

2. Analysis at the county level reveals that on average, the program group earned more than the control group during most quarters, but this finding was statistically significant only in San Bernardino County. Los Angeles County program participants earned slightly less than the controls.

3. The difference in time on AFDC for the controls and experimentals varied by county. Alameda County had no differences during the first 24 months, but a significant decrease in the number of months on aid for the program group during the following 18 months. Los Angeles experimentals were significantly more likely to remain on AFDC than the controls during the first three years. There was no difference at all between the groups in San Bernardino.

4. Alameda had the only detectable demographic variation in relation to leaving AFDC. White and African-American experimental households in the county left at a higher rate than Hispanic and Asian participants.

TIME TRENDS IN FINDINGS: No consistent patterns found.

DESIGN ISSUES: None apparent.

REPLICABILITY: Treatment documentation is available through the UC DATA web site, http://ucdata.berkeley.edu.

GENERALIZABILITY: Given the large sample and diverse sites within the state, the findings should apply at least to California as a whole, and, to some extent, probably to the U.S. as a whole.

FUNDING SOURCE: California Department of Social Services. Key personnel: Werner Schink and Lois VanBeers.

TREATMENT ADMINISTRATOR: County welfare agencies.

EVALUATOR: Welfare Policy Research Group, UCLA School of Public Policy and Social Research. Key personnel: Rosina Becerra, Vivian Lew, Michael Mitchell, and Hiromi Ono.

INFORMATION SOURCE: Rosina Becerra, Vivian Lew, Michael Mitchell, and Hiromi Ono, *Final Report: California Work Pays Demonstration Project,* Welfare Policy Research Group, UCLA School of Public Policy and Social Research, 1998.

PUBLIC-USE ACCESS TO DATA: Available at http://ucdata.berkeley.edu.

Georgia Preschool Immunization

SUMMARY: This demonstration, conducted from 1993 to 1996, tested the impact of sanctions for failure to immunize young children against childhood diseases on a large sample of AFDC recipient families. Subjects were followed for four years.

COST: Research only, $1,129,343.

TIME FRAME: Demonstration period, January 1993–December 1996; data collected, same period.

TREATMENTS TESTED: On application for AFDC and at every eligibility recertification, experimentals were informed that they must present proof of immunization for any children 6 years old or younger. The penalty for failing to present such proof, after both oral and written warnings, unless good cause exceptions were allowed for religious objections and known allergic reactions, was the loss of AFDC benefits normally provided for that child.

Controls "were encouraged to immunize" their children, but were not informed about sanctions nor subject to them.

OUTCOMES OF INTEREST: (1) Immunization rates; (2) AFDC participation; and (3) Sanctions.

SAMPLE SIZE: Experimentals, 1,500 families (1,725 children); controls, 1,000 families (1,076 children).

TARGET POPULATION: AFDC recipient families with children 6 years old or younger.

NUMBER OF TREATMENT GROUPS: Two (with one control group).

NUMBER AND LOCATION OF SITES: One—Muscogee County.

RESEARCH COMPONENTS:
- Process analysis: Review of actual application of sanctions in case records; brief telephone survey of small sample of experimentals on issue of client burden; interviews with caseworkers.
- Impact analysis: Up-to-date immunization status means adjusted through logit regressions.
- Benefit–cost analysis: Not conducted.

MAJOR FINDINGS:
1. Assignment to experimental resulted in higher probability of immunization against polio; diphtheria, pertussis, and tetanus; and measles, mumps, and rubella in all four years of follow-up, with a p-value of .02 or less.

2. The differences in immunization rates are typically 6 to 7 percentage points.
3. Assignment to experimental status raised the probability of immunization against hepatitis B in the last three years of follow-up, and against Haemophilus influenzae type B (Hib) in the last two years of follow-up, with a p-value of .01 or less.
4. Of the children who were in the study long enough to undergo the complete childhood immunization series, 72.4 percent of the experimental group and 60.6 percent of the control group completed the series. This difference is statistically significant at a p-value of less than .001.
5. Typical client burden was on the order of 40 minutes and 41 cents for transportation cost.
6. Total number of families sanctioned was 11, less than 0.5 percent.
7. Statistically significant reductions in AFDC usage in the experimental group were noted in three of the four follow-up years, amounting to a difference of 4.8 percentage points in the first and fourth years.

TIME TRENDS IN FINDINGS: Immunization impacts rose over time for Hib and hepatitis B.

DESIGN ISSUES:
1. Written consent to access medical records was not obtained for roughly 37 percent of experimental children and 41 percent of control children. Families providing consent had more children and were more likely to be black than families withholding consent.
2. Various implementation issues were noted in the study, among them (a) caseworkers did not remember receiving much training; (b) in a few cases controls were incorrectly sanctioned; and (c) unrelated immunization promotion activities occurred in the community at the same time.

REPLICABILITY: Replicable.

GENERALIZABILITY: Muscogee County, in southwestern Georgia, contains the city of Columbus (population 186,000) and the Fort Benning military reservation. A significant concern is the high attrition rate stemming from failure to obtain parental consent to access the records. Evaluation of the Maryland Primary Prevention Initiative (p. 104), a similar intervention, found no significant effects in a much larger sample. The evaluators of this demonstration and the Maryland experiment do not agree on which results are more generalizable. Implementation of the intervention was clearly superior in Georgia, the focus on immunization was narrower, and responsibility for children's health was almost entirely with the public sector (the county health department) rather than mixed between public and private health care providers.

FUNDING SOURCES: Georgia Department of Human Services and U.S. Department of Health and Human Services. Key personnel: Diane Simms for Georgia and Peter Germanis for HHS.

TREATMENT ADMINISTRATOR: Georgia Department of Human Resources, Division of Family and Children Services.

EVALUATOR: Abt Associates. Key personnel: Larry Kerpelman and David Connell.

INFORMATION SOURCE: Larry C. Kerpelman, David B. Connell, and Walter J. Gunn, "Effect of a Monetary Sanction on Immunization Rates of Recipients of Aid to Families with Dependent Children," *Journal of the American Medical Association*, 2000, 284(1): 53–59.

PUBLIC-USE ACCESS TO DATA: Not available.

FIRST CLINTON ADMINISTRATION

Iowa Family Investment Program

SUMMARY: This demonstration, conducted between 1993 and 1999, tested the effects of eligibility reforms, mandatory employment services, and financial incentives on a large sample of AFDC recipients. Subjects were followed for up to five years.

COST: Core impact evaluation, $1,404,000; child impact evaluation, $1,389,000; process study, $546,000; cost-benefit study, $138,000.

TIME FRAME: Demonstration period, September 1993–March 1996; child impacts study, 1997; data collected through 1999; final report, June 2002.

TREATMENTS TESTED: Welfare reform in Iowa, implemented October 1, 1993, as the Family Investment Program (FIP), was tested against the standard policies of the AFDC program. Relative to AFDC, FIP increased the amount adult recipients could earn without grant reduction. It also expanded eligibility for two-parent families. FIP tested a strong work requirement and sharply reduced exemptions for required participation in PROMISE JOBS, Iowa's employment and training program. A critical PROMISE JOBS activity was the development and signing of a Family Investment Agreement (FIA) outlining a strategy for self-sufficiency. Failure to comply with the FIA requirement could result in a temporary reduction or elimination of the family's cash grant. Control group members were subject to the policies governing AFDC.

Families were grouped by time of entry. Ongoing families were active on welfare in September 1993. Applicant families were divided into three cohorts: cohort I applied for benefits between October 1993 and September 1994; cohort II applied between October 1994 and September 1995; and cohort III applied between October 1995 and March 1996.

OUTCOMES OF INTEREST: (1) Employment; (2) Earnings; (3) Welfare participation; (4) Benefit receipt; and (5) Measures of child well-being.

SAMPLE SIZE: Experimentals, 11,567 (ongoing recipients, 4,952; new applicants, 6,615); controls, 5,778 (ongoing, 2,466; applicants, 3,312).

TARGET POPULATION: AFDC recipient and new applicant families.

NUMBER OF TREATMENT GROUPS: Two (with one control group).

NUMBER AND LOCATION OF SITES: Nine—five urban county sites (Black Hawk, Linn, Polk, Pottawattamie, and Woodbury) and four rural county sites (Clinton, Des Moines, Jackson, and Jones).

RESEARCH COMPONENTS:
- Process analysis: Administrative records, client survey, and site visits.
- Impact analysis: Conducted using multivariate regression.
- Benefit–cost analysis: Conducted based on data from first two years of the evaluation.

MAJOR FINDINGS:
1. FIP increased employment among ongoing cases and cohort I applicant cases, but increased earnings for these two groups were only statistically significant in years one and two for ongoing cases and year one for cohort I applicants.
2. There were no statistically significant impacts on employment and earnings among cohort II applicants.
3. On average, experimentals in cohort III had lower employment rates and lower quarterly earnings than the controls. However, the impact estimates were generally not statistically significant and may be biased because control cases were subject to reform policies during this period. (See "Design Issues.")
4. In general, FIP significantly increased welfare participation and the rate of combining welfare and work.
5. Among single-parent applicant cases, FIP significantly increased the proportion of household heads who did not marry and significantly reduced their total household earnings and income compared with controls.
6. FIP had mixed, statistically significant effects on measures of child well-being. Ongoing treatment group children were less likely to change their place of residence. However, among applicant families, FIP increased the placement of children in foster care and doubling up with

other households. Among applicant children age 5–12, FIP led to a decline in school engagement and an increase in school tardiness. Among both ongoing and applicant cases, FIP increased the incidence of domestic abuse.
7. Overall, FIP produced benefits to society in the first two years of the program. From the recipient perspective, applicants benefited substantially in the first year, but ongoing recipients received only small benefits over the two-year period. For applicant cases, FIP produced net costs to all branches of government. For ongoing cases, FIP benefited government overall, but there were small net costs to state and local governments in the first year.

TIME TRENDS IN FINDINGS: Among ongoing cases and cohort I applicant cases, FIP initially increased employment and earnings but there is little significant evidence of long-run FIP impacts on employment and earnings for either ongoing or any cohort applicant cases. However, as discussed in "Design Issues," changing the policies that governed the control group in 1997 may have biased the long-run impact estimates.

DESIGN ISSUES: The policies that governed the control group became subject to federal welfare reform policies beginning in April 1997. Although some of the control cases had already left welfare, the policy changes probably resulted in underestimating the effects of the program after April 1997.

REPLICABILITY: Replicable.

GENERALIZABILITY: Designed to generalize to the FIP population in the nine research counties. Baseline characteristics of research sample are generally similar to comparable Iowa and national populations.

FUNDING SOURCES: Iowa Department of Human Services; U.S. Department of Health and Human Services (HHS), Administration for Children and Families.

TREATMENT ADMINISTRATOR: Iowa Department of Human Services, Division of Financial, Health and Work Supports. Key personnel: Robert Krebs, project officer.

EVALUATOR: Mathematica Policy Research, Inc. Key personnel: Thomas M. Fraker, project director.

ENABLING LEGISLATION: In August 1993, HHS granted the state of Iowa waivers from certain AFDC regulations under Section 1115 of the Social Security Act, and the U.S. Department of Agriculture granted the state waivers from certain Food Stamps Program regulations under Section 17(b) of the Food Stamp Act.

INFORMATION SOURCES: Thomas M. Fraker, Christine M. Ross, Rita A. Stapulonis, Robert B. Olsen, Martha D. Kovac, M. Robin Dion, and Anu Rangarajan, *The Evaluation of Welfare in Iowa: Final Impact Report,* Mathematica Policy Research, Inc., June 2002; Anne R. Gordon and Thomas J. Martin, *Cost-Benefit Analysis of Iowa's Family Investment Program: Two-Year Result,* Mathematica Policy Research, Inc., February 1999.

PUBLIC-USE ACCESS TO DATA: A public-use file can be obtained by contacting Tom Fraker at Mathematica Policy Research, Inc.

New Jersey Family Development Program

SUMMARY: This demonstration, conducted from October 1993 to 1996, tested the effects of selected changes in welfare policy—a "family cap"; a higher earnings disregard; an extension of Medicaid benefits; strengthened sanctions; and mandatory participation in education, training, and job search—on a large sample of AFDC recipients. Subjects were followed for four years.

COST: $1.3 million for evaluation.

TIME FRAME: Demonstration period, 1993–96; data collected, same period.

TREATMENTS TESTED: Ongoing and new AFDC recipients in the treatment group were subject to all provisions and waivers under the Family Development Plan. Program elements included the "family cap" provision, which denied additional benefits to children conceived while the mother was on AFDC; an earnings disregard (up to 50 percent of the welfare grant) for those women whose grants were capped and who found employment; participation in educational, training, and job search activities; a strengthening of the sanctioning process; and an extension of Medicaid benefits for up to two years after leaving the AFDC rolls for employment. In addition, the programs instituted intensive case management services for the entire family of AFDC recipients, as opposed to the head of the family only.

The control group, made up of ongoing and new AFDC cases, was not subject to any of the waiver elements.

OUTCOMES OF INTEREST: (1) Employment; (2) Earnings; (3) Births; (4) Abortions; and (5) Welfare receipt.

SAMPLE SIZE: Experimentals, 5,519 (3,286 ongoing, 2,233 new recipients); controls, 2,892 (1,607 ongoing, 1,285 new recipients).

TARGET POPULATION: New Jersey AFDC recipients.

NUMBER OF TREATMENT GROUPS: Two (with one control group).

NUMBER AND LOCATION OF SITES: Ten—Atlantic, Camden, Cumberland, Essex, Hudson, Mercer, Middlesex, Monmouth, Passaic, and Union counties.

RESEARCH COMPONENTS:
■ Process analysis: Conducted.
■ Impact analysis: Regression.
■ Benefit–cost analysis: Conducted.

MAJOR FINDINGS:
1. The Family Development Program did not significantly improve employment prospects and earnings. Experimentals earned less, on average, over the evaluation period than the control group.
2. The program did have a statistically significant impact on birth, abortion, and family planning decisions. *Ongoing* recipients in the treatment group experienced a birth rate that was about

9 percent lower than the control group birth rate, used family planning services about 10 percent more than the control group, and had about 28 percent more sterilizations than the control group. There was no statistically significant difference between treatment group and the control group in abortions.

3. *New* recipients in the treatment group experienced a birth rate that was 12 percent lower than the control group birth rate, an abortion rate that was 14 percent higher than the control group abortion rate, and a contraception use rate that was 21 percent higher than the control group contraception rate. There were no statistically significant differences between the groups in family planning use or sterilizations.

4. The program had minimal impact on welfare recipiency. Ongoing recipients in the treatment group were about 2 percent more likely than controls to have moved off the welfare rolls during the study period. Among new recipients, the difference between the treatment and controls was about 4 percent.

5. Among ongoing AFDC recipients, program costs exceeded program benefits from all perspectives. Over four years, society lost on average $1,042 per experimental relative to the counterfactual control, largely because of lower treatment group earnings.

6. Among new recipients, average net benefits (i.e., benefits–costs) to society were −$1,600 per case, owing in part to lower earnings and in part to higher service costs for the treatment group. From the participant perspective, however, higher cash, food stamp, and Medicaid assistance transfers resulted in a four-year average net benefit of +$468.

TIME TRENDS IN FINDINGS: None apparent.

DESIGN ISSUES:

1. The program received very wide publicity. Critics (such as Glen Loury and Peter Rossi) contend that this publicity might have confused the controls, who might have thought the family cap applied to them, and have cited survey results indicating confusion among both controls and experimentals about treatment status. The evaluators (Camasso et al. 2003) report that experimentals who gave answers indicating confusion in fact had a higher abortion rate than experimentals who answered correctly, while controls indicating confusion did not display abortion behavior significantly different from unconfused controls. The evaluators contend that survey error may merely prove that "poor measures of contamination do perform poorly"—that the survey instrument was flawed.

2. A handful of control subjects may have been inadvertently made subject to the family cap provision.

3. There were dramatic variations in implementation in terms of program structure, policies, and services at the county level. These differences were attributable to local conditions as well as to differences in leadership styles across counties.

REPLICABILITY: Replicable, taking into account the design issues above.

GENERALIZABILITY: Given the large sample size and the differences in the treatment sites, there are no apparent limits to generalizability outside New Jersey of the effects of the family cap.

FUNDING SOURCES: U.S. Department of Health and Human Services, New Jersey Department of Human Services, and the Kaiser Foundation. Key personnel: Rudy Myers for New Jersey.

TREATMENT ADMINISTRATOR: New Jersey Department of Human Services, Division of Family Development.

EVALUATORS: Michael J. Camasso and Carol Harvey, Rutgers University.

ENABLING LEGISLATION: New Jersey Family Development Act of 1992.

INFORMATION SOURCES: Michael J. Camasso, Carol Harvey, Radha Jagannathan, and Mark Killingsworth, *The Final Report on the Impact of*

New Jersey's Family Development Program, New Jersey Department of Human Services, October 1998.

Michael J. Camasso, Carol Harvey, and Radha Jagannathan, *Cost-Benefit Analysis of New Jersey's Family Development Program,* New Jersey Department of Human Services, October 1998.

Michael J. Camasso, Radha Jagannathan, Carol Harvey, and Mark Killingsworth, "The Use of Client Surveys to Gauge the Threat of Contamination in Welfare Reform Experiments," *Journal of Policy Analysis and Management* 22(2): 207–23.

PUBLIC-USE ACCESS TO DATA: Not available.

Colorado Personal Responsibility and Employment Program (CPREP)

SUMMARY: This demonstration, conducted between 1994 and 1997, tested the effects of consolidated services, mandatory employment services, and financial incentives on a large sample of AFDC recipients. Subjects were followed up to three years.

COST: Unavailable.

TIME FRAME: Demonstration period, April 1994–March 1996; data collected through June 30, 1997.

TREATMENTS TESTED: The Colorado Personal Responsibility and Employment Program (CPREP) consolidated cash assistance, Food Stamps, and child care benefits into a single cash benefit package. Relative to AFDC, CPREP increased the amount adult recipients could earn and save without grant reductions. New case managers were added and the capacity of the JOBS program was increased to provide services to a higher proportion of clients. Sanctions for noncompliance were strengthened. Further, CPREP provided a $500 cash incentive for the completion of high school or GED attainment for JOBS participants. The control group received services subject to the policies and provision of the existing AFDC system.

OUTCOMES OF INTEREST: (1) Employment; (2) Earnings; (3) Educational achievement; (4) Welfare receipt; (5) Welfare recidivism; and (6) Children's immunization rates.

SAMPLE SIZE: Experimentals, 5,035; controls, 5,005.

TARGET POPULATION: AFDC recipients and new applicants.

NUMBER OF TREATMENT GROUPS: Two (with one control group).

NUMBER AND LOCATION OF SITES: Five—Adams, Jefferson, El Paso, Mesa, and Logan counties.

RESEARCH COMPONENTS:
- Process analysis: Administrative records, administrator interviews, a client survey, and focus groups.
- Impact analysis: Comparison of means.
- Benefit–cost analysis: Not conducted.

MAJOR FINDINGS:
1. Overall, more experimentals were enrolled in JOBS sometime between June 1994 and June 1997 than were controls over the same period (56 percent compared with 36 percent). A nonexperimental comparison indicated that in all the study counties, JOBS program impacts were greater for the experimentals in the original sample (comprising ongoing welfare recipients) than for the experimentals in the second sample (comprising mainly new applicants). Over half of the original sample (54 percent) received JOBS services compared with 41 percent of the second, a statistically significant difference.
2. Experimentals (in both samples) received welfare assistance for significantly longer periods than did controls. There was a small but statistically significant reduction in welfare recidivism among experimentals: 16.5 percent of the

experimental group returned to welfare after leaving, compared with 18.5 percent of the control group.

3. There were little or no statistically significant differences between experimentals and controls in employment, earnings, and child care arrangements.

TIME TRENDS IN FINDINGS: None, but see "Design Issues."

DESIGN ISSUES: The program was discontinued after the implementation of national welfare reform legislation in 1997. The original plan called for an evaluation over a period of five years (1994–99). The program ended before most of the impacts on employment and earnings from the JOBS program would be expected to appear among later participants.

REPLICABILITY: Replicable.

GENERALIZABILITY: The sample is reasonably representative of the entire state of Colorado.

FUNDING SOURCE: Colorado Department of Human Services. Key personnel: Maynard Chapman. There was a federal matching grant from the U.S. Department of Health and Human Services.

TREATMENT ADMINISTRATOR: Colorado Department of Human Services. Key personnel: Maynard Chapman.

EVALUATOR: The Centers of the University of Colorado at Denver and the Center for Policy Research. Key personnel: Peggy Cuciti.

ENABLING LEGISLATION: Pursuant to section 1115 of the Social Security Act.

INFORMATION SOURCE: The Centers of the University of Colorado at Denver and The Center for Policy Research, *Evaluation of the Colorado Personal Responsibility and Employment Program: Final Report,* June 1998.

PUBLIC-USE ACCESS TO DATA: Not available.

Minnesota Family Investment Program (MFIP)

SUMMARY: This demonstration, conducted between 1994 and 1998, tested the effects of financial incentives and mandatory training on a large sample of welfare recipients and new applicants. Subjects were followed for three years.

COST: $5,090,300 for research.

TIME FRAME: Demonstration period, April 1994–March 1996; data collected, same period and for 12-month and 36-month follow-up periods.

TREATMENTS TESTED: The Minnesota Family Investment Program (MFIP) provided a 20 percent grant increase when recipients became employed, increased the level of income that would be disregarded in grant calculation, and paid the child care subsidy directly to caregiver. Two-parent families were not subject to work history requirements or to the 100-hour rule. Both single-parent and two-parent families assigned to MFIP were subject to mandatory participation in employment services. Rules and procedures were simplified by combining Food Stamps, AFDC, and Minnesota's Family General Assistance (FGA) to form a single cash benefit program.

Subjects assigned to the MFIP incentives-only group received identical benefits as MFIP, but were not required to participate in training services.

In the AFDC system, benefits were reduced by an amount almost equal to earned income. Participation in STRIDE (Minnesota's version of JOBS) was voluntary for most AFDC recipients: only recipients in two-parent families were subject to mandatory participation.

The AFDC no services group is essentially the same as the AFDC group except that families in this group were not eligible to receive STRIDE services. The AFDC no services group was created strictly for the purpose of evaluating the effect of the STRIDE program within AFDC and not for comparing outcomes between MFIP and AFDC.

OUTCOMES OF INTEREST: (1) Employment; (2) Earnings; (3) Welfare receipt;[1] (4) Total family income; and (5) Other measures of child and family well-being.

SAMPLE SIZE: MFIP, 5,275; MFIP incentives-only, 1,933; AFDC, 5,634; AFDC, no services, 1,797.

TARGET POPULATION: AFDC recipient and recent applicant families.

NUMBER OF TREATMENT GROUPS: Four (with one control group).

NUMBER AND LOCATION OF SITES: Seven—three urban counties (Hennepin, Anoka, and Dakota) and four rural counties (Mille Lacs, Morrison, Sherburne, and Todd).

RESEARCH COMPONENTS:
- Process analysis: Administrative records, baseline data, 12- and 36-month client surveys, staff attitude surveys, fiscal records, and field research. Program was implemented as intended.
- Impact analysis: Conducted using regression adjusted means.
- Benefit–cost analysis: Conducted.

MAJOR FINDINGS:
Results were weighted to reflect the composition of the caseload in the seven pilot counties. Average income from earnings and welfare for two-parent families is adjusted to account for differences in separation and divorces between the MFIP and the AFDC groups (see tables here and on page 119).

1. From government and recipient perspectives, MFIP was most efficient at increasing financial well-being for long-term single-parent families.
2. Financial gains were similar for long-term single-parent recipients whether they lived in urban or rural counties. However, the annual cost was about $700 more per family in the rural counties.
3. MFIP costs among two-parent long-term recipient families were about $3,800 per family annually, but the financial gain per family was only about $1,400 over five years. Two-parent recent applicant families experienced little financial gain, but the program cost about $2,500 per family over five years.
4. Estimates from the three-year follow-up survey of a sample subset indicate that MFIP recipients were more likely than AFDC recipients to be married and remain married, have health care coverage, and be homeowners. MFIP is estimated to reduce domestic abuse by 18 percent among single-parent recipients with young children.
5. The subgroup of families receiving federal housing assistance is responsible for nearly the entire measured impact of MFIP. A study confirming this finding should be available

Findings for Long-Term Recipients

Work, welfare, and income per quarter over 9 quarters	Single-Parent Families				Two-Parent Families			
	MFIP	AFDC	Impact	Change (%)	MFIP	AFDC	Impact	Change (%)
Percent with at least one parent employed	49.9	36.9	12.9***	35.0	60.2	62.5	−2.3	−3.7
Average family earnings ($)	955	779	176***	22.6	2,193	2,682	−489***	−18.2
Average welfare benefits ($)	1,745	1,569	176***	11.2	1,889	1,367	522***	38.2
Average income from earnings and welfare ($)	2,700	2,348	352***	15.0	3,958	3,769	189*	5.0
Percent combining work and welfare	42.4	26.1	16.3***	62.7	45.8	37.6	8.2***	21.9

Findings for Recent Applicants

Work, welfare, and income per quarter over 9 quarters	Single-Parent Families				Two-Parent Families			
	MFIP	AFDC	Impact	Change (%)	MFIP	AFDC	Impact	Change (%)
Percent with at least one parent employed	55.3	52.0	3.3***	6.3	78.6	78.4	0.1	0.2
Average family earnings ($)	1,470	1,509	−39	−2.6	4,057	4,492	−435*	−9.7
Average welfare benefits ($)	1,060	823	237***	28.8	783	433	350***	81.0
Average income from earnings and welfare ($)	2,530	2,332	198***	8.5	4,840	4,924	−85	−1.7
Percent combining work and welfare	32.5	21.2	11.2***	53.0	33.1	24.9	8.2***	32.8

* = finding significant at the $p < .10$ level; ** = finding significant at the $p < .05$ level; *** = finding significant at the $p < .01$ level.

from the Office of Policy Development and Research, U.S. Department of Housing and Urban Development, by the time this edition of the *Digest* is published.

TIME TRENDS IN FINDINGS: None reported.

DESIGN ISSUES:
1. MFIP case managers reported that only one-quarter of recipients were "well-informed" about the financial incentives. Financial workers reported that time constraints made it difficult for staff to explain the details fully.
2. MFIP financial workers were more likely than their AFDC counterparts to encourage work, because the MFIP design better rewarded work than the AFDC design did.

REPLICABILITY: Replicable.

GENERALIZABILITY: Several factors limit the generalizability of the demonstration. At the time of the evaluation, Minnesota's economy was notably strong. Compared with recipients nationally, Minnesota recipients were more likely to be white and to have graduated from high school. Minnesota's AFDC program provides higher benefits than the national average.

FUNDING SOURCES: Minnesota Department of Human Services, the Ford Foundation, the U.S. Department of Health and Human Services, the U.S. Department of Agriculture, Charles Stewart Mott Foundation, Annie E. Casey Foundation,

McKnight Foundation, and Northwest Area Foundation.

TREATMENT ADMINISTRATOR: Minnesota Department of Human Services (DHS). Key personnel: Chuck Johnson and Joel Kvamme, directors.

EVALUATOR: Manpower Demonstration Research Corporation. Key personnel: Barbara Goldman.

ENABLING LEGISLATION: None.

INFORMATION SOURCE: Virginia Knox, Cynthia Miller, and Lisa A. Gennetian, *Reforming Welfare and Rewarding Work: A Summary of the Final Report on the Minnesota Family Investment Program,* Manpower Demonstration Research Corporation, September 2000; Cynthia Miller, Virginia Knox, Lisa A. Gennetian, Martey Dodoo, Jo Anna Hunter, and Cindy Redcross, *Final Report on the Minnesota Family Investment Program,* Manpower Demonstration Research Corporation, September 2000.

PUBLIC-USE ACCESS TO DATA: Available from Manpower Demonstration Research Corporation.

Note

1. The term *welfare* is defined for families in the AFDC groups as the combined benefit receipt from AFDC income, Food Stamp benefits, and General Assistance payments. For families in the MFIP groups, *welfare* refers to MFIP payments, including the cash replacement of Food Stamp benefits.

Post-Employment Services Demonstration (PESD)

SUMMARY: This demonstration, conducted between spring 1994 and fall 1996, tested the effectiveness of providing case-management services to a large sample of newly employed welfare recipients. Subjects were followed for two years.

COST: Evaluation, $1.3 million.

TIME FRAME: Demonstration period, spring 1994–fall 1996; final report, April 1999.

TREATMENTS TESTED: Post-Employment Services Demonstration (PESD) case managers provided clients with counseling and support; job search assistance; help with applying for benefits and resolving eligibility problems; service referrals; and payments for temporary work-related expenses. Control group members received the regular services provided for employed welfare recipients.

OUTCOMES OF INTEREST: (1) Employment; (2) Earnings; and (3) Welfare receipt.

SAMPLE SIZE: Chicago: Experimentals, 552; controls, 993. Portland: Experimentals, 425; controls, 379. Riverside: Experimentals, 500; controls, 1,006. San Antonio: Experimentals, 386; controls, 392.

TARGET POPULATION: Welfare recipients for whom participation was mandatory in Job Opportunities and Basic Skills and who had recently been hired as full- or part-time workers.

NUMBER OF TREATMENT GROUPS: Two (with one control group).

NUMBER AND LOCATION OF SITES: Four— Chicago, Illinois; Portland, Oregon; Riverside, California; and San Antonio, Texas.

RESEARCH COMPONENTS:
- Process analysis: Conducted. The program evolved over time as case managers discovered that some components of the program were not needed and other components were added to address unanticipated needs of clients. PESD case managers were new to the clients and had to initiate contact with them.
- Impact analysis: Conducted. Comparison of means and subgroup analysis
- Benefit–cost analysis: Not conducted.

MAJOR FINDINGS:
1. The PESD treatment had little effect on employment, earnings, or welfare receipt.
2. Some clients needed minimal assistance or short-term assistance (e.g., finding child care) to remain employed. Other clients had serious or multiple barriers and required more assistance on an ongoing basis.
3. Although the PESD programs offered to provide clients with employer mediation to help them retain their jobs, and many clients experienced job-related problems that made it difficult for them to remain employed, most clients did not want their case managers to intervene on their behalf. The clients did not want their employers to know of their welfare connection and to feel that they required mediation assistance from others.
4. The PESD treatment was not more effective for some subgroups than for others.

TIME TRENDS IN FINDINGS: None.

DESIGN ISSUES:
1. The impacts of the programs might have been reduced by the strong economic conditions that prevailed during the demonstration, the pioneering nature of the program, and the evolutionary character of the experiment.
2. The four sites had various levels of preexisting services for welfare recipients who had recently been hired and different post-employment services for experimentals.
3. Case managers had little guidance on what their roles were, what services they were to deliver, and how they were to deliver services.
4. The PESD programs provided all clients with case management services, regardless of client needs.

5. The services received by control group members in Portland and Riverside were very similar to the services received by experimental group members at those sites.

6. The programs in Riverside and Portland adhered closely to the requirements of serving the target population. In contrast, 25 to 35 percent of the clients at the San Antonio and Chicago sites were JOBS-exempt welfare recipients.

REPLICABILITY: Replicable. See Haimson, Hershey, and Rangarajan (1995).

GENERALIZABILITY: Generalizable. The final report suggested that similar case management–based programs working with like populations would not be more successful than the PESD.

FUNDING SOURCE: Funding was provided by grants from the Administration for Children and Families of the U.S. Department of Health and Human Services.

TREATMENT ADMINISTRATOR: Illinois Department of Human Services. Key personnel: David Gruenenfelder.

EVALUATOR: Mathematica Policy Research, Inc. Key personnel: Anu Rangarajan.

INFORMATION SOURCES: J. Haimson, A. Hershey, and A. Rangarajan, *Providing Services to Promote Job Retention,* Mathematica Policy Research, Inc., October 1995; Anu Rangarajan and Tim Novak, *The Struggle to Sustain Employment: The Effectiveness of the Postemployment Services Demonstration, Final Report,* Mathematica Policy Research, Inc., April 1999.

PUBLIC-USE ACCESS TO DATA: Not available.

Vermont Welfare Restructuring Project (WRP)

SUMMARY: This demonstration, conducted from 1994 to 2001, tested the effects of financial incentives and work requirements on a large sample of welfare recipients. Subjects were followed for six years.

COST: $3,349,661 for evaluation.

TIME FRAME: Demonstration period, July 1994–2001; data collected, same period.

TREATMENTS TESTED: Parents applying for or receiving welfare in Vermont between July 1994 and December 1996 were randomly assigned to three groups:

1. The Welfare Restructuring Project (WRP) group members received cash assistance for 30 months for single-parent families and 15 months for two-parent families and were subject to work requirements. Families were required to work in a wage-paying job after they had received cash assistance for the specified period as a condition for further assistance. Financial incentives included enhanced earnings disregard and permission to own a more valuable car and to accumulate more savings from earnings without losing eligibility for assistance. The demonstration further provided three years of transitional Medicaid coverage and child care.

2. The WRP incentives-only group was not subject to the work requirement but was eligible for the financial incentives.

3. Controls, the Aid to Needy Families with Children (ANFC) group, were not subject to the incentives or the work requirement.

OUTCOMES OF INTEREST: (1) Employment; (2) Income, and (3) Welfare receipt.

SAMPLE SIZE: WRP group, 6,382; WRP incentives-only group, 2,127; ANFC group, 2,127.

TARGET POPULATION: Statewide welfare recipients in Vermont.

NUMBER OF TREATMENT GROUPS: Three (with one control group).

NUMBER AND LOCATION OF SITES: Six—Burlington, Barre, Rutland, St. Albans, Newport, and Springfield districts.

RESEARCH COMPONENTS:
- Process analysis: Conducted.
- Impact analysis: Regression.
- Benefit–cost analysis: Conducted.

MAJOR FINDINGS:
1. At the beginning of the fourth year, the employment rate for the full WRP group was 10 percentage points higher than for the ANFC group (58 percent compared with 48 percent).
2. Over the six-year demonstration period, WRP increased average annual earnings by 9 percent ($508).
3. Midway through the follow-up period, the program began to reduce the number of families receiving cash assistance. By the end of the follow-up period, only 18 percent of the WRP group was receiving assistance, compared with 24 percent of the ANFC group. WRP reduced cash assistance by $449 (28 percent) per year during the last two years of the demonstration.
4. WRP's financial incentives alone did not lead to increases in employment or income, probably because the incentives were only marginally different from incentives under the old rules. In fact, WRP's enhanced earnings disregard during the first four months of work was less generous than the disregard under prior rules.
5. Few recipients received welfare sufficiently long to become subject to the work requirement. Less than half of the single-parent families in the WRP group accumulated 30 or more months of cash assistance receipt during the entire six-year study period.

TIME TRENDS IN FINDINGS: Employment gains and reductions in cash assistance grew larger over time, peaking at the beginning of the fourth year of the demonstration period.

DESIGN ISSUES: None apparent.

REPLICABILITY: Replicable.

GENERALIZABILITY: Generalizable, taking into account Vermont's exceptional environment:
1. The demonstration was implemented during a healthy economic climate. Vermont's annual unemployment rate remained lower than the national average throughout the demonstration period.
2. Vermont is predominantly rural but offers welfare grant levels that are among the highest in the country.
3. Baseline data show that Vermont's welfare caseload was less disadvantaged than recipients in many other states. Almost all sample members (92 percent) had at least some work experience.
4. Vermont provides generous child care and health insurance subsidies for all low-income working families.

FUNDING SOURCES: The U.S. Department of Health and Human Services; the Vermont Department of Prevention, Assistance, Transition, and Health Services (PATH)—formerly the Department of Social Welfare; and the Ford Foundation. Key personnel: Jane Kitchel, Eileen Elliot, and Sandra Dooley for PATH.

TREATMENT ADMINISTRATORS: The Vermont Department of PATH and Manpower Demonstration Research Corporation (MDRC).

ENABLING LEGISLATION: None.

INFORMATION SOURCE: Susan Scrivener, Richard Hendra, Cindy Redcross, Dab Bloom, Charles Michalopoulos, and Johanna Walter, *Final Report on Vermont's Welfare Restructuring Project*, MDRC, September 2002.

PUBLIC-USE ACCESS TO DATA: Available on request at MDRC: phone 212-532-3200 or send e-mail to public_use_files@mdrc.org.

Florida Family Transition Program (FTP)

SUMMARY: This demonstration, conducted from 1994 to 1999, tested the effects of time limits and earnings disregards on a large sample of families receiving welfare. Subjects were followed for four years.

COST: Net cost of the program was $11,200,000 over five years.

TIME FRAME: Demonstration period, 1994–99; data collected, same period.

TREATMENTS TESTED: Family Transition Program (FTP) experimentals could only receive welfare benefits for 24 months out of any 60-month period, unless they were deemed "least job-ready," in which case the time limit was 36 out of any 72-month period. These subjects also received an enhanced earnings disregard of the first $200 plus half of their earnings. FTP subjects also received intensive case management and other job-related support services and were subject to increased requirements to participate in employment-related activities. Controls remained under the preexisting AFDC policy, which did not include time limits and did not disregard earnings of longer-term recipients.

OUTCOMES OF INTEREST: (1) Effects on earnings; (2) Welfare benefit receipts; and (3) Outcomes for children.

SAMPLE SIZE: Experimentals, 1,400; controls, 1,400.

TARGET POPULATION: Families on AFDC.

NUMBER OF TREATMENT GROUPS: Two (with one control group)

NUMBER AND LOCATION OF SITES: Two—Escambia and Alachua counties.

RESEARCH COMPONENTS:
- Process analysis: Surveys and interviews were conducted to gather staff and client reactions.
- Impact analysis: Regression analysis.
- Benefit–cost analysis: Conducted from the government and participant perspectives.

MAJOR FINDINGS (see table):
1. Children of FTP members in the subgroup least at risk for long-term dependence demonstrated impaired school performance, most notably 6.4 percent more treatment children exhibited below-average achievement than control children. 12.3 percent more treatment than control children, ages 10 and older, had ever been suspended from school. Both results are statistically significant. There were no impact trends from children in the medium-risk and most at risk for long-term dependence subgroups.
2. FTP resulted in a net cost to the government of approximately $6,300 per FTP member. There is no evidence to suggest that this effect would change in the long term.

TIME TRENDS IN FINDINGS: Effects on earnings, employment, and benefit receipt decrease over time as controls catch up.

DESIGN ISSUES:
1. FTP was implemented just prior to the change in federal law imposing time-limited welfare.

Major Findings

Outcome	FTP group	AFDC group	Difference
Average quarterly employment rate (%)	48.3	43.8	4.5
Average months receiving AFDC/TANF	15.4	17.1	−1.7
Received more than 36 months of AFDC/TANF (%)	6.1	16.5	−10.4
Average total earnings ($)	16,666	14,288	2,378
Average total AFDC/TANF benefits ($)	3,987	4,698	−711
Average total Food Stamp benefits ($)	6,121	6,621	−499
Combined income from earnings, AFDC/TANF, and Food Stamps ($)	26,774	25,606	1,167
At least 50% of income from earnings (%)	50.1	44.7	5.4
Ever quit job/school/training because of problems with child care (%)	19.7	23.6	−3.9
Informed about transitional child care subsidies (%)	67.1	53.7	13.5

Note: All outcomes are statistically significant at the .01 level, except for income, which is significant at the .10 level.

As a result, many controls were exposed to the debate surrounding time-limited welfare and this may have affected their behavior.

2. The authors note that the results may have been influenced by a strong economy and a lower average unemployment rate in Escambia County than the rest of the nation. Also, Escambia County is largely rural, with no large urban areas.

REPLICABILITY: Replicable.

GENERALIZABILITY: This study does not seem to generalize well. The results in the evaluation report were confined to Escambia County, which is not particularly representative of the rest of Florida or the nation. Also, cost outcomes may not be generalizable because FTP received exceedingly generous funding to attempt to ensure that no one would reach the experimental time limit without some form of employment or support. Such funding is unlikely to be more generally available.

FUNDING SOURCES: Florida Department of Children and Families, through the U.S. Department of Health and Human Services. Additional funding from The Ford Foundation, Centers for Disease Control, National Institute of Child Health and Human Development, and the U.S. Department of Agriculture.

TREATMENT ADMINISTRATOR: Florida Department of Children and Families. Key personnel: Don Winstead, welfare reform administrator.

EVALUATOR: Manpower Demonstration Research Corporation. Key personnel: Barbara Goldman.

ENABLING LEGISLATION: None.

POLICY EFFECTS: Shortly after FTP's inception, the federal government imposed time-limited welfare reforms. FRP provided some information about the potential effects of this policy change.

INFORMATION SOURCE: Dan Bloom, James J. Kemple, Pamela Morris, Susan Scrivener, Nandita Verma, and Richard Hendra, *The Family Transition Program: Final Report on Florida's Initial Time-Limited Welfare Program,* Manpower Demonstration Research Corporation, June 2000.

PUBLIC-USE ACCESS TO DATA: Available through MDRC.

Arkansas Welfare Waiver Demonstration

SUMMARY: This demonstration, conducted from July 1994 to June 1997, tested the effects of imposing a family cap on AFDC benefits on a large sample of AFDC families. Participants were followed for two and a half years.

COST: $700,000 for research.

TIME FRAME: Demonstration period, July 1994–June 1997; data collected, July 1994–December 1996; final report, June 1997.

TREATMENTS TESTED: The treatment group was subject to a family cap on their AFDC benefits, i.e., the incremental increases in AFDC benefits otherwise granted at the birth of another child were eliminated. The treatment also emphasized family planning services to try to prevent additional births. Controls were subject to existing AFDC rules, which meant that they were eligible for higher AFDC benefits at the birth of another child.

OUTCOMES OF INTEREST: (1) Number of births; (2) Employment; (3) Income; (4) Education; (5) AFDC and Food Stamp receipt; (6) Medicaid use; (7) Exits from and entry to AFDC; (8) Paternity establishment; (9) Use of foster care; (10) Time devoted to family planning activities; and (11) Number of family moves.

SAMPLE SIZE: Total 4,168, with approximately half each in the experimental and control groups.

TARGET POPULATION: AFDC recipients not already pregnant when the program began.

NUMBER OF TREATMENT GROUPS: Two (with one control group).

NUMBER AND LOCATION OF SITES: Ten—Ashley, Clark, Independence, Izard, Lincoln, Pope, St. Francis, Stone, Union, and Yell counties. These are all small, rural counties.

RESEARCH COMPONENTS:
- Process analysis: Surveys and interviews of caseworkers and surveys of heads of families in the sample population.
- Impact analysis: Comparisons of means, simple correlations.
- Benefit–cost analysis: Not conducted.

MAJOR FINDINGS:
1. No differences between the experimental and control groups in the number of births, or in any other of outcomes, were found.
2. Eighty-two percent of the sample families indicated when surveyed that benefit amounts had no influence on their decision to have another child.
3. Seventy-eight percent of the sample families indicated when surveyed that they would not use abortion as a method of birth control in the event of pregnancy.

TIME TRENDS IN FINDINGS: None.

DESIGN ISSUES:
1. The controls often believed they were included in the treatment. This most likely occurred due to feedback effects from the program group, the fact that the rest of the state was covered under the cap, and media attention, although confusion on the part of the providers cannot be discounted.
2. The treatment was not implemented as planned, in that neither control nor experimental families knew what the effects of an additional child would be on welfare benefits. Survey data indicated that the information provided to both treatment and control families was often vague and misleading. Consequently, they were often unaware of the differences in the program rules applied to control and treatment household. "I tell them all that a cap on benefits may apply to them" (Turturro et al. p. 22).

3. Telephone surveys of case heads were used to obtain outcome data. This might have introduced some bias if those with phones differed from other sample members.

REPLICABILITY: Replicable.

GENERALIZABILITY: The design issues noted suggest that the findings do not generalize.

FUNDING SOURCES: Split between the Arkansas Department of Human Services and the U.S. Department of Health and Human Services (HHS). Key personnel: Peter Germanis for HHS.

TREATMENT ADMINISTRATOR: Arkansas Department of Human Services. Key personnel: Joie Wallis, Linda Greer, and Lori Williams.

EVALUATOR: The University of Arkansas at Little Rock, School of Social Work. Key personnel: Carolyn Turturro, Brent Benda, and Howard Turney.

INFORMATION SOURCE: Carolyn Turturro, Brent Benda, and Howard Turney, *Arkansas Welfare Waiver Demonstration: Final Report,* University of Arkansas, June 1997.

PUBLIC-USE ACCESS TO DATA: Not available.

Cal-Learn

SUMMARY: This demonstration, conducted from 1994 to 1999, tested the effects of financial incentives and intensive case management on a large sample of pregnant and parenting teenagers on welfare. Subjects were followed for five years.

COST: The experiment was embedded in a larger program that cost $10 million.

TIME FRAME: Demonstration period, October 1994–October 1999; data collected, same period.

TREATMENTS TESTED: Participants in four counties in California were randomly assigned to one of four research groups: full Cal-Learn; financial incentives only; case management only, and a no-treatment control group.

In addition to case managements, the full Cal-Learn and financial incentives only groups were subject to the following financial incentives: a bonus of $500 upon graduation and a progress bonus of $100; and sanctions of $100 for a missing or "inadequate" report card and $50 for a late report card. Control group members received no case management, bonuses, or sanctions. All teenagers in the evaluation were offered supportive services consisting of child care, transportation, and ancillary expenses.

OUTCOMES OF INTEREST: (1) Graduation rates; (2) Persistence in high school; (3) Employment; and (4) Welfare receipt.

SAMPLE SIZE: Samples used varied with outcome. The largest sample was 3,803: Full Cal-Learn, 978; financial incentives only, 937; case management only, 939; controls, 949.

TARGET POPULATION: Custodial parents under age 19, on welfare, who did not have a high school diploma.

NUMBER OF TREATMENT GROUPS: Four (with one control group).

NUMBER AND LOCATION OF SITES: Four—Alameda, Los Angeles, San Bernardino, and San Joaquin counties.

RESEARCH COMPONENTS:
- Process analysis: Operational challenges (including interagency coordination, client identification, and declining case loads) were analyzed, based on interviews conducted with state and county agency staff.
- Impact analysis: Conducted as difference in means.
- Benefit–cost analysis: Not conducted.

MAJOR FINDINGS:
1. Full Cal-Learn program participants were more likely to graduate than the control group. Among teenagers age 18 and over, 32 percent of the full Cal-Learn group graduated compared with 24 percent of the control group. By age 20, an estimated 47 percent of the full Cal-Learn group and 33 percent of the control group graduated.

2. The effect of full Cal-Learn was greater than either of its constituent treatments alone. Nearly 18 percent of teenagers out of school at Cal-Learn entry who were assigned to full Cal-Learn earned a GED, while only 10 percent of those only receiving financial incentives and only 7 percent under case management earned a GED.

3. There were no significant benefits in terms of more employment, higher earnings, or less dependence on welfare.

TIME TRENDS IN FINDINGS: None apparent.

DESIGN ISSUES:
1. Cal-Learn caseload steadily declined from 21,184 cases statewide in January 1996 to 11,744 cases in September 1999, reflecting a sharp drop in the teen birth rate in California.

2. A combination of administrative and survey data was used for the evaluation. Survey data were available for 58 percent of the program participants. Non-surveyed teenagers were somewhat different from the surveyed teenagers.

REPLICABILITY: Replicable.

GENERALIZABILITY: Intended to generalize to the entire state of California. The four research counties accounted for about half of the California Cal-Learn caseload; Los Angeles accounted for 38 percent.

FUNDING SOURCES: California Departments of Education, Health Services, and Social Services–Cal-Learn Program. Key personnel: Ronda Simpson-Brown for Education, Sharlyn Hansen for Health, and Nancy Remley for Social Services–Cal-Learn.

TREATMENT ADMINISTRATOR: California Department of Social Services Research and Evaluation Branch. Key personnel: J. Oshi Ruelas.

EVALUATOR: University of California, Berkeley. Key personnel: Jane Mauldon and Jan Malvin.

ENABLING LEGISLATION: California Senate Bills 35 and 1078, 1993.

INFORMATION SOURCES: Jane Mauldon, Jan Malvin, Jon Stiles, Nancy Nicosia, and Eva Seto, *Impact of California's Cal-Learn Demonstration Project: Final Report,* University of California, Berkeley, June 2000; James Cunniff, Diane Hirshberg, and Janet Malvin, *Implementation of California's Cal-Learn Demonstration Project: A Process Evaluation,* University of California, Berkeley, April 1998.

PUBLIC-USE ACCESS TO DATA: Not available.

LA Jobs-First GAIN Evaluation

SUMMARY: This demonstration, conducted from 1995 to 1996, tested Los Angeles County's new work-first program on a large sample of welfare recipients. Subjects were followed for two years.

COST: Net administrative costs were approximately $16.1 million for single parents over two years and approximately $4.8 million for couples over two years.

TIME FRAME: Demonstration period, January 1995–March 1998; data collected, same period.

TREATMENTS TESTED: Members of the treatment group were enrolled in Jobs-First GAIN. These subjects were required to participate in at least one of the job search activities, including job clubs and other informational services and job search training sessions. Experimentals were also exposed to Jobs-First GAIN's intensive work-first message. Sanctions were imposed, usually in the form of partial reductions in welfare benefits, for failure to participate. Controls were not exposed to any of Jobs-First GAIN's services, the intensive work-first message, or sanctions. Controls could still receive assistance from other agencies and were subject to existing welfare rules.

OUTCOMES OF INTEREST: (1) Effects on employment; (2) Effects on earnings; (3) Welfare benefits; (4) Outcomes for children; and (5) Incremental effects compared with previous Los Angeles GAIN program.

SAMPLE SIZE: Single parents: Experimentals, 11,521; controls, 4,162. Couples: Experimentals, 4,039; controls, 1,009.

TARGET POPULATION: Single-parent (AFDC-FG) and two-parent (AFDC-U) welfare families in Los Angeles County.

NUMBER OF TREATMENT GROUPS: Two (with one control group).

NUMBER AND LOCATION OF SITES: One—Los Angeles County.

RESEARCH COMPONENTS:
■ Process analysis: Surveys were administered to clients.
■ Impact analysis: Impact estimates were regression-adjusted.
■ Benefit–cost analysis: Conducted from welfare recipient and government perspectives.

MAJOR FINDINGS:
1. AFDC-FG experimentals experienced a 10 percentage point increase in employment and an average increase in earnings of $1,627 compared with AFDC-FG controls.
2. AFDC-FG experimentals experienced a 5 percentage point decrease in welfare receipt compared with controls. Welfare payment also decreased by 10 percent, or $972 per treatment group member.
3. AFDC-FG experimentals earned more and received more earned income tax credit (EITC) payments than controls, although this was almost perfectly counterbalanced by the reduction in welfare and food stamp payments they received, resulting in an increase in net income of only about 2 percent.
4. 53 percent of AFDC-FG experimentals reported conditions of food insecurity, approximately 5 percentage points more than controls. 19 percent of AFDC-FG experimentals reported food insecurity with hunger, again approximately 5 percentage points above controls. Only the latter result was statistically significant.
5. AFDC-FG experimentals reported a 13 percent increase over controls in the use of child

care. Experimentals also reported an increase in the incidence of problems with child care that resulted in missed workdays or other employment problems.

6. The only statistically significant impact on AFDC-FG children was a 3.6 percentage point decrease in treatment children ever suspended or expelled from school.

7. Jobs-First GAIN increased earnings by more than $1,700 for AFDC-FG treatments with similar background characteristics to those in the previous Los Angeles GAIN, while the previous GAIN program increased earnings by only $200. Both programs produced similar reductions in average welfare expenditure per group member, about $1,000.

8. AFDC-U experimentals experienced an increase in employment of 10 percentage points and an increase in two-year earnings of $2,050, or 31 percentage points, more than AFDC-U controls.

9. Jobs-First GAIN resulted in a reduction in the two-year welfare payments of approximately $1,429, or 12 percent, per AFDC-U treatment group member.

10. The demonstration resulted in a net benefit of approximately $1,868 in earnings and benefits over the two-year project period for experimental group members.

11. The program also resulted in an average net benefit to the government budget of $1,613 through reduced AFDC/TANF, food stamp, and Medi-Cal payments over the two-year period.

12. Jobs-First GAIN staff had enforced formal sanctions on approximately 30 percent of the AFDC-FG treatment group and 23 percent of the AFDC-U treatment group for noncompliance during the two-year follow-up.

TIME TRENDS IN FINDINGS: None reported.

DESIGN ISSUES:

1. Outcomes were measured with administrative data, such as unemployment insurance records, that capture only in-state employment, earnings, and benefit receipts.

2. Outcomes were also measured with the Two-Year Client Survey, which used a much smaller report sample. Results may have been influenced by recall error, nonreporting, and exaggeration.

3. Earnings and employment outcomes measured with administrative data cover only one parent in each AFDC-U family, which may result in underestimation of Jobs-First GAIN's true effect for this group.

4. AFDC-Us were not included in the Two-Year Client Survey, thus all impacts for them can be measured only with administrative data.

REPLICABILITY: The demonstration is a replication of the GAIN demonstration in Riverside County, California (p. 72).

GENERALIZABILITY: This study was intended to generalize to other large, urban areas. The authors note that economic conditions and demographics are similar to those of other urban areas. Note that the sanctions for noncompliance in work activities in this demonstration were partial, not a complete elimination of benefits to the family.

FUNDING SOURCES: Los Angeles Department of Public Social Services; U.S. Department of Health and Human Services, Administration for Children and Families; and the Ford Foundation.

TREATMENT ADMINISTRATOR: Los Angeles County Department of Public Social Services. Key personnel: Lynn Bayer.

EVALUATOR: Manpower Demonstration Research Corporation (MDRC).

ENABLING LEGISLATION: None.

INFORMATION SOURCES: Steven Freedman, Marisa Mitchell, and David Navarro, *The Los Angeles Jobs-First GAIN Evaluation: First-Year Findings on Participation Patterns and Impacts,* MDRC, June 1999; Steven Freedman, Jean Tansey Knab, Lisa A. Gennetian and David Navarro, *The Los Angeles Jobs-First GAIN Evaluation: Final Report on a Work First Program in a Major Urban Center,* MDRC, June 2000.

PUBLIC-USE ACCESS TO DATA: MDRC had no plans for a public-use file.

Teenage Parent Home Visitor Services Demonstration

SUMMARY: This demonstration, conducted from 1995 to 1997, tested the effects of paraprofessional home visitor services on a large sample of teenage parents receiving AFDC. Subjects were followed for up to 27 months.

COST: $1.18 million for research and implementation combined.

TIME FRAME: Demonstration period, March 1995–September 1997; data collected, same period.

TREATMENTS TESTED: Experimentals received weekly home visits from paraprofessionals lasting 45 minutes to an hour, during which child development, parenting, employment, and support needs were supposed to be addressed, in accordance with a prescribed curriculum. The visitors did not hold degrees in nursing, college, or social work and were often former welfare recipients; they each took a one-week training course before the demonstration began, followed up by an in-service training program. Persistent noncompliance with scheduled visits constituted grounds for financial sanction ranging from $50 to $160 per month, depending on the state. Controls received regular JOBS services for teenage parents in their states.

OUTCOMES OF INTEREST: (1) School attendance; (2) Degree attainment; (3) Job training; (4) Employment; (5) Income; (6) Assistance receipt; (7) Sexual activity; (8) Contraceptive use; (9) Pregnancies; and (10) Births.

SAMPLE SIZE: Experimentals, 1,103; controls, 1,293. Only 708 of 975 sample members randomly selected for follow-up completed the survey (392 experimentals and 316 controls).

TARGET POPULATION: First-time parents 19 years or younger, either newly applying for AFDC or members of a family already receiving AFDC who qualified as head of a new case by virtue of pregnancy or bearing a child.

NUMBER OF TREATMENT GROUPS: Two (with one control group). The design involved one control and two treatment groups, with 31 percent of sample members randomly assigned to home visitor services through the welfare agency and 15 percent to home visitor services provided by community agencies. The two treatment groups are combined for purposes of evaluation.

NUMBER AND LOCATION OF SITES: Three—South Chicago, Illinois; Dayton, Ohio; and Portland, Oregon.

RESEARCH COMPONENTS:
- Process analysis: Review of welfare case records.
- Impact analysis: Multivariate regression.
- Benefit–cost analysis: Not conducted.

MAJOR FINDINGS:
Differences that are statistically significant at the $p < .10$ level are denoted with an asterisk.

1. Only one out of three scheduled home visits actually took place during the first six months of the demonstration.
2. Forty-five percent of experimentals lost benefits through sanctions, while only 35 percent of controls did.*
3. Experimentals spent 24 percent of their time in school, while controls spent 21 percent.*
4. There was no overall effect on degree attainment.
5. Experimentals were less likely to participate in job training than controls.*
6. Experimentals were employed for 36 percent of months observed compared with 41 of months for controls.*
7. Experimentals had higher earnings than controls.*
8. There were no significant effects on receipt of AFDC, Food Stamps, or Medicaid.
9. The treatment had no impact on sexual activity. It had positive impacts on use of condoms* and Norplant® or Depo-Provera contraceptives.*

10. The treatment had no impact on pregnancy or abortion.

11. Evaluators conclude that three factors are responsible for the limited success of the demonstration:
    a Challenges in identifying and serving the needs of adolescents;
    b. Limitations of working in the home environment;
    c. Charging relatively unskilled workers with important and demanding tasks.

12. Experimentals were randomly assigned to home visitors employed either by a welfare agency or a local nonprofit community agency, but the evaluators find no evidence that the employer of the visitor made any difference.

TIME TRENDS IN FINDINGS: The evaluators report that a "mid-course correction" in the visitors' training appeared to raise the rate of degree completion and lower the rate of pregnancy among younger experimentals.

DESIGN ISSUES: None apparent.

REPLICABILITY: Replicable. Training and curricular materials were developed for the demonstration.

GENERALIZABILITY: Reasonably generalizable, with some limitations. Sites are diverse, but the sample that completed the survey is not large. Process analysis indicates that maintaining strength and uniformity of the intervention using paraprofessionals with this target population is difficult.

FUNDING SOURCES: Henry J. Kaiser Family Foundation, and the Administration for Children and Families, U.S. Department of Health and Human Services. Key personnel: Dennis Beatrice and Felicia Stewart for Kaiser and Nancye Campbell for HHS.

TREATMENT ADMINISTRATORS: State welfare agencies in Illinois, Ohio, and Oregon. Key personnel: Denise Simon, Jackie Martin, and Erma Hepburn, respectively.

EVALUATORS: University of Pennsylvania and Mathematica Policy Research. Key personnel: Meredith Kelsey and Rebecca Maynard for U-Pennsylvania, and Amy Johnson and Ellen Kisker for Manpower.

INFORMATION SOURCES: Meredith Kelsey, Ann Johnson, and Rebecca Maynard, *The Potential of Home Visitor Services to Strengthen Welfare-to-Work Programs for Teenage Parents on Cash Assistance,* July 2001.

Meredith Kelsey, "The Role of Home Visitation in Improving Outcomes for Teenage Mothers and Their Children." Doctoral dissertation, Philadelphia, The University of Pennsylvania, 2000.

Amy Johnson, "The Teenage Parent Home Visitor Services Demonstration: Providing Home Visitor Services to Teen Parents on Welfare: An Analysis of Key Implementation Features," Philadelphia, The University of Pennsylvania, 1999.

PUBLIC-USE ACCESS TO DATA: Not known.

Indiana Welfare Reform Evaluation

SUMMARY: This demonstration, conducted from 1995 to 1999, tested the effects of welfare reform on two large samples of AFDC recipients. Subjects were followed for five years and two years, respectively.

COST: Net operating cost for the first cohort was estimated at $288 per household, or $18.2 million total. Total research cost was about $5 million.

TIME FRAME: Demonstration period, 1995–2000: first sample selected May 1995–April 1996; second sample selected March 1998–February 1999; data collected through 2000.

TREATMENTS TESTED: Experimentals were subject to new welfare reform polices: assisted job search, broader mandatory work participation, earned income disregard, time limits for cash assistance, a revised system of child care provision, family benefit cap, and parental responsibility (such as immunizing children). Financial sanction for failure to comply either with work requirements or parental responsibility was generally $90 per month until compliance. Controls continued under the traditional AFDC policies.

OUTCOMES OF INTEREST: (1) Work participation; (2) Earnings; (3) Receipt of cash welfare and food stamps; (4) Income; (5) Health insurance; and (6) Parental responsibility.

SAMPLE SIZE: First cohort: Experimentals, 63,223; controls, 3,217. Second cohort: Experimentals, 3,863; controls, 1,091.[1]

TARGET POPULATION: Indiana families on welfare.

NUMBER AND LOCATION OF SITES: The entire State of Indiana—all 92 counties statewide for the first-year cohort and 12 counties for the second cohort.

RESEARCH COMPONENTS:
- Process analysis: Conducted.
- Impact analysis: Regression-adjusted.
- Benefit–cost analysis: Conducted.

MAJOR FINDINGS:

First Cohort (1995–96)

1. The program reduced TANF receipt and payments, and the effect grew over the five-year follow-up period. Payments were reduced by 18.1 percent in the first year and 41.1 percent in the fifth year. The program also reduced food stamp payments, but the effects were smaller and did not grow with time. The effects were statistically significant.
2. The program increased earnings and employment rates in each of the follow-up years. Over five years, average earnings were approximately $2,100 higher for the experimental group than for the control group for single-parent families. The experimental group's average total earnings

increased by approximately 9 percent per year over the five-year period. Quarterly employment rates were on average 3.5 percentage points higher for the experimental group than for the control group. Effects grew slightly over the five-year follow-up period. Earnings and employment effects were largest for clients with no recent work experience at the time of random assignment. The effects were statistically significant.

3. The program had no significant impact on health insurance coverage for either adults or children.
4. Benefit–cost analysis indicates a gain of $897 in net income to treatment households and net savings to taxpayers of $2,015 over the five-year period.

Second Cohort (1998–99)

1. Over the first two follow-up years, average TANF payments to single-parent families were $446 (about 17 percent) lower for the experimental group than for the control group, a statistically significant change. Most of the food stamp effects were smaller and statistically insignificant.
2. The demonstration increased average employment rates across the two years (the average quarterly employment rate was 56 percent, 2.7 percentage points above the rate for the control group) but did not increase earnings.
3. The demonstration did not produce effects on income, measured as a sum of earnings, welfare payments, and food stamps. Over the two years, income from these sources was $187 (about 2 percent) lower for the experimental group than for the control group, a small and not statistically significant difference.

TIME TRENDS IN FINDINGS: Employment and earnings rose over the demonstration period for both cohorts.

DESIGN ISSUES:
1. Impacts included in the study did not include effects of the demonstration on the decision to

apply for welfare. The more stringent program rules might have deterred some families from applying for welfare.

2. Evidence from the process study and client survey suggests that some control group members mistakenly believed they were subject to some of the same requirements as the experimental group members.

REPLICABILITY: Replicable.

GENERALIZABILITY: Generalizable, with the caveat that a strong economy with low levels of unemployment at the time of welfare reform might have contributed to higher employment and earnings impacts.

FUNDING SOURCES: Division of Family and Children (DFC), Family and Social Services Administration (FSSA), Indiana, and the U.S. Department of Health and Human Services, Administration for Children and Families (ACF). Key personnel: Jim Hmurovich and John Boyce for DFC and Howard Rolston and Alan Yaffe for ACF.

TREATMENT ADMINISTRATOR: FSSA Indiana. Key personnel: Jim Hmurovich and John Boyce.

EVALUATORS: Abt Associates and the Urban Institute. Key personnel: Erik Beecroft, Wang Lee, and David Long for Abt Associates Inc. and Pamela Holcomb, Terri Thomson, Nancy Pindus, Carolyn O'Brien, and Jenny Bernestin for the Urban Institute.

ENABLING LEGISLATION: None.

INFORMATION SOURCE: Erik Beecroft, Wang Lee, David Long, Pamela Holcomb, Terri Thomson, Nancy Pindus, Carolyn O'Brien, and Jenny Bernestin, *The Indiana Welfare Reform Evaluation: Five-Year Impacts, Implementation, Costs, and Benefits,* Abt Associates Inc., December 2002.

PUBLIC-USE ACCESS TO DATA: A public-use file is available from Erik Beecroft at Abt Associates.

Note

1. The first and second cohorts differed substantially in the length of time they were on cash assistance prior to random assignment. The second cohort was defined as AFDC applicants who had not received cash assistance since May 1995, when Indiana's welfare reform began.

Ohio Children of Opportunity: Learnfare

SUMMARY: This demonstration, conducted from 1995 to 1998, tested the effects of monetary sanctions on a large sample of students from families receiving public assistance in two Ohio counties. Subjects were followed for three years.

COST: Not available.

TIME FRAME: Demonstration period, 1995–98; data collected, same period; final report, June 1999.

TREATMENTS TESTED: Experimentals were subject to financial sanctions—payments reduced by the amount of the student's benefit—if they had more than two unexcused absences in a month on at least two occasions during a school year. Controls were not subject to the sanctions.

OUTCOMES OF INTEREST: (1) School attendance and (2) School performance.

SAMPLE SIZE: Experimentals, 1,622 (Allen County, 1,376, Shelby, 246); controls, 857 (Allen County, 695, Shelby, 162).

TARGET POPULATION: School-age children of families on public assistance.

NUMBER AND LOCATION OF SITES: Two—Allen and Shelby counties in western Ohio. Allen County is urban and has a population of over 100,000. Shelby County is more rural and has a population of under 50,000.

RESEARCH COMPONENTS:
▪ Process analysis: Conducted.

■ Impact analysis: Regression.

■ Benefit–cost analysis: Conducted.

MAJOR FINDINGS: In both Allen and Shelby counties, the demonstration had a statistically significant effect on students' school attendance: an improvement of .07 days per month in Allen and .17 days in Shelby. Experimental groups had significantly fewer unexcused absences than the control groups.

TIME TREND IN FINDINGS: By the third year, there was no significant relationship between exposure to the program and absences in Allen County. In Shelby County, the trend was toward improved attendance.

DESIGN ISSUES:

1. The original research design called for combining data from both counties. Because of differences in county size and caseloads, as well as in program implementation approaches, the impact analyses for the two counties were performed separately. Shelby County's smaller size and smaller sample reduced the power of the test to detect an impact.
2. Although students were randomly assigned to one group or the other, a consent form was required to obtain information from the school system about absenteeism. Experimental group members were required to sign consent forms but control group members were not, and many control groups members did not sign the forms. That might have created a selection bias if the control group members who did not sign were those who were most often absent.

REPLICABILITY: Replicable.

GENERALIZABILITY: Generalizable, taking into account the design issues highlighted above.

FUNDING SOURCE: Ohio Department of Human Services. Key personnel: Jackie Martin.

TREATMENT ADMINISTRATORS: Ohio Department of Human Services and the Ohio Department of Education.

EVALUATOR: Macro International. Key personnel: JoAnn Kuchak and Michael Errecart.

ENABLING LEGISLATION: None.

INFORMATION SOURCE: JoAnn Kuchak, Michael Errecart, Hellen Jennings, Richard Mantovani, Ellen Marks, and Michael Svilar, *Final Report: Children of Opportunity: Learnfare,* Macro International, June 1999.

PUBLIC-USE ACCESS TO DATA: Not available.

Virginia Independence Program (VIP)

SUMMARY: This demonstration, conducted from 1995 to 1997, tested the effects of eligibility reforms, time limits, work requirements, and work and savings incentives on a large sample of AFDC recipients. Subjects were followed for 42 months.

COST: Approximate evaluation costs: $300,000 for both the early impact evaluation and the final evaluation.

TIME FRAME: Demonstration period, July 1995–September 1997; data collected, July 1995–December 1998.

TREATMENTS TESTED: The program consisted of two components:

1. Virginia Independence Program (VIP) eligibility reforms were implemented statewide in July 1995. VIP requirements departed from Aid to Families with Dependent Children (AFDC) with stronger requirements for child support; a cap on benefits for children born more than 10 months after assistance was authorized; and eligibility criteria for two-parent families identical to the single-parent criteria.
2. The Virginia Initiative for Employment not Welfare (VIEW) replaced the Job Opportunity and Basic Skills (JOBS) program in the experimental group. The VIEW component

was phased in by locality beginning with Lynchburg in October 1995 and followed by Prince William in April 1996; Petersburg in January 1997; and Portsmouth and Wise in October 1997. VIEW included a work search requirement; earned income and savings disregard; and a two-year limit on cash assistance. In addition, VIEW reduced exemptions for parents of young children. Participants had to sign an agreement of personal responsibility. Noncompliance could result in full family sanctions.

Controls remained subject to the old AFDC policies and received employment services under JOBS.

OUTCOMES OF INTEREST: (1) Employment; (2) Earnings; (3) Welfare participation; and (4) Benefit receipt.

SAMPLE SIZE: Experimentals, 3,715; controls, 3,853. Total sample at each site: Lynchburg, 1,019; Petersburg, 1,227; Portsmouth, 2,577; Prince William, 1,864; and Wise, 881. Final evaluation conducted on total sample of 2,444; experimentals, 1,237; controls, 1,207.

TARGET POPULATION: Welfare recipients.

NUMBER OF TREATMENT GROUPS: Two (with one control group).

NUMBER AND LOCATION OF SITES: Five—Lynchburg, Petersburg, Portsmouth, Prince William, and Wise.

RESEARCH COMPONENTS:
- Process analysis: Administrative records of the Virginia Department of Social Services (VDSS) and the Virginia Employment Commission (VEC) reviewed.
- Impact analysis: Conducted using difference in means and regression.
- Benefit–cost analysis: Not conducted.

MAJOR FINDINGS:
1. The early impact evaluation showed no significant impacts on employment, earnings, welfare participation, or benefit receipt from VIP alone.
2. The VIEW evaluation is based solely on cases in the three sites that had implemented VIEW at some point during the experimental period—Lynchburg, Petersburg, and Prince William. In addition, the sample includes only cases with characteristics that were consistent with mandatory VIEW participation.
3. Generally, there were no effects on employment or welfare receipt among new applicant cases (who had little exposure to VIEW); the final evaluation is conducted only on the experiences of those already receiving services at random assignment.
4. In Lynchburg, VIEW increased the average employment rate but had no significant effect on earnings, welfare participation, or benefit receipt.
5. In Petersburg, the experimentals had consistently higher rates of employment and earnings, and lower rates of welfare participation and benefit receipt, than did the controls. These findings are significant in quarters two through nine. Since VIEW wasn't implemented in Petersburg until the seventh quarter, much of the observed impact occurred before VIEW policies were in place.
6. Follow-up interviews with caseworkers revealed that Lynchburg and Petersburg differed in their implementation strategies. Lynchburg caseworkers emphasized the work requirement and encouraged working clients to take advantage of the earning disregard and use the two years they were permitted to stay on welfare to prepare for self-sufficiency. In contrast, caseworkers in Petersburg encouraged clients to close their cases once they became employed in order to "bank" their time.
7. In Prince William, VIEW had little significant impact on employment rates and no impact on welfare participation or benefit receipt. VIEW increased earnings significantly only in quarters 8 and 10. (The experimental period ended after the ninth quarter.)

8. The increase in overall employment rates in the three VIEW sites was largely attributed to those clients who combined welfare and work.

TIME TRENDS IN FINDINGS: Overall, modest increases in employment and earnings persisted during the follow-up period. However, comparisons between the experimentals and controls in quarters 10–14 of the follow-up period no longer indicate the full effects of VIP/VIEW because the control group was gradually brought under VIEW policies beginning in October 1997. In addition, the positive effect on combining welfare and work decreased as members in the treatment group reached their two-year limit.

DESIGN ISSUES:

1. Publicity concerning national welfare reforms and VIP may have affected controls. For example, some members in the control group may have anticipated being subject to time limits (or other changes).
2. Observations in the follow-up period included both the impact of VIEW's time limits (treatment members left welfare), as well as the gradual "contamination" as controls were brought under VIEW policy.

REPLICABILITY: Replicable.

GENERALIZABILITY: The three VIEW sites are reasonably representative of the geographical diversity of Virginia. The diversity in caseworker philosophy among the sites is representative of the profusion of localized approaches to welfare reform in the U.S., especially in states like Virginia, with a tradition of significant devolution to local government. The interaction of geographic with philosophical diversity makes these results difficult to generalize.

FUNDING SOURCES: U.S. Department of Health and Human Services, Administration for Children and Families, and VDSS.

TREATMENT ADMINISTRATOR: VDSS.

EVALUATOR: Mathematica Policy Research, Inc., under contract with Virginia Polytechnic Institute and State University.

ENABLING LEGISLATION: Federal AFDC waiver, March 20, 1995.

INFORMATION SOURCES: Anne Gordon and Roberto Agodini, *Early Impacts of the Virginia Independence Program: Final Report,* Mathematica Policy Research, Inc., November 1999; Anne Gordon and Susanne James-Burdumy, *Impacts of the Virginia Initiative for Employment Not Welfare: Final Report,* Mathematica Policy Research, Inc., January 2002.

PUBLIC-USE ACCESS TO DATA: Not available.

Delaware: A Better Chance

SUMMARY: This demonstration, conducted from 1995 to 1997, tested the effects of employment assistance, income incentives, and personal responsibility requirements on a large sample of welfare recipients in Delaware. Subjects were followed for two years.

COST: Research, approximately $1.6 million.

TIME FRAME: Demonstration period, October 1995–February 1997; data collected, same period.

TREATMENTS TESTED: Experimentals were required to participate in rapid job entry activities. The sanction for noncompliance with either work or job search or short-term training requirements was a one-third reduction in benefits for the first occurrence, two-thirds reduction for the second, and permanent loss for the third. The tax (benefit rate reduction) on earned income cooperation was cut roughly in half through "fill the gap" budgeting rules (deducting income from a standard of need substantially higher than the maximum welfare benefit). A time limit of 24 months on cash assistance was imposed; subjects were eligible for a "pay for performance" program after 24 months. Experimentals were also subject to a family cap (no increase in the grant for child conceived while the mother was on welfare). Controls remained under traditional AFDC rules.

OUTCOMES OF INTEREST: (1) Employment; (2) Earnings; (3) Welfare receipt; and (4) Child neglect.

SAMPLE SIZE: Experimentals, 2,138; controls, 1,821.

TARGET POPULATION: Delaware welfare recipients.

NUMBER AND LOCATION OF SITES: Five—Carroll's Plaza, Georgetown, Hudson, Thatcher, and Williams.

RESEARCH COMPONENTS:
▪ Process analysis: Conducted.
▪ Impact analysis: Regression.
▪ Benefit–cost analysis: Conducted.

MAJOR FINDINGS:
1. There were no statistically significant employment or earnings impacts even in the presence of benefit reductions.
2. In the last quarter of the second year, 31 percent of the experimental group was receiving cash assistance compared with 39 percent of the control group.
3. The incidence of child neglect increased by around 1 percentage point among experimentals.

TIME TRENDS IN FINDINGS: The program had little effect on welfare receipt during the first year of follow-up, but it substantially reduced welfare participation thereafter. Impacts on average total welfare payments were statistically significant in the first year, with payments to the experimentals $140 lower than for the control group (a 6 percent difference). Payment impacts grew to $364 (a 26 percent difference) in the second year.

Follow-up data were collected for only 18 months, beyond which it is not possible to measure the demonstration's impact.

DESIGN ISSUES: None apparent.

REPLICABILITY: Replicable.

GENERALIZABILITY: Generalizable.

FUNDING SOURCE: Delaware Department of Health and Social Services, Division of Social Services (DSS). Key personnel: Elaine Archangelo.

TREATMENT ADMINISTRATORS: Delaware Department of Health and Social Services DSS and Maximus, Inc. Key personnel: Dave Meara.

EVALUATOR: Abt Associates. Key personnel: David J. Fein and David Long.

POLICY EFFECTS: After February 1997, the program continued without the experimental design.

INFORMATION SOURCE: David Fein, David Long, Joy Behrens, and Wang Lee, *Turning the Corner: Delaware's A Better Chance Welfare Program at Four Years,* Abt Associates, January 2001.

PUBLIC-USE ACCESS TO DATA: None.

Connecticut Jobs First

SUMMARY: This demonstration, conducted from 1996 to 2002, tested the effect of a time limit, earnings disregard, and mandatory job search activities on a large sample of AFDC recipients. Subjects were followed for four years.

COST: Evaluation, $5,376,684.81.

TIME FRAME: Demonstration period, January 1996–February 1997. Data collected, same period, as well as over a four-year follow-up period.

TREATMENTS TESTED: Experimental group members were limited to a cumulative total of 21 months of cash assistance receipt (with certain exceptions). All earnings that fell below the federal poverty level were disregarded in calculating the grant amount. Most individuals were required to search for work or participate in Job Search Skills Training (JSST). Parents were exempt when caring for a child under the age of 1 year. Sanctions for noncompliance during the first 21 months could result in a reduction or interruption of the grant. After the time limit, sanctions could result in permanent discontinuance of the entire grant.

Control group members were not subject to a time limit. In general, earned income reduced grant levels. Parents were exempt from work search activities if caring for a child under the age of 2 years. Sanctions for noncompliance reduced the family grant only by the amount calculated for one adult.

OUTCOMES OF INTEREST: (1) Employment; (2) Earnings; (3) Benefit receipt; and (4) Other measures of child well-being.

SAMPLE SIZE: Experimentals, 2,396; controls, 2,407.

TARGET POPULATION: AFDC recipients.

NUMBER OF TREATMENT GROUPS: Two (with one control group).

NUMBER AND LOCATION OF SITES: Two—New Haven and Manchester.

RESEARCH COMPONENTS:
- Process analysis: Baseline data, administrative records, site visits, staff and client surveys. Owing to start-up problems, the program's main components were not implemented as intensively as planned.
- Impact analysis: Conducted with ordinary least squares (OLS) regression.
- Benefit–cost analysis: Conducted.

MAJOR FINDINGS:
1. On average, the experimental group earned roughly $1,800 more than the control group over the four-year study period. Experimentals received an average of $2,400 more total income from earnings, cash assistance, and food stamps than did the controls.
2. The program's impacts on employment and earnings were concentrated among individuals with greater barriers to employment (i.e., long-term recipients, no high school diploma, and

no recent work history). Compared with controls, experimentals in this subgroup had a 37 percent increase in earnings. There was little effect on employment and no effect on earning among individuals facing few employment barriers.
3. Roughly half of the experimental group reached the time limits during the four-year period, two-thirds of which received an extension.
4. The program had mixed effects on living conditions. Compared to the control group, experimentals reported fewer neighborhood problems, but more were likely to be homeless.
5. There were few program effects on various measures of child well-being.
6. From the government perspective, Jobs First cost more (roughly $4,200) than AFDC per person over five years. Recipients in the treatment group benefited from increases in income, food stamps, child care assistance, Medicaid benefits, earned income tax credit, and other employment benefits. Participants' gains (including child care assistance and other benefits plus employment "fringe" benefits) exceeded the program costs. Over five years, the net gain per person in the experimental group was roughly $1.30 for every net dollar invested in the program.

TIME TRENDS IN FINDINGS: During the first two years of the follow-up period, Jobs First increased total average income by 12 percent and average cash assistance by 16 percent. But as experimental group members began to reach the time limit, income gains diminished. In the final three months of the study period, average income from earnings, cash assistance, and food stamps was essentially the same for experimentals and controls.

DESIGN ISSUES: Because of the extensive media coverage of the Jobs First Program, it is likely that many AFDC group members were influenced by the Jobs First message. This may have diminished the estimated impacts of the program.

REPLICABILITY: Replicable.

GENERALIZABILITY: The sample sites were chosen to represent two distinctly different communities. Baseline characteristics of research sample are generally consistent with comparable populations in Connecticut.

FUNDING SOURCES: Connecticut Department of Social Services, U.S. Department of Health and Human Services, the Ford Foundation, the Smith Richardson Foundation, and support from other federal agencies and numerous private foundations.

TREATMENT ADMINISTRATOR: Connecticut Department of Social Services. Key personnel: Mark Heuschkel.

EVALUATOR: Manpower Demonstration Research Corporation. Key personnel: Barbara Goldman.

ENABLING LEGISLATION: None.

INFORMATION SOURCES: Dan Bloom, Susan Scrivener, Charles Michalopoulos, Pamela Morris, Richard Hendra, Diana Adams-Ciardullo, and Johanna Walter, *Final Report on Connecticut's Welfare Reform Initiative: Summary Report,* Manpower Demonstration Research Corporation, February 2002; Dan Bloom, Laura Melton, Charles Michalopoulos, Susan Scrivener, and Johanna Walter, *Implementation and Early Impacts of Connecticut's Welfare Reform Initiative,* Manpower Demonstration Research Corporation, March 2000.

PUBLIC-USE ACCESS TO DATA: Available at http://www.mdrc.org.

San Diego School Attendance Demonstration Project (SADP)

SUMMARY: This demonstration, conducted from 1996 to 1998, tested the effects of financial penalties and social services on a sample of high school students from families on welfare. Subjects were followed for approximately two years.

COST: Approximately $800,000 on administration of treatment.

TIME FRAME: Demonstration period, January 1996–March 1998; data collected, same period.

TREATMENTS TESTED: Experimentals had their families' welfare grants reduced if their school attendance fell below the 80 percent minimum requirement for two consecutive months and they did not attend an orientation leading to eligibility to receive social services. The services requested by students were academic and medical help; child care; family counseling; family planning and pregnancy; financial and employment assistance; transportation (bus passes); and treatment for drug or alcohol problems. The most frequent requests were for academic help, followed by requests for transportation. SADP primarily provided case management.

Controls were not penalized for nonattendance but were required to be enrolled in school or registered in the GAIN/Jobs program if they wished to avoid reductions in their families' welfare grants. Controls also did not attend the orientation meetings and were not eligible for demonstration services.

OUTCOMES OF INTEREST: (1) School attendance rates and (2) School completion.

SAMPLE SIZE: Changed from month to month, as students graduated, left welfare, became pregnant, left school or jurisdiction, or transferred to private schools. It ranged from 1,499 to 1,766 with about two-thirds experimentals and one-third controls.

TARGET POPULATION: Sixteen- through eighteen-year-old welfare recipients who attend school less than 80 percent of school days in each month.

NUMBER OF TREATMENT GROUPS: Two (with one control group).

NUMBER AND LOCATION OF SITES: Two—San Diego Unified School District and Charter Schools, and Sweetwater School District.

RESEARCH COMPONENTS:
- Process analysis: An organizational analysis of the project was conducted; project staff was

interviewed, case files were reviewed, and service recipients were interviewed.
- Impact analysis: Regression.
- Benefit–cost analysis: Conducted.

MAJOR FINDINGS:

1. The treatment had a significant positive impact on school attendance. In the last year of the demonstration, the number of experimental teens in any month who met the attendance requirement ranged from 75.9 percent to 86.0 percent. In the same time frame, 67.9 percent to 78.5 percent of controls met the requirement.
2. Orientation leading to providing services to sanctioned students did not significantly improve school attendance.
3. There was no significant difference between experimental and control groups in graduation rates.

TIME TRENDS IN FINDINGS: None.

DESIGN ISSUES: Department of Social Services data for the experimental group were missing. Reporting on some variables by the DSS and school district staff was also incomplete. The SADP workers treated "no attendance records" as nonattendance, which was not always the case.

REPLICABILITY: Replicable.

GENERALIZABILITY: There are no obvious limits on generalizability, but note that families of teens in the control group were subject to sanctions if the teens were not enrolled in school.

FUNDING SOURCE AND TREATMENT ADMINISTRATOR: San Diego Department of Social Services. Key personnel: Lynn Titalii, project officer.

EVALUATOR: San Diego State University, School of Social Work. Key personnel: Loring Jones.

ENABLING LEGISLATION: None.

INFORMATION SOURCE: Loring Jones, *San Diego's School Attendance Demonstration Project: Final Reports of the Impact and Process Study,* San Diego Department of Social Services, 2001.

PUBLIC-USE ACCESS TO DATA: None.

The Achieving Change for Texans (ACT) II Experiments

INTRODUCTION: This complex demonstration assessed the impact of welfare reform policies by comparing the outcomes of 44,852 TANF cases assigned to experimental or control groups in one of three experiments: Responsibilities, Employment, and Resources (RER)–Non-Choices; Time Limits Pilot; and RER Choices. The demonstration was designed to measure the impacts of these policies separately and in combination with each other.

Common Elements for the Three Experiments

COST: We have no information about cost.

OUTCOMES OF INTEREST: (1) Welfare dependency; (2) Child health and support; and (3) Education and employment.

TARGET POPULATION: AFDC (later TANF) recipients in the state of Texas.

RESEARCH COMPONENTS:
- Process analysis: Conducted.
- Impact analysis: Regression-adjusted.
- Benefit–cost analysis: Conducted.

TIME TREND IN FINDINGS: None apparent.

GENERALIZABILITY: These studies were conducted on large samples over geographically diverse areas. Nonetheless, a major question remains. The total welfare population of Texas fell by roughly 44 percent during the demonstration period (the rest of the country experienced comparable changes). How can the findings of the experiment be reconciled with this trend? More specifically, the experimental findings indicate that the explicit policies adopted by Texas account for only a very small part of this reduction. It is widely believed that economic changes such as reduced unemployment, although favorable, account for only a portion of the decline in recipiency. If so, how can the caseload reductions be explained?

FUNDING SOURCE: Texas Department of Human Resources. Key personnel: Kent Gummerman and Ellen Montgomery.

TREATMENT ADMINISTRATOR: Texas Department of Human Resources. Key personnel: Kent Gummerman and Ellen Montgomery.

EVALUATOR: Ray Marshall Center for the Study of Human Respires, Lyndon B. Johnson School of Public Affairs at the University of Texas at Austin. Key personnel: Deanna T. Schexnayder.

ENABLING LEGISLATION: Texas HB 1863.

INFORMATION SOURCES: Deanna T. Schexnayder, Daniel G. Schroder, Jerome A. Olson, and Hyunsub Kum, *Achieving Change for Texans Evaluation: Final Impact Report,* November 2002.

Deanna T. Schexnayder, Daniel G. Schroder, Jerome A. Olson, Alicia M. Besinger, and Saho-Chee Sim, *Achieving Change for Texans Evaluation: Net Impacts through December 1997,* December 1998.

"Welfare Reform Information: Choices Program," from http://www.twc.state.tx.us/welref/welrefinfo.html, accessed March 17, 2003.

PUBLIC-USE ACCESS TO DATA: We have no information about public-use files for these demonstrations.

Responsibilities, Employment, and Resources (RER)–Non-Choices

SUMMARY: This demonstration, conducted from January 1997 to September 2000, tested the effects of expanded eligibility and expanded caretaker responsibilities on a large sample of families on Temporary Assistance for Needy Families (TANF). Subjects were followed for four years.

TREATMENTS TESTED: Experimental group members were subject to RER provisions: expanded TANF eligibility and a Personal Responsibility Agreement (PRA). Expanded TANF eligibility comprised disregarding children's income; permitting increased resource limits for eligibility determination; and eliminating the work history requirement and 100-hour work rule for two-parent families. The PRA required caretaker recipients to cooperate with child support enforcement; ensure immunizations and regular health checkups for children; participate in an employment services program; participate in parenting skills training if referred; provide proof of school attendance for each dependent child; refrain from voluntarily quitting a paying job; and refrain from drug use and alcohol abuse. Clients who failed to comply with PRA requirements were sanctioned $25 to $75 per month in one-parent families, or up to $125 in two-parent families. (In Texas the maximum TANF benefit in January 2000 for a family of three was $200 per month.) Signing the PRA was a condition for TANF eligibility.

The old AFDC rules applied to control group members. Neither group was subject to time limits.

TIME FRAME: Demonstration period, January 1997–September 2000; data collected, same period.

SAMPLE SIZE: Experimentals, 842; controls, 842.

NUMBER OF TREATMENT GROUPS: Two (with one control group).

NUMBER AND LOCATION OF SITES: Four offices in four counties in the state of Texas.

MAJOR FINDINGS:
Unless otherwise indicated, the following differences are statistically significant at the 5 percent level.
1. Caretakers in the experimental group spent significantly more time receiving TANF: 1.4 percentage points, or 5 days per year, more than controls.
2. Caretakers in the experimental group also spent significantly more time receiving Medicaid than controls (1.9 percentage points, or one additional week per year).
3. Experimental group families received food stamps 3.2 percentage points, or 12 days per year, less than controls.

4. The earnings and total income from all sources of the experimental group caretakers were not significantly different from those of controls.

5. Experimental group members used subsidized child care significantly more (0.5 percentage points, or two days per year) than controls.

6. There were no overall differences between the groups in school attendance or child support measures.

DESIGN ISSUES: None apparent.

Time Limits Pilot

SUMMARY: This demonstration, conducted from June 1996 through September 2000, tested the effects of time-limiting benefits on a large sample of families receiving Aid to Families with Dependent Children (AFDC) and, later, Temporary Assistance for Needy Families (TANF). Subjects were followed for five years.

TREATMENTS TESTED: Prior to randomization, welfare recipients were sorted into three groups based on their educational attainment, work history, and work readiness. They were then randomly assigned to treatment and control status. In the experimental group, the most work-ready were subject to the shortest time limit (12 months), a middle category to a 24 month-limit, and the least ready to the longest limit (36 months). Controls were not subject to time limits. Both experimentals and controls were subject to RER policies described for the treatment group in the previous summary. Both groups were provided increased transitional Medicaid and child care.

After their time limits run out, the experimentals were provided opportunities from the Choices program, a work development program with three main components: job readiness preparation, job search assistance, and mandatory community service for TANF assistance recipients who could not obtain immediate employment. The mandatory requirements exempted teens in school.

TIME FRAME: Demonstration period, June 1996–September 2000; data collected, same period.

SAMPLE SIZE: Experimentals, 14,818; controls, 14,977. Sample size by time limit: 12 months experimentals, 6,877; controls 6,969. 24 months experimentals, 3,030; controls 3,113. 36 months experimentals, 4,844; controls 4,828.

NUMBER OF TREATMENT GROUPS: Two (with one control group).

NUMBER AND LOCATION OF SITES: One—Bexar County, which includes San Antonio.

MAJOR FINDINGS:
Unless otherwise indicated, the following differences are statistically significant at the 5 percent level.

1. After 36 months of operation the demonstration revealed small, statistically insignificant reductions in TANF receipt, coupled with small increases in the use of other benefits relative to controls. Experimentals spent about two fewer days per year than controls on TANF, or 0.6 percentage points less.

2. There were very small increases in employment, alongside small declines in self-sufficiency measured by a combination of family earnings and caretaker employment rates, and a few impacts on workforce development participation. Experimentals had employment rates of 46.2 percent versus 45.8 percent for controls, a small but statistically significant difference. The treatment had no effect on total earnings, and only slightly decreased the amount of time that experimentals earned wages equal to or exceeding official state poverty level income. Very few families generated enough income to become independent of welfare (income 155 percent above the state poverty level).

3. Reduced TANF use, employment gains, and child support collection gains among the experimentals were greatest among those best prepared to enter the workforce.

4. For members of the experimental and control groups, about 17 percent of the time on TANF

after random assignment was spent in sanction penalty status, with a small reduction in the sanction rate for those in the 12-month limit treatment group.

5. TANF recipients subject to time limits were significantly more likely to have used Medicaid than control group members. However, these effects were very small (0.2 percentage points, or about 1 day per year).

6. Imposition of time limit policies also led to increased use of transitional benefits, including both Medicaid and subsidized child care, but had no impact on food stamp use. These impacts were small (.08 and .01 percentage points).

7. No significant differences were observed in student education measures and the need for child protective services between experimental and control groups.

DESIGN ISSUES: None apparent.

REPLICABILITY: Replicable.

Responsibilities, Employment, and Resources (RER)–Choices

SUMMARY: This demonstration, conducted from June 1996 through September 2000, tested the combined effects of time limits and RER provisions on a large sample of welfare recipients. Subjects were followed for four years.

TREATMENTS TESTED: As in the RER Non-Choices demonstration, members of the treatment group were subjected to RER interventions that included expanded TANF eligibility and a Personal Responsibility Agreement (PRA). As in the Time Limits Pilot, experimentals were subject to time limits and those who hit their time limits had access to Choices. The mandatory requirements exempted teens in school. Controls continued on old AFDC rules. Both groups were provided increased transitional Medicaid and child care.

TIME FRAME: Demonstration period, June 1996–September 2000; data collected, same period.

SAMPLE SIZE: Experimentals, 6,899; controls, 6,474.

NUMBER OF TREATMENT GROUPS: Two (with one control group).

NUMBER AND LOCATIONS OF SITES: Four—Beaumont County, Odessa County, the Dillon office in Corpus Christi, and the Clint office in El Paso.

MAJOR FINDINGS:
Unless otherwise indicated, the following differences are statistically significant at the 5 percent level.

1. Adults in the control group received TANF benefits for 27 percent of the possible months after enrollment in the RER choices experiment, or just over three months per year. Caretakers in the experimental group spent significantly more time on TANF than those in the control group, a difference of 1.5 percentage points, or about five additional days per year. The difference reflects a statutory difference: sanctioned caretakers in the experimental group were still treated as welfare recipients, while sanctioned caretakers under the old AFDC rules were not.

2. Children in the experimental group families received TANF for slightly *less* time than controls (1.1 percentage points less, or four days less per year), which indicates a slight reduction in total welfare receipt.

3. Twenty-nine percent of families in the experimental group were sanctioned at least once for failure to comply with some PRA requirement, while less than 5 percent of the control group were sanctioned.

4. Experimentals received Medicaid 38 percent of the time compared with 36 percent of the time by controls. Adults in the experimental group made use of transitional Medicaid and transitional child care at a rate 21 percent higher than the adults in the control group.

5. Caretakers in the experimental group were employed at a slightly higher rate (0.8 percentage points, or about three days more per year) and families earned slightly higher wages ($27 per quarter) than members of the control group.

6. Experimentals participated slightly less (by 1.8 percentage points) than controls in workforce development services. Experimentals and controls participated in postsecondary education equally, 9 percent of each group.

7. Child support was collected for the experimental group members significantly more often, and in greater amounts, than for the members of the control group—1 percentage point, an additional $2 per month.

8. There were no significant differences in immunization rates of preschool children in the experimental and control groups, and there were no significant differences in educational indicators, such as school attendance, for children in the experimental and control groups.

DESIGN ISSUES: None apparent.

Wisconsin Self-Sufficiency First/Pay for Performance Program

SUMMARY: This demonstration, conducted from 1996 to 1997, tested the effects of mandatory job search or other employment-related activity on a large sample of AFDC families. Subjects were followed for one year.

COST: Evaluation only, $193,000.

TIME FRAME: Demonstration period, March 1996–April 1997; data collected, same period.

TREATMENTS TESTED:

1. Subjects in the SSF (Self-Sufficiency First) treatment group were required to complete an interview with a "financial planning resource specialist" upon applying for AFDC. Within the 30-day AFDC processing period, subjects were also required to participate in the state's JOBS job search assistance program for a minimum of 60 hours, including 30 hours of direct employer contact. Only upon meeting these requirements could the applicant enter AFDC.

2. Subjects in the PFP (Pay for Performance) treatment group were required to meet a minimum level of participation in the JOBS program, between 20 and 40 hours weekly. Each hour of participation missed resulted in a deduction from the AFDC grant equal to federal hourly minimum wage until the grant was reduced to zero, at which point the penalty fell on the food stamp benefit.

3. SSF controls were exempted from the SSF requirements and thus were not subject to the elevated AFDC entry requirements.

4. PFP control subjects were exempted from the PFP requirements and were instead subject to the prior penalty for noncompliance with the JOBS program, a reduced AFDC grant.

OUTCOMES OF INTEREST: (1) AFDC participation and benefits; (2) Food stamp participation and benefits; and (3) Earnings and income.

SAMPLE SIZE: SSF experimentals, 1,560; SSF controls, 1,413; PFP experimentals, 1,139; PFP controls, 1,132.

TARGET POPULATION: AFDC participants and new applicants.

NUMBER OF TREATMENT GROUPS: Four (with two control groups).

NUMBER AND LOCATION OF SITES: Four—Dane, Dodge, Jefferson, and Waukesha counties.

RESEARCH COMPONENTS:

- Process analysis: Interviews were conducted with staff and officials in each county and the responses later coded.
- Impact analysis: Comparison of means.
- Benefit–cost analysis: None conducted

MAJOR FINDINGS:

1. By the end of the demonstration, approximately 72 percent of PFP experimental cases

had exited AFDC and did not return, compared with roughly 67 percent of controls, indicating that PFP had the expected effect.

2. There was no statistically significant difference in benefit amounts received by PFP experimental and control subjects, except during the third quarter of the experiment, when experimentals received significantly higher benefits than controls.

3. There was no significant difference between controls and PFP experimentals in exit from food stamps, or in food stamp benefits over the life of the demonstration.

4. There was no statistically significant difference in the employment and earnings of PFP treatment and control subjects.

5. Only about 35 percent of SSF experimentals reentered AFDC in the 18-month follow-up, compared with 45 percent of controls. The result is statistically significant.

6. There is no consistent, statistically significant difference in the earnings of SSF experimental and control subjects.

7. Because of the design issues described below, only limited confidence should be placed in these findings.

TIME TRENDS IN FINDINGS: None reported.

DESIGN ISSUES:

1. The demonstration was originally intended to run for four years, from March 1996 until 2000. The state terminated the experiment partly due to the impending implementation of the W-2 program. In addition, in terminating the experiment, Wisconsin also terminated the contract with the evaluator, MAXIMUS, leaving most of the existing data unanalyzed.

2. "While the initial assignment was random, the ultimate placement of individuals into the control or experiment groups may have been nonrandom."

3. Random assignment to the control group depended on the applicant's check digit in the Request-for-Assistance number, which made an individual 10 percent more likely to be selected as a control subject. This conflicted with the policy of keeping the control group small, and yielded unequal experimental and control groups.

4. A lack of management reports made it impossible to evaluate staff understanding of the database system. As a result, staff difficulty with new SSF/PFP screens resulted in many examples of missing or inconsistent data entries and also led some staff members to deviate from standard procedure in assignment of cases to experimental or control group status.

5. Because the database system had not been fully developed by the beginning of the program, staff members often had to use their own discretion in assignment status for applicants. This resulted in placing different members of the same family in different groups, assigning people to the study who did not meet the requirements, and deleting individuals from the SSF extract when corrections were attempted.

6. In some instances, members of the same family were assigned to different groups. This may have contaminated control subjects. Also, there were problems in assigning cases in closely knit immigrant communities, which may have also contaminated controls. Staff members were ill-equipped to explain why some clients were placed in the experimental group and subjected to more rigorous requirements than their friends or family members.

7. Assignment to the control group was disproportionately large in the smaller counties of Dodge, Jefferson, and Waukesha. Dane County, which contained 70 percent of the AFDC caseload for the experiment, only had 28 percent of the AFDC controls.

8. Because of the abrupt cancellation of the demonstration and the uncertain end date, many controls were informed that they should prepare themselves for "an imminent conclusion to their control status and a requirement to participate in W-2."

REPLICABILITY: The extent and severity of administrative difficulties suggest that this experiment is not replicable.

GENERALIZABILITY: Because of the design issues noted above, this study is not generalizable.

FUNDING SOURCE: U.S. Department of Health and Human Services.

TREATMENT ADMINISTRATOR: Wisconsin Department of Workforce Development, Wisconsin Department of Health and Social Services.

EVALUATOR: Institute for Research on Poverty, University of Wisconsin–Madison. Key personnel: Maria Cancian, Thomas Kaplan, and Ingrid Rothe.

ENABLING LEGISLATION: None.

INFORMATION SOURCE: Maria Cancian, Thomas Kaplan, and Ingrid Rothe, *Wisconsin's Self-Sufficiency/Pay for Performance: Results and Lessons from a Social Experiment,* Institute for Research on Poverty, University of Wisconsin–Madison, March 2000.

PUBLIC-USE ACCESS TO DATA: None.

SECOND CLINTON ADMINISTRATION

Work-First Profiling Demonstration

SUMMARY: This demonstration, conducted from 1998 to 2000, tested the effects of a referral system in which clients were referred to various service providers based on a statistical employability assessment, on a large group of unemployed welfare recipients. Subjects were followed for up to two years.

COST: Program costs, $145,000.

TIME FRAME: Demonstration period, January 1998–March 2000.

TREATMENTS TESTED:

1. A statistical assessment was used to compute an employability score for all welfare clients enter-

ing Michigan's welfare-to-work program, Work-First. Each participant was assigned to one of three employability groups based on her score relative to others: the lowest 40 percent were assigned to the low group, the next 20 percent to the middle group, and the highest 40 percent to the high group. Participants in each employability group were then randomly assigned to either the control group or the experimental group. Each service provider was believed to be best matched with a particular employability group: Goodwill was considered most appropriate for the low group, Youth Opportunities Unlimited (YOU) for the middle group, and Behavioral Foundation for the high group. Experimental group members were assigned to the appropriate provider for their employability group.

2. Control group members were randomly assigned to one of the three service providers. As a result, control group members formed a number of possible combinations of employability groups and providers. In the combination designated as gyk, the control members for each employability group were assigned to the same combination of service providers as the treatment group, (i.e., the low group to Goodwill, the middle group to YOU, and the high group to Behavioral Foundation) and therefore had the expected "optimal assignment combination." Estimates for the overall retention rates of a total of six combinations, including the optimal assignment combination, were ranked to determine if there was a comparative advantage to the optimal assignment combination.

OUTCOME OF INTEREST: Job retention rates of six possible combinations of service providers.

SAMPLE SIZE: Experimentals, 998; controls, 992. By employability group: low, 782; middle, 377; high, 831.

TARGET POPULATION: Single-parent welfare recipients.

NUMBER OF TREATMENT GROUPS: Two (with one control group).

NUMBER AND LOCATION OF SITES: One—Kalamazoo, Michigan.

RESEARCH COMPONENTS:

- Process analysis: Not conducted. However, the program intake system was monitored using administrative data.
- Impact analysis: Logit estimation.
- Benefit–cost analysis: Conducted from the participant perspective.

MAJOR FINDINGS:

1. The combination gyk yielded the highest estimates for job retention (defined as the participant working for at least 90 consecutive days). As expected, this was the same combination as the predetermined assignment of participants to providers in the treatment group. As shown in table 1, the differences in 10 of the 15 pairs of combinations were statistically significant.

Estimates were obtained as follows: Within each employability group, the retention rate for control members assigned to one service provider was multiplied by the total number of control group members in the employability group. For example, in the combination gyk, the control group in the low employability group that was assigned to Goodwill had a retention rate of 0.153. When multiplied by the total number of low control group members, 380, this yields 58. The same calculation was performed on the middle and high groups, yielding 68 and 96, respectively. Summing the results gives the estimated retention rates if all control group members were assigned to the service provider combination gyk. Notice that this finding is experimental. Although it depends only on comparisons of outcomes for the control

Table 1 Estimated Retention Rates by Combinations of Providers and Differences in Retention Rates between Pairs of Combinations

Provider combination	Total	Ranking	gyk	gky	ygk	ykg	kyg	kgy
gyk	222	1		0.066**	0.034**	0.046**	0.026**	0.080**
gky	156	5			−0.031**	−0.019*	−0.039**	0.014
ygk	188	3				0.012	−0.008	0.045**
ykg	175	4					−0.020	0.033**
kyg	195	2						0.053**
kgy	142	6						

Note: Combination designations order: low, middle, and high.
g = Goodwill; y = YOU; k = foundation
** = finding significant at the $p < .05$ level.

Table 2 Number of Participants and Retention Rates by Provider and Employability Group

	Low				Middle				High			
Provider	Control retention rate	No.	Experimental retention rate	No.	Control retention rate	No.	Experimental retention rate	No.	Control retention rate	No.	Experimental retention rate	No.
Goodwill	0.153	144	0.154	402	0.219	73			0.226	164		
YOU	0.136	59			0.370**	26	0.170**	194	0.167	54		
Foundation	0.079	177			0.145	83			0.223	211	0.234	402
Average	0.116				0.208				0.217			
Total number assigned		380		402		182		194		429		402

** = finding significant at the $p < .05$ level.

group, these persons were randomly allocated across providers.

2. As expected, in both the experimental and the control groups, the average retention rates increased from the lowest employability group to the highest. This is not an experimental comparison.

3. To check the validity of the random assignment technique, the retention rates of those within the control group who were randomly assigned to a provider were compared with those in the experimental group who were purposely assigned to the predetermined provider. As shown in table 2, the only significant difference in the retention rates for the experimental and control groups assigned to the same provider was among the middle group.

4. Benefit-to-cost ratio ranged from 3.25 to 5.8, depending on assumptions about the length of time the difference in earnings persisted.

TIME TRENDS IN FINDINGS: None.

DESIGN ISSUES:

1. Roughly half the individuals attending each orientation were excluded from the study because either they were in a two-parent family (not included in the study) or their records were missing. As a result, the distributions of actual study participants may differ from the model, which was based on the overall Work-First population in a year.

2. The mean of the score distributions varied from one session to another; therefore, a given employability score could fall into the high group one day and the middle or low group on another day.

3. There were significant differences for the middle group in the validity test mentioned under point 3 of the "Findings" section. Nonetheless, the evaluators argue that this is not a serious concern because the test was based on only 26 individuals in the control group (there were 194 in the experimental group).

REPLICABILITY: Replicable.

GENERALIZABILITY: There are several factors that limit generalizability:

1. Participants in the high group did not have particularly good retention rates, suggesting that the assignment instrument needs further work.

2. The ability to determine the provider that is best suited for participants in each of the three groups identified by employability scores is not strongly confirmed and might not generalize to other communities.

3. The town of Kalamazoo is unlikely to have a population that is representative of national populations.

FUNDING SOURCE: U.S. Department of Labor, Employment and Training Administration.

TREATMENT ADMINISTRATOR: Kalamazoo-St. Joseph Work First, Workforce Development Boards.

EVALUATOR: W. E. Upjohn Institute for Employment Research. Key personnel: Randall W. Eberts.

ENABLING LEGISLATION: None.

INFORMATION SOURCES: Randall W. Eberts, *Design, Implementation, and Evaluation of the Work First Profiling Pilot Project,* Employment and Training Administration, U.S. Department of Labor, Occasional Paper 2002-07, March 2002; Randall W. Eberts, "Using Statistical Assessment Tools to Target Work First Participants," in Randall W. Eberts, Christopher J. O'Leary, and Stephen A. Wandner (editors), *Targeting Employment Services,* W. E. Upjohn Institute for Employment Research, 2002, pp. 221–44.

PUBLIC-USE ACCESS TO DATA: The Upjohn Institute will prepare a public-use file, which will be available at the Employment Data Research Center on the web site http://www.upjohninstitute.org.

W-2 Child Support Demonstration Evaluation

SUMMARY: This demonstration, conducted from 1998 to 2000, tested a liberalized pass-through of child support payments on a large sample of families receiving welfare. Subjects were followed for two years.

COST: Research, $6.6 million.

TIME FRAME: Demonstration period, July 1998–July 2000; data collected, same period.

TREATMENTS TESTED: Mothers in the W-2 experimental group received a full pass-through of child support payments. W-2 controls received only a partial pass-through, the greater of $50 per month or 41 percent of child support paid.

OUTCOMES OF INTEREST: (1) Formal child support payments and receipts; (2) Paternity establishment; (3) Child support orders; (4) Mothers' welfare program participation and employment; (5) Family incomes; (6) Government costs; and (7) Fathers' employment and income.

SAMPLE SIZE: Experimentals, 1,438; controls, 1,446.

TARGET POPULATION: Mothers who participate in Wisconsin Works (W-2), the reformed welfare program; the fathers of their children; and the children themselves.

NUMBER OF TREATMENT GROUPS: Two (with one control group).

NUMBER AND LOCATION OF SITES: Statewide.

RESEARCH COMPONENTS:
- Process analysis: In-person interviewers met with the field coordinator weekly to review cases and deliver completed data. Shift supervisors monitored telephone interviewers regularly and a complete interview was monitored every four weeks. Supervising staff also conducted verification interviews. Tracing, incentives and pre-notification letters were used to reduce nonresponse.
- Impact analysis: Impact estimates were regression-adjusted.
- Benefit–cost analysis: Conducted from government perspective.

MAJOR FINDINGS:
1. Fathers in the experimental group were more likely to pay child support and also to have made higher payments in 1999. The effect on payments, although statistically significant, was less than a 10 percent increase in the likelihood of paying and in the amount paid. On average, mothers in the treatment group received $142 more in 1998 and $123 more in 1999 than control mothers.
2. Paternity establishment rates increased for children in the experimental group in 1998. In 1999, paternity establishment rates were significantly higher only for children whose mothers had high amounts of child support payments in the past.
3. The demonstration did not produce statistically significant long-term effects on mothers' program participation. There were no discernible effects on participation in other related programs.
4. Results do not clearly indicate increased or decreased labor force participation rates among mothers. Effect on mothers' incomes was inconsistent.
5. There were no significant differences in overall family income or economic hardship.
6. Informal employment of experimental group fathers fell, but there was no significant impact on formal employment or earnings. Fathers' incomes and hardship were also unaffected.
7. No change in the frequency of child support orders was detected. Also, there was no evidence of increases in revisions of existing orders and some evidence to the contrary.
8. "There is no significant difference between the experimental and the control groups in average net governmental costs."
9. The demonstration did not produce any substantial effect on fathers' social interaction with their children. No effects on child well-being, health, parenting, or education were found.

TIME TRENDS IN FINDINGS: Decreased differences in child support payments. Increased paternity establishment.

DESIGN ISSUES:

1. Information initially distributed to caseworkers did not make any distinction between full and partial pass-through status. Some Milwaukee agencies continued to use the old draft for several months after the distribution of a corrected draft. One Milwaukee agency was unaware of any form until January 1999. This may have contributed to the lack of understanding of pass-through status among many participating families.

2. Although Milwaukee agencies served almost 80 percent of W-2 participants, staff within these agencies demonstrated a lower level of understanding of the program than staff in agencies outside Milwaukee. This also may have contributed to the lack of understanding among participating families.

3. A code error on July 9, 1998, prompted the exclusion of all Milwaukee cases assigned to the demonstration between July 9, 1998, and December 31, 1998. Only Milwaukee cases assigned prior to July 9, 1998, and after January 1, 1999, could be included in the study.

REPLICABILITY: Replicable

GENERALIZABILITY: The demonstration may understate the statewide effects. More adequately trained staff in highly concentrated areas, such as Milwaukee, may produce greater statewide effects. The demonstration was designed to generalize to other states; however, greater possible effects than those achieved in Wisconsin are potentially possible.

FUNDING SOURCES: The Joyce Foundation of Chicago and the U.S. Department of Health and Human Services, Office of the Assistant Secretary for Planning and Evaluation.

TREATMENT ADMINISTRATOR: Bureau of Child Support through the Wisconsin Works Offices.

EVALUATORS: Institute for Research on Poverty, University of Wisconsin–Madison. Key personnel: Daniel R. Meyer and Maria Cancian.

ENABLING LEGISLATION: TANF block grant.

INFORMATION SOURCES: Daniel R. Meyer and Maria Cancian, *W-2 Child Support Demonstration Evaluation, Phase 1: Final Report. Volume I: Effects of the Experiment,* and *Volume III: Technical Reports,* Institute for Research on Poverty, University of Wisconsin–Madison, April 2001; Daniel R. Meyer and Maria Cancian, *The Two-Panel Survey of Milwaukee Families and the Wisconsin Works Welfare Program: An Update,* March 2001.

PUBLIC-USE ACCESS TO DATA: Available in 2003; contact evaluators.

EXPERIMENTS ONGOING AT PUBLICATION

New Visions: College as a Job Advancement Strategy

STARTING YEAR/YEAR FINAL REPORT EXPECTED: 1997/2005.

INFORMATION SOURCE: David Fein, Erik Beecroft, David Long, and André Rose Catalfamo, *The New Visions Evaluation: College as a Job Advancement Strategy: An Early Report of the New Visions Self-Sufficiency and Lifelong Learning Project,* Abt Associates Inc., May 2000. The New Visions evaluation is being funded by the Administration for Children and Families, Department of Health and Human Services.

PRINCIPAL INTERVENTIONS: Academic instruction and career guidance. New Visions participants enter a 24-week core program of academic instruction and career guidance. The program offers classes in remedial math, English, and reading; basic computer skills; and career life guidance, which concentrates on critical thinking and problem-solving skills, as well as study and communication skills, needed at college and the workplace.

The core program offers a flexible schedule and individualized instruction in classes taught in three-hour blocks each day, four days a week. After students graduate from the core program, New Visions staff help them choose occupational programs. These programs last from one to five months and are available in occupations such as corrections, human services, early childhood education, manufacturing and construction, medical technician, nursing, office administration, and police dispatching.

TARGET POPULATION: Welfare recipients in Riverside County, California.

OUTCOMES OF INTEREST: Employment, education, and welfare.

New Jersey Substance Abuse Research Demonstration (SARD)

STARTING YEAR/YEAR FINAL REPORT EXPECTED: 1999/2004.

INFORMATION SOURCE: J. Morganstern, A. Riodan, B. S. McCrady, K. Blanchard, K. H. McVeigh, and T. W. Irwin, *Barriers to Employability Among Women on TANF With a Substance Abuse Problem,* Mount Sinai School of Medicine, New Jersey Department of Human Services, Rutgers University, January 2001. State/SARD Program director: Mercedes Kennedy. Contact: Jon Morganstern, Mount Sinai School of Medicine.

PRINCIPAL INTERVENTIONS: TANF recipients found to be in need of substance abuse treatment are randomly assigned to one of two treatments: (1) care coordination (CC), which represents the standard substance abuse treatment available for welfare recipients in New Jersey; (2) intensive case management (ICM), which adds intensive case management and contingency interventions to the standard treatment.

TARGET POPULATION: TANF recipients in need of substance abuse treatment.

OUTCOMES OF INTEREST: Employment, welfare dependency, substance abuse, and child welfare.

Employment Retention and Advancement Project

STARTING YEAR/YEAR FINAL REPORT EXPECTED: 2000/2007.

INFORMATION SOURCE: Dan Bloom, Jacquelyn Anderson, Melissa Wavelet, Karen Gardiner, and Michael Fishman, "New Strategies to Promote Stable Employment and Career Progression: An Introduction to the Employment Retention and Advancement Project," Manpower Demonstration Research Corporation, February 2002.

PRINCIPAL INTERVENTION: This project consists of 15 separate experiments at 23 sites. The interventions use case management as a means of delivering other services, which may include education or training, financial incentives to remain on the job, career planning, rehabilitation services, or job search assistance, depending on the demonstration.

SITES: Los Angeles and Riverside counties, California; Duval and Leon counties, Florida; Cook and St. Clair counties, Illinois; Medford, Portland, Salem, and Eugene, Oregon; Hennepin County, Minnesota; New York City, New York; Chesterfield, Darlington, Dillon, Florence, Marion, and Marlboro counties, South Carolina; Shelby County, Tennessee; Corpus Christi, Fort Worth, and Houston, Texas.

TARGET POPULATION: Current or recent TANF recipients, but within those broad categories each demonstration has a different targeting rule.

OUTCOMES OF INTEREST: Employment, earnings, and welfare receipt.

Welfare to Work Housing Voucher Demonstration

STARTING YEAR/FINAL REPORT EXPECTED: 2000/2003.

INFORMATION SOURCE: No published source. This project is sponsored by the U.S. Department of Housing and Urban Development. Key personnel: Paul Dornan and Mark Shroder. Abt Associates' Michelle Wood and David Long were project directors at the initiation of the demonstration, and Greg Mills and Larry Orr are the current project director and principal investigator, respectively.

An interim report of findings should be available from the U.S. Department of Housing and Urban Development, Office of Policy Development and Research, by the time of publication.

PRINCIPAL INTERVENTION: Access to tenant-based rental assistance.

TARGET POPULATION: Families that have received TANF in the previous two years or are TANF-eligible.

OUTCOMES OF INTEREST: Employment, earnings, welfare receipt and benefits, and housing assistance.

2

Public Assistance Recipients
Food Stamps and Medicaid

Food Stamp Work Registration and Job Search Demonstration

SUMMARY: This demonstration, conducted from 1981 to 1983, tested the effects of eight models of mandatory job search on a large sample of applicants for food stamps. Subjects were followed for two years.

COST: Research only, roughly $3–$4 million (1983).

TIME FRAME: Demonstration period, October 1981–December 1983; data collected through June 1984; final report, June 1986.

TREATMENTS TESTED: Although a total of eight treatments were tested, only one treatment was tested at each demonstration site. The first four treatments were tested during the initial demonstration period (October 1981–March 1983), a recessionary period. The remaining four treatments were tested during the expanded demonstration period (October 1982–June 1984), a recovery period. Eight kinds of treatments were tested:

1. In-person registration model (Cheyenne, Colorado Springs, Sarasota, and Washington). All members of a recipient household who were not exempt from work were required to register for work in person at the State Employment Security Agency (SESA) and to report evidence of registration to the Food Stamp Agency (FSA). In three out of four cases, the SESA added a requirement for certain numbers of job contacts to be made within a specified period of time.

2. Job Club model (Tucson, Albuquerque, and Detroit). Work registration occurred at the FSA. Nonexempt household members were then called in for assessment by the SESA; job-ready registrants were assigned to a standard Job

Club group job search model, which lasted two or three weeks.

3. In-person registration/Job Club model (Austin). Work registration occurred at the SESA, and nonexempt job-ready persons were assigned to the Job Club model. Findings for this treatment are combined with those of model 2, because only one site implemented it.

4. Food Stamp Agency/Job Club model (Schenectady, Niagara County, and Toledo). All work registration and job search requirements were completed at the FSA. A special FSA Employment Unit (EU) performed registration, assessment, and supervision. Job-ready registrants were required to make up to 24 employer contacts in an eight-week period, reporting regularly to the EU.
   [Note: The next four treatments were not initiated until after October 1982 and, consequently, involve the FSA only, because by 1982 SESAs had been removed from the work registration process by legislation.]

5. Applicant search model (Nassau and Fresno counties). Before applicants were certified to receive food stamps, household members not exempt from work registration were required to complete a specified number of employer contacts. Following certification, the EU monitored continuing employer contacts.

6. Job Club model (Portland, Lewiston, Augusta, Pensacola, and Portsmouth). All job-ready work registrants were assigned to a two-, three-, or four-week Job Club. In Pensacola, subjects were also required to complete six employer contacts in a two-week period prior to assignment to the Job Club.

7. Group job search assistance model (Clark and Madison counties). A two-day employability skills training workshop was followed by an eight-week job search requirement with bi-weekly group monitoring meetings.

8. Job Club/Workfare model (San Diego County). After a three-week Job Club, job-ready registrants who did not find a job were assigned to Workfare, under which they were required to repay the household food stamp allotment with work at the minimum wage.

Controls were not subject to any work requirements.

OUTCOMES OF INTEREST: (1) Employment; (2) Earnings; and (3) Transfer payments.

SAMPLE SIZE: Sample sizes for the initial demonstration were not reported in the 1986 final report, but 31,000 people were randomly assigned. Key findings (e.g., earnings, employment) are based on follow-up interviews with randomly selected subsamples of the experimental and control populations. Applicant search model: experimentals, 4,396; controls, 4,116; Job Club model: experimentals, 2,333; controls, 1,633; group job search: experimentals, 870; controls, 586; Job Club with Workfare: experimentals, 2,070; controls, 422.

TARGET POPULATION: All recipients of food stamps who were not exempt from work registration (i.e., able-bodied people 18–65 years of age, not enrolled at least half-time in school or training programs, not working 30 or more hours per week, not otherwise incapacitated, and not caring for children under 12). In Nassau and Fresno counties, subjects applying for food stamps and meeting the above criteria had to meet job search requirements before they were certified.

NUMBER OF TREATMENT GROUPS: Sixteen: one experimental and one control group for each model.

NUMBER AND LOCATION OF SITES: Twenty-one— Tucson, Arizona; Fresno and San Diego counties, California; Colorado Springs, Colorado; Washington, D.C.; Pensacola and Sarasota, Florida; Clark and Madison counties, Kentucky; Portland, Lewiston, and Augusta, Maine; Detroit, Michigan; Albuquerque, New Mexico; Nassau and Niagara counties, and Schenectady, New York; Toledo, Ohio; Austin, Texas; Portsmouth, Virginia; and Cheyenne, Wyoming.

RESEARCH COMPONENTS:

■ Process analysis: Conducted. The analysis found that the treatments were implemented as planned, although treatments involving groups (models 2, 3, 4, 6, 7, and 8) sometimes had difficulty matching staff to clients. On average, FSA staff terminated benefits to 23 percent of experimentals for noncompliance, compared with 9 percent of controls. According to the project report, "Contrary to the conventional view of policy analysts, agency staff are indeed willing to conduct assessment interviews, provide job search assistance, and sanction those who fail to comply."

■ Impact analysis: Conducted by site with tobit, and the results were then pooled.

■ Benefit–cost analysis: Conducted from taxpayer, recipient, and social perspectives.

MAJOR FINDINGS:

1. Impacts are reported by quarter (Q) following random assignment; "transfers" refers to all transfers:

Model	Earnings (1st Q)	Earnings (2nd Q)	Food Stamps (2nd Q)	Transfers (2nd Q)
1	−$8	+$113	−$53	−$62
2 and 3	+53	+59	−41	−93
4	+11	+6	−4	−17
5	+126	+117	−20	−111
6	+76	+29	−13	−31
7	−23	+54	−33	−60
8	+136	+208	−59	−117

2. Benefit–cost analysis showed positive social net benefits for all models except 4. Net social benefits per experimental ranged from −$55 for 4 to +$471 for 8. Taxpayers had a net benefit from all models except 4, with transfer savings greater than administrative costs. Recipients had a net loss of income in models 2, 3, 4, and 7, but a net income gain in models 1, 5, 6, and 8. Since models 2, 3, and 6 are

identical in concept, implementation may matter. Implementation was also felt to be important with respect to model 8: "Given San Diego's extensive experience with Workfare, coupled with its high priority on rigorous implementation of job search and work requirements, the success of the Job Club/Workfare model might be attributed to factors specific to San Diego as well as to the attributes of the model." Models 1 and 5, however, were effective in a wide range of sites.

TIME TRENDS IN FINDINGS: As shown.

DESIGN ISSUES:

1. Previous research had found that many registrants faced little or no actual treatment, owing to agency policy, administrative failure, insufficient resources, or other reasons, despite the legislative mandates for work registration and job search. This accounts for the decision that controls should face no work requirement. However, it might well be the case that the typical U.S. food stamp recipient did face some requirement, however small.

2. All the demonstration sites volunteered to participate in the experiment. Clearly, the findings of the experiment do not apply to agencies that would refuse to administer these treatments or that lacked the resources. In that sense, there is a site-selection bias. According to Kowal, managers at some sites were motivated by the prospect of savings in county payments to General Assistance, which is sometimes administered jointly with Food Stamps, and in others were simply strongly motivated to establish model programs. Thus, the results are best interpreted as predictions of the probable impact of an experimental treatment if local agency managers chose to implement it thoroughly, rather than enforce no requirement whatever.

3. The Food Stamp program interacts with other support programs (such as Unemployment Insurance and Aid to Families with

Dependent Children [AFDC]). There is no discussion in the final report about what the consequences would be if the recipients of more than one income maintenance program were then subject to more than one work search requirement.

4. There is no discussion in the final report on the reasons for basing the employment and earnings findings on follow-up interviews rather than administrative records, such as are maintained for unemployment insurance. Follow-up interviews were only planned for about a sixth of the total sample, and the response rate was only 61 percent. The authors attempt to correct for potential nonresponse bias, but no consistent technique exists for dealing with it.

REPLICABILITY: Replicable.

GENERALIZABILITY: Site self-selection bias is critical. Local agency managers will not always have the motivation or the ability to implement these programs as well as the agencies that ran them in this demonstration.

FUNDING SOURCE: U.S. Department of Agriculture, Food and Nutrition Service. Key personnel: Boyd Kowal.

TREATMENT ADMINISTRATORS: State employment security and social service agencies in 21 locations.

EVALUATORS: Brandeis University, Center for Human Resources; Abt Associates. Key personnel: Leonard Hausman, research design; Jane Kulik, project director; Robert Lerman and Barry Friedman, principal authors.

ENABLING LEGISLATION: None.

POLICY EFFECTS: Boyd Kowal has stated that the Agriculture Department had recommended that states be allowed flexibility in enforcing work registration and job search requirements. The act reauthorizing the Food Stamps Program in 1985 allowed for such flexibility, and the experimental findings might have influenced the congressional authors.

INFORMATION SOURCE: Robert Lerman and Barry Friedman, with Shari Ajemian, Charles K. Fairchild, JoAnn Jastrzab, Jane Kulik, Christopher Logan, Cecile Papirno, and Adam Seitchik, *Food Stamp Work Registration and Job Search Demonstration: Final Report,* July 1986.

PUBLIC-USE ACCESS TO DATA: We have no information about a public-use file for this demonstration.

Illinois Monthly Reporting Food Stamp Demonstration

SUMMARY: This demonstration, conducted from October 1981 to September 1982, tested the effects of monthly reporting of household circumstances on a large sample of joint Aid to Families with Dependent Children (AFDC)/food stamp recipients. Subjects were followed for one year.

COST: Evaluation costs, $1.2 million.

TIME FRAME: Demonstration period, October 1981–September 1982; final report, June 1985.

TREATMENTS TESTED: Recipients of AFDC/food stamps were required to submit monthly reports documenting their income and family composition. They were not required to appear at a welfare office for recertification. Both sets of benefits were determined retrospectively by the content of their monthly reports. The control group households were recertified in the conventional manner, by appearing in-person after a specified period of time.

OUTCOMES OF INTEREST: (1) Food stamp caseloads and benefits; (2) Food stamp accuracy and error rates; (3) Administration costs; and (4) Experiences of food stamp recipients.

SAMPLE SIZE: Experimentals, 7,000; controls, 3,600.

TARGET POPULATION: Joint AFDC/food stamp recipients.

NUMBER OF TREATMENT GROUPS: Three: a treatment group, a control group, and a variant group.

The variant group was to be identical to the treatment group, but was scheduled to undergo in-person annual eligibility reviews. Since this rarely occurred, this group was usually combined with the treatment group for analysis.

NUMBER AND LOCATION OF SITES: One welfare office in Chicago, Illinois—the Southeast District Office. The demonstration also occurred in the Peoria office; however, data were not examined for this site.

RESEARCH COMPONENTS:

- Process analysis: Focused on the problems created by the computer system and the effects of monthly reporting on staff and recipients.
- Impact analysis: Effects on payments and caseload were studied, as well as the effect on food stamp payment accuracy. Conducted using comparison of means.
- Benefit–cost analysis: Conducted.

MAJOR FINDINGS:

1. Benefits paid to monthly reporting cases (the treatment group) were approximately 5.5 percent greater than those issued to cases under the conventional system (the control group). This effect was concentrated entirely in the first six months of the demonstration.
2. Comparisons of aggregate benefits for selected subgroups of the food stamp caseload showed that the treatment did not lead to significant payment savings within any of the identified subgroups. Positive, though not significant, effects were shown for large households, households in which the youngest child was between 16 and 18 years old, households with no adults, and households in which the head was at least 40 years old. All of these subgroups had consistent (but not statistically significant) payment savings throughout the demonstration, or had payment increases that were generally smaller than the average increase for the entire caseload.
3. The treatment did not lead to increased payment accuracy. Because of the computer problems, the incidence of errors increased by between 11 percent and 14 percent relative to the conventional system. Aside from the computer problems, error rates were largely unaffected.
4. The treatment did not affect recipients in any major way (e.g., changes in time and out-of-pocket expenses).

TIME TRENDS IN FINDINGS: As mentioned above, administration costs were significantly higher for the treatment group during the first six months owing to computer problems, but not during the last six months.

DESIGN ISSUES:

1. The new data processing system developed to handle the increased volume of information created by the program was difficult to implement. Problems existed throughout most of the project period, but mostly during the first six months. This led to incorrect benefits being issued and to inadvertent closings of some cases. Thus, caseworker activity and administrative costs increased.
2. The group most often expected to show net benefits from monthly reporting, the cases with earned income, was not addressed by this evaluation. All such cases were subject to monthly reporting during the administration regardless of the treatment group to which they were assigned.

REPLICABILITY: Replicable.

GENERALIZABILITY: Designed to generalize to the entire state of Illinois. Results from this demonstration are generally supported by similar experiments in Massachusetts, Colorado, New York, and Michigan (the Colorado experiment showed significant AFDC payment reductions in the first year, but these effects dissipated in the second year).

FUNDING SOURCES: U.S. Department of Agriculture, Food and Nutrition Service, and U.S. Department of Health and Human Services.

TREATMENT ADMINISTRATOR: Illinois Department of Public Aid. Key personnel: Stephen Spence.

EVALUATOR: Abt Associates. Key personnel: Jean Wood, project director.

ENABLING LEGISLATION: None.

INFORMATION SOURCE: Jean C. Wood, *Summary of Final Results of the Illinois Monthly Reporting Food Stamp Demonstration,* Abt Associates, June 1985.

PUBLIC-USE ACCESS TO DATA: No public-use file exists.

Program for Prepaid Managed Health Care (PPMHC)

SUMMARY: This demonstration, conducted from 1986 to 1992, tested the effects of incentives for using HMO plans on a large sample of Medicaid recipients. The evaluation of the demonstration was successfully implemented as planned at one site but not the other. Subjects were followed for one year.

COST: Evaluation costs, approximately $2 million.

TIME FRAME: Demonstration period, 1986–92; data collected through 1997.

TREATMENTS TESTED: The treatment group received a guarantee of at least six months of Medicaid eligibility if they agreed to enter a capitated health plan. In New York, the treatment group also qualified for generous health care options (not otherwise covered by Medicaid) if they chose capitation. The control group remained in a fee-for-service (FFS) system.

OUTCOMES OF INTEREST: Health care costs and utilization were the primary economic outcomes. Health and satisfaction outcomes were also measured.

SAMPLE SIZE: Random assignment only. New York: experimentals, 811; controls, 1,077. Florida: experimentals, 1,240; controls, 1,061.

TARGET POPULATION: Medicaid recipients eligible through participation in the AFDC pro-

gram. Samples were selected from Medicaid eligibility files.

NUMBER OF TREATMENT GROUPS: There were two experimental (randomly assigned) groups: Program for Prepaid Managed Health Care (PPMHC) and FFS. There were also two self-selected groups at the experimental sites.

NUMBER AND LOCATION OF SITES: Two—New York and Florida. A total of 10 sites were in the demonstration.

RESEARCH COMPONENTS:
- Process analysis: Focus groups were used to develop informed consent materials. A number of forms and interviews with participants were used at various stages of the evaluation to determine eligibility, language ability (primarily for Spanish-speaking participants), and health status.
- Impact analysis: Conducted using logistic and OLS regression models. An intention to treat analysis is used.
- Benefit–cost analysis: The cost to the state of allowing Medicaid beneficiaries to voluntarily enroll in capitated plans was calculated and contrasted with per-beneficiary costs in the FFS system.

MAJOR FINDINGS:
1. Participants in New York who were assigned to the PPMHC group but did not enroll had higher use and higher costs than either PPMHC enrollees or the control (FFS) group. Average per-person monthly expenditures were $61 for the randomly assigned PPMHC enrollees, $90 for the randomly assigned FFS group, and roughly $100 for those assigned to PPMHC but who did not enroll. The lower use of the PPMHC participants while they were in the plan appears to be entirely accounted for by selection effects because total costs for those assigned to the PPMHC (including non-enrollees) averaged more than total costs for people assigned to FFS.
2. In Florida, estimated monthly health care use was lower for the PPMHC groups (both randomly assigned and self-selected) than for their

FFS counterparts. By assigned plan, average monthly per-person expenditures were as follows: self-selected FFS, $37; randomly assigned FFS, $36; self-selected PPMHC, $27; and randomly assigned PPMHC, $31.

TIME TRENDS IN FINDINGS: None.

DESIGN ISSUES:

1. At the New York site, PPMHC enrollment was very difficult. Of the original 811 people assigned to this group, over half (427) refused to participate upon learning of their assignment or were refused by the PPMHC program. Of the remaining 384 who accepted, only 185 eventually enrolled. The evaluators felt that the experimental portion of the design failed in New York. Those who refused study participation were significantly different from those who accepted (they were somewhat healthier and younger but had been on Medicaid longer). Enrollment was generally more successful in Florida.
2. Participation in the study was voluntary, so individuals did not necessarily agree to their assignment and others who agreed did not necessarily remain in their assigned groups. Therefore, some participants actually used both systems of care (PPMHC and FFS) during the study. For the major analyses, use was combined and attributed to the "assigned" group.

REPLICABILITY: Replicable.

GENERALIZABILITY: Although the demonstration was designed to generalize to the national AFDC Medicaid population, the design issues in New York discourage generalization from findings in that state.

FUNDING SOURCES: Robert Wood Johnson Foundation and the U.S. Department of Health and Human Services, Health Care Financing Administration. Key personnel: Alan Cohen for Robert Wood Johnson; Spike Duzor, Arne Anderson, and Sid Trieger for HCFA. Technical assistance was provided by the National Governors Association.

TREATMENT ADMINISTRATOR: Technical oversight of the demonstration was contracted to a group at the New England Medical Center.

EVALUATOR: The New England Medical Center was responsible for health outcomes, physical outcomes, and satisfaction measures. The RAND Corporation was responsible for cost and utilization components as well as the case studies.

ENABLING LEGISLATION: None.

INFORMATION SOURCE: Joan L. Buchanan, Arleen Leibowitz, Joan Keesey, Joyce Mann, and Cheryl Damberg, *Cost and Use of Capitated Medical Services: Evaluation of the Program for Prepaid Managed Health Care,* RAND Corporation, 1992.

PUBLIC-USE ACCESS TO DATA: Available through the RAND Corporation.

Food Stamp Employment and Training Program

SUMMARY: This demonstration, conducted in 1988, tested the effects of the Food Stamp Employment and Training (E&T) program on a large sample of food stamp recipients. Subjects were followed for one year.

COST: Expenditures on participants, fiscal year 1988, $1.76 million. Total costs, including evaluation, approximately $3.5 million.

TIME FRAME: Demonstration period, 1988; final report, June 1990.

TREATMENTS TESTED: The E&T program included job search, job search training, Workfare and work experience, and education and vocational skills training.

OUTCOMES OF INTEREST: (1) Employment; (2) Earnings; and (3) Public assistance receipt.

SAMPLE SIZE: Experimentals, 6,376; controls, 6,710.

TARGET POPULATION: All eligible food stamp recipients between the ages of 17 and 59, not exempted by the Food Stamp Administration (FSA).

NUMBER OF TREATMENT GROUPS: Two (with one control group) at each site.

NUMBER AND LOCATION OF SITES: Fifty-three sites in 23 states. Sites were local FSA offices, usually counties (Puma et al. 1990, pp. 4–11 list the sites).

RESEARCH COMPONENTS:
- Process analysis: Conducted. Participant monitoring was used to ensure the accuracy of assignment, as well as the accuracy and timeliness of information flow; and to identify instances of noncompliance.
- Impact analysis: Conducted, using multivariate regression models.
- Benefit–cost analysis: Conducted.

MAJOR FINDINGS:
1. Although substantial gains in employment were observed over the 12-month period among both treatment and control group members, E&T had no discernible effect on aggregate earnings, probability of finding work, amount of time worked, or average wages. That is, there were no significant treatment–control group differences.
2. There were treatment–control group differences in the receipt of Food Stamp benefits, with a reduction in the treatment group of $65 per household. Some of this difference, however, was accounted for by the termination of benefits for noncompliance with E&T requirements. No differences in cash assistance were produced.
3. Despite being a low-cost program, the program was not found to be cost-effective, owing to its limited impact on employment and welfare receipt.
4. Some sites had heavy caseloads and/or limited staffing, which led to large percentages (up to 75 percent) of registrants who never received their initial appointment letters.

In general, there were participation rates of approximately 50 percent. Males living alone, the largest group of participants, were the least likely to comply with program requirements.
5. Many control group members were able to find services on their own. Of treatment group members, 43 percent received services, whereas 31 percent of control group members received comparable services.
6. Because the evaluation was of an actual program as it operated in response to legislative and regulatory guidelines, treatment was dictated by local operating agencies rather than by the researchers. The flexibility afforded states, and their decentralized administrative arrangements, complicated the evaluation.

TIME TRENDS IN FINDINGS: Reduction in the receipt of food stamps came mostly in the second and third quarters after random assignment.

DESIGN ISSUES:
1. Because multiple service models do not normally exist in the same site, it was not possible to compare effects of different service models.
2. The period studied was the first year of the program. Start-up effects may confound the observed results.
3. Due to extreme mobility on the part of the sample, difficulty obtaining addresses from the local Food Stamp office, and a large homeless contingent, full 12-month follow-up data were obtained for only 50 percent of the sample. Although statistical adjustments were developed to account for survey nonresponse, this raises questions about reliability.

REPLICABILITY: There were wide variations in service delivery across sites. Many states dropped or added components (usually the training component) during the study.

GENERALIZABILITY: Designed to generalize to the entire nation. This was close to a nationally representative sample of sites. Sites were selected as a probability sample of the national population of Food Stamp offices. Characteristics of the sample closely matched the population of food stamp recipients as a whole. However, high attrition from the sample may bias the results.

FUNDING SOURCE: U.S. Department of Agriculture, Food and Nutrition Service. Key personnel: Boyd Kowal.

TREATMENT ADMINISTRATORS: Local FSAs acting under the U.S. Department of Agriculture, Food and Nutrition Service.

EVALUATOR: Abt Associates. Key personnel: Jean Wood and Michael Puma.

ENABLING LEGISLATION: Food Security Act of 1985.

INFORMATION SOURCE: Michael J. Puma, Nancy R. Burstein, Katie Merrell, and Gary Silverstein, *Evaluation of the Food Stamp Employment and Training Program: Final Report,* June 1990.

PUBLIC-USE ACCESS TO DATA: Available at U.S. Department of Agriculture.

San Diego Food Stamp Cash-Out Demonstration

SUMMARY: This demonstration, conducted in 1989 and 1990, tested the effects of issuing food stamp benefits by check rather than coupon on a large sample of Food Stamp Program (FSP) participants.

COST: Evaluation cost, $1,507,114.

TIME FRAME: Phase I, experimental: July 1989–August 1990; data collected, May–August 1990. Phase II, a saturation program, was begun in September 1990 and is currently in operation.

TREATMENTS TESTED: The treatment group received Food Stamp Program benefits in check form, rather than by coupon. The control group continued to receive the coupon form.

OUTCOMES OF INTEREST: (1) Food purchasing and food use patterns and (2) Administrative costs.

SAMPLE SIZE: Experimentals, 613; controls, 613. The final sample used for analysis was reduced to 1,078; experimentals, 542; controls, 536.

TARGET POPULATION: Food stamp recipients.

NUMBER OF TREATMENT GROUPS: Two (with one control group).

NUMBER AND LOCATION OF SITES: One—San Diego County, California.

RESEARCH COMPONENTS:
- Process analysis: Planning process for design and implementation. Detailed analysis of work activities that were changed in the implementation of cash-out. Analysis of data on lost or stolen benefits.
- Impact analysis: Comparison of means. Analysis of regression-adjusted means was also conducted, but did not prove to be substantially more precise than the simple difference-in-means estimates.
- Benefit–cost analysis: Not highly formalized, though integrated into analysis of administrative cost outcomes.

MAJOR FINDINGS:
1. Cash-out had a relatively small, but statistically significant, downward impact on household food use. The money value of food used at home was 4 percent to 7 percent lower (depending on the specific measure of food use) for check recipients than for coupon recipients. This finding suggests that cash-out reduced the effectiveness of the FSP in stimulating food use.
2. The reductions in the money value of food used at home resulting from cash-out were accompanied by decreases in the amounts of food energy and protein contained in the food that was used. These reductions, although relatively small (roughly 5 percent each) are statistically significant.
3. There was no significant impact on households running out of food during the month, nor was the impact on the purchase of food used away from home significant.

4. There were statistically significant increases for cash-out households in three expenditure categories: housing, medical costs, and education.
5. Cash-out led to clear reductions in administrative costs incurred at the state and county levels associated with the issuing of food stamp benefits. Savings of $2.21 per issuance were realized for recipients who also received Aid to Families with Dependent Children (AFDC) (one check was issued for both). Savings of $1.19 per issuance were realized for cases not on AFDC.

TIME TRENDS IN FINDINGS: No long-term follow-up has been conducted.

DESIGN ISSUES:

1. The evaluators reported no significant problems with design or implementation. They stated that the administration in San Diego has been very active in trying innovative programs and that department personnel are "old hands" at these types of evaluations.
2. The data source is an after-the-fact questionnaire administered to the head of household. This could be subject to recall error or other problems.

REPLICABILITY: Replicable. Procedures are well documented in the report.

GENERALIZABILITY: San Diego County is highly urban. A high proportion of the Food Stamp caseload also receives AFDC relative to the nation as a whole. Because AFDC income is relatively high, food stamp benefit levels, relative to household income, are lower in San Diego than the national average (12 percent versus 23 percent, respectively).

For a more complete picture of the impacts of cash-out, these findings should be considered along with those from similar demonstrations. The Alabama Food Stamp Cash-Out Demonstration is a comparably "pure" cash-out. Those findings showed few significant impacts on recipients. Alabama's Avenues to Self-Sufficiency through Employment and Training Services (ASSETS)

and Washington's Family Independence Program (FIP) are "mixed" programs, with cash-out being only one component.

FUNDING SOURCE: U.S. Department of Agriculture (USDA), Food and Nutrition Service. Key personnel: Boyd Kowal.

TREATMENT ADMINISTRATOR: San Diego County Department of Social Services. Key personnel: Jerry Hughs and Susan Gardner.

EVALUATOR: Mathematica Policy Research. Key personnel: James C. Ohls (project director), Thomas Fraker, Alberto Martini, Michael Ponza, and Anne Ciemnecki.

ENABLING LEGISLATION: Food Stamp Act of 1977, as amended.

POLICY EFFECTS: The USDA presented these findings to Congress. Robert Greenstein, of the Center on Budget and Policy Priorities, predicted that the finding of a negative impact on food purchases would kill congressional cash-out proposals. The USDA has, in fact, moved in a different direction—toward electronic benefit transfers.

INFORMATION SOURCE: James C. Ohls, Thomas M. Fraker, Alberto P. Martini, and Michael Ponza, *The Effects of Cash-Out on Food Use by Food Stamp Program Participants in San Diego*, Mathematica Policy Research, 1992.

PUBLIC-USE ACCESS TO DATA: Available through Mathematica Policy Research.

Alabama Food Stamp Cash-Out Demonstration

SUMMARY: This demonstration, conducted in 1990, tested the effects of paying food stamp benefits by check on a large sample of food stamp recipients. Subjects were followed for six months.

COST: Evaluation cost, $1,835,415.

TIME FRAME: Demonstration period, May 1990–December 1990; data collected, same period; final report, September 1992.

TREATMENTS TESTED: For the treatment group, food stamp benefits were paid in the form of checks, rather than coupons. The control group continued to receive food stamps in coupon form.

OUTCOMES OF INTEREST: (1) Food purchasing and food use patterns and (2) Administrative costs.

SAMPLE SIZE: Experimentals, 2,253; controls, 2,233. Sample used for analysis: experimentals, 1,255; controls, 1,131.

TARGET POPULATION: Recipients of food stamp benefits.

NUMBER OF TREATMENT GROUPS: Two (with one control group).

NUMBER AND LOCATION OF SITES: Twelve—two urban and 10 rural Alabama counties.

RESEARCH COMPONENTS:
- Process analysis: Planning and implementation outcomes were an integral part of the overall evaluation.
- Impact analysis: Comparison of means.
- Benefit–cost analysis: Conducted as an integral part of the evaluation.

MAJOR FINDINGS:
1. For almost all outcome measures, the difference in mean values between check and coupon recipients was small and not statistically significant. There were no significant differences in the money value of food used at home, nutrient availability, running out of food, or the purchase of food used away from home.
2. Check recipients did report a significantly larger (1.1 percent) expenditure share than coupon recipients on utilities. It is not clear whether this difference was caused by cash-out.
3. In Alabama, most Food Stamp Program coupons are issued in person. The cash-out checks were primarily mailed to recipients.

Issuance-system vulnerabilities increased with cash-out because of the issuance of checks by mail. This is considered less a cost of cash-out than of the change in mode of delivering benefits. In general, costs were lower under check issuance. Overall check issuance cost $1.03 per case-month compared to $2.05 per case-month for coupons. Three-quarters of these savings accrued to the federal government and one-quarter accrued to the state government.

TIME TRENDS IN FINDINGS: No long-term follow-up was conducted.

DESIGN ISSUES:
1. Development of the computer software for the check-issuance system absorbed considerable resources and required more labor hours than expected. This is one reason that implementation was delayed for four months.
2. It is important to note some of the differences between this demonstration and the other cash-out programs. The San Diego cash-out was the only other "pure" cash-out (no other programmatic changes were being measured) and was also an experimental design. Alabama ASSETS and Washington FIP were quasi-experimental designs. In Alabama, joint Food Stamp Program and AFDC households received two checks; they received only one check in San Diego. San Diego normally issued coupons by mail, so there was less difference in issuance procedures compared to Alabama. The San Diego program ran longer than in Alabama. The evaluators suggest that the Alabama program may have been too short to capture impacts.
3. The data source is an after-the-fact questionnaire administered to the head of household. This could be subject to recall error or to other problems.

REPLICABILITY: Replicable. The final report and its appendixes provide great detail regarding procedures and implementation.

GENERALIZABILITY: Designed to generalize to the entire state of Alabama. Alabama is more rural than the United States as a whole, and residents are more likely to be unemployed or to have low income. Only six states and Washington, D.C., have a higher percentage of food stamp users, and average food stamp benefits are 10 percent higher than the U.S. average. Alabama has lower levels of cash assistance (e.g., AFDC) than the nation as a whole. Food stamp recipients are more likely to be elderly.

The findings from the San Diego Food Stamp Cash-Out Demonstration showed a small but significant negative impact on food expenditures, on the nutritional value of food, and on other outcome variables. This suggests that cash-out impacts may depend on context and implementation.

FUNDING SOURCE: U.S. Department of Agriculture (USDA), Food and Nutrition Service. Key personnel: Pat McKinney, project officer.

TREATMENT ADMINISTRATOR: Alabama Department of Human Resources (DHR). Key personnel: Andrew Hornsby, commissioner; Gene Gandy and Bill Mintz, project facilitators. DHR county directors were also involved in administration.

EVALUATOR: Mathematica Policy Research. Key personnel: Thomas Fraker (project director), Alberto Martini, James Ohls, Michael Ponza, Elizabeth Quinn, and Anne Ciemnecki.

ENABLING LEGISLATION: None.

POLICY EFFECTS: After findings of a negative impact on food purchases in San Diego were presented to Congress (see San Diego Food Stamp Cash-Out Demonstration on page 161), the USDA moved in another direction—toward electronic benefit transfers.

INFORMATION SOURCE: Thomas M. Fraker, Alberto P. Martini, James C. Ohls, Michael Ponza, and Elizabeth A. Quinn, *The Evaluation of the Alabama Food Stamp Cash-Out Demonstration: Volume I: Recipient Impacts* and *Volume II: Administrative Outcomes, Overall Conclusions, and Appendices,* Mathematica Policy Research, 1992.

PUBLIC-USE ACCESS TO DATA: Available through Mathematica Policy Research.

3

Firms and Organizations

POWER CUSTOMERS

Southern California Edison Electricity Pricing Experiment

SUMMARY: This experiment, conducted from 1980 to 1982, tested the effects of varying time-of-use electricity rates on a medium-sized sample of commercial and industrial customers. Subjects were followed for up to 21 months.

COST: Unavailable.

TIME FRAME: Demonstration period, October 1980–October 1982; data collected, same period.

TREATMENTS TESTED: There were a total of six experimental treatments. There were two experimental rate structures: time-varying energy rates and time-varying demand rates. "Energy" pricing varies by kilowatt-hours (kWh) of usage; "demand" pricing varies by reserved capacity or "maximum instantaneous load." For each of these rate structures, there were three absolute differences in rate levels: (1) a small difference between peak and off-peak rates ($0.01 per kWh for energy rates, $1 for demand rates); (2) a moderate difference between peak and off-peak rates ($0.03 and $3.50); and (3) an extreme difference between peak and off-peak rates ($0.06 and $6.00). The control group faced the conventional rates.

OUTCOMES OF INTEREST: (1) Energy usage (substitution between peak and off-peak consumption) and (2) Costs.

SAMPLE SIZE: Total, 733; experimentals, 574; controls, 159.

TARGET POPULATION: Commercial and industrial electricity customers with summer monthly demands between 20 kW and 500 kW.

NUMBER OF TREATMENT GROUPS: Seven (with one control group).

NUMBER AND LOCATION OF SITES: Subjects were all customers of the Southern California Edison Company, Rosemead, California.

RESEARCH COMPONENTS:
■ Process analysis: Customer participation and compensation were monitored.
■ Impact analysis: Conducted using analysis of covariance and econometric analyses.
■ Benefit–cost analysis: Conducted.

MAJOR FINDINGS:
1. The time-of-use demand rate was more effective in eliciting substitution of peak and off-peak usage than was the time-of-use energy rate, especially in the summer season.
2. A small, but statistically significant, elasticity of substitution between peak and off-peak kWh consumption was estimated for the summer season in the overall sample for firms facing the time-of-use demand rate. A substantially larger response was estimated for the subgroup of "large" firms (200–500 kWh) in the experiment that faced the demand rate.
3. A small welfare gain of 1.1 percent was estimated when moving from the conventional, non-time-of-use (control) rate to a 2.5:1 effective energy-to-price ratio, which is suggestive of the time-of-use demand rate that might prevail were time-of-use pricing to be applied to this group of firms. For large customers, this more than offsets additional metering costs.

TIME TRENDS IN FINDINGS: Usage levels declined for all groups from 1981 to 1982. This likely reflects a response to the rising average price of electricity over the life of the experiment.

DESIGN ISSUES:
1. To attempt to nullify the divergence of impact on the customers in this heterogeneous sample, variable compensation payments were made to customers whose bills under time-of-use rates exceeded bills under normal rates by more than 10 percent. This offset some of the incentive to adjust usage patterns.
2. Since firms could elect to participate when initially contacted or could drop out during the course of the experiment, some self-selection bias was present. High-peak-usage customers tended not to participate.

REPLICABILITY: Replicable.

GENERALIZABILITY: Designed to generalize to the entire region (Southern California). However, the experiment was voluntary, and customers with high-peak usage were underrepresented.

FUNDING SOURCE: Southern California Edison Company. Key personnel: Leo Gargan.

TREATMENT ADMINISTRATOR: Southern California Edison Company.

EVALUATORS: Dennis J. Aigner and Joseph G. Hirschberg, University of Southern California.

ENABLING LEGISLATION: None.

INFORMATION SOURCE: Dennis J. Aigner and Joseph G. Hirschberg, "Commercial/Industrial Customers' Response to Time-of-Use Electricity Prices: Some Experimental Results," *Rand Journal of Economics* 16(1985): 341–55.

PUBLIC-USE ACCESS TO DATA: Not available.

Niagara Mohawk Hourly Integrated Pricing Program (HIPP)

SUMMARY: This demonstration, conducted from 1987 to 1989, tested the effects of real-time pricing (RTP) on a small sample of large industrial consumers of electricity.

COST: Unavailable.

TIME FRAME: Project period, June 1987–1989. Baseline data extend back to July 1986.

TREATMENTS TESTED: The treatment group paid for electricity using real-time pricing, a "dynamic, fully time-differentiated marginal cost-based electricity rate" (Herriges et al. 1993). RTP bases the price of electricity on the production and transmission costs of electricity at various times. These costs are highest at peak times (e.g., 10:00 AM), less at shoulder periods (e.g., 6:00 PM), and least at off-peak times (e.g., midnight). The control group continued to use standard "time-of-use" tariffs, with on-peak and off-peak hourly rates.

OUTCOME OF INTEREST: Electricity usage by time period.

SAMPLE SIZE: Total, 21 large industrial clients; 9 treatment and 6 control clients were used for analysis.

TARGET POPULATION: Large, industrial customers of electric power.

NUMBER OF TREATMENT GROUPS: Two (with one control group).

NUMBER AND LOCATION OF SITES: Customers were located throughout western New York State. Niagara Mohawk Power Corporation is located in Syracuse.

RESEARCH COMPONENTS:
▪ Process analysis: Not formally conducted.
▪ Impact analysis: Comparison of means, price index analysis, and econometric analysis.
▪ Benefit–cost analysis: Conducted.

MAJOR FINDINGS:
1. The hourly integrated pricing program (HIPP) resulted in a decrease in total energy consumed. The control group load growth was 5.1 percent, compared to that of the treatment group growth of –1.5 percent.
2. The treatment group's average price was more than 6 percent lower under HIPP than under the standard rate. This difference suggests an ability to shift loads away from high-priced hours.
3. At the peak system hour, the treatment group reduced loads from their baseline level by 13.2 percent. The control group increased loads by 4.5 percent. At the HIPP price peak hour, the treatment group reduced loads by 36.2 percent compared to the control group reduction of only 4.4 percent.
4. The response to RTP was not uniform. That is, two customers were able to shift usage more than others and thus provided the bulk of the measured response.

TIME TRENDS IN FINDINGS: None.

DESIGN ISSUES: Because of unspecified data problems, only nine treatment and six control customers were available for the analysis. In other energy experiments, the sheer size of the data set—energy usage at every hour of the day for a considerable number of days—has forced analysts to be selective about how much data they use.

REPLICABILITY: Replicable, though the project report provides no details about operations, such as how customers were notified of the prices.

GENERALIZABILITY: Participants were voluntary. The sample was very small, although the participating clients account for a large amount of electricity use. The large users in this study are more likely than smaller firms or individuals to generate benefits from RTP that exceed administration costs. Large users are also more likely to invest the resources required to understand and profit from the HIPP tariff.

FUNDING SOURCE: Niagara Mohawk Power Corporation. Key personnel: Mike Kalleher.

TREATMENT ADMINISTRATOR: Niagara Mohawk Power Corporation.

EVALUATORS: Joseph A. Herriges, Iowa State University; S. Mostafa Baladi and Douglas W. Caves, Laurits R. Christensen Associates; and Bernard F. Neenan, Niagara Mohawk Power Corporation.

ENABLING LEGISLATION: None.

INFORMATION SOURCES: Joseph A. Herriges, S. Mostafa Baladi, Douglas W. Caves, and Bernard F. Neenan, "The Response of Industrial Customers to Electric Rates Based upon Dynamic Marginal Costs," *Review of Economics and Statistics* 75(1993): 446–54.

PUBLIC-USE ACCESS TO DATA: Not available.

EMPLOYERS

Wage-Subsidy Variation Experiment

SUMMARY: This demonstration, conducted in 1980, tested the effects of a wage subsidy paid to employers on a medium-sized sample of private-sector businesses. Subjects were followed for less than one year.

COST: Cannot be separated from Youth Incentive Entitlement Pilot Project (YIEPP), a large nonexperimental demonstration, of which this experiment was a small component.

TIME FRAME: Demonstration period, January–May 1980; data collected, same period; final report, March 1981.

TREATMENTS TESTED:
1. A 100 percent wage subsidy was offered to businesses that would employ disadvantaged 16–19-year-olds who would be assigned by the project. Youths were guaranteed minimum wage employment if they stayed in school and maintained satisfactory school performance.
2. A 75 percent wage subsidy was offered.

A list of over 1,000 possible employers was compiled, and the firms were randomly assigned to one treatment or the other. Payroll was handled by the project administrator.

OUTCOME OF INTEREST: Agreement to participate in youth employment.

SAMPLE SIZE: Group 1, 519 businesses; group 2, 569 businesses.

TARGET POPULATION: Private-sector businesses within commuting distance of the impact neighborhoods of the project.

NUMBER OF TREATMENT GROUPS: Two (with one control group).

NUMBER AND LOCATION OF SITES: One—Detroit, Michigan.

RESEARCH COMPONENTS:
- Process analysis: Interviews with subjects on reasons for participating or not participating.
- Impact analysis: Difference in means; also some logit.
- Benefit–cost analysis: Not conducted.

MAJOR FINDINGS:

Treatment	Contacted	Agreed to participate	Rate
75 percent subsidy	569	44	7.7%
100 percent subsidy	519	81	15.6%

1. The difference is statistically significant, but "wage considerations did not appear to be a first priority for most businesses."
2. Most important reasons for agreeing: "Chance to do something for disadvantaged youth; cheap or no-cost labor."
3. Most important reasons for not agreeing: "Not enough work for them to do; work inappropriate for teenagers."

TIME TRENDS IN FINDINGS: Not applicable.

DESIGN ISSUES:
1. The project could not offer wage subsidies beyond August 1980.
2. "Both local economic conditions and the diligence of the call-back effort (to employers) appeared to affect the yield (of participants)."
3. Current or former YIEPP employer participants were excluded from the sample. The bias could be in either direction (current participants are presumably positive responders, former participants presumably negative), but since current participants exceeded former participants, the probable direction of the bias was to reduce participation rates in both treatments.

4. The experiment occurred during a serious recession in Detroit.
5. Displacement bias is a virtual certainty, and the project authors concluded that the more real work a job involved, the more likely it was that a wage-subsidy placement would displace an unsubsidized worker.

REPLICABILITY: Replicable.

GENERALIZABILITY: Very limited, since only two levels of the subsidy were tested and, moreover, were tested in the context of a serious local recession. Diaz has argued, however, that the results point to a very limited efficacy for a subminimum wage.

FUNDING SOURCE: U.S. Department of Labor, Employment and Training Administration, Office of Youth Programs. Key personnel: Robert Taggart.

TREATMENT ADMINISTRATOR: Detroit Employment and Training Department.

EVALUATOR: Manpower Demonstration Research Corporation. Key personnel: Joseph Ball and Carl Wolfhagen. Primary author of the project evaluation was William Diaz.

ENABLING LEGISLATION: The Youth Employment and Demonstration Projects Act of 1977 authorized YIEPP.

INFORMATION SOURCE: Joseph Ball and Carl Wolfhagen, *The Participation of Private Businesses as Work Sponsors in the Youth Entitlement Demonstration,* Manpower Demonstration Research Corporation, 1981.

PUBLIC-USE ACCESS TO DATA: Public-use file does not exist.

Wilkes-Barre Job Search Voucher Project

SUMMARY: This demonstration, conducted in 1981, tested the effects of employer subsidies on a medium-sized sample of area employers. Subjects were followed for less than one year.

COST: Cost of operations, $181,044 (1981).

TIME FRAME: Demonstration period, January–December 1981; data collected, same period; final report, September 1982.

TREATMENTS TESTED:
1. Voucher and Targeted Jobs Tax Credit (TJTC), a wage subsidy in the form of a reduction on personal or corporate federal income tax available for employers of low-income 18–24-year-olds. Job developers visited these employers, informed them about the TJTC, and also made available to them a special subsidy (the voucher) for hiring 16- and 17-year-olds. The voucher subsidy was $1.80 per hour for the first three months a youth worked for the firm, and $1.00 per hour for the next five months. The intention was to stimulate the hiring of youths from the Wilkes-Barre YES Workshop Program (see p. 255), although the TJTC could not be restricted to them.
2. TJTC only. Job developers visited these employers, informed them of the availability of the TJTC, and encouraged them to hire program youths.
3. Control employers were not contacted by job developers.

A sample of 375 employers was drawn and stratified according to size, location, and the intensity of youth employment in their industries. Random assignment was performed within strata. Program youths attended individual and group counseling sessions to develop career goals and job search skills.

OUTCOME OF INTEREST: Employment of low-income youths by employers who received wage subsidies.

SAMPLE SIZE: Total, 375; group 1, 125; group 2, 125; group 3, 125.

TARGET POPULATION: Potential employers.

NUMBER OF TREATMENT GROUPS: Three (with one control group).

NUMBER AND LOCATION OF SITES: One—Wilkes-Barre, Pennsylvania.

RESEARCH COMPONENTS:

- Process analysis: Conducted. The program was affected by high staff turnover. The turnover itself was increased by the near certainty that the Labor Department would terminate the program at the end of the period.
- Impact analysis: Not conducted, for reasons obvious in "Major Findings," below.
- Benefit–cost analysis: Not conducted.

MAJOR FINDINGS:

1. Of 125 firms contacted, three took advantage of the voucher. Another firm, outside the sample, asked to use the subsidy and was allowed to do so; the four firms hired five workers.
2. Precisely one firm from each group used the TJTC. The voucher-group firm employed seven youths; the other two firms hired one each.

TIME TRENDS IN FINDINGS: None.

DESIGN ISSUES: It is not clear why the Wilkes-Barre YES organization was selected to run this experiment. The previous Workshop experiment, run by YES and evaluated by the same team from Brandeis (see page 255), was poorly implemented. The program was plagued by many of the same factors that are discussed in the process analysis of this experiment, and ceased operation when the Labor Department grant ended in December 1981.

REPLICABILITY: Replicable.

GENERALIZABILITY: The unemployment rate in Wilkes-Barre in December 1981 was 11.7 percent. High unemployment among all workers would in any case have resulted in poor job prospects for teenagers. ("On the average employers report 11 applicants for each entry level opening . . . among all ages.")

FUNDING SOURCE: U.S. Department of Labor, Employment and Training Administration, Office of Youth Programs. Key personnel: Robert Taggart.

TREATMENT ADMINISTRATOR: Youth Employment Service. Key personnel: Frank Hines and Richard Borofsky.

EVALUATOR: Center for Employment and Income Studies, Brandeis University. Key personnel: Cecilia Rivera-Casale, Barry Friedman, and Robert Lerman.

ENABLING LEGISLATION: Funded under the Youth Employment and Demonstration Projects Act of 1977.

INFORMATION SOURCE: Cecilia Rivera-Casale, Barry Friedman, and Robert Lerman, *Can Employer or Worker Subsidies Raise Youth Employment? An Evaluation of Two Financial Incentive Programs for Disadvantaged Youth,* Center for Employment and Income Studies, Florence Heller Graduate School for Advanced Studies in Social Welfare, Brandeis University, September 1982.

PUBLIC-USE ACCESS TO DATA: We have no information about a public-use file for this demonstration.

HEALTH CARE PROVIDERS

NCHSR Nursing Home Incentives Demonstration

SUMMARY: This demonstration, conducted between 1980 and 1983, tested the effects of incentive payments on a small sample of proprietary nursing homes. Subjects were followed for 30 months.

COST: The evaluators are unable to separate evaluation and program costs. Total costs, approximately $4.6 million.

TIME FRAME: Demonstration period, May 1981–April 1983; data collected, November 1980–April 1983.

TREATMENTS TESTED: The use of incentive payments made to nursing homes for reaching admission, outcome, and discharge goals. Incentives were in addition to Medicaid reimbursement. Control group homes did not receive incentive payments.

OUTCOMES OF INTEREST: Admissions, discharges, and outcome patterns for Medicaid patients in nursing homes.

SAMPLE SIZE: Nursing homes were the unit of analysis. There were a total of 36 homes: 18 experimental and 18 control. The number of individual patients varied by outcome. The total number of individual patients observed was 3,215.

TARGET POPULATION: Proprietary, Medicaid-certified nursing homes in San Diego County.

NUMBER OF TREATMENT GROUPS: Two (with one control group).

NUMBER AND LOCATION OF SITES: Thirty-six Medicaid-certified nursing homes in San Diego County, California.

RESEARCH COMPONENTS:
- Process analysis: Special effort went into the definition and classification of all components within the experiment.
- Impact analysis: Conducted using multivariate regression methods, as well as simple comparisons of means.
- Benefit–cost analysis: Not conducted.

MAJOR FINDINGS: For admissions outcomes, the study investigated the number of harder-to-care-for patients who were admitted. Patients were classified as A, B, C, D, or E; C was the "break-even" patient, and disbursements (incentives) were made for D and E patients. There was a negative incentive for B patients.
1. During the first half of the treatment period, there were no statistically significant differences in Medicaid admissions between the experimental and control facilities. During the second half, however, the experimental facilities admitted significantly fewer B patients and significantly more E patients. There was no effect on the admission of D patients.
2. Experimental facilities admitted patients with significantly higher average activities of daily living (ADL) scores (a measure of dependency and need for care—a higher ADL score indicates a higher need for care). Experimental facilities also had significantly higher average management minutes than did control facilities.
3. There were no statistically significant differences in patient outcomes, as measured by goal achievement, between experimental and control facilities.
4. Discharge results are less clear than those for admissions and outcomes because there was no comparable discharge planning process in control facilities. Nevertheless, the results suggest that the discharge incentive payment did little to encourage the experimental facilities to identify their patients for possible discharge, but did increase the likelihood of placing appropriate discharge candidates in a lower level of care.

TIME TRENDS IN FINDINGS: Admissions incentives appear to have had a greater impact in the second half of the project period. It may have taken some time for the facilities to adjust some of their admissions policies and practices.

DESIGN ISSUES: The design of the discharge component of the experiment precluded the generation of meaningful results. Research team nurses felt that little effort was expended on the discharge process. The study requirements for discharge planning and implementation may have been a barrier to participation.

REPLICABILITY: Replicable. The reports furnish detailed information regarding the calculation of incentives and other operations.

GENERALIZABILITY: Designed to generalize to, at least, San Diego County. The sample is representative of those found throughout the state of California. Roughly three-fourths of nursing homes in California are proprietary (rather than nonprofit). Thirty-six of the 41 skilled nursing facilities in San Diego County participated in the study. However, the two-year project duration is an inadequate test of a permanent, widespread change in this system. It is hypothesized that many homes were reluctant to make changes that would affect them for years after the experiment's termination.

FUNDING SOURCE: U.S. Department of Health and Human Services, National Center for Health Services Research.

TREATMENT ADMINISTRATOR: Applied Management Sciences was responsible for data collection, training and supervising a local field team of nurses, and disbursing incentive payments. (Admission, discharge, assessment, goal setting, and care planning of residents remained the responsibility of the nursing homes.)

EVALUATOR: National Center for Health Services Research and Health Care Technology Assessment. Key personnel: William Weissert and Mark Meiners.

ENABLING LEGISLATION: None.

INFORMATION SOURCES: William G. Weissert, William J. Scanlon, Thomas T. H. Wan, and Douglas E. Skinner, "Care for the Chronically Ill: Nursing Home Incentive Payment Experiment," *Health Care Financing Review* 5(1983): 41–49.

Mark R. Meiners, Phyllis Thorburn, Pamela C. Roddy, and Brenda Jones, *Nursing Home Admissions: The Results of an Incentive Reimbursement Experiment,* Long-Term Care Studies Program Research Report, DHHS Pub. No. 86-3397, October 1985.

Phyllis Thorburn and Mark R. Meiners, *Nursing Home Patient Outcomes: The Results of an Incentive Reimbursement Experiment,* Long-Term Care Studies Program Research Report, DHHS Pub. No. 86-3400, March 1986.

Brenda J. Jones and Mark R. Meiners, *Nursing Home Discharges: The Results of an Incentive Reimbursement Experiment,* Long-Term Care Studies Program Research Report, DHHS Pub. No. 86-3399, August 1986.

Edward C. Norton, "Incentive Regulation of Nursing Homes," *Journal of Health Economics* 11(1992): 105–28.

PUBLIC-USE ACCESS TO DATA: Available through National Technical Information Service, Springfield, Virginia.

National Home Health Prospective Payment Demonstration—Phase I

SUMMARY: This demonstration, conducted between 1990 and 1994, tested the effects of a prospective per-visit rate for home health visits on a small sample of nongovernmental home health agencies. Subjects were followed for three years.

COST: Evaluation costs, $3.1 million.

TIME FRAME: Demonstration period, October 1990–October 1994; data collected, same period; final report, December 1995.

TREATMENTS TESTED: Home health care agencies in the treatment group were paid a predetermined per-visit rate for each type of home health visit. There were six types of visit: skilled nursing; home health aide; physical therapy; occupational therapy; speech therapy; and medical/social services. Rates were set at an agency's pre-demonstration costs per visit times expected inflation rates. Profits and losses were shared with the Health Care Financing Administration (HCFA).

Control group agencies continued with the current payment method, paying agencies as services were rendered and reconciling payments to actual costs later.

OUTCOMES OF INTEREST: Principal outcomes were agency cost per visit, volume of services, quality of care provided, and agency profitability. Patient outcomes included functional ability, hospitalizations, and satisfaction with care.

SAMPLE SIZE: Total, 47 health care agencies; 26 treatments; 21 controls.

TARGET POPULATION: Nongovernmental home health agencies that had been in operation for at least three years. There were 41 urban agencies in three strata: freestanding proprietary, freestanding voluntary or nonprofit, and facility-based. The six rural agencies formed a separate stratum.

NUMBER OF TREATMENT GROUPS: Two (with one control group).

NUMBER AND LOCATION OF SITES: Forty-seven agencies in five states: California, Florida, Illinois, Massachusetts, and Texas.

RESEARCH COMPONENTS:

▪ Process analysis: Case studies and analysis of primary and secondary data were used to determine agency response to demonstration incentives. Agency staff at both treatment and control agencies were interviewed.

▪ Impact analysis: Conducted using fixed effects and other regression models.

▪ Benefit–cost analysis: Not conducted.

MAJOR FINDINGS:

1. There was no significant difference between groups on costs per visit, on the number of visits that agencies provided, or on patients' needs for other Medicare-covered services. Thus, total costs to Medicare were unaffected by prospective rate setting.

2. A rapid growth in visits occurred over the period for all agencies, although average total visits for both groups grew at a similar rate (21.3 percent for the treatment group and 23.6 percent for the control group).

3. There was a statistically significant difference in the length of home health aide visits. Average visit lengths were substantially shorter for the treatment group—65 minutes compared to 83 minutes for the control group. The evaluators pointed out that this finding was inconsistent with the finding of no effects on the average costs of aide visits and was probably not due to the demonstration.

4. The subset of treatment group agencies that serve predominantly Medicare patients and were not controlled by hospitals or hospices were significantly more likely than their control agency counterparts to hold their visit cost increases below inflation rates. As a result, net revenues on services to Medicare patients were positive for 77 percent of agency years for the treatment group. Only 40 percent of control group agencies would have earned profits had their actual costs been compared to revenues calculated under demonstration rules. The difference in cost growth was small, however (about 4 percent less for the treatment group). Treatment group agencies on average earned about $197,000 more in net revenues from Medicare than the average hypothetical net revenues for control group agencies.

5. There were no differences between groups on almost all measures of patient outcomes. Quality of care, access to home health care, and patient health and functioning were not significantly affected by the treatment.

TIME TRENDS IN FINDINGS: None reported.

DESIGN ISSUES:

1. There was a skewed distribution of agency size. Demonstration agencies delivered anywhere from 120 to 330,000 visits per year. This disparity led to problems in the analysis of patient level data. Patient observations were weighted to represent agencies equally, sometimes leading to anomalous estimates.

2. A sizeable number of observations in the individual-level analyses were lost owing to the inability to link data from the treatment forms, patient intake forms, and Medicare claims files to the demonstration claims files and the survey files. Identification numbers were often recorded incorrectly, and many agencies did not submit all patient intake forms. This reduced precision levels of the analyses.

REPLICABILITY: Replicated in Phase II, below.

GENERALIZABILITY: Designed to generalize to the entire nation, with sites in five large states. However, the sample size was small. Specifically, there were too few observations on facility-based and rural agencies to estimate impacts for each group separately. Thus, the results are mainly indicative of the effects of prospective rate setting on urban, freestanding agencies. Also, there were a number of differences between the sample agencies and a random sample of home health care agencies nationally. The proportion of for-profit agencies was significantly higher and the proportion of hospital-based agencies significantly lower in the sample than in home health agencies generally. Area characteristics, such as urbanicity, population, and hospital wage index, differed considerably from national averages, mostly because of the small proportion of rural agencies.

FUNDING SOURCE: HCFA. Key personnel: Elizabeth Mauser, Office of Research and Demonstration.

TREATMENT ADMINISTRATOR: Abt Associates was the implementation contractor for the demonstration. Key personnel: Henry Goldberg. (Actual home health care was administered by the individual agencies.)

EVALUATOR: Mathematica Policy Research. Key personnel: Randall S. Brown, Barbara R. Phillips, and Christine Bishop (Brandeis University).

ENABLING LEGISLATION: Section 4027 of the Omnibus Budget Reconciliation Act of 1987 and Section 4207(c) of the Omnibus Reconciliation Act of 1990.

INFORMATION SOURCE: Randall Brown, Barbara Phillips, Christine Bishop, Amy Klein, Grant Ritter, Craig Thornton, Peter Schochet, and Kathleen Skwara, *The Effects of Predetermined Payment Rates for Home Health Care,* Mathematica Policy Research, December 1995.

PUBLIC-USE ACCESS TO DATA: HCFA has data tapes, but they are not set up for public use.

National Home Health Prospective Payment Demonstration—Phase II

SUMMARY: This demonstration, conducted from 1995 to 1998, tested the effects of a predetermined per-episode payment rate on the delivery of Medicare funded home health care on a small sample of home health agencies. Subject agencies were followed for over three years.

COST: Evaluation, approximately $4 million.

TIME FRAME: Demonstration period, June 1995–December 1998; extended for the demonstration group to October 2000; data collected, same period.

TREATMENTS TESTED: Experimentals: Agencies received per-episode payment, allowing for profit from-cost containment. Controls: Continued to operate under the existing cost-reimbursement payment system.

OUTCOMES OF INTEREST: (1) Visits to patients by home health nurses and physical therapists; (2) Patient outcomes; and (3) Direct and indirect Medicare expenditures.

SAMPLE SIZE: Experimentals, 48; controls, 43.

TARGET POPULATION: Home health agencies providing services to Medicare-funded users.

NUMBER OF TREATMENT GROUPS: Two (with one control group).

NUMBER AND LOCATION OF SITES: Five—California, Florida, Illinois, Massachusetts, and Texas.

RESEARCH COMPONENTS:
- Process analysis: Looked at provider characteristics, patient characteristics, and service area characteristics.
- Impact analysis: Regression.
- Benefit–cost analysis: Conducted from agency and government budget perspectives.

MAJOR FINDINGS:
1. The per-episode payment system reduced the number of patient visits in the first 120 days of care by 17 percent. Control agency patients averaged 45 visits; treatment agency patients averaged 37 visits. Prospectively paid agencies also reduced the average number of visits provided over a patient-year by 24 percent.
2. Per-episode payment method did not adversely affect patient outcomes; the experimental and

control groups' mortality rates during the year after admission were the same.

3. Reductions in home health services did not lead to an increase in the expenditures for and use of other Medicare services.

4. Medicare expenditure on every experimental subtype of home health facility recorded reductions in total visits and length of service relative to the levels in similar control group agencies. However, the expenditure reductions occurred during a time of "unprecedented decline in the use of Medicare home health services" as a result of federal legislative changes to Medicare benefits. The average prospectively paid agency's Medicare revenue was 20 percent lower than that of the average cost-reimbursed agency, resulting in greater savings for the Medicare program.

TIME TRENDS IN FINDINGS: Home health utilization progressively declined. During the last year of the demonstration it reached its lowest point but without significantly impacting patient outcome measures.

Agency profits under the prospective payment system fell in the first three years of the demonstration, apparently because the agencies were unaware that their cost per visit was increasing. Despite efficiency-enhancing measures, costs per visit rose because of the fixed-cost component of home health services.

DESIGN ISSUES: None apparent.

REPLICABILITY: Replicable.

GENERALIZABILITY: Generalizable. The demonstration agencies were reasonably representative of home health agencies nationwide, with the following caveats:

1. The range of participants did not precisely reflect the range of agencies across the country. The typical demonstration agency was large.

2. The sample underrepresented hospital-based and non-urban area agencies.

3. Demonstration sites had a slightly younger population and a higher per capita income than the national average for health agencies.

FUNDING SOURCE: U.S. Department of Health and Human Services, Health Care Financing Administration (now the Centers for Medicare & Medicaid Services). Key personnel: Ann Meadow.

TREATMENT ADMINISTRATOR: U.S. Department of Health and Human Services, Health Care Financing Administration (now the Centers for Medicare & Medicaid Services). Key personnel: Ann Meadow.

EVALUATOR: Valerie Cheh and Cheryl Pedersen, Mathematica Policy Research.

ENABLING LEGISLATION: None.

INFORMATION SOURCE: Valerie Cheh and Cheryl Pedersen, *The Final Evaluation Report on the National Home Health Prospective Payment Demonstration: Agencies Reduce Visits While Preserving Care,* Mathematica Policy Research, April 2001.

PUBLIC-USE ACCESS TO DATA: Contact Ann Meadow, Centers for Medicare & Medicaid Services.

4

Middle-Class and Employee Populations

POWER CUSTOMERS

Introduction

During the 1970s, the former Federal Energy Administration, which subsequently was absorbed by the U.S. Department of Energy, funded 16 residential electricity rate experiments in the following locations: Arizona, Arkansas, California, Connecticut, Los Angeles, Michigan, New Jersey, New York, North Carolina, Ohio, Oklahoma, Puerto Rico, Rhode Island, Vermont, Washington, and Wisconsin. These experiments tested different combinations of pricing plans on residential users. All used declining block rates, with lower prices per kilowatt-hour for greater quantities of usage, as the control group treatment. Time-of-use rates, in which the prices are higher (or lower) according to whether the electricity is consumed during peak (or off-peak) hours, was the experimental treatment for all but the Michigan and Washington experiments. We were able to locate detailed information on only the Connecticut and Los Angeles experiments. Thus, only these two experiments are summarized here.

We traced the Connecticut and Los Angeles reports through subsequent references in academic journals. We have not found any subsequent use of the other experiments. Some reports on them are available through the Electric Power Research Institute in Palo Alto, California; however, they are available only on microfiche and are quite expensive.

Comments from Hausman and Wise (1985)[1] have illustrated some limitations to the generalizability of these experiments. The utilities were given little guidance in their designs—a haphazard approach that led each project to define its universe differently. Coverage of the stated target population was often low, and the time-horizon was too short to allow households to adjust their stock of electricity-using equipment.

Note

1. For a brief summary of these experiments, see Jerry Hausman and David Wise, *Social Experimentation* (Chicago: University of Chicago Press, 1985), 1401–3.

Connecticut Peak Load Pricing Experiment

SUMMARY: This experiment, conducted from 1975 to 1976, tested the effects of peak load pricing (PLP) on a medium-sized sample of residential energy customers. Subjects were followed for two years.

COST: Unavailable.

TIME FRAME: Demonstration period, October 1975–October 1976; data collected, October 1974–November 1976.

TREATMENTS TESTED: PLP is the adjustment of electricity rates to reflect the cost of supply at various times of the day. The experimental rates used in this experiment (per kilowatt-hour) were $0.16 for peak periods, $0.03 for intermediate periods, and $0.01 for off-peak periods. The control group customers were billed using the existing rate structure (declining block rate, wherein rates are not affected by supply costs or seasonal variations).

OUTCOME OF INTEREST: Changes in electricity use.

SAMPLE SIZE: A total of 250 residential customers were randomly selected for the treatment group; 199 of these agreed to participate in the experiment. For the control group, 195 customers were selected.

TARGET POPULATION: Residential energy customers.

NUMBER OF TREATMENT GROUPS: Two (with one control group).

NUMBER AND LOCATION OF SITES: Connecticut Light and Power (CLP) covers 60 percent of the state, serving 52 percent of the electric customers in Connecticut.

RESEARCH COMPONENTS:

■ Process analysis: Customer interviews were designed to assess attitudes and demographic characteristics, and to provide information about energy consumption and its modification.

■ Impact analysis: Comparison of means.

■ Benefit–cost analysis: Not conducted.

MAJOR FINDINGS:

1. Peak hour consumption represented 13 percent of total electricity use by the test customers during the baseline year, but only 10 percent during the test year. During the test year, test customers consumed a smaller percentage of their electricity requirements during peak hours and a larger percentage during off-peak hours relative to both their own prior-year usage and to consumption by controls during the test year (see table below). Information regarding statistical significance of these findings was not provided.

Major Findings

	Test group prior year kWh	Percentage	Test group test year kWh	Percentage	Control group test year kWh	Percentage
Peak	1,058.1	12.8	822.0	10.0	1,120.4	13.0
Shoulder	4,021.1	48.8	3,890.5	47.6	4,270.8	49.6
Off-peak	3,166.3	38.4	3,467.3	42.4	3,221.6	37.4
Total	**8,245.6**	**100.0**	**8,180.0**	**100.0**	**8,612.9**	**100.0**

Note: Numbers may not add to totals because of rounding.

2. Survey data indicated that the test participants preferred the time-of-day test rate to the declining-block rate. More than 80 percent of the test customers made schedule and/or activity changes in their living patterns (e.g., cleanup, laundry, bathing). More changes were made by high-use customers than by low-use customers.

TIME TRENDS IN FINDINGS: None.

DESIGN ISSUES:

1. Significant selection bias is possible due to the nonparticipation of roughly 20 percent of those selected for the treatment group.
2. Savings by customers (and their enthusiastic response) were likely exaggerated by the high (16:1) ratio of peak to off-peak prices.
3. Since the rate was in effect for only one year, findings do not reflect long-term impacts such as changing appliance stocks.

REPLICABILITY: Replicable.

GENERALIZABILITY: Designed to generalize to the entire state. The Connecticut Light and Power service area from which the sample was drawn includes a cross-section of the urban, suburban, and rural areas of the state as well as all types of residential users of electricity. However, design issue 3 may reduce generalizability.

FUNDING SOURCE: The project was partially funded by the former Federal Energy Administration.

TREATMENT ADMINISTRATOR: Connecticut Light and Power Company, a subsidiary of Northeast Utilities.

EVALUATORS: Research Triangle Institute and Northeast Utilities. Key personnel: H. Donald Burbank.

ENABLING LEGISLATION: None.

INFORMATION SOURCE: H. Donald Burbank, "The Connecticut Peak-Load Pricing Experiment," in *Forecasting and Modeling Time-of-Day and*

Seasonal Electricity Demands, edited by Anthony Lawrence, Special Report EA-578-SR, Electric Power Research Institute, December 1977 (1–3 to 1–31).

PUBLIC-USE ACCESS TO DATA: Not available.

Los Angeles Peak Load Pricing Experiment for Electricity

SUMMARY: This demonstration, conducted from 1976 through 1980, tested the effects of alternative electricity pricing structures on a large sample of residential electric consumers. Subjects were followed for 30 months.

COST: The entire project cost approximately $4.3 million. More than half the cost was for the evaluation design and analysis.

TIME FRAME: Demonstration period, summer 1976–1980; data collected, same period.

TREATMENTS TESTED: Treatment households were enrolled in one of 34 different experimental time-of-use (TOU) electricity tariffs. These rates are designed to reflect the cost of supplying electricity at different times of the day. TOU prices ranged from $0.05 to $0.13 per kilowatt-hour (kWh) during peak hours and $0.01 or $0.02 during off-peak hours. Control groups had either seasonal and time invariant tariffs (flat rates of $0.02 to $0.08 per kWh) or the standard declining-block rate structure available to all nonexperimental customers in the Los Angeles area.

OUTCOMES OF INTEREST: (1) Energy consumption in each period of the day and (2) Total energy consumption.

SAMPLE SIZE: A total of 1,286 households were used for the analysis; 931 were assigned to one of 34 TOU rates; 337 faced seasonal, time-invariant or declining-block rates.

TARGET POPULATION: Residential electricity consumers.

NUMBER OF TREATMENT GROUPS: Forty (with six control groups).

NUMBER AND LOCATION OF SITES: One—Los Angeles, California.

RESEARCH COMPONENTS:
- Process analysis: Demographic, economic, and attitudinal data were obtained through household interviews at several points in the study.
- Impact analysis: Conducted using analysis of covariance and econometric modeling.
- Benefit–cost analysis: Conducted.

MAJOR FINDINGS:

1. For all households, weather was the primary cause of variation in electricity consumption. This variation was largely independent of the price of electricity.
2. Relative to the control groups, the TOU rates reduced the share of electricity use during peak periods in all experimental groups. Most of the estimated effects were statistically significant. In most cases, higher TOU rates resulted in greater reductions.
3. The higher experimental rates per kWh also reduced overall electricity use for 28 of the 34 treatment groups, although the difference was statistically significant for only 1 group.
4. Price responsiveness was markedly greater in households having certain types of appliances (e.g., those appliances associated with swimming pools).
5. The benefit–cost analysis suggested that, for all households, the average gain in welfare exceeded the metering costs only when consumption was above 1,100 kWh per month. This is the case for only 4 percent of residential users in the area. These users account for 17 percent of residential use.

TIME TRENDS IN FINDINGS: None.

DESIGN ISSUES: A classical stratified random sample was not used. Instead, the stratification was purposive, with deliberate overrepresentation of high-usage customers. The effect was then accounted for in the statistical analysis. Whereas this is a widely accepted practice today, the evaluators say that it required considerable explanation when they first proposed it.

REPLICABILITY: Replicable.

GENERALIZABILITY: Participation was voluntary. Eligible participants were offered the chance to join the study, and over 92 percent of eligible households accepted the experimental rate plans. Some households were offered compensation in the form of "participation payments" so that they would not be made worse off under the experimental treatment.

Considering the importance of weather, generalizability would be limited to Los Angeles or other urban areas with similar weather patterns and similar patterns of electricity use.

FUNDING SOURCES: Los Angeles Department of Water and Power and U.S. Department of Energy.

TREATMENT ADMINISTRATOR: Los Angeles Department of Water and Power. Key personnel: Michael T. Moore, project officer.

EVALUATOR: The RAND Corporation. Key personnel: Jan Paul Acton, Bridger Mitchell, and Willard G. Manning.

ENABLING LEGISLATION: None.

INFORMATION SOURCES: Bridger M. Mitchell and Jan Paul Acton, *Electricity Consumption by Time of Use in a Hybrid Demand System*, RAND Corporation, December 1980.

Jan Paul Acton and Bridger Mitchell, *Evaluating Time-of-Day Electricity Rates for Residential Customers*, RAND Corporation, November 1979.

Willard G. Manning Jr., Bridger M. Mitchell, and Jan Paul Acton, *Design of the Los Angeles Peak-Load Pricing Experiment for Electricity*, RAND Corporation, November 1976.

PUBLIC-USE ACCESS TO DATA: Public-use access does not exist.

HEALTH CARE CONSUMERS

RAND Health Insurance Study

SUMMARY: This demonstration, conducted from 1974 to 1982, tested the effects of universal health insurance (at various deductibles and copayment rates) on a large sample of nonelderly, noninstitutionalized households. Subjects were followed for up to five years.

COST: $136 million (in 1984 dollars).

TIME FRAME: Demonstration period, November 1974–January 1982; data collected, same period.

TREATMENTS TESTED: Insurance benefits varied over two dimensions, the maximum dollar expenditure (MDE) and the coinsurance rate (CR). The MDE was the upper limit on the annual out-of-pocket medical expenses for which the family was responsible. It was set at 5 percent, 10 percent, or 15 percent of income, up to a maximum of $1,000 (1973 dollars; this limit was held constant in real terms). The coinsurance rate was the percentage of expenditures below the MDE for which the family was responsible. It was set at 0 percent (free care), 25 percent, 50 percent, and 95 percent. An "individual deductible" (ID) plan had a coinsurance rate of 95 percent for outpatient care only, but the MDE was limited to $150 per person (fixed in nominal terms), or $450 per family. Inpatient care was free in the ID plan.

To obtain uniformity in the experiment, all participant families were induced to sign over the benefits from their existing insurance plan to the experiment. The inducement was the financial maintenance (where necessary) of the plan by the administrator and a guaranteed payment equal to the difference between the MDE assigned to the family and the maximum deductible of their previous coverage. Families therefore could not be financially worse off by participating and would in most cases have somewhat higher incomes.

Participant families were randomly assigned to three-year or five-year treatments. The experiment also randomly assigned Seattle participants between a health maintenance organization (HMO) and a fee-for-service (FFS) plan.

OUTCOMES OF INTEREST: (1) Total expenditures on health care; (2) Relative demand for services by poor and nonpoor; (3) Quantifiable health differences; and (4) Effect of HMO organizational structure on expenditures and care.

SAMPLE SIZE: Numbers are individuals. Free care: 1,893; 25 percent coinsurance: 1,137; 50 percent coinsurance: 383; 95 percent coinsurance: 1,120; ID plan: 1,276; total, 5,809.

TARGET POPULATION: Representative samples of the populations of the site areas with the following exclusions: (1) people over 61 years, (2) people with incomes in excess of $25,000 (1973 dollars), (3) those in jails or institutionalized, (4) those eligible for the Medicare disability program, (5) military personnel and their dependents, and (6) veterans with service-connected disabilities.

NUMBER OF TREATMENT GROUPS: Fourteen (for most analyses; however, for some analyses these 14 groups were combined into 5).

NUMBER AND LOCATION OF SITES: Six—Dayton, Ohio; Seattle, Washington; Fitchburg, Massachusetts; Franklin County, Massachusetts; Charleston, South Carolina; and Georgetown County, South Carolina.

RESEARCH COMPONENTS:
- Process analysis: Careful analysis of characteristics of persons who refused to participate in the experiment. Although the rate of refusal rose with the coinsurance rate, the project report authors stated that the refusers do not appear statistically different from the participants. Attrition was very small. There was no analysis of the content of medical care received.
- Impact analysis: Conducted with sample means and sophisticated analyses using regression and other methods.

Table 1 Predicted Annual per Capita Use of Medical Services

Plan	Likelihood of any use (%)	One or more admissions to hospital (%)	Medical expenses (1984 dollars)
Free care	86.7 (0.67)	10.37 (0.42)	777 (32.8)
25 percent coinsurance rate (CR)	78.8 (0.99)	8.83 (0.379)	630 (29.0)
50 percent CR	74.3 (1.86)	8.31 (0.4)	583 (32.6)
95 percent CR	68.0 (1.48)	7.75 (0.354)	534 (27.4)
Individual deductible (ID)	72.6 (1.14)	9.52 (0.529)	623 (34.6)

Benefit–cost analysis: Not conducted, but see "Generalizability."

MAJOR FINDINGS:

1. The predicted annual per capita use of medical services by plan appears in table 1 (from a four-equation system designed to reduce the effects of individual catastrophic cases on the estimates; sample means generally show the same patterns; standard errors in parentheses).

   "Our findings decisively reject the hypothesis that increased coverage of outpatient services, holding constant the coverage of inpatient services, will reduce expenditure" (Manning et al. 1987).

2. The predicted annual use of medical services by income group is shown in table 2.

3. For the sample as a whole, the only statistically significant health gains from the free-care plan over the cost-sharing plans were for high blood pressure and the correction of nearsightedness. For the 25 percent of the sample judged to be in the poorest health, there was a 10 percent greater risk of dying in the cost-sharing plans than in the free-care plan, other things being equal.

   The project evaluators noted that gains in health were mostly due to improved control of blood pressure, and that a targeted program of free hypertension screening could accomplish the same result.

Table 2 Predicted Annual Use of Medical Services

Plan	Lowest third	Middle third	Highest third	Corrected t[a]
Likelihood of any use (%)				
Free care	82.8	87.4	90.1	5.90
25 percent CR	71.8	80.1	84.8	6.28
50 percent CR	64.7	76.2	82.3	4.86
95 percent CR	61.7	68.9	73.8	4.64
ID	65.3	73.9	79.1	7.09
Likelihood of one or more hospital admissions (%)				
Free care	10.6	10.1	10.4	−0.35
25 percent CR	10.0	8.4	8.0	−2.75
50 percent CR	9.1	8.1	7.8	−1.66
95 percent CR	8.8	7.4	7.1	−2.46
ID	9.3	9.4	9.9	0.68
Medical expenditures ($1984)				
Free care	788	736	809	0.53
25 percent CR	680	588	623	−1.47
50 percent CR	610	550	590	−0.49
95 percent CR	581	494	527	−1.41
ID	609	594	670	1.38

a. "Corrected t" is the t-test on the hypothesis that the population value for the upper third of households is the same as the population value for the lower third of households, corrected for intertemporal and intrafamily correlation. An absolute value of 1.96 or higher indicates that the probability of this hypothesis being true is 5 percent or less.

4. Valdez et al. (1985) reported: "For the typical child participant, we could not discern significant differences in health status between those who received free care and those insured by the cost-sharing plans. . . . Taking all the measures together, the direction of estimated effects favored neither the free plan nor the cost-sharing plans."

5. Ware et al. (1986) reported: "1,673 individuals aged 14 to 61 were randomly assigned to one HMO or FFS plan in Seattle. For nonpoor individuals assigned to the HMO who were initially in good health, there were no adverse effects. Health outcomes in the two systems of care differed for high- and low-income individuals who began the experiment with health problems. For the high income initially sick group, the HMO produced significant improvements in cholesterol levels and in general health ratings by comparison with free FFS care. The low income initially sick group assigned to the HMO reported significantly more bed-days per year due to poor health and more serious symptoms than those assigned free FFS care, and a greater risk of dying by comparison with pay FFS plans."

6. Table 3 shows the annual use of medical services per capita, by HMO and FFS status.

Table 3 Annual per Capita Use of Medical Services

Plan	Likelihood of any use (%)	One or more admissions to hospital (%)	Imputed expenditures (1984 dollars)
HMO experimental	87.0	7.1	434
HMO control	91.1	6.4	432
Free FFS	85.3	11.2	640

HMO critics have long claimed that the apparent cost savings from the HMO organizational mode were partly due to self-selection; persons less likely to demand care are more likely to choose HMOs. To test this, HMO experimentals were randomly assigned to the HMO; HMO controls were assigned to it randomly but had already been enrolled in it anyway; the randomly assigned FFS group included people who had been HMO members before the experiment.

The project report stated: "Our results . . . show no evidence of selection in the single HMO that we studied; those previously enrolled at the HMO (the Controls) used services at approximately the same rate as those who were not previously enrolled (the Experimentals)."

TIME TRENDS IN FINDINGS: No differences between three-year and five-year groups were reported.

DESIGN ISSUES:

1. "There are no easy, quantitative measures of health in large populations" (A. S. Relman, in editorial accompanying Brook et al. 1983).

2. Poor families in this study reached their MDE quickly, since it was a function of income, and thereafter care was free. This will distort any projections from these findings to the effects of cost sharing on the poor when the deductible is set at a higher level and/or is not a function of income. These reservations do not apply to comparisons between the free-care plan and the ID plan, where the limit was not a function of income; however, the ceiling in the ID plan was still fairly low.

3. "The fact that there was greater variation in the amount of care used by children between sites than between payment groups suggests that very different types of care were provided in different places. Unless one knows what care was delivered, it is difficult to come to conclusions about its relation to outcomes" (R. J. Haggerty, in editorial accompanying Valdez et al. 1985).

4. Although the refusal group was not statistically different from the participant group in observed characteristics, the rate of refusal rose with the coinsurance rate (25 percent of those offered the 95 percent plan refused), leaving

open the question of differences in unobserved characteristics.

5. Published reports do not generally report the effects of differing levels of MDE on the variables of interest. Given the experimental design, this omission is strange.

6. The HMO study is clearly dependent on the characteristics of the HMO used, and perhaps on the characteristics of competing FFS physicians in Seattle as well.

REPLICABILITY: Replicable.

GENERALIZABILITY:

1. The key finding of the experiment is that the price elasticity of health care is substantial, even when price changes are compensated (in this case, overcompensated) by income supplements. Under standard economic theory, the provision of subsidized medical care will therefore result in an important loss in social welfare owing to the use of resources in medical care that have less value to the consumer than the money it costs to provide them. This has a clear bearing on the design of any national health insurance plan. Using strong assumptions, such as competitive medical care prices and no externalities, Manning et al. (1987) calculated the "dead-weight" loss in wasted resources in moving from a national 95 percent plan with $1,000 MDE to a national free-care plan. Their estimate is between $37 billion and $60 billion; expenditures on these services in 1984 by the under-65 population were around $200 billion.

2. In an early article (Newhouse et al., *New England Journal of Medicine* 305[25, December 17, 1981]: 1501–7) the authors noted some limits to generalizability. An increase in subsidy to ambulatory care would result in increases in the quantity of services demanded sufficient to exceed the short-run capacity of the medical-care delivery system; this might well lead to a non-price rationing of care, which would upset many of the conclusions in these articles. Large, long-run increases in capacity might not be allowed by the government for cost reasons, so this generalizability problem might be a long-run problem as well. On the other hand, a slackening in services demanded brought on by increased cost-sharing would in some theories cause physicians to "induce demand" by suggesting more costly therapies to their patients; this theory, however, is controversial.

FUNDING SOURCE: U.S. Department of Health and Human Services, Office of the Assistant Secretary for Planning and Evaluation. Key personnel: Larry L. Orr and James Schuttinga.

TREATMENT ADMINISTRATOR: RAND Corporation. Key personnel: Rae Archibald.

EVALUATOR: RAND Corporation. Key personnel: Joseph P. Newhouse.

ENABLING LEGISLATION: None.

INFORMATION SOURCES: Joseph P. Newhouse and The Insurance Experiment Group, *Free for All? Lessons from the RAND Health Insurance Experiment,* Harvard University Press, 1993.

Willard G. Manning, Joseph P. Newhouse, Naihua Duan, et al., "Health Insurance and the Demand for Medical Care: Evidence from a Randomized Experiment," *American Economic Review* 77(3, June 1987): 251–77.

Robert H. Brook, John E. Ware Jr., William H. Rogers, Emmett B. Keeler, et al., "Does Free Care Improve Adults' Health? Results from a Randomized Controlled Trial," *New England Journal of Medicine* 309 (December 8, 1983): 1426–34.

John E. Ware Jr., Robert H. Brook, William H. Rogers, Emmett B. Keeler, et al., "Comparison of Health Outcomes at a Health Maintenance Organization with Those of Fee-for-Service Care," *Lancet,* May 3, 1986: 1017–22.

R. Burciaga Valdez, Robert H. Brook, William H. Rogers, John E. Ware Jr., et al., "Consequences of Cost-Sharing for Children's Health," *Pediatrics* 75(5): 952–61.

PUBLIC-USE ACCESS TO DATA: Public-use file available through RAND Corporation or National Technical Information Service, Springfield, Virginia.

United Healthcare Gatekeeper Plan Experiment

SUMMARY: This demonstration, conducted in 1979, tested the effects of a gatekeeper on health care usage and costs for a large sample of health care users. Subjects were followed for one year.

COST: Not available.

TIME FRAME: Data were collected on participants who enrolled in a health care plan in 1979.

TREATMENTS TESTED: The sample was randomly assigned to either a health care plan with a gatekeeper (physicians who control health care services and charges) or to a plan without a gatekeeper.

OUTCOMES OF INTEREST: Health care usage and costs.

SAMPLE SIZE: Treatments (gatekeeper plan), 555 subscribers and their dependents (1,419 enrollees); controls (no gatekeeper), 558 subscribers and their dependents (1,408 enrollees).

TARGET POPULATION: Washington State employees in the Seattle metropolitan area enrolling for the first time in a health care plan with United Healthcare (UHC), excluding retirees.

NUMBER OF TREATMENT GROUPS: Two (with one control group).

NUMBER AND LOCATION OF SITES: One—Seattle metropolitan area.

RESEARCH COMPONENTS:
- Process analysis: None.
- Impact analysis: Comparison of means and analysis of covariance. (Since the adjusted and unadjusted results were essentially the same, unadjusted rates are presented in the report.)
- Benefit–cost analysis: Not conducted.

MAJOR FINDINGS:
1. People in the gatekeeper plan had 6 percent more visits to the primary care physician (PCP) and 9 percent fewer visits to a specialist.
2. There was no reported difference between plans in enrollees' use of other health insurance plans, in the proportion of claims submitted, or in out-of-pocket expenses.
3. On average, total charges were 6 percent less for the gatekeeper plan than for controls ($239 per person, per year versus $254.) The gatekeeper plan had lower ambulatory charges per enrollee, per year ($146 versus $167), primarily due to lower use of specialists. The gatekeeper plan had little impact on hospital use or charges. In fact, the gatekeeper plan had slightly higher charges ($93 versus $87).

TIME TRENDS IN FINDINGS: None reported.

DESIGN ISSUES:
1. The use of claims data precluded certain categories of examination. For example, the evaluators had no way of knowing who initiated a visit to the PCP, or whether a patient was seeing a particular provider as a PCP or as a specialist.
2. This 12-month study may not be representative of the plans' or enrollees' experiences over time.

REPLICABILITY: Replicable.

GENERALIZABILITY: The evaluation does not address this issue. This was a voluntary program, and subscribers who chose United Healthcare rather than another state health insurance plan had the opportunity to familiarize themselves with the standard UHC plan. They may have been oriented to use PCPs more than the general population.

FUNDING SOURCE: Health Care Financing Administration.

TREATMENT ADMINISTRATOR: United Healthcare, operated by SAFECO Insurance Company.

EVALUATOR: Diane Martin, University of Washington–Seattle, School of Public Health and Community Medicine.

ENABLING LEGISLATION: None.

INFORMATION SOURCE: Diane P. Martin, et al., "Effect of a Gatekeeper Plan on Health Services Use and Charges: A Randomized Trial," *American Journal of Public Health* 79(1989): 1628–32.

PUBLIC-USE ACCESS TO DATA: Not available.

OTHER

Minnesota Income Tax Compliance Experiment

SUMMARY: This experiment, conducted in 1995, tested the effects of four separate strategies to increase tax compliance on a large sample of Minnesota taxpayers. Subjects were followed for one year.

COST: This was an in-house evaluation, and most costs were borne internally. There were other direct evaluation costs of approximately $50,000 to $80,000.

TIME FRAME: Demonstration period, 1995; data were collected for previous and current tax years; final report, 1996.

TREATMENTS TESTED: There were four separate treatments: (1) an increased examination and audit rate of both state and federal tax returns with prior notice to taxpayers, (2) enhanced taxpayer services, (3) redesign of the standard Minnesota state tax form, and (4) letters to taxpayers with information messages on the importance of voluntary compliance.

OUTCOMES OF INTEREST: (1) Change in reported taxable federal income and (2) Change in state taxes paid from previous tax year.

SAMPLE SIZE: Approximately 47,000 taxpayers were assigned to the four treatments; control groups numbered approximately 23,500.

TARGET POPULATION: Minnesota taxpayers whose 1994 taxes were filed and processed by the Department of Revenue by the end of November 1995.

Specific eligibility criteria were applied to individual treatments.

NUMBER OF TREATMENT GROUPS: Eight: four treatment and four control (one control group was shared by the audit and service treatments, one control group was used for the letter treatment, and two control groups were used for the tax form treatment).

NUMBER AND LOCATION OF SITES: Throughout the state of Minnesota.

RESEARCH COMPONENTS:
- Process analysis: Implementation was carefully monitored and documented.
- Impact analysis: Conducted using analysis of variance and linear regression.
- Benefit–cost analysis: Not conducted.

MAJOR FINDINGS:
1. Low- and mid-income taxpayers facing higher examination and audit rates reported significantly more income and paid more taxes relative to the control group. As a whole, the treatment group reported $1,131 more income and paid $87 more in Minnesota state taxes than controls. Increases were generally larger among taxpayers who had business income and paid estimated taxes in 1993. Certain small groups of taxpayers who were especially responsive to the threat of an examination accounted for most of the group differences. High-income taxpayers had a mixed reaction to the examination threat—the net effect on them was slight.
2. The service offer, which was an incremental expansion of existing services, did not have a net effect on reported income or taxes paid. Only 14 percent of taxpayers who were offered the service telephoned the Department of Revenue—slightly below the normal rate.
3. One of the two information messages had a modest positive effect on reported income and taxes paid. This message refuted the idea that many taxpayers cheat on their taxes and reinforced social norms about tax compliance.

4. The experiment had little effect on timeliness of tax filings, on the rate of adjustments made to tax filings during the department's machine processing of returns, or on taxpayers' use of a tax practitioner.

TIME TRENDS IN FINDINGS: None.

DESIGN ISSUES:
1. The use of multiple control groups was overly complex. Some treatments shared the same control group, whereas other treatments had more than one control group. There was also a "quasi-control group" that received a simple letter advising them of available telephone numbers for assistance, which technically amounts to another treatment.
2. Although not part of the design or implementation, an important issue was the printing of a story in the *St. Paul Pioneer Press* (1995), reporting that many members of the treatment group were upset over the letters that hinted at an audit. The story was subsequently printed in several other newspapers. It is uncertain what effect this may have had on the results of the experiment.

REPLICABILITY: Replicable—all forms and letters are included in the report.

GENERALIZABILITY: Designed to generalize to the entire state. The strategy showing the greatest impact, the threat of examination or audit, may not be practical or cost-effective on a large scale. In general, the findings point to greater effectiveness for small subgroups than for taxpayers as a whole.

FUNDING SOURCE: Minnesota Department of Revenue.

TREATMENT ADMINISTRATOR: Minnesota Department of Revenue.

EVALUATOR: Minnesota Department of Revenue. Key personnel: Stephen Coleman, project director.

ENABLING LEGISLATION: None.

INFORMATION SOURCE: Stephen Coleman, *The Minnesota Income Tax Compliance Experiment:*

State Tax Results, Minnesota Department of Revenue, April 1996.

PUBLIC-USE ACCESS TO DATA: Not available.

Seed Money Experiment

SUMMARY: This demonstration, conducted in 1999, tested the effects of seed money and refunds on charitable giving on a large group of Florida households.

COST: $6,000.

TIME FRAME: Letters of solicitation sent between November 29 and December 3, 1999; response data collected through December 31, 1999.

TREATMENTS TESTED: Two types of treatment were applied through the University of Central Florida's capital campaign to fund computers for a new Center for Environmental Policy Analysis (CEPA). Potential donors were told that CEPA had already obtained either 10, 33, or 67 percent of the amount needed to purchase a particular computer and that they were soliciting donations to cover the remaining amount, rounded to $2,700, $2,000, or $1,000, respectively.

Half of all potential donors were also assigned to the refund group, in which the individuals were told that the policy was to refund donors' gifts if CEPA failed to raise sufficient funds to purchase the computer. Individuals who were not assigned to the refund group were told that, in that event, their gifts would be put toward CEPA operating expenditures. All potential donors were told that revenue in excess of the threshold amount would be used to fund other CEPA needs.

Treatment Groups by Seed Money Level

Possible refund	10%	33%	67%
No	Group 10	Group 33	Group 67
Yes	Group 10R	Group 33R	Group 67R

OUTCOME OF INTEREST: Charitable donations.

SAMPLE SIZE: Total, 3,000; 500 in each group.

TARGET POPULATION: Households in central Florida with an annual income above $70,000 that are known to have previously contributed to charity.

NUMBER OF TREATMENT GROUPS: Six.

NUMBER AND LOCATION OF SITES: One—University of Central Florida (Orlando).

RESEARCH COMPONENTS:
▓ Process analysis: Not conducted.
▓ Impact analysis: Comparison of means.
▓ Benefit–cost analysis: Conducted.

MAJOR FINDINGS:

	10%	33%	67%
Average donation	$15.42	$26.12	$39.87
Participation rate	3.7%	6.4%	8.2%

1. Higher levels of seed money increased both participation rates and the average donation. The combined impact of the two 67 percent treatments yielded a statistically significant 560 percent increase ($3,260) in donations compared with the combined yield of the two 10 percent groups ($581).
2. The refund treatment appears to have a positive impact on the average donation size in all three levels. However, the largest and only statistically significant impact was at the 10 percent level. There were no effects on participation rates from the refund treatment.
3. There was a net loss of more than $1,000, which was a smaller loss than expected.

   (Authors note that direct mail fundraising usually results in a net loss on first contact with potential donors, with subsequent renewals providing a positive net cash flow.)

TIME TRENDS IN FINDINGS: None.

DESIGN ISSUES: None noted.

REPLICABILITY: Replicable.

GENERALIZABILITY: The experiment tested propositions in economic theory on charitable giving. Seed-money results appear robust and generally applicable; refund results might not be repeated in other tests. Attitudes toward the particular charity are likely to influence outcomes. The researchers note that this experiment had a high response rate and yielded substantially more in revenue than an experiment for a different type of charity conducted two weeks earlier with another 3,000 people from the same target population.

FUNDING SOURCE: University of Central Florida.

TREATMENT ADMINISTRATORS: John A. List, University of Maryland and David Lucking-Reiley, University of Arizona.

EVALUATORS: John A. List, University of Maryland and David Lucking-Reiley, University of Arizona.

ENABLING LEGISLATION: None.

INFORMATION SOURCE: John A. List and David Lucking-Reiley, "The Effects of Seed Money and Refunds on Charitable Giving: Experimental Evidence from a University Capital Campaign," *Journal of Political Economy* 110(2002, 1).

PUBLIC-USE ACCESS TO DATA: Available by writing to David Lucking-Reiley, Department of Economics, University of Arizona, 401CC McClelland Hall, Tucson, Arizona 85721.

Employee Monitoring

SUMMARY: This quasi-experimental demonstration, conducted from 1993 to 1994, tested the effects of employee monitoring on telephone solicitation employees at a small sample of sites. Subjects were followed for 14 months.

COST: We have no information about cost.

TIME FRAME: Pre-experiment period, April 1993–May 1994, audit data collected. Demonstration period, June 1 to roughly mid-October 1994; audit data collected throughout. Survey data collected from four treatment sites in week 60.

TREATMENTS TESTED: Subjects were employed by a marketing firm conducting telephone solicitation for nonprofit organizations. Employees were salaried but received an incentive bonus for every pledge reported above their targets. (On average they received four genuine pledges per hour.) Managers at the company's central headquarters checked a proportion of reported pledges with callbacks. Suspicious bad calls (SBC) (i.e., donations reported by employees that were found to be invalid) were deducted from the individual's incentive pay. Callback frequency (audit rate) was not reported to the employees, but any employee making false pledge reports could infer it from the SBC deductions at the end of the week.

An audit rate of 25 percent held at all sites for weeks 1–25 of the demonstration, 15 percent in weeks 26–44, and 10 percent in weeks 45–59. In week 60, the control site audit rate fell to 5 percent; at treatment sites, the actual audit rate was 25 percent, but the managers suppressed some SBCs to create the following "observed" audit rates:

Site	Weeks 60–67	Weeks 68–74
A	2%	0%
B	5%	2%
C	10%	10%
D	0%	10%

OUTCOMES OF INTEREST: Number and rate of SBCs (defined above).

SAMPLE SIZE: 16 sites; 4 treatments, 12 controls.

TARGET POPULATION: Telephone solicitation employees.

NUMBER OF TREATMENT GROUPS: Five (with one control group).

NUMBER AND LOCATION OF SITES: Sixteen.

RESEARCH COMPONENTS:
- Process analysis: Survey of employee attitudes.
- Impact analysis: OLS regression and grouped logit.
- Benefit–cost analysis: None reported.

MAJOR FINDINGS:
1. The mean ratio of SBCs to good calls across all sites in all weeks was .02. OLS of this ratio on "observed" audit rates *by site, including control sites,* from the previous week yielded the following:

Audit rate in week $t-1$	Increase (above the average) in SBC/ good call ratio	Adjusted t-statistic
0%	.031	2.69
2%	.006	2.81
5%	.019	6.29
10%	.002	1.36
15%	.002	1.20

2. Thus, the greatest increase in suspicious bad calls is at the zero observed monitoring level. Relative size and statistical significance of effects at the higher levels of audit rate are sensitive to specification.
3. Analysis at the individual worker level (with a separate dummy variable for each worker) shows that for each suppressed SBC in the previous week, the number of SBCs in the current week rose by about 0.7. The authors find that the number of SBCs was higher among employees with negative attitudes about the employer, especially among those who thought it would be difficult to find a different job if they were laid off.
4. More than half of all employees had zero SBCs.

TIME TRENDS IN FINDINGS: None noted.

DESIGN ISSUES: While the treatment sites were randomized, individual employee assignment was not.

Hence differences across sites arising from local labor markets are not controlled.

REPLICABILITY: Replicable.

GENERALIZABILITY: The experiment was limited to one company. The authors note that this organization's "small employment rents, short expected tenures, and brief one-time interactions with customers" might not encourage high levels of intrinsic motivation. They believe, however, that there is a general trade-off between monitoring employees who are inclined to "shirk" and alienating workers not so inclined.

FUNDING SOURCE: None acknowledged.

TREATMENT ADMINISTRATOR: Anonymous firm.

EVALUATORS: Daniel Nagin and James Rebitzer, Carnegie-Mellon and Case Western Reserve Universities.

INFORMATION SOURCE: Daniel S. Nagin, James B. Rebitzer, Seth Sanders, and Lowell J. Taylor, "Monitoring, Motivation, and Management: The Determinants of Opportunistic Behavior in a Field Experiment," *American Economic Review* 92(2002): 850–61.

PUBLIC-USE ACCESS TO DATA: We have no information about a public-use file.

Lifelong Learning Demonstration

SUMMARY: This demonstration, conducted from March 1995 to June 1998, tested the effects of a targeted direct-mail campaign promoting continuing education and training and the Federal Direct Student Loan program on a large sample of mature incumbent workers. Participants were followed for two years.

COST: Administrative, $570,000; evaluation, $2,200,000.

TIME FRAME: Demonstration period, November 1995–March 1997; data collected through December 1998; final report, June 1999.

TREATMENTS TESTED: Members of the treatment group were sent two mailings that gave limited information on available programs and allowed them to call a toll-free number or return a postcard to obtain further information from any of 12 participating educational institutions. These institutions, which included two- and four-year public and private colleges, as well as private career schools, provided interested workers with information regarding available education and training opportunities and the Federal Direct Student Loan as a source of financial aid. Controls did not receive any mailings.

OUTCOMES OF INTEREST: (1) School enrollment; (2) Number of credits earned; and (3) Receipt and amount of financial aid.

SAMPLE SIZE: Total, 208,400; treatments, 104,668; controls, 103,732. A subsample of 3,601 was interviewed in a follow-up survey.

TARGET POPULATION: Mature incumbent workers, defined as individuals 25 or older, who were currently employed and who earned more than $1,105 per quarter in at least six of the last eight quarters prior to sample selection.

NUMBER OF TREATMENT GROUPS: Two (with one control group).

NUMBER AND LOCATION OF SITES: One—Greater Baltimore, Maryland.

RESEARCH COMPONENTS:

- Process analysis: Interviews were conducted with admissions and financial aid staff at participating institutions, and focus groups were conducted with public information campaign respondents. The findings indicate that implementation occurred as planned.
- Impact analysis: OLS and logistic regression.
- Benefit–cost analysis: Not conducted.

MAJOR FINDINGS: The treatment had no significant impact on educational outcomes or the use of financial aid, either at participating institutions or at non-participating institutions in the area. Participants reported that the intervention was not strong enough to encourage pursuit of further information. They also indicated that significant barriers (such as time, information, and cost) kept them from following up.

TIME TRENDS IN FINDINGS: None reported.

DESIGN ISSUES: None apparent.

REPLICABILITY: Replicable.

GENERALIZABILITY: There are no apparent limits to generalizability.

FUNDING SOURCE: U.S. Department of Labor.

TREATMENT ADMINISTRATOR: U.S. Department of Labor. Key personnel: Jon Messenger.

EVALUATOR: Abt Associates, Inc. Key personnel: Steve Bell, Larry Buron, Larry Orr, Satyendra Patrabansh, Michelle Wood, and Terri Thompson. Subcontracted with Cygnet Associates and Battelle Memorial Institute.

INFORMATION SOURCE: Larry Buron, Larry Orr, and Satyendra Patrabansh, *The Lifelong Learning Demonstration: Final Evaluation Report on the Experimental Site,* Abt Associates, Inc., June 1999.

PUBLIC-USE ACCESS TO DATA: Data available at the Upjohn Institute Employment Data Research Center web site, http://www.upjohninst.org/erdc/index.htm.

Retirement Plan Decisions Experiment

SUMMARY: This demonstration, conducted from August 2000 to October 2001, tested the effects of an attendance incentive and informal information dissemination about employee retirement plans on a large sample of a non-faculty university staff. Subjects were followed for 12 months.

COST: Approximately $20,000.

TIME FRAME: Demonstration period, August 2000–October 2001. Data were collected in three waves: September 2000, March 2001, and October 2001.

TREATMENTS TESTED: All non-faculty employees of a large university were invited to a retirement plan fair. However, prior to the fair, randomly selected employees of randomly selected departments received an inducement of $20 for fair attendance. Thus, there were two levels of random assignment:

1. Treatment departments versus control departments: some employees of treatment departments received the $20 offer. No employees of control departments received the offer.
2. Experimental employees versus control employees: Within treatment departments, experimental employees received the offer and control employees did not receive the offer.

OUTCOMES OF INTEREST: Fair attendance and retirement-plan enrollment (treatment vs. control departments; treatment vs. control employees).

SAMPLE SIZE: Total departments, 220; treatments, 110; controls, 110. Total employees, 6,211: experimental employees in treated departments, 2,039; control employees in treated departments, 2,129; employees of control departments, 2,043.

TARGET POPULATION: Non-faculty employees of a large university.

NUMBER OF TREATMENT GROUPS: Three: treatment department experimental employees, treatment department control employees, and control department employees.

NUMBER AND LOCATION OF SITES: One (unnamed large university).

RESEARCH COMPONENTS:
- Process analysis: Conducted.
- Impact analysis: Regression.
- Benefit–cost analysis: Not conducted.

MAJOR FINDINGS:

1. The offer had a strong effect on attendance: in treatment departments, 21.4 percent of individuals attended the fair. In control departments, fewer than 5 percent of individuals attended the fair.

2. The fair attendance rate for treatment department experimentals was 28 percent versus 15.1 percent for treatment department controls. The difference in the attendance rate between treatment department controls and control department employees was 10.2 percent (highly significant).

3. At 4.5 months, employees in treatment departments were significantly more likely to be enrolled in a retirement plan than employees in control departments (4.9 percent versus 4 percent), a 24 percent increase in the enrollment rate. However, the difference between treatment department experimentals and treatment department controls was an insignificant 1.26 percentage point.

4. At 11 months, there was a significant 1.4 percentage point difference in retirement plan enrollment rates between treatment departments and control departments.

5. The incentive scheme had a large effect on fair participation of treatment departments, as well as a significant effect on enrollment in a retirement plan. However, within treated departments, there is no difference in enrollment between those who received a letter and the $20 inducement for fair attendance and those who did not.

TIME TRENDS IN FINDINGS: None.

DESIGN ISSUES: None apparent.

REPLICABILITY: Replicable.

GENERALIZABILITY: Findings are derived from a large sample and appear to have internal validity. The target population—non-faculty employees of a university—is a mixture of blue-collar and generally lower-salary white-collar employees whose retirement savings behavior is of great interest. The single-employer/single-site character of the experiment might limit the generalizability of the specific parameter estimates.

FUNDING SOURCE: National Science Foundation.

TREATMENT ADMINISTRATOR: Benefits office of the unnamed university.

EVALUATORS: Esther Duflo, Massachusetts Institute of Technology and National Bureau of Economic Research, and Emmanuel Saez, Harvard University and National Bureau of Economic Research.

ENABLING LEGISLATION: None.

INFORMATION SOURCE: Esther Duflo and Emmanuel Saez, *The Role of Information in Social Interactions in Retirement Plan Decisions: Evidence from a Randomized Experiment,* Working paper 02-23, March 21, 2002.

PUBLIC-USE ACCESS TO DATA: Not available (confidential university benefits records).

5

Low-Income Households (General)

New Jersey Income Maintenance Experiment

SUMMARY: This demonstration, conducted from 1968 to 1972, tested the effects of negative income tax (NIT) at various levels of income guarantee and tax rate on a large sample of low-income households. Subjects were followed for three years.

COST: $7.8 million (1971); research and administrative costs only, $5.4 million.

TIME FRAME: Demonstration period, August 1968–September 1972; data collected, same period; final report, December 1973 (to Department of Health, Education, and Welfare).

TREATMENTS TESTED: The negative income tax consists of an income guarantee accompanied by a tax rate on other income. Eight combinations of guarantees and tax rates (partial reductions in payments as other income rises) were tested: (1) 50 percent (of poverty level) guarantee, 30 percent tax rate (on earnings); (2) 50 percent guarantee, 50 percent tax rate; (3) 75 percent guarantee, 30 percent tax rate; (4) 75 percent guarantee, 50 percent tax rate; (5) 75 percent guarantee, 70 percent tax rate; (6) 100 percent guarantee, 50 percent tax rate; (7) 100 percent guarantee, 70 percent tax rate; and (8) 125 percent guarantee, 50 percent tax rate.

All families were paid for participating in interviews; controls otherwise received only a small monthly fee for mailing in a postcard with current address.

OUTCOMES OF INTEREST: (1) Reduction in work effort and (2) Lifestyle changes.

SAMPLE SIZE: By payment group: (1) 46; (2) 76; (3) 100; (4) 117; (5) 85; (6) 77; (7) 86; and (8) 138. Total experimentals, 725; controls, 632.

TARGET POPULATION: Households with one nondisabled male between 18 and 59 years old, at least one other member, and a total family income not exceeding 150 percent of the poverty level.

NUMBER OF TREATMENT GROUPS: Nine (with one control group).

NUMBER AND LOCATION OF SITES: Four— Trenton, Jersey City, and Paterson, New Jersey; and Scranton, Pennsylvania.

RESEARCH COMPONENTS:

▪ Process analysis: Two important questions considered in the project report (volume 2, chapter 11; and volume 3, chapter 12) were the extent to which experimentals understood program parameters and the extent to which state welfare changes contaminated the results. In January 1969, New Jersey instituted an Aid to Families with Dependent Children (AFDC) plan allowing benefits to two-parent families (AFDC-UP), and until July 1971 these benefits were among the highest in the country. Thus, differences between controls and experimentals did not have the same meaning that they were expected to have; low-guarantee experimentals found that AFDC-UP offered higher payments.

▪ Impact analysis: Conducted by regression.

▪ Benefit–cost analysis: Not conducted.

MAJOR FINDINGS:

1. Average nominal payments rose 6.4 percent over three years, but real payments decreased because the cost of living rose between 11 percent and 17 percent. Unemployment also increased during this period, from 4.4 percent to 7.1 percent (weighted average).

2. The number of hours of employment reduction for male family heads was not statistically significant. However, a significant experimental elasticity was calculated; the experimental variable was defined as the ratio of the guarantee to the net wage. At the experimental mean, the regression results imply that experimentals worked 1–1.6 percent fewer hours than controls.

3. Experimental wives worked 23 percent fewer hours per week than controls; differences in labor-force participation were highly significant. Differences were concentrated in white families. However, the reduction was from a fairly small base, since large families with non-working wives dominated the sample.

4. Teenagers enrolled in the treatment were (for the medium-generosity plans) 25 to 50 percent more likely to complete high school than controls, other things being equal. Specifically, the higher the tax rate, the more likely was high-school completion; but the higher the guarantee rate, the less likely was high-school completion. Experimental status was associated with lower teen earnings.

5. Observed lifestyle changes were mostly negligible. Some increase in the ownership of both homes and major appliances by experimentals over controls was noted.

TIME TRENDS IN FINDINGS: Findings reported are typically for the middle period of the experiment because of the learning curve expected in the early quarters and the possibility of gaming behavior in the later quarters.

DESIGN ISSUES:

1. Although assignments to treatment were random, given pretreatment income, they were not independent of income. Sample designs resulted in experimentals with very low incomes being directed mainly into low-guarantee programs or into the control group. Families at 100 percent of the poverty level or less are overrepresented in the control group.

2. The evaluators suggest that the long-term labor-supply effects of a permanent national program might differ from the effects of a three-year experiment. The biases are believed to be the following: effects on adult males are underestimated, and effects on adult females and young people are overestimated.

3. No attempt was made to verify the income reports, so a misreporting of earnings may have occurred. Simultaneous, inappropriate receipts of both experimental transfers and AFDC payments are known to have occurred in several cases.

4. Experimentals also reported income more frequently than controls and are believed to have learned to report gross rather than net income

more quickly; as a consequence, early months of data from all sites are contaminated for purposes of comparison.

5. The sample is truncated by total family income, rather than by the income of husbands, leading to a substantial underrepresentation of working wives.

6. A set of anomalous results for black households (essentially, male hours of labor) appears to be a product of unexpected labor-supply reductions in the black control group. Labor hours changed little among experimentals but fell sharply among controls.

7. Reported results are for intact families. Experimental families were slightly more likely to break up.

REPLICABILITY: Designed for replicability through the Internal Revenue Service.

GENERALIZABILITY:

1. Blacks were deliberately overrepresented in this study, to test the culture-of-poverty hypothesis.

2. Large numbers of Puerto Ricans in the sample do not correspond to their numbers in the United States as a whole.

3. The sample was drawn from areas of concentrated poverty; poor people (principally white) living in nonpoor areas were not represented.

4. The concentration of findings on two-parent families limits current applicability.

5. The more generous treatment plans would have potentially applied to large numbers of nonpoor families, especially to nonpoor two-earner families, who were excluded from the sample design. Thus, potential negative income tax effects on the behavior of married women who work full-time cannot be estimated from this experiment.

FUNDING SOURCE: Office of Economic Opportunity. Key personnel: James Lyday and Robert Levine.

TREATMENT ADMINISTRATOR: Mathematica Policy Research. Key personnel: David N. Kershaw.

EVALUATORS: Institute for Research on Poverty, University of Wisconsin–Madison, and Mathematica Policy Research. Key personnel: Harold Watts.

ENABLING LEGISLATION: None. The experiment did require an Internal Revenue Service ruling that program payments were not taxable income.

POLICY EFFECTS: The Nixon administration's proposed Family Assistance Plan was related in concept to this experiment. A preliminary data report, which showed the negative income tax as increasing work effort, was prepared for hearings on this proposal. Dennis Coyle and Aaron Wildavsky's "Social Experimentation in the Face of Formidable Fables," in *Lessons from the Income Maintenance Experiments,* edited by Alicia H. Munnell (Federal Reserve Bank of Boston and Brookings Institution, 1987), stated that this finding was cited by NIT supporters such as then-Senator Fred Harris and House Ways and Means Committee (former) Chairman Wilbur Mills.

INFORMATION SOURCES: David N. Kershaw and Jerilyn Fair, *The New Jersey Income-Maintenance Experiment, Volume 1: Operations, Surveys and Administration;* Harold Watts and Albert W. Rees, ed., *Volume 2: Labor-Supply Responses;* Kershaw and Fair, *Volume 3: Expenditures, Health, and Social Behavior;* and Kershaw and Fair, *The Quality of the Evidence,* Academic Press, 1976, 1977.

PUBLIC-USE ACCESS TO DATA: We have no information about a public-use file for this demonstration.

Rural Income Maintenance Experiment

SUMMARY: This demonstration, conducted from 1970 to 1972, tested the effects of a negative income tax (at various levels of income guarantee and tax rate) on a medium-sized sample of rural low-income families. Subjects were followed for three years.

COST: $6.1 million (1971); research and administrative costs only, $3.7 million.

TIME FRAME: Demonstration period, 1970–72; data collected, 1969–73; final report, 1976.

TREATMENTS TESTED: Five negative income tax plans were tested: (1) a 50 percent of poverty line income guarantee with a 50 percent tax rate; (2) a 75 percent guarantee with 30 percent tax rate; (3) a 75 percent guarantee with 50 percent tax rate; (4) a 75 percent guarantee with a 70 percent tax rate; and (5) a 100 percent guarantee with a 50 percent tax rate.

Controls only received small payments for survey participation.

OUTCOMES OF INTEREST: (1) Work behavior; (2) Health, school, and other effects on poor children; and (3) Savings and consumption behavior.

SAMPLE SIZE: Although formally there were 809 families in the experiment, only 587 were families headed by working-age males whose behavior was of primary interest. (The others were female-headed families or those with an aged male head.) Of the 587, 318 were controls. Of the 269 experimentals, the allocation among the negative income tax (NIT) plans listed above was (1) 37, (2) 67, (3) 75, (4) 30, and (5) 60.

TARGET POPULATION: Rural, low-income families, in which the male head was 18–58 years of age and not disabled.

NUMBER OF TREATMENT GROUPS: Six (with one control group).

NUMBER AND LOCATION OF SITES: Three—Duplin County, North Carolina; and Pocahontas and Calhoun counties, Iowa.

RESEARCH COMPONENTS:
- Process analysis: Conducted. Fifty-four percent did not know their guarantee within 20 percent; 23 percent did not know earnings were taxed; 8 percent thought the tax on earnings was 100 percent. Attrition bias was studied and found not likely to affect results.
- Impact analysis: Conducted with sophisticated regression techniques.
- Benefit–cost analysis: Not conducted.

MAJOR FINDINGS:
1. For a weighted average of the sample, family income of experimentals compared to controls fell by 13 percent, family wage income by 13 percent, and family wage hours by 13 percent. The employment rate of wives fell 28 percent and that of dependents by 46 percent; changes in male work efforts were small (a 1 percent reduction in hours).
2. "An income maintenance scheme which must administer a program to the self-employed will entail more cost from income reporting problems than cost from disincentives in labor supply" (Primus, in Palmer and Pechman 1978).
3. Among renters, the probability of buying a home was .06 percent higher among experimentals than among controls.

TIME TRENDS IN FINDINGS: Farm incomes among experimental families dropped sharply in the last year of the experiment, possibly a deferral of sales of storable commodities to an untaxed year.

DESIGN ISSUES:
1. "The sample size was probably too small to provide definitive answers to some of the relevant policy questions" (Bawden and Harrar, in Palmer and Pechman 1978).
2. More than one-fourth of the households in the sample had no relevance to the question under investigation because they were female-headed or aged. This is one of the reasons that many effects of a large magnitude but no statistical significance were found.
3. The heterogeneity of responses was much larger than the planners expected. Investigators found it necessary to disaggregate the sample of 587 by state, race, farm, and nonfarm. After they had performed this disaggregation, most effects were statistically insignificant, though some were large in size. Effects that were significant were just as often anomalous (coefficient had the wrong sign) as not.
4. As a group, farmers substantially under-reported their incomes and probably manipulated loopholes in the payment rules.

REPLICABILITY: Replicable, but the elaborate carry-over-income concept developed for the self-employed is complex.

GENERALIZABILITY: Intended for generalization to rural poverty populations in the South and Midwest. Generalizations based on this experiment would be suspect, however, because of the small sample size and the internal heterogeneity of the sample groups.

FUNDING SOURCES: The Ford Foundation and the Office of Economic Opportunity; subsequently, Assistant Secretary for Planning and Evaluation, U.S. Department of Health, Education, and Welfare. Key personnel: Larry L. Orr for HEW.

TREATMENT ADMINISTRATOR: Institute for Research on Poverty, University of Wisconsin–Madison. Key personnel: D. Lee Bawden, Philip Salisbury, and William S. Harrar.

EVALUATOR: Institute for Research on Poverty. Key personnel: D. Lee Bawden.

ENABLING LEGISLATION: None.

INFORMATION SOURCES: U.S. Department of Health, Education, and Welfare, *Summary Report: Rural Income Maintenance Experiment,* November 1976; John L. Palmer and Joseph A. Pechman, eds., *Welfare in Rural Areas: the North Carolina-Iowa Income Maintenance Experiment,* Brookings Institution, 1978. A six-volume, unpublished final report is on file at the Institute for Research on Poverty, University of Wisconsin–Madison.

PUBLIC-USE ACCESS TO DATA: We have no information about a public-use file for this demonstration.

Seattle-Denver Income Maintenance Experiment

SUMMARY: This demonstration, conducted from 1970 to 1977, tested the effects of both a negative income tax (NIT) (at various levels of income guarantee and tax rate) and subsidized vocational counseling and training on a large sample of low-income families. Subjects were followed for up to five years.

COST: $77.5 million (1975); research and administrative costs only, $57.1 million.

TIME FRAME: Demonstration period, October 1970–August 1977; data collected, October 1970–December 1978; final report, May 1983.

TREATMENTS TESTED: There were two types of treatment. One consisted of a negative income tax plan. In this plan, some treatments had a declining rate of benefit reductions (tax rate) as nonprogram income rose. The other treatment was a subsidy to vocational counseling and training.

1. Financial treatments (income guarantee as a percentage of poverty line, tax rate, and change in tax rate for each $1,000 of nonprogram income): (1) 95 percent, 50 percent, 0 percent; (2) 95 percent, 70 percent, 0 percent; (3) 95 percent, 70 percent, −2.5 percent; (4) 95 percent, 80 percent, −2.5 percent; (5) 120 percent, 50 percent, 0 percent; (6) 120 percent, 70 percent, 0 percent; (7) 120 percent, 70 percent, −2.5 percent; (8) 120 percent, 80 percent, −2.5 percent; (9) 140 percent, 50 percent, 0 percent; (10) 140 percent, 70 percent, 0 percent; and (11) 140 percent, 80 percent, −2.5 percent. Experimental subjects were randomly assigned to programs that were either three or five years in duration in order to test for effects owing solely to the temporary nature of the experiment. (Ninety-three Denver families were switched without warning into a 20-year plan in the third year of their NIT participation for the same reason.)

2. Counseling/training treatments: (1) Control, no treatment; (2) Free, nondirective, vocational counseling of a standardized form provided by staffs of the community colleges; (3) Free counseling plus a 50 percent tuition subsidy for either career-related training or enrollment at any institution the student wished to attend; (4) Free counseling plus a 100 percent tuition subsidy.

Pure controls received neither the financial nor the counseling treatments.

OUTCOMES OF INTEREST: (1) Effects on labor supply; (2) Marital stability; and (3) Other lifestyle changes.

SAMPLE SIZE: Two presentations of sample sizes are relevant. Numbers are households.

1. Financial/counseling
   Control/control: 1,041
   Control/experimental: 1,012
   Experimental/control: 946
   Experimental/experimental: 1,801
2. Second-year (after attrition) distribution of experimentals by the financial treatments listed above in "Treatments Tested":
   (1) 346, (2) 184, (3) 204, (4) 163, (5) 237, (6) 278, (7) 241, (8) 224, (9) 93, (10) 193, and (11) 251. There were 1,715 controls in the second year.

TARGET POPULATION: Families who met all of the following requirements: (1) either married couples (with or without children) or single heads of households with at least one dependent child younger than 18; (2) either earning less than $9,000 per year (if just one worker in the family) or less than $11,000 per year (if two workers), in 1971 dollars; and (3) either includes a nondisabled husband, 18 to 58 years old, or a single, nondisabled, female head of household, 18 to 58.

NUMBER OF TREATMENT GROUPS: Forty-eight (with one pure control group).

NUMBER AND LOCATION OF SITES: Two—Seattle, Washington; and Denver, Colorado.

RESEARCH COMPONENTS:
■ Process analysis: Investigators extensively tested the verbally articulated degree of comprehension of the program among experimentals, but did not find that the degree of comprehension was associated with any labor-supply effects. They also tested for Hawthorne effects by paying half of the Denver controls to report income on a monthly basis, as all experimentals had to do, and did not find any significant effects in interview data between reporting and nonreporting controls. The investigators did not, however, expect the surprising results for the counseling program, which are discussed below, and no interview data with experimentals or counselors are available to explain them.
■ Impact analysis: Conducted with sophisticated regression techniques.
■ Benefit–cost analysis: Not conducted.

MAJOR FINDINGS:

1. According to the project report, "A universal NIT program without any work requirements in which the mean guarantee level [is] about 110 percent of the poverty level and the mean tax rate is about 50 percent would lead to significant reductions in virtually every major dimension of labor supply."

   Mean second-year experimental response across 11 NIT treatments compared with the control mean:

Variable	Husbands (%)	Wives (%)	Female heads (%)
Annual hours of work	−9	−21	−14
Annual weeks worked	−7	−19	−14
Probability of working at all during the year	−7	−19	−11
Earnings	−8	−20	−16

The major effect of the experiment was not a marginal reduction in hours worked per week but a lengthening of unemployment spells. Among youths, the experimental effect was a major reduction in hours worked. The project report stated: "There is no evidence that the work effort reduction is accompanied by any increase in school attendance."

LOW-INCOME HOUSEHOLDS (GENERAL) 199

2. The counseling-only program did not significantly increase years of schooling. The 50 percent subsidy had significant effects on schooling only among female heads. The 100 percent subsidy significantly affected the schooling of husbands, wives, and female heads: the average increase in schooling was .11 to .27 years.

3. The counseling/training programs had a negative impact, as anticipated, on hours and earnings in the first year. The unexpected finding was that the impact on wages and earnings of the counseling/training programs, where significant, was negative in the subsequent years of the program and in the postexperimental data, for both husbands and wives. Single-female heads consistently showed a positive earnings and wage effect from the counseling-only program (not necessarily significant), but the same generally consistent (not necessarily significant) negative impact from the subsidy programs as husbands and wives. The effects appear independent of participation in the NIT experiment.

   Disaggregated regressions suggest that the negative effect of counseling was largest for the following groups: (1) Husbands who were, before the experiment, unemployed or members of families with normal incomes below $5,000, and who were eligible for counseling only—they earned $1,600 to $1,700 less than their control counterparts in the year following the five-year experiment; (2) Wives who, before the experiment, were employed; they earned $500 to $650 less than their control counterparts under all three counseling/training plans in the year following the five-year experiment.

   The investigators believed that non-directive counseling led some husbands and some wives to enter into unduly ambitious academic programs, which they either did not finish or could not use to good effect in the labor market.

4. According to the project report, "The negative income tax . . . plans tested in SIME/DIME dramatically increased the rates at which marriages dissolved among white and black couples, and decreased the rate at which Chicano women entered marriages." Twenty-eight percent of marriages among black experimentals broke up in the first three years, compared with 21 percent among black controls; 20 percent of marriages among white experimentals broke up, compared with 15 percent of marriages among white controls. (These results are controversial; see "Time Trends" and "Design Issues.")

5. The project report stated: "SIME/DIME probably did not affect the health of participants"; "no experimental effect on psychological distress"; and "SIME/DIME . . . does not appear to have had an effect on infant health status." For married women, the experiment seems to have raised fertility rates among Chicanos, to have had no effect on blacks, and to have had inconsistent effects on whites. Effects on the fertility rate of single women were insignificant.

   Other reported findings: "SIME/DIME resulted in increased debt"; "white migrants receiving experimental treatments were more likely than controls to move to destinations with a better climate"; and "SIME/DIME had little effect on intracity residential mobility and no effect on integration."

TIME TRENDS IN FINDINGS:

1. Labor-supply effects tended to grow after the first year; to diminish as the program neared an end; and vanished in the year after NIT program-eligibility expired. An exception was single-female heads, who continued to work fewer hours after the program ended.

2. The marital-stability findings are controversial; one reason for this is that the experimental/control differential at an early point in the treatment was greater than the subsequent differential.

DESIGN ISSUES:

1. A portion of the labor-supply difference between experimentals and controls comes from

a systematic underreporting of earnings and hours by experimentals. This problem was known at the time of the final report and does not appear to substantively change the report's conclusions.

2. Marital-dissolution effects are strongest in the first two years of the experiment and seem to be sensitive to the presence of the counseling experiment, the preexperimental income, and the guarantee level. The higher the guarantee level, the lower the experimental effect. Since assignment to guarantee levels was not independent of preexperimental income (low-income families were more likely to be assigned to low-guarantee plans), the marital-dissolution findings may be in part an artifact of the assignment system. The marital-dissolution findings remain controversial, partly because of the time trend noted above, because dissolution is a relatively rare event, and because attrition bias in the controls is difficult to evaluate. But there is no evidence that the NIT increased the stability of marriages, which was the expected outcome.

3. Much of the benefit to be derived from the extremely large sample was dissipated by the excessive number of treatments. Cell sizes are then reduced further by race, marital status, previous employment history, and so on.

REPLICABILITY: NIT plans were designed for national replication. The methodology of the counseling program is summarized in the final report and does not appear very different from vocational-counseling programs in common use.

GENERALIZABILITY:
1. Findings may have been affected by the serious recession in Seattle in the early 1970s. The experiment was extended to Denver, a city with low unemployment rates, for this reason.
2. All participants were, at least initially, residents of low-income communities. SIME/DIME does not address the effects of an NIT on dispersed poverty, as opposed to concentrated poverty.

3. Other studies in the 1970s reported very low rates of return from schooling in the labor market. The counseling/training findings may be specific to that era.
4. SIME/DIME is the best available source for income-substitution and leisure-substitution parameter estimates that can be applied to project the effects of national policy proposals affecting low-income people.

FUNDING SOURCES: U.S. Department of Health, Education, and Welfare; and U.S. Department of Health and Human Services (HHS), Office of the Assistant Secretary for Planning and Evaluation. Key personnel: Joseph Corbett.

TREATMENT ADMINISTRATORS: Mathematica Policy Research (MPR) for payments and data collection; Seattle Central Community College and Community College of Denver for vocational counseling. Key personnel: David N. Kershaw (deceased) and Gary Christopherson for MPR, N. John Andersen for Seattle CCC.

EVALUATOR: SRI International. Key personnel: Robert G. Spiegelman.

ENABLING LEGISLATION: None.

POLICY EFFECTS: The experiment data were used to estimate labor-supply parameters that, in turn, were incorporated into microsimulation models. These models were used to cost out and predict the future effects of various welfare-reform proposals under consideration by policymakers. In addition, the marital-stability findings were widely circulated at a time when policymakers were seriously considering NIT-based welfare reform.

INFORMATION SOURCES: SRI International, *Final Report of the Seattle-Denver Income Experiment, Volume 1: Design and Results*; Gary Christopherson, *Volume 2: Administration,* SRI International, May 1983.

U.S. Department of Health and Human Services, Assistant Secretary for Planning and Evaluation, Office of Income Security Policy, *Overview of the Seattle-Denver Income Maintenance*

Experiment Final Report, Summary Report, May 1983.

Robert G. Spiegelman, K. E. Yaeger, Michael C. Keeley, Philip K. Robins, Richard W. West, Nancy Brandon Tuma, Arden R. Hall, Yoram Weiss, Fred Dong, and Lyle P. Groeneveld, articles in *Journal of Human Resources,* Fall 1980.

PUBLIC-USE ACCESS TO DATA: We have no information about a public-use file for this demonstration.

Gary Income Maintenance Experiment

SUMMARY: This demonstration, conducted from 1971 to 1974, tested the effects of a negative income tax (at various levels of income guarantee and tax rate) on a large sample of low-income African-American families. Subjects were followed for three years.

COST: $20.3 million (1973); research and administrative costs only, $14.8 million.

TIME FRAME: Demonstration period, 1971–74; data collected, 1971–74; final report, 1980.

TREATMENTS TESTED: Four combinations of guarantee and tax rate were tested: (1) 75 percent of poverty level guarantee, 40 percent tax rate; (2) 75 percent and 60 percent; (3) 100 percent and 40 percent; and (4) 100 percent and 60 percent. (Experimental treatments with social service access and day care were terminated early for lack of participation.)

Controls did not receive income maintenance payments.

OUTCOMES OF INTEREST: (1) Employment; (2) Schooling; (3) Infant mortality and morbidity; (4) Educational achievement; and (5) Housing consumption.

SAMPLE SIZE: Total experimentals, 1,028; controls, 771. Experimentals by treatment plans: (1) 313, (2) 314, (3) 203, and (4) 198.

TARGET POPULATION: Black families with at least one child under the age of 18.

NUMBER OF TREATMENT GROUPS: Five (with one control group).

NUMBER AND LOCATION OF SITES: One—Gary, Indiana.

RESEARCH COMPONENTS:
■ Process analysis: Conducted.
■ Impact analysis: Conducted through sophisticated regression and other analytical models.
■ Benefit–cost analysis: Not conducted.

MAJOR FINDINGS:
1. Statistically significant reductions in the employment rate of experimental husbands (2.7 percent to 4.9 percent) and female heads of households (25.8 percent to 26.8 percent), compared with controls. No significant effects on married women's labor-market participation.
2. No significant effects of the experimental tax rate were found.
3. Experimental teenagers were significantly more likely to continue schooling and less likely to enter the labor market than controls. The effect was concentrated in lower-income experimentals.
4. Significantly fewer low-birth-weight infants were born to high-risk experimental mothers than to high-risk control mothers. The high-risk group consists of women who smoke and had previously given birth within 16 months or less. The experimental effect is consistently greater the higher the risk.
5. Experimental children in grades four through six had significantly better reading achievement than the controls. The effect is limited to the third or fourth year after enrollment in the experiment. No effects were found for students in grades seven through ten.
6. Experimentals increased their rent payments about 4.3 percent above the rent levels paid by controls. Six percent of the net increase in income was spent on rent; an elasticity of rent payment with respect to income of about 0.3 was calculated. There was a small, statistically significant increase in the probability of an

experimental buying a home compared with a control.

TIME TRENDS IN FINDINGS: As noted above.

DESIGN ISSUES:

1. The Gary experiment also intended to test two other treatments. One of these was a social service access worker (a personal ombudsman); the other was the expansion of day-care services in one neighborhood. Both services were undersubscribed and subsequently discontinued.
2. The Gary findings are probably highly conditional on the specific Gary labor market. See "Generalizability."
3. The Gary sample was not selected on the basis of total family income and therefore does not have the truncation bias found in the New Jersey and rural experiments against two-earner families.

REPLICABILITY: Replicable.

GENERALIZABILITY: The Gary labor market at the time of the experiment was heavily dominated by the steel industry, which offered almost exclusively full-time jobs. Opportunities for part-time work and for other marginal adjustments in hours such as overtime and moonlighting appear to have been rare. This probably explains (a) the absence of responses to the experimental tax rate, (b) the absence of experimental responses among wives, and (c) the relatively high experimental responses among married men and female heads of households. Instead of a marginal choice about how many hours to work, many in the sample probably faced a discrete choice about whether to be employed full time or not at all.

FUNDING SOURCE: U.S. Department of Health, Education, and Welfare, Assistant Secretary for Planning and Evaluation. Key personnel: Joseph Corbett.

TREATMENT ADMINISTRATOR: Indiana University. Key personnel: Kenneth C. Kehrer and John Maiolo.

EVALUATORS: Indiana University and Mathematica Policy Research. Key personnel: Kenneth C. Kehrer and Andy Anderson.

ENABLING LEGISLATION: None.

POLICY EFFECTS: The results of all four income maintenance experiments were discussed in the context of the Carter welfare reform proposal, which did not pass Congress.

INFORMATION SOURCES: Kenneth C. Kehrer, Barbara H. Kehrer, Charles M. Wolin, Rebecca A. Maynard, Richard J. Murnane, Robert A. Moffitt, John F. McDonald, Stanley P. Stephenson Jr., and Richard L. Kaluzny, 1979, five articles in *Journal of Human Resources*, 14 (4, Fall): 431–506; Kenneth C. Kehrer, John F. McDonald, and Robert A. Moffitt, *Final Report of the Gary Income Maintenance Experiment: Labor Supply*, Mathematica Policy Research, 1980.

PUBLIC-USE ACCESS TO DATA: We have no information about a public-use file for this experiment.

Housing Allowance Demand Experiment

SUMMARY: This demonstration, conducted from 1973 to 1977, tested the effects of two forms of housing subsidy on a large sample of low-income renter households. Subjects were followed for two years.

COST: $31.2 million (1976); payments, $3.6 million; administration, $2 million; research and monitoring, $25.6 million.

TIME FRAME: Demonstration period, April 1973–February 1977; data collected, April 1973–February 1976; final report, June 1980.

TREATMENTS TESTED: The principal treatments tested were payments to households based on a "housing gap" and payments based on a percentage of the rent.

For the housing gap treatment, a panel of experts at each site estimated the cost of housing meeting certain standards in modest neighborhoods in that city. This number was C^*. Payment (P) was based on the formula $P = dC^* - bY$, where Y was disposable income less $300 per year for each working member of the family, and d and b were experimental parameters (higher d and lower b imply a greater generosity). Treatments also varied in housing requirements: a minimum rent requirement, set at 0.7 or 0.9 of C^*, or a minimum standards requirement, under which occupied units would be inspected for conformity with standards for health and safety. Households living in units that did not meet the standard specified for the treatment to which they were assigned could not receive payments.

Treatment	d	b	Housing requirement
1	1	.15	Minimum standards
2	1.2	.25	Minimum standards
3	1	.25	Minimum standards
4	0.8	.25	Minimum standards
5	1	.35	Minimum standards
6	1.2	.25	Minimum rent (.7)
7	1	.25	Minimum rent (.7)
8	0.8	.25	Minimum rent (.7)
9	1.2	.25	Minimum rent (.9)
10	1	.25	Minimum rent (.9)
11	0.8	.25	Minimum rent (.9)
12	1	.25	No requirements

In the percentage-of-rent treatments, payment (P) was determined by the formula $P = aR$, where R is rent and a is a program parameter. There were no housing requirements.

Treatment	a
13	.6
14	.5
15	.4
16	.3
17	.2

Controls were paid $10 a month for filling out a monthly form and $25 for periodic interviews. Experimentals were not paid for interviews. The payment system for experimentals lasted three years. Information was collected for two years.

OUTCOMES OF INTEREST: (1) Enrollment; (2) Rate of participation (actual receipt of payment); and (3) Effects on housing expenditures, quality, and residential segregation.

SAMPLE SIZE: The number of households invited to enroll either as experimentals or as controls was 3,600 (1,800 in each city). The numbers actually enrolling (not necessarily receiving payments) were recorded for the initial enrollment offer and two years later. The difference between the second and third columns below is attrition, which in this experiment was of independent interest.

Treatment	Initial	Two years
1	212	181
2	91	63
3	133	77
4	128	82
5	137	75
6	85	58
7	132	89
8	124	79
9	88	60
10	145	88
11	137	78
12	145	103
13	66	49
14	235	190
15	265	179
16	258	176
17	176	111
Controls	950	603

A different way of presenting the second-year numbers is as follows:

Treatment type	Phoenix	Pittsburgh	Total
Housing gap (minimum standards)	174	204	378
Housing gap (minimum rent)	207	245	452
Housing gap (no requirements)	40	63	103
Percentage of rent	298	407	705
Controls	282	321	603
Total	**1,001**	**1,240**	**2,241**

TARGET POPULATION: Renter households with two or more people, meeting the following tests: (1) disposable income less than four times the C^* figure for households of that size in that city; (2) assets of under $5,000 (under $10,000 if 62 or older); (3) either two or more related persons of any age or with a household head who was handicapped, disabled, 62 or older, or displaced by an urban renewal project; (4) resident in unsubsidized housing—public housing tenants were only eligible if they moved.

NUMBER OF TREATMENT GROUPS: Nineteen (with two control groups).

NUMBER AND LOCATION OF SITES: Two—Pittsburgh, Pennsylvania; and Phoenix, Arizona.

RESEARCH COMPONENTS:

- Process analysis: Obtained reasons for refusal to enroll, choice not to participate, and condition of initial housing units.
- Impact analysis: By comparison of means and various response-surface estimation techniques.
- Benefit–cost analysis: A relative cost-effectiveness study was conducted comparing costs of housing allowances and public subsidies to housing construction.

MAJOR FINDINGS:

1. Many families refused to enroll (see table 1), a finding that is important in estimating the costs of a national program; refusal to enroll did not seem related to the variables in the experiment, but to a disinterest in receiving public assistance. Many of those who did enroll did not participate (receive a payment), and this non-participation was substantially affected by the stringency of the housing requirements, the household's race, and the relative availability of housing meeting the minimum requirements (which varied between the sites). Participation is stated as the percentage of those enrolling (all of whom were eligible for immediate payments on income grounds) who received one or more payments.

   Higher payments increased participation. At an average monthly payment level of $43, one-fourth of all renters who had to meet housing requirements participated; at twice that level, twice as many participated.

Table 1 Enrollment and Participation Ratio (percent)

Treatment/Site	Enrollment	Participation
No housing requirements Percentage of rent		
Pittsburgh	82	100
Phoenix	87	100
Housing gap		
Pittsburgh	78	100
Phoenix	90	100
Minimum standards		
Pittsburgh	75	40
Phoenix	84	54
Minimum rent (.7)		
Pittsburgh	74	81
Phoenix	82	74
Minimum rent (.9)		
Pittsburgh	73	58
Phoenix	81	54

2. Table 2 shows the estimated experimental effect on housing expenditures and services among households meeting the eligibility requirements two years after enrollment (services measured with "hedonic index" based on characteristics of the housing unit).

Table 2 Changes in Expenditures and Services (percent)

Site/Treatment	Change in expenditures	Change in expenditures as share of payment	Change in services
Pittsburgh			
No restriction	2.6	5.7	3.4
Percentage of rent	8.0	14.0	3.0
Minimum rent (.7)	−3.6	−7.8	0
Minimum rent (.9)	8.5*	23.3	0.9
Minimum standards	4.3	8.6	3.1
Phoenix			
No restriction	16.0*	19.0	12.6*
Percentage of rent	8.0	23.7	−1.0
Minimum rent (.7)	15.7	25.5	11.0*
Minimum rent (.9)	28.4*	41.3	18.9*
Minimum standards	16.2*	27.4	10.2*

* Statistically significant difference from zero.

3. The impact on housing expenditures in the housing gap treatments differs according to whether the household initially occupied a unit satisfying the minimum standards at enrollment (see table 3). Of those whose units did not, most who ended up participating satisfied the requirements by moving. The numbers of those who moved and the distances they moved were such that the impact on residential segregation would have been negligible.

Table 3 Effects on Housing Expenditures (percent)

	Estimated Experimental Effects		
Site/Treatment	Change in expenditures	As share of payment	Change in services
Pittsburgh			
Satisfactory			
Minimum rent (.7)	2.4	5.7	0.5
Minimum rent (.9)	4.6	13.7	−0.7
Minimum standards	1.1	2.3	0.8
Unsatisfactory			
Minimum rent (.7)	8.7	15.4	−0.9
Minimum rent (.9)	15.8*	38.8	3.1
Minimum standards	7.5*	14.2	5.6
Phoenix			
Satisfactory			
Minimum rent (.7)	−1.2	−2.7	2.5
Minimum rent (.9)	7.4	15.4	4.2
Minimum standards	−0.7	−2.1	8.2*
Unsatisfactory			
Minimum rent (.7)	42.0*	41.7	20.2*
Minimum rent (.9)	42.6*	50.0	26.0*
Minimum standards	23.6*	32.8	10.5*

* Statistically significant difference from zero.

4. Estimates of income elasticity ranged from .29 to .34 in Pittsburgh and from .26 to .44 in Phoenix. Estimates of price elasticity ranged from −.11 to −.18 in Pittsburgh and from −.23 to −.24 in Phoenix.

TIME TRENDS IN FINDINGS: Only two years of data were collected.

DESIGN ISSUES:

1. Payments guaranteed over three years may not induce the same behavioral changes as a permanent program. For instance, a family that would need to move in order to receive payments might also realize that a second move would be necessary at the close of the experiment because they could not afford the unit the experiment had subsidized.

2. The measure of housing services, a hedonic quality index, was developed for this experiment and is not completely satisfactory.

3. The least-generous plans were assigned only to very low-income members of the sample, because otherwise many enrolled persons would have been eligible only for very small payments or none at all, limiting their benefits from participating in the experiment. However, this tends to confound the treatment effect with the characteristics of households assigned to the treatment.

4. "The price elasticity per se is unlikely to be of much use in designing a housing-allowance program. A percent-of-rent formula offers such attractive opportunities for mutually beneficial fraud on the part of landlords and renters that [it] is hard to imagine it ever being implemented" (Harvey Rosen, in Bradbury and Downs 1981).

5. Most households change their housing units infrequently, and the effect of the experiment will occur with some lag; however, the timing of the lag is not known with certainty and requires modeling assumptions.

REPLICABILITY: Replicable.

GENERALIZABILITY:

1. The single most important finding from this experiment is that the income elasticity of housing demand among low-income people is quite low. This result was confirmed in the "Supply" portion of the Experimental Housing Allowance Program (EHAP). One implication of this finding is that housing allowances would

not result in large inflation of rents. Another implication is that in meeting the objectives of a housing-allowance program, there is a trade-off between assisting large numbers of people and improving the quality of the existing housing stock.

2. Results of this experiment and the other components of the EHAP were used by the Urban Institute to project total costs of housing-allowance programs using microsimulation techniques.

FUNDING SOURCE: U.S. Department of Housing and Urban Development, Assistant Secretary for Policy Development and Research. Key personnel: Jerry Fitts and Terrence Connell.

TREATMENT ADMINISTRATOR: Abt Associates. Key personnel: Ellen Bakeman.

EVALUATOR: Abt Associates. Key personnel: Stephen D. Kennedy and James Wallace.

ENABLING LEGISLATION: Housing and Urban Development Act of 1970, title V; amended in 1974 for additional funding. The experiment was one component of the EHAP, which included a supply experiment and an administrative agency experiment; these other components were not random-assignment treatment evaluations.

INFORMATION SOURCES: A large number of unpublished reports are available from Abt Associates. The following are published sources: Raymond J. Struyk and Mark Bendick Jr., eds., *Housing Vouchers for the Poor: Lessons from a National Experiment,* Urban Institute, 1981.

Katharine L. Bradbury and Anthony Downs, eds., *Do Housing Allowances Work?* Brookings Institution, 1981.

U.S. Department of Housing and Urban Development (HUD), *Experimental Housing Allowance Program: A 1979 Report of Findings,* 1979.

HUD, *The Experimental Housing Allowance Program: Conclusions,* 1980.

PUBLIC-USE ACCESS TO DATA: No public-use file exists.

Freestanding Housing Voucher Demonstration

SUMMARY: This demonstration, conducted from 1985 to 1988, tested the effects of housing vouchers with an experimental payment formula on a large sample of low-income families. Subjects were followed for one year.

COST: Roughly $3 million (1987).

TIME FRAME: Demonstration period, April 1985–September 1988; data collected, same period; final report, May 1990.

TREATMENTS TESTED:

1. Certificate program (controls). The preexisting Section 8 program paid a monthly stipend to the landlord on behalf of a tenant living in privately owned existing housing. The amount of the payment was the difference between the rent (plus certain scheduled utility allowances, if they are not included in the rent) and the tenant's contribution, which was essentially 30 percent of adjusted income. Tenants must live in a unit meeting housing quality criteria set by the Department of Housing and Urban Development (HUD), and the rent must be less than or equal to the local fair market rent (FMR) (set by HUD) and judged "reasonable" by the Public Housing Agency (PHA). From the time of enrollment into the program, tenants have two to four months to find acceptable housing under the program.

2. Housing voucher program (experimentals). This treatment differed from the existing program in the payment formula; the housing unit still had to meet HUD quality criteria. The housing assistance payment is equal to $P - .3Y$, where P is the local rental payment standard, initially set equal to the FMR and Y is income. Thus, the PHA no longer sets a ceiling on gross rent. The tenant has, on the one hand, an incentive to obtain housing at a lower cost than the FMR, if it can be found, and, on the other hand, the option to secure housing that costs

more than the PHA would allow under the certificate program.

OUTCOMES OF INTEREST: (1) Success rate (percentage of those enrolled who find acceptable units and become recipients); (2) Rent payments; (3) Rent burdens; (4) Program payments; and (5) Administrative costs.

SAMPLE SIZE: 12,390, evenly divided. Many analyses, however, used subsamples of about 4,500.

TARGET POPULATION: Lower-income families certified as eligible for Section 8 who live in large urban areas.

NUMBER OF TREATMENT GROUPS: Two (with one control group).

NUMBER AND LOCATION OF SITES: Nineteen—Atlanta, Georgia; Boston, Massachusetts; Buffalo and New York City, New York; Cleveland and Dayton, Ohio; Los Angeles, Oakland, and San Diego, California; Minneapolis, Minnesota; Montgomery County, Maryland; New Haven, Connecticut; Omaha, Nebraska; Pittsburgh, Pennsylvania; St. Petersburg, Florida; San Antonio, Texas; Seattle, Washington; and state-wide public housing authorities in Michigan and New Jersey.

RESEARCH COMPONENTS:
- Process analysis: Not conducted.
- Impact analysis: Comparison of means and ordinary least squares (OLS).
- Benefit–cost analysis: Not conducted.

MAJOR FINDINGS:
Regressions on housing quality appear to show that roughly half of the higher rent payments under the voucher plan go to improved housing quality, with the other half increasing landlord income (see table).

TIME TRENDS IN FINDINGS: As noted in table under "Rent burden" and "Monthly assistance payments."

DESIGN ISSUES: The most obvious problem is the absence of a process analysis. The voucher program changes the budget constraint of the Public Housing Agency as well as that of the subjects, and the absence of a process analysis means that we do not know how the PHAs responded or whether their responses affected the experimental results.

REPLICABILITY: Replicable.

GENERALIZABILITY: Designed for generalizability to the population of large urban PHAs. Two special caveats are (1) the sample is drawn from applicants to the current Section 8 program and (2) more important, many experimentals were renting from landlords with substantial Section 8 experience. If the entire program changed over to vouchers, landlord rent-setting behavior might change as well. PHAs may have effective monopoly power with respect to a group of Section 8 landlords that tenants shopping individually cannot match.

FUNDING SOURCE: HUD, Office of Policy Development and Research. Key personnel: David Einhorn.

TREATMENT ADMINISTRATORS: Nineteen Public Housing Agencies (PHAs).

Major Findings

	Voucher	Certificate
Success rate, overall (%)	64.6	61.0*
Success rate when P = FMR (PHAs had some discretion about changing P)	64.4	59.5*
Total rent paid by recipients	$463	$437*
Rent burden as percentage of income:		
At initial payment	34	31
At annual recertification	35	31*
Among recipients who		
Did not move	28	31**
Moved	39	31
Monthly assistance payments, overall average	$310	$293**
Initial assistance payment	307	287**
Payment at recertification	304	298
Administrative cost per slot:		
Initial eligibility	$579	$598
Annual ongoing	257	261

* Difference significant at .05 percent level.
** Difference significant at .01 percent level.

EVALUATOR: Abt Associates. Key personnel: Mireille L. Leger and Stephen D. Kennedy.

ENABLING LEGISLATION: Housing and Urban/Rural Recovery Act of 1983, PL 98–181.

POLICY EFFECTS: The results of the experiment show that vouchers are both more flexible (serve more people) and more expensive (for recipients and the government alike) than certificates; there was no clear-cut winner. While the experiment was being conducted, the Reagan and Bush administrations took various incremental actions to increase the number of vouchers through administrative action. Subsequent policy has adopted a hybrid of the certificate and voucher designs, which allows tenants to choose gross rents above the payment standard at their own expense but does not pay greater subsidy if the rent is below the payment standard.

INFORMATION SOURCE: Mireille L. Leger and Stephen D. Kennedy, *Final Comprehensive Report of the Freestanding Housing Voucher Demonstration,* 2 vols., U.S. Department of Housing and Urban Development, Office of Policy Development and Research, May 1990.

PUBLIC-USE ACCESS TO DATA: HUD possesses the data, but has not created a public-use file.

National Job Training Partnership Act (JTPA) Study

SUMMARY: This demonstration, conducted from 1987 to 1991, tested the effects of the Job Training Partnership Act (JTPA) Title II program's employment and training services on a large sample of economically disadvantaged adults and youths. Subjects were followed for 30 months.

COST: Total evaluation costs were approximately $23 million from 1986 to 1994.

TIME FRAME: Enrollment period, November 1987–September 1989; data collected through December 1991; final report, 1994.

TREATMENTS TESTED: Access to Title II-A services under the JTPA. Participants were divided into three groups by local staff according to which services were deemed appropriate. They were then randomly assigned to a treatment or control group for each service strategy. Specific services varied widely across sites, but could include the following:

Specific program service	Classroom training group	On-the-job training (OJT)/ job search assistance group	Other activities group
Classroom training in occupational skills	Yes	No	Yes
OJT	No	Yes	Yes
Job search assistance	Yes	Yes	Yes
Basic education	Yes	Yes	Yes
Work experience	Yes	Yes	Yes
Miscellaneous	Yes	Yes	Yes

The control group was not allowed to receive services for 18 months.

OUTCOMES OF INTEREST: (1) Earnings; (2) Employment; (3) Welfare receipt; and (4) Attainment of educational credentials and occupational competencies.

SAMPLE SIZE: Full experimental sample, 20,602. Classroom training group, 7,090; on-the-job training group, 7,412; other activities group, 6,100. Sample size includes both treatment and control group members. On average, 68 percent of sample members were randomly assigned to treatment groups.

TARGET POPULATION: Eligible JTPA Title II adults and out-of-school youth. The study focused on four subgroups: adult women, adult men, female out-of-school youths, and male out-of-school youths.

NUMBER OF TREATMENT GROUPS: Two groups (with one control) in each of the three service subgroups.

NUMBER AND LOCATION OF SITES: Sixteen—Butte, Montana; Cedar Rapids, Iowa; Coosa Valley, Georgia; Corpus Christi, Texas; Decatur, Illinois; Fort Wayne, Indiana; Heartland, Florida; Jackson, Mississippi; Jersey City, New Jersey; Larimer County, Colorado; Marion, Ohio; Oakland, California; northwest Minnesota; Omaha, Nebraska; Providence, Rhode Island; and Springfield, Missouri;

RESEARCH COMPONENTS:

▨ Process analysis: Examined sample and participant characteristics, patterns of enrollment and participation, and the random assignment process.

▨ Impact analysis: Conducted using multiple regression.

▨ Benefit–cost analysis: Conducted.

MAJOR FINDINGS: Because the control group was able to receive employment and training services from non-JTPA providers, impacts reflect the incremental effect of JTPA services beyond what sample members could have accomplished without access to JTPA. Impacts were estimated separately by subgroups: adult men; adult women; female youth; male youth, nonarrestees; and male youth, arrestees.

Adults

1. The treatment group received significantly ($p = .01$) more employment and training services than did the control group; on average, men received 169 more hours of service and women received 136 more hours.

2. For adult women, average earnings over the 30-month period following random assignment were $1,176 (9.6 percent) greater for the treatment group than the control group. This is significant at the .01 level. For men, earnings were $978 (5.3 percent) greater for the treatment group. This is significant at the .10 level.

3. Earnings gains came more from an increase in hours worked (an employment effect), than from an increase in average hourly earnings (a wage effect). This was especially true for women.

4. JTPA resulted in a substantial and statistically significant impact on the attainment of a high school credential (diploma or equivalent) for adult female dropouts. The findings for adult males were also positive, although not statistically significant.

5. The greatest earnings impact was estimated for women in the OJT/JST and other activities subgroups.

6. For adult women, there was no significant program impact on Aid to Families with Dependent Children (AFDC) or food stamp receipt. For men, there was a small but significant *increase* in AFDC receipt for the treatment group.

Youth

1. JTPA resulted in a significant increase in the amount of employment and training services for all categories of youth. (Female youth in the treatment group received, on average, 182 more hours than their control group counterparts; male youth nonarrestees received 175 more hours; and male youth arrestees received 127 more hours.)

2. There were no significant treatment–control group differences for the quarterly earnings of female youths and male youth nonarrestees. For male youth arrestees, there was a great discrepancy between survey data and data using unemployment wage records. The former suggests significantly lower earnings for the treatment group. The wage record data suggest no significant treatment–control group difference.

3. JTPA had a significant positive effect on the attainment of a high school credential for female youths (7.7 percent more treatment group females, compared to their control group

counterparts, had a high school diploma or GED 30 months after random assignment), but not for male youths.

4. No significant treatment–control group differences were found for welfare receipts for male or female youths.

TIME TRENDS IN FINDINGS: There was a gradual increase in the earnings of all adult participants—treatment and control group—over time.

DESIGN ISSUES:

1. Impacts are reported per assignee, but 34 percent of women and 38 percent of men in the treatment group did not actually receive JTPA services. Therefore, this reflects the impact of *offering* JTPA services, rather than receiving them. Impacts per participant were not estimated directly from the experimental data, but were inferred using an extension of the data. The estimates reported above are in terms of impact per assignee, rather than per participant.

2. Site participation was voluntary. Service delivery areas (SDAs) were not mandated to participate. Many were reluctant because they feared political fallout from random assignment, they found the design too complex, or they could not obtain agreement among all local participants.

3. Because JTPA program staff often recommend more than one program service for an applicant, the study was designed to measure impacts of clusters of program services, not single services in isolation, such as classroom training, on-the-job training, or job search assistance.

4. Formal agreements with some of the SDAs excluded certain small groups of applicants from the study (and from random assignment) owing to logistical reasons, recruitment difficulties, and/or the nonvoluntary nature of certain applications.

REPLICABILITY: Replicable.

GENERALIZABILITY: Site selection was not a probability sample, and the SDAs that volunteered to be part of the study may differ from the national population in unobservable ways. They differed in two observable ways: (1) No large, central cities were included owing to the decentralized nature of service in these locations, and (2) The study sites tended to emphasize classroom training and job search assistance more, and OJT and miscellaneous services less, than their counterparts nationally.

FUNDING SOURCE: U.S. Department of Labor. Key personnel: David Lah.

TREATMENT ADMINISTRATORS: Local service delivery areas (SDAs) in the 16 sites. See Orr et al. (1996: ix–x) for key personnel at each site.

EVALUATORS: Manpower Demonstration Research Corporation (MDRC) and Abt Associates. Key personnel: Larry Orr and Howard Bloom for Abt and Judith Gueron for MDRC.

ENABLING LEGISLATION: Job Training Partnership Act of 1982.

POLICY EFFECTS: Following the results and recommendations of the National JTPA study, the U.S. Department of Labor proposed a 47 percent reduction in funding for Title II-C (the program for out-of-school youth) and a modest increase for Title II-A (the adult program). Congress responded by applying a large reduction for Title II-C and allowing the 11 percent increase in funding for the adult program.

INFORMATION SOURCES: Larry L. Orr, Howard S. Bloom, Stephen H. Bell, Fred Doolittle, Winston Lin, and George Cave, *Does Training for the Disadvantaged Work? Evidence from the National JTPA Study,* Urban Institute Press, 1996.

Larry L. Orr, Howard S. Bloom, Stephen H. Bell, Winston Lin, George Cave, and Fred Doolittle, *The National JTPA Study: Impacts, Benefits, and Costs of Title II-A,* Abt Associates, 1994.

Fred Doolittle and Linda Traeger, *Implementing the National JTPA Study,* Manpower Demonstration Research Corporation, 1990.

PUBLIC-USE ACCESS TO DATA: Available through U.S. Department of Labor.

Emergency Food and Homelessness Intervention Project

SUMMARY: This demonstration, conducted between 1988 and 1990, tested the effects of in-home case management on a medium-sized sample of low-income families. Subjects were followed for six months.

COST: The evaluation cost approximately $5,000, but there was a considerable amount of donated services. Service cost per treatment family was estimated at $700.

TIME FRAME: October 1988–October 1990.

TREATMENTS TESTED: Home-based case management that included assessment, agency referrals (for counseling or health services), home visits, and transportation. The control group received food and referrals with no additional follow-up.

OUTCOMES OF INTEREST: (1) Employment; (2) Income; and (3) Welfare receipt.

SAMPLE SIZE: Total, 394; treatments, 199; controls, 195.

TARGET POPULATION: Low-income families requesting emergency food.

NUMBER OF TREATMENT GROUPS: Two (with one control group).

NUMBER AND LOCATION OF SITES: One—Lincoln, Nebraska.

RESEARCH COMPONENTS:
- Process analysis: Conducted with attention given to intake and assignment procedures, attrition, and follow-up.
- Impact analysis: Conducted—comparison of means.
- Benefit–cost analysis: Conducted.

MAJOR FINDINGS:
1. The project group had significantly higher wages compared to the control group. Average wages for project group increased $192 per month; control group wages increased $124 per month.
2. Treatment group families had a significantly greater reduction (9.3 percent) in their level of poverty compared with the control families.
3. Repeat requests for emergency food and the risk of homelessness were unaffected by the intervention.
4. Families with a male head of household and no evidence of alcohol or drug abuse showed the greatest gains.
5. Benefit–cost analysis suggests that the rate of return on investment of case management was excellent (intervention cost per family, per year, $696; income gain in wages by project families over control families, $812 per year).

TIME TRENDS IN FINDINGS: No long-term follow-up was done.

DESIGN ISSUES: The evaluators felt that the instrument used to assess outcomes such as risk of homelessness and self-sufficiency was unduly subjective and made some outcomes difficult to measure.

REPLICABILITY: Replicable. The Lincoln Action Program has replicated this model in other agency projects.

GENERALIZABILITY: The project was voluntary and offered only to those families requesting emergency food. This may represent a distinct subgroup of low-income families. Few participant demographic characteristics are reported, so the representativeness of the sample (e.g., age, ethnicity, and educational level are not given) cannot be judged.

FUNDING SOURCE: U.S. Department of Health and Human Services (HHS), Administration for Children and Families, Office of Community Services, Demonstration Partnership Program. Key personnel: Anna Guidery.

TREATMENT ADMINISTRATOR: Lincoln Action Program. Key personnel: Beatty Brasch and Mary Barry-Magsamen.

EVALUATOR: SRI Gallup. Key personnel: Gary Hoeltke.

ENABLING LEGISLATION: Demonstration Partnership Program under Section 408 of the Human Services Reauthorization Act of 1986, as amended.

INFORMATION SOURCE: U.S. Department of Health and Human Services, *Demonstration Partnership Programs: Summaries and Findings, FY 1988 and 1989,* 1991.

PUBLIC-USE ACCESS TO DATA: Available through Office of Community Services, DHHS.

Operation INC (Incubator for New Companies)

SUMMARY: This demonstration, conducted from 1989 to 1991, tested the effects of a self-employment and small business startup program on a small sample of low-income individuals. Subjects were followed for one year.

COST: $250,000 in loan funds was made available. We have no information on administrative or research costs.

TIME FRAME: Demonstration period, May 1989–October 1991; data collected, same period.

TREATMENTS TESTED: Subjects in the treatment group received training, if necessary, and technical assistance to develop a business plan and apply for a bank loan. They were advised and monitored after receipt of the loan to ensure that payments were made and their business operated according to plan. Operation INC was able to set aside $20,000 in loan guarantee funds for some experimentals. Control subjects did not receive any of INC's services.

OUTCOME OF INTEREST: Startup and maintenance of a struggling business.

SAMPLE SIZE: Total, 78; treatments, 40; controls, 38.

TARGET POPULATION: (1) Displaced farmers and farm workers; (2) Struggling farmers; (3) Single female heads of families, particularly those in public or assisted housing; (4) Owners of existing struggling service-providing businesses who met the Community Service Block Grant poverty guidelines.

NUMBER OF TREATMENT GROUPS: Two (with one control group).

NUMBER AND LOCATION OF SITES: One—Appleton, Missouri.

RESEARCH COMPONENTS:
▪ Process analysis: Questionnaires were utilized to evaluate program implementation and operational performance.
▪ Impact analysis: Comparison of means.
▪ Benefit–cost analysis: None conducted.

MAJOR FINDINGS:
1. Of treatment subjects, 38 percent received funding for business endeavors, compared with 33 percent of controls contacted. The remaining controls, 53 percent of the original 38 individuals in the control group, were not contacted and were assumed to not be in business.
2. At the conclusion of the study, 86.6 percent of the treatment businesses were still operational. One treatment subject closed her business and paid off her loan. Inclusion of this subject as a success increases the percentage of successful endeavors to 93.4.
3. The program had considerable trouble attaining loans from banks as they deemed the subjects to be too risky. Many subjects were either unable or unwilling to put up collateral for their loans. The limited loan guarantee funds restricted the number of attainable loans.

TIME TRENDS IN FINDINGS: None reported.

DESIGN ISSUES:
1. The sample was very small and the control group suffered from a 53 percent attrition rate.

2. Participants on welfare risked losing their benefits if they experienced any increase in assets as a result of participating in the program. INC was never able to resolve this issue with the Missouri Division of Family Services.

REPLICABILITY: Replicable.

GENERALIZABILITY: The idiosyncratic target population, the small sample, and the attrition rate jointly suggest that the demonstration is not generalizable.

FUNDING SOURCE: U.S. Department of Health and Human Services, Administration for Children and Families, Office of Community Services.

TREATMENT ADMINISTRATOR: West Central Missouri Community Action Agency, Director Charles Braithwait.

EVALUATORS: John Wandless and Wayne Thomas, no listed affiliation.

ENABLING LEGISLATION: Demonstration Partnership Program, under section 508 of the Human Services Reauthorization Act of 1986, as amended.

INFORMATION SOURCE: U.S. Department of Health and Human Services, Administration for Children and Families, Office of Community Service, *"Operation INC (Incubator for New Companies)" Summary of Final Evaluation Findings from FY 1989,* Demonstration Partnership Program Projects, Monograph Series 100-89, Micro-Business and Self-Employment, June 10, 1992, pp. 200-1-1 to 200-1-16.

PUBLIC-USE ACCESS TO DATA: We have no information about a public-use file for this demonstration.

Project Hope (Head Start Opportunities for Parents through Employment)

SUMMARY: This demonstration, conducted from 1989 to 1991, tested the effects of intensive case management, life-skills, and job-readiness training on a small sample of parents with children enrolled in Head Start. Serious failures occurred in attempts to obtain follow-up information from the sample.

COST: $250,000, of which $25,000 was for evaluation.

TIME FRAME: October 1989–April 1991.

TREATMENTS TESTED: All treatment subjects received intensive case management and were enrolled in a six-week program of life-skills and job-readiness training. In addition, they could receive child care, tuition assistance, entrepreneur training workshops, or bus fare, depending on their needs and goals. Controls were referred to other agencies.

OUTCOMES OF INTEREST: (1) Employment and (2) Enrollment in training.

SAMPLE SIZE: Total, 140; treatments, 73; controls, 67.

TARGET POPULATION: Parents of children enrolled in Head Start (i.e., low-income—three-quarters received public assistance).

NUMBER OF TREATMENT GROUPS: Two (with one control group).

NUMBER AND LOCATION OF SITES: One—Columbus, Ohio.

RESEARCH COMPONENTS:
- Process analysis: Mailed questionnaire with telephone follow-up on employment, sense of progress, participation, and helpfulness of staff.
- Impact analysis: Telephone interview.
- Benefit–cost analysis: Not conducted.

MAJOR FINDINGS: Only 75 total subjects were reached (by telephone) for the impact analysis, and only 24 of them were willing to be interviewed. Among respondents, the 13 controls were more likely to be employed and were less likely to be in training or educational programs than the 11 experimentals.

TIME TRENDS IN FINDINGS: None.

DESIGN ISSUES:

1. The sample was too small at the outset. Furthermore, the evaluator only attempted to contact 116 of the 140 in the sample; of the 116, 55 telephone numbers were disconnected; of the 61 connections, only 24 responded.
2. The "formative analysis" (questionnaire followed up with a telephone call) shed less light on what actually happened in the program than the usual observation and record keeping for a process analysis would have.
3. The follow-up period for the evaluation was inadequate.

REPLICABILITY: There is always a question as to whether "intensive case management" is replicable. Presumably, there were written materials for the life-skills and job-readiness courses, but there was no treatment manual.

GENERALIZABILITY: There were no findings to generalize.

FUNDING SOURCE: U.S. Department of Health and Human Services (HHS), Administration for Children and Families, Office of Community Services, Demonstration Partnership Program.

TREATMENT ADMINISTRATOR: Columbus Metropolitan Area Community Action Organization. Key personnel: Robert Day.

EVALUATOR: Robert Ransom, Ohio State University.

ENABLING LEGISLATION: Demonstration Partnership Program under Section 408 of the Human Services Reauthorization Act of 1986, as amended.

INFORMATION SOURCE: U.S. Department of Health and Human Services, Office of Community Services, *Demonstration Partnership Programs Projects: Summary of Final Evaluation Findings from FY 1989,* Monograph Series 100-89: Case Management Family Intervention Models, 1992.

PUBLIC-USE ACCESS TO DATA: Available through HHS, Office of Community Services.

North Dakota Self-Reliance Program

SUMMARY: This demonstration tested the effects of case management on a small sample of low-income individuals. Subjects were followed for six months.

COST: Not available.

TIME FRAME: Demonstration period not clear from report.

TREATMENTS TESTED: Treatment subjects received emotional support from an individual case manager, who also provided referrals and guidance for the subject in receiving assistance from various service agencies. Controls did not receive any of the individual case management services.

OUTCOMES OF INTEREST: Effects on self-reliance, as measured by welfare program participation and coping with stress.

SAMPLE SIZE: Treatments, 61; controls, 71.

TARGET POPULATION: Individuals with an income below 125 percent of the federal poverty level and receiving one or more forms of direct assistance (fuel assistance, AFDC, or food stamps).

NUMBER OF TREATMENT GROUPS: Two (with one control group).

NUMBER AND LOCATION OF SITES: One—Southeastern North Dakota.

RESEARCH COMPONENTS:
 Process analysis: None conducted.
 Impact analysis: Comparison of means.
 Benefit–cost analysis: None conducted.

MAJOR FINDINGS:

1. Welfare program participation for treatment subjects was significantly lower than for controls, although there was no statistical difference in welfare program participation for treatment subjects at intake into the study and six months later.

2. Several measures of coping with stress, the Family Hardiness Index, the Social Support Index, the Family Strains Index, and the Family Stressors Index showed no significant difference between groups or within groups over the life of the experiment.

TIME TRENDS IN FINDINGS: None.

DESIGN ISSUES: The sample size was quite small and the experimental group had a high attrition rate because subjects moved out of state. The control group did not suffer the same high attrition rate.

REPLICABILITY: The design issue noted above suggests failed randomization, and that this study may not be replicable.

GENERALIZABILITY: The sample was too small to support generalizations, even within North Dakota.

FUNDING SOURCE: North Dakota Department of Human Services, Office of Intergovernmental Assistance.

TREATMENT ADMINISTRATOR: Southeastern North Dakota Community Action Agency. Key personnel: James Kappel, director.

EVALUATOR: North Dakota State University, Department of Child Development and Family Science, Fargo, North Dakota. (The document listed below does not report the name of any individual responsible for the evaluation. Current faculty of the Department of Child Development and Family Science did not recognize the study and were unable to identify the author.)

ENABLING LEGISLATION: None.

INFORMATION SOURCE: "North Dakota Self-Reliance Program. Southeastern North Dakota Community Action Agency (SENDCAA). Fargo, North Dakota," *Summaries and Findings FY 1987. Demonstration Partnership Program Projects,* U.S. Department of Health and Human Services, Family Support Administration, Office of Community Services, pp. V-1 through V-25.

PUBLIC-USE ACCESS TO DATA: None.

Wisconsin New Hope Project

SUMMARY: This demonstration, conducted from 1994 to 1997, tested a program of earnings supplements and other work supports in Wisconsin on a large sample of low-income individuals. Subjects were followed for two years.

COST: Net cost over two years, $5,499,936.

TIME FRAME: Demonstration period, July 1994–January 1997; data collected, same period.

TREATMENTS TESTED: Treatment group subjects were required to work a minimum of 30 hours weekly to qualify for New Hope benefits. These benefits included an earnings supplement designed to raise the worker's income to the poverty level; a health insurance plan, in which subjects would pay a co-pay amount determined on a sliding scale; and child care subsidies. Treatment subjects were also eligible for a subsidized community service job, if unsubsidized work could not be found after three weeks (if the subject was employed when enrolled in New Hope) or after eight weeks (if the subject was unemployed upon enrollment). Controls were not eligible for any New Hope benefits.

OUTCOMES OF INTEREST: (1) Effects on earnings; (2) Employment; (3) Welfare receipt; (4) Income; (5) Material hardship; (6) Emotional well-being; (7) Parent-child relations; (8) Child care use; and (9) Child outcomes.

SAMPLE SIZE: Total, 1,357; treatments, 678; controls, 679.

TARGET POPULATION: Families with income at or below 150 percent of the poverty level.

NUMBER OF TREATMENT GROUPS: Two (with one control group).

NUMBER AND LOCATION OF SITES: Two low-income neighborhoods in Milwaukee, Wisconsin.

RESEARCH COMPONENTS:

- Process analysis: Surveys and interviews were conducted to obtain staff and participant reactions.

- Impact analysis: Comparison at means.
- Benefit–cost analysis: Conducted from participant and social perspectives.

MAJOR FINDINGS:

1. Key findings are summarized in the table.

Outcome	Program group	Control group	Difference
Ever employed (%)			
Year 1	90.8	83.0	7.8
Year 2	86.8	81.3	5.5
Both years	95.5	90.0	5.5
Number of quarters employed			
Year 1	3.0	2.6	0.4
Year 2	2.9	2.7	0.2
Both years	5.9	5.4	0.5
Earnings ($)			
Year 1	6,833	6,250	583
EIC ($)			
Year 2	1,170	1,022	148
Earnings-related income ($)			
Year 1	8,210	7,130	1,080
Year 2	9,457	8,818	639
Both years	17,667	15,949	1,718
Earnings-related income plus AFDC and food stamps ($)			
Year 1	12,303	11,287	1,016
Both years	24,449	22,838	1,611
Earnings-related income above the federal poverty level (%)			
Year 1	26.1	20.6	5.5
Year 2	34.5	26.8	7.7
During the follow-up, reported any (%)			
Unmet medical needs	16.2	20.1	−3.9
Unmet dental needs	24.2	29.4	−5.2
Periods without health insurance	48.2	59.1	−10.9
Stressed much or all of the time	43.5	49.9	−6.4
Worried "quite a bit" or "a great deal about"			
Medical care	40.7	47.9	−7.2
Affordable housing	32.8	38.5	−5.7
General financial health	55.5	62.2	−6.7

Note: All impacts shown are statistically significant at the .01 or .05 level.

2. In the Child and Family Study (CFS), parents in the program group had lower minimal educational standards for their children, but this was the only statistically significant parent attitudinal finding. Findings varied depending on parent's employment status at random assignment and the child's gender.

3. In the CFS, 10 percent more program group children were ever in formal care, compared with control children. Program group children, aged 9–12, spent 0.4 more hours watching television on weekends than control group children, and 9.8 percent more program children attended clubs or youth groups.

4. There were few statistically significant impacts on children's education. In general, program boys were reported by teachers to be better students than control boys, with higher academic achievement, social skills, and behavioral skills. The only significant impact for program group girls was decreased emphasis on academics for girls age 9–12.

5. There were no significant trends on children's psychological well-being. However, teachers reported improved positive behavior for program group boys and increased problem behavior for program group girls.

6. New Hope produced approximately $4,613 in benefits for participants but incurred costs of approximately $7,232 to program funders and nonparticipants, resulting in a net cost to society of approximately $2,619 over the two-year period.

TIME TRENDS IN FINDINGS: Time trends are reported in a September 2003 report received too late for summary.

See MDRC web site at http://www.mdrc.org/publications/345/full.pdf.

DESIGN ISSUES:

1. Staff had difficulty explaining eligibility rules and requirements to participants. The supplement amount proved exceptionally confusing. As a result, many participants did not take advantage of New Hope's benefits, or at times did not receive their supplement check due to noncompliance.

2. New Hope staff had difficulty satisfactorily explaining to some participants why they were control group members. As a result, many controls discouraged other potentially eligible individuals from participating.

REPLICABILITY: Replicable.

GENERALIZABILITY: New Hope was conducted in the two areas of Milwaukee with the highest concentrations of poverty. These areas also have high concentrations of minority groups, particularly African Americans in the Northside location and Hispanics in the Southside location.

FUNDING SOURCES: The John D. and Catherine T. MacArthur Foundation, the Helen Bader Foundation, the Ford Foundation, the Wisconsin Department of Workforce Development, the William T. Grant Foundation, the U.S. Department of Health and Human Services, and the National Institute of Child Health and Human Development.

TREATMENT ADMINISTRATOR: New Hope offices in Milwaukee. Key personnel: Julie Kerksick, executive director.

EVALUATORS: Thomas Brock and Johannes Bos, Manpower Demonstration Research Corporation.

ENABLING LEGISLATION: None.

INFORMATION SOURCES: Thomas W. Brock, Fred Doolittle, Veronica Fellerath, and Michael Wiseman, *Creating New Hope: Implementation of a Program to Reduce Poverty and Reform Welfare,* MDRC, October 1997; Johannes M. Bos, Aletha C. Huston, Robert C. Granger, Greg J. Duncan, Thomas W. Brock, and Vonnie C. McLoyd, *New Hope for People with Low Incomes: Two-Year Results of a Program to Reduce Poverty and Reform Welfare,* MDRC, August 1999.

PUBLIC-USE ACCESS TO DATA: There is no public-use file at this time. However, check MDRC web site, http://www.mdrc.org/rsch_publicuse.htm.

Parents' Fair Share (PFS) Demonstration

SUMMARY: This demonstration, conducted between 1994 and 1996, tested the effects of employment services, training services, and modified child support enforcement on a large sample of low-income noncustodial fathers who were delinquent in child support payments. Subjects were followed for two years.

COST: Evaluation only, approximately $8.3 million.

TIME FRAME: Demonstration period, 1994–96; data collected, same period; final report, November 2001.

TREATMENTS TESTED:

Experimentals: Participation in PFS core services was mandatory. Fathers were expected to participate until they found a job and started paying child support. Those who failed to participate were referred back to the child support agency for follow-up, which sometimes led to an additional court hearing. Participants received employment and training services, peer support groups, voluntary mediation between parents, and modified (typically lowered) child support obligations.

Controls: Received no employment, training, or other services from the program, and child support orders were not changed.

OUTCOMES OF INTEREST: (1) Employment; (2) Earnings; and (3) Parental involvement with children.

SAMPLE SIZE: Total, 5,500; treatments, 2,641; controls, 2,859.

TARGET POPULATION: Low-income noncustodial fathers who were underemployed or unemployed, were not paying child support, and owed support for children who were receiving or had received welfare.

NUMBER OF TREATMENT GROUPS: Two (with one control group).

NUMBER AND LOCATION OF SITES: Seven—Dayton, Ohio; Grand Rapids, Michigan; Jacksonville, Florida; Los Angeles, California; Memphis, Tennessee; Springfield, Massachusetts; and Trenton, New Jersey.

RESEARCH COMPONENTS:

Process analysis: An analysis of participation was conducted. Most participants had limited education and had arrest records; many lived on the edge of poverty and had little or no access to public assistance or training and employment programs. They were difficult to reach.

Impact analysis: Regression adjusted.

Benefit–cost analysis: Not conducted.

MAJOR FINDINGS:

1. Participation in the demonstration increased employment and earnings for the least employable men, but not for the men who were able to find work on their own.
2. Treatment fathers' involvement with their children did not increase relative to controls' involvement.
3. Assignment to program slightly increased child support payments. Over the two-year program period; experimentals contributed $27 more than the controls.
4. Most sites had difficulty enrolling a sufficient number of fathers into the program. However,

the Dayton site achieved a high appearance rate because of a more effective outreach effort.

TIME TRENDS IN FINDINGS: Program impacts on finding and retaining jobs declined over time.

DESIGN ISSUES:

1. Smaller-than-expected enrollments affected program group activities and sites' funding streams.
2. Sites experienced interagency relationship difficulties.

REPLICABILITY: Replicable.

GENERALIZABILITY: The seven sites involved in the demonstration represented diverse settings.

FUNDING SOURCES: Linda Mellgren at the Office of Assistant Secretary at the U.S. Department of Health and Human Services, The Pew Charitable Foundation, the W. K. Kellogg Foundation, the Charles Stewart Mott Foundation, the U.S. Department of Agriculture, the Annie E. Casey Foundation, the U.S. Department of Labor, the Smith Richardson Foundation, the Ford Foundation, The McKnight Foundation, and the Northwest Area Foundation.

TREATMENT ADMINISTRATORS: Child support agencies, employment and training providers, and community-based service organizations.

EVALUATOR: Manpower Demonstration Research Corporation.

ENABLING LEGISLATION: None.

INFORMATION SOURCES: Cynthia Miller and Virginia Knox, *The Challenge of Helping Low-Income Fathers Support Their Children: Final Lessons from Parents' Fair Share,* 2001; Fred Knox, Cynthia Miller, and Sharon Rowser, *Building Opportunities, Enforcing Obligations: Implementation and Interim Impacts of Parents' Fair Share,* 1998.

PUBLIC-USE ACCESS TO DATA: Public-use file available. Contact Virginia Knox at MDRC.

EXPERIMENTS ONGOING AT PUBLICATION

Moving to Opportunity (MTO)

STARTING YEAR/YEAR FINAL REPORT EXPECTED: 1994/2009.

INFORMATION SOURCES: *Expanding Housing Choices for HUD-Assisted Families: First Biennial Report to Congress—Moving to Opportunity for Fair Housing Demonstration,* U.S. Department of Housing and Urban Development, Office of Policy Development and Research, April 1996.

John Goering, Joan Kraft, Judith Feins, Debra McInnis, Mary Joel Holin, and Huda Elhassan, *Moving to Opportunity for Fair Housing Demonstration Program: Current Status and Initial Findings,* U.S. Department of Housing and Urban Development, Office of Policy Development and Research, September 1999.

Jens Ludwig, Greg J. Duncan, and Paul Hirschfield, "Urban Poverty and Juvenile Crime: Evidence from a Randomized Housing-Mobility Experiment," *Quarterly Journal of Economics* (May 2001): 655–79.

Lawrence F. Katz, Jeffrey R. Kling, and Jeffrey B. Liebman, "Moving to Opportunity in Boston: Early Results of a Randomized Mobility Experiment," *Quarterly Journal of Economics* (May 2001): 607–54.

Mark Shroder, "Locational Constraint, Housing Counseling, and Successful Lease-up in a Randomized Housing Voucher Experiment," *Journal of Urban Economics* 51(2, March 2002): 315–38.

John Goering, Judith D. Feins, and Todd M. Richardson, "A Cross-Site Analysis of Initial Moving to Opportunity Demonstration Results," *Journal of Housing Research* 13(1, 2002): 1–30.

John Goering and Judith Feins, editors, *Choosing a Better Life: Evaluating the Moving to Opportunity Social Experiment,* Urban Institute Press, 2003.

Larry Orr, Judith D. Feins, Robin Jacob, Erik Beecroft, Lisa Sanbonmatsu, Lawrence F. Katz, Jeffrey B. Liebman, and Jeffrey R. Kling, *Moving to Opportunity Interim Impacts Evaluation,* U.S. Department of Housing and Urban Development, Office of Policy Development and Research, September 2003.

Other papers from the demonstration may be found at a special web site, http://www.wws.princeton.edu:80/~kling/mto/.

FUNDING SOURCES: The U.S. Department of Housing and Urban Development, Office of Policy Development and Research is the principal funder. Key personnel: John Goering, Todd Richardson, and Mark Shroder. Two other federal agencies and at least 10 private foundations have also contributed to the research.

EVALUATORS: Abt Associates and the National Bureau of Economic Research. Key personnel: Judith Feins and Larry Orr for Abt Associates, Jeffrey Kling for Princeton University, and Jens Ludwig for Georgetown University.

PRINCIPAL INTERVENTIONS: (1) Rental housing vouchers that may only be used in low-poverty (i.e., middle-class) neighborhoods, with search assistance to find appropriate units and (2) Rental housing vouchers without location restrictions.

TARGET POPULATION: Very low-income families with children who live in public housing or Section 8 project-based housing located in central-city neighborhoods with high concentrations of poverty in Baltimore, Boston, Chicago, Los Angeles, and New York City.

OUTCOMES OF INTEREST: The evaluation hopes to answer two questions: (1) What are the impacts of the treatment on families' location choices and on their housing and neighborhood conditions? and (2) What are the impacts of neighborhood conditions on the employment, income, educational achievement, health, crime, risky behavior, and social well-being of the demonstration families?

Bridges to Work

STARTING YEAR/YEAR FINAL REPORT EXPECTED: 1996/?

INFORMATION SOURCES: Beth Z. Palubinsky and Bernardine H. Watson, "Getting from Here to There: The Bridges to Work Demonstration First Report to the Field," Field Report Series, Public/Private Ventures, Philadelphia, spring 1997; Mark Elliott, Beth Palubinsky, and Joseph Tierney, *Overcoming Roadblocks on the Way to Work: Bridges to Work Field Report*, Field Report Series, Public/Private Ventures, summer 1999.

Fact sheets are located at http://www.huduser .org/publications/povsoc/btw/demo.html and http://www.huduser.org/publications/povsoc/btw/ fact.html.

FUNDING SOURCES: The demonstration was funded by HUD and the Department of Transportation.

PRINCIPAL INTERVENTIONS: Provides job placement, transportation, and supportive services such as child care and counseling in order to place participants in suburban jobs. This demonstration operated in five sites: Baltimore, Chicago, Denver, Milwaukee, and St. Louis.

TARGET POPULATION: Work-ready, low-income, inner-city residents.

OUTCOMES OF INTEREST: Earnings, employment, and dependence on government support.

NOTE: The final report is long overdue from Public/Private Ventures, the evaluator. It is known that the treatment failed to have significant impacts.

Chicago Housing Voucher Lottery

STARTING YEAR/YEAR FINAL REPORT EXPECTED: 1997/2004.

INFORMATION SOURCE: Brian Jacob and Jens Ludwig, "Neighborhood Effects on Low Income Families: Evidence from a Housing-Voucher Lottery in Chicago," paper presented at 2002–2003 HHS-ASPE/Census Bureau Research Development Grants Conference, Washington, D.C., Sept. 4–5.

FUNDING SOURCE: National Consortium on Violence Research at the Heinz School of Public Policy, Carnegie Mellon University.

EVALUATORS: Jens Ludwig, Georgetown University; Timothy Bray, University of Missouri–St. Louis; Michael Johnson, Carnegie Mellon University; James Rosenbaum and Greg Duncan, Northwestern University; Brian Jacob, Harvard University; and Jeffrey Kling, Princeton University.

PRINCIPAL INTERVENTIONS: Section 8 rental subsidies (housing vouchers).

TARGET POPULATION: All low-income families who are income and otherwise eligible for standard Section 8 rental subsidies.

OUTCOMES OF INTEREST: Criminal offending, employment, earnings, welfare receipt, children's educational outcomes, utilization of child protective services (including foster care), health.

Community Action Program of Tulsa County (CAPTC) American Dream Demonstration

STARTING YEAR/YEAR OF FINAL REPORT: 1998/2003.

INFORMATION SOURCE: Donna DeMarco and Gregory Mills, *Evaluation of the American Dream Demonstration, Semi-Annual Progress Report*, July–December 1999. This demonstration is being evaluated by Abt Associates, Inc.

PRINCIPAL INTERVENTION: Individual Development Accounts (IDAs), which are dedicated savings accounts that can only be used for purchasing a first home, paying for postsecondary education, or capitalizing a business. Matching funds and interest accrue to the participant in a separate custodial account. For each account year, up to $750 in deposits made by a participant are subject to match, when withdrawn for an allowable use. Participants making full use of their accounts over three years will accumulate $6,750 if planning a home purchase ($2,250 of their own savings plus $4,500 in matching funds) or $4,500 for other allowable uses.

TARGET POPULATION: Low-income individuals and families in the Tulsa, Oklahoma, metropolitan area. Participants must be employed and have incomes below 150 percent of the federal poverty guideline.

OUTCOMES OF INTEREST: Asset accumulation and self-sufficiency.

Jobs-Plus

STARTING YEAR/YEAR FINAL REPORTED EXPECTED: 1998/2003.

INFORMATION SOURCES: James Riccio, *A Research Framework for Evaluating Jobs-Plus, a Saturation and Place-Based Initiative for Public Housing Residents,* MDRC, 1998; James Riccio, *Mobilizing Public Housing Communities for Work: Origins and Early Accomplishments of the Jobs-Plus Demonstration,* MDRC, 1999.

FUNDING SOURCES: The project is sponsored at the national level by the Department of Housing and Urban Development and the Rockefeller Foundation. Key personnel: Garland Allen and Jennifer Stoloff for HUD and Julia Lopez for Rockefeller.

EVALUATOR: MDRC. Key personnel: James Riccio.

PRINCIPAL INTERVENTIONS: Jobs-Plus is a quasi experiment. Public housing projects were randomly assigned. Treatment projects receive a three-pronged intervention strategy: (1) saturation availability of employment support activities, including job search assistance, child care, transportation, some education and training; (2) financial incentives, which tend to break the connection between earnings and public housing rent; and (3) activities to strengthen social capital, including support groups and child care cooperatives.

TARGET POPULATION: Residents of large family public housing projects with high levels of welfare receipt and unemployment.

OUTCOMES OF INTEREST: Employment, earnings, welfare benefits and food stamp receipt.

6

Lower-Income Homeowners

Counseling for Delinquent Mortgagors

SUMMARY: This demonstration, conducted in 1974, tested the effects of counseling on a large sample of defaulting or delinquent borrowers under a subsidized homeownership program. Subjects were followed for six to 12 months.

COST: Unavailable.

TIME FRAME: Demonstration period July 1974–January 1975; analysis was conducted of loan status as of July 1975.

TREATMENTS TESTED: Controls received no counseling and were subject to the usual procedures for Section 235 mortgagors who fell behind on their payments. Experimentals received an offer of financial counseling; the fact that a household was being counseled might or might not affect lender forbearance.

TARGET POPULATION: Section 235 mortgagors in delinquency or default.

OUTCOME OF INTEREST: Mortgage repayment.

SAMPLE SIZE: Experimentals, 605; controls, 705.

NUMBER OF TREATMENT GROUPS: Two (with one control group).

NUMBER AND LOCATION OF SITES: Five—Atlanta, Georgia; Columbia, South Carolina; Detroit, Michigan; Los Angeles, California; and Seattle, Washington.

RESEARCH COMPONENTS:
  Process analysis: Very limited.
  Impact analysis: Comparison of unadjusted means.
  Benefit–cost analysis: Conducted.

MAJOR FINDINGS:

1. There were 10 agencies in the five sites. They differed in emphasis on home versus office counseling, debt collection services (offered to build support from creditors), and interest in referral to other social services.

2. Only one-quarter of those referred were actually counseled. Almost one-quarter of those referred could not be contacted, and over half (334) declined to make counseling appointments, although 184 of the latter went through a pre-counseling interview. Those who declined counseling, as a group, had a lower foreclosure rate than the controls.

3. As of July 1975, financial counseling had a significant positive impact on loan repayment by experimentals.

Good Outcomes Loan Status (percent)

	Current	Fewer months in default	Total improvement
Referred (for counseling)	41.3	19.7	61.0
Not referred	38.8	14.6	53.4
Difference	+2.5	+5.1	+7.6

Bad Outcomes Loan Status (percent)

	Foreclosed	More months in default	Total decline
Referred (for counseling)	14.0	12.1	26.1
Not referred	21.7	9.3	31.0
Difference	−7.7*	+2.8	−4.9*

* Statistically significant at the .05 level.

4. In-home counseling appeared substantially more effective than in-office counseling.

5. Counseling has net benefits of $174.82 to $440.32 per case, depending on the benefit–

cost model chosen. The higher figure reflects the net *social* benefits; costs to the taxpayer of continued Section 235 subsidies (which is a transfer from one party to another, not a social cost) and to the government of foregone tax revenues from debt forgiveness as a consequence of foreclosure (which also is not a social cost) constitute most of the difference among the models.

DESIGN ISSUES: Assignment in Los Angeles was nonrandom. Los Angeles data should not have been included in the analysis; one of the three agencies in Los Angeles was conspicuously ineffective, so the direction of any bias is unclear.

REPLICABILITY: Not replicable from the text, which does not fully characterize the criteria for eligibility of the target population or define the counseling intervention.

GENERALIZABILITY: The study was intended to generalize to other urban areas with high default rates. Note, however, that these are defaults on a subsidized loan program that is no longer offered.

FUNDING SOURCE: U.S. Department of Housing and Urban Development (HUD).

EVALUATORS: Les Rubin and Eugene Johnson, HUD Office of Policy Development and Research.

INFORMATION SOURCE: U.S. Department of Housing and Urban Development, Office of Policy Development and Research, *Counseling for Delinquent Mortgagors II: A Staff Study,* Washington, DC, January 1977.

PUBLIC-USE ACCESS TO DATA: None.

Detroit Default Counseling Demonstration

SUMMARY: This demonstration, conducted from 1976 to 1977, tested the effects of counseling on a large sample of delinquent or defaulting FHA-insured mortgagors, although the findings are based on a medium-sized sample of the total. Subjects were followed for three to four years.

COST: Administration and evaluation costs, approximately $420,000.

TIME FRAME: Demonstration period, October 1976–October 1977; data collected, same period.

TREATMENTS TESTED: Experimentals received counseling with emphasis on money management: they were randomly assigned to one of four counseling agencies. Controls were not offered counseling.

OUTCOME OF INTEREST: Mortgage repayment.

SAMPLE SIZE: Experimentals, approximately 4,400; controls, approximately 4,600. A smaller random sample, 195 experimentals and 185 controls, was used in the impact analysis.

TARGET POPULATION: Delinquent or defaulting mortgagors in FHA programs in the Detroit area.

NUMBER OF TREATMENT GROUPS: Two (with one control group).

NUMBER AND LOCATION OF SITES: One—Detroit, Michigan.

RESEARCH COMPONENTS:
- Process analysis: Conducted.
- Impact analysis: Comparison of means.
- Benefit–cost analysis: Not conducted (components for cost-effectiveness calculations were assembled).

MAJOR FINDINGS:
1. The process analysis found just 787 (about 19.7 percent of experimentals who were contacted) actually received counseling; most of the remainder refused it. However, one agency had a rate of actual counseling that was three times higher than the other three agencies.
2. Impact analysis. "The counseling demonstration did not result in a higher rate of 'saved' mortgages."

Mortgage Status as of August 1, 1980—Analytic Sample
Loan Status (percent)

	Current	In default	Foreclosed
Experimentals (195)	56.4	16.4	27.2
Controls (185)	62.7	17.8	19.5

TIME TRENDS IN FINDINGS: None.

DESIGN ISSUES:
1. The intake procedures resulted in a very large proportion of experimentals being referred more than once for counseling.
2. The small sample actually analyzed (380 out of 9,000 randomly assigned) was an enormous waste of potential information.

REPLICABILITY: Replicable.

GENERALIZABILITY: Poor. Detroit was ground zero for an explosion of default on FHA-insured mortgages in the 1970s. For example, in 1972 the national rate of default was 2.75 percent (an unacceptably high rate), while in Detroit, in June 1971, the default rate was 10.5 percent. Underlying the deterioration were the decline of the city itself, with huge declines in auto industry and related factory employment, and gross administrative deficiencies at the Detroit FHA office. High levels of default could be readily traced to inadequate property inspections, issuance of insurance for buyers who failed to meet underwriting standards, and mortgages well in excess of real market value of the collateral. At the time of the demonstration, 3.7 percent of all dwelling units in Detroit were abandoned, and HUD owned two-thirds of them. Counseling might well be ineffective in this situation without any necessary implications for more normal conditions.

FUNDING SOURCE: The Department of Housing and Urban Development. Key personnel: Les Rubin.

TREATMENT ADMINISTRATORS: Four private counseling agencies.

EVALUATOR: Sol Jacobson, Morgan Management Systems, Inc.

ENABLING LEGISLATION: None.

INFORMATION SOURCE: Morgan Management Systems, Inc., *A Report on the Detroit Default Counseling Demonstration: An Assessment of Counseling as a Default Remedy,* September 1980.

PUBLIC-USE ACCESS TO DATA: None.

Prepurchase Homeownership Counseling Demonstration

SUMMARY: This 1978–79 demonstration tested the effects of prepurchase counseling on a large sample of low- and moderate-income households that were interested in buying a first home. Subjects were followed for no more than one year.

TIME FRAME: Demonstration period, June 1978–June 1979; data collected, June–September 1979.

COST: Unavailable.

TREATMENTS TESTED: The controls only received a written Homebuyers Information Package (HIP). Experimentals were assigned to one of three treatment groups, which made the following services available:
1. Group I (low intensity): Three group counseling sessions, for up to seven hours total, with 6–10 households per session, and the HIP.
2. Group II (medium intensity): Three group counseling sessions, with some individual counseling, for up to 10 hours total, and the HIP.
3. Group III (high intensity): Individual advocacy counseling including housing inspections, attendance at closings, and other individualized services, for up to 14 hours total, and the HIP.

TARGET POPULATION: First-time prospective homebuyers whose income profiles matched Section 235 income limits (low and moderate income).

OUTCOMES OF INTEREST: (1) Participation and (2) Home purchases. The demonstration was also intended to measure the ultimate impact on mortgage default.

SAMPLE SIZE: Experimentals, 949; controls, 292.

NUMBER OF TREATMENT GROUPS: Four (with one control group).

NUMBER AND LOCATION OF SITES: Three—Philadelphia, Pennsylvania; Atlanta, Georgia; and Phoenix, Arizona. There were two counseling agencies at each site.

RESEARCH COMPONENTS:
- Process analysis: Conducted.
- Impact analysis: Conducted through regression and comparison of means.
- Benefit–cost analysis: Not conducted.

MAJOR FINDINGS:
1. An intensive and expensive outreach campaign was conducted at the three sites. It had poor results. The evaluators estimated that if there were a national prepurchase counseling program with a comparable outreach effort, then for every 10,000 households that would consider buying a home, 1,960 would learn that a counseling program existed, 1,390 would inquire about it, 740 would enroll, and 477 would actually be counseled. In other words, less than 5 percent of the target population would be reached.
2. About two-thirds of households that were assigned to experimental treatments used them.
3. Although no limit was placed on the number or length of contacts for individual counseling, the average amount actually received was 2.2 hours.
4. Since the take-up was far below the anticipated level, it was not worthwhile to continue data collection to investigate the impact of prepurchase counseling on the default rate. Default is a relatively rare event; a productive analysis requires large samples.
5. Group counseling (treatments I and II) reduced the home purchase rate. These groups had a

combined home purchase rate of 21.6 percent, while individual counseling (treatment III) had a 23.7 percent rate, and the controls had a 29.1 percent rate. The difference between the group rate and the control rate is statistically significant at the .05 level.

6. Among those who bought homes, "housing expenditures . . . show no statistically significant variation by Demonstration treatment group."

DESIGN ISSUES: The major question is the effectiveness of the outreach, which is extensively documented in the reference cited below. "The outreach message for the Demonstration was not perceived as relevant by more than half the eligible homebuyers who had heard of the program." A second question is the provision of the HIP to the controls. The HIP probably contained much of the information that the subjects could have expected to obtain from the counseling, and the process analysis showed that many subjects read it and liked it; this in turn suggests some redundancy in offering counseling as well to an audience that is motivated to read the information for itself.

REPLICABILITY: All outreach, eligibility for inclusion, and treatment elements are documented.

GENERALIZABILITY: See "Design Issues."

FUNDING SOURCE: HUD. Key personnel: Les Rubin.

EVALUATOR: Abt Associates. Key personnel: Judith Feins.

INFORMATION SOURCE: Judith D. Feins, L. Dixon Bain Jr., and Charles S. White Jr., *Outreach and Participation in the Prepurchase Homeownership Counseling Demonstration: Interim Report,* Abt Associates, Cambridge, July 1979.

PUBLIC-USE ACCESS TO DATA: None.

7

Low-Income Children and Their Families

Perry Preschool Program

SUMMARY: This demonstration, begun in 1962, tested the effects of a structured preschool program on a small sample of low-income children and their families. Subjects have been followed up to age 27 and will be followed in the future up to ages 39–41.

COST: Estimated program costs per child, $1,589 ($92,000 total). Evaluation costs have been approximately $2 million, over a considerable period of time, in nominal dollars.

TIME FRAME: The intervention began in 1962 and continued through five annual "waves" of children. Follow-up has been extensive and ongoing. The most recent available results are for the 27-year follow-up, published in 1993.

TREATMENTS TESTED: The treatment was a "high-quality preschool program" offered for two and one-half hours daily for seven and one-half months. Four waves received two years of preschool, whereas wave 0 (the first wave) received only one year. Controls received no preschool.

OUTCOMES OF INTEREST: (1) Cognitive development; (2) Academic achievement; (3) Delinquent behavior; (4) Employment; and (5) Welfare receipt.

SAMPLE SIZE: Total, 123; treatments, 58; controls, 65.

TARGET POPULATION: Low-income children and their families. All participants were African American and from one neighborhood.

NUMBER OF TREATMENT GROUPS: Two (with one control group).

NUMBER AND LOCATION OF SITES: One—the Perry School in Ypsilanti, Michigan.

RESEARCH COMPONENTS:

▪ Process analysis: Conducted. Much has been written on this program over the years, with different reports focusing on different aspects of implementation.

▪ Impact analysis: In most cases, conducted with simple comparison of means.

▪ Benefit–cost analysis: Conducted.

MAJOR FINDINGS:

1. At age 19:

Category	Number responding	Preschool group	Control group	Two-tailed p values
Employed	121	59%	32%	.032
High school graduate or equivalent	121	67%	49%	.034
College or vocational training	121	38%	21%	.029
Ever detained or arrested	121	31%	51%	.022
Total teen pregnancies, per 100 (females only)	49	64	117	.084
Functional competence (out of 40)	109	24.6	21.8	.025
Years in special education (%)	112	16%	28%	.039

In addition, the treatment group had significantly greater median earnings ($2,772 versus $1,070) per year and received less welfare than controls. This last finding is statistically significant based on interviews, although not significant based on official social service records.

2. At age 27 (95 percent of original sample responding):

	Treatment (%)	Control (%)
Completed twelfth grade	71	54
Had five or more arrests	7	35
Earned $2,000+/month	29	7
Owned a home	36	13
Ever received welfare	59	80

Note: All findings are statistically significant at the .05 level.

TIME TRENDS IN FINDINGS: IQ differences between treatment and control group members were found in the early follow-up but diminished with time and were no longer significant by second grade. Similar trends were found for other measures of academic aptitude.

DESIGN ISSUES:

1. The initial design began as a local evaluation and then grew beyond the original intent. This has not caused major problems, although it required more funding and resources than originally planned.

2. The design was essentially random assignment, with some small compromises. Two children with employed mothers were reassigned rather than dropped. Also, children from the same family were assigned to the same treatment.

REPLICABILITY: Tracking the subjects over two decades has been difficult, although the evaluators have been very successful. They attribute this to having an excellent, dedicated interviewer who lived in the community and had the respect of the families involved. Further, the families tended to stay in the community, rather than move on to other cities or neighborhoods. This may be difficult to replicate.

GENERALIZABILITY: The sample size was small and not representative of the state or the nation. All children were African American and from one neighborhood.

FUNDING SOURCES: Core funding was provided by the Carnegie Foundation. Key personnel:

Barbara Finberg. Additional funding was provided by the U.S. Office of Special Education and Rehabilitative Services, the Spencer Foundation, the Ford Foundation, the National Institute of Mental Health, the Rosenberg Foundation, the Levi-Strauss Foundation, and the State Department of Education of Michigan, supplemented by the Ypsilanti schools.

TREATMENT ADMINISTRATOR: David Weikart, director of special education for Ypsilanti Public Schools.

EVALUATOR: High/Scope Educational Research Foundation. Key personnel: David Weikart and Larry Schweinhart. Ann Epstein, Steve Barnett, Ellen Barnes, and many others played a part in various stages of evaluation.

ENABLING LEGISLATION: None.

INFORMATION SOURCES: Six monographs have been published by High/Scope Press that cover the various follow-up periods. Numerous journal publications have also addressed this study, including: Lawrence J. Schweinhart and David P. Weikart, "Success by Empowerment: The High/Scope Perry Preschool Study through Age 27," *Young Children,* November 1993. Various publications are available at the web site, http://www.highscope.org.

PUBLIC-USE ACCESS TO DATA: Available through High/Scope Press.

Washington, D.C., Mobile Unit for Child Health Care

SUMMARY: This experiment, conducted between 1965 and 1972, tested the effects of mobile intensive prenatal and infant care on a small sample of low-income families. Subjects were followed for up to six years.

COST: The evaluators were not available to provide any cost figures.

TIME FRAME: Demonstration period, 1965–72; data collected through 1976.

TREATMENTS TESTED: Intensive prenatal and infant care was provided by a pediatrician and a public health nurse. Care was provided by appointment in a mobile coach parked in front of the home. Prenatal care was begun at least by the seventh month of pregnancy and continued until the child's third birthday. Mothers also had telephone access to the nurse and pediatrician at any time. Care included routine medical examinations, immunizations, nutritional guidance, counseling, and a cognitive stimulation program. The control group was referred to area health clinics.

OUTCOMES OF INTEREST: (1) Child health, behavioral, and cognitive outcomes and (2) Parental behaviors, including parenting skills and employment stability.

SAMPLE SIZE: Treatments, 47 infants and their parents; controls, 48 infants and their parents.

TARGET POPULATION: First-born African American infants from low-income families. Mothers were unmarried school girls age 15–18.

NUMBER OF TREATMENT GROUPS: Two (with one control group).

NUMBER AND LOCATION OF SITES: One—Washington, D.C. (neighborhoods surrounding Children's Hospital).

RESEARCH COMPONENTS:
 Process analysis: None.
 Impact analysis: Comparison of means.
 Benefit–cost analysis: Not conducted.

MAJOR FINDINGS:
1. A very large number of child outcome variables were measured (approximately 300). Statistically significant differences were found for 32 of these variables—all but 3 favored the treatment group. These 29 included a more nutritious diet and healthier eating habits, fewer maladaptive behaviors such as thumb-

sucking or extreme shyness, and higher levels of confidence and assurance.

2. Mothers in the experimental group, when compared with their control group counterparts, demonstrated significantly more instances of positive parenting skills such as spending more time outdoors with the child, use of storybooks at home, and appropriate handling of child's misbehavior. They also were more likely to have taken some type of schooling during the first three years of the study, and significantly more were in some type of schooling at the four-year follow-up. Fathers in the experimental group were significantly less likely to have changed jobs during the three-year intervention period.

3. Compared with the control group children, the children in the experimental group showed significantly higher cognitive development on a standardized intelligence test at age three (IQ = 99.3 versus 91.2 for the control group children).

TIME TRENDS IN FINDINGS: The majority of findings persisted through the follow-up period.

DESIGN ISSUES:

1. Although attrition was low throughout the project intervention period (the first three years), by the end of the six-year follow-up, 9 treatment and 22 control group children were lost (had moved, broken contact with the evaluators, or had developed significant health problems). The excess loss of control subjects caused some bias in the results.

2. The staff of the project inadvertently provided the first group of mothers admitted to the program considerably more counseling and attention than was possible with the second half of the mothers. Outcomes were more favorable for this group.

REPLICABILITY: Replicable, though the evaluators cautioned that the medical professionals in this study were especially dedicated and talented counselors and that there was an enthusiasm for change among poor families in the 1960s.

GENERALIZABILITY: The sample was drawn from 16 census tracts in urban Washington, D.C., where crowded, rundown housing was the norm. Mothers were typically heads of households. Generalizability may be hindered, even to this population, for two reasons: (1) the sample size was quite small, especially for the outcomes regarding father's employment and (2) the experiment was conducted more than 30 years ago.

FUNDING SOURCE: National Institute of Mental Health.

TREATMENT ADMINISTRATOR: Children's Hospital of Washington, D.C.

EVALUATORS: Department of Child Health and Development, George Washington University School of Medicine, and Research Foundation of Children's Hospital, Washington, D.C.

ENABLING LEGISLATION: None.

INFORMATION SOURCE: Margaret F. Gutelius, Arthur D. Kirsh, Sally MacDonald, Marion R. Brooks, and Toby McErlean, "Controlled Study of Child Health Supervision: Behavioral Results," *Pediatrics* 60(1977): 294–304.

PUBLIC-USE ACCESS TO DATA: Not available.

Carolina Abecedarian Project

SUMMARY: This demonstration, which began in 1972, tested the effects of a developmental daycare program and a school-age intervention on a small sample of at-risk children and their families. Subjects have been followed up to 21 years of age, and further follow-up is planned.

COST: Cost figures are not available. The National Institute for Child Health and Human Development (NICHHD), the primary funder, contributed approximately $6 million over the life of the project. Some of the evaluation costs were included in this figure. There were many other funding sources, however, and also considerable donated time.

TIME FRAME: Pilot work began in 1971; treatment period, 1972–85; data collection, continuing.

TREATMENTS TESTED:

1. Preschool intervention: A systematic, developmental day-care program and educational day-care services. The curriculum emphasized language development and appropriate and adaptive social behavior.
2. School-age intervention: Increased and enhanced parent involvement. Treatment group families were assigned a home/school resource teacher (HST) who provided home curriculum activities that reinforced concepts taught in school. The HST also helped families with non-school-related problems.

The control group children received no preschool intervention and received the existing school curriculum when they reached school age.

OUTCOMES OF INTEREST: (1) Children's cognitive development; (2) Maternal attitudes; and (3) Maternal employment.

SAMPLE SIZE: Total, 111; preschool treatments, 57; preschool controls, 54. Roughly one-half of these initial groups were then randomly assigned to a school-age intervention as they entered school.

TARGET POPULATION: Infants and children believed to be at high risk for school failure. Criteria for selection included maternal IQ, family income, parent education, and intactness of family. All but one sample family were African American.

NUMBER OF TREATMENT GROUPS: Four (with one control group).

NUMBER AND LOCATION OF SITES: One—Orange County, North Carolina.

RESEARCH COMPONENTS:

▪ Process analysis: Service delivery was closely monitored, as was the admission of families to the sample.
▪ Impact analysis: Comparison of means.
▪ Benefit–cost analysis: Not conducted.

MAJOR FINDINGS: Findings have been summarized at various points in this experiment, highlighting a wide variety of outcomes. Maternal outcomes were examined formally at the 54-month follow-up and informally at the 12-year follow-up. The evaluators hope to look more closely at these outcomes in a future publication; they will also be studying the economic outcomes of the children themselves when data become available. Those interested in child development and academic outcomes are referred to the information sources below.

1. At the 54-month follow-up, mothers of day-care children (treatment group) had significantly more formal education (11.9 years) than the mothers of the control group children (10.3 years), although the groups were equivalent in the year of the children's births.
2. At 54 months, significantly more mothers with children in the treatment group held semiskilled or skilled jobs (55 percent) than did the control-group mothers (26 percent). Conversely, significantly more control-group mothers were unemployed or unskilled (65 percent) than were day-care mothers (36 percent). (Note: The remaining mothers not counted above were considered students.)
3. Whereas the parental data from the 12-year follow-up have not yet been analyzed, the evaluators reported that it appears that mothers of treatment group children still had more years of education, were less likely to be on welfare, and were more likely to own their own homes than mothers of control-group children.
4. At the age-21 follow-up, those with treatment were significantly more likely to still be in school; 40 percent of the intervention group compared with 20 percent of the control group.
5. At age 21, a significant difference was also found for the percent of young adults who ever attended a four-year college. About 35 percent of the young adults in the intervention group had either graduated from or were

attending a four-year college or university at the time of the assessment. In contrast, only about 14 percent in the control group had done so.

6. At age 21, employment rates were higher (65 percent) for the treatment group than for the control group (50 percent), although the difference was not statistically significant.

TIME TRENDS IN FINDINGS: None reported for maternal outcomes. There was some fluctuation among cognitive development test scores.

DESIGN ISSUES:

1. At the 54-month follow-up (the point when maternal interviews were conducted), less than half of the sample was available for analysis. However, some subjects earlier lost to attrition were relocated and participated in the 12-year follow-up, increasing the follow-up rate to 81 percent of the original infants.

2. The subsample analysis is based on very small numbers because the original sample infants were further divided into four groups.

REPLICABILITY: Replicable. The information sources provide information regarding teacher training, curriculum, and so on.

GENERALIZABILITY: The sample, especially for maternal outcomes, was quite small, though other similar experiments tend to support these findings. On average, 72 percent of this sample had a female head of household, a mean income of $(1972) $1,455, mother's education was roughly 10 years, and all but one family was black. In terms of academic achievement and cognitive ability, this experiment had comparable findings to other similar experiments (e.g., the Perry Preschool Project).

FUNDING SOURCES: National Institute for Child Health and Human Development; the Spencer Foundation; the Carnegie Foundation; the Office of Special Education, U.S. Department of Education; the Department of Human Re-

sources of the State of North Carolina; and the Department of Social Services of Orange County, North Carolina.

TREATMENT ADMINISTRATOR: The curriculum developers and the day-care director were responsible for direct administration of the treatment. These positions have changed personnel many times over the life of the project.

EVALUATOR: Frank Porter Graham Child Development Center, University of North Carolina at Chapel Hill. Key personnel: Craig Ramey and Frances Campbell.

ENABLING LEGISLATION: None.

INFORMATION SOURCES: Craig T. Ramey, Keith Owen Yeates, and Elizabeth J. Short, "The Plasticity of Intellectual Development: Insights from Preventive Intervention," *Child Development* 55(1984): 1913–25.

Craig T. Ramey, David MacPhee, and Keith Owen Yeates, "Preventing Developmental Retardation: A General Systems Model," in *Facilitating Infant and Early Childhood Development,* edited by Lynne A. Bond and Justin M. Joffe, University Press of New England, 1982.

Frances A. Campbell and Craig T. Ramey, "Cognitive and School Outcomes for High-Risk African-American Students at Middle Adolescence: Positive Effects of Early Intervention," *American Educational Research Journal* 32(1995): 743–72.

Frances A. Campbell and Craig T. Ramey, "Effects of Early Intervention on Intellectual and Academic Achievement: A Follow-up Study of Children from Low-Income Families," *Child Development* 65(1994): 684–98.

Frances A. Campbell, Craig T. Ramey, E. P. Pungello, J. Sparling, and S. Miller-Johnson, "Early Childhood Education: Young Adult Outcomes from the Abecedarian Project," *Applied Developmental Science* 6(2002): 42–57.

PUBLIC-USE ACCESS TO DATA: The researchers are still collecting data and they are not yet public information.

New York Nurse Home Visitation Experiment: 15-Year Follow-Up

SUMMARY: This demonstration, conducted between 1978 and 1980, tested the effects of a visiting nurse program on a medium-sized sample of disadvantaged pregnant women and their children. Subjects were followed for up to 15 years.

COST: Unknown.

TIME FRAME: Demonstration period, April 1978 to September 1980; data collected over program period; follow-up data collected at 4 and 15 years following the child's birth.

TREATMENTS TESTED: Treatment 1, sensory and developmental screening of the study child at ages 12 and 24 months; treatment 2, same as treatment 1 plus free transportation for prenatal and well-child care through the second birthday; treatment 3, same as treatment 2 plus nurse visits during pregnancy; treatment 4, same as treatment 3 plus additional nurse visits through the second birthday. Treatments groups 1 and 2 were combined to form a single control group.

OUTCOMES OF INTEREST: (1) Welfare receipt; (2) Maternal employment; (3) Subsequent pregnancies; (4) Interval between first and second birth; (5) Child behavior; and (6) Other non-economic outcomes.

SAMPLE SIZE: Total, 400; treatment group 1, 90; group 2, 94; group 3, 100; group 4, 116.

TARGET POPULATION: Low-income pregnant women with no previous births, who were less than 26 weeks of gestation and met any of the following criteria: (1) under 19 years of age, (2) unmarried, (3) low socioeconomic status.

NUMBER OF TREATMENT GROUPS: Three (with one control group).

NUMBER AND LOCATION OF SITES: One—Chemung County (Elmira), New York.

RESEARCH COMPONENTS:

■ Process analysis: The program was closely monitored and nurses used computerized forms to comment on program implementation, participation rates, attrition, and service delivery.

■ Impact analysis: Generalized linear models and analysis of covariance were used.

■ Benefit–cost analysis: Conducted.

MAJOR FINDINGS:

Four-Year Findings

1. At the sixth-month postpartum follow-up, among women who had not graduated from high school at registration, 59 percent of the nurse-visited groups (treatments 3 and 4) and 27 percent of the control group had either graduated or enrolled in an educational program. By the 10th month, the effects of the program held only for unmarried women, and no treatment effects were found at the 46th month follow-up.

2. Between birth and the 22nd month postpartum, nurse-visited poor unmarried older women had worked 2.5 times longer than their counterparts in the control group (9.27 months versus 3.61 months). By the 46th month, the nurse-visited poor unmarried teenagers also had begun to work more than their counterparts (14.9 months versus 10.03 months). There was an 83 percent increase in the number of months worked by the treatment group mothers (older and teenagers) in contrast to poor unmarried women in the control group (average months of employment, 31.31 versus 17.17).

3. During the first two years after delivery, the nurse-visited poor unmarried older women were on public assistance 157 fewer days than their control counterparts (a 40 percent reduction). This effect did not extend into the two-year period following the end of the intervention.

4. The program produced significant savings (due to increased maternal employment, reductions in unintended pregnancies, and lower child health costs) for the sample families during the 24- to 48-month period after delivery, although not for the first two years. The savings for the whole four-year period were not statistically significant (savings per family: 0–24 months, $325; 24–48 months, $1,448).

Fifteen-Year Findings (with treatment group as group 4 only)

Outcome measured	Treatment	Control	P-value
Subsequent pregnancies	1.5	2.2	.03
Average months between birth of first and second child	65	37	.001
Average months of AFDC receipt	60	90	.005
Average months of Food Stamp receipt	46.7	45.04	.001

Overall, there were no differences between the nurse-visited women and their control group counterparts on measures of welfare receipt, employment, and subsequent pregnancies. However, in a subgroup analysis of poor and unmarried women, there were several enduring program effects, including effects on some measures of family abuse, child behavior, and other outcomes not reported here.

TIME TRENDS IN FINDINGS: Early program impacts generally diminished in the first two years following the end of the program intervention. By the 15-year follow-up period, the only enduring program effects are reported among those in the subsample of poor and unmarried women (see above).

DESIGN ISSUES:

1. There were two deviations from random assignment. In six cases, women who lived in the same household as others who had already been assigned were assigned to the same treatment. Treatment group four was expanded (more people were randomly selected for this group) during the last six months of the enrollment period.

2. Of the sample (both treatment and control), 20 to 25 percent reported that they discussed pregnancy or child care matters with nurse-visited women. In other words, people in groups 3 and 4 talked about the program with women in groups 1 and 2. This could be a source of horizontal diffusion.

REPLICABILITY: Replicable. Information on program replication is available at the National Center for Children, Families and Communities at the University of Colorado Health Sciences Center.

GENERALIZABILITY: Several factors limit generalizability: no urban participants; only white participants' outcomes used for analysis; nurses were specially hired and trained for the program and probably had more manageable caseloads than might be possible in an ongoing program.

FUNDING SOURCES: Bureau of Community Health Services, National Center for Nursing Research, the Robert Wood Johnson Foundation, the William T. Grant Foundation, and the Ford Foundation. Key personnel: Gontran Lamberty for the Bureau of Community Health Services, Ruby Hearn for Robert Wood Johnson, Robert Haggerty for William T. Grant, and Oscar Harkary for Ford.

TREATMENT ADMINISTRATOR: Comprehensive Interdisciplinary Development Service. Key personnel: John Shannon.

EVALUATORS: Harriet Kitzman, University of Rochester; David Olds, University of Colorado.

ENABLING LEGISLATION: None.

INFORMATION SOURCES: D. L. Olds, "Prenatal and Infancy Home Visiting by Nurses: From Randomized Trials to Community Replication," *Prevention Science* (2002); J. Eckenrode, C. R. Henderson, E. Smith, J. Powers, R. Cole, H. Kitzman, and K. Sidora, "Preventing Child Abuse and Neglect with a Program of Nurse Home Visitation," *Journal of the American Medical Association* 284(2000): 1385–91.

PUBLIC-USE ACCESS TO DATA: Not available.

Increasing the Immunization of Preschool Children

SUMMARY: This experiment, conducted in 1981, tested the effects of various incentives to visit a clinic for immunization on a medium-sized sample of the parents of immunization-deficient preschool children. Subjects were followed for three months.

COST: This experiment was done as a master's thesis project; costs are not available.

TIME FRAME: The project was conducted over a three-month period in 1981; data collected, same period.

TREATMENTS TESTED: There were six treatments—four experimental incentives and two control groups: (1) a mailed general prompt to bring the child into the clinic for immunization; (2) a more client-specific prompt, which mentioned the target child by name and his or her specific immunization needs; (3) the same specific prompt plus increased clinic access ("off-hours" clinics); (4) the specific prompt plus a monetary incentive (a lottery ticket for a cash prize); (5) control—telephone contact with no prompt; and (6) control—no contact. The control groups did receive prompts after the conclusion of the study.

OUTCOMES OF INTEREST: (1) Clinic attendance. Increased attendance is a desired outcome in itself. By getting families into the clinic, doctors not only complete the immunizations but also see other family members, make appointments, etc., and (2) Inoculations.

SAMPLE SIZE: The parents of 1,133 children were the total sample. Some parents had more than one child who needed immunization. Numbers of children by treatment: treatment 1, 195; treatment 2, 190; treatment 3, 185; treatment 4, 183; treatment 5, 189; treatment 6, 191.

TARGET POPULATION: Parents of an identified group of immunization-deficient preschool children who were clients of the public health clinic. Children were five years of age or younger and in need of one or more inoculations.

NUMBER OF TREATMENT GROUPS: Six (with two control groups).

NUMBER AND LOCATION OF SITES: One public health clinic in Akron, Ohio.

RESEARCH COMPONENTS:
- Process analysis: Efforts were made to ensure that target parents received prompts, that information (names, addresses, and inoculation records) was correct, and that the correct inoculations were actually given. Random samples were used to check the reliability.
- Impact analysis: Comparison of means.
- Benefit–cost analysis: A cost-effectiveness analysis was conducted.

MAJOR FINDINGS: Findings for attendance and inoculations are presented separately. Since some children needed more than one inoculation, one visit does not necessarily equal one inoculation. Further, some families brought in by the prompts made appointments and returned to the clinic for other services.

1. After two weeks, the specific prompt plus monetary incentive had significantly increased both clinic attendance (by 20.9 percent) and the number of inoculations (by 28.6 percent) compared with the control group. The specific prompt plus access had produced significantly more inoculations (20.7 percent), but not attendance.

2. At two months, all treatment groups except the general prompt had produced significantly more inoculations. The prompt plus treatments (treatments 3 and 4) also produced greater attendance.
3. As expected by the evaluators, the monetary incentive produced the greatest effects, followed by the increased access and the specific prompt without incentives. The general prompt produced slight (not significant) attendance and inoculation gains. This ranking persisted throughout the three-month period.
4. Secondary effects were produced, in that parents of target children also brought nontarget children to the clinic, some of whom received needed inoculations.

TIME TRENDS IN FINDINGS: The monetary incentive appeared to be the most cost-effective intervention in the short run (after two weeks) because of its immediate significant impact. In the long run, the specific prompt alone proved the most cost-effective intervention capable of demonstrating evidence of statistical significance.

DESIGN ISSUES:
1. Families, rather than children, were randomly assigned to prevent confounding due to different types of prompts being mailed to parents with two or more children.
2. The second follow-up measure was taken after three months. Data gathered after two months must be evaluated with caution because some inoculations are required again after two months. Experimental groups were compared on cost-effectiveness after the first follow-up period (two months).

REPLICABILITY: Replicable.

GENERALIZABILITY: The evaluation did not address this issue. No data were provided about the representativeness of the sample to Akron, Ohio, or the nation as a whole. Children of the sample parents were 50 percent male, 64 percent white, averaged roughly three years old, and lacked an average of 5.2 inoculations. Findings from this study are consistent with some studies but at odds with others.

FUNDING SOURCES: Akron Department of Health, B. F. Goodrich Company, and Kent State University, Department of Psychology. Key personnel: C. William Keck for Akron, Thomas Duke for B. F. Goodrich, and Roy Lilly for Kent State.

TREATMENT ADMINISTRATOR: James M. Yokley, in conjunction with the Akron, Ohio, Department of Health.

EVALUATORS: James M. Yokley and David S. Glenwick, Kent State University, Department of Psychology.

ENABLING LEGISLATION: None.

INFORMATION SOURCE: James M. Yokley and David Glenwick, "Increasing the Immunization of Preschool Children: An Evaluation of Applied Community Interventions," *Journal of Applied Behavior Analysis* 17(1984): 313–25.

PUBLIC-USE ACCESS TO DATA: Not available.

Infant Health and Development Program

SUMMARY: This study, conducted from January 1985 to the present, tested the effects of early intervention services on a medium-sized sample of low birth-weight, premature children and their families. Subjects were followed for up to eight and one-half years.

COST: The evaluators are unable to separate evaluation and project costs. They estimate that approximately $15,000 per child was spent over the three years of the intervention ($5.7 million for the sample of 377 children).

TIME FRAME: Intervention, January 1985–89 (when last child reached the age of three years). Follow-up was done at five years and eight and one-half years. This last phase of the project is not yet published.

TREATMENTS TESTED: The treatment group received early intervention services including home visits, parent support and training groups, and a child development center program in addition to pediatric follow-up. The control group received pediatric follow-up only.

OUTCOMES OF INTEREST: (1) Child development outcomes, including cognitive development, behavioral competence, and health; and (2) Maternal outcomes, including employment, education, and welfare receipt.

SAMPLE SIZE: Total, 985; treatments, 377; controls, 608.

TARGET POPULATION: Low birth-weight (LBW), premature children and their families.

NUMBER OF TREATMENT GROUPS: Two (with one control group). The intervention group was subdivided into lighter LBW (< 2,000 g) and heavier LBW (2,001–2,500 g).

NUMBER AND LOCATION OF SITES: Eight—University of Arkansas, Albert Einstein College of Medicine, Harvard Medical School, University of Miami, University of Pennsylvania, University of Texas Health Science Center at Dallas, University of Washington, and Yale University.

RESEARCH COMPONENTS:
- Process analysis: Conducted. Care was given to maintain both standardization across sites and the integrity of the experimental design.
- Impact analysis: Conducted with multiple linear regression.
- Benefit–cost analysis: Not conducted, though such an analysis may be done after the eight and one-half-year follow-up.

MAJOR FINDINGS:
1. Mothers in the intervention group were employed for a greater number of months than the control group mothers at the end of phase I.
2. When controlling for employment and education, the treatment group was more likely to receive public assistance. That is, in the treatment group, mothers who had some college education and/or were employed received more months of welfare benefits than similar control group mothers.
3. Participation in the program had a positive effect on the children's cognitive development.

TIME TRENDS IN FINDINGS: At the five-year follow-up, significant cognitive differences were found only for the heavier LBW subgroup. No long-term follow-up was reported for the maternal measures (employment and welfare receipt).

DESIGN ISSUES: There were no significant problems with the design or implementation of this project.

REPLICABILITY: Replicable. The Centers for Disease Control is currently doing an effectiveness study based on this project.

GENERALIZABILITY: The sites were chosen for their ability to conduct good research, rather than based on a probability sample, but findings should otherwise be generalizable to the national population of low birth-weight children and their families.

FUNDING SOURCES: Primary funding came from the Robert Wood Johnson Foundation. Additional support came from the Pew Charitable Trusts, the Bureau of Maternal and Child Health and Resource Development at the Health Resources Service Administration, the National Institute of Child Health and Human Development, and the March of Dimes Foundation.

TREATMENT ADMINISTRATOR: Infant Health and Development Program, Program Development and Implementation Office, Frank Porter Graham Child Development Center, University of North Carolina at Chapel Hill. Key personnel: Craig Ramey, director.

EVALUATOR: National Study Office, Stanford University. Key personnel: Ruth Gross, MD. Other key personnel: Cecilia McCarton, Albert Einstein College of Medicine; James Tonascia, Johns Hopkins University.

ENABLING LEGISLATION: None.

INFORMATION SOURCES: Infant Health and Development Program Staff, "Enhancing the Outcomes of Low-Birth-Weight, Premature Infants: A Multisite, Randomized Trial," *Journal of the American Medical Association* 263(1990): 3035–42; J. Brooks-Gunn, C. M. McCarton, P. H. Casey, M. C. McCormick, C. R. Bauer, J. C. Bernbaum, J. Tyson, M. Swanson, F. C. Bennett, and D. T. Scott, "Early Intervention in Low-Birth-Weight, Premature Infants: Results through Age 5 Years from the Infant Health and Development Program," *Journal of the American Medical Association* 272(1994): 1257–62.

PUBLIC-USE ACCESS TO DATA: Available through Frank Porter Graham Child Development Center.

Memphis Nurse Home Visitation

SUMMARY: This demonstration, conducted between 1990 and 1994, tested the effects of a visiting nurse program on a medium-sized sample of disadvantaged pregnant women. Subjects were followed for up to four and a half years.

COST: Unknown.

TIME FRAME: Demonstration period, June 1990–April 30, 1994; data collected, same period.

TREATMENTS TESTED: Treatment group 1, free transportation to prenatal care; group 2, same as group 1 plus developmental screening for the child at ages 6, 12, and 24 months; group 3, same as group 2 plus one postpartum nurse visit in the hospital and one home visit after hospital discharge; group 4, same as group 3 plus postnatal home visits through the child's second birthday.

OUTCOMES OF INTEREST: (1) Rate of subsequent pregnancy; (2) Interval between first and second birth; (3) Employment; (4) Welfare receipt; and (5) Child development and other noneconomic outcomes.

SAMPLE SIZE: Total, 1,139; group 1, 166; group 2, 515; group 3, 230; and group 4, 228. Only groups 2 and 4 were used in postpartum assessments.

TARGET POPULATION: Low-income pregnant women with no previous births, living in an urban setting. The experiment was only open to women who had less than 29 weeks of gestation and who had at least two of the three following characteristics: unemployed, unmarried, and less than 12 years of education. Women who were not at risk but who asked to participate were allowed to do so.

NUMBER OF TREATMENT GROUPS: Four, but only group 2 (control) and group 4 (treatment) were used in this assessment.

NUMBER AND LOCATION OF SITES: One—Memphis/Shelby County, Tennessee.

RESEARCH COMPONENTS:
- Process analysis: Adherence to program protocols was closely monitored.
- Impact analysis: Generalized linear models and analysis of covariance were used.
- Benefit–cost analysis: Not conducted.

MAJOR FINDINGS:
1. During the first year following the child's birth, there were no program impacts on welfare receipt. At 24 months, nurse-visited women reported fewer second pregnancies than controls (36 percent compared with 47 percent, $p = .006$) and fewer person-months of welfare receipt (7.8 compared with 8.4, $p = .07$).
2. At the 4.5-year follow-up, there were small, but statistically significant, program effects among the nurse-visited women. See table next page.
3. There were no statistically significant program effects on maternal educational achievement, employment, or Medicaid use.

TIME TRENDS IN FINDINGS: Overall, many program effects diminished after the program ended.

Major Findings at Four and One-Half Year Follow-Up

Outcome measured	Treatment n = 224	Control n = 515	P-value
Subsequent pregnancies	1.15	1.34	.03
Rate of closely spaced pregnancies	0.22	0.32	.03
Average months between birth of first and second child	30.25	26.6	.004
Average months of AFDC receipt	32.55	36.19	.01
Average months of Food Stamp receipt	41.57	45.04	.005

However, the authors report that enduring program effects were concentrated in the higher risk groups.

DESIGN ISSUES: As a result of a nurse shortage, the staff turnover rate was 50 percent during the first two years of the program, causing a disruption in the relationship with the originally assigned nurse for 37 percent of all families. Moreover, 6 percent of the treatment group members did not receive the number of visits deemed necessary to achieve a clinical impact.

REPLICABILITY: Replicable. Information on program replication is available at the National Center for Children, Families and Communities at the University of Colorado Health Sciences Center.

GENERALIZABILITY: The study was designed to measure program effects on primarily high-risk African American women living in an urban setting. The sample was composed almost entirely (92 percent) of African American women: 98 percent were not married, 65 percent were age 18 or younger, and 85 percent had household incomes at or below federal poverty guidelines.

FUNDING SOURCES: The Administration for Children and Families of the Department of Health and Human Services, Robert Wood Johnson Foundation, Carnegie Corporation, and a Senior Research Scientist Award to Dr. Olds.

TREATMENT ADMINISTRATOR: Memphis/Shelby County Health Department.

EVALUATORS: Harriet Kitzman, University of Rochester, and David Olds, University of Colorado.

ENABLING LEGISLATION: None.

INFORMATION SOURCES: H. Kitzman, D. L. Olds, K. Sidora, C. R. Henderson, C. Hanks, R. Cole, D. W. Luckey, J. Bondy, K. Cole, and J. Glazner, "Enduring Effects of Nurse Home Visitation on Maternal Life Course: A 3-Year Follow-Up of a Randomized Trial," *Journal of the American Medical Association* 283(2000): 1983–89; David L. Olds, "Prenatal and Infancy Home Visiting by Nurses: From Randomized Trials to Community Replication," *Prevention Science* 3(2002): 153–72.

PUBLIC-USE ACCESS TO DATA: Public-use file deposited with the Inter-University Consortium for Political and Social Research at http://www.icpsr.umich.edu:8080/ICPSRSTUDY/06782.xml.

Even Start Family Literacy Program

SUMMARY: This demonstration, conducted from 1991 to 1994, tested the effects of early childhood education, adult literacy or basic skills training, and parenting education on a medium-sized sample of low-income families. Subjects were followed for 18 months. The experimental portion of this evaluation, summarized below, was part of a larger nationwide evaluation involving more than 20,000 families.

COST: Evaluation costs, $2.9 million.

TIME FRAME: Demonstration period, fall 1991–spring 1994; data collected, same period; final report, January 1995.

TREATMENTS TESTED: Even Start projects must provide families with an integrated program of early childhood education, adult literacy or basic skills training, and parenting education. However, there is flexibility in devising projects to meet local needs. Even Start both coordinates existing services and directly provides services when they are not locally available. Control group families did not receive Even Start services but could find similar services elsewhere in the community.

OUTCOMES OF INTEREST: (1) Child outcomes—school readiness and literacy; and (2) Family outcomes—parental educational level, literacy, attainment of a general equivalency diploma (GED), employment, and income.

SAMPLE SIZE: There were 565 families participating at all 10 sites that contributed data to the experimental component of the evaluation. Of these 10 sites, five implemented random assignment. At the five sites that implemented random assignment, there were 101 Even Start families (treatment) and 98 control group families.

TARGET POPULATION: Low-income families with at least one adult who is eligible for adult education programs under the Adult Education Act and who is a parent of a child less than 8 years old living in a Chapter 1 elementary school attendance area.

NUMBER OF TREATMENT GROUPS: Two (with one control group).

NUMBER AND LOCATION OF SITES: Although the treatment was implemented at 10 sites, random assignment occurred only at five—Albuquerque, New Mexico; Birmingham, Alabama; Golden, Colorado; Phoenix, Arizona; and Reading, Pennsylvania.

RESEARCH COMPONENTS:
■ Process analysis: Site visits were conducted in 1991 and again in 1993. Staff interviews and observation provided details about program activities and sample characteristics.
■ Impact analysis: Conducted using a comparison of unweighted means as well as regression models.
■ Benefit–cost analysis: Not conducted.

MAJOR FINDINGS:
1. From pretest to the second posttest, both treatment and control group children showed significant gains on a measure of school readiness. However, the gain for the treatment group children was not significantly greater than the gain for the control group children. Likewise, there was no significant program effect on a measure of child literacy.
2. Similarly, parents in both treatment and control groups showed significant pretest/posttest gains on a measure of adult literacy. Again, there was not a significant difference between groups. There was a significant program effect on the attainment of a GED. Of treatment group adults, 22.4 percent attained a GED during the study period compared with 5.7 percent of control group adults.
3. There were no significant program effects on quantifiable measures of social support, adequacy of financial resources, income level, and employment status.

TIME TRENDS IN FINDINGS: Treatment group children gained significantly more than their control group counterparts on a measure of school readiness between the pretest and the first posttest (9 months), but the effect had dissipated at the second posttest (18 months).

DESIGN ISSUES: Sites varied considerably in their size, participant and staff characteristics, and program components. Because of small sample sizes at individual sites, participants were aggregated for the analysis.

REPLICABILITY: Replicable.

GENERALIZABILITY: Designed to generalize to all Even Start families in the selected projects, including those that drop out early. Even Start recruits and serves families that are willing to participate. The sample may be more motivated to succeed than the population served by less-demanding social programs such as Head Start. The 10 projects were selected purposively, based on geographic location, level of program implementation, and willingness to participate. They differ in a number of ways from the national Even Start sample used in the larger evaluation (e.g., a far greater number of Hispanics who speak Spanish as their primary language).

FUNDING SOURCE: U.S. Department of Education, Office of Planning and Evaluation Service. Key personnel: Nancy Rhett, project officer.

TREATMENT ADMINISTRATOR: The treatment was administered locally by the staff at each Even Start project site.

EVALUATOR: Abt Associates. Key personnel: Robert St. Pierre, Janet Swartz, and Beth Gamse.

ENABLING LEGISLATION: The Hawkins-Stafford Elementary and Secondary School Improvement Amendments of 1988, Part B of Chapter 1 of Title 1 (PL 100–297) and the National Literacy Act of 1991 (PL 102–73).

INFORMATION SOURCE: Robert St. Pierre, Janet Swartz, Beth Gamse, Stephen Murray, Dennis Deck, and Phil Nickel, *National Evaluation of the Even Start Family Literacy Program—Final Report*, U.S. Department of Education, Office of Planning and Evaluation Service, January 1995.

PUBLIC-USE ACCESS TO DATA: Available through RMC Research Corporation, Portland, Oregon. Contact Dennis Deck.

National Evaluation of the Comprehensive Child Development Program (CCDP)

SUMMARY: This demonstration, conducted from 1990 to 1995, tested the effects of providing supplemental community support services on a large sample of low-income families. Subjects were followed for five years.

COST: Administrative cost was $14,984 per program family per year, or about $30 million. The impact evaluation cost approximately $12.5 million and the process evaluation $1.9 million.

TIME FRAME: Demonstration period, February 1990–September 1995; data collected, November 1991–January 1996; final report, June 1997.

TREATMENTS TESTED: Supplemental support services were offered to low-income families with children. They were built around those already present in the community or added where deficiencies existed. Paraprofessional case managers with low caseloads made home visits to provide or refer families to required services, which included early childhood education, health screening, immunizations, nutritional services, and other early intervention programs. Parents could receive prenatal care, education in child development, and health care. The control group had no access to these supplemental services but could access programs that had been present prior to the implementation of the program.

OUTCOMES OF INTEREST: (1) Child cognitive and social development; (2) Child health; (3) Maternal employment; (4) Average family income; (5) Mother's participation in education; (6) Number of subsequent births; (7) Use of prenatal care; (8) Birth outcomes; (9) Pregnancy risks; (10) Self-esteem; (11) AFDC receipt; and (12) Food Stamp receipt.

SAMPLE SIZE: Total, 3,961 families; treatments, 1,981; controls, 1,980.

TARGET POPULATION: Families with income below the poverty level that included a pregnant woman or a child under the age of one.

NUMBER OF TREATMENT GROUPS: Two (with one control group).

NUMBER AND LOCATION OF SITES: Twenty-one CCDP projects nationwide, in many different states, both urban and rural. Names of the sites are not listed in official documents.

RESEARCH COMPONENTS:

- Process analysis: Performed through analysis of administrative data, quarterly compliance reports, monthly telephone contacts, regular national meetings, and annual site visits. The evaluators found that consistency was maintained in design and delivery throughout the various sites.
- Impact analysis: OLS and logistic regression, longitudinal growth curve analysis, and subgroup analyses.
- Benefit–cost analysis: None conducted.

MAJOR FINDINGS:

1. CCDP had no statistically significant impacts on parenting skills or the economic self-sufficiency of participating mothers, or on child cognitive or social development. Length of enrollment had no effect.
2. Control families accessed many of the same services that were provided to the CCDP families on their own. CCDP families received significantly more of some services than the controls, but the overall pattern of service receipt was quite similar.
3. Families agreed to participate for the full five years, but there was no way to enforce participation. The resultant average participation was 3.3 years.
4. Based on the process analysis, the evaluators conclude that CCDP had a clear design and was implemented as conceived. They conclude that the case management model tested in this demonstration is ineffective for obtaining the desired improvement in family outcomes.
5. Only one site had statistically significant and somewhat large positive effects for multiple outcomes—children's cognitive development, families' employment, income, use of federal benefits, and parenting attitudes.

DESIGN ISSUES: None apparent.

REPLICABILITY: Replicable. Manuals prepared by CSR included regulations and standards for each CCDP site.

GENERALIZABILITY: CCDP was designed for nationwide generalizability, having been implemented in a wide variety of settings representative of areas with large numbers of low-income families. The evaluation of the comparable Even Start Family Literacy Program also found no measurable impact.

FUNDING SOURCE: U.S. Department of Health and Human Services, Administration on Children, Youth, and Families. Key personnel: Michael Lopez.

TREATMENT ADMINISTRATOR: Administration on Children, Youth, and Families. Grantees included universities, hospitals, public and private nonprofit organizations, and school districts.

EVALUATOR: Abt Associates, Inc. Key personnel: Robert St. Pierre.

INFORMATION SOURCES: Robert St. Pierre, Jean Layzer, Barbara Goodson, and Lawrence Bernstein, *The Effectiveness of Comprehensive Case Management Interventions: Findings from the National Evaluation of the Comprehensive Child Development Program*, Abt Associates, Inc., September 1997.

Robert St. Pierre, Jean Layzer, Barbara Goodson, and Lawrence Bernstein, *National Impact Evaluation of the Comprehensive Child Development Program: Final Report*, Abt Associates, Inc., June 1997.

Comprehensive Child Development Program: A National Family Support Demonstration. Interim Report to Congress. CSR, Inc., May 1994.

Comprehensive Child Development Program: A National Family Support Demonstration. Process Evaluation Final Report. CSR, Inc., March 1997.

PUBLIC-USE ACCESS TO DATA: Available from Westat; contact Kwant Kim at 301-517-4078.

Maryland Guardianship Assistance Program Demonstration

SUMMARY: This demonstration, conducted from 1998 to 1999, tested a new guardianship program on a medium-sized sample of foster children and caregivers. Subjects were followed for approximately two years (22–28 months). Additional demonstrations are ongoing.

COST: $714,000 over five years.

TIME FRAME: Demonstration period, September 1998–January 1999; data collected, September 1998–January 2001.

TREATMENTS TESTED: The demonstration allowed members of the experimental group to be eligible for a guardianship subsidy of $300 per month until the child reached the age of 18, or 21 if in formal schooling. Controls were not eligible for the subsidy but received normal monthly foster-child maintenance payments.

OUTCOMES OF INTEREST: Effects on exits from foster care.

SAMPLE SIZE: Total, 442; experimentals, 228; controls, 214.

TARGET POPULATION: Children younger than 17, committed to state care or kinship care, who have lived with the caregiver for at least six months and are adjusting well to the home. "Adoption and reunification must not be likely or anticipated." The caregiver must be able to provide a safe and healthy home and be financially solvent without the subsidy.

NUMBER OF TREATMENT GROUPS: Two (with one control group).

NUMBER AND LOCATION OF SITES: Statewide, with a focus on Baltimore City.

RESEARCH COMPONENTS:
- Process analysis: Focus on implementation and themes about child welfare and subsidized guardianship. Implementation analyzed through group interviews with Department of Social Services staff.
- Impact analysis: Conducted using Cox proportional hazard models.
- Benefit–cost analysis: Cost-effectiveness analysis conducted from government and caregivers' perspectives.

MAJOR FINDINGS:
1. "Eligibility for the guardianship subsidy reduced the estimated median time to exit from foster care for females by approximately seven months (217 days) and for males by more than six months (192 days)."
2. Kinship caregivers gain approximately $130 per month with the experimental subsidy; but restricted foster caregivers, who receive the foster care board payment of $600, potentially lose $300 a month by assuming guardianship with the experimental subsidy. This suggests that the program would need to at least equal the foster care board payment to induce both groups to seek guardianship.
3. A simulation suggests that the program saves the state approximately $622 per month per child in administrative costs, but this examination is limited to the kinship caregivers.

TIME TRENDS IN FINDINGS: None reported.

DESIGN ISSUES:
1. There were too few children in the restricted foster care group in the sample, and thus they could not be included in the study. Analysis was limited to kinship care children, which was not the original aim of the demonstration.
2. Subjects had been in foster care for varying lengths of time. Numerical estimates do not apply to a given entry cohort, but only to the group in kinship care at the time the subsidy was made available.
3. The short duration of the study does not address the issue of reentry into foster care. Study also does not address whether eligibility for the subsidy affects adoption as an alterna-

tive to guardianship. This also brings into question the formal legal status of children.

4. Study does not address the children's and caregivers' levels of satisfaction with placement.

REPLICABILITY: Replicable.

GENERALIZABILITY: The study does not generalize well because of the focus on Baltimore City. Although Baltimore City demographics are not representative of the rest of Maryland, similar demonstrations are being conducted across the state. This study only examined African American children in kinship care. Baltimore also has a much higher concentration of poverty than the rest of the state or the nation.

FUNDING SOURCES: Maryland Department of Human Resources, Social Services Administration.

TREATMENT ADMINISTRATOR: Baltimore City Department of Social Services.

EVALUATORS: University of Maryland–Baltimore, and University of Maryland–Baltimore County.

ENABLING LEGISLATION: None.

INFORMATION SOURCES: Marv Mandell, *The Effect of Subsidized Guardianship on Exits from Kinship Care: Results from Maryland's Guardianship Assistance Demonstration Project,* Policy Sciences Graduate Program, UMBC, March 2001; Malinda Orlin and University of Maryland School of Social Work GAP Research Team, *Maryland Subsidized Demonstration Project Evaluation. Interim Report,* October 2000.

PUBLIC-USE ACCESS TO DATA: None.

School Vouchers

TIME FRAME: Demonstration period, 1997–98.

TREATMENTS TESTED: In the experimental group, families received vouchers that could be used to pay private school tuition. In New York, the maximum amount of a voucher was $1,400. In Dayton, the ceiling was $1,200 or 60 percent of tuition, whichever was less. In Washington, it was $1,700 or 60 percent of the tuition. The control group (applicants who did not win the voucher lottery) did not receive these vouchers.

OUTCOME OF INTEREST: Achievement test scores.

SAMPLE SIZE: Total, 2,724 students.

TARGET POPULATION: Low-income families in New York City (e.g., income below $21,320 for a family of four) and families with less than 2 and 2.7 times the federal poverty level in Dayton, Ohio, and Washington, D.C., respectively (e.g., $35,985 in Dayton and $44,932 in Washington for a family of four).

NUMBER AND LOCATION OF SITES: Three— New York City, New York; Dayton, Ohio; and Washington, D.C.

SUMMARY OF THE EVALUATION: The demonstration began in 1997 in New York City and in 1998 in Ohio and Washington, D.C. The intervention was tested on a total of 2,724 students in three sites. Treatment and control students were both invited back for testing, one and two years after randomization. These tests provided the key outcome measures used to estimate the impacts of the vouchers. The participation of the sample in the follow-up testing was as follows:

	New York City	Dayton	Washington, DC
Grades at baseline	1–4	K–12	K–8
Baseline sample	1,960	803	1,582
Took test after 1st year	82%	56%	63%
Took test after 2nd year	66%	49%	50%

In Howell et al. (2002), the methods adopted to motivate students to take the follow-up tests are described as follows (footnotes are in parentheses):

> To promote high response rates, the voucher programs conditioned the renewal of scholarships on participating in these sessions. (While program administrators included this provision to boost

response rates, ultimately they did not drop any voucher recipients for not attending follow-up sessions.) In addition, they provided modest financial incentives to encourage families in the control group and members of the treatment group who remained in public schools to return for follow-up testing. (In New York and Washington, families in the control group who attended follow-up testing sessions after both 1 and 2 years were automatically entered in a new lottery. In Dayton, control group families were entered in a new lottery only after the first year of the program. For the second year, they were instead offered higher compensation for attending testing sessions.)

Thus, the mechanism for inclusion in the data follow-up strongly encouraged selection bias. In the treatment group, voucher users who were not interested in returning to (or entering) private schools had little reason to participate. In the control group, families that had lost interest in private schools or lacked faith in their chances in the lottery after the first failure had small interest in the return test.

On the basis of attrition alone, the results from Washington in the second year and from Dayton in either year are of little interest. The first-year and second-year New York City results and the first-year Washington results might be of interest if one could be sure they were unaffected by selection bias, but one cannot be.

For the sample as a whole, the evaluators found no statistically significant effect of the voucher in any year in New York or Dayton; a positive significant effect on the combined math and reading score was found in Washington in

the second year. The first two articles cited below report significant positive effects in the African American subgroup in New York in both the first and second years. Krueger and Zhu's paper reports that statistical significance for this subgroup disappears when students with missing baseline test scores (most of whom were in kindergarten at random assignment) are added to the sample.

TREATMENT ADMINISTRATORS: Private foundations at the three sites.

EVALUATORS: Mathematica Policy Research conducted the tests. Howell, Wolf, Campbell, and Peterson are affiliated with the University of Wisconsin, Georgetown University, Princeton University, and Harvard University, respectively. The Harvard Program on Education Policy and Governance was responsible for the analysis.

INFORMATION SOURCES: William Howell, Patrick Wolf, David Campbell, and Paul Peterson, "School Vouchers and Academic Performance, Results from Three Randomized Field Trials," *Journal of Policy Analysis and Management* 21(2002, 2): 191–217.

William Howell, Patrick Wolf, David Campbell, and Paul Peterson, *Test Scores Effects of School Vouchers in Dayton, Ohio, New York City, and Washington, DC: Evidence from Randomized Field Trials,* September 2000.

Alan Krueger and Pei Zhu, *Another Look at the New York City School Voucher Experiment,* Princeton University, August 2002.

8

Low-Income Youth

Public- versus Private-Sector Jobs Demonstration Project

SUMMARY: This demonstration, conducted from 1978 to 1980, tested the effects of subsidized work experience with either public or private employers on a large sample of low-income youth. Subjects were followed for one to eight months.

COST: About $600,000.

TIME FRAME: Demonstration period, summer 1978–spring 1979; data collected, spring 1980; final report, 1981.

TREATMENTS TESTED: Participating public- and private-sector employers were assigned youths fully subsidized by the program at 100 percent of the minimum wage for 25 weeks. Employers were encouraged to place the young worker in an unsubsidized position at program's end, but where this was infeasible, program operators attempted to develop a different unsubsidized job with another employer. Young people from the same site were grouped according to age, race, sex, and a reading test score, and were randomly assigned to either a public- or private-sector job slot.

OUTCOME OF INTEREST: Employment.

SAMPLE SIZE: Public-sector workers, 1,366; private-sector workers, 1,470.

TARGET POPULATION: 16–21-year-old low-income youths who were not in school.

NUMBER OF TREATMENT GROUPS: Two (with no control group).

NUMBER AND LOCATION OF SITES: Five—Portland, Oregon; St. Louis, Missouri; Philadelphia, Pennsylvania; New York City; and rural Minnesota.

RESEARCH COMPONENTS:

▪ Process analysis: Conducted. The analysis concluded that a much greater effort was needed to develop private-sector worksites for the demonstration.

▪ Impact analysis: Conducted by comparison of means and ordinary least squares (OLS).

▪ Benefit–cost analysis: Not conducted.

MAJOR FINDINGS: All findings are subject to some doubt because of heavy attrition in responses to follow-up surveys, and attrition may not have been random across treatments. Sixty percent of the sample could not be found at the first follow-up, which occurred 90 days after program termination. At the second follow-up, 240 days after termination, the nonresponse rate was 65 percent. In the comparison of means, Gilsinan's report (1984) does not state that any differences were statistically significant, although some of them appear to be.

1. Program flow data:

Stage	Public	Private
1. Random assignment	1,366	1,470
2. Starting program	1,034	1,092
3. Reporting to worksite	892	879
4. Early termination	530	675
(percentage of line 2)	(51.3)	(61.8)
5. Completing program	504	417
(percentage of line 2)	(48.8)	(38.2)

Thus, subjects assigned to the private sector were more likely to quit or be fired than their public counterparts.

2. Outcomes for those completing the program, at completion:

	Public (%)	Private (%)
Unsubsidized employment	39.2	52.5
Other positive (schooling, etc.)	12.6	5.1
"Nonpositive" outcomes	47.1	40.4

3. Outcomes for completers, 90 days after program completion:

	Public responses (%)	Total (%)	Private responses (%)	Total (%)
Unsubsidized full-time job	50.2	28.6	64.0	32.4
Unsubsidized part-time job	16.0	9.1	16.6	8.4
Education or training	25.6	14.7	17.5	8.9
"Nonpositive" outcomes	8.0	4.6	1.9	1.0
Unknown		43.1		49.4

Thus, private-sector experience was more likely to lead directly to employment than to public-sector experience for those who completed the program. This is confirmed in OLS regressions using discrete outcomes (employment, etc.) as the dependent variables. For example, private-sector assignment raised the probability of unsubsidized employment immediately after completion by 14 percent, an effect that is statistically significant at the 5 percent level.

TIME TRENDS IN FINDINGS: The 240-day follow-up results are similar to the 90-day results.

DESIGN ISSUES: According to the project report, "The high dropout rate clouds the issue of whether those who dropped out of the program and were never heard from again failed to gain meaningful employment." The failure to collect data on the subsequent experience of those terminated is a flaw in the experimental design; some of them may have dropped out in favor of better jobs, for example, and there is no information on whether the private-sector group of dropouts had a better career path than the public-sector group.

REPLICABILITY: Replicable.

GENERALIZABILITY: This project is unique; it is the only source of experimental information on the relative effects of job creation in government as opposed to business. The findings seem to indicate a trade-off between a higher attrition rate in business and lower prospects of a permanent job in government. However, the flawed design, discussed above in "Design Issues," limits the confidence that can be placed in the findings.

FUNDING SOURCE: U.S. Department of Labor, Office of Youth Programs. Key personnel: Robert Taggart and Joseph Seiler.

TREATMENT ADMINISTRATOR: Comprehensive Employment and Training Act, prime sponsors in five sites.

EVALUATOR: Center for Urban Programs, Saint Louis University. Key personnel: James F. Gilsinan and E. Allen Tomey.

ENABLING LEGISLATION: Youth Employment and Demonstration Projects Act of 1977.

INFORMATION SOURCE: James F. Gilsinan, "Information and Knowledge Development Potential," *Evaluation Review* June 1984: 371–88.

PUBLIC-USE ACCESS TO DATA: We have no information about a public-use file for this demonstration.

Cambridge Job Factory

SUMMARY: This demonstration, conducted from 1979 to 1980, tested the effects of job clubs, supervised job search assistance, and a bonus for finding a job quickly on a medium-sized sample of unemployed youth. Subjects were followed for one year.

COST: $202,940 (1979).

TIME FRAME: Demonstration period, June 1979–July 1980; data collected through October 1980; final report, 1981.

TREATMENTS TESTED:
1. Experimentals. A four-week cycle in which participants were "hired and paid to get a job."

The program components included minimum-wage payments for attendance (which could be docked or terminated); a one-week Job Club program with special group problem-solving exercises; three weeks of supervised job search; and a bonus (two days' pay) for finding a job within the first three weeks.
2. Controls were told that because of funding limitations, no slots were open for them.

OUTCOMES OF INTEREST: (1) Employment and (2) Earnings.

SAMPLE SIZE: Experimentals, 203; controls, 165.

TARGET POPULATION: Unemployed youth ages 15–21. Recent high school graduates, dropouts, and graduating seniors (no in-school youth) from CETA-eligible (low-income) families.

NUMBER OF TREATMENT GROUPS: Two (with one control group).

NUMBER AND LOCATION OF SITES: One—Cambridge, Massachusetts.

RESEARCH COMPONENTS:
- Process analysis: Conducted. It showed that enrollment targets for graduating seniors were difficult to meet (some of those enrolled were only temporarily unemployed), but that graduate and dropout participation targets were feasible. It also showed that without stipends paid to participants, it was not feasible to run the program. (However, this was shown only for a cycle of graduating seniors.)
- Impact analysis: Comparison of means, logit, and ordinary least squares (OLS).
- Benefit–cost analysis: Not conducted.

MAJOR FINDINGS:
(The data source used was follow-up surveys. The authors attempted to control for differential attrition bias by reporting both the results for all respondents and the results for respondents who completed all surveys. The pattern of response among the latter was much the same as among the former. Follow-ups were sent roughly once a

quarter. The question asked was essentially, "Have you found a job since intake?" The percentage answering yes can decrease as well as increase because of a less-than-complete response on each follow-up.)

Job Finding Rates (percent)

Survey	Experimentals	Controls
First	63.6	47.7
Second	77.1	73.2
Third	79.3	78.0
Fourth	79.2	81.8

(The question asked here was, "Are you now employed?")

Employment Rates (percent)

Survey	Experimentals	Controls
First	63.1	47.7
Second	55.1	55.1
Third	56.4	51.4
Fourth	64.7	50.0

Logit and OLS confirmed that the experimental effect on job-finding was statistically significant in the first quarter.

Cost per experimental was $715. Cost per one net new job (where new jobs are the expected experimental/control differential at the close of the first quarter) was $4,468.

TIME TRENDS IN FINDINGS: Apparent above.

DESIGN ISSUES: The first graduating seniors cycle included many students who either planned to go on to other education or had (before the program started) signed up for CETA-subsidized employment commencing shortly after the treatment ended.

REPLICABILITY: Replicable.

GENERALIZABILITY: The sample is probably a representative low-income urban population, but the size is small and the targeting of graduating seniors problematic.

FUNDING SOURCE: U.S. Department of Labor, Office of Youth Programs. Key personnel: Robert Taggart, Joseph Seiler, and Gordon Berlin.

TREATMENT ADMINISTRATOR: Cambridge Job Factory Program. Key personnel: Joseph Fisher.

EVALUATOR: Center for Employment and Income Studies, Florence Heller Graduate School. Key personnel: Andrew Hahn and Barry Friedman.

ENABLING LEGISLATION: Youth Employment and Demonstration Projects Act of 1977.

INFORMATION SOURCE: Andrew Hahn and Barry Friedman with the assistance of Cecilia Rivera-Casale and Robert Evans, *The Effectiveness of Two Job Search Assistance Programs for Disadvantaged Youth,* Center for Employment and Income Studies, Florence Heller Graduate School for Advanced Studies in Social Welfare, Brandeis University, Waltham, Massachusetts, 1981.

PUBLIC-USE ACCESS TO DATA: We have no information about a public-use file for this demonstration.

Career Advancement Voucher Demonstration Project

SUMMARY: This demonstration, conducted from 1979 to 1980, tested the effects of financial support for postsecondary education on a medium-sized sample of low-income youth. Some subjects were followed for at least one college semester.

COST: $1.8 million (1980).

TIME FRAME: The period covered by the cited report is April 1, 1979–March 31, 1980; data collected, unknown; date of final report, unknown.

TREATMENTS TESTED: The experimental treatment was financial support for two years of a full-time college program (accredited, offering Associate of Arts, Bachelor of Arts, or both) plus counseling. In principle, the support was limited to schools charging $2,500 or less in tuition and located within commuting distance of the project site; but in practice, this was waived in Little Rock. Four variants of this treatment were randomly assigned in all five sites: (1) Voucher (no counselor approval for academic program required) plus assistance with involvement in college life; (2) Voucher without such assistance; (3) Non-voucher (counselor approval required for academic program) plus assistance with involvement in college life; and (4) Non-voucher, but no assistance with involvement in college life. The variants were to test the ability of the subjects to choose realistic programs without guidance (guidance would be more expensive and would reduce diversity) and the sociological finding that dropouts had little contact with the campus apart from attendance in class. The control treatment was designed to be regular CETA-subsidized employment.

OUTCOMES OF INTEREST: (1) College attendance; (2) Employment; (3) Earnings; and (4) Effectiveness of strategies to integrate subjects into ordinary college life.

SAMPLE SIZE: Experimentals, 490; controls, 205. Experimentals by treatment: treatment 1, 125; treatment 2, 120; treatment 3, 125; treatment 4, 120.

TARGET POPULATION: CETA-eligible low-income youth, 16–21 years old, who were out of school, had obtained a high school diploma or general equivalency diploma (GED), had had at most eight months of participation in other CETA programs, and had a desire to attend college. (The last condition is emphasized because it critically affected the experiment.) In some sites there were additional screens. In Atlanta and Washington, subjects had to have a test score of 80 or better on an aptitude test (GATB). In El Paso, subjects needed proof of legal residency, letters of recommendation, and SAT or ACT scores. In Little Rock, they needed at least a C average in high school. In Pittsburgh, there were no additional requirements.

NUMBER OF TREATMENT GROUPS: Five (with one control group).

NUMBER AND LOCATION OF SITES: Five—Atlanta, Georgia; El Paso, Texas; Little Rock, Arkansas; Pittsburgh, Pennsylvania; and Washington, D.C. The effectiveness of the experimental treatment was hypothesized to vary with the unemployment rate. El Paso and Pittsburgh had fairly high rates; the other three cities had fairly low rates.

RESEARCH COMPONENTS:

- Process analysis: Control group youths failed to enroll in CETA programs. To be exact, only 20 out of 205 controls enrolled in CETA. The experiment, therefore, could not shed any light on whether college was more likely than subsidized employment to raise wages and employment among some representative group of low-income youths. The reasons for this failure were the recruitment sources and the identity of the program operators. Most subjects were recruited by high school guidance counselors; many of them had no particular interest in subsidized employment or noncollege training. With the exception of Pittsburgh, the Career Advancement Voucher Demonstration (CAVD) projects were "semiautonomous" from the local CETA programs. The local projects did not have any CETA jobs to provide, and the coordination problem with the CETA prime sponsors was apparently not solved. According to the interim report we obtained, "The current manner in which the local sites relate to their respective regional offices does not particularly facilitate learning how to fit the CAVDP into the existing CETA system."
- Impact analysis: None.
- Benefit–cost analysis: None.

MAJOR FINDINGS: The major substantive finding that could be drawn from this experiment would be the effect of the scholarship offer on enrollment. This turned out to be significant but was not a focus of the report.

The following figures are calculated from the interim report.

1. Attending college, October 1979:

	Experimentals	Controls
Atlanta	78 (89%)	22 (82%)
El Paso	109 (98%)	36 (77%)
Little Rock	103 (100%)	12 (50%)
Pittsburgh	77 (85%)	6 (32%)
Washington, DC	94 (95%)	15 (56%)

The control percentages have been calculated as percentages of controls whose status was known. The project had no information on about 30 percent of the controls. About 5 percent of the experimentals were attending college without support from the project, usually because they had chosen colleges that they could not commute to from the project city.

2. First-semester dropout rates from college among experimentals were reported to be low, but they were not compared with those of controls or of first-semester freshmen in general.

3. The effects of the voucher/non-voucher experimental treatments on the diversity of colleges chosen were inconsistent.

TIME TRENDS IN FINDINGS: None.

DESIGN ISSUES: This experiment tested an interesting idea on a large population. It then dissipated much of its value with a needlessly complex experimental design, an inadequate data collection strategy, and a severely flawed implementation.

REPLICABILITY: Both the experimental treatment and the control treatment are replicable, but it is doubtful whether the two treatments can be simultaneously assigned to different members of the same population with reasonable results. It appears that low-income young people who are primarily interested in college and low-income young people who are primarily interested in subsidized employment are fundamentally different groups.

GENERALIZABILITY: This is the only experiment of its kind. The findings indicate that a substantial population of young poor people exists that would attend college if they received scholarships. The findings do not indicate whether they would finish their programs if they received such scholarships.

FUNDING SOURCE: U.S. Department of Labor, Office of Youth Programs. Key personnel: Robert Taggart.

TREATMENT ADMINISTRATORS: Negro Scholarship Service-Fund for Negro Students (Atlanta); CETA, prime sponsor (Pittsburgh); three "semi-autonomous" projects in Little Rock, Arkansas; Washington, D.C.; and El Paso, Texas.

EVALUATOR: Clark, Phipps, Clark, and Harris.

ENABLING LEGISLATION: None.

INFORMATION SOURCES: Clark, Phipps, Clark, and Harris, "Advanced Education and Training—Interim Report on the Career Advancement Voucher Demonstration," U.S. Department of Labor (DOL), Employment and Training Administration, *Youth Knowledge Development Report 5.3*, May 1980. The names of the authors are not given in this report, which was obtained from William Showler of DOL. The only copy of the final report known to exist is in the files of Kenneth Clark and Associates (615 Broadway, Hastings-on-Hudson, NY 10706; 914-478-1010). The position of the firm is that its reports are proprietary to the client; on application to Dr. Clark, permission might be granted to inspect the report, but not to copy it. All copies sent to the funding agency, the Department of Labor's Office of Youth Programs, have apparently been lost. As of this writing, we have not been able to inspect this report.

PUBLIC-USE ACCESS TO DATA: We have no information about a public-use file for this demonstration.

Wilkes-Barre YES Workshop Program

SUMMARY: This demonstration, conducted from 1979 to 1980, tested the effects of career counseling and job search assistance on a medium-sized sample of unemployed low-income youth. Subjects were followed for about one year.

COST: $164,162 (1980).

TIME FRAME: Demonstration period, May 1979–October 1980; data collected, same period; final report, 1981.

TREATMENTS TESTED:
1. Individual career counseling and job placement services (job bank only). The job bank included a job developer who would actively look for jobs for youths from employers in the community and would try to locate specific kinds of jobs sought by youths if they were not already listed.
2. Career counseling, job placement services, and special job search skills workshops (job bank and workshop).
3. Career counseling and job search skills workshops (workshop only). No subjects were paid for participating.

OUTCOME OF INTEREST: Employment.

SAMPLE SIZE: Job bank only, 138; job bank and workshop, 140; workshop only, 123.

TARGET POPULATION: Youths age 16–21, unemployed, and from low-income families (Comprehensive Employment and Training Act [CETA]–eligible).

NUMBER OF TREATMENT GROUPS: Three (with no control group).

NUMBER AND LOCATION OF SITES: One—Wilkes-Barre, Pennsylvania.

RESEARCH COMPONENTS:
- Process analysis: Conducted. Focused on (1) low levels of enrollment, which were attributed to problems with outreach to targeted population, completion of income verification forms, and competition with CETA-subsidized jobs; (2) actual levels of participation, which were low in the group workshops, with typically only two or three young people present, apparently owing to lack of interest; and (3) effects of personnel turnover. The treatment organization was not fully in place prior to the commencement of the experiment, so difficulties in starting up may have affected the impact analysis.
- Impact analysis: Comparison of means, logit, and ordinary least squares (OLS).
- Benefit–cost analysis: Not conducted.

MAJOR FINDINGS:
(The data source used was follow-up surveys. The project report authors attempted to control for differential attrition bias by reporting both the results for all respondents and the results for respondents who completed all surveys. The pattern of response among the latter was much the same as among the former. Follow-ups were sent roughly once a quarter. The question being asked was essentially, "Have you found a job since intake?" The percentage answering yes could go down as well as up because of a less-than-complete response on each follow-up.)

Job-Finding Rates (percent)

Survey	Job Bank only	Job Bank and workshop	Workshop only
First	70.7	70.8	70.8
Second	77.4	68.9	76.0
Third	89.5	90.2	84.2
Fourth	92.3	83.3	89.5

Logit and OLS confirm that differences in outcome among the experimental groups were statistically insignificant.

Available data seem to indicate that individuals in the job bank and workshop group, despite their apparent lack of incremental success in finding jobs, were more likely to have first-time jobs that were full-time and unsubsidized, and that their median earnings were higher; but the data were too incomplete for statistical testing.

TIME TRENDS IN FINDINGS: Data too incomplete; response to surveys declines over time.

DESIGN ISSUES: Treatment administrators believed that individual counseling was the most effective component of their program; however, all three groups received individual counseling and therefore this component is untested.

REPLICABILITY: It is not clear that there was a prescribed workshop format with content different from the individual counseling available to all subjects. In this sense, the treatment is not replicable.

GENERALIZABILITY: Probably none.

FUNDING SOURCE: U.S. Department of Labor, Office of Youth Programs. Key personnel: Robert Taggart, Joseph Seiler, and Gordon Berlin.

TREATMENT ADMINISTRATOR: Youth Employment Service. Key personnel: Joey Kelly.

EVALUATOR: Center for Employment and Income Studies, Florence Heller Graduate School. Key personnel: Andrew Hahn and Barry Friedman.

ENABLING LEGISLATION: Youth Employment and Demonstration Projects Act of 1977.

INFORMATION SOURCE: Andrew Hahn and Barry Friedman, with the assistance of Cecilia Rivera-Casale and Robert Evans, *The Effectiveness of Two Job Search Assistance Programs for Disadvantaged Youth,* Center for Employment and Income Studies, Florence Heller Graduate School for Advanced Studies in Social Welfare, Brandeis University, Waltham, Massachusetts, 1981.

PUBLIC-USE ACCESS TO DATA: We have no information about a public-use file for this demonstration.

Alternative Youth Employment Strategies (AYES) Project

SUMMARY: This demonstration, conducted from 1980 to 1982, tested the effects of various combinations of work experience, training, and placement assistance on a large sample of low-income unemployed youth. Subjects were followed for eight months.

COST: $4.8 million (1981) for implementation; research only, roughly $1.5 million (1981).

TIME FRAME: Demonstration period, July 1980–September 1981; data collected through May 1982; final report, August 1983.

TREATMENTS TESTED: All subjects receiving one of three experimental treatments could remain in the program for up to 26 weeks.

Model 1. Full-time work experience with counseling and placement services. The work was in entry-level jobs with, on the one hand, government or nonprofit agencies or, on the other hand, in a supported work environment in which crews of participants performed building rehabilitation, landscape, and clean-up work for community organizations. Jobs were 35 hours per week.

Model 2. Basic education or vocational education or prevocational training with counseling and placement services. Educational option selected by the subject, in consultation with counselors. Payment was based on 30 hours per week participation, equivalent to payment in model 1 because the stipend was not taxed.

Model 3. Balanced and complementary part-time work experience and part-time training, with counseling and placement services. Payment based on 30 hours per week participation.

Controls. Received no services from the project, but $10 for completing the intake interview. Both controls and experimentals received $10 per follow-up interview.

The assignment process was complex. Subjects were randomly assigned to be either controls or experimentals (where experimentals would be in any of the three models). The first 225 experimentals in each of the three sites chose which model they wanted for themselves, with guidance from a counselor. In every case, the client received either his first or second choice. The remaining experimentals in each site were randomly assigned.

OUTCOMES OF INTEREST: (1) Employment; (2) Earnings; and (3) Arrests.

SAMPLE SIZE: Experimentals, 1,082; controls, 1,137. Of the experimentals, 357 were in model 1, 355 in model 2, and 370 in model 3. The experimentals assigned randomly were 186 in New York, 151 in Miami, and 70 in Albuquerque.

TARGET POPULATION: Persons 16–21 years old, unemployed, Youth Employment Training Program (YETP)–eligible (low-income), out of school, and "high-risk" (defined as having a prior involvement with the juvenile or criminal justice systems or "a substantial likelihood for such involvement in the future"). At least 50 percent of subjects, by design, were to be referred from the juvenile or criminal justice systems.

NUMBER OF TREATMENT GROUPS: Four (with one control group).

NUMBER AND LOCATION OF SITES: Three— Albuquerque, New Mexico; Miami, Florida; and New York City.

RESEARCH COMPONENTS:
- Process analysis: Conducted. Probation officers in Albuquerque were uncooperative about referring clients to a random-assignment program where half of those referred received no services. Fifty-six percent of the New York subjects were justice-system referrals, as were 49 percent of the Miami subjects, but only 29 percent of the Albuquerque subjects. The Albuquerque sample is therefore unrepresentative of the target population: it was 41 percent female (compared with 26 percent in New York and 35 percent in Miami) and 43 percent had high school diplo-

mas or GEDs (compared with 11 percent in New York and 16 percent in Miami).

Documentation of low-income status tended to screen out the high-risk target population. Criminal justice referrals were more likely than referrals from other sources to fail to bring documents with them and to fail to keep subsequent intake appointments. There was no starting-up period prior to intake; the initial cohort received lower-quality services as a consequence. Model 3 in most cases could not be implemented as designed, owing to insufficient preparation time; most participants received either mostly training or mostly work experience. The Labor Department's budget commitment to the experiment was uncertain throughout the life of the project; according to the project report, "no provision was made for assuring program staff of employment beyond the end of the data collection period," and "an atmosphere of imminent doom developed in the last few months," which probably affected the quality of service delivery, especially when important staff left the project early. (This would have been most serious in Albuquerque; funding from other sources continued for a while in New York and Miami.) Budget uncertainties caused job developer positions, vital to the placement service, to go unfilled for long periods in Miami, and they were never filled in Albuquerque or New York.
- Impact analysis: Conducted as difference in means, and with ordinary least squares (OLS) and logit.
- Benefit–cost analysis: Not conducted.

MAJOR FINDINGS:
1. "Have you worked in the eight months since . . . [for experimentals, "exit from the program"; for controls, "intake"]?" See table, next page.

The overall difference was statistically significant and was significant at all individual sites except Miami (the only site where job development was properly implemented).

Employment Data from Eight-Month Follow-Up (percent)

	Overall	Albuquerque	Miami	New York City
Experimentals	51	64.4	47.2	43.9
Controls	41	55.3	41.6	27.1

2. Weekly earnings, most recent job (includes zeros for those who had no jobs):

	Overall ($)	Albuquerque ($)	Miami ($)	New York City ($)
Experimentals	63.16	68.39	62.37	59.12
Controls	47.67	52.82	56.12	32.78

The overall difference was statistically significant. The difference was due almost entirely to higher employment rates for experimentals, not to higher wages for those employed.

3. Percentage of the eight-month follow-up spent working: experimentals, 26.2 percent; controls, 19.2 percent. The difference was highly significant.

4. In a regression, the effects of the three different models were insignificantly different from each other, except that those model 1 subjects who were employed had higher earnings during the follow-up than both model 2 and model 3 subjects who were employed.

5. There was no effect on arrests. Three-quarters of both experimentals and controls were not arrested during the data collection period.

TIME TRENDS IN FINDINGS: Only data from an eight-month follow-up were available for analysis.

DESIGN ISSUES:

1. One could argue that the selection of the treatment model by experimentals themselves almost necessarily prevented the evaluation from distinguishing true treatment effects from unobserved participant attributes; thus, the results of the experiment could not have substantially illuminated program design choices, even if the three different models had produced significantly different results. In designing the experiment, however, "the research staff came to believe that random assignment to model would substantially increase the rate at which participants failed to show up or dropped out of the program prematurely. . . . this would result in fewer people having a meaningful experience with the program. Moreover, since there was no reason to assume that the increased dropout rates would be uniform for the three models, there was no theoretical assurance of group equivalence at the start of the program."

2. The contradiction between the positive effects of model 1, compared with controls, and the findings of the National Supported Work Demonstration (NSWD) (see page 389) on the employment and earnings of young dropouts and ex-offenders in supported work is striking. The contradiction is even more striking because in New York City the same agency was administering both the NSWD and the Alternative Youth Employment Strategies (AYES) treatments. The project report did not address this discrepancy.

3. The labor market in the country was steadily worsening throughout the course of the experiment, especially for young, unskilled workers.

4. Using logit on the dichotomous variable "have you worked in the past 8 months?" models 2 and 3 did significantly better than model 1. According to the project report: "The different conclusions reflect the fact that the logistic regression was applied to the entire eight-month sample ($N > 1,300$) and is a more powerful statistical technique. Statistical significance is not hard to achieve with so large an N, but the size of the effect seems quite small." It might also reflect self-selection, given the assignment process.

REPLICABILITY: Replicable.

GENERALIZABILITY: The AYES project was reviewed with other Youth Employment and Demonstration Projects Act (YEDPA) projects by a committee from the National Academy of Sciences (see Richard F. Elmore, "Knowledge Development under the Youth Employment and Demonstration Projects Act, 1977–1981," in *Youth Employment and Training Programs,* edited by Charles L. Betsey, Robinson B. Hollister Jr., and Mary R. Papgeorgiou [Washington, DC: National Academy Press, 1985]). Their primary reaction was to the finding of no significant differences among the three experimental models. "In several other studies, similar null findings for alternative treatments were also found. Indeed, this is the one finding that was fairly robust throughout the studies of labor market preparation programs we reviewed." Comparing the results of the 26-week program with the 10–12-week program, they found evidence, subject to some caveats, that "the same marginal gains in employment can be achieved as well by a shorter program."

FUNDING SOURCE: U.S. Department of Labor, Office of Youth Programs. Key personnel: Robert Taggart.

TREATMENT ADMINISTRATORS: Three agencies—in Albuquerque, New Mexico (Office of Comprehensive Employment and Training Administration); in Miami, Florida (South Florida Employment and Training Consortium); and in New York City (Court Employment Project).

EVALUATOR: Vera Institute of Justice. Key personnel: Susan Sadd and Claire Haaga.

ENABLING LEGISLATION: YEDPA of 1977.

INFORMATION SOURCE: Susan Sadd, Mark Kotkin, and Samuel R. Friedman, "Alternative Youth Employment Strategies Project Final Report," Vera Institute of Justice, August 1983.

PUBLIC-USE ACCESS TO DATA: We have no information about a public-use file for this demonstration.

Cambridge Job Search Voucher Program

SUMMARY: This demonstration, conducted from 1980 to 1982, tested the effects of job search assistance and a wage supplement on a medium-sized sample of low-income youth. Subjects were followed for up to 20 weeks.

COST: Administration, $272,625 (1981).

TIME FRAME: Demonstration period, November 1980–February 1982; data collected, April 1982; final report, September 1982.

TREATMENTS TESTED: Full-treatment experimentals received a Job Club model treatment over four weeks; the treatment combined a weeklong workshop in job search skills with a supervised group job search organized around a telephone bank. For each hour spent in this job factory, subjects received the minimum wage. Those who obtained jobs were paid a supplemental bonus of $1.50 an hour (up to 48 hours per week) for the first two weeks on the job, and $1.00 an hour for the following 10 weeks. If the subject left one job for another during the 12 weeks, the subsidy would carry over to the new job.

Voucher-only experimentals received no help with job search but were entitled to the same 12-week subsidy if they found a job.

Controls received neither job search assistance nor a subsidy.

Hours worked were verified by pay stubs or special employer records. There was generally a four-week lag in voucher payments.

OUTCOMES OF INTEREST: (1) Employment and (2) Earnings.

SAMPLE SIZE: Full-treatment experimentals, 161; voucher-only, 130; controls, 108.

TARGET POPULATION: CETA-eligible (low-income) Boston area youth, ages 16 to 22.

NUMBER OF TREATMENT GROUPS: Three (with one control group).

NUMBER AND LOCATION OF SITES: One—Cambridge, Massachusetts.

RESEARCH COMPONENTS:
- Process analysis: Conducted. Later intake cycles were affected by turnover of top staff and office relocation. Payment of wages to subjects for attendance in the job factory treatment was believed to have brought in a number of "program hustlers" with no real interest in finding unsubsidized employment.
- Impact analysis: Conducted with ordinary least squares (OLS) and logit.
- Benefit–cost analysis: Cost per new job calculated.

MAJOR FINDINGS:
Data come from three follow-up surveys, taken at 4, 12, and 20 weeks after intake.
1. Difference in probability of having worked at all since the previous follow-up (or since intake), logit estimation:

	1st follow-up	2nd follow-up	3rd follow-up
Experimentals (both groups) versus controls	.035	.123*	.190*
Full-treatment versus voucher-only	.142*	.008	−.150*
Actual control mean	.343	.446	.512

* Statistically significant at one-tail, 5 percent–level test.

"A voucher paid to workers consistently raised employment of disadvantaged youth. . . . the voucher impacts rose over time. . . . the combined Job Factory plus voucher treatment produced employment gains in the initial period after program start-up, but the combined treatment did no better and sometimes worse than the voucher alone in later periods."

2. Effect on wage rates of those who worked, OLS estimate, in dollars:

	1st follow-up	2nd follow-up	3rd follow-up
Experimentals dummy variable	−0.1183	−0.4620	−0.7830*
Full-treatment dummy	0.1997	0.5570*	0.5150*
Actual control mean	3.81	4.07	4.40

Notes: "Experimentals dummy" is a measure of the effect of the voucher alone. "Full-treatment dummy" is a measure of the additional effect of the Job Factory. The number of observations are 90, 72, and 89 among the three follow-ups, respectively. Asterisk (*) denotes statistically significant at one-tail 5 percent–level test.

The only data on job retention and hours worked come from voucher payments to experimentals. Differences between full-treatment and voucher-only groups are not significant.

3. Cost per new job (net over controls):

Full-treatment, 1st follow-up	$6,739
Ever found job	$8,611
Voucher-only, 1st follow-up	$2,220
Ever found job	$793

According to the project report, "the evidence from this experiment does not suggest any positive long-term benefits" from the Job Factory treatment, although short-term employment effects were noted.

TIME TRENDS IN FINDINGS: As noted above.

DESIGN ISSUES:
1. Findings about the job factory did not generalize to Job Club treatments where participants were not paid to attend.
2. No attention was paid to potential attrition bias, and sample attrition was considerable.

REPLICABILITY: Replicable.

GENERALIZABILITY: Findings are for one job market only.

FUNDING SOURCE: U.S. Department of Labor, Office of Youth Programs. Key personnel: Robert Taggart.

TREATMENT ADMINISTRATOR: Cambridge Office of Manpower Affairs (CETA), primary sponsor. Key personnel: Patricia Tankard and Timothy Reidy.

EVALUATOR: Center for Employment and Income Studies, Florence Heller Graduate School, Brandeis University. Key personnel: Cecilia Rivera-Casale, Barry Friedman, and Robert Lerman.

ENABLING LEGISLATION: Funded under the Youth Employment and Demonstration Projects Act of 1977.

INFORMATION SOURCE: Cecilia Rivera-Casale, Barry Friedman, and Robert Lerman, *Can Employer or Worker Subsidies Raise Youth Employment? An Evaluation of Two Financial Incentive Programs for Disadvantaged Youth,* Center for Employment and Income Studies, Florence Heller Graduate School for Advanced Studies in Social Welfare, Brandeis University, September 1982.

PUBLIC-USE ACCESS TO DATA: We have no information about a public-use file for this demonstration.

Summer Experimental Youth Transition Project

SUMMARY: This demonstration, conducted in 1980, tested the effects of different forms of subsidized job search on a medium-sized sample of graduating low-income high school seniors. Subjects were followed for one month.

COST: Not available. Payments to participants must have been at least $130,000.

TIME FRAME: Demonstration period, July 1980–September 1980; data collected, same period; final report, May 1981.

TREATMENTS TESTED: Model 1 received a standard Job Club treatment: one week of job search skills workshop followed by three weeks of supervised group job search using a telephone bank. Model 2 also received a one-week skills workshop, followed by three weeks of individual job search assisted by a professional job developer. Model 3 was the same as the last three weeks of model 2 (i.e., no workshop). Model 4 received three weeks of "standard . . . transition services," mostly counseling, if desired. Experimentals in models 1–3 received minimum wage payments over the duration of the experiment.

OUTCOME OF INTEREST: Employment.

SAMPLE SIZE: Model 1, 65; model 2, 110; model 3, 110; model 4, 100.

TARGET POPULATION: Graduating low-income high school seniors who had at least six months' experience in the Youth Incentive Entitlement Pilot Project (YIEPP). YIEPP was a major non-experimental project guaranteeing full-time summer and part-time school-year jobs to disadvantaged youths, provided they remained in school.

NUMBER OF TREATMENT GROUPS: Four (with one control group).

NUMBER AND LOCATION OF SITES: One—Baltimore, Maryland.

RESEARCH COMPONENTS:

- Process analysis: Conducted. The observers noted that the staff assigned to the workshop phase of the group 2 model did not adhere to the prescribed presentation. Thus, the intended pure test of the effectiveness of supervised group job search compared with individual job search did not occur.
- Impact analysis: Conducted as a difference in means.
- Benefit–cost analysis: Unknown.

MAJOR FINDINGS:

1. For all subjects, the job-finding rates by the end of four weeks were
   Model 1: 26 percent*

Model 2: 12 percent

Model 3: 10 percent

Model 4: 7 percent

* The difference from the combined job-finding rate of the three other groups is statistically significant at the $p < .01$ level.

2. Of those who were functionally illiterate, the job-finding rates were

Model 1: 50 percent

Model 2: 26 percent

Model 3: 17 percent

Model 4: 0 percent

Bruml (1981) did not provide the gross number of those who were functionally illiterate.

TIME TRENDS IN FINDINGS: Only four weeks of data collected.

DESIGN ISSUES: See "Process analysis" under "Research Components."

REPLICABILITY: This is a replication.

GENERALIZABILITY: Impossible to evaluate. Findings can be compared with those of the Cambridge Job Factory, a similar intervention with a similar population.

FUNDING SOURCE: U.S. Department of Labor, Office of Youth Programs.

TREATMENT ADMINISTRATOR: City of Baltimore, Mayor's Office of Manpower Resources.

EVALUATOR: City of Baltimore, Mayor's Office of Manpower Resources. Key personnel: Susan Radcliffe.

ENABLING LEGISLATION: None.

INFORMATION SOURCE: The original report appears to have been lost. It is by Susan Radcliffe, *Summer Experimental Youth Transition Project Analysis and Evaluation Report,* Mayor's Office of Manpower Resources, Research and Evaluation, Baltimore, May 1981. The data are discussed in an unpub-

lished paper by Elise Bruml, "Self-Directed Group Job Search: The Results," July 13, 1981.

PUBLIC-USE ACCESS TO DATA: We have no information about a public-use file for this demonstration.

JOBSTART

SUMMARY: This demonstration, conducted between 1985 and 1992, tested the effects of education, training, and supportive services on a large sample of economically disadvantaged school dropouts. Subjects were followed for four years.

COST: The entire demonstration cost $6.2 million. Of this amount, $350,000 was paid to the sites and $800,000 was paid to operations staff who were providing assistance to the sites. The remainder was research cost.

TIME FRAME: Demonstration period, 1985–1988; data collected through 1992; final report, October 1993.

TREATMENTS TESTED: Education and vocational training, support services, and job placement assistance. Support services included assistance with transportation, child care, counseling, and incentive payments. Controls did not receive these services from the demonstration.

OUTCOMES OF INTEREST: (1) Educational attainment; (2) Employment; (3) Earnings; and (4) Welfare receipt.

SAMPLE SIZE: Total, 2,312 (1,941 used for analysis—see "Design Issue" 3); experimentals, 1,163; controls, 1,149.

TARGET POPULATION: Economically disadvantaged school dropouts age 17–21 who read below the eighth grade level and were eligible for Job Training Partnership Act (JTPA) Title IIA programs or the Job Corps. Some sites screened out youth with problems that the program was not equipped to handle. These problems included emotional problems, drug and alcohol abuse, health problems, unstable living conditions, poor motivation, and those who were likely to prove dangerous or disruptive.

NUMBER OF TREATMENT GROUPS: Two (with one control group).

NUMBER AND LOCATION OF SITES: Thirteen— Atlanta, Georgia; Buffalo and New York, New York; Chicago, Illinois; Dallas and Corpus Christi, Texas; Denver, Colorado; Hartford, Connecticut; San Jose, Monterey Park, and Los Angeles, California; Phoenix, Arizona; and Pittsburgh, Pennsylvania.

RESEARCH COMPONENTS:
- Process analysis: Conducted. Separate publications are available from Manpower Demonstration Research Corporation (MDRC) addressing implementation, site selection, and participation patterns.
- Impact analysis: Conducted using comparison of regression-adjusted means.
- Benefit–cost analysis: Conducted.

MAJOR FINDINGS:
1. Significantly more experimental group youths completed high school or equivalent compared with the control group (42 percent versus 28.6 percent). This impact was fairly large for all subgroups studied.
2. Employment was significantly greater for the control group in the first year of follow-up. In the second year, significantly more experimental group youths were employed. There were no significant differences in the third and fourth years regarding this variable.
3. Similarly, control group members earned more in the first two years after follow-up, whereas the experimental group earned more in the third and fourth years. This finding was statistically significant only for year one.
4. Few significant findings are found in subgroup analyses regarding employment. Trends are similar to those for the full sample.
5. For women who had no children when the program started, those in the experimental group were less likely to have children and to

receive AFDC payments at follow-up than were women in the control group. For custodial mothers (those with children at the start of the program), this finding was reversed; those in the experimental group were more likely to have more children at follow-up. However, this finding was not statistically significant.
6. There is some indication that JOBSTART led to a reduction in criminal activity (arrests and drug use), although impacts are generally not significant.
7. The San Jose site had higher earnings impacts than any other site. This finding was significant at the .01 level. The reasons for this are unclear. At the San Jose site, training and placement efforts were closely linked to the labor market, education and training efforts were coordinated, and the program had a clear organizational mission. Any or all of these factors may have affected program impacts.

TIME TRENDS IN FINDINGS: Experimental group payoffs did not usually occur until after year two.

DESIGN ISSUES:
1. The intake process was quite lengthy at some sites. Some youth who were eventually assigned to the experimental group had already found other opportunities or had lost interest.
2. At some sites, assessment was performed after random assignment. This led to the inclusion of some participants with reading levels higher than eighth grade.
3. Roughly 84 percent of the sample responded to the 48-month follow-up survey. These 1,941 youths were used for the analysis. There were significant differences between respondents to the follow-up survey and nonrespondents, although respondents were not more likely to be experimentals than controls.

REPLICABILITY: Replicable. The U.S. Department of Labor is currently funding a large-scale replication of the San Jose program for youth (see CET Replication Study, page 286).

GENERALIZABILITY: Designed to generalize to the entire nation. Site selection was not a probability sample. Sites were chosen for their ability to meet program guidelines, assemble operational funding, and yield sufficient sample members. At some sites, the assessment process screened out youths with significant problems. Despite this, the JOBSTART sample still appears to be slightly more disadvantaged than the majority of youth served nationwide by JTPA Title IIA programs, but the JOBSTART sample had slightly fewer barriers to employment than those in Job Corps.

FUNDING SOURCES: Funding was through a consortium of the U.S. Department of Labor, the Rockefeller Foundation, the Ford Foundation, Charles Stewart Mott Foundation, the William and Flora Hewlett Foundation, National Commission for Employment Policy, the AT&T Foundation, Exxon Corporation, ARCO Foundation, Aetna Foundation, the Chase Manhattan Bank, and Stuart Foundations.

TREATMENT ADMINISTRATORS: Local Service Delivery Areas (SDAs) at the 13 sites. The final report (p. 20) lists all treatment administrators.

EVALUATOR: MDRC. Key personnel: George Cave, Fred Doolittle, Hans Bos, and Cyril Toussaint.

ENABLING LEGISLATION: Job Training Partnership Act of 1982.

INFORMATION SOURCE: George Cave, Hans Bos, Fred Doolittle, and Cyril Toussaint, *JOBSTART: Final Report on a Program for School Dropouts,* Manpower Demonstration Research Corporation, October 1993.

PUBLIC-USE ACCESS TO DATA: Contact MDRC.

Summer Training and Education Program (STEP)

SUMMARY: This demonstration, conducted from 1985 to 1988, tested the effects of a combined work and educational remediation program on a large sample of low-income youth. Subjects were followed for up to four and one-half years.

COST: Total program costs, approximately $12 million. Research costs, approximately $7 million over eight years.

TIME FRAME: Demonstration period, 1985–88; data collected, 1984–93.

TREATMENTS TESTED: The intervention took place over two consecutive summers, with approximately 200 hours of program involvement each summer. The treatment consisted of a half-day job and a half day of remedial reading and math. In addition, two sessions per week dealt with decisionmaking and responsible social and sexual behavior. The control group was involved in the local Summer Youth Employment and Training Program (SYETP), which provided a job but no other services.

OUTCOMES OF INTEREST: (1) School dropout rates; (2) Academic achievement; (3) Employment and earnings; and (4) Parenting outcomes.

SAMPLE SIZE: The total original sample was 4,800, with 2,400 in both the experimental and control groups. Only cohorts 2 and 3 were used in the analysis. This total was 2,968.

TARGET POPULATION: Fourteen- and 15-year-olds from poor urban families who were seriously behind academically.

NUMBER OF TREATMENT GROUPS: Two (with one control group).

NUMBER AND LOCATION OF SITES: Five—Boston, Massachusetts; Fresno and San Diego, California; Portland, Oregon; and Seattle, Washington.

RESEARCH COMPONENTS:
- Process analysis: Examined planning, coordination, and operations through structured observations, as well as data from application forms, questionnaires, and program records.
- Impact analysis: Comparison of means conducted using standardized test scores, school records, and participant interviews.

Benefit–cost analysis: Not conducted, though some detail was provided about program costs.

MAJOR FINDINGS: The analysis was conducted only for the second and third cohorts. It compares STEP to SYETP, rather than to no program at all.

1. Over the first summer, STEP significantly boosted the experimental group's academic competence and knowledge of responsible sexual behavior. STEP had a net impact of .5 grade equivalents in reading, .6 equivalents in mathematics, and a 2-point increase on the 9-point contraceptive-knowledge scale.
2. The gains of the first summer did not translate into changes over the school year. No overall impacts on reading or mathematics, on credits earned, or on dropout behavior were found.
3. Second-summer impacts were again positive for academics and contraceptive knowledge, but were not as strong.
4. At follow-up (54 months after enrollment for cohort 2, 42 months for cohort 3), no significant impacts were found for any educational, employment, or parenting outcomes.

TIME TRENDS IN FINDINGS: As can be seen above, STEP produced immediate positive effects yet had no measurable long-term impact.

DESIGN ISSUES:

1. Due to a fast start-up schedule, it was difficult to establish significant cooperation between employment and training agencies and local school districts. Thus, over 85 percent of the educational remediation costs were borne by the employment and training system.
2. During the second summer, the evaluators came to believe that the remedial component for the first cohort was of substantially lower quality. They revised the curriculum and added a third cohort, treating the first cohort as an extension of the pilot period.
3. Intensive outreach efforts were necessary at all sites to enroll the required number of STEP participants and ensure their return for the second summer (the return rate was 75 percent).

4. The program design called for a school-year component between summers. The students were to be contacted and assistance was to be provided as necessary. In practice, the school component had little substantive connection to the summer activities and low participation rates.

REPLICABILITY: The program is highly structured and detailed. This project was replicated in approximately 100 U.S. cities.

GENERALIZABILITY: Designed to generalize to the entire nation. However, only 15 of the potential 595 employment and training agencies applied to take part in STEP. The financial burden was cited as a reason for this lack of interest. Of the five cities selected, four were on the West Coast. The sample was similar to those youth eligible for JTPA programs: they all met JTPA low-income standards; approximately 86 percent were ethnic minorities; and they were split roughly evenly for gender.

FUNDING SOURCES: Primary funding came from the Ford Foundation. Additional funding was provided by the U.S. Department of Labor, the Robert Wood Johnson Foundation, the U.S. Department of Health and Human Services, William T. Grant Foundation, the Edna McConnell Clark Foundation, the Hewlett Foundation, Lilly Endowment, the Ahmanson Foundation, Aetna Life and Casualty Foundation, and James C. Penney Foundation.

TREATMENT ADMINISTRATORS: Local agencies at each site administered the programs. Lead agencies were: Boston—Mayor's Office of Jobs and Community Services; Fresno—Fresno Private Industry Council; Portland—Portland Private Industry Council; San Diego—San Diego Regional Employment and Training Consortium; Seattle—Seattle Department of Human Resources. Key personnel changed over the life of the project.

EVALUATOR: Public/Private Ventures. Key personnel: Jean B. Grossman and Cynthia Sipe.

ENABLING LEGISLATION: None.

POLICY EFFECTS: In large part due to the STEP program, and appearances before the U.S. Congress by Public/Private Ventures staff, amendments were made to the SYETP program (e.g., funding and a requirement for remediation were added to SYETP).

INFORMATION SOURCES: Alvia Y. Branch, Julita Milliner, Susan Phillipson Bloom, and Jon Bumbaugh, *Summer Training and Education Program: Report on the Pilot Experience,* Public/Private Ventures, March 1985.

Alvia Y. Branch, Julita Milliner, and Jon Bumbaugh, *Summer Training and Education Program (STEP): Report on the 1985 Summer Experience,* Public/Private Ventures, April 1986.

Cynthia L. Sipe, Jean Baldwin Grossman, and Julita A. Milliner, *Summer Training and Education Program (STEP): Report on the 1986 Experience,* Public/Private Ventures, April 1987.

Cynthia L. Sipe, Jean Baldwin Grossman, and Julita A. Milliner, *Summer Training and Education Program (STEP): Report on the 1987 Experience,* Public/Private Ventures, Summer 1988.

Jean Baldwin Grossman and Cynthia L. Sipe, *Summer Training and Education Program (STEP): Report on Long-Term Impacts,* Public/Private Ventures, Winter 1992.

Gary Walker and Frances Vilella-Velez, *The Summer Training and Education Program (STEP): From Pilot through Replication and Post-Program Impacts,* Public/Private Ventures, 1992.

PUBLIC-USE ACCESS TO DATA: Available through Public/Private Ventures, Philadelphia, Pennsylvania.

New Orleans and Philadelphia Nonresidential Job Corps Centers

INFORMATION SOURCE: Terry R. Johnson, Sally Leiderman, and Susan Philipson Bloom, *Review of Experiences and Outcomes of the New Orleans and Philadelphia Non-residential Job Corps Centers: Final Report,* Bloom Associates, October 1991.

SUMMARY FROM ABOVE SOURCE: This demonstration, conducted from 1988 to 1990, was designed to test the effects of offering Job Corps services on a nonresidential basis to a large sample of economically and educationally disadvantaged youth.

Basic Job Corps services provided at both sites included an academic program of reading, mathematics, general equivalency diploma (GED) classes and a small Advanced Career Training program; vocational training classes; and other services such as counseling and health services.

Initially, the evaluators intended to evaluate this program using an experimental design. Subjects were randomly assigned to either a nonresidential Job Corps program (the treatment) or a traditional residential program (the control). Unfortunately, the subjects had strong feelings about the type of program in which they wanted to participate, and take-up rates for both treatment and control groups were unacceptable. Many of those assigned did not adhere to their assignments. The evaluators were left with very low sample sizes, and the experimental portion of the program was terminated before outcomes were measured.

The final report provides some qualitative and quantitative data concerning issues related to the types of youth served in the pilot centers, the services provided, and the outcomes achieved during the first few years of operations.

NUMBER AND LOCATION OF SITES: Two—New Orleans, Louisiana, and Philadelphia, Pennsylvania.

TREATMENT ADMINISTRATORS: New Orleans Job Corps Center—Maryetta Cunningham, project manager. Philadelphia Satellite Job Corps Center—Jim Kennedy, project manager.

EVALUATORS: A joint research effort involving Bloom Associates, Battelle Human Affairs Research Centers, and Abt Associates.

PUBLIC-USE ACCESS TO DATA: We have no information about a public-use file for this demonstration.

Alternative Schools

SUMMARY: This demonstration, conducted from 1988 to 1990, tested the effects of enrolling high-risk students in alternative high schools. It followed participants for three years.

COST: The evaluation cost $1.8 million. Federal funding for the demonstration school was $800,000 per year for two years, with local matching.

TIME FRAME: Demonstration period, 1988–90 school years; data collected, 1990–93 school years for Wichita and Stockton and 1993–96 school years for Cincinnati; final report, April 1997.

TREATMENTS TESTED: Students volunteered for the experiment after referral. Experimentals attended alternative high schools rather than a traditional setting. Services offered included an intensive reading program, on-site child care, limited extracurricular activities, and mentoring by teachers and peer meetings. Controls were not offered admission to the Alternative Schools Demonstration program (ASDP).

OUTCOMES OF INTEREST: School-related: (1) Attendance; (2) Graduation rates; (3) Credits earned; (4) Academic skills; (5) Diploma versus GED rates; and (6) Postsecondary education. Other measures: employment, wages, gang involvement, arrests, drug use, pregnancies, and welfare receipts.

SAMPLE SIZE: Stockton: treatments, 616; controls, 308. Wichita: treatments, 241; controls, 117. Cincinnati: treatments, 622; controls, 290.

TARGET POPULATION: Youth in economically disadvantaged areas who wanted a high school diploma but had been unsuccessful in a regular school setting.

NUMBER OF TREATMENT GROUPS: Two (with one control group).

NUMBER AND LOCATION OF SITES: Three—Stockton, California; Wichita, Kansas; and Cincinnati, Ohio. Analysis of Cincinnati subjects was limited.

RESEARCH COMPONENTS:

■ Process analysis: Evaluated adherence to study design. Performed quantitative analysis using administrative data, interviews with program staff, classroom observation, a data collection survey of all students completed by school personnel, and a survey of student perceptions of various school components.

■ Impact analysis: Impacts were estimated using regression models to adjust for differences in baseline characteristics between the research groups, using samples that alternatively included and excluded control group members who spent one or more semesters enrolled in the ASDP schools during the first two follow-up years. The data used included school records, GED records from the Ohio Department of Education, follow-up student surveys (see "Design Issues"), and the Test of Adult Basic Education.

■ Benefit–cost analysis: Costs for treatment and control regimes were collected, but the evaluators did not attempt to monetize benefits.

MAJOR FINDINGS:

1. Stockton: Students in the program were significantly more likely to graduate, although the overall rates were still very low (12 to 15 percent). They attended school more and earned more credits. At the end of the third follow-up year, 43 percent of the treatment group versus 53 percent of the control group had not earned degrees and were no longer pursuing them. At this time, there was also less likelihood that the treatment group was using illegal drugs. All of these findings are significant at the .10 level. There was also a significant wage increase noted for the program group, but the evaluators consider this result an anomaly, rather than a finding. No other significant impacts on outcomes of interest were obtained. Program impacts increased somewhat when controls who received the treatment were excluded from the analysis.

2. Wichita: No significant improvements. Treatment students scored lower on reading and math than the controls by about one grade level, a difference that was significant at the .10 level. The three-year follow-up showed that 51 percent of the treatment versus 30 percent of the control had dropped out before receiving either a diploma or a GED.

3. Trends for both sites: Gang membership was reduced for the treatment groups over all three years, but there was no reduction in the arrest rate. A GED was more likely to be obtained than a high school diploma at all three sites although the schools had been set up specifically to encourage students to earn a diploma. College attendance was equally likely between treatment and control groups.

4. Cincinnati: The limited analysis showed that in the second follow-up year, 7 percent of the treatment group versus 6 percent of the control had earned either a diploma or a GED. Very high dropout rates were shown with 83 percent of the program group and 88 percent of the control group leaving school before completion of a degree. When diplomas and GEDs are combined, the shares are 80 and 83 percent, respectively.

5. The evaluators compared the dollars spent per student in the alternative versus regular district schools. The Stockton treatment was found to cost approximately the same, and the Wichita ASDP was somewhat less expensive.

TIME TRENDS IN FINDINGS: None reported.

DESIGN ISSUES:

1. Some control group students were not kept out of alternative schools for the three years of the evaluation. Wichita had 13 percent of controls attending ASDP within two years and Stockton had 39 percent. The analysis adjusted for this deviation from the design, but the analysts acknowledged it may still have resulted in an underestimation of the true effects of the program.

2. School records and follow-up student surveys were relied upon to check high school completion. School district records were only valid if students remained within the same districts. Surveys could not be conducted for 10–20 percent of students in the Stockton and Wichita samples and were not conducted at all in Cincinnati.

REPLICABILITY: This program is itself a replication. The Alternative Schools program was designed to mirror the High School Redirection program that operates in Brooklyn, New York. The Department of Labor set up guidelines that programs funded through ASDP had to meet to be included.

GENERALIZABILITY: Designed to generalize to high-risk students across the country. Self-selection of staff members to the demonstration programs often resulted in highly motivated and especially knowledgeable providers in the area of alternative education. Some designs also involved staff members making themselves available to students and their families on weekends and during the evening. This could not be expected to occur with regularity in other locations.

FUNDING SOURCES: U.S. Department of Labor paid for the first two years. School districts that established the schools contributed some matching funds in the first two years and were expected to fully fund the program beginning in the third year.

TREATMENT ADMINISTRATOR: U.S. Department of Labor. Key personnel: David Lah, project officer.

EVALUATORS: Mathematica Policy Research, Inc. Key personnel: Mark Dynarski, project director, and Robert Wood. Academy for Educational Development subcontracted for the process evaluation. Key personnel: Alexandra Weinbaum and Anita Baker.

INFORMATION SOURCES: Mark Dynarski and Robert Wood, *Helping High-Risk Youths: Results from the Alternative Schools Demonstration Program*,

Mathematica Policy Research, Inc., April 1997; Alexandra Weinbaum, Ph.D., and Anita Baker, Ph.D., *Final Implementation Report: High School Redirection Replication Project,* Academy for Educational Development, June 1991.

PUBLIC-USE ACCESS TO DATA: Available on CD-ROM from Mark Dynarski at Mathematica Policy Research, Inc., 609-275-2397.

High-Risk Youth Demonstration Project—Yolo County, California

SUMMARY: This demonstration, conducted between 1989 and 1991, tested the effects of a self-esteem-building/motivational curriculum on a small sample of high-risk youth. Subjects were followed for two years.

COST: Exact costs are not available, though the average evaluation cost for Demonstration Partnership Program projects is between $35,000 and $50,000.

TIME FRAME: Demonstration period, July 1989–August 1991; final report, 1992.

TREATMENTS TESTED: The treatment was a 190-hour curriculum implemented in a classroom setting in a public school. The curriculum focused on social and emotional goals, rather than academic ones. Additional services included counseling and preemployment skills training. The control group continued with the traditional class structure offered at Yolo High School.

OUTCOMES OF INTEREST: (1) Self-esteem; (2) Academic achievement; and (3) Employment.

SAMPLE SIZE: Total initial sample, 113; treatments, 30; controls, 83. A considerably smaller sample was used for analysis.

TARGET POPULATION: High-risk youth between ages 16 and 18.

NUMBER OF TREATMENT GROUPS: Two (with one control group).

NUMBER AND LOCATION OF SITES: One—Yolo High School in West Sacramento, California.

RESEARCH COMPONENTS:
- Process analysis: Attention was paid to attrition rates and the maintenance of the design integrity.
- Impact analysis: Comparison of means.
- Benefit–cost analysis: Not conducted.

MAJOR FINDINGS:
1. No significant differences were found between the treatment and control groups nor between pre- and posttest scores for either group on self-esteem or school attitude.
2. Grade-point average and academic unit completion rate were significantly greater for the treatment group at the end of the project compared with the control group. Attendance was also better for the treatment group, though the difference was not significant.
3. The dropout rate was lower for the treatment group. A greater percentage of the treatment group had either graduated or was still enrolled in an educational program.
4. Treatment group students were more likely than controls to be employed, more likely to be employed full-time, and more likely to have a history of work experience.

TIME TRENDS IN FINDINGS: None reported.

DESIGN ISSUES:
1. Attrition rates were high, with only 16 youth from the treatment group and 8 from the control group completing posttest measures of self-esteem and school attitude. Slightly larger numbers were available for analysis on educational and employment measures (80 and 59, respectively). High attrition also led to additional students being drawn (randomly) from the control group to receive the intervention.

2. Data collection was difficult due to a lack of computerization as well as budgetary and staff shortages.

3. Since intervention was offered in a school environment, it was necessary to structure the curriculum to meet state and school district guidelines and graduation requirements. This required a change in teacher for the second year of the project. It also caused considerable inconvenience for the counseling component of the program.

REPLICABILITY: Replicable.

GENERALIZABILITY: Generalizing from this small sample would be speculative. Further, the experimental and control groups differed significantly on several demographic variables at the start of the program. This is likely owing to the small sample size, for there is no indication that the randomization procedure was contaminated. Finally, some students were excluded due to "hard-core drug use and/or violent behavior." Thus, this program may not generalize to some at-risk students.

FUNDING SOURCE: Demonstration Partnership Program, Office of Community Services, U.S. Department of Health and Human Services.

TREATMENT ADMINISTRATOR: Yolo County (California) Community Partnership Agency. Key personnel: Alexander M. Laiewski, agency director.

EVALUATOR: Gerald C. Shelton and Bill Kirby, University of Sacramento, Department of Economics.

ENABLING LEGISLATION: Demonstration Partnership Program under section 408 of the Human Services Reauthorization Act of 1986, as amended.

INFORMATION SOURCE: Department of Health and Human Services, Office of Community Services, *Summary of Final Evaluation Findings from FY 1989: Demonstration Partnership Program Projects Monograph Series 400-89*, 1992.

PUBLIC-USE ACCESS TO DATA: Available through U.S. Department of Health and Human Services, Office of Community Services.

Quantum Opportunities Program (QOP) Pilot

SUMMARY: This demonstration, conducted from 1989 to 1993, tested the effects of a comprehensive package of educational services, case management, and financial incentives on a medium-sized group of low-income high school students. Subjects were followed for four years.

COST: Total program costs (including evaluation) were $1,180,000 over four years.

TIME FRAME: Demonstration period, summer 1989–fall 1993; data collected, same period; final report, 1994.

TREATMENTS TESTED: The Quantum Opportunities Program (QOP) is a comprehensive program that can last up to four years. Program components include basic education; LifeSkills and cultural enrichment curricula; community service; mentoring; summer activities (including a part-time job and summer school for those who need it); and financial incentives (a stipend for participation and a bonus for completion of major blocks of activities). There was also a financial incentive for staff to meet program participation rates. The control group received no demonstration services.

OUTCOMES OF INTEREST: Achievement of academic and social competencies such as high school graduation, postsecondary attendance, academic achievement (grades and test scores), involvement in community service, teen pregnancy, and employment.

SAMPLE SIZE: Total: 200. There were 50 students at each site: 25 treatments and 25 controls.

TARGET POPULATION: High school students from low-income families (receiving public assistance).

NUMBER OF TREATMENT GROUPS: Two (with one control group).

NUMBER AND LOCATION OF SITES: Four—Oklahoma City, Oklahoma; Philadelphia,

Pennsylvania; Saginaw, Michigan; and San Antonio, Texas.

RESEARCH COMPONENTS:
▪ Process analysis: Focused on participation rates and "team-building" (the ability to form a group identity) at each site.
▪ Impact analysis: Conducted using comparison of means.
▪ Benefit–cost analysis: Conducted.

MAJOR FINDINGS: Although the samples from four sites were pooled for analysis, the majority of the overall impacts was attributable to the Philadelphia site. The implementation at this site was superior, creating a group identity among QOP members. It offered a more reliable menu of program offerings and provided stable, consistent relationships between youth and staff.
1. By the end of the fourth year, when most participants were leaving high school, average treatment group scores on all 11 academic and functional skills were much higher than control group scores, and all were statistically significant. Average academic skill levels had increased more than three grade levels for 27 percent of the treatment group compared with 14 percent of the control group.
2. Treatment group members were more likely to be high school graduates than were control group members (63 percent versus 42 percent), and they were more likely to enter postsecondary schools (42 percent versus 16 percent).

TIME TRENDS IN FINDINGS: Group differences did not appear until the second year of the program and continued to widen for the next two years.

DESIGN ISSUES:
1. The treatment varied considerably across sites and within sites over time. It is unclear what services were actually provided to participants and by whom. Implementation seemed to work best at the Philadelphia site, it failed at the Milwaukee site (which was dropped from the experiment), and it was somewhere in between for the remaining three sites.

2. Sample size was small, especially at individual sites. This makes it difficult to compare results across sites.

REPLICABILITY: Replicable, though clarification is needed regarding the exact services provided. This project was considered a pilot. The full QOP demonstration is discussed on page 282.

GENERALIZABILITY: Designed to generalize to the entire nation. However, the sample size was very small, especially at individual sites, and the majority of the impacts are based on the success of one site. An enhancement to generalizability is that the sample was randomly selected from lists of eighth grade students rather than from a prescreened group of volunteers.

FUNDING SOURCE: The Ford Foundation. Key personnel: Inca Mohamed, project officer.

TREATMENT ADMINISTRATOR: Opportunities Industrial Centers of America (OIC). Key personnel: Ben Lattimore and Ruben Mills.

EVALUATOR: Brandeis University, Center for Human Resources. Key personnel: Andrew Hahn.

ENABLING LEGISLATION: None.

INFORMATION SOURCE: Andrew Hahn, *Evaluation of the Quantum Opportunities Program (QOP): Did the Program Work?* Brandeis University, Center for Human Resources, June 1994.

PUBLIC-USE ACCESS TO DATA: Not available.

Brothers

INFORMATION SOURCE: U.S. Department of Health and Human Services, *Summary of Final Evaluation Findings from FY 1991: Demonstration Partnership Program Projects—Monograph Series 500-91—Minority Male*, 1995.

SUMMARY FROM ABOVE SOURCE: This demonstration, which began in October 1991, sought to use volunteer mentors to help low-income, primarily African American, males ages 14 to 16. The mentors were to meet with the youth at least two hours each week to increase their educational success and self-esteem and improve their attitudes toward drug use, sexual responsibility, and work. Interested youth were randomly assigned to either be matched with a mentor or be in the control group.

There were significant implementation problems, and far fewer mentor–youth matches were made than expected. Less than 15 percent of the referred mentors actually became mentors. At the six-month follow-up, there were only 23 participants in the treatment group with data available for analysis. At one year, the sample had shrunk to less than 10. The program director cited "systematic barriers in the community and political opposition" as reasons for the failed implementation. Also, a 25-member policy board responsible for planning, design, and oversight of the project had difficulty agreeing on program direction. Further, the evaluators had difficulty acquiring data from schools, mentors, and youth subjects.

COST: Treatment, approximately $30,000 to $35,000.

NUMBER AND LOCATION OF SITES: One—Lexington, Kentucky, serving Fayette County.

TREATMENT ADMINISTRATOR: Community Action Council. Key personnel: Jack E. Burch, director; Mary Twitty, project director.

EVALUATOR: Bennie Robinson, Kentucky State University; and David Royse, University of Kentucky.

PUBLIC-USE ACCESS TO DATA: We have no information about a public-use file for this demonstration.

Homeless Youth Self-Sufficiency Project

INFORMATION SOURCE: U.S. Department of Health and Human Services, Office of Community Services, *Homeless and Youth at Risk: Demonstration Partnership Program Projects: Summary of Final Evaluation Findings from 1990,* 1993.

SUMMARY FROM ABOVE SOURCE: This demonstration, conducted from 1991 through 1994, tested the effects of long-term transitional housing, case management, counseling, and a preemployment training and work experience program on a small sample of homeless youth. Subjects were to be followed for six months beyond the termination of services (the program period was to be at least 12 months). The initial sample size was 76, with 53 in the treatment group and 23 in the control group—the program was considered completed after two years if the youth was living in a stable residence and was either working or attending school.

There was a very high rate of attrition, with most program dropouts occurring in the treatment group. At the two-year follow-up, only 27 youth from both groups had completed the program and only 12 were available for interviews. Although there is some indication that the program led to more youth living off the streets (i.e., in housing) and being involved in educational programs or employment, there are insufficient data to make any meaningful claims regarding program effectiveness.

COST: Unavailable, although the average Demonstration Partnership Program project evaluation costs are between $35,000 and $50,000.

NUMBER AND LOCATION OF SITES: One—Multnomah County (Portland), Oregon.

TREATMENT ADMINISTRATOR: Multnomah County Community Action Program Office and the Outside In Agency. Key personnel: William B. Thomas, project director.

EVALUATOR: Robert Donough and Patricia Freeman, Tri-County Youth Services Consortium.

PUBLIC-USE ACCESS TO DATA: We have no information about a public-use file for this demonstration.

Success Connection

SUMMARY: This demonstration, conducted from 1991 through 1993, tested the effects of adventure-based counseling and exposure to college on a small sample of at-risk rural youth. Subjects were followed for 18 months.

COST: Program costs, $350,000.

TIME FRAME: Demonstration period, October 1991–October 1993; data collected, same period.

TREATMENTS TESTED: The treatment group received up to 377 hours of services over 18 months consisting of (1) ongoing support groups with an "adventure-based" curriculum (an "Outward Bound" type of experience where participants learn trust, self-esteem, and teamwork by working together to overcome physical obstacles); (2) one-day leadership retreats; (3) two-week on-campus college experience; and (4) a goal-setting experience for their parents. The controls attended an initial orientation; thereafter, they received nothing from the program except $10 fees for cooperating with evaluation interviews.

OUTCOMES OF INTEREST: (1) Employment; (2) Wage rates; and (3) Welfare receipt.

SAMPLE SIZE: Total, 227; treatments, 107; controls, 120.

TARGET POPULATION: At-risk youth, defined as those age 17–22 with at least two of the following characteristics: school dropout; unemployed and not enrolled in job training; employed but below minimum wage; ward of the court; AFDC-qualified or public assistance recipient; or referred to as "at-risk" by teachers, counselors, or agency personnel.

NUMBER OF TREATMENT GROUPS: Two (with one control group).

NUMBER AND LOCATION OF SITES: One—Yakima Valley, Washington.

RESEARCH COMPONENTS:
- Process analysis: Contact forms, activity logs, assessment portfolio; implemented as designed, with 88 members of the treatment group completing the program.

- Impact analysis: Comparison of raw totals at conclusion of 18-month program.
- Benefit–cost analysis: Not conducted.

MAJOR FINDINGS: Evaluator compared the experience of control group members with the experience of 88 participating treatment group members. The participating treatment group members had significantly higher career aspirations than controls. Qualitatively, their jobs were more diverse and had greater potential for upward mobility; it is difficult to tell from the summary whether there was any difference in wages. Eleven controls received or applied for public assistance, whereas only one participant did, but the evaluator did not test for statistical significance because he did not feel the data were meaningful. Participating treatment group members also had a 94 percent high school graduation rate compared with 78 percent in the control group, but this finding was apparently not statistically significant.

TIME TRENDS IN FINDINGS: None.

DESIGN ISSUES: The evaluation was clearly compromised by the exclusion of nonparticipating treatment group members. The report attributed non-participation to "the transitory nature of migrancy in rural Washington" (many of the participants are the children of migrant farmworkers).

REPLICABILITY: Designed for replicability.

GENERALIZABILITY: Findings of modest impact might generalize to other migrant farmworker children, although the fairly small sample size and the design and implementation issues discourage attempts at generalization.

FUNDING SOURCE: Office of Community Services, Administration for Children and Families, U.S. Department of Health and Human Services.

TREATMENT ADMINISTRATOR: Yakima Valley Opportunities Industrialization Center. Key personnel: Raul Sital.

EVALUATOR: William Hansen, an independent consultant.

ENABLING LEGISLATION: Demonstration Partnership Program, under section 408 of the Human Services Reauthorization Act of 1986, as amended.

INFORMATION SOURCE: U.S. Department of Health and Human Services, *Summary of Final Evaluation Findings from FY 1991: Demonstration Partnership Program Projects, Monograph Series 400-91, Youth at Risk,* April 1995: 2-25 to 2-40.

PUBLIC-USE ACCESS TO DATA: Available through BHM International, contractor for the Office of Community Services.

Austin Youth Leadership Development

SUMMARY: This demonstration, conducted from October 1991 to September 1993, tested the effects of enhanced services on a sample of at-risk youth. Subjects were followed for nine months.

COST: Not available.

TIME FRAME: Demonstration period, October 1991–September 1993; data collected, same period.

TREATMENTS TESTED: Experimentals received targeted family outreach services—job training and employment assistance. They also received "usual services": leadership development activities to help youth participate in policymaking and program planning with agencies, and better coordinated youth services delivery system. Controls received usual services only.

OUTCOME OF INTEREST: Self-sufficiency: income from a job and skills to keep a job.

SAMPLE SIZE: Total, 74; experimentals, 28; controls, 46.

TARGET POPULATION: At-risk youth.

NUMBER OF TREATMENT GROUPS: Two (with one control group).

NUMBER AND LOCATION OF SITES: One—Austin, Texas.

RESEARCH COMPONENTS:
- Process analysis: Conducted.
- Impact analysis: Comparison of means.
- Benefit–cost analysis: Not conducted.

MAJOR FINDINGS: Thirty-six percent of youth who received the family outreach services versus only 24 percent of the youth who received usual services improved their self-sufficiency index, a combination of income from a job, skills to solve life problems and get and keep a job, ability to withstand stress, and a disposition to support success. Authors do not discuss statistical significance.

TIME TRENDS IN FINDINGS: Youth receiving family outreach services showed a slight but steady improvement in their average self-sufficiency scores, which rose from 4.60 at intake to 4.94 after three months, then to 5.18 at nine months. In contrast, average scores for controls fluctuated over the period. They declined from 4.43 at intake to 4.27 at three months and then rose to 4.58 at nine months.

DESIGN ISSUES:
1. Sample recruitment failed; only 74 youth took part in the study whose design demanded at least 200 cases.
2. Assignment to treatment was not random in all cases. In order to have 74 cases, recruitment into the control group continued well into the study.

REPLICABILITY: Not replicable. At-risk targeting criteria are not defined, and the self-sufficiency index is not specified.

GENERALIZABILITY: Poor, because of the design issues noted above.

FUNDING SOURCE: U.S. Department of Human Services, Administration for Children and Families, Office of Community Services.

TREATMENT ADMINISTRATOR: City of Austin, Health and Human Services Division. Key personnel: Sandi Steinfield, project coordinator.

EVALUATORS: Cindy Roberts-Gray and Sandra Wells. No affiliation listed in the document.

ENABLING LEGISLATION: None.

INFORMATION SOURCE: "Summary of Final Evaluation Findings from 1991: Demonstration Partnership Program Projects," *Monograph Series 400-91 Youth-At-Risk,* April 1995.

PUBLIC-USE ACCESS TO DATA: We have no information about a public-use file for this demonstration.

School Dropout Demonstration Assistance Program

SUMMARY: This demonstration, conducted from September 1992 to June 1995, tested the effectiveness of varying dropout prevention programs on a large sample of at-risk youth. Follow-up lasted for up to 4 years.

COST: Evaluation, $7.4 million.

TIME FRAME: Demonstration period, September 1991–August 1996; data collected, September 1991–June 1998; final report, June 1998.

TREATMENTS TESTED: See table below.

Controls attended school as they normally would and had access to other education programs in their area.

OUTCOMES OF INTEREST: (1) Dropout rates; (2) Attendance; (3) Test scores; (4) Alcohol and drug use; (5) Pregnancies; (6) Parent involvement in education; (7) College enrollment; and (8) Employment. (Because the impact of the tested treatments on outcomes 1–7 were so small for high school students, effects on employment were not actually estimated, although the evaluators originally planned to do so.)

SAMPLE SIZE: See table.

TARGET POPULATION: Students in impoverished areas who meet specific criteria (see table).

NUMBER OF TREATMENT GROUPS: Two (with one control group).

NUMBER AND LOCATION OF SITES: Sixteen middle schools and high schools throughout the country—Albuquerque, New Mexico; Atlanta, Georgia; Boston, Massachusetts; Chicago, Illinois; Chula Vista, California; Flint, Michigan; Las Vegas,

Location/Grantee (program name)	Sample size exp/control	Grades served	Characteristics of target population	Treatment	GED vs. diploma
Albuquerque, NM/ Youth Development Inc. (Middle School Leadership Program)	215/119	8	Low math and English grades Poor attendance Suspension in previous year Leadership potential	Counseling Career awareness Leadership workshop Supplement to regular school	NA
Atlanta, GA/ Georgia Cities in Schools (Griffing-Spalding Middle School Academy)	80/77	7, 8	Behind grade level	Counseling services Attendance monitoring Social services Alternative school, separate building	NA
Boston, MA/ Jobs for Youth (JFY High School and University High)	62/38	9–12	Dropped out or on verge of dropping out	Counseling services Career awareness Social services Challenging curricula Accelerated learning Alternative school, separate building	Diploma

(continued)

Location/Grantee (program name)	Sample size exp/control	Grades served	Characteristics of target population	Treatment	GED vs. diploma
Chicago, IL/ Chicago Teachers & Chicago Public Schools (Northeastern Illinois University Dropout Prevention Partnership Program)	106/65	8–12	Low test scores Behind grade level	Counseling services Attendance monitoring Team teaching Outreach to families Challenging curricula Interschool linkages School within a school	Diploma
Chula Vista, CA/ Sweetwater Union High School District (Twelve Together Program)	259/235	7	Poor attendance Low grades Disciplinary problems	Counseling services Attendance monitoring Annual weekend retreat Supplement to regular school	NA
Flint, MI/ Flint Community Schools District (Accelerated Academies Academy)	113/79	6–8	Behind by two grade levels	Counseling services Attendance monitoring Family outreach Challenging curricula Social services Alternative school, separate building	NA
Las Vegas, NV/ Clark County School District (Horizon High Schools)	287/197	9, 10	Low grades Low standardized test scores Behind grade level Ever dropped out	Counseling services Attendance monitoring Social services Accelerated learning Alternative school, separate building	Diploma
Long Beach, CA/ Long Beach Unified School District (Up with Literacy)	168/114	6–8	Low standardized test scores	Counseling services Attendance monitoring Accelerated learning Outreach to families Supplement to regular school	NA
Miami, FL/ Cities in Schools of Miami, Inc. (COMET Program)	122/67	5	Poor attendance Low motivation Behavioral problems	Counseling services Attendance monitoring Outreach to families Challenging curricula Career awareness School within a school	NA
Miami, FL/ Cities in Schools of Miami, Inc. (Corporate Academy)	77/65	9–12	Two or more of: Low grades, low test scores, poor attendance, behind grade level, ever dropped out, pregnant/parent	Counseling services Social services Attendance monitoring Career awareness Outreach to families Alternative school, separate building	Diploma

Location/Grantee (program name)	Sample size exp/control	Grades served	Characteristics of target population	Treatment	GED vs. diploma
Newark, NJ/ Newark Public School District (Project ACCEL)	348/203	6, 7	Behind grade level Sufficiently high skill and motivation levels	Counseling services Attendance monitoring Outreach to families Accelerated learning Team teaching School within a school	NA
Queens, NY/ Flowers with Care Youth Services (Flowers with Care)	106/60	9–12	Dropped out	Counseling services Attendance monitoring Career awareness Community-based	GED
Rockford, IL/ Rockford Public Schools (Early Identification and Intervention Project)	393/210	6–8	Low standardized test scores Poor attendance Behind grade level Dysfunctional family	Outreach to families Interschool linkages Counseling services Daily skill-building class Supplement to regular school	NA
Seattle, WA/ Seattle Public Schools (Middle College High School)	322/193	9–12	Ever dropped out Poor attendance	Counseling services Career awareness Attendance monitoring Alternative school, separate building	Diploma
St. Louis, MO/ Human Development Corporation of Metropolitan St. Louis (Metropolitan Youth Academy)	223/149	9–12	Dropped out Drug abuse or delinquency Low family income Welfare receipt	Counseling services Social services Attendance monitoring Career awareness Community-based	GED
Tulsa, OK/ Tulsa County Area Vocational-Technical School District No. 18 (Student Training and Reentry STAR)	258/149	9–12	Dropped out or on the verge of dropping out	Counseling services Attendance monitoring Career awareness Outreach to families Accelerated learning Community-based	Both

Note: NA = not available.

Nevada; Long Beach, California; Miami, Florida (two programs); Newark, New Jersey; Queens, New York; Rockford, Illinois; Seattle, Washington; St. Louis, Missouri; and Tulsa, Oklahoma.

RESEARCH COMPONENTS:

▪ Process analysis: Extensive, including classroom observation and student focus groups.

▪ Impact analysis: Logit and OLS.

▪ Benefit–cost analysis: Not conducted.

MAJOR FINDINGS:

Middle Schools

Intensive programs (full-day participation) were located in Atlanta, Flint, Newark, and Miami. Low-intensity programs were located in Albuquerque, Long Beach, Rockford, and Chula Vista.

1. In Atlanta, experimentals received significantly higher average grades. Dropout rates in Flint

experimentals were significantly lower for the first cohort. Grade and dropout impacts were otherwise insignificant.

2. Three out of four intensive programs had higher absenteeism and did not have higher test scores or English or math grades.

3. Low-intensity schools had no significant effect on any outcomes.

High Schools

1. GED programs helped students obtain certificates, but two out of every three students still dropped out.

2. Alternative high schools had no impact on dropping out or other outcomes, with the exception of Las Vegas, where the treatment group had a significantly higher dropout rate than the controls.

3. High school programs had no significant effect on personal and social outcomes.

4. Programs had no significant impact on increasing high school completion.

5. Looking at combined high school diploma and GED receipt, the evaluators find two programs, St. Louis and Tulsa, that had significant positive impacts.

TIME TRENDS IN FINDINGS: None reported.

DESIGN ISSUES:

1. Small sample size for some treatments would have made statistical significance hard to obtain.

2. Comparison of relative effectiveness cannot be made between treatments due to many differences in programs and populations served.

REPLICABILITY: Not all treatment programs had documented protocols.

GENERALIZABILITY: "The limited success of the eight programs we studied suggests that we do not know how to promote educational success among most high school age students who have dropped out or are on the verge of doing so" (Dynarski et al. 1998).

FUNDING SOURCE: U.S. Department of Education. Key personnel: Audrey Pendleton, project officer, and John Fiegel.

TREATMENT ADMINISTRATORS: School districts listed in table.

EVALUATOR: Mathematica Policy Research, Inc. Key personnel: Mark Dynarski, project director.

INFORMATION SOURCES: Mark Dynarski and Phil Gleason, "How Can We Help? What We Have Learned from Evaluations of Federal Dropout Prevention Programs," *Journal of Education for Students Placed At Risk* 7(1, 2002): 43–69.

Mark Dynarski, Philip Gleason, Anu Rangarajan, and Robert Wood, *Impacts of Dropout Prevention Programs,* Mathematica Policy Research, Inc., Princeton, NJ, June 1998.

Alan Hershey, Nancy Adelman, and Steven Murray, *Helping Kids Succeed: Implementation of the School Dropout Demonstration Assistance Program,* Mathematica Policy Research, Inc., Princeton, NJ, September 1995.

PUBLIC-USE ACCESS TO DATA: Available on CD-ROM from Mark Dynarski. Contact at MDynarski @Mathematica-mpr.com.

American Conservation and Youth Services Corps

SUMMARY: This demonstration, conducted from 1993 to 1994, tested the effects of a standard youth corps program—a nonresidential program employing groups of 5 to 10 young people in community service projects—on a medium-sized sample of out-of-school 18- to 25-year-old youth. Subjects were followed for 15 months.

COST: Treatment costs, $8.25 million.

TIME FRAME: Demonstration period 1993–94; data collected, same period; final report, August 1996.

TREATMENTS TESTED: Experimentals received typical youth corps services for a period of 14 months, temporary paid employment in service sectors, job training, job search, basic and remedial education, and life skills training. Controls did not receive the services.

OUTCOMES OF INTEREST: (1) Education and training achievements; (2) Personal development; (3) Involvement in community and other social services; and (4) Employment and earnings.

SAMPLE SIZE: Total, 626; experimentals, 313; controls, 313.

TARGET POPULATION: Unemployed out-of-school youth, 18 to 25 years old.

NUMBER OF TREATMENT GROUPS: Two (with one control group).

NUMBER AND LOCATION OF SITES: Four—Washington State Service Corps; City Volunteer Corps, New York City; Greater Miami Service Corps; and Santa Clara District, California Conservation Corps.

RESEARCH COMPONENTS:
 Process analysis: Conducted.
 Impact analysis: Regression.
 Benefit–cost analysis: Conducted.

MAJOR FINDINGS:

1. The program increased employment by 26 percentage points, from 73 percent to 99 percent. Much of the positive employment-related impact is attributable to work while still in the corps. Typically, participants stay in the corps for a year.
2. Experimentals worked almost 40 percent more hours over the follow-up period than controls.
3. The most dramatic employment and earning impacts were for African American males. Treatment group members' average monthly earnings were over one-and-a-half times larger than those of controls.
4. The positive impacts on employment for minority males of limited skills may reflect the difficult job market for members of this group; the corps appears to provide a critical source of employment and earnings for minority males.
5. Experimentals were less likely to earn a technical certificate or diploma (8 versus 13 percent for controls).

6. The most dramatic positive impacts on education were on African American males. For example, nearly 66 percent of experimentals versus less than 40 percent of controls indicated they would like to graduate from college.

TIME TREND IN FINDINGS: None.

DESIGN ISSUES: The demonstration did not measure possible long-term effects because of its limited follow-up period. In particular, it captured little of the post-program period.

REPLICABILITY: Replicable.

GENERALIZABILITY: The impact study sites were larger than average, both in budgetary terms and in terms of number of participants. There are no other clear limits on generalizability.

FUNDING SOURCE: Corporation for National Service. Key personnel: Lance Porter.

TREATMENT ADMINISTRATOR: Corporation for National Service. Key personnel: Lance Porter.

EVALUATOR: Abt Associates. Key personnel: JoAnn Jastrzab and Julie Masker.

ENABLING LEGISLATION: None.

INFORMATION SOURCE: JoAnn Jastrzab, Julie Masker, John Blomquist, and Larry Orr, *Final Report on Evaluation of American Conservation and Youth Service Corps*, Abt Associates, August 1996.

PUBLIC-USE ACCESS TO DATA: Not available.

Illinois Youth Employment and Training Initiative (YETI)

SUMMARY: This demonstration, conducted from 1994 to 1997, tested the effects of providing social and supplemental vocational skills on a medium-sized sample of students from TANF households. Subjects were followed for three years.

COST: Total federal and state funding was $957,503; evaluation costs, $215,847.

TIME FRAME: Demonstration period, 1994–98; data collected, 1994–99; final report, October 2000.

TREATMENTS TESTED: Experimentals received educational and vocational counseling and training, drug avoidance and sex education, and job readiness training from public and private organizations. Controls did not receive the services.

OUTCOMES OF INTEREST: (1) Graduation and (2) Employment.

SAMPLE SIZE: Total, 773; experimentals, 424; controls, 349.

TARGET POPULATION: High school students from households receiving public assistance.

NUMBER OF TREATMENT GROUPS: Two (with one control group).

NUMBER AND LOCATION OF SITES: Three—Bowen, Harper, and Crane high schools in Chicago.

RESEARCH COMPONENTS:
- Process analysis: Conducted; major emphasis on students' attitudes toward the program.
- Impact analysis: Regression.
- Benefit–cost analysis: Conducted.

MAJOR FINDINGS:
1. The program had a modestly positive impact on the graduation rate; 48 percent of the served group graduated (130 of 272), while only 38 percent of the control group graduated (46 of 120). For the class of 1977, 45 percent more students in the experimental group graduated than in the control group, a significant difference at the .10 level.
2. No overall significant differences were observed between the experimental and control groups for wages earned or public cash assistance during the period.

TIME TRENDS IN FINDINGS: None.

DESIGN ISSUES:
1. Evaluators reported receipt of YETI services by some control group members that was "neither trivial nor pervasive." Survey responses by controls suggest some compromise in the integrity of random assignment.
2. The demonstration did not have provision for medium- to long-term follow-up of program participants. Students in the program were more likely to continue their education, less likely to be working, and more likely to be receiving public aid.

REPLICABILITY: Replicable.

GENERALIZABILITY: Generalizable to urban areas with significant population on public assistance.

FUNDING SOURCES: Illinois Department of Human Services and the U.S. Department of Human and Health Services. Key personnel: Ken Manha.

TREATMENT ADMINISTRATOR: Illinois Department of Human Services. Key personnel: David Gruenenfelder.

EVALUATORS: Quintin E. Sullivan and Dennis Crowell, School of Social Work, Illinois State University, Normal, Illinois.

ENABLING LEGISLATION: None.

POLICY EFFECTS: Now an official program of the State of Illinois, the program has been expanded and renamed Youth Opportunity Program (YOP).

INFORMATION SOURCE: Quintin E. Sullivan, Dennis Crowell, Cheryl Stampley, and Katherine Jones, *Final Report for the Enhancement to the Process and Impact Analysis of the Youth Employment and Training Initiative (YETI)*, October 2000.

PUBLIC-USE ACCESS TO DATA: Not yet available.

National Job Corps Study

SUMMARY: This study, conducted from 1994 to 1996, tested the effects of vocational training, academic instruction, residential living, and other social and health education services on a large sample of eligible disadvantaged youths. Subjects were followed for four years.

COST: $18,740,050.29, evaluation only, plus $2,847,152 for increased Job Corps recruitment and administrative costs.

TIME FRAME: Data collected November 1994–February 1996, and at 12, 30, and 48 months after random assignment.

TREATMENTS TESTED: All eligible Job Corps applicants nationwide were randomly assigned to either the treatment group (permitted to enroll in Job Corps services) or the control group (not permitted to enroll in Job Corps services for three years). Job Corps centers provided vocational training, academic instruction, health care, social skills training, and counseling. The number and types of trades for which vocational training was provided varied from site to site. Placement agencies provided post-program services for all program participants for a period of six months. The majority of participants (88 percent) lived at the centers, which are usually located in rural areas at some distance from the participants' urban homes. Nonresidential participants were primarily females with children.

OUTCOMES OF INTEREST: (1) Employment; (2) Earnings; (3) Education and job training; (4) Welfare receipt; (5) Criminal behavior; (6) Drug use; (7) Health factors; and (8) Household status.

SAMPLE SIZE: Total, 15,386; treatments, 9,409; controls, 5,977.

TARGET POPULATION: Disadvantaged men and women between the ages of 16 and 24.

NUMBER OF TREATMENT GROUPS: Two (with one control group).

NUMBER AND LOCATION OF SITES: 110 Job Corps centers in all 50 states, the District of Columbia, and Puerto Rico.

RESEARCH COMPONENTS:

- Process analysis: Telephone survey of Job Corps Outreach and Admissions (OA) counselors, mail survey of all Job Corps centers, and weeklong site visits to 23 centers. The study reports that the program had been successfully implemented.
- Impact analysis: Conducted with multivariate regression and comparison of means.
- Benefit–cost analysis: Conducted.

MAJOR FINDINGS:

Impact on Education and Training Enrollment

	Percentage enrolled	Average percentage of total weeks spent in education or training
Treatment group	93	24
Control group	72	18
Estimated impact per eligible applicant	21	6

Impact on Credential Receipt

	Percentage who received GED	Percentage who received vocational certificate
Treatment group	42	38
Control group	27	15
Estimated impact	15	23

1. Job Corps had no effect on college attendance, illegal drug use, child support payments, custody of children, or fertility rates.
2. Placement services were insufficient. Few program participants received assistance in securing employment in the six-month post-program period.
3. Approximately two years following random assignment, the program group surpassed the control group in earnings. In the fourth year there was a 12 percent earnings gain for program participants. However, there was no increase in employment and earnings for 18- to 19-year-olds or for Hispanic program participants of any age.
4. The program group received an estimated $639 less per participant in combined cash assistance and food stamps benefits than did the control group.

5. The program group had 16 percent reduction in the overall number of arrests. The impact was greater on reducing arrests for less serious crimes.

6. The benefit–cost analysis suggests that the program returns about $2 to society for every dollar spent, due to the combination of increased participant output in years two to four; reduced use of other programs and services; reduced crime and the output produced during program vocational training.

TIME TRENDS IN FINDINGS: Early in the follow-up period, the control group had higher earnings and rates of employment because many of the program group members were enrolled in Job Corps services. Beginning about two years after random assignment, the average earnings for program group members gradually grew to be higher than the average earnings of control group members and persisted through the fourth year follow-up period.

DESIGN ISSUES: None apparent.

REPLICABILITY: Replicable.

GENERALIZABILITY: This study is based on a fully national random sample of all eligible applicants to Job Corps with services delivered nationwide. Since many members of the control group received training and education from outside sources, the findings of the study should be interpreted as the incremental effects of Job Corps services.

FUNDING SOURCE: U.S. Department of Labor, Employment and Training Administration. Key personnel: Daniel Ryan.

TREATMENT ADMINISTRATOR: Local Job Corps centers.

EVALUATOR: Mathematica Policy Research and Battelle Memorial Institute. Key personnel: John Burghardt for Mathematica and Terry Johnson for Battelle.

ENABLING LEGISLATION: None.

INFORMATION SOURCES: John Burghardt, Peter Z. Schochet, Sheena McConnell, Terry Johnson, R. Mark Gritz, Steven Glazerman, John Homrighausen, and Russell Jackson, *Does Job Corps Work? Summary of the National Job Corps Study*, Mathematica Policy Research, Inc., 2001, and the references listed there.

PUBLIC-USE ACCESS TO DATA: Available through the Department of Labor.

Quantum Opportunity Program (QOP) Demonstration

SUMMARY: This demonstration, conducted from July 1995 through September 2001, tested the effects of intensive and comprehensive services on a medium-sized sample of youth with low grades entering high schools with high dropout rates. Subjects were followed for nine years.

COST: The total treatment cost per enrollee over the full five-year demonstration period was $18,000 to $22,000 for DOL-funded sites, $23,000 for the Yakima site, and $49,000 for the Philadelphia site.

TIME FRAME: Demonstration period, July 1995–September 2001; data collected, 1999–2004.

TREATMENTS TESTED: The Quantum Opportunity Program (QOP) was an after-school program providing case management and mentoring, supplemental education, developmental activities, community service, and support services. Incentives for participation included stipends, bonuses, and contributions to accrual accounts for postsecondary education or training.

These services were provided year-round for five years to enrollees who had not graduated from high school. Typically, each case manager was assigned between 15 and 25 enrollees. The program prescribed an annual participation goal of 750 hours for each enrollee who had not graduated. The control group was not allowed to participate in QOP activities.

OUTCOMES OF INTEREST: (1) High school graduation and (2) Enrollment in postsecondary education or training. Secondary outcomes include grades, achievement test scores, substance abuse, crime, and teen parenting.

SAMPLE SIZE: Total, 1,069; treatments, 580; controls, 489.

TARGET POPULATION: Youth with low grades entering high schools with high dropout rates.

NUMBER OF TREATMENT GROUPS: Two (with one control group).

NUMBER AND LOCATION OF SITES: Through community-based organizations, five Department of Labor–funded sites—Cleveland, Ohio; Fort Worth and Houston, Texas; Memphis, Tennessee; and Washington, D.C.—and two Ford Foundation–funded sites—Philadelphia, Pennsylvania; and Yakima, Washington.

RESEARCH COMPONENTS:
■ Process analysis: Conducted.
■ Impact analysis: Difference-of-means and regression-adjusted impact estimates.
■ Benefit–cost analysis: Cost analysis conducted, but benefit–cost analysis not conducted based on first round of impact estimates.

MAJOR FINDINGS: From data collected through the fifth year of the demonstration:
1. The demonstration increased the likelihood of graduation from high school with a diploma by 7 percentage points. The increase was statistically significant.
2. The demonstration increased the likelihood of engaging in postsecondary education or training. The size and statistical significance of the impact, however, depended on how the outcome was measured and how the impact was estimated.
3. The demonstration did not improve grades or achievement test scores.
4. The demonstration did not reduce risky behaviors.

TIME TREND IN FINDINGS: Data collection to measure the demonstration's longer-term impacts will be conducted approximately seven years and nine years after enrollment in high school.

DESIGN ISSUES:
1. Every site implemented a version of the demonstration. However, two sites implemented a version of the demonstration that deviated substantially from the program model, and the other five sites implemented versions that deviated moderately from the model.
2. No site fully implemented the education component, and most sites did not meet—directly or through referrals—enrollees' needs for child care or physical and mental health services. No site implemented the community service component as prescribed.
3. Both beneficial and detrimental impacts for the whole demonstration were substantially—but not entirely—attributable to the impacts of the Philadelphia site alone or the Philadelphia and Yakima sites (the Ford-funded sites) together. One site—Cleveland—had significant beneficial impacts and no significant detrimental impacts. Three sites—Washington, D.C., Houston, and Memphis—had significant detrimental impacts and no significant beneficial impacts. The significant detrimental impacts on risky behaviors might have been due to differences between treatment- and control-group youth in how accurately they reported risky behaviors or to purely random differences in baseline characteristics for which the evaluators could not adjust.

REPLICABILITY: The model is replicable, but the program actually implemented at the sites is not replicable.

GENERALIZABILITY: Generalizability was undercut by lack of fidelity to the program model in all sites.

FUNDING SOURCES: U.S. Department of Labor and the Ford Foundation. Key personnel: Eileen Pederson for Labor and Benjamin Lattimore for Ford.

TREATMENT ADMINISTRATOR: Opportunities Industrialization Centers of America, Inc.

EVALUATOR: Mathematica Policy Research, Inc. Key personnel: Allen Schirm, project director.

ENABLING LEGISLATION: The research and evaluation demonstration authority under the Job Training Partnership Act.

INFORMATION SOURCE: Myles Maxfield, Allen Schirm, and Nuria Rodriguez-Planas, *The Quantum Opportunity Program Demonstration: Implementation and Short-Term Impacts,* Mathematica Policy Research Reference No. 8279-093, December 2002.

PUBLIC-USE ACCESS TO DATA: Not available.

Carrera Model

SUMMARY: This demonstration, conducted from 1997 to 2000, tested the effects of a pregnancy prevention program on a large sample of high-risk youth. Subjects were followed for three years.

COST: Research costs, approximately $850,000 over four years.

TIME FRAME: Demonstration period, January 1997–November 1997; data collected through 2001.

TREATMENTS TESTED: The Children's Aid Society (CAS)–Carrera Program was implemented in schools, Boys and Girls clubs, Settlement Houses, and other community-based organizations. The treatment included a work-related intervention, an educational component, family life and sex education, self-expression through art, and sports. Comprehensive health care services were provided. Control group members were assigned to the regular youth programming offered by the participating organization.

OUTCOMES OF INTEREST: (1) Pregnancy; (2) Education; (3) Drug use; (4) Job readiness; and (5) Program participation.

SAMPLE SIZE: Total, 1,163; treatments, 589; controls, 574.

TARGET POPULATION: Thirteen- to 15-year-old adolescents.

NUMBER OF TREATMENT GROUPS: Two (with one control group).

NUMBER AND LOCATION OF SITES: Twelve sites in seven cities. Six sites in New York City—Bronx, South Bronx, Lower East Side Manhattan, Queens, Harlem, and Brooklyn. Other sites—Baltimore, Maryland; Broward County, Florida; Houston, Texas; Portland, Oregon; Rochester, New York; and Seattle, Washington.

RESEARCH COMPONENTS:
- Process analysis: Administrative records, annual surveys, and staff interviews.
- Impact analysis: Regression.
- Benefit–cost analysis: Not conducted.

MAJOR FINDINGS:
1. By the end of the third year, 70 percent of the treatment group was still involved with their CAS–Carrera program, but only 35 percent of the control group was regularly participating in an after-school program (see table).
2. Compared with the control group, treatment group students were significantly more likely to have made a college visit.
3. In the six sites that administered the PSAT (New York only), the scores were slightly higher for the treatment group than for the control group. There was no other program impact on education.
4. Treatment group males were less likely to begin using marijuana than their control group counterparts. There were no other impacts on drug use.

TIME TRENDS IN FINDINGS: Reproductive knowledge gains were increasingly greater among the experimentals than among the controls.

DESIGN ISSUES: None noted.

REPLICABILITY: Replicable.

GENERALIZABILITY: Sites were selected to include widely diverse settings. Analysis showed no significant site influence. Implementation of the program appears to have been successful and consistent.

FUNDING SOURCES: Charles Stewart Mott Foundation and the Robin Hood Foundation.

TREATMENT ADMINISTRATORS: Directors and staff of the community-based organizations that participated in the experiment.

EVALUATOR: Philliber Research Associates. Key personnel: Jackie Kaye.

ENABLING LEGISLATION: None.

INFORMATION SOURCE: Susan Philliber, Jackie Kaye, and Scott Herrling, *The National Evaluation of the Children's Aid Society Carrera–Model Program to Prevent Teen Pregnancy,* Philliber Research Associates, May 2001.

PUBLIC-USE ACCESS TO DATA: Not available.

EXPERIMENTS ONGOING AT PUBLICATION

Career Academies

STARTING YEAR/YEAR FINAL REPORT EXPECTED: 1993/2008.

INFORMATION SOURCE: James Kemple, *Executive Summary, Career Academies: Impacts on Students' Initial Transitions to Post-Secondary Education and Employment,* Manpower Demonstration Research Corporation, December 2001.

PRINCIPAL INTERVENTIONS: (1) a school-within-a-school organizational structure to create a supportive and personalized learning environment, (2) curricula that combine academic and career or

Three-Year Reproductive Health and Work Readiness Outcomes

	Total Sample (percent)		Females (percent)		Males (percent)	
	Treatment	Control	Treatment	Control	Treatment	Control
Reproductive health outcomes						
Changes in knowledge	22	12***	24	14***	19	9***
Has had vaginal intercourse	63	68	59	65	69	73
Used Depo-Provera at last intercourse	12	5**	22	9**	1	2
Used a condom at last intercourse	85	86	79	80	91	92
Pregnant or caused pregnancy	12	18**	15	25**	10	11
Actual births	4	6	5	10*	4	2
Work readiness outcomes						
Has a bank account	59	32***	60	31***	57	32***
Has had work experience	89	77***	90	78***	87	76**
Computer use outcomes						
Uses computer often	68	62	71	62*	64	63
Uses word processing	81	74**	87	77**	75	70
Uses Internet	81	75*	77	74	86	76*
Uses e-mail	58	49*	55	46*	61	53
Three or four of the computer outcomes	66	57**	68	57**	63	57**

* $p < .05$, ** $p < .01$, *** $p < .001$ for the difference between the program and control groups.

technical courses, and (3) partnerships with local employers to increase career awareness and provide work-based learning opportunities.

TARGET POPULATION: Initial focus was on keeping students at high risk of dropping out enrolled in high school; later focus broadened to include preparing high-performing and high-risk students for college and employment.

OUTCOMES OF INTEREST: High school graduation rates and early college and work experiences.

Upward Bound

STARTING YEAR/YEAR FINAL REPORT EXPECTED: 1994/2005.

INFORMATION SOURCE: David Myers and Allen Schirm, "The Impacts of Upward Bound: Final Report for Phase 1 of the National Evaluation." Mathematica Policy Research Reference No. 8046–515, April 1999.

PRINCIPAL INTERVENTIONS: Students enrolled in Upward Bound projects are offered traditional academic instruction, tutoring, mentoring, counseling, career planning, cultural programs, and college planning activities. The programs also offer intensive instruction in summer, typically lasting six weeks.

TARGET POPULATION: High school students from low-income families without a history of college attendance.

OUTCOMES OF INTEREST: Student academic and personal development, college access and retention, and employment and earnings.

Center for Employment Training (CET) Replication Study

STARTING YEAR/YEAR FINAL REPORT EXPECTED: 1995/2005.

INFORMATION SOURCE: Manpower Demonstration Research Corporation (MDRC) web site, http://www.mdrc.org.

FUNDING SOURCE: U.S. Department of Labor Employment and Training Administration.

EVALUATOR: Manpower Demonstration Research Corporation.

SITES: Camden and Newark, New Jersey; Chicago, Illinois; El Centro, Oxnard, Riverside, San Francisco, and Santa Maria, California; New York, New York; Orlando, Florida; Reidsville, North Carolina; and Reno, Nevada.

PRINCIPAL INTERVENTIONS: This experiment tests whether the CET model (which is highlighted in both the JOBSTART and Minority Single Female Parent experiments) can achieve success at other sites. The model focuses on occupational training and offers training for a selection of occupations based on area employer demand. Clients' basic skills needs are linked to the occupational training classes. The program is full-time, with peer training and behavioral expectations that reflect the workplace. Job placement is emphasized, and clients are considered to have graduated when they have found employment.

TARGET POPULATION: Economically disadvantaged youth age 18–22 not currently attending school.

OUTCOMES OF INTEREST: Employment and earnings, welfare receipt, training credentials received, health, household status, and involvement in the criminal justice system.

9

Low-Income Single/Teen Parents

Minority Female Single-Parent (MFSP) Demonstration

SUMMARY: This demonstration, conducted from 1984 to 1987, tested the effects of education and training on a large sample of minority female single parents. Subjects were followed for up to five years.

COST: Evaluation costs, approximately $3 million.

TIME FRAME: Demonstration period, November 1984–December 1987; data collected, same period, with follow-up of up to five years (San Jose only).

TREATMENTS TESTED: The four centers used different approaches, but all included assessment, education, job training, and support services such as counseling and child care assistance. The control group was not eligible to receive services at the centers, but could seek services elsewhere.

OUTCOMES OF INTEREST: (1) Earnings; (2) Employment; and (3) Welfare receipt.

SAMPLE SIZE: Total applicants, 3,965. Total used in analysis, 3,175; treatments, 1,841; controls, 1,334. Atlanta: treatments, 373; controls, 299. San Jose: treatments, 440; controls, 329. Providence: treatments, 346; controls, 163. Washington, D.C.: treatments, 682; controls, 543.

TARGET POPULATION: Minority, single mothers.

NUMBER OF TREATMENT GROUPS: Two (with one control group) at each site.

NUMBER AND LOCATION OF SITES: Four—Atlanta, Georgia (Atlanta Urban League, AUL); San Jose, California (Center for Employment Training, CET);

Providence, Rhode Island (Opportunities Industrialization Center, OIC); and Washington, D.C. (Wider Opportunities for Women, WOW).

RESEARCH COMPONENTS:

■ Process analysis: Program operations, participant characteristics, and service delivery at the four sites were analyzed.

■ Impact analysis: Comparison of regression-adjusted means.

■ Benefit–cost analysis: Conducted.

MAJOR FINDINGS: The San Jose CET, unlike the three other sites, immediately provided job-specific skill training to all trainees and integrated basic literacy and mathematics skills into the job-training curriculum. Participants at this site demonstrated the greatest employment and earnings gains. In contrast, the other sites provided more traditional remedial education and training.

1. The CET program generated the greatest gains in employment and earnings, and these lasted over the full 60-month period (only CET had a five-year follow-up; the other three sites were followed for only 30 months). During the fifth year after program application, treatment group members earned an average of $95 per month more than did control group members, a statistically significant impact equal to 17 percent of control group mean earnings.

2. CET's impact on welfare receipt at 30 and 60 months was small and not statistically significant.

3. Over the five-year period, CET produced a positive return from the perspectives of both society and program participants (in 1986 dollars, $975 and $2,500 per participant, respectively). From a government-budget perspective, costs exceeded benefits by about $1,600 per participant.

4. WOW generated modest and significant gains in employment rates, but not in average earnings. Reductions in welfare receipts were small and not significant.

5. The investment in WOW did not produce a positive return from either the social or the government-budget perspective.

6. The projects at AUL and OIC had no significant impacts on any of the outcome variables.

7. No programs had significant long-term impacts on measures of psychological well-being, including depression and locus of control, or on fertility or marriage behavior.

TIME TRENDS IN FINDINGS: At the 30-month follow-up in the CET program, all treatment group members showed significant gains in employment and earnings. At five years, only sample members with 12 or more years of schooling showed significant gains. Impacts on general equivalency diploma (GED) attainment were significant for the treatment group at 30 months, but had dissipated at 60 months.

DESIGN ISSUES: The Minority Female Single-Parent (MFSP) demonstration consisted of four projects in different locations. The impacts of each project may be due to the characteristics of each site. Differences in impacts across sites should be treated cautiously.

REPLICABILITY: Replicable.

GENERALIZABILITY: Designed to generalize to the entire nation. MFSP projects were operated by community-based organizations independent from the local welfare offices. MFSP participation was entirely voluntary. MFSP participants were more disadvantaged than national samples of minority single mothers; on average, they were younger, had younger children, had less employment experience, and had less education.

FUNDING SOURCE: The Rockefeller Foundation. Key personnel: Phoebe Cunningham.

TREATMENT ADMINISTRATORS: AUL key personnel: Lyndon Wade and Edna Crenshaw; CET key personnel: Russ Tershey, Carmen Ponce, and Carmen Placido; OIC key personnel: Michael van Leesten and Kathy May; WOW key personnel: Cindy Marano and Barbara Makris.

EVALUATOR: Mathematica Policy Research. Key personnel: John Burghardt and Stuart Kerachsky.

ENABLING LEGISLATION: None.

POLICY EFFECTS: The Rockefeller Foundation was active in disseminating the results of the CET findings and entering them into the policy debate. The U.S. Department of Labor has funded CET to replicate their model in other programs, see CET Replication Study, page 286.

INFORMATION SOURCES: John Burghardt, Anu Rangarajan, Anne Gordon, and Ellen Kisker, *Evaluation of the Minority Female Single Parent Demonstration: Summary Report,* Mathematica Policy Research, October 1992; Amy Zambrowski and Anne Gordon, *Evaluation of the Minority Female Single Parent Demonstration: Fifth-Year Impacts at CET,* Mathematica Policy Research, December 1993.

PUBLIC-USE ACCESS TO DATA: Available through Mathematica Policy Research.

Young Families Can Project

SUMMARY: This demonstration, conducted from 1987 through 1990, tested the effects of case management and counseling on a medium-sized sample of teenage mothers. Subjects were followed for up to two years.

COST: Total evaluation costs over three years, approximately $50,000, plus substantial in-kind services.

TIME FRAME: Demonstration period, September 1987–June 1990; final report, July 1991.

TREATMENTS TESTED: The program consisted of intensive case management and counseling. Case management included assessment, agency referrals, and cash resources for short-term resolution of individual issues. The control group received no demonstration services.

OUTCOMES OF INTEREST: The project measured 15 social, educational, family, and financial "client stressors," including high school graduation, employment, and money management.

SAMPLE SIZE: Total, 204; experimentals, 104; controls, 100.

TARGET POPULATION: Teenage mothers. Eligibility based on the following: 19 years old or younger; the custodial parent of at least one child; and a recipient of, or eligible for, AFDC benefits.

NUMBER OF TREATMENT GROUPS: Two (with one control group).

NUMBER AND LOCATION OF SITES: One—Phoenix, Arizona.

RESEARCH COMPONENTS:

■ Process analysis: Some attention paid to implementation issues, the partnership process, and staff behaviors.
■ Impact analysis: Comparison of means—experimental versus control, pretest versus posttest.
■ Benefit–cost analysis: Not conducted.

MAJOR FINDINGS:

1. For the total sample, there were no significant differences between experimental and control groups on posttest measures on any outcomes. Further, there were no statistically significant improvements in any of the 15 stress areas in either group (in fact, there was some statistically significant deterioration in the experimental group on measures of money management, parenting knowledge, and isolation).
2. Women who spent two years in the program made progress in some areas. (There were two cohorts in the project; only those who enrolled at the beginning were in the program for two full years.) Education, family planning, career planning, housing, household maintenance, and self-esteem factors improved for these women. The experimental group had higher employment rates (mostly part-time) than the

control group, though this finding was not statistically significant. There was a significant difference, in favor of the experimental group, in rates of high school graduation (or its equivalent), as well as in junior college enrollment.

TIME TRENDS IN FINDINGS: Improvements were seen only for those women who had received the intervention for two years.

DESIGN ISSUES:
1. There was some friction between city and state workers during the first year. This caused some difficulties in accessing data and providing uniform services.
2. Higher-than-expected client needs in education and housing led to some program changes.
3. There was high staff (caseworker) turnover due to high caseloads.

REPLICABILITY: Replicable, with cautions regarding the above issues.

GENERALIZABILITY: Designed to generalize to the city of Phoenix. The sample was largely Hispanic and the evaluator referred to a distinct Southwest culture. However, he stated that the program ideas are found in many similar programs, and he felt there is some generalizability.

FUNDING SOURCE: U.S. Department of Health and Human Services, Office of Community Services, Demonstration Partnership Program.

TREATMENT ADMINISTRATORS: City of Phoenix Human Resources Department (HRD) and Arizona Department of Economic Security (DES). Key personnel: Nancy McLeod and Alnita McClure for Phoenix HRD and Karen Novachek for DES.

EVALUATORS: Arizona State University School of Social Work. Key personnel: Robert Moroney, Gwat Yong Lie, and Peter Kettner.

ENABLING LEGISLATION: Demonstration Partnership Program under section 408 of the Human Services Reauthorization Act of 1986, as amended.

POLICY EFFECTS: This program was modified and subsequently continued with Arizona state and local funding.

INFORMATION SOURCE: U.S. Department of Health and Human Services (DHHS), Office of Community Services, *Demonstration Partnership Program: Summaries and Findings, FY 1988 and 1989*, 1991.

PUBLIC-USE ACCESS TO DATA: Available through the Office of Community Services, DHHS.

Single-Parent Economic Independence Demonstration (SPEID)

SUMMARY: This demonstration, conducted from 1988 to 1990, tested the effects of unpaid internships and mentoring on a medium-sized sample of single parents. Subjects were followed for up to one year. The random assignment design was not faithfully implemented, as program dropouts were removed from the treatment group in analysis.

COST: Evaluation costs, approximately $70,000.

TIME FRAME: Demonstration period, July 1988–November 1990; data collected, same period; final report, July 1991.

TREATMENTS TESTED: Unpaid internships with local businesses. Interns were also assigned a mentor at the business site. Control group participants were referred to other service agencies and received some supportive services.

OUTCOMES OF INTEREST: (1) Employment; (2) Earnings; (3) Welfare receipt; and (4) Other noneconomic indicators such as self-esteem and motivation.

SAMPLE SIZE: Total, 571; treatments, randomly assigned (RA), 197; not randomly assigned (non-RA), 67; controls, 182. An additional 125 interns entered the program after the initial evaluation phase.

TARGET POPULATION: Single parents. Participants were required to have a high school diploma or equivalent and a prior history of participation in preemployment training.

NUMBER OF TREATMENT GROUPS: Three (with one control group). Initially, all eligible applicants were placed in internships (non-RA interns). In a second phase, participants were randomly assigned to a treatment (RA interns) or a control group.

NUMBER AND LOCATION OF SITES: Nine service delivery areas throughout Utah.

RESEARCH COMPONENTS:

- Process analysis: Included a review of measurement tools, organizational structure, and implementation.
- Impact analysis: For economic outcomes, a comparison of means was conducted without employing tests of statistical significance. Analysis of variance was used in comparing pre- and posttest scores on measures of non-economic outcomes.
- Benefit–cost analysis: Not conducted.

MAJOR FINDINGS: In the analysis, treatment group dropouts are examined as a separate category, violating the random assignment design.

1. Interns (both RA and non-RA) had higher overall percentages of positive employment placements than did controls or dropouts. Over 50 percent of interns were employed full-time at the conclusion of SPEID compared with less than 30 percent of controls or dropouts.
2. Interns who were working were employed in jobs that brought them higher salaries and greater benefits than controls were receiving. For participants who had worked within Utah during the 12 months prior to intake and who were employed at posttreatment, general wage increases were seen. Non-RA interns' average salary increased by $.92 per hour; RA interns gained $1.50 per hour; controls gained $.54 per hour; and dropouts gained $.40 per hour.
3. Approximately 50 percent of employed interns were receiving medical benefits compared with 24 percent of employed controls.
4. There is some indication that involvement in SPEID had a positive influence on participant attitudes. Interns scored significantly higher on two of three posttreatment (compared to pretreatment) measures of self-esteem and assertiveness.

TIME TRENDS IN FINDINGS: Little or no long-term follow-up was done. Only 20 percent of the sample was contacted at 12 months.

DESIGN ISSUES:

1. There was a high attrition rate. There was difficulty obtaining posttreatment and follow-up information for controls and those not serving internships. Only 53 percent of the sample was contacted at the 6-month follow-up, and only 20 percent at the 12-month point.
2. The random assignment component created negative repercussions. Some staff were reluctant to refer clients to the program, and some applicants were also hesitant to enroll.
3. As noted above, dropouts were not considered part of the treatment group. Their employment and earnings were analyzed separately, creating a selection bias.
4. There were several salient differences between program dropouts and program completers. Dropouts were receiving higher salaries and had received less preemployment training during the year prior to SPEID intake.

5. Because the program was not initially designed as a treatment-versus-no-treatment study and tests of statistical significance were not employed, it is difficult to discern the true import of the findings.

REPLICABILITY: This project was replicated in Boise, Idaho, and New York State.

GENERALIZABILITY: The project was designed to generalize to the entire state, and the sample did reflect the population of single parents in Utah. However, design and implementation issues discourage attempts at generalization. In addition, the evaluators feel that SPEID applicants likely represented a segment of the population that was more difficult to place in employment than other low-income single parents.

FUNDING SOURCE: U.S. Department of Health and Human Services (HHS), Office of Com-munity Services, Administration on Children and Families. Key personnel: Marianne Mackenzie.

TREATMENT ADMINISTRATOR: Davis County Employment and Training. Key personnel: Richard Nelson, agency director, and Susan Sheehan, project director.

EVALUATORS: Lenore Shisler and Garth Mangum, University of Utah.

ENABLING LEGISLATION: Demonstration Partnership Program under section 408 of the Human Services Reauthorization Act of 1986, as amended.

INFORMATION SOURCE: U.S. Department of Health and Human Services, *Demonstration Partnership Program: Summaries and Findings, FY 1988 and 1989,* 1991.

PUBLIC-USE ACCESS TO DATA: Available through HHS, Office of Community Services.

10
Unemployed Workers

General Education in Manpower Training

SUMMARY: This demonstration, conducted from 1964 to 1966, tested the effects of technical and general education in a small sample of unemployed males. Subjects were followed for one year.

COST: $1.75 million; research only, roughly 25 percent.

TIME FRAME: Demonstration period, January 1964–June 1965; data collected through June 1966; final report, 1966.

TREATMENTS TESTED:
1. Controls received no treatment.
2. Placebos received "simulated type of occupational information and guidance" daily. No further description in report, and the evaluator does not remember.
3. Technical education group members received one half-day of technical education, and one hour per day of supervised (but not guided) study. Classes were in auto mechanics, sheet metal, masonry, electronics, and maintenance technology (upkeep of buildings). They received $30 per week stipend. The program placed graduates with employers.
4. General education group members went to the same courses as group 3 and, in addition, one half-day of systematic instruction in reading improvement, language arts, number skills, and occupational information. They received $30 per week stipend. There was considerable stress on making work in reading and mathematics both job-related and adult-oriented. Special materials were prepared. The program placed graduates with employers.

OUTCOMES OF INTEREST: (1) Employment; (2) Salary per week; and (3) Mobility.

SAMPLE SIZE: Total, 180; 45 in each of the four groups.

TARGET POPULATION: Men, unemployed for three months or more, laid off from previous work, typically for automation-related reasons.

NUMBER OF TREATMENT GROUPS: Four (with one control group).

NUMBER AND LOCATION OF SITES: One—Norfolk, Virginia.

RESEARCH COMPONENTS:

■ Process analysis: In follow-up surveys, some group 4 participants attributed their subsequent success to reading, language, and mathematics courses.

■ Impact analysis: Conducted. Comparison of means.

■ Benefit–cost analysis: Not conducted.

MAJOR FINDINGS: Average gains of three years in reading and arithmetic were found for the general education group.

From follow-up interviews, one year later:

Group	Employment rate (%)	Average weekly salary ($)	Percentage promoted
General education	95	83*	31
Technical education	74	71	25
Placebo	63	50	12
Control	59	46	12

* Statistically significant difference from technical education group at the 1 percent level.

TIME TRENDS IN FINDINGS: Only one follow-up reported; Brazziel does not know if any were conducted subsequently.

DESIGN ISSUES: None apparent.

REPLICABILITY: In principle, fully replicable. Principles are use of job-related materials in general education, an educational approach that recognizes the experience that adults bring to the classroom, and adequate stipends.

GENERALIZABILITY: Several challenges to generalizability: (1) small sample; (2) self-selection of site by an enthusiastic faculty who developed special instructional materials; (3) the evaluator says having the program on a college campus seemed to make a positive difference in subject attitudes; (4) jobs were available in Norfolk but were mismatched to worker skills. The results may not generalize to the common inner-city situation in which transportation to jobs is costly.

FUNDING SOURCES: U.S. Department of Labor, Office of Automation; U.S. Department of Health, Education & Welfare (HEW), Office of Education; and an anonymous donor. Key personnel: David Kerrico for Office of Education.

TREATMENT ADMINISTRATOR: Norfolk Division, Virginia State College. Key personnel: William Cooper, Hampton University.

EVALUATOR: Norfolk Division, Virginia State College. Key personnel: William F. Brazziel.

ENABLING LEGISLATION: None.

INFORMATION SOURCES: William F. Brazziel, "Effects of General Education in Manpower Programs," *Journal of Human Resources* 1(1966): 39–44; HEW, Office of Education, "Re-educating Unemployed Workers," in *Cooperative Research*.

PUBLIC-USE ACCESS TO DATA: We have no information about a public-use file for this demonstration.

Carbondale Job-Finding Club

SUMMARY: This demonstration, conducted in 1973, tested the effects of supervised group job search assistance on a small sample of the unemployed. Subjects were followed for three months.

COST: Estimate of $200 per experimental cost increment (administration only), or $12,000.

TIME FRAME: Demonstration period, 1973; data collected, 1973; final report, 1975.

TREATMENTS TESTED:

1. Controls received no treatment.
2. Experimentals attended daily group meetings to teach job search methods and develop positive job search attitudes through group reinforcement. Subjects received supervision in job search until successful. Elements of the treatment included the buddy system, secretarial services for résumés and letters of recommendation, a telephone bank, and job leads from other clients.

Experimentals were matched one-for-one with controls by an overall criterion of probable employability based on age, sex, race, education, marital status, desired position and salary level, number of dependents, and current financial resources. Once matched, a coin flip determined which member of the pair would be a control and which an experimental.

OUTCOME OF INTEREST: Employment.

SAMPLE SIZE: Experimentals, 60; controls, 60.

TARGET POPULATION: Unemployed people not receiving unemployment benefits.

NUMBER OF TREATMENT GROUPS: Two (with one control group).

NUMBER AND LOCATION OF SITES: One—Carbondale, Illinois.

RESEARCH COMPONENTS:

- Process analysis: To eliminate attrition bias, those experimentals matched with nonresponding controls were dropped from the sample for reporting purposes.

Major Findings

	Experimentals	Controls
Employed (more than 20 hours/week) within two months of beginning treatment	90%	55%
Employed within three months of beginning treatment	92%	60%
Mean starting hourly wage	$2.73	$2.01
Median time until job found (includes those who did not find jobs during the period)	14 days	53 days

Note: These figures exclude experimentals who attended fewer than five sessions and their matched controls. No data are available on those excluded. All differences shown are statistically significant.

- Impact analysis: Conducted as difference in means or medians.
- Benefit–cost analysis: Not conducted.

MAJOR FINDINGS: See table above.

TIME TRENDS IN FINDINGS: Results are only reported through three months of treatment.

DESIGN ISSUES:

1. Results are probably biased by self-selection, since only data on those who chose to attend five or more sessions were presented. The matching process did not control for self-selection except to the degree that the observed variables captured it.
2. The sample was small and quite heterogeneous.
3. Success of the Job Club method probably varies with the size of the informal (unadvertised) job market, and this may vary among communities.

REPLICABILITY: The treatment has been replicated in subsequent studies scattered throughout this book, and a training manual for counselors has been published.

GENERALIZABILITY: Findings are striking, since Carbondale was a high-unemployment community. The sample excluded people receiving unemployment insurance benefits because the project report authors believed some individuals were likely to lack motivation to find employment until their benefits ran out. They suggested, however, that if participation were a condition of receiving benefits, it would motivate job search in this group too.

FUNDING SOURCE: Illinois Department of Mental Health. Key personnel: None.

TREATMENT ADMINISTRATOR: Anna Mental Health Center. Key personnel: Nathan H. Azrin.

EVALUATOR: Anna Mental Health Center. Key personnel: Nathan H. Azrin.

ENABLING LEGISLATION: None.

INFORMATION SOURCE: Nathan H. Azrin, T. Flores, and S. J. Kaplan, "Job-Finding Club: A Group-Assisted Program for Obtaining Employment," *Behavior Research and Therapy* 13(1975): 17–27.

PUBLIC-USE ACCESS TO DATA: We have no information about a public-use file for this demonstration.

Carbondale Handicapped Job-Finding Club

SUMMARY: This demonstration, conducted from 1974 to 1975, tested the effects of supervised group job search assistance on a small sample of handicapped unemployed individuals. Subjects were followed for six months.

COST: Not available (experiment was one activity of an ongoing research laboratory).

TIME FRAME: Demonstration period, 1974–75; data collected, same period; final report, 1979.

TREATMENTS TESTED:
1. Controls received two days of group lectures, discussions, and role-playing in job search. The project report authors stated that this is the common format of the only other standardized method of job counseling.
2. Experimentals received daily group job search training and supervised job search until a job was obtained. A fuller description is in the preceding Carbondale Job-Finding Club summary.

OUTCOME OF INTEREST: Employment.

SAMPLE SIZE: Experimentals, 80; controls, 74.

TARGET POPULATION: Unemployed people with "severe employability problems": physical or mental handicaps, ex-prisoners or mental patients, welfare clients, substance abusers, and alcoholics; and other long-term job seekers.

NUMBER OF TREATMENT GROUPS: Two (with one control group).

NUMBER AND LOCATION OF SITES: One—Carbondale, Illinois.

RESEARCH COMPONENTS:
- Process analysis: The project report stated that "a principal difference between the two programs was that the comparison clients were informed of the need for (certain) actions; the Job Club clients were required to perform them under supervision."
- Impact analysis: Conducted as a difference in means or medians.
- Benefit–cost analysis: Not conducted.

MAJOR FINDINGS: See table next page. According to the project report, "the program was found superior to an alternative program, but the salaries were not extraordinary, and some clients required weeks and months of continued diligent supervision and guidance."

TIME TRENDS IN FINDINGS: There was no tendency for differences to narrow between two months and six months.

DESIGN ISSUES:
1. Experimental design eliminates any possibility of self-selection bias (because both experimentals and controls had to attend at least two sessions to be included in the sample), but the six-month follow-up is probably vulnerable to attrition bias.
2. The sample is small, and the clients' problems, although severe, are heterogeneous.

Major Findings

	Experimentals	Controls
Employed after two months at a job over 20 hours/week (based on survey with 100 percent response rate)	90%	20%
Employed after six months (based on survey with 32 percent response rate)	95%	28%
Mean starting hourly wage	$3.01	$3.08
Median starting hourly wage	$2.61	$2.20
Median time to find job (successful seekers only)	10 days	30 days
Percentage of days worked out of all available days over a three-month period	89%	23%

Notes: Table data exclude both experimentals and controls who attended fewer than two sessions. Differences in employment are significant. The difference between mean and median starting wages is due to a single high-wage control. All jobs found were unsubsidized.

REPLICABILITY: See Carbondale Job-Finding Club summary, page 294.

GENERALIZABILITY: See Carbondale Job-Finding Club summary, page 294.

FUNDING SOURCE: Illinois Department of Mental Health.

TREATMENT ADMINISTRATOR: Anna Mental Health Center. Key personnel: Nathan H. Azrin.

EVALUATOR: Anna Mental Health Center. Key personnel: Nathan H. Azrin.

ENABLING LEGISLATION: None.

INFORMATION SOURCE: Nathan H. Azrin and Robert A. Philip, "The Job Club Method for the Job Handicapped: A Comparative Outcome Study," *Rehabilitation Counseling Bulletin* 23 (December 1979): 144–155.

PUBLIC-USE ACCESS TO DATA: We have no information about a public-use file for this demonstration.

U.S. Employment Service Effectiveness of Counseling Pilot Study

SUMMARY: This demonstration, conducted from 1975 to 1976, tested the effects of employment counseling on a medium-sized sample of U.S. Employment Service (ES) clients. Subjects were followed for up to 10 months.

COST: Roughly $250,000 (1976).

TIME FRAME: Demonstration period, November 1975–February 1976; data collected, August 1976; final report, August 1977.

TREATMENTS TESTED:

1.a. People determined by U.S. Employment Service interviewers to need counseling and who received it (ES experimentals).

1.b. People determined by ES interviewers to need counseling who did not receive it (ES controls).

2.a. People determined by Stanford Research Institute (SRI) interviewers (not ES interviewers) to need counseling and who then received it from the usual ES counselors (SRI experimentals).

2.b. People determined by SRI interviewers (not ES interviewers) to need counseling and who did not receive it (SRI controls).

Random assignment occurred after determination of need. The reason for the second set of experimentals/controls was the investigators' belief that ES interviewers tend to refer people to counseling not on the basis of need but on the basis of their low placement potential. People with a higher placement potential might need counseling to achieve that potential, whereas low-potential individuals still might not benefit from employment counseling.

OUTCOME OF INTEREST: Duration of unemployment.

SAMPLE SIZE: Experimentals, 481; controls, 439.

TARGET POPULATION: Clients of the U.S. Employment Service determined by interviewers to need employment counseling.

NUMBER OF TREATMENT GROUPS: Four (with two control groups).

NUMBER AND LOCATION OF SITES: Three—Salt Lake City, Utah; Minneapolis, Minnesota; and West Palm Beach, Florida.

RESEARCH COMPONENTS:
- Process analysis: Not conducted.
- Impact analysis: Conducted with ordinary least squares regressions. Other analytical methods were also used.
- Benefit–cost analysis: Not conducted.

MAJOR FINDINGS:
1. Counseling had no significant impact on the duration of unemployment. This finding was the same for both ES and SRI subjects.
2. Counseling also had no significant impact on wages, job prestige, percentage of observation period employed, job satisfaction, or the number of job search methods used.

TIME TRENDS IN FINDINGS: Data series were too short to find any.

DESIGN ISSUES: Because this study was explicitly designed as a pilot for a more ambitious evaluation, the period for which the investigators had data was no more than 10 months for any subject and as little as 6 months for some.

REPLICABILITY: None. The experiment was undertaken to demonstrate the feasibility of a larger study, which was never funded. The investigators did not inquire into the content of the counseling.

GENERALIZABILITY: The sites selected were not representative of the U.S. Employment Service nationally.

FUNDING SOURCE: U.S. Department of Labor, Employment and Training Administration. Key personnel: William Showler.

TREATMENT ADMINISTRATOR: U.S. Employment Service, three locations.

EVALUATOR: Stanford Research Institute. Key personnel: Jacob Benus.

ENABLING LEGISLATION: None.

INFORMATION SOURCE: Jacob Benus, Arden R. Hall, Patty Gwartney-Gibbs, Marilyn Coon, Caren Cole, Diane Leeds, and Doug Brent, *The Effectiveness of Counseling in the U.S. Employment Service: A Pilot Study; Analytic Results,* Stanford Research Institute, August 1977.

PUBLIC-USE ACCESS TO DATA: We have no information about a public-use file for this demonstration.

Job Club Behavioral Supervision Test

SUMMARY: This demonstration, conducted from 1980 to 1981, tested the effects of supervised job search activities on a medium-sized sample of the unemployed. Subjects were followed for six months.

COST: Not possible to separate from other research.

TIME FRAME: Demonstration period, roughly 1980–81; data collected, roughly the same period; final report, March 1982.

TREATMENTS TESTED:
1. Controls were taught all skills and techniques used in the job search under the Job Club model. See Carbondale Job-Finding Club summary, p. 294.
2. Experimentals received this information and were supervised in using it—for example, in telephoning employers and friends and writing résumés.

OUTCOME OF INTEREST: Employment.

SAMPLE SIZE: Experimentals, 186; controls, 133.

TARGET POPULATION: Unemployed people of all sorts, especially (but not solely) referrals from the local employment service.

NUMBER OF TREATMENT GROUPS: Two (with one control group).

NUMBER AND LOCATION OF SITES: One—Carbondale, Illinois.

RESEARCH COMPONENTS:
- Process analysis: None.
- Impact analysis: Conducted as a difference in means.
- Benefit–cost analysis: Not conducted.

MAJOR FINDINGS:
Six months after enrollment:

	Controls	Experimentals
Obtained jobs of 20⁺ hours/week	70.6%	87.6%*
Mean hours/week worked	33.6	36.9
Days required to find job	60.7	32.1*
Mean salary/hour	$3.93	$4.99

* Difference is statistically significant.

TIME TRENDS IN FINDINGS: Only six-month data are reported.

DESIGN ISSUES:
1. Attrition was higher in the controls than in the experimentals, and there was no analysis of it. (The initial sample included 196 experimentals and 150 controls.)
2. This study in particular would have benefited from a benefit–cost analysis, to show whether the experimental difference was worth the supervision cost.
3. See also the comments on the other Job Club experiments.

REPLICABILITY: Replicable. See Carbondale Job-Finding Club summary, page 294.

GENERALIZABILITY: Apparently generalizable; there does not seem to be any community-specific effect here.

FUNDING SOURCE: Illinois Department of Mental Health. Key personnel: None.

TREATMENT ADMINISTRATOR: Anna Mental Health Center. Key personnel: Nathan H. Azrin.

EVALUATOR: Anna Mental Health Center. Key personnel: Nathan H. Azrin.

ENABLING LEGISLATION: None.

INFORMATION SOURCE: Nathan H. Azrin, V. A. Besalel, I. Wisotzek, M. McMorrow, and R. Bechtel, "Behavioral Supervision versus Informational Counseling of Job Seeking in the Job Club," *Rehabilitation Counseling Bulletin*, 25 (March 1982): 212–18.

PUBLIC-USE ACCESS TO DATA: We have no information about a public-use file for this demonstration.

Buffalo Dislocated Worker Demonstration Program

SUMMARY: This demonstration, conducted from 1982 to 1984, tested the effects of employment services (job search assistance, training, on-the-job training) on a medium-sized sample of laid-off workers. Subjects were followed for six months.

COST: The impact analysis was conducted as part of a six-site program evaluation, most of which was nonexperimental. It was not possible to separate the experimental and nonexperimental costs.

TIME FRAME: Demonstration period, October 1982–September 1983; data collected through July 1984; final report, March 1985.

TREATMENTS TESTED: The experiment took place in the context of factory shutdowns and large-scale layoffs in the Buffalo area. Laid-off workers from six large "target plants" were recruited for reemployment-related services. Because resources were limited, treatment administrators rationed these services through a lottery system; at random, workers were either notified or not notified of the availability of program slots. The program offered testing and assessment, a four-day job search workshop, a job search resource center, classroom training for new careers, on-the-job training, job development services, relocation assistance, and Targeted Jobs Tax Credit eligibility determination. These component services were not assigned randomly.

OUTCOMES OF INTEREST: (1) Participation; (2) Employment; (3) Wages; and (4) Receipt of transfer payments.

SAMPLE SIZE: Analysis sample: Experimentals, 586; controls, 210.

TARGET POPULATION: Laid-off workers from four steel plants, an automobile assembly plant, and a petroleum refinery. Workers over the age of 55 were excluded ex post from the analysis sample, because no such workers opted to receive the services offered.

NUMBER OF TREATMENT GROUPS: Two (with one control group).

NUMBER AND LOCATION OF SITES: One— Buffalo, New York.

RESEARCH COMPONENTS:

■ Process analysis: Conducted. Some unexpected differences in background variables between experimentals and controls were noted, but they were judged not to affect the results. The treatment was an expensive one, averaging $1,975 per participant. Participation was fairly low, with 27.7 percent of experimentals choosing to receive services.

■ Impact analysis: Conducted with ordinary least squares and a Heckman selection term for participation. The inverse Mills ratio was set equal to zero for controls; a probit analysis was performed on the discrete choice to participate or not to participate among experimentals, and the inverse Mills ratio was derived for each experimental from that probit. The impact of the experimental treatment per participant was then calculated as the coefficient on a dummy variable (one if experimental participant, zero if experimental nonparticipant or control) in an equation that included, among other variables,

the inverse Mills ratio. The project report authors presented alternative estimation models and argued that the one they used is the most efficient. Also, because of significant nonresponse rates, the observations were weighted so that the analysis sample of experimentals resembled the population of controls.

■ Benefit–cost analysis: Not conducted.

MAJOR FINDINGS:

Impacts on participant experimentals in the first six months after recruitment:

	Impact estimate	Mean for participants
Proportion of time employed	+0.33**	0.57
Probability of ever being employed	+0.31**	0.72
Average hours employed per week	+13.6**	23.7
Average weekly earnings	$115**	$174
Weekly amount of food stamps	−$5.10*	$3.60
Percentage of time receiving public assistance	−10.7*	2.3
Weekly amount of public assistance	−$9.20*	$1.10

* Significant at the 90 percent level with a one-tail test. Public assistance includes Aid to Families with Dependent Children, Supplemental Security Income, and general assistance.
** Significant at the 95 percent level with a one-tail test.

Effects on unemployment insurance receipt and Supplemental Unemployment Benefit are not significant.

TIME TRENDS IN FINDINGS: Experimental/control employment differences narrow over time.

DESIGN ISSUES:

1. The most serious problem is the high nonresponse rate, nearly 46 percent among controls, over one-third of them refusals. The rate of refusals is higher among controls than among experimentals; nonresponse bias might well exist, and the weighting method will not eliminate it.

2. One of the great advantages of random-assignment experiments is that they do not require the use of econometric adjustments for self-selection like the Heckman procedure, which is not robust to deviations from

the assumptions of the model concerning the distribution of the random disturbance.

REPLICABILITY: Replicable.

GENERALIZABILITY: Limited by the possibility of nonresponse bias and the particularly depressed condition of the local economy. The Buffalo economy was quite depressed at the time of the experiment, with the unemployment rate rising from 9.7 percent to 12.6 percent over the course of 1982.

FUNDING SOURCE: U.S. Department of Labor, Employment and Training Administration. Key personnel: Beverly Bachemin and George Koch.

TREATMENT ADMINISTRATOR: Worker Re-employment Center. Key personnel: Harry Reeverts, Mark Cosgrove, and Edie Rifenburg.

EVALUATOR: Mathematica Policy Research. Key personnel: Walter Corson, Sharon Long, and Rebecca A. Maynard.

ENABLING LEGISLATION: None.

INFORMATION SOURCE: Walter Corson, Sharon Long, and Rebecca A. Maynard, *An Impact Evaluation of the Buffalo Dislocated Worker Program,* Mathematica Policy Research, March 1985.

PUBLIC-USE ACCESS TO DATA: Public-use file available; contact National Technical Information Service, Springfield, Virginia.

Claimant Placement and Work Test Demonstration

SUMMARY: This demonstration, conducted in 1983, tested the effects of a deadline to register for work with the Employment Service, mandatory supervised job search, and job placement services on a large sample of unemployment insurance (UI) claimants. Subjects were followed for less than one year.

COST: Administration, $25,000; research only, roughly $200,000.

TIME FRAME: Demonstration period, February–December 1983; data collected, same period; final report, July 31, 1984.

TREATMENTS TESTED:

Group A—Controls. The treatment of controls differed slightly from prior practice in that prior practice theoretically required Employment Service (ES) registration. Controls had no ES registration requirement and did not receive special job development efforts, although they could use the ES services voluntarily. They were required (as were experimentals) to come in periodically for eligibility reviews at the UI office.

Group B—Improved work test, but regular ES services. These experimentals were mailed notices coincidentally with their first week's UI check to come to the Employment Service office to register their availability for work. This practice differed from prior practice in that the registration requirement was delayed so that those who never received a check did not come into ES offices, and the registration was required as of some definite date. In general, failure to register would be taken as possible evidence of unavailability for work and, therefore, ineligibility for UI payments. New procedures were implemented to match ES and UI records so that this rule would be routinely enforced.

Group C—Improved work test and enhanced placement interviewer services. These experimentals received the same notice as group B. In addition, when the subject reported to the ES, an interviewer would attempt to develop a job for the subject unless he or she was a union member, was not job-ready, or was on layoff for some definite period. Group C subjects were also called in for a renewed job-placement attempt if still unemployed after nine weeks.

Group D—Improved work test, enhanced placement interviewer services, and job search workshops. In addition to group C experimentals, three-hour job search workshops were mandated for group D experimentals who were still receiving UI benefits four to five weeks after receiving enhanced placement interviewer services.

OUTCOMES OF INTEREST: (1) Employment and (2) UI payment reductions.

SAMPLE SIZE: Group A, 1,485; group B, 1,493; group C, 1,666; group D, 1,277.

TARGET POPULATION: New UI claimants who had received an initial UI check, excluding those whose employers said they were on layoff for some definite period.

NUMBER OF TREATMENT GROUPS: Four (with one control group).

NUMBER AND LOCATION OF SITES: One—Charleston, South Carolina.

RESEARCH COMPONENTS:
- Process analysis: Conducted. The process analysis indicates that the experiment was conducted essentially as planned. Roughly 25 percent of the experimentals failed to register on time with the ES the first time, and among experimentals subject to subsequent call-ins, about 9 percent of those eligible failed to respond. Nonresponse was more common among men than women and varied inversely with age and education. Nonresponses by men and women were not homogeneous (i.e., could not be captured simply by an intercept term), and there was a cohort effect (the longer the call-in policy was in effect, the more likely subjects were to respond). Eighty-five percent of experimentals received some ES service, compared with 35 percent of controls. Over 62 percent of group C and D members received some attempt at job development, compared with 33 percent of group B and 9 percent of group A members.

- Impact analysis: Ordinary least squares (OLS), comparison of means.
- Benefit–cost analysis: Cost-effectiveness analysis.

MAJOR FINDINGS:

	Group A	Group B	Group C	Group D
Percentage of subjects with nonmonetary determination (eligibility ruling)	5.8	13.4	16.7	18.4
Percentage of subjects with a denial (ruled ineligible)	4.2	7.4	9.2	8.7

1. OLS confirms that all experimental treatments had a statistically significant positive effect on the denial rate compared with the experience of controls. This effect was substantially higher in C and D than in B, but differences between C and D were negligible.
2. Treatment effects on employment and wages as recorded in the UI wage reporting system were weak, inconsistent, and usually not statistically significant.
3. Effects on weeks of UI payments (coefficients of OLS dummy variables for treatment group—this measures the treatment effect on experimentals by comparison with controls):

	Group B	Group C	Group D
Men	−0.83*	−1.15*	−1.14*
Women	−0.20	0.31	−0.15

* Statistical significance at 95 percent confidence level, on a two-tail test. OLS results control for cohort (week applying for UI).

Much of the difference between men and women results from the strong treatment effect on construction workers, who are mostly male. The experimental treatments reduced the weeks of UI received by male construction workers by about two weeks (the effects on female construction workers are about the same, but are not statistically significant because of small numbers). "A possible explanation for this result may relate to the casual, part-time nature of some construction employment (particularly during slack periods) and to the relatively low wage replacement rates that UI provides to construction workers."

All experimental treatments were inexpensive: $4.72, $13.17, and $17.58 per subject increments for treatments B, C, and D, respectively. The corresponding average reductions in UI payments were $52.93, $58.71, and $73.14. All experimental treatments are therefore cost-effective, with the most cost-effective being treatment D.

TIME TRENDS IN FINDINGS: The variable representing cohort has a negative and statistically significant effect on weeks of unemployment. However, it is not possible to distinguish between the effect of falling unemployment rates and the effect of learning about new registration requirements for UI. Since the experimental treatments differ in the times at which interventions occur, treatment effects are also indistinguishable from time effects.

DESIGN ISSUES:

1. Unemployment in Charleston fell from 8.9 percent to 6.6 percent in 1983. The improving economy reduced UI claims and increased job orders at the ES office.

2. If a claimant stated that he or she had failed to report as required because of illness or lack of transportation, there would have been a denial of UI on the grounds that the claimant was unable to work or was unavailable for work. On the other hand, claims that the summons to register at the ES had been lost in the mail were always accepted, even when there had been no difficulty receiving the UI check sent under a separate cover. The summons was sent under a separate cover only because of the experimental character of the demonstration (controls were not supposed to receive a call-in, and it was apparently too complex to insert

a call-in with some checks and not with others); experimental denial rates therefore slightly understate what could be expected upon implementation of the policy.

3. If the treatment effect is primarily centered on construction workers, it would not be surprising if no wage or employment effects were noted from UI data, because much of the industry is not covered or escapes reporting requirements.

4. In the cost-effectiveness analysis, instead of estimating the reduction in UI payments directly, the authors take the average UI weekly payment ($96.24) and multiply it by the experimental treatment effect on weeks of receipt. This procedure fails to take into account the possibility that the part of the population whose behavior is changed by the treatment will not have the same average weekly benefit as the overall population.

REPLICABILITY: Replicable.

GENERALIZABILITY: The project report authors were cautious about generalizability. South Carolina Job Service/UI procedures are similar to those in most other states, but other factors vary considerably: the Charleston labor force has a higher percentage of blacks than the U.S. labor force; the importance of the construction industry, where much of the treatment impact was concentrated, varies across the country; and most states have higher maximum weekly UI payments than South Carolina's, which was $118 in 1983.

FUNDING SOURCE: U.S. Department of Labor, Employment and Training Administration. Key personnel: Norm Harvey and William Showler.

TREATMENT ADMINISTRATOR: South Carolina Employment Security Agency.

EVALUATORS: SRI International, Mathematica Policy Research, and Bloom Associates. Key personnel: Terry R. Johnson for SRI, Walter Corson and Walter Nicholson for Mathematica, and Susan Philipson Bloom for Bloom.

ENABLING LEGISLATION: None.

INFORMATION SOURCES: Terry R. Johnson, Jennifer M. Pfiester, Richard W. West, and Katherine P. Dickinson, *Design and Implementation of the Claimant Placement and Work Test Demonstration,* SRI International, May 1984; Walter Corson, David A. Long, and Walter Nicholson, *Evaluation of the Charleston Claimant Placement and Work Test Demonstration,* Mathematica Policy Research, July 1984.

PUBLIC-USE ACCESS TO DATA: We have no information about a public-use file for this demonstration.

Delaware Dislocated Worker Pilot Program

SUMMARY: This demonstration, conducted in 1983, tested the effects of job search assistance and employment counseling on a small sample of unemployment insurance (UI) claimants. Subjects were followed for up to six months.

COST: Research only, $10,000 (1983).

TIME FRAME: Demonstration period, January 1983–July 1983; data collected through December 1983; final report, 1984.

TREATMENTS TESTED: Experimentals received four basic services in sequence: job search workshops, regular individual counseling sessions, services of job developers, and retraining. The retraining services were a last resort, and only 13 out of 65 experimentals received them.

Controls received the usual services for the unemployed in Delaware.

OUTCOMES OF INTEREST: (1) UI benefit payments and (2) Earnings.

SAMPLE SIZE: Experimentals, 65; controls, 110.

TARGET POPULATION: Volunteers were taken from the population of all UI claimants who had been receiving benefits for 7 to 12 weeks, attended an orientation, and applied for entry in the program. Those without at least 10 years of education or access to transportation were screened out, as were those who expected to be recalled by their most recent employer. Separate assignment lotteries were held in each of the state's three counties to even out the workload of program staff in the different locations.

NUMBER OF TREATMENT GROUPS: Two (with one control group).

NUMBER AND LOCATION OF SITES: All three counties in Delaware.

RESEARCH COMPONENTS:
- Process analysis: An analysis of participation was conducted; it generally found that nonparticipants had better-than-average employment prospects than participants, and that early dropouts had higher past earnings than did completers, but lower earnings after the program started. Program staff also commented unfavorably on one of the key concepts of the program, that of having high school guidance counselors with very limited special training perform the counseling tasks. The program was also evaluated with no preliminary start-up period.
- Impact analysis: Conducted with OLS.
- Benefit–cost analysis: Not conducted.

MAJOR FINDINGS: The program had no statistically significant impact on UI payments or earnings.

TIME TRENDS IN FINDINGS: None.

DESIGN ISSUES: The sample size was too small, but in this case, the underlying population also appeared small—only 965 workers in the entire state had been unemployed for 7 to 12 weeks, and those who applied for program services were only about a third of the total. Statistically significant results could not have been expected from a sample this size unless the treatment impacts were quite large.

REPLICABILITY: Replicable.

GENERALIZABILITY: Probably none, because the sample is too small and the implementation, specifically the use of high school guidance counselors, seems questionable.

FUNDING SOURCE: U.S. Department of Labor, Employment and Training Administration.

TREATMENT ADMINISTRATOR: Delaware Department of Labor. Key personnel: Dennis Carey.

EVALUATOR: Bloom Associates. Key personnel: Howard S. Bloom and Susan Philipson Bloom.

ENABLING LEGISLATION: None.

INFORMATION SOURCE: Howard S. Bloom, "Lessons from the Delaware Dislocated Worker Pilot Program," *Evaluation Review* (April 1987): 157–77.

PUBLIC-USE ACCESS TO DATA: We have no information about a public-use file for this demonstration.

Illinois Unemployment Insurance Incentive Experiment

SUMMARY: This demonstration, conducted from 1984 to 1985, tested the effects of a reemployment bonus incentive on a large sample of unemployment insurance (UI) clients. Subjects were followed for up to one year.

COST: $800,000; research only, $200,000.

TIME FRAME: Demonstration period: mid-1984 to early 1985; data collected, mid-1984 to mid-1985; final report, February 1987.

TREATMENTS TESTED:
1. Claimant experiment. A $500 bonus was offered to an eligible claimant of UI payments if he or she could find a job within 11 weeks and hold that job for four months.
2. Employer experiment. The same, except that the $500 bonus would be paid to the claimant's employer.

3. Controls. Standard UI eligibility.

OUTCOMES OF INTEREST: (1) Reductions in unemployment spells and (2) Net program savings.

SAMPLE SIZE: Claimant experimentals, 4,186; employer experimentals, 3,963; controls, 3,963.

TARGET POPULATION: People who were (1) eligible for 26 weeks of UI benefits; (2) between 20 and 55 years of age; and (3) registrants with Job Service offices who were not on definite layoff, ineligible for a union hiring hall, or not recent veterans or federal employees.

NUMBER OF TREATMENT GROUPS: Three (with one control group).

NUMBER AND LOCATION OF SITES: Twenty-two Job Service offices in northern and central Illinois.

RESEARCH COMPONENTS:
■ Process analysis: Not conducted.
■ Impact analysis: Conducted as difference in means.
■ Benefit–cost analysis: Conducted from a budgetary perspective.

MAJOR FINDINGS:
1. A $194 reduction in 52-week benefit payments to the average claimant experimental was found, compared with the average control. The comparable $61 reduction for employer experimentals was not statistically significant.
2. A 1.15-week reduction in insured unemployment over 52 weeks was found for the average claimant experimental. The 0.36-week reduction for employer experimentals was not statistically significant.
3. The experimental treatments did not appear to curtail productive job search activity, because no statistically significant change in subsequent earnings was found between the control and experimental groups.
4. The employer experiment did result in a $164 reduction per claimant in benefit payments to white women, which was statistically

significant. The effects of the employer experimental treatment among blacks (male and female) and white males were not significantly different from zero. The claimant experimental response was statistically significant for whites of both sexes, but not for blacks of either sex.

5. Of claimant experimentals, 13.6 percent received a bonus; 25 percent qualified for one. Of employer experimentals, 2.8 percent obtained a bonus for their employers; 22.8 percent of them could have obtained one for their employers.

6. The ratio of benefit payments reductions to bonus cost for the claimant experiment was 2.32, which is statistically significant. The ratio for the employer experiment was 4.29 (not significant). If 100 percent of those eligible for bonuses had claimed them, the benefit–cost ratio would have been 1.26 for claimant experimentals and 0.53 for employer experimentals.

TIME TRENDS IN FINDINGS: Reductions in the initial unemployment spell may be slightly offset by increases in subsequent unemployment, but this is not statistically significant.

DESIGN ISSUES: The low rate at which those who qualified for bonuses claimed them is puzzling.

REPLICABILITY: The treatments are clearly replicable.

GENERALIZABILITY: The 22 sites involved in the experiment represented very diverse labor markets, so locality effects should not be present. Spiegelman noted that roughly the first half of workers subject to the experiment would have been eligible for extended (38-week) federal unemployment payments if their unemployed status had lasted longer than 26 weeks, whereas subsequent claimants were ineligible for them. Experimental response seems to have been stronger in the first group, but this was not conclusively established.

FUNDING SOURCES: Illinois Department of Employment Security (DES; using federal Wagner-Peiser grants) and W. E. Upjohn Institute for Employment Research. Key personnel: Sally Ward for DES and Robert G. Spiegelman for Upjohn.

TREATMENT ADMINISTRATOR: Illinois DES. Key personnel: Sally Ward.

EVALUATOR: W. E. Upjohn Institute for Employment Research. Key personnel: Robert G. Spiegelman and Stephen A. Woodbury.

ENABLING LEGISLATION: None.

INFORMATION SOURCES: Stephen A. Woodbury and Robert G. Spiegelman, "Bonuses to Workers and Employers to Reduce Unemployment: Randomized Trials in Illinois," *American Economic Review* (September 1987): 513–30; Stephen A. Woodbury and Robert G. Spiegelman, *The Illinois Unemployment Insurance Incentive Experiments,* final report to Illinois Department of Employment Security, W. E. Upjohn Institute, February 1987.

PUBLIC-USE ACCESS TO DATA: We have no information about a public-use file for this demonstration.

Texas Worker Adjustment Demonstration

SUMMARY: This demonstration, conducted from 1984 to 1985, tested the effects of assisted job search, job clubs, and training on a large sample of unemployed/displaced workers. Subjects were followed for one year.

COST: Total project costs, approximately $2 million; evaluation costs, under $500,000.

TIME FRAME: Demonstration period, April 1984–July 1985.

TREATMENTS TESTED: Two-tiered intervention. Tier I included assisted job search and job clubs. Tier II included classroom and on-the-job occupational training. Transportation services were available at all sites. Child care was provided only at the Houston site. Controls did not receive these services.

OUTCOMES OF INTEREST: (1) Earnings; (2) Employment; and (3) Unemployment insurance (UI) benefits.

SAMPLE SIZE: Total, 2,259; tier I only (Houston site), 332; tiers I/II (all sites), 1,113; controls (all sites), 814.

TARGET POPULATION: Unemployed and displaced workers. There were also site-specific guidelines targeting certain industries and/or specific occupations.

NUMBER OF TREATMENT GROUPS: Three in Houston (tier I only, tier I/II, control); two in both El Paso sites (tier I/II, control).

NUMBER AND LOCATION OF SITES: Three—Texas Employment Commission/Houston Community College (TEC/HCC); El Paso School for Educational Enrichment (SEE); and Greater El Paso SER Jobs for Progress (SER/JOBS).

RESEARCH COMPONENTS:
- Process analysis: Focus on implementation, variation across sites, participation, and operations. Also, special care was taken to reduce control group crossovers and treatment group no-shows.
- Impact analysis: Conducted using multiple regression models (ordinary least squares regression and maximum likelihood logit models).
- Benefit–cost analysis: A formal benefit–cost analysis was not conducted, but a cost-effectiveness study was done.

MAJOR FINDINGS:
1. Program impacts for displaced female workers were substantial and sustained throughout the one-year follow-up. Female participants experienced a $1,148 (34 percent) average annual program-induced earnings gain. Correspondingly, these participants received 19 percent less in UI benefits during their first 30 weeks after entering the program.
2. Impacts for men were appreciable, but were much smaller and shorter-lived than for women. Male participants experienced an average annual program-induced earnings gain of $673 (8 percent), most of which occurred in the second quarter, when earnings gains averaged $329, or 16 percent. Impacts were statistically significant only in this quarter.
3. UI data suggested a statistically significant, though declining over time, increase in the likelihood of employment for women. No large or statistically significant effects on this outcome were suggested for men.
4. Average costs per participant varied considerably across sites but were comparable to the Job Training Partnership Act (JTPA) Title III national average. Measured earnings impacts for women exceeded program costs.
5. Findings from the TEC/HCC site suggest that essentially no additional gains accrued from adding tier II services to job-search assistance. In fact, during the first year after random assignment, the tier I group had a significantly higher earnings gain than the tier I/II group ($403 versus $320).

TIME TRENDS IN FINDINGS: All program impacts declined over time.

DESIGN ISSUES:
1. Initial recruitment at both El Paso sites was done through industry referrals and walk-ins. These strategies did not produce sufficient enrollment, and it was necessary to contract with the El Paso TEC office for UI claimant referrals.
2. Original demonstration plans specified that all sites identify target occupations, but SEE and SER/JOBS did not implement this feature.
3. TEC/HCC had a predominantly white-collar sample, yet offered mostly blue-collar-oriented classroom training. This could explain the weak impacts for the tier I/II group. Additional courses were added to help correct this mismatch.
4. Sites varied in their training focus. TEC/HCC focused overwhelmingly on classroom training, SER/JOBS focused overwhelmingly on on-the-job training, and SEE reflected an even mix of these activities.

REPLICABILITY: Replicable.

GENERALIZABILITY: The typical sample member was an experienced worker who had recently lost a relatively good job and was using the UI system to help meet substantial family responsibilities. The TEC/HCC program targeted specific occupations that produced a mostly white-collar demonstration sample. This sample differed markedly from the local pool of unemployed workers and even more so from JTPA IIA (disadvantaged) counterparts. The El Paso sites better reflected the existing pool of the insured unemployed.

Population characteristics between Houston and El Paso also differed. Houston's population is more ethnically diverse and better educated. El Paso is predominantly Hispanic and less well educated. Houston wage rates are much higher than El Paso's. El Paso also had higher unemployment (10 percent versus 7 percent during the project period).

FUNDING SOURCE: Texas Department of Community Affairs (TDCA). Key personnel: Christopher King, Mary Jane Leahy, and Saundra Kirk.

TREATMENT ADMINISTRATOR: TDCA. Key personnel: Jean Wood for TEC/HCC, Iris Burnham for SEE, and Ruben Villalobos for SER/JOBS.

EVALUATOR: Abt Associates. Key personnel: Howard Bloom, Jane Kulik, and Linda Sharpe.

INFORMATION SOURCE: Howard Bloom, *Back to Work: Testing Reemployment Services for Displaced Workers,* W. E. Upjohn Institute, 1990.

PUBLIC-USE ACCESS TO DATA: Not available.

New Jersey Unemployment Insurance Reemployment Demonstration

SUMMARY: This demonstration, conducted from 1986 to 1987, tested the effects of job search assistance, training, and a reemployment bonus payment on a large sample of dislocated (unemployed) workers. Subjects were followed for six years.

COST: Research only, $1.27 million (1987).

TIME FRAME: Demonstration period, July 1986–fall 1987; data collected through July 1988; final report, April 1989. Six-year follow-up and summary report, January 1996.

TREATMENTS TESTED:

1. Job search assistance (JSA) only. Four weeks after subjects received their first weekly unemployment insurance (UI) payment, they were directed to come to an orientation and testing session. The following week, subjects were (with certain exceptions) expected to attend a job search workshop lasting five days (half-day sessions). The week thereafter they were to attend individual sessions with counselors to assess their employment prospects. An employment resource center with job listings, telephones, and literature was set up in the UI office and subjects were expected to use it regularly. If they failed to do so, they would be recontacted every two weeks and reminded of this obligation. Failure to comply with these expectations would be grounds for termination of UI payments.

2. JSA plus training and relocation. The same treatment as JSA only, but in addition, at the individual counseling session subjects were informed of the availability of funds for vocational training courses or expenses of relocation and job search in another area. (The option was training or relocation, but not both.) Counseling on training options was provided to those interested. As anticipated, less than 1 percent of those offered the relocation option accepted assistance for that purpose; the incremental effect of this treatment over JSA only is essentially the training effect.

3. JSA plus reemployment bonus. The same treatment as JSA only, but, in addition, at the individual counseling session, subjects were offered a reemployment bonus. The maximum bonus was equal to half of the remaining UI entitlement at the time of the interview (the

average of the maximum bonus was $1,644). The bonus declined at the rate of 10 percent per week until UI was no longer available to the subject. The bonus was not available if the new job was with the subject's last employer or a relative, or if it was temporary, seasonal, or part-time. The subject received 60 percent of the bonus if employed 4 weeks, and the balance if employed 12 weeks.

4. Controls faced the usual obligation to look for work, but the use of existing job search services was voluntary.

OUTCOMES OF INTEREST: (1) UI payments; (2) Employment; and (3) Earnings.

SAMPLE SIZE: JSA only, 2,416; JSA plus training and relocation, 3,810; JSA plus reemployment bonus, 2,449; controls, 2,385.

TARGET POPULATION: The treatments were intended for dislocated workers. The following types of UI claimants were therefore screened out of the sample: those who never received the first payment (they found work or were ineligible), those who had worked less than three years for their previous employer, those less than 25 years old, those who had definite recall dates from the last employer, those hired through a union hiring hall, and certain types of special claimants (e.g., ex-armed forces, ex-federal government, interstate movers).

NUMBER OF TREATMENT GROUPS: Four (with one control group).

NUMBER AND LOCATION OF SITES: Ten—UI offices in Bloomfield, Burlington, Butler, Deptford, Elizabeth, Hackensack, Jersey City, Newark, Paterson, and Perth Amboy.

RESEARCH COMPONENTS:

- Process analysis: Conducted. Essentially the treatments were delivered as planned. Many subjects were excused from portions of the JSA treatments because they could not read, speak, or understand English well enough to benefit from them.
- Impact analysis: Conducted with ordinary least squares (OLS), logit.
- Benefit–cost analysis: Conducted from claimant, agency budget, government budget, and social perspectives.

MAJOR FINDINGS:

	JSA only	JSA plus training/ relocation	JSA plus bonus
Change in UI benefits	−$87*	−$81*	−$170*
Change in weeks of UI payments, benefit year	−0.47*	−0.48*	−0.97*
Change in probability of exhausting benefits	−0.028*	−0.017	−0.037*
Change in weeks employed, benefit year:			
1st quarter	2.3*	1.9*	2.8*
2nd quarter	4.9*	2.8*	5.0*
3rd quarter	4.2*	2.2	2.3
4th quarter	2.8	1.7	0.6
Change in earnings ($)			
1st quarter	125*	82	160*
2nd quarter	263*	103*	278*
3rd quarter	171	83	131
4th quarter	49	77	22

* An effect significantly different from zero at a two-tailed 90 percent confidence level, and often at higher confidence levels.

1. Subgroup analysis indicates that "the treatments were less successful for individuals who faced hard-core, structural unemployment problems, such as blue-collar workers, workers from durable-goods manufacturing industries, and permanently separated workers."

2. The six-year follow-up found further significant reductions in regular UI receipt two years after the initial benefit year for the JSA-only group (−$94 and −0.53 weeks paid) and for the JSA plus bonus group (−$78 and −0.44 weeks paid). The JSA plus bonus group also received

significantly fewer dollars in the third year (−$65). No statistically significant long-term effects on employment and earnings were found.

3. Claimants who received on-the-job training experienced high levels of employment and earnings throughout the period following the initial claim relative to the JSA-only claimants. Those who received classroom training initially experienced relatively lower earnings and less employment in the first three quarters, but higher employment and earnings in subsequent quarters.

4. Long-term findings suggest that all treatment components may have contributed to longer-term impacts. It is suggested that the treatments generated jobs that were more stable than those found by control group members.

5. When longer-term impacts from the six-year follow-up are included in the benefit–cost analysis, the results were more favorable than they were initially. The results suggest that all three treatments offered positive net benefits to claimants and to society as a whole, relative to existing services. The JSA-only treatment and the JSA plus bonus treatment also led to net gains for the government. The JSA plus training and relocation treatment was expensive for the government sector, resulting in net losses.

TIME TRENDS IN FINDINGS: As shown above.

DESIGN ISSUES: The major issue is covered under "Generalizability," below. Subgroup analysis seems to consist mostly of the use of interaction terms (e.g., a dummy for industry multiplied by a dummy for treatment) in the regression. This type of analysis assumes that the slope coefficients on continuous variables, like prior earnings, are identical for all groups. Separate regressions for distinct groups might have been useful.

REPLICABILITY: Replicable.

GENERALIZABILITY: It is unlikely that a real social program would be set up using the particular eligi-bility criteria selected for this experiment. Only about one-quarter of the UI claimant population was eligible for the experiment. It is noteworthy that the treatments were less successful for the sub-groups most typical of the population the experi-mental treatments were intended to assist (older workers and blue-collar workers).

FUNDING SOURCE: U.S. Department of Labor, Employment and Training Administration. Key personnel: Stephen Wandner and Wayne Zajac.

TREATMENT ADMINISTRATOR: New Jersey Depart-ment of Labor. Key personnel: Frederick Kniesler, Nancy Snyder, and Roger Emig.

EVALUATOR: Mathematica Policy Research. Key personnel: Walter Corson, Paul T. Decker, and Shari Miller Dunstan.

ENABLING LEGISLATION: None.

POLICY EFFECTS: Stephen Wander has stated that this experiment related to an ongoing debate in Congress over the appropriate government response to dislocated workers: a passive income maintenance approach or an active intervention approach. Elements of the New Jersey model (early identification of dislocated workers, referrals to job search assistance) were adopted in the Economic Dislocation and Worker Adjustment Assistance Act. To encourage early intervention, needs-based stipends under that act are available to workers after the 13th week of a UI claim only if they are in a training program. MPR found that the additional costs per claimant from adding the reemployment bonus as designed in New Jersey to the Job Search Assistance program were greater than the additional UI savings. This finding has led to other experiments with different bonus designs.

INFORMATION SOURCES: Walter Corson, Paul T. Decker, Shari Miller Dunstan, and Anne R. Gordon, with Patricia Anderson and John Homrighausen, *The New Jersey Unemployment*

Insurance Reemployment Demonstration Project: Final Evaluation Report, U.S. Department of Labor, Employment and Training Administration, Unemployment Insurance Occasional Paper 89-3, April 1989; Walter Corson and Joshua Hamilton, *The New Jersey Unemployment Insurance Reemployment Demonstration Project: Six-Year Follow-Up and Summary Report,* rev. ed., U.S. Department of Labor, Employment and Training Administration, Unemployment Insurance Occasional Paper 96-2, January 1996.

PUBLIC-USE ACCESS TO DATA: Public-use file available; contact National Technical Information Service, Springfield, Virginia.

Washington State Alternative Work Search Experiment

SUMMARY: This demonstration, conducted from 1986 through 1988, tested the effects of alternative work-search policies on a large sample of unemployment insurance (UI) claimants. Subjects were followed for one year.

COST: Battelle Human Affairs Research Centers reported that they received approximately $70,000

for the evaluation. Washington State Employment Security Department (ESD) reported program costs of approximately $100,000. Both sources acknowledge considerable donated services on this project.

TIME FRAME: Enrollment period, July 1986–August 1987; data collected for one year from enrollment; final report, January 1991.

TREATMENTS TESTED: Four variations of work-search policies. See table below.

OUTCOMES OF INTEREST: (1) UI benefit receipt; (2) Employment; and (3) Earnings.

SAMPLE SIZE: Total, 9,634. By treatment group: A, 2,246; B, 2,871; C, 1,964; D, 2,553.

TARGET POPULATION: Unemployed individuals filing new claims for UI benefits. Claimants with employer or referral-union attachment were excluded.

NUMBER OF TREATMENT GROUPS: Four (with one control group).

NUMBER AND LOCATION OF SITES: One—Tacoma, Washington.

Treatments Tested

Activity or service	A	B (control)	C	D
Presentation of benefit rights	Special group interview	Regular group interview	Regular group interview	Regular group interview
Continued-claims process	By telephone, as necessary	Submit forms biweekly	Submit forms biweekly	Submit forms biweekly
Initial work search directive	Active search for work	Active search for work	Active search for work	Active search for work
Subsequent work search directive	None	Three contacts per week; later to report for ERI	Directed to report for ERI 4 or 5 weeks into claim period	Directed to attend job search workshop after about 4 weeks; later to report for ERI
Eligibility review interview (ERI)	None	13–15 weeks after filing claim; focus on UI eligibility	Individualized timing of ERI, with possible increase in work search requirements	13–15 weeks after filing claim; focus on employability development

RESEARCH COMPONENTS:

▪ Process analysis: Looked at specific behaviors of local office staff related to ESD services.

▪ Impact analysis: Comparison of means, regression, and probit models.

▪ Benefit–cost analysis: Conducted, though not in-depth. All information and calculations are not presented in the cited report.

MAJOR FINDINGS:

1. Claimants in the exception-reporting group (group A) received significantly greater average UI benefits (+$265) than did control group members. They also received benefits for a significantly longer period (+3.3 weeks) than the control group. Further, they were significantly more likely to exhaust their benefits.

2. The intensive work search group (group D) members received $68 less than controls in total UI benefits; however this is only significant at about the .11 level. They received payments for .5 fewer weeks than controls, significant at the .1 level.

3. Very small differences in UI payments and in period of receipt between group C and control group members were observed. None were statistically significant.

4. Few significant differences were noted among group members concerning employment and earnings. The more rapid reemployment of group D members did not result in lower earnings or hourly wage rates.

TIME TRENDS IN FINDINGS: There was a significant difference in the earnings for group A. Individuals in that group earned hourly wages that were 3 percent higher than controls, though they were less likely to be working during the first quarter following their claim. These results dissipate when examined over the complete year.

Overall impacts for groups A and D tend to be smaller for the full benefit year than for the first spell of UI receipt.

DESIGN ISSUE: As of May 1987, no additional claimants were assigned to group A, owing to preliminary findings suggesting that the costs of this treatment to the UI Trust Fund were substantial. For the remainder of the study, these claimants were assigned to group D. This required minor adjustments in the modeling.

REPLICABILITY: Replicable.

GENERALIZABILITY: The demonstration was conducted only in the Tacoma office, which serves Pierce County, the second most populated county in Washington. The county did have a diverse labor market and unemployment rates similar to the state average (8.6 percent in 1985 and declining during the period of study). Racial/ethnic composition was "reasonably representative" of the state as a whole, although African Americans are overrepresented (Pierce County— 86.5 percent white, 6.8 percent African American; Washington State—90.5 percent white, 2.9 percent African American).

Although difficult to generalize from one site, these findings fit well with those from similar demonstration projects.

FUNDING SOURCES: U.S. Department of Labor, Washington State Employment Security Department, and the W. E. Upjohn Institute for Employment Research. Key personnel: Gary Bodeutsch, Kathy Countryman, and Judy Johnson.

TREATMENT ADMINISTRATOR: Tacoma Job Service Center.

EVALUATOR: Battelle Human Affairs Research Centers. Key personnel: Terry Johnson and Daniel Klepinger, project directors.

ENABLING LEGISLATION: None reported.

POLICY EFFECTS: According to the project evaluator, these results were "definitely used" in the federal policy debate regarding alternative plans in the area of unemployment. Testimony regarding the project results was submitted in 1991 to a U.S. Senate subcommittee and was partly responsible for decisions not to implement exception reporting methods (treatment A in this project).

INFORMATION SOURCE: Terry R. Johnson and Daniel H. Klepinger, *Evaluation of the Impacts of the Washington Alternative Work Search Experiment: Final Report,* Unemployment Insurance Occasional Paper 91-4, U.S. Department of Labor, 1991.

PUBLIC-USE ACCESS TO DATA: Available through U.S. Department of Labor.

Nevada Concentrated Employment Program (CEP)

SUMMARY: This demonstration, conducted from 1988 to 1989, tested the effects of enhanced employment services and training on a large sample of unemployed workers. Subjects were followed for one year.

COST: Total project costs, $312,948. Evaluation costs were limited because automated administrative data systems were used.

TIME FRAME: Demonstration period, July 1988–June 1989; data collected, same period.

TREATMENTS TESTED: The Concentrated Employment Program (CEP) included the development of an employment plan, job search assistance (workshops, referrals, and placements), and training, if necessary. The control group received normal Employment Service (ES) and unemployment insurance (UI) services.

OUTCOMES OF INTEREST: (1) Unemployment insurance benefits and (2) Duration of unemployment.

SAMPLE SIZE: Total, 2,962; treatments, 1,424; controls, 1,538.

TARGET POPULATION: Unemployed workers.

NUMBER OF TREATMENT GROUPS: Two (with one control group).

NUMBER AND LOCATION OF SITES: Two—Sparks and North Las Vegas, Nevada.

RESEARCH COMPONENTS:
- Process analysis: Special attention was paid to sample characteristics, participation rates, and service delivery.
- Impact analysis: Comparison of means.
- Benefit–cost analysis: Conducted.

MAJOR FINDINGS:
1. CEP significantly reduced the average duration of UI benefits for all treatment subgroups. For the entire sample, excluding trainees, the program reduced average weekly duration by 2.1 weeks (11.9 weeks for the treatment group versus 14 weeks for the control group). Including the trainees increased the average duration of the treatment group, though treatment–control differences remained statistically significant (treatment, 12.4 weeks; control, 14 weeks).
2. CEP had the greatest impact on females and claimants over 55 years of age.
3. For every dollar spent on providing enhanced services (excluding training), CEP reduced UI payout by $2.39. Although more complicated to measure, estimated benefit–cost ratios when training was included ranged from 1.1 to 1.64, depending on the assumptions made.

TIME TRENDS IN FINDINGS: None.

DESIGN ISSUES:
1. Due to high CEP workloads, the "one-to-one" random assignment design was altered. After assignments to treatment and control groups had been made, all claimants remaining in the selection pool were put into the control group. Although the larger number of control participants did not present a problem, the alteration of random assignment led to some significant differences between the groups. A total of 120 older males were randomly removed from the control group to rectify the problem. The resulting groups were then not significantly different, but could have still differed on unobservable characteristics.
2. One hundred and thirty CEP claimants who received training were excluded from the test,

which assessed the non-training impact on UI duration. Similar exclusions were not made with the control group owing to the difficulty in ascertaining training status. This probably introduces an upward bias on the CEP program impact.

3. The design did not incorporate a control group for CEP trainees, thus making it difficult to assess long-term training impacts. This does not cause problems in comparing *all* controls with *all* experimentals.

REPLICABILITY: Replicable.

GENERALIZABILITY: Designed to generalize to the entire state. Findings are supported by a prior Nevada study of the JTPA Title II program and the Nevada Claimant Placement Program. Although claimant characteristics were provided (claimants had an average age of 41 years, 17.4 percent were ethnic minorities, 38.2 percent were female, and they averaged 12.4 years of education), these characteristics were not compared with any larger population.

FUNDING SOURCE: UI Penalty and Interest Fund of the Nevada Employment Security Department. Key personnel: Stan Jones, executive director.

TREATMENT ADMINISTRATOR: Nevada Employment Security Department. Local Job Training Partnership Act (JTPA) entities were responsible for the training component. Key personnel: Stan Jones.

EVALUATOR: Nevada Employment Security Department. Key personnel: Jim Hanna and Zina Turney.

ENABLING LEGISLATION: None.

POLICY EFFECTS: When these results were presented to the Nevada legislature, they decided to levy a .05 percent tax on state payrolls to fund the continuation of the program. The CEP remains a standard component of the UI program. The evaluators also testified before the U.S. Congress, and other states have adopted similar programs.

INFORMATION SOURCES: James Hanna and Zina Turney, "The Economic Impact of the Nevada Claimant Employment Program," in U.S. Dept. of Labor, Unemployment Insurance Service, *UI Research Exchange: Information on Unemployment Research,* Unemployment Insurance Occasional Paper 90-4, Washington, D.C., 1990, 79–92; "Nevada Claimant Employment Program," in Esther R. Johnson, editor, *Reemployment Services to Unemployed Workers Having Difficulty Becoming Reemployed,* Unemployment Insurance Occasional Paper 90-2, U.S. Dept. of Labor, Unemployment Insurance Service, Washington, D.C., 1990, 150–63.

PUBLIC-USE ACCESS TO DATA: Not available.

Pennsylvania Reemployment Bonus Demonstration

SUMMARY: This demonstration, conducted in 1988 and 1989, tested the effects of a reemployment bonus payment on a large sample of unemployment insurance (UI) recipients. Subjects were followed for one year.

COST: Design and evaluation costs, approximately $990,000. Per-claimant expenditures range from $70 per claimant for treatment 1 to $180 per claimant for treatment 4.

TIME FRAME: Demonstration period, July 1988–89; data collected, same period; final report, September 1991.

TREATMENTS TESTED: Five combinations of bonus amount and qualification period (time allotted to get a job and receive a bonus) were tested. A sixth group did not receive the job search assistance (JSA) component to test the effects of this component. See table next page.

OUTCOMES OF INTEREST: (1) UI receipt; (2) Employment; and (3) Earnings.

SAMPLE SIZE: Total selected, 15,005; analysis sample, 14,086; controls, 3,392. Group 1, 1,395;

Treatments Tested

Group	Bonus amount	Qualification period	JSA workshop offered
0 (control)	0	0	No
1	3 × WBA	6 weeks	Yes
2	3 × WBA	12 weeks	Yes
3	6 × WBA	6 weeks	Yes
4	6 × WBA	12 weeks	Yes
5	6 × WBA, declining	12 weeks	Yes
6	6 × WBA	12 weeks	No

WBA = Weekly benefit amount.

group 2, 2,456; group 3, 1,910; groups 4 and 6 (combined for analysis), 3,073; group 5, 1,860.

TARGET POPULATION: Eligible UI claimants. Demonstration excluded those with a definite recall date, union attachment, filers of transitional claims, and filers separated from their jobs due to labor disputes.

NUMBER OF TREATMENT GROUPS: Seven (with one control group).

NUMBER AND LOCATION OF SITES: Twelve—local UI/JS (Job Service) offices in Butler, Coatesville, Connellsville, Erie, Lancaster, Lewistown, McKeesport, Philadelphia North, Philadelphia Uptown, Pittston, Reading, and Scranton.

RESEARCH COMPONENTS:
- Process analysis: Conducted, with special attention given to eligibility, JSA workshop, and verification of bonus amounts and claims.
- Impact analysis: Conducted using comparison of means with regression.
- Benefit–cost analysis: Conducted.

MAJOR FINDINGS:
1. Bonus offers significantly reduced UI receipt during the benefit year. Estimated impacts were generally larger for the more generous bonus offers.
2. Evidence suggests that the treatment increased employment and earnings. However, the significance of these findings differs for wage record data versus interview data. The latter provides stronger evidence of a positive effect.
3. Bonus offers yielded net benefits to claimants and to society as a whole. From the perspective of the UI system, bonus offers were not cost-effective, generating net losses for the UI trust fund. Some treatments generated positive net benefits for the government (treatments 2 and 3), and the government either broke even or incurred a modest loss for the other treatments.
4. Reemployment bonuses can be implemented successfully as part of the existing UI system. However, the job search component was ineffective due to very low participation rates.

TIME TRENDS IN FINDINGS: None.

DESIGN ISSUES: The low participation rate (less than 3 percent) for the job search workshop, due to lack of interest among claimants, led to the combining of two treatment groups for analysis. According to the final report, the bonus "may have provided a disincentive to participate in the workshop."

REPLICABILITY: Replicable.

GENERALIZABILITY: Designed to generalize to the entire state. UI/JS offices were selected randomly with a probability of selection proportional to caseload size. Site characteristics closely matched statewide characteristics in many salient respects. The local economy was quite strong during the demonstration and the unemployment rate was low (4.5 percent). Effects of the bonus and the ability of participants to meet qualification requirements may differ under more adverse economic conditions. Examining the four similarly designed bonus experiments together suggests generalizability across states.

FUNDING SOURCE: U.S. Department of Labor (DOL). Key personnel: William Coyne and Wayne Zajac.

TREATMENT ADMINISTRATOR: Pennsylvania Department of Labor and Industry. Key personnel: Frances Curtin and Robert Peebles.

EVALUATOR: Mathematica Policy Research. Key personnel: Walter Corson and Stuart Kerachsky.

ENABLING LEGISLATION: None.

POLICY EFFECTS: The DOL cited this study in 1994, proposing to allow states to change their UI laws, but the legislation was not enacted.

INFORMATION SOURCE: Walter Corson, Paul Decker, Shari Dunstan, and Stuart Kerachsky, *Pennsylvania Reemployment Bonus Demonstration: Final Report,* Mathematica Policy Research, September 1991.

PUBLIC-USE ACCESS TO DATA: Available through DOL.

Reemploy Minnesota (REM)

SUMMARY: This demonstration, conducted from 1988 to 1990, tested the effects of intensive case management services on a large sample of unemployed workers. Subjects were followed for two years.

COST: Total program cost, $835,000. The evaluation was done in-house. Evaluation costs were not separated other than hiring a research analyst for three months at $10,000.

TIME FRAME: Demonstration period, July 1988–June 1990; data collected, same period.

TREATMENTS TESTED: More personalized and intensive unemployment insurance (UI) services, including case management, intensive job search assistance and job matching, claimant targeting for special assistance, and a job-seeking skills seminar. The control group received regular UI services.

OUTCOMES OF INTEREST: Duration and amount of UI benefits.

SAMPLE SIZE: Treatment, 4,212. The control group was roughly 10 times as large as the treatment group. Those randomly selected were in the treatment group; all claimants not chosen and not excluded were in the control group.

TARGET POPULATION: Unemployed workers. A number of claimants were screened out, including those on short-term layoff, union-attached workers, and claimants enrolled in training.

NUMBER OF TREATMENT GROUPS: Two (with one control group).

NUMBER AND LOCATION OF SITES: Ten—eight offices in the Minneapolis/St. Paul area and one each in Duluth and Mankato (out of state).

RESEARCH COMPONENTS:
- Process analysis: Job services database and a survey were used to examine client characteristics, satisfaction, and participation.
- Impact analysis: Regression analysis.
- Benefit–cost analysis: Not conducted, though cost savings are reported.

MAJOR FINDINGS:
1. During the first year of the program, the treatment group's average claim duration was 11.16 weeks, compared with 15.24 weeks for the control group. Multiplied by the average weekly benefit amount for the treatment group, the result was an estimated $1,476,000 cost savings for the UI Trust Fund.
2. Over the two-year period, the average claim reduction for the treatment group was 4.32 weeks. This translates to a gross savings of $3,285,554 and a net savings (subtracting administrative costs) of $1,570,554.
3. In the metro area, among clients who attributed their reemployment to area office services, the Reemploy Minnesota (REM) group was reemployed at a significantly higher rate than were regular clients (35 percent versus 25 percent). In the out-of-state offices, there was no significant difference in the reemployment rate (both REM and regular client rates were approximately 35 percent).

TIME TRENDS IN FINDINGS: None.

DESIGN ISSUES:

1. There were problems with program coordination between the intake staff and the case managers. Without the cooperation and vigilance of the intake staff, the case managers could not keep their caseloads (40 clients) full.

2. Because caseloads were full at times, there were occasional breaches of the random assignment design. There was no purposeful selection of clients based on any client characteristics, but not all individuals had an equal chance of being selected at all times of the year.

3. The REM case managers were all volunteers and were eager to do well with this program. They were the "best and brightest," because there was a push to make an impression on the administration. This group may well have been different from the staff that worked on the control cases.

4. People coming in with large severance packages were put into the control group rather than excluded. They differed from the treatment group participants in a number of ways. They did not begin receiving benefits right away and usually came from higher-paying jobs. Although it is unclear how many claimants were in this category, this could pose a threat to internal validity.

REPLICABILITY: Replicable. Forms and procedures are available from the Minnesota Department of Jobs and Training.

GENERALIZABILITY: Designed to generalize to the entire state. Approximately 50 percent of all new claims went into the sample (treatment and control). The remainder were excluded for reasons mentioned above. The REM sample differed from regular UI clients on gender (10 percent more women), salary (earned 10 percent less), and occupation. Also, several of the design and implementation issues mentioned above may affect generalizability.

FUNDING SOURCE: Unemployment Insurance Contingent Account of the Minnesota Department of Jobs and Training.

TREATMENT ADMINISTRATOR: Minnesota Department of Jobs and Training. Key personnel: Tom Romens.

EVALUATOR: Minnesota Department of Jobs and Training. Key personnel: Tom Romens and Steve Scholl.

ENABLING LEGISLATION: None.

INFORMATION SOURCES: Steven R. Scholl, *Data Analysis: Reemploy Minnesota Evaluation,* Research and Statistics Office, Minnesota Department of Jobs and Training, October 1989; U.S. Department of Labor, Employment and Training Administration, *Reemployment Services to Unemployed Workers Having Difficulty Becoming Reemployed,* Unemployment Insurance Occasional Paper 90-2, 1990.

PUBLIC-USE ACCESS TO DATA: Not available.

Washington State Reemployment Bonus Experiment

SUMMARY: This demonstration, conducted from 1988 through 1990, tested the effects of a reemployment bonus on a large sample of the unemployed who were applying for unemployment insurance (UI) benefits. Subjects were followed for one year.

COST: Approximately $450,000 for design and evaluation.

TIME FRAME: Demonstration period, February 1988–January 1990; final report, 1992.

TREATMENTS TESTED: The reemployment bonus had two parts: the bonus amount and the qualification period (the time allotted for applicant to find a job in order to receive a bonus payment). This demonstration varied these two components as shown in the table on the next page.

OUTCOMES OF INTEREST: (1) Weeks of insured unemployment and (2) UI receipt.

Treatments Tested by Qualification Period

Bonus amount	.2 × Duration + 1[a]	.4 × Duration + 1[b]
2 × WBA	Treatment 1	T4
4 × WBA	T2	T5
6 × WBA	T3	T6

Notes: Duration refers to the number of weeks that a claimant would be eligible for UI benefits. The control group received no bonus payment. WBA = weekly benefit amount.
a. Longest period, 7 weeks.
b. Longest period, 13 weeks.

SAMPLE SIZE: Treatments, 12,451 (T1, 2,239; T2, 2,343; T3, 1,577; T4, 2,380; T5, 2,344; T6, 1,530); controls, 3,083.

TARGET POPULATION: Eligible UI claimants filing new claims. Contrary to previous studies, claimants waiting to be recalled to their previous employer and union hiring hall members were not excluded (though they were not paid a bonus if they accepted employment under these conditions). Filers of interstate claims were excluded.

NUMBER OF TREATMENT GROUPS: Seven (with one control group).

NUMBER AND LOCATION OF SITES: Twenty-one of Washington's 31 regional Job Service Centers (JSCs) located throughout the state. The project's final report (p. 26) provides a complete listing of sites.

RESEARCH COMPONENTS:
- Process analysis: Operations were closely monitored through computer checks and personal visits.
- Impact analysis: Conducted using regression.
- Benefit–cost analysis: Conducted.

MAJOR FINDINGS:
1. High-level bonus treatments produced substantial and statistically significant reductions in UI compensation and weeks of insured unemployment.
2. Three of the four low- and middle-level bonus treatments (treatments 1, 2, and 5) failed to produce statistically significant effects.
3. There were few statistically significant differences in the subgroup analyses, although estimates suggest that males respond more than females to bonus incentives; that whites and Hispanics respond more than blacks but less than other racial/ethnic groups; and that older claimants respond more than younger claimants.
4. No significant impacts on overall earnings were produced.
5. From a societal perspective, the bonus program had large net benefits. From the perspective of the UI system, net losses were incurred. For the government as a whole, the bonus program was roughly a break-even proposition.

TIME TRENDS IN FINDINGS: None reported; the follow-up period is relatively short.

DESIGN ISSUES:
1. Despite the use of random assignment, few impacts were statistically significant prior to the introduction of control variables due to differences among the treatment groups. The evaluators do not feel that random assignment was compromised.
2. There was always a question of adequate communication and understanding of the program by the subjects. Approximately 45 percent of those eligible for the bonus payment did not take advantage of the program (i.e., claim their bonus).
3. Entry and displacement effects, which would be likely to occur in a fully operational program, were not captured by the design in this demonstration. Also, to avoid a negative employment effect, some bonuses were paid to claimants who may not have been eligible for nonmonetary reasons (e.g., attachment to a previous employer or union hall).

REPLICABILITY: Replicable; the final report provides great detail regarding implementation and design.

GENERALIZABILITY: Designed to generalize to the entire state. The 21 JSCs handled 85 percent of the state's claimant population. Eligible claimants were included in the sample even if they did not receive any UI benefits. A large number of claimants (33 percent) assigned to the experiment did not participate. The cost of a fully implemented program could be substantially increased if wide knowledge of the bonuses led to larger rates of participation.

The findings of this demonstration are consistent with the other reemployment bonus experiments that have been conducted. Therefore, results should be considered generalizable across states as well.

FUNDING SOURCES: Alfred P. Sloan Foundation and U.S. Department of Labor, Employment and Training Administration. Key personnel: Albert Rees for Sloan and Stephen Wandner for Labor.

TREATMENT ADMINISTRATOR: State of Washington Employment Security Department. Key personnel: Jim Wolfe, Gary Bodeutsch, Kathy Countryman, and Patricia Remy.

EVALUATOR: W. E. Upjohn Institute for Employment Research. Key personnel: Robert Spiegelman and Christopher O'Leary.

ENABLING LEGISLATION: None.

INFORMATION SOURCE: Robert G. Spiegelman, Christopher J. O'Leary, and Kenneth J. Kline, *The Washington Reemployment Bonus Experiment: Final Report,* Unemployment Insurance Occasional Paper 92-6, U.S. Department of Labor, Unemployment Insurance Service, Washington, 1992.

PUBLIC-USE ACCESS TO DATA: Available through W. E. Upjohn Institute.

Washington and Massachusetts Unemployment Insurance Self-Employment Work Search Demonstrations

SUMMARY: This demonstration, conducted from 1989 to 1991, tested the effects of business start-up services, including financial assistance, counseling, and workshop sessions, on a large sample of the recently unemployed. Subjects were followed for three years.

COST: Research component, approximately $2 million.

TIME FRAME: Demonstration period—Washington State: September 1989–March 1991; Massachusetts: May 1990–April 1993; data collected, same period; final report, December 1994.

TREATMENTS TESTED: Washington State experimentals were offered four business training sessions; they continued to receive regular unemployment insurance (UI) payments and, in addition, were eligible for a lump-sum payment after achieving five program milestones (e.g., completion of training sessions and development of an acceptable business plan). Massachusetts experimentals attended a one-day training session, an individual counseling session, and six workshop sessions on a variety of business topics. They continued to receive regular UI benefits and were exempted from UI work search requirements.

Controls in both states remained eligible for regular UI benefits.

OUTCOMES OF INTEREST: (1) Self-employment; (2) Combined self-employment and wage and salary employment; and (3) Earnings.

SAMPLE SIZE: Washington: Treatments, 755; controls, 752. Massachusetts: Treatments, 614; controls, 608.

TARGET POPULATION: New UI claimants. Filers of interstate claims, filers who were employer-attached (i.e., on standby to return to their former employer), and those who were under 18 were excluded. Massachusetts also excluded new claimants with a low predicted probability of exhausting UI benefits.

NUMBER OF TREATMENT GROUPS: Two (with one control group) in each state.

NUMBER AND LOCATION OF SITES: Six sites in Washington State—King County, Olympia, Snohomish County, Vancouver, Wenatchee, and Yakima. Seven sites in Massachusetts—Gloucester, Greenfield, Lowell, New Bedford, Roxbury, Springfield, and Woburn.

RESEARCH COMPONENTS:
- Process analysis: Conducted. Focused on recruitment and intake procedures as well as the timing of service delivery.
- Impact analysis: Conducted. Comparison of means.
- Benefit–cost analysis: Conducted.

MAJOR FINDINGS: Results based on the longer of two observation periods (33 months in Washington, 31 months in Massachusetts).

1. Treatment group members in both states were much more likely than controls to have had a self-employment experience (+22 percent in Washington; +12 percent in Massachusetts) and to have spent more time per year in self-employment (+2 months in Washington; +0.8 months in Massachusetts). The Washington group was more likely to be still self-employed at the time of the second follow-up survey (the experimental–control difference was not statistically significant).
2. Annual self-employment earnings increased significantly in Washington (+$1,675). These earnings also increased in Massachusetts, though not significantly.
3. In Washington, claimants' likelihood of working in wage and salary employment, and their earnings from that employment, were significantly reduced. Wage and salary earnings for the Massachusetts group increased significantly.

4. Combining self- and wage employment, the treatment groups in both states significantly increased their likelihood of employment and time employed compared with control groups. Further, a significant increase in total annual earnings was seen in Massachusetts (+$3,053).
5. The Washington treatment had a significant positive impact on the employment of non-participants (family and nonfamily employees).
6. The Washington demonstration significantly increased total program benefit payments. Taking into account both regular UI benefits and the lump-sum payment, total benefits were increased by approximately $1,000. In contrast, the Massachusetts demonstration significantly reduced receipt of total benefits by nearly $900.
7. The Massachusetts treatment generated large net gains from each of several benefit–cost perspectives (participant, nonparticipant, society, and government). The Washington treatment generated net gains from the perspective of participants and society, but resulted in net losses from nonparticipants and government perspectives.

TIME TRENDS IN FINDINGS: In Massachusetts, treatment group members were more likely than controls to have had a self-employment experience, but there was no difference in the percentage of self-employment after 33 months (at the time of the second follow-up survey). No time trends were reported for the Washington group.

DESIGN ISSUES:
1. In both states, only a small fraction (3.6 percent in Washington, 1.9 percent in Massachusetts) of targeted UI claimants met the initial requirements of attending an orientation meeting and submitting an application. Random assignment occurred at this point.
2. Massachusetts had legislative requirements to focus on UI claimants who were likely to exhaust their UI benefits. Sample selection was based on a statistical model that predicted claimants' likelihood of benefit exhaustion.

Those with low predicted probability were eliminated from the target group. There were no comparable requirements in Washington.

REPLICABILITY: Replicable. Note design differences between the two states (e.g., lump-sum payment in Washington, not Massachusetts).

GENERALIZABILITY: Interest in self-employment is concentrated in a specific subgroup of the unemployed (males, ages 36–55, better educated, and with experience in professional, managerial, and technical occupations). Washington used a purposive site selection method based on an index of representativeness. Selected sites had the characteristics and diversity to enhance generalizability. Massachusetts's sites were self-selected, though they represented a wide geographic distribution and mix of salient characteristics.

FUNDING SOURCE: U.S. Department of Labor, Employment and Training Administration, Unemployment Insurance Service. Key personnel: Jon Messenger and Stephen Wandner.

TREATMENT ADMINISTRATORS: Massachusetts—Department of Employment and Training (DET); Washington—State Employment Security Department (ESD). Key personnel: Bonnie Dallinger for DET and Judy Johnson for ESD.

EVALUATORS: Abt Associates and Battelle Memorial Institute. Key personnel: Jacob Benus for Abt and Terry Johnson for Battelle.

ENABLING LEGISLATION: Section 9152 of the Omnibus Budget Reconciliation Act of 1987 (Massachusetts only).

POLICY EFFECTS: According to the researchers, this demonstration had a "great impact" on the policy debate. It was cited by Congress, as part of the North American Free Trade Agreement, in the decision to authorize states to implement self-employment programs.

INFORMATION SOURCE: Jacob M. Benus, Terry R. Johnson, Michelle Wood, Neelima Grover, and Theodore Shen, *Self-Employment Programs—*

A New Reemployment Strategy: Final Impact Analysis of the Washington and Massachusetts Self-Employment Demonstrations, U.S. Department of Labor, Employment and Training Administration, Unemployment Insurance Occasional Paper 95-4, Washington, 1995.

PUBLIC-USE ACCESS TO DATA: Available through the U.S. Department of Labor.

Minority Male Opportunity and Responsibility Program

SUMMARY: This demonstration, conducted between 1991 and 1994, tested the effects of intensive case management on a small sample of unemployed minority males. Subjects were followed for up to 12 months. The design was not implemented as planned, owing to a number of difficulties.

COST: Evaluation funded at $12,500, although the evaluator felt the actual cost was greater owing to considerable donated services.

TIME FRAME: Demonstration period, November 1991–August 1994; final report, 1995.

TREATMENTS TESTED: Program services included intensive case management, educational skills development, job search and placement activities, and Job Club. Control participants received limited services and engaged in independent job search.

OUTCOMES OF INTEREST: (1) Employment and wages; (2) Educational levels; (3) Health; and (4) Family functioning.

SAMPLE SIZE: Analysis sample, 168; treatments, 79; controls, 89.

TARGET POPULATION: Unemployed minority males age 18–34. Additional selection criteria included: low income, at least one child, and low academic achievement.

NUMBER OF TREATMENT GROUPS: Two (with one control group).

NUMBER AND LOCATION OF SITES: One— Milwaukee, Wisconsin.

RESEARCH COMPONENTS:
- Process analysis: A participant observer attended several sessions and interviewed program participants and staff members to check implementation of the program.
- Impact analysis: Conducted with multivariate regression analysis.
- Benefit–cost analysis: Not conducted.

MAJOR FINDINGS:
1. The treatment group was significantly more likely to be employed at closure (treatment group, 28 percent; control group, 10 percent) and at follow-up (treatment, 47 percent; control, 12 percent) than was the control group. There was little difference between the groups in the nature of the employment or the wages received.
2. No significant differences were found between groups on educational achievement or health status. Only one significant change was found (baseline to follow-up) on measures of family relationships. The treatment group reported an increase in family conflicts, a finding counter to program hypotheses. The project report offered no explanation for this finding.
3. Frequency of case manager contacts and past employment experience were significantly related to the probability of current employment. Educational achievement was also found to be predictive of employment.

TIME TRENDS IN FINDINGS: There were insufficient data to document any time trends.

DESIGN ISSUES:
1. Overall implementation of program and services was "far less intensive" than planned, owing to higher than expected caseloads and minimal compliance from some participants. Further, the follow-up return rate was low, with only 38 percent of participants returning for interviews and testing.
2. Data on approximately 100 participants entering the project prior to June 1992 were discarded owing to design contamination and inconsistent data collection and reporting. Thus, the first year of the project was treated as an unevaluated pilot effort, and results are based on participation during the final year (summer 1992–June 1993).
3. Some problems arose due to evaluation issues. The number of clients needed for evaluation purposes exceeded the capacity of the program. The evaluator "concluded that attempting an experimental design was inappropriate given the level of funding," and the design was "resented and (possibly) sabotaged at first."
4. In general, the evaluator felt that the funder's expectations were unrealistic given the level of funding.

Given the considerable difficulty encountered in the design implementation of this project, the findings should be interpreted cautiously.

REPLICABILITY: Replicable.

GENERALIZABILITY: The small sample size and the design and implementation issues discourage attempts at generalization.

FUNDING SOURCE: U.S. Department of Health and Human Services (HHS), Administration for Children and Families, Office of Community Services. Key personnel: John Tabori.

TREATMENT ADMINISTRATOR: Social Development Commission of Milwaukee, Wisconsin. Key personnel: George Gerharz and Janice Wilberg.

EVALUATOR: D. Paul Moberg, Center for Health Policy and Program Evaluation, University of Wisconsin–Madison.

ENABLING LEGISLATION: Demonstration Partnership Program under section 408 of the Human Services Reauthorization Act of 1986.

INFORMATION SOURCE: U.S. Department of Health and Human Services, *Demonstration Partnership Program: Summary of Final Evaluation Findings From FY 1991*, 1995.

PUBLIC-USE ACCESS TO DATA: Available at Office of Community Services, DHHS.

Maryland Unemployment Insurance Work Search Demonstration

SUMMARY: This demonstration, conducted from 1994 to 1995, tested the effect of four alternative work search policy requirements on a large sample of new unemployment insurance (UI) claimants. Subjects were followed for one year.

COST: Approximately $250,000.

TIME FRAME: Random assignment, January 1994–December 1994; data collected for 12 months after assignment.

TREATMENTS TESTED: The demonstration tested four alternatives to the Maryland UI eligibility policy, which at the time of the demonstration required claimants to search for work and document two employer contacts per week. Employer contacts were not verified.

1. Group A. Increased the required number of employer contacts from two to four per week.
2. Group B. Maintained the two contact requirements, but eliminated the documentation requirement.
3. Group C. Required claimants to attend a four-day job search workshop early in the unemployment period. No change to the normal work search requirements.
4. Group D. No change to the normal work search requirement, but claimants were informed that their employer contacts would be verified.

Two control groups were included to test the Hawthorne effect. Both groups followed the normal requirements, but one group (group E) was informed that its administrative records would be included in the evaluation of the demonstration project.

OUTCOMES OF INTEREST: (1) UI payments in terms of weeks and dollars; (2) Continuing eligibility; (3) Employment; and (4) Earnings.

SAMPLE SIZE: Treatments: group A, 3,510; group B, 3,455; group C, 3,680; group D, 3,400; controls: group E, 4,812; group F, 4,901.

TARGET POPULATION: New UI claimants.

NUMBER OF TREATMENT GROUPS: Five (with one combined control group).

NUMBER AND LOCATION OF SITES: Five—Baltimore, College Park, Eastern Shore, Glen Burnie, and Hagerstown.

RESEARCH COMPONENTS:

- Process analysis: A monitoring protocol was developed to ensure that all the parties involved, including the state, the research contractor, and DOL, consistently followed the procedures manual. The protocol was designed to collect information during site visits by observing key demonstration activities and interviewing staff members. Results indicated that the procedures were followed closely.
- Impact analysis: Ordinary least squares (OLS); logit was used for binary outcome variables.
- Benefit–cost analysis: Not conducted.

MAJOR FINDINGS:

1. Overall, the three treatments that imposed greater stringency or additional requirements upon claimants (A, C, and D) had a negative impact on total UI benefits paid and the length of time claimants received benefits (see table next page). The treatment that eliminated the requirement of reporting employer contacts (B) did not affect UI payments but did increase the weeks of UI payments. With one exception, the treatments did not affect the likelihood of claimants having a second spell of UI receipt or the amount of UI benefits during a second spell. The exception was group C, which received a statistically significant $64 more than the control group during a slightly longer second spell. However, group C was no more likely to have a second spell.

Impact Estimates by Treatment

	Group A	Group B	Group C	Group D	Control group means
Full benefits year					
Total UI benefits paid ($)	−116**	34	−75**	−113**	2,085
Number of weeks of benefits	−.7**	.4*	−.6**	−.9**	11.9
Percent that exhausted benefits	−2.6**	1.6*	−1.1	−3.0**	28.3
First spell					
Percent who received at least one UI payment	−2.4**	2.1**	−1.7	−3.5**	68.8
Number of weeks in first spell	−.8**	.3	−.8**	−.9**	10.9
Total UI benefits paid in first spell ($)	−143**	14	−115**	−121*	1,894
Second spell					
Percent with second spell	1.1	0.0	1.2	.6	15.0
Number of weeks in second spell	.2	.1	.3**	.1	1.5
Total benefits paid in second spell ($)	38	25	64**	24	254

* Significantly different from control group at the .05 level.
** Significantly different from control group at the .01 level.

2. Findings show no statistically significant differences between any of the four treatment groups and the control group in the number of denials of payment, the number of appeals, or the number of conditional payments. However, results show significantly fewer overpayments and significantly less in dollars were received by claimants in the workshop group (C) than those in the control group. No significant differences in overpayments were found between any of the other treatment groups and the control group.

3. Claimants in groups A, C, and D are significantly more likely to exit UI during the first spell than claimants in the control group. The log hazard estimates indicate that claimants in group B are less likely to exit; however, this result is not significant.

4. Treatments had little impact on earnings.

5. In the employer verification treatment (group D) the actual verification rate of the reported employer contacts was low. Only half of the claimants in this group were selected for verification of even one reported contact. In addition, UI staff was largely unsuccessful in reaching employers to verify claimants' employer contact reports.

6. In the Eastern Shore and other rural offices, transportation problems were a major impediment to claimants' ability to get to the offices and workshops.

7. A test to determine the existence of a Hawthorne effect showed that there was no observable difference between the informed control group (group E) and the uninformed group (group F). Since no Hawthorne effect was detected, the two control groups were subsequently combined for the work search treatment analyses.

TIME TRENDS IN FINDINGS: As noted, there was no impact on second unemployment spells.

DESIGN ISSUES: In the Hagerstown and Eastern Shore sites, assigning claimants to the additional contacts group (A) was inappropriate because there were too few employers to enable claimants to fulfill the requirement. Consequently, all claimants assigned to group A were from sites with a high proportion of black claimants and where claimants had higher prior year earnings. The evaluators note that the analyses are conducted controlling for a number of factors including site, race, and prior earnings; hence, the analysis yielded unbiased estimates of treatment impacts.

REPLICABILITY: Replicable.

GENERALIZABILITY: Site selection was designed to represent a range of geographical and labor market conditions within the state. The authors suggest the interpretation of work search services from the Maryland demonstration may not be applicable to programs that supply services only to claimants who have been determined to be in need of such services.

FUNDING SOURCE: The U.S. Department of Labor. Key personnel: Wayne Gordon and Stephen Wandner.

TREATMENT ADMINISTRATOR: Maryland Department of Labor, Licensing and Regulation. Key personnel: Lucy Smith and Ornetta Craig.

EVALUATOR: Battelle Memorial Institute. Key personnel: Dan Klepinger.

INFORMATION SOURCE: Daniel H. Klepinger, Terry R. Johnson, Jutta M. Joesch, and Jacob M. Benus, *Evaluation of the Maryland Unemployment Insurance Work Search Demonstration,* final report to the Maryland Department of Labor, Licensing and Regulation, Battelle Memorial Institute in conjunction with Abt Associates Inc., November 1997.

PUBLIC-USE ACCESS TO DATA: We have no information about a public-use file for this demonstration.

Kentucky Worker Profiling and Reemployment Services (WPRS) Experiment

SUMMARY: This evaluation, conducted from 1994 to 1999, used a unique "tie-breaking" experimental design to estimate the impacts of the Worker Profiling and Reemployment Services system on a large sample of unemployment insurance (UI) claimants. Subjects were followed for two years.

COST: Treatment, $11.93 for each UI claimant assigned to the treatment group, or about $15,000. This figure does not include the cost of training that some participants received from outside the Department of Employment Services. No explicit evaluation costs; the evaluation was done as part of the evaluators' normal academic research.

TIME FRAME: Demonstration period, October 1994–June 1996; data collected for two years after the beginning of each UI claimant's spell of unemployment; final report, 1999.

TREATMENTS TESTED: The national Worker Profiling and Reemployment Services (WPRS) system requires UI claimants who are predicted through an econometrically estimated profiling model to have a high probability of exhausting their benefit eligibility to receive employment and services early in their spell of unemployment. Treatment group members were notified by letter that they were required to participate in reemployment services (e.g., structured job search activities, employment counseling, and retraining) as a condition for continuing to receive benefits.

Control group members were exempt from this requirement and, hence, did not receive the letter.

OUTCOMES OF INTEREST: (1) Earnings; (2) Length of benefit receipt; and (3) Amount of UI benefits received.

SAMPLE SIZE: Total, 1,981; treatments, 1,236; controls, 745.

TARGET POPULATION: UI benefit claimants.

NUMBER OF TREATMENT GROUPS: Two (with one control group). This experiment is apparently the first to use a so-called "tie-breaking" design for purposes of random assignment. Use of this design was possible because, from time to time, local UI offices in Kentucky face a capacity constraint on the number of UI claimants they can provide with reemployment services. The Kentucky profiling scheme assigned values between 1 and 20 to claimants, with higher scores predicting a higher probability of benefit exhaustion. Thus, if capacity was reached at a score of 17 and 19 claimants had this score, but only 8 slots remained, then 8 claimants would be randomly assigned to the treatment group and the remaining 11 claimants would be assigned to the control group.

NUMBER AND LOCATION OF SITES: UI offices throughout Kentucky.

RESEARCH COMPONENTS:
- Process analysis: Participation rates in reemployment services were examined.
- Impact analysis: Conducted using ordinary least squares regressions, weighted regressions, and hazard models.
- Benefit–cost analysis: Conducted from the perspective of the UI program.

MAJOR FINDINGS:
1. On average, the program reduced mean weeks of UI benefit receipt by about 2.2 weeks and mean UI benefits received by $143. Both estimates are statistically significant, the latter at only the .10 level.
2. The earnings of experimentals were $1,054 higher than those of controls. This result is statistically significant.
3. Given its low cost, the WPRS system results in cost savings for the UI program.
4. Treatment impacts do not appear to be higher for those with higher profiling scores, suggesting that the Kentucky system of "profiling does not increase the efficiency of treatment allocation."

TIME TRENDS IN FINDINGS: Much of the impacts resulted from an increase in early return to work and early UI exits by the treatment group relative to controls. Indeed, most of the treatment response occurred prior to members of the treatment group receiving any reemployment services. The evaluators interpret this as indicating that the program effects mainly result from the requirement to participate in services (a deterrent effect), rather than from the actual receipt of services.

DESIGN ISSUES: Because of the experimental design, it is possible that the random assignment ratio is correlated across local UI offices with the outcome measures. The evaluators attempted to control for bias resulting from this possibility by estimating fixed effect regression models.

REPLICABILITY: The treatment and evaluation is replicable. However, not all states administer their WPRS systems in a manner that would allow a "tie-breaking" experiment to be conducted.

GENERALIZABILITY: The evaluation results should be fairly generalizable. However, because some local UI offices within Kentucky were more likely to reach capacity constraints than others, the sample is not distributed across offices in proportion to their caseload. But the research sample had characteristics similar to those of the statewide population of UI claimants. Moreover, because of the experimental design, claimants with the highest predicted probabilities of UI exhaustion tended to be excluded from the sample. However, there was no evidence that treatment impact differed systematically by profiling scores. In generalizing to other states, it is important to recognize that UI programs and WPRS systems both vary considerably among states.

FUNDING SOURCE: The evaluators conducted the evaluation as part of their normal academic research.

TREATMENT ADMINISTRATOR: The Kentucky Department of Employment Services. Key personnel: Bill Burris, Donna Long, and Ted Pilcher.

EVALUATORS: Dan Black (Center for Policy Research, Syracuse University), Jeffrey Smith (Department of Economics, University of Maryland–College Park), Mark C. Berger (Economics Department, University of Kentucky), and Brett J. Noel (American Express–TRS).

INFORMATION SOURCE: Dan Black, Jeffrey Smith, Mark C. Berger, and Brett J. Noel, "Is the Threat of Reemployment Services More Effective Than the Services Themselves? Evidence from Random Assignment in the UI System," *American Economic Review* (September 2003): 1313–27.

PUBLIC-USE ACCESS TO DATA: Available subject to privacy restrictions. Contact the evaluators. Public-use file may be available at http://www.upjohn.org by time of publication of this book.

Job Search Assistance Demonstration

SUMMARY: This demonstration, conducted between 1995 and 1996, tested the effects of three reemployment service packages on a large sample of unemployment insurance (UI) claimants. Subjects were followed for two years.

COST: $2.68 million.

TIME FRAME: Demonstration period, March 1995–June 1996.

TREATMENTS TESTED:
1. Structured job search assistance (SJSA). This treatment required claimants to participate in a sequence of services when six or seven weeks had passed since their initial claim: orientation, testing, job search workshop, and individual assessment interview. Claimants were required to have two additional contacts with demonstration staff thereafter.
2. Individualized job search assistance (IJSA). In this treatment the required orientation was followed by an individual assessment interview, in which claimants and demonstration staff developed an individual service plan. When the plan included demonstration-specific services (testing or job search workshop), these services became mandatory.
3. Individualized job search assistance with Training (IJSA+). This treatment was identical to the IJSA treatment but included a co-

ordinated effort with Economic Dislocation and Worker Adjustment Act (EDWAA) staff to enroll interested claimants in training. In all treatments, EDWAA training opportunities were explained during the orientation, but in this treatment the opportunities were presented by EDWAA staff whenever possible, and more extensively than in the other treatments. Special effort was made to arrange for interested claimants to meet with EDWAA staff in the Jobs Service office immediately after the assessment interview.

OUTCOMES OF INTEREST: UI benefit receipt in (1) weeks and (2) dollars; (3) Whether claimants exhausted their benefits; (4) Employment; and (5) Earnings.

SAMPLE SIZE: D.C.: SJSA, 2,026; IJSA, 2,022; IJSA+, 2,011; controls, 2,012. Florida: SJSA, 3,032; IJSA, 3,007; IJSA+, 2,989; controls, 3,014.

TARGET POPULATION: UI claimants who had been identified at an early point of contact as likely to have long UI spells. Claimants must have worked a minimum of 126 weeks for $30 or more per week during the previous three years, have no definite date for recall to their former employment, and not be searching for work through a union hiring hall.

NUMBER OF TREATMENT GROUPS: Four (with one control group).

NUMBER AND LOCATION OF SITES: In the District of Columbia (D.C.), the demonstration operated in a single office, but random selection was made from the entire eligible UI population. In Florida, random selection to all four groups was made from the 10 offices selected: Clearwater, Davie, Fort Lauderdale, Fort Pierce, Hialeah, Lakeland, Miami, Orlando, Pensacola, and St. Augustine.

RESEARCH COMPONENTS:
- Process analysis: The participant tracking system; UI program data and wage records; and a follow-up survey were used to examine the timing and sequence of service delivery,

satisfaction, and the variation between D.C. and Florida in participation rates and use of sanctions.

- Impact analysis: Conducted as difference in means.
- Benefit–cost analysis: Conducted from claimant, agency budget, government budget, and society perspectives.

MAJOR FINDINGS:

1. Overall, the treatments had a positive impact on training participation (see table below). However, claimants in the IJSA+ treatment did not receive any more training services than did the claimants in the other treatment groups. This issue is covered under "Design Issues."

2. Subgroup analysis suggests that more restrictive eligibility criteria would not substantially affect the average impact of the treatments. Subgroup analysis found particularly large impacts in D.C. for young people in all three treatments and for whites in both IJSA treatments. In Florida, impacts were particularly large for women in both IJSA treatments and for those who had previous been employed in trade industries in the SJSA treatment.

3. In D.C., all three treatments had generally positive impacts on earnings; with the SJSA treatment having the largest impact ($2,005).

Treatments had uneven impacts on employment rates in D.C. Only the SJSA treatment had consistently positives estimates, but they were only significant in six of the ten observation quarters.

4. In the 12-quarter observation period in Florida, there is no evidence that any of the three treatments had any impact on earnings. The treatments had little or no impact on employment rates in Florida, as well.

5. Although participation in EDWAA training was low among demonstration participants, the training rate was increased by the demonstration.

6. The JSA treatments affected neither the likelihood that claimants would change occupations nor the quality of jobs accepted.

7. None of the treatments in either D.C. or Florida was cost-effective from the agency perspective. However, in D.C., all the treatments were cost-effective from the claimant, government, and society perspectives. In Florida, none of the treatments was cost-effective.

8. There is not enough evidence to determine the most cost-effective of the three treatments.

TIME TRENDS IN FINDINGS: Treatments did not have significant impacts beyond the first benefit year.

Estimated Impact during Initial Benefit Year

	District of Columbia			Florida		
	SJSA	IJSA	IJSA+	SJSA	IJSA	IJSA+
Weeks of UI benefits received	−1.13***	−0.47**	−0.61**	−0.41**	−0.59***	−0.52**
	(0.29)	(0.28)	(0.28)	(0.23)	(0.23)	(0.23)
Dollars of UI benefits received	−182**	−56	−37	−39	−100**	−73*
	(84)	(84)	(84)	(52)	(51)	(51)
Rate of UI benefit exhaustion (percent)	−4.8***	−2.4*	−3.9***	−1.8*	−2.4**	−2.8**
	(1.6)	(1.6)	(1.6)	(1.3)	(1.3)	(1.3)

Notes: Estimates are based on differences in outcomes between the control group and each of the treatment groups. Standard errors are in parentheses.
* Statistically significant at the $p < .10$ level in a one-tailed test.
** Statistically significant at the $p < .05$ level in a one-tailed test.
*** Statistically significant at the $p < .01$ level in a one-tailed test.

DESIGN ISSUES: In practice, the IJSA+ treatment did not differ from the IJSA treatment. Despite the IJSA+ design, the EDWAA staff did not appear to provide greater access to training for IJSA+ claimants, and the training rate was generally no higher among claimants in the IJSA+ treatment than among claimants in the other two treatments.

REPLICABILITY: Replicable.

GENERALIZABILITY: Generalizable to the entire eligible population, in both Florida and D.C. The authors of the report caution that the eligible claimants in D.C. and Florida are less likely to be from the manufacturing sector than claimants nationwide.

FUNDING SOURCE: U.S. Department of Labor, Employment and Training Administration. Key personnel: Wayne Gordon, Jon Messenger, and Stephen Wandner.

TREATMENT ADMINISTRATORS: D.C. Department of Employment Services and Florida Department of Labor and Employment Security. Key personnel: Barbara Hawkins for D.C. and Texalia Karl for Florida.

EVALUATORS: Mathematica Policy Research and Battelle Memorial Institute. Key personnel: Walter Corson for Mathematica and Terry Johnson for Battelle.

ENABLING LEGISLATION: The Emergency Unemployment Compensation Act of 1991.

INFORMATION SOURCE: Paul T. Decker, Lance Freeman, and Robert B. Olsen with Daniel H. Klepinger, *Assisting Unemployment Insurance Claimants: The Long-Term Impacts of the Job Search Assistance Demonstration,* U.S. Department of Labor, Employment and Training Administration, Office of Workforce Security Occasional Paper 2000-02, February 2000.

PUBLIC-USE ACCESS TO DATA: Available through the W. E. Upjohn Institute web site, http://www.upjohninstitute.org/erdc/index.htm.

EXPERIMENT ONGOING AT PUBLICATION
Individual Training Accounts

STARTING YEAR/YEAR FINAL REPORT EXPECTED: 2001/2005.

INFORMATION SOURCE: Irma Perez-Johnson and Paul Decker, *Customer Choice or Business As Usual? Promoting Innovation in the Design of WIA Training Programs Through the Individual Training Account Experiment,* Mathematica Policy Research, Inc., June 2001. Mathematica Policy Research, Inc., is evaluating the demonstration; Irma Perez-Johnson and Paul Decker, project directors.

PRINCIPAL INTERVENTIONS: Three widely different approaches to individual training accounts with respect to resources expended on trainees: (1) structured trainee choice in which counselors play a central role directing trainees to specific high-return training costing up to $8,000, (2) guided trainee choice in which the counselors play a less central role with a fixed training account of up to $3,000, and (3) wide trainee choice, essentially a voucher program of up to $3,000. Trainees will be free to spend allotted resources on any state-approved training program and on related expenses approved by local counselors.

TARGET POPULATION: Unemployed adults and dislocated workers in six sites across the United States.

OUTCOMES OF INTEREST: Training outcomes, employment and earnings, return on investment, and trainee satisfaction.

11 Homeless People

Homeless Employment Partnership (HEP)

SUMMARY: This demonstration, conducted from 1989 through 1992, tested the effects of intensive case management and employment services on a medium-sized sample of homeless men. Subjects were followed for six months.

COST: Approximately $36,000–$45,000.

TIME FRAME: May 1989–December 1992; final report, December 1993.

TREATMENTS TESTED: The Homeless Employment Partnership (HEP) treatment, or case management (CM), group received all normal services available at the Metropolitan Development Council resource center (personal maintenance, job referrals, and bus tokens) plus "employment intensive services" (wraparound case management, job development, and housing subsidy). The case management included financial aid for transportation and identity card assistance, job counseling, résumé assistance, and client/employer liaison.

The control, or information and referral (I&R), group members received the normal facility services and were eligible for intensive services after a 90-day waiting period. Because very few of these subjects returned to enroll in the CM group after this period, the eligibility of controls for CM had little impact on the analysis.

OUTCOMES OF INTEREST: (1) Employment; (2) Income; and (3) Homelessness.

SAMPLE SIZE: Total, 254; CM group, 127; I&R group, 127.

TARGET POPULATION: Homeless men who were judged "employable."

NUMBER OF TREATMENT GROUPS: Two (with one control group).

NUMBER AND LOCATION OF SITES: One—Tacoma, Washington.

RESEARCH COMPONENTS:

- Process analysis: Service delivery data were collected throughout the intervention period. Demographic characteristics and required services of the clients were monitored. This led to a change in intervention focus from training to job search and retention services.
- Impact analysis: Analysis varied with outcome being measured. Regression and analysis of variance were used.
- Benefit–cost analysis: Not conducted.

MAJOR FINDINGS:

1. CM group members were significantly more likely to have had an employment experience in the week prior to follow-up than were I&R group members (80 percent versus 48 percent). The intervention appears to have a slightly stronger effect on this outcome for the higher-risk client. Further, the CM group's employment was more likely to be permanent, rather than temporary, compared with the I&R group's employment.
2. The CM group worked significantly more hours in the week prior to follow-up than did the I&R group (28.09 versus 16.16).
3. The CM group members were more likely to have job benefits such as insurance and sick leave than were I&R group members.
4. The CM group members had significantly higher pay than did I&R group members ($159.61/week versus $95.46).
5. The CM group was more likely to be living in a house or an apartment (not homeless) than the I&R group (46 percent versus 23 percent).

TIME TRENDS IN FINDINGS: Long-term follow-up was not conducted. Follow-up at six months suggested that individuals who were more "job-ready" at the start of the program were more likely to retain employment and other benefits at follow-up.

DESIGN ISSUES:

1. After random assignment, there were statistically significant differences between groups on several "barriers to employment" variables. Although the evaluator reported that "painstaking measures were taken to ensure random assignment," he questioned whether the assignment procedure may have been compromised. It is likely that some selection bias was present when one agency had difficulty excluding some participants from the control group. This partner was replaced and the intended design was maintained.
2. In a very few cases, intervention services were offered to control group members felt to be "in desperate need." The evaluator feels this deviation is small and not likely to affect outcomes.
3. The follow-up rate was only 59 percent. However, a comparison of those with follow-up data and those lost to follow-up shows few significant differences.

REPLICABILITY: Replicable.

GENERALIZABILITY: Design and implementation issues discourage attempts at generalization. In addition, the program was voluntary and a screening process was used to assess educational background, employment history, mental health, drug/alcohol abuse, and financial eligibility. Those admitted to the program were drug/alcohol free, mentally stable, and motivated to find employment. The project report's authors cited several studies showing that roughly 50 percent of the homeless population would not fit these characteristics. The evaluator agreed that the sample "is certainly not representative of all the homeless," but represents "a sizable portion."

FUNDING SOURCE: U.S. Department of Health and Human Services (HHS), Office of Community Services, Demonstration Partnership Program. Key personnel: John Buckstead.

TREATMENT ADMINISTRATOR: Metropolitan Development Council, Tacoma, Washington. Key personnel: Doug Swanberg, project director.

EVALUATOR: Dennis McBride, Puget Sound Research Associates.

ENABLING LEGISLATION: Demonstration Partnership Program under section 408 of the Human Services Reauthorization Act of 1986.

INFORMATION SOURCE: U.S. Department of Health and Human Services, Administration for Children and Families, Office of Community Services, *Homeless and Youth at Risk: Demonstration Partnership Program Projects— Summary of Final Evaluation Findings from 1990,* 1993.

PUBLIC-USE ACCESS TO DATA: Available through Office of Community Services, DHHS.

Boston McKinney Demonstration Project

SUMMARY: This demonstration, conducted from October 1990 to April 1992, contrasted the effects of group and independent living on a small sample of formerly homeless mentally ill adults. Subjects were followed for 18 months.

COST: We have no information about research cost. Costs for treatment and housing assistance to the sample, both experimental and control, appear to have totaled about $7.5 million, but a large fraction of this total might have been spent in the absence of the experiment.

TIME FRAME: Demonstration period, October 1990–April 1992; data collected, same period.

TREATMENTS TESTED: Clients in the Boston McKinney demonstration project were randomly assigned to two housing arrangements: individual public housing units or group living.

OUTCOMES OF INTEREST: (1) Housing stability; (2) Consumption of mental health services; and (3) Hospitalization.

SAMPLE SIZE: Total, 112; single-occupancy apartments, 56; group living, 62. Six subjects who began the study were lost to follow-up.

TARGET POPULATION: Homeless mentally ill adults.

NUMBER OF TREATMENT GROUPS: Two (with no control group).

NUMBER AND LOCATION OF SITES: One—Boston, Massachusetts.

RESEARCH COMPONENTS:
- Process analysis: Conducted.
- Impact analysis: Regression.
- Benefit–cost analysis: A cost-effectiveness study (Dickey et al. 1996) was conducted.

MAJOR FINDINGS:
1. One-third of the group house clients moved out of their units compared with nearly half (47 percent) of the clients assigned to single apartments. In context, those who move out are assumed to have returned to the streets.
2. There was no significant hospitalization difference between the apartment group and the group-home group.
3. There was no significant difference in the amount or type of services used by the apartment group and the group-home group.
4. Cost of services to the group-home group averaged $56,000 annually, while the apartment group averaged $30,000. Most of this difference is in the cost of housing.

TIME TRENDS IN FINDINGS: None apparent.

DESIGN ISSUES: The sample was quite small. The authors state that because of the small sample size, the findings could be skewed by the hospitalization of one client from a group home for more than a year.

REPLICABILITY: Replicable.

GENERALIZABILITY: The small size of the sample limits generalizability. Residents in both housing types were supported by extensive community services that exceeded those customarily available at group homes. The treatment administrator assured the public housing authority of the availability of these services when needed. Moreover, the group homes operated on a new "consumer-oriented" model that appears to have been inconsistently implemented.

FUNDING SOURCE: National Institute of Mental Health.

TREATMENT ADMINISTRATOR: The Massachusetts Department of Mental Health.

EVALUATOR: Barbara Dickey, Department of Psychiatry, Harvard Medical School.

ENABLING LEGISLATION: None.

INFORMATION SOURCE: Barbara Dickey, Olinda Gonzalez, Stephene Goldfinger, Eric Latimer, Karen Powers, and Russell Schutt, "Use of Mental Health Services by Formerly Homeless Adults Residing in Group and Independent Housing," *Psychiatric Services* 47(1996, 2): 152–58.

PUBLIC-USE ACCESS TO DATA: None.

Philadelphia Micro-Enterprise Development Program

SUMMARY: Beginning in October 1990, the Micro-Enterprise Development Program sought to provide entrepreneurial training, developmental activities, unconventional capital, and various support services to homeless individuals to encourage progress toward self-sufficiency. Each training cycle consisted of a feasibility phase and an entrepreneurial training phase. Only the first two cycles used a fully randomized design.

Early in the project, Philadelphia's nationally publicized financial crisis contributed to a delay in fully implementing the project as intended. In addition, there were two changes in the position of project director and a change in the third-party evaluator. The first two project directors lacked full control over the project. Midway through the third training cycle, the project was under control, but by then the design model had been changed to a "waiting control." This meant that individuals in the control group were assigned to treatment in the next cycle.

Despite the original experimental design, there was no apparent attempt to compare the outcomes of the treatment group to those of the control. Findings are stated relative to the goals of the program.

INFORMATION SOURCE: Mayor's Office of Community Services, *Summary of Final Evaluation Findings from FY 1992–1999*, Demonstration Partnership Program Projects, Chapter 6, U.S. Department of Health and Human Services, Administration for Children and Families, reported March 1995, published December 1996.

PUBLIC-USE ACCESS TO DATA: We have no information about a public-use file for this demonstration.

Critical Time Intervention

SUMMARY: This demonstration, conducted from 1991 to 1993, contrasted the effects of informal and formal services on a small sample of severely mentally ill men discharged from institutions. Subjects were followed for 18 months.

COST: Unavailable.

TIME FRAME: Demonstration period, 1991–93; data collected, same period.

TREATMENTS TESTED: Individually tailored formal and informal support services (Critical Time Intervention, or CTI) to mentally ill men on discharge from institutions. Formal services included follow-up by CTI workers. Informal services consisted of assistance in finding and using community services, relating to people, help with medication adherence, and money management.

The control group received usual services only (USO): reference to community services and mental and health rehabilitation programs; non-active and unsystematized participation by program workers in the client's care.

The CTI group received nine months of CTI plus usual services and then only usual services for the following nine months. The USO group received usual services only for the entire 18 months of the study.

OUTCOME OF INTEREST: Recurrent homelessness.

SAMPLE SIZE: Total, 96; CTI services, 48; USO, 48.

TARGET POPULATION: Inner-city men with severe mental illness discharged from institutions such as shelters and jails.

NUMBER OF TREATMENT GROUPS: Two (with one control group).

NUMBER AND LOCATION SITES: One—New York City region.

RESEARCH COMPONENTS:
- Process analysis: Conducted.
- Impact analysis: Regression.
- Benefit–cost analysis: Not conducted.

MAJOR FINDINGS:
1. Compared with the USO group, the CTI group had one-third the number of homeless nights (30 nights versus 91 nights), a significant difference. In the last month of the study, 8 percent of men in the CTI group were homeless compared with 23 percent of men in the USO group.
2. Compared with the USO group, the CTI group had half the risk of extended homelessness (21 percent versus 40 percent).

TIME TRENDS IN FINDINGS: Differences between the groups widened over the course of the study. The risk of major homelessness was significantly lower in the CTI than in the USO group.

DESIGN ISSUES: None apparent.

REPLICABILITY: Replicable.

GENERALIZABILITY: The sample size was very small. Moreover, the intervention was tested among men who had completed an on-site shelter program. Since participation in the demonstration was conditional on completed on-site treatment, some of the most intractable patients were probably excluded from the study sample.

FUNDING SOURCE: National Institute for Mental Health.

TREATMENT ADMINISTRATOR: Psychiatry Shelter Program, New York.

EVALUATOR: Ezra Susser, Columbia University/New York State Psychiatric Institute, New York.

ENABLING LEGISLATION: None.

INFORMATION SOURCE: Ezra Susser, Elie Valencia, Sarah Conover, Alan Felix, Wei-Yann Tsai, and Richard Jed Wyatt, "Preventing Recurrent Homelessness among Mentally Ill Men: A 'Critical Time' Intervention after Discharge from a Shelter," *American Journal of Public Health* 87(2): 256–62.

PUBLIC-USE ACCESS TO DATA: Available on request. Contact Ezra Susser, Columbia University/New York State Psychiatric Institute, 722 W 168th St., Box 24, New York, NY 10032.

San Diego Homeless Research Demonstration

SUMMARY: This demonstration, conducted from 1991 to 1994, tested the effects of Section 8 housing vouchers and comprehensive case management on a medium-sized sample of severely mentally ill homeless people. Subjects were followed for three years.

COST: Total program and evaluation cost, $3.4 million.

TIME FRAME: Demonstration period, 1991–94; data collected, same period.

TREATMENTS TESTED: (1) Comprehensive case management, provided by a private mental health service, with access to a Section 8 voucher; (2) traditional case management, provided by the county, with access to a Section 8 voucher; (3) comprehensive case management without access to a Section 8 voucher; and (4) traditional case management without access to a Section 8 voucher.

Comprehensive case management differed from traditional management in several respects: comprehensive case managers had smaller maximum caseloads (22 versus 40); were available to clients 24 hours a day, seven days a week; and had higher salaries. In addition, they worked to establish housing support groups for the clients and to get them jobs.

OUTCOMES OF INTEREST: (1) Length of time to achieve stable housing and (2) Housing patterns.

SAMPLE SIZE: Total, 362; 91 or 90 individuals in each treatment category.

TARGET POPULATION: Severely mentally ill homeless people.

NUMBER OF TREATMENT GROUPS: Four (with one control group).

NUMBER AND LOCATION OF SITES: One—San Diego County, California.

RESEARCH COMPONENTS:
- Process analysis: Conducted.
- Impact analysis: Regression.
- Benefit–cost analysis: Not conducted.

MAJOR FINDINGS:
1. There were no statistically significant differences in the time it took to achieve housing "consistency" (defined as the first interval at which a client was consistently housed for the remaining time in the two year follow-up period) and stable housing across the four experimental treatment groups.
2. Among individuals achieving some type of stable housing (independent or community), access to Section 8 vouchers significantly increased the likelihood of achieving stable independent living. Clients with access to Section 8 vouchers were 7.56 times more likely to obtain stable independent living arrangements than clients without access to the vouchers.

TIME TRENDS IN FINDINGS: Time trends were built into the outcomes. The period it took to achieve the outcomes was central to measurement of outcomes.

DESIGN ISSUES: According to the lead author, in practice, the difference between comprehensive case management and traditional case management was minimal.

REPLICABILITY: Replicable, but note the design issue above.

GENERALIZABILITY: The participation criteria excluded the most difficult and sickest individuals, especially those with severe drug and alcohol abuse problems or criminal histories. It is also worth noting that the climate in San Diego is conducive to living on the streets.

FUNDING SOURCES: The National Institute of Mental Health and Center for Mental Health Services.

TREATMENT ADMINISTRATORS: San Diego County Mental Health Services and San Diego State University.

EVALUATORS: Richard L. Hough, Department of Sociology, San Diego State University; Michael S. Hurlburt, Department of Psychology, University of California, San Diego; and Patricia A. Wood, Homeless Research Project, San Diego State University.

ENABLING LEGISLATION: None.

INFORMATION SOURCE: Michael Hurlburt, Patricia A. Wood, and Richard L. Hough, "Providing Independent Housing for the Homeless Mentally Ill: A Novel Approach to Evaluating Long-Term Longitudinal Housing Patterns," *Journal of Community Psychology* 24(1996, 3): 291–310.

PUBLIC-USE ACCESS TO DATA: Available on request. Contact Richard L. Hough, The Homeless Research Project, 1202 Morena Blvd., Suite 100, San Diego, CA 92110. E-mail Rhough@casrc.org.

New Orleans Homeless Substance Abusers Project

SUMMARY: This demonstration, conducted from 1991 to 1993, tested the effects of a residential alcohol and drug treatment program on a medium-sized sample of homeless alcoholics and drug abusers. Subjects were followed for 18 months.

COST: Research and administrative costs, $3.1 million.

TIME FRAME: Demonstration period, 1991–93; data collected, same period.

TREATMENTS TESTED: One experimental group received a two-phase intervention: social detoxification—a seven-day pretreatment screening program focused on detoxification and introduction to sobriety groups—and transitional care—a 21-day treatment involving extensive client assessment and case management. A second experimental group received a third phase of treatment after transitional care, extended care/independent living—a 12-month program that continued and intensified transitional care. The control group received the first phase intervention only (detoxification).

OUTCOMES OF INTEREST: (1) Drug- and alcohol-free existence; (2) Residential stability; (3) Economic independence; and (4) Social functioning.

SAMPLE SIZE: Total, 670; treatments, 164 (transitional care only 107, transitional care with extended care/independent living, 57); controls, 506.

TARGET POPULATION: Homeless alcoholics and drug abusers.

NUMBER OF TREATMENT GROUPS: Three (with one control group).

NUMBER AND LOCATION SITES: One—Greater New Orleans.

RESEARCH COMPONENTS:
- Process analysis: Conducted (data collected over one-year period; extensive interviews with key members of the treatment staff, including staff who left the organization; formal and informal contacts with clients in the three phases of the program).
- Impact analysis: Regression.
- Benefit—cost analysis: Not conducted.

MAJOR FINDINGS:
1. Process analysis led to finding that the control group had been compromised. See "Design Issues."
2. Treatment had positive and significant impact on sobriety and housing stability: 2.3 more days and 1.8 more days, respectively, than the controls in the previous 30 days.
3. After correcting for both nonrandom assignment into treatment and research attrition, the impact was enhanced and indicated that treatments had 3.7 more days of sobriety and 4.9 more days of housing stability than controls. (This result is ironic. If the treatment staff had correctly picked those who were most likely to benefit from treatment, the impact estimates would have gone *down* after the correction was made. As it was, the staff's selection criteria seem to have been worse than random.)
4. Extended care/independent living had no significant impact (using corrected and uncorrected estimates) on employment.

TIME TRENDS IN FINDINGS: None.

DESIGN ISSUES:
1. According to the authors, the project staff subverted randomization into treatment by placing only the names of clients they considered sufficiently motivated on the selection lists. Only 32 percent of the 164 clients entering transitional care and 25 percent of the clients going on to treatment in extended care/independent living were randomized. The impact assessment corrected for the nonrandomization (selection bias) using the two-step estimation approach developed by Heckman and others.
2. The size of the experimental groups was too small to measure modest impacts.

REPLICABILITY: Replicable.

GENERALIZABILITY: Given the small sample size and the violation of random assignment, the general applicability of the findings is doubtful.

FUNDING SOURCE: National Institute of Alcohol Abuse and Alcoholism. Key personnel: Dan McMillen.

TREATMENT ADMINISTRATOR: The New Orleans Homeless Substance Abusers Project.

EVALUATORS: Joel A. Devine, James D. Wright, and Charles J. Brody, Tulane University.

ENABLING LEGISLATION: None.

INFORMATION SOURCE: Joel A. Devine, James D. Wright, and Charles J. Brody. "Evaluating an Alcohol and Drug Treatment Program for the Homeless: An Econometric Approach," *Evaluation and Program Planning* 20(1997, 2): 205–15.

PUBLIC-USE ACCESS TO DATA: Not available.

HUD-VA Supported Housing Program (HUD-VASH)

SUMMARY: This demonstration, conducted from 1992 to 1999, tested the effects of HUD Section 8 vouchers and intensive case management on a medium sample of homeless veterans with psychiatric and/or addictive disorders. Subjects were followed for three years.

COST: Evaluation costs are not available. Costs-per-case information presented below suggests at least $2 million in administrative costs.

TIME FRAME: Demonstration period, 1992–99; data collected, same period.

TREATMENTS TESTED: (1) Section 8 vouchers and case management; (2) Case management without access to Section 8 vouchers; and (3) Standard veterans care—typically focusing on linkage with Veterans Administration (VA) health care services. Veterans in the case management–only group were not barred from accessing Section 8 vouchers from other sources.

OUTCOMES OF INTEREST: (1) Housing stability; (2) Health status; and (3) Community functioning.

SAMPLE SIZE: Total, 460; vouchers with case management, 182; case management without vouchers, 90; standard VA care, 188.

TARGET POPULATION: Homeless veterans with psychiatric and/or addictive disorders.

NUMBER OF TREATMENT GROUPS: Three (with one control group).

NUMBER AND LOCATION OF SITES: Four—Cleveland, Ohio; New Orleans, Louisiana; San Diego, California; and San Francisco, California.

RESEARCH COMPONENTS:
- Process analysis: Conducted.
- Impact analysis: Regression.
- Benefit–cost analysis: Conducted.

MAJOR FINDINGS:
1. Over the three-year follow-up period, veterans in the vouchers and case management group achieved 25 percent more nights (in the previous 90 days) in accommodation than the standard care group and 17 percent more nights than the case management–only group. These differences were statistically significant.
2. There were no significant differences between the groups on any clinical or community adjustment outcome.
3. The total three-year costs for the vouchers plus case management group were $8,009 (28 percent) greater than for the standard care group, while the costs of the case management–only group were $6,580 greater than for the standard care group. Those differences were statistically significant.

TIME TRENDS IN FINDINGS: The differences across the three groups were significant for the first two years and then decreased in the third year.

DESIGN ISSUES: There was substantial and differential follow-up attrition across treatment groups.

REPLICABILITY: Replicable.

GENERALIZABILITY: This study was conducted within the VA health care system, which has a predominantly male clientele.

FUNDING SOURCES: U.S. Department of Housing and Urban Development and the Veterans Health Administration, Department of Veterans Affairs.

TREATMENT ADMINISTRATORS: Local public housing agencies and the Veterans Health Administration.

EVALUATORS: Northeast Program Evaluation Center, Veterans Administration Medical Center, West Haven, CT. Key personnel: Robert Rosenheck.

ENABLING LEGISLATION: None.

INFORMATION SOURCES: Robert Rosenheck, Wesley Kaprow, Linda Frisman, Wen Liu-Mares, Diane Dilella, David Dausey, and Haiqun Lin, *Integrating Health Care and Housing Supports from Federal Agencies: An Evaluation of the HUD-VA Supported Housing Program (HUD-VASH)*, National Program Evaluation Center, VA Medical Center, West Haven, CT; Robert Rosenheck, Wesley Kasprow, Linda Frisman, and Wen Liu-Mares, "Cost-Effectiveness of Supported Housing for Homeless Persons with Mental Illness," *Archives of General Psychiatry* 60(2003, 9): 940–51.

PUBLIC-USE ACCESS TO DATA: Not available.

EXPERIMENTS ONGOING AT PUBLICATION

Phoenix, Arizona, Homeless Study

STARTING YEAR/YEAR FINAL REPORT EXPECTED: 2001/2004.

INFORMATION SOURCE: Grant Proposal for Phoenix, Arizona Homeless Study (project director: Michael S. Shafer). A grant from the U.S.

Department of Health and Human Services, Substance Abuse and Mental Health Services Administration is funding the project.

PRINCIPAL INTERVENTION: Intensive team case management approach using the principles of motivational learning.

TARGET POPULATION: Homeless women who have a mental health or substance abuse disorder and children.

OUTCOMES OF INTEREST: Housing stability, health, and employment.

St. Louis, Missouri, Community Alternatives

STARTING YEAR/YEAR FINAL REPORT EXPECTED: 2001/2004.

INFORMATION SOURCE: *Multi-Dimensional Assistance for Homeless Families,* Center for Mental Health Services and the Center for Substance Abuse Treatment, The Homeless Families Coordinating Center, Vanderbilt University Institute for Public Policy Studies, 1999.

PRINCIPAL INTERVENTION: Housing assistance, mental health services, substance abuse treatment, trauma recovery services, education and employment, and health services.

TARGET POPULATION: Homeless mothers with their children in St. Louis County and St. Louis City.

OUTCOMES OF INTEREST: Housing, school attendance (children), and health.

Westchester County, New York, Homeless Study

STARTING YEAR/YEAR FINAL REPORT EXPECTED: 2001/2004.

INFORMATION SOURCE: "Homeless Families in Westchester County, New York," Center for the Study of Issues in Public Mental Health, http://www.rfmh.org/csipmh/projects/hm5.htm. Principal investigator: Judith Samuels, Nathan Kline Institute for Psychiatric Research, Orangeburg, NY.

PRINCIPAL INTERVENTION: Family Critical Time Intervention, which couples rapid placement in transitional housing with intensive short-term case management.

TARGET POPULATION: Homeless mothers entering the family shelter system with psychiatric and/or substance abuse disorders who are caring for their dependent children.

OUTCOMES OF INTEREST: Housing stability, health, employment, and school attendance.

12

Charged/Convicted Individuals

Living Insurance for Ex-Offenders (LIFE)

SUMMARY: This demonstration, conducted from 1972 to 1975, tested the effects of temporary financial assistance and job placement services on a medium-sized sample of male ex-offenders. Subjects were followed for one year.

COST: $230,000; research only, $30,000.

TIME FRAME: Demonstration period, fiscal years 1972–74; data collected, 1972–75; final report, 1978.

TREATMENTS TESTED:
1. Financial aid. Sixty dollars a week for 13 weeks, conditional on not being reimprisoned. If the subject had earnings above $40 a week, 50 percent of those earnings was subtracted from the weekly payment and deferred to a later week, thus slightly extending the 13-week period.
2. Job placement services. Staff members worked full-time finding job openings, chauffeuring experimentals to interviews and helping them fill out job applications, and advocating on experimentals' behalf with employers and bureaucrats.
3. Financial aid and job placement. Experimentals received both job services and financial aid.
4. Controls received no treatment.

OUTCOMES OF INTEREST: (1) Rearrest; (2) Employment; and (3) Earnings.

SAMPLE SIZE: Group 1, 108; group 2, 108; group 3, 108; group 4, 108.

TARGET POPULATION: Male ex-offenders returning to Baltimore from prison; nonaddicts, with records of multiple prior offenses, at least one of them for theft; under age 45; and with less than $400 in savings.

NUMBER OF TREATMENT GROUPS: Four (with one control group).

NUMBER AND LOCATION OF SITES: One—Baltimore, Maryland.

RESEARCH COMPONENTS:
- Process analysis: Extensive interviews of experimentals.
- Impact analysis: Conducted both as difference in means and by regression and probit.
- Benefit–cost analysis: Conducted from several perspectives with upper and lower bounds on confidence.

MAJOR FINDINGS:
1. Job placement services had no statistically significant impacts. The remaining findings are reported for financial experimentals (groups 1 and 3) versus financial controls (groups 2 and 4).
2.

	Experimentals (n = 216)	Controls (n = 216)
New arrests, all theft crimes	48	66
Estimated new arrests, from regression with other factors	48.6	66
Estimated new arrests, from probit with other factors	45.5	66
New arrests, all crimes	107	123
In school or training, first quarter	3.7%	1.4%
Second quarter	4.2%	2.0%
Employed full-time, fourth quarter	54.7%	49%

Note: All differences above are statistically significant; however, schooling differentials are not significant after the second quarter, and employment differentials are not significant in the first, second, and third quarters. There are no statistically significant differences in weekly earnings in any quarter.

3. Benefit–cost analysis from a social perspective: Lower bound—$108,565 benefits, $27,000 costs; 4.02 benefit–cost ratio. Upper bound—$870,431 benefits, $16,200 costs; 53.73 benefit–cost ratio.

Benefit–cost ratio from other perspectives:

	Lower	Upper
Budgetary	0.49	2.67
Nonparticipant	0.77	3.99
Participant	1.93	3.76

TIME TRENDS IN FINDINGS: The difference in arrests was 16 in the second year, compared with 18 in the first year, indicating the effect did not disappear. However, the second-year data are lower in quality since they rely on Baltimore area court records, and some subjects had left the area.

DESIGN ISSUES: None apparent.

REPLICABILITY: Replicable.

GENERALIZABILITY: The sample is not large, and the sample selection criteria were deliberately chosen to assemble a group that was likely to show a strong response. Since a policy would necessarily embrace a larger group, the Transitional Aid Research Project (TARP) (page 343) was funded to determine whether the experimental effects would be repeated in a wider population. Lenihan (1978) noted that Baltimore had fairly inexpensive inner-city housing at the time of the experiment, and thus the experimental response was obtainable there at a lower cost than in some other cities.

FUNDING SOURCE: U.S. Department of Labor, Employment and Training Administration. Key personnel: Howard Rosen.

TREATMENT ADMINISTRATOR: Bureau of Social Science Research. Key personnel: Kenneth J. Lenihan.

EVALUATORS: Bureau of Social Science Research (BSSR) and Mathematica Policy Research (MPR).

Key personnel: Kenneth J. Lenihan for BSSR; Charles D. Mallar and Craig Thornton for MPR.

ENABLING LEGISLATION: None.

POLICY EFFECTS: Kenneth Lenihan has stated that a California legislator, citing LIFE results, eventually obtained financial assistance for released prisoners.

INFORMATION SOURCES: Charles D. Mallar and Craig Thornton, "Transitional Aid for Released Prisoners: Evidence from the LIFE Experiment," *Journal of Human Resources* Spring 1978: 208–36; Kenneth J. Lenihan, *Unlocking the Second Gate: The Role of Financial Assistance in Reducing Recidivism among Ex-Prisoners,* R&D Monograph 45, U.S. Department of Labor, Employment and Training Administration, 1978.

PUBLIC-USE ACCESS TO DATA: We have no information about a public-use file for this demonstration.

Transitional Aid Research Project (TARP)

SUMMARY: This demonstration, conducted from 1975 to 1977, tested the effects of a temporary negative income tax (at various levels of income guarantee and tax rate) on a large sample of released prisoners. Subjects were followed for up to two years.

COST: $3.4 million ($2.6 million federal; the rest is an estimate of the states' administrative expenses).

TIME FRAME: Demonstration period, January–December 1976; data collected, December 1975–June 1977; final reports for each state were submitted in 1978.

TREATMENTS TESTED: Treatments varied in regard to whether there were guaranteed incomes to subjects for a period following release. Payment treatments varied by the number of weeks of payments guaranteed and by the tax rate on earnings. Georgia and Texas unemployment insurance rules applied, accounting for differences in the size of payments and the maximum amount of untaxed, earned income permitted (weekly forgiveness amount). The Georgia and Texas unemployment rules are summarized as a 100 percent tax rate above the forgiveness amount; this is an oversimplification. See table below for treatments 1, 2, and 3.

4. Job placement services in both states, with grants up to $100 for tools, work clothes, and the like. No eligibility for payment.
5. Interviewed controls in both states. Fifteen-dollar payment for each of the four interviews in Georgia; $10 average payment for each of the four interviews in Texas; no other payments.
6. Noninterviewed controls in both states, followed through arrest and FICA earnings records; no payments, did not know they were part of an experiment.

OUTCOMES OF INTEREST: (1) Recidivism and (2) Employment and earnings.

SAMPLE SIZE: Georgia: group 1, 176; group 2, 199; group 3, 201; group 4, 200; group 5, 200; group 6, 1,031. Texas: group 1, 175; group 2,

Treatments Tested

Treatment	State	Maximum weekly payment ($)	Maximum weeks	Maximum allowance ($)	Forgiveness	Tax rate (%)
1.	Georgia	70	26	1,820	8	100
	Texas	63	26	1,638	15.75	100
2.	Georgia	70	13	910	8	100
	Texas	63	13	819	15.75	100
3.	Georgia	70	13	910	—	25
	Texas	63	13	819	—	25

200; group 3, 200; group 4, 200; group 5, 200; group 6, 1,000.

TARGET POPULATION: All prisoners released from state prisons with the following exceptions: (1) those returning to a small number of remote rural counties; (2) those returning to some other state or country; (3) those for whom arrest warrants or detainers for other offenses were pending prior to release.

NUMBER OF TREATMENT GROUPS: Six (with two control groups).

NUMBER AND LOCATION OF SITES: Georgia and Texas, statewide, with limited exceptions.

RESEARCH COMPONENTS:

■ Process analysis: Wide-ranging interviews with members of the first five groups were conducted, in some cases with their family members. However, the researchers do not have any data about the content of the subjects' interactions with the employees of the employment security agencies. This is important for group 4, where virtually nothing is known except expenditures for tools and work clothes; it is also important for group 3, the low-tax group, because interviews showed no particular understanding of the tax system by that group or the others. Tests were also performed on the possibility of underreporting of employment by the payment groups against unemployment insurance records; no such pattern was found.

■ Impact analysis: Conducted both as difference in means and with regression and other statistical techniques.
■ Benefit–cost analysis: Not conducted.

MAJOR FINDINGS:
1. No statistically significant differences in recidivism were found.
2. Employment and earnings, Georgia: See table below. In general, experimental groups have statistically significant differences from control group 5 in rows 1, 2, and 4.
3. Employment and earnings, Texas: See table below. In general, experimental-group differences from group 5 are statistically significant for all rows except the last one.
   "The TARP payments, as administered, did not decrease arrests for property-related offenses in either state. . . . TARP payment eligibility exerted a clear and strong work-disincentive effect."
4. The project report authors set up and tested an elaborate multiple-equation system with the experimental data. They concluded that the payments themselves reduced recidivism, but the negative effects of the high tax rate led to low employment, which in turn led to higher recidivism.

TIME TRENDS IN FINDINGS: Data are for one year.

DESIGN ISSUES: In Georgia, a "speeded-up" commutation procedure went into effect shortly before the experiment began. This change increased the

Employment and Earnings

Variable	Group 1	Group 2	Group 3	Group 4	Group 5	Group 6
Georgia						
Mean weeks worked, first year after release	12.3	17.4	17.7	19.6	24.3	NA
Mean weeks worked, first 14 weeks	2.4	2.8	3.1	4.9	5.9	NA
Mean weeks worked, weeks 15–24	2.5	4.0	4.5	5.2	6.5	NA
Percentage with some earnings	53.7	60.8	62.4	62.5	65.2	61.2
Mean earnings ($)	1,064	1,525	1,433	1,088	1,553	1,531
Texas						
Mean weeks worked, first year after release	20.8	27.1	24.6	29.3	28.3	NA
Mean weeks worked, first 14 weeks	4.0	4.9	5.2	7.0	7.1	NA
Mean weeks worked, weeks 15–24	4.5	7.3	6.8	7.4	7.6	NA
Percentage with some earnings	67.4	78.6	69.7	73.1	66.1	66.2
Mean earnings ($)	1,922	2,215	2,242	2,069	1,960	2,043

number of prisoners in the Georgia sample who would be expected to exhibit an experimental effect if one existed; it tended to accelerate the release of older offenders with more than one prior theft conviction.

REPLICABILITY: Replicable.

GENERALIZABILITY: This experiment was planned to generalize the results of the Living Insurance for Ex-Offenders (LIFE) experiment (page 341). It did not confirm those results.

FUNDING SOURCES: U.S. Department of Labor (DOL), Employment and Training Administration, and Department of Justice, Law Enforcement Assistance Administration. Key personnel: Howard Rosen for DOL.

TREATMENT ADMINISTRATORS: Texas Department of Corrections, Georgia Department of Corrections, and the Employment Security Agency.

EVALUATORS: Social and Demographic Research Institute, University of Massachusetts at Amherst, and the Group for Research on Social Policy, University of California–Santa Barbara. Key personnel: Peter H. Rossi and Richard A. Berk.

ENABLING LEGISLATION: None.

INFORMATION SOURCE: Peter H. Rossi, Richard A. Berk, and Kenneth J. Lenihan, *Money, Work and Crime: Experimental Evidence,* Harcourt Brace Jovanovich, 1980.

PUBLIC-USE ACCESS TO DATA: We have no information about a public-use file for this demonstration.

Court Employment Project

SUMMARY: This demonstration, conducted from 1977 to 1979, tested the effects of case dismissal in exchange for acceptance of counseling and employment-related services on a medium-sized sample of individuals charged with felonies. Subjects were followed for one year.

COST: $750,000.

TIME FRAME: Demonstration period, January 1977–March 1978; data collected through 1979; final report, June 1981.

TREATMENTS TESTED: Prosecutors would refer people charged with felonies to the project, and an "approximately" random assignment, described below, would occur. Experimentals were offered a delay and eventually a dismissal of their cases if they agreed to attend counseling sessions over a four-month period and if they complied with the agreement. The counseling included job referral and placement services, needs assessment, and referral to services in experimentals' neighborhoods (for general equivalency diploma [GED] tutoring, substance abuse, etc.). This option was not open to controls. The approximately random process was adopted to make the experiment politically acceptable. The experimental period was randomly divided into time periods of varying length, and project staff did not know when the current subperiod would expire. Quotas were preset, proportional to the length of the subperiods: new participants who entered before the quota was reached were experimentals; the overflow were controls.

OUTCOMES OF INTEREST: (1) Disposition of case; (2) Employment; and (3) Education or training activity.

SAMPLE SIZE: Experimentals, 410; controls, 256.

TARGET POPULATION: Persons charged with felonies selected by prosecutors. Three-quarters of the felonies were property crimes.

NUMBER OF TREATMENT GROUPS: Two (with one control group).

NUMBER AND LOCATION OF SITES: Two—Brooklyn and Manhattan, New York.

RESEARCH COMPONENTS:
- Process analysis: Conducted through interviews with prosecutors, implementation staff, and subjects.
- Impact analysis: Conducted as a difference in means. OLS findings were not qualitatively different and were not reported.
- Benefit–cost analysis: Not conducted.

MAJOR FINDINGS:

1. The key finding in the process analysis was that large numbers of controls either would not have been prosecuted; or, if prosecuted, would not have been convicted; or, if both prosecuted and convicted, would have faced minor penalties. Prosecutors used pretrial diversion to skim off a group who were not in serious trouble but "needed supervision." Defense attorneys cooperated with the tactic partly to economize on their own scarce resources. A second finding was that the Court Employment Project (CEP) staff felt they had not been successful in job development.

2. Charges were dropped against 72 percent of experimentals, and 46 percent of controls. However, only 6.6 percent of controls were convicted of criminal charges, whereas 1.9 percent of experimentals were. Thus, the experimental treatment did not significantly conserve court resources. Effects on employment were negligible. At a six-month follow-up, the average experimental had been employed for 1.29 months, the average control for 1.41 months. Effects on education and training were negligible.

TIME TRENDS IN FINDINGS: A 12-month follow-up also found no effects of treatment.

DESIGN ISSUES: The assignment process was accepted as effectively random by a national panel of referees.

REPLICABILITY: Replicable.

GENERALIZABILITY: The final report emphasized that the CEP, set up by the Vera Institute of Justice, was one of the earliest pretrial diversion programs; its policies conformed to standards set by a national professional organization. Thus, there is no obvious reason that the finding that pretrial diversion is ineffective and conceptually flawed should not have general validity.

FUNDING SOURCE: National Institute of Justice. Key personnel: Joel Garner.

TREATMENT ADMINISTRATOR: CEP. Key personnel: Ennis J. Olgiati, Bruce Eichner, and Rae Linefsky.

EVALUATOR: Vera Institute of Justice. Key personnel: Sally Hillsman Baker and Susan Sadd.

ENABLING LEGISLATION: None.

POLICY EFFECTS: Sally Hillsman Baker believed these findings caused pretrial diversion, as a strategy, to be largely abandoned in New York City. It has not had the same effect in the rest of the country, although Hillsman Baker feels the experiment has exposed pretrial diversion as conceptually flawed.

INFORMATION SOURCE: Sally Hillsman Baker and Susan Sadd, *Diversion of Felony Arrests. An Experiment in Pretrial Intervention: An Evaluation of the Court Employment Project*, Summary Report, Department of Justice, National Institute of Justice, June 1981.

PUBLIC-USE ACCESS TO DATA: We have no information about a public-use file for this demonstration.

Ex-Offender Research Project

SUMMARY: According to Lafayette Grisby of the Employment and Training Administration, this experiment was intended to determine the effects of guaranteed jobs on the behavior of ex-offenders on their release from prison. It was located in Baltimore, the contractor was Blackstone Associates, and $2.5 million (1981) was initially allocated to the project. The project was terminated within a few months of initiation because of a funding cutback, long before any results could have been observed.

FUNDING: U.S. Department of Labor, Employment and Training Administration.

INFORMATION SOURCE: None is known to exist.

PUBLIC-USE ACCESS TO DATA: No data.

13

Substance Abusers

Wildcat Experiment

SUMMARY: This demonstration, conducted from 1972 to 1978, tested the effects of supported work experience on a medium-sized sample of adult substance abusers. Subjects were followed for three years.

COST: $36.2 million for administration and payments to treatment participants who were not in the initial sample.

TIME FRAME: Demonstration period, July 1972–June 1976; data collected, July 1972–June 1978; final report, 1978.

TREATMENTS TESTED: Experimentals were randomly selected for work from volunteers. They were placed in small work crews with people of similar background and were confronted with graduated demands for productivity, graduated rewards for performance, sympathetic but firm supervision, and consistent daily communication of management expectations. One crew member was the designated crew chief, and there were additional supportive services. Typical work: office/clerical, messenger, and building maintenance; usually the work was performed for the city government. Controls received no services from the demonstration.

OUTCOMES OF INTEREST: (1) Employment; (2) Earnings; (3) Rearrest; and (4) Drug and alcohol use.

SAMPLE SIZE: Experimentals, 194; controls, 207.

TARGET POPULATION: Substance abusers, at least 18 years old, enrolled in drug abuse treatment for at least three months, currently unemployed, receiving public assistance, unemployed at least 12 of the past 24 months, and not intoxicated at interview.

NUMBER OF TREATMENT GROUPS: Two (with one control group).

NUMBER AND LOCATION OF SITES: One—New York City.

RESEARCH COMPONENTS:
- Process analysis: Conducted with open-ended interviewing. Self-reported earnings, arrests, and drug use tested against data available from tax, police, and drug treatment clinic sources.
- Impact analysis: Conducted as a difference in means.
- Benefit–cost analysis: Conducted from a taxpayer perspective.

MAJOR FINDINGS:

	Experimentals	Controls
Weeks worked in three years	101	46
Earnings	$12,236	$4,968
Weekly earnings (if working) in unsubsidized jobs	$133	$108
Never received welfare payments over three years	46%	6%
Probability of arrest, first year	19%	31%

Note: All differences are statistically significant.

1. No significant impact was found on drug or alcohol use.
2. Experimentals were more likely to marry and to stay married.
3. Average taxpayer expenditures on experimentals: $13,127; average taxpayer benefits: $15,405; benefit–cost ratio: 1.12.

TIME TRENDS IN FINDINGS: All experimental effects diminished over time. For example, at the end of the first year, 74 percent of experimentals were working, compared with 30 percent of controls; at the end of three years, 49 percent of experimentals were working, compared with 36 percent of controls. Rearrest differences also vanish.

DESIGN ISSUES: None apparent.

REPLICABILITY: Crew chiefs required special training. Project supervisors apparently had to possess entrepreneurial skills of a high order.

GENERALIZABILITY: Sample is not large and New York City is a special environment. The National Supported Work Demonstration (NSWD) (page 389) was performed to determine whether the findings could be generalized. Wildcat and NSWD participants were mostly addicted to heroin and were receiving methadone maintenance.

FUNDING SOURCES: New York City Addiction Services Agency, Department of Employment; U.S. Department of Health and Human Services, National Institute on Drug Abuse; U.S. Department of Justice, Law Enforcement Assistance Administration; and the U.S. Department of Labor, Labor, Employment, and Training Administration.

TREATMENT ADMINISTRATOR: Vera Institute of Justice, which set up the Wildcat Service Corporation. Key personnel: Herbert Sturz and Kenneth Marion.

EVALUATOR: Vera Institute of Justice. Key personnel: Lucy N. Friedman.

ENABLING LEGISLATION: Waiver of regulations to permit diversion to wages of welfare funds otherwise payable to participants.

POLICY EFFECTS: The findings from this experiment led the Ford Foundation and the Department of Labor, with support from other sources, to initiate the creation of the Manpower Demonstration Research Corporation to oversee a national experimental evaluation of the supported work concept.

INFORMATION SOURCE: Lucy N. Friedman, *The Wildcat Experiment: An Early Test of Supported Work in Drug Abuse Rehabilitation,* National Institute on Drug Abuse, 1978.

PUBLIC-USE ACCESS TO DATA: We have no information about a public-use file for this demonstration.

Job Seekers' Workshop

SUMMARY: This demonstration, conducted from 1976 to 1979, tested the effects of an employment-related workshop and modified job club on three small samples of heroin abusers. Subjects were followed for three months.

COST: Roughly $120,000 (1979) for the latter two studies.

TIME FRAME: First study demonstration period, 1976; second and third studies demonstration period, 1978–1979; data collected, three-month follow-ups only; final report, 1981.

TREATMENTS TESTED: There were three experiments:
1. A (Hall et al. 1977). Random assignment was performed by use of the date of the workshop the subject chose, relying on the fact that experimental and control workshops alternated randomly according to a schedule not known at intake. Controls attended a three-hour meeting during which they learned about available employment resources (e.g., union halls); they discussed their job interests with group leaders, and leaders made appropriate suggestions. Experimentals attended a similar meeting. They then attended a workshop lasting eight hours over three days, corresponding to the initial phases of the Job Club model but with much less supervised job search. Much more attention was placed on appropriate interview behavior than on obtaining interviews (probably because of the favorable local job market). Interviews in which participants role-played were set up two days after the workshop for both groups.

2. B (Hall, Loeb, Coyne, et al. 1981). Subjects were stratified according to sex, parole/probation status (yes or no), and past job history. Members of each stratum were randomly assigned to experimental or control treatments. These treatments were the same as in A, although the experimental treatment took 12 hours over four days.
3. C (Hall, Loeb, LeVois, et al. 1981). The pilot study had simple random assignment, with an experimental treatment that was a little longer than that in A or B, mostly because of two days at the end with no preset structure, where subjects could identify areas in which they wanted more work.

In all three experiments, self-reported employment was verified with other sources.

OUTCOMES OF INTEREST: (1) Employment and (2) Performance at simulated interview.

SAMPLE SIZE: Experiment A: Experimentals, 35; controls, 20. Experiment B: Experimentals, 30; controls, 30. Experiment C: Experimentals, 23; controls, 26.

TARGET POPULATION: For experiment A, the target population was parolees or those on probation with documented histories of heroin abuse. Those who were psychotic, illiterate, or anticipated serving jail time in the next three months were screened out. For experiments B and C, the target populations were patients at methadone maintenance clinics, with the same exclusion criteria as in A.

NUMBER OF TREATMENT GROUPS: Two (with one control group).

NUMBER AND LOCATION OF SITES: One—San Francisco, California.

RESEARCH COMPONENTS:
- Process analysis: Not conducted.
- Impact analysis: Conducted as a difference in means.
- Benefit–cost analysis: Not conducted.

MAJOR FINDINGS:

1. Experiment A. Eighty-six percent of experimentals found full- or part-time employment over the three-month follow-up, compared with 54 percent of controls. This difference is significant at the .01 level.
2. Experiment B. At the end of three months, 52 percent of experimentals had found jobs, compared with 30 percent of controls. The difference is not quite significant. "Regardless of [experimental or control] condition, subjects who reported no job history in the 5 years prior to the study start failed to find employment."
3. Experiment C. At three-month follow-up, 50 percent (9 of 18) of experimentals were employed, compared with 14 percent (3 of 23) of controls, a statistically significant difference. This difference may be partly biased by the dropping of three experimentals who failed to attend workshops from the sample.

TIME TRENDS IN FINDINGS: "Life Tables" are presented in Hall, Loeb, Coyne, et al. (1981) and Hall, Loeb, LeVois, et al. (1981), showing the differences in job-finding success over 12 weeks for each group. In A, the difference continues to increase up to 10 weeks; in B, the difference is stable after 3 weeks. There is no follow-up beyond three months.

DESIGN ISSUES: Differences in job-finding success were reported, but not in relative wages or tenure on the job.

REPLICABILITY: Replicable.

GENERALIZABILITY: The samples were small, and the San Francisco job market was very favorable to job seekers.

FUNDING SOURCE: U.S. Department of Health and Human Services, National Institute on Drug Abuse, U.S. Public Health Service.

TREATMENT ADMINISTRATOR: University of California, Behavioral Treatment Research. Key personnel: Sharon Martinelli Hall.

EVALUATOR: University of California, Behavioral Treatment Research. Key personnel: Sharon Martinelli Hall.

INFORMATION SOURCES: Sharon Martinelli Hall, Peter Loeb, Joseph Norton, and Ray Yang, "Improving Vocational Placement in Drug Treatment Clients: a Pilot Study," *Addictive Behaviors* 2(1977): 227–34.

Sharon Martinelli Hall, Peter Loeb, Kristin Coyne, and James Cooper, "Increasing Employment in Ex-Heroin Addicts I: Criminal Justice Sample," *Behavior Therapy* 12(1981): 443–52.

Sharon Martinelli Hall, Peter Loeb, Michel LeVois, and James Cooper, "Increasing Employment in Ex-Heroin Addicts II: Methadone Maintenance Sample," *Behavior Therapy* 12(1981): 453–60.

PUBLIC-USE ACCESS TO DATA: We have no information about a public-use file for this demonstration.

Transition Project

SUMMARY: This demonstration, conducted from 1980 to 1981, tested the effects of job orientation meetings on a medium-sized sample of substance abusers. Subjects were followed for up to one year.

COST: Research only, $187,000 (1980).

TIME FRAME: Demonstration period, 1980; data collected through 1981; final report, 1982.

TREATMENTS TESTED: Experimentals were able to attend two meetings a week over seven weeks, one at their own drug-treatment site, one at a corporation to which their group had been assigned. Company personnel would explain what types of jobs were available in that firm, the entry-level job requirements, what they looked for in job applications and interviews, how job performance was evaluated, and opportunities for advancement and benefits. Experimentals practiced interviewing people who made hiring decisions and observed employees at work. Lessons were reinforced at counseling sessions at the treatment site. Five corporations (a bank, a pharmaceutical, and three insurance companies) participated. There was no expectation that the corporation would hire the experimentals; the purpose was orientation to the rewards and demands of corporate life. Controls were not eligible for these services, although they were told about job-placement services offered by the administrator. All subjects were paid for their time in research interviews.

OUTCOMES OF INTEREST: (1) Employment; (2) Wages; (3) Education or training activity; (4) Drug or alcohol use; and (5) Criminal behavior.

SAMPLE SIZE: Experimentals, 146; controls, 78.

TARGET POPULATION: Substance abusers who (1) had been involved in drug treatment for at least six months, (2) were in good standing within treatment program guidelines (e.g., no evidence of recent substance abuse), (3) had no major time conflicts with participation (child care, criminal justice, medical), (4) could read at least on a sixth-grade level, (5) had no more than 6 months' work experience in the previous 12 months, (6) were considered nearing job readiness by counselors, but still having substantial barriers to employability, and (7) volunteered to participate.

NUMBER OF TREATMENT GROUPS: Two (with one control group).

NUMBER AND LOCATION OF SITES: One—New York City.

RESEARCH COMPONENTS:
- Process analysis: Evaluations of the value of the program by participants, corporate staff, and treatment center staff. Attendance at sessions was on average about 50 percent of planned attendance.
- Impact analysis: Used ordinary least squares, but reported only unadjusted means to facilitate exposition.
- Benefit–cost analysis: Not conducted.

MAJOR FINDINGS:
1. Treatment effects on employment and wages were not significant.
2. Comparing only employed experimentals and employed controls, experimentals earned higher wages at their longest full-time job ($212 versus $193) and were more likely to work in a company with over 100 employees (36 percent versus 21 percent). These results are not statistically significant, possibly because only 52 experimentals and 25 controls who had held full-time jobs were reached during the follow-up.
3. Differences in enrollment in academic or vocational training were insignificant, but experimentals were more likely to choose academic training, whereas controls were more likely to choose vocational training.
4. Subgroup analysis did not find statistically significant differences. The evaluators came to believe that the experimental/control differences were greatest in subgroups where controls had the poorest outcomes (i.e., were the most disadvantaged).
5. Controls were more likely than were experimentals to report that their principal activity in the previous year was illegal (10 percent versus 3 percent, a significant difference). The most common illegal activity was drug dealing.
6. There was no significant difference in alcohol or drug use. Most participants were in methadone maintenance, which inhibits only heroin use, but the majority in both groups had used cocaine since treatment. There was no significant difference in self-reported criminal activity.

TIME TRENDS IN FINDINGS: The patterns in 6-month and 12-month follow-ups are similar.

DESIGN ISSUES: Treatment counselors were usually not well trained in group counseling skills, which limited the usefulness of the clinic sessions.

REPLICABILITY: Replicable.

GENERALIZABILITY: Small sample size does not permit finding statistical significance for subtle effects, if they are present.

FUNDING SOURCE: U.S. Department of Labor, Employment and Training Administration.

TREATMENT ADMINISTRATOR: National Association on Drug Abuse Problems (NADAP). Key personnel: Holly Robinson.

EVALUATOR: NADAP. Key personnel: Don Des Jarlais.

ENABLING LEGISLATION: None.

INFORMATION SOURCE: Ellen Rossman, Don Des Jarlais, Sherry Derren, and Holly Robinson, *An Evaluation of a Corporate-Based Job Preparation Training Program, the Transition Project,* National Association on Drug Abuse Problems, 1982.

PUBLIC-USE ACCESS TO DATA: We have no information about a public-use file for this demonstration.

14

Frail Elderly

INTRODUCTION

Since the 1960s, a number of home and community care studies have been conducted as social experiments. In addition to the criteria set forth in the introduction to this volume, these studies all met four other criteria: (1) they tested the effects of providing a home- and community-based alternative to existing long-term care services (which may have included other home- and community-based services as well as services provided in an institution); (2) they used the individual as their primary unit of analysis; (3) they served primarily an elderly population; and (4) one of their outcomes was institutionalization (nursing home placement).

We include these experiments with some misgivings. We have tried to exclude experiments with only health status outcomes. Some institutionalization is dictated by health need—the patient might die or suffer grievous harm in its absence. However, some institutionalization is truly a choice for the patient—a choice that may be affected by his or her endowment with community services.

Most of the information contained in the following summaries comes from the paper by Weissert, Cready, and Pawelak (1988), who reviewed 13 long-term care studies and discussed many of the cost and targeting issues they contain. Targeting success is measured by the percentage of the control group that was institutionalized during the study, for this is an indication of the number of experimentals who would have been institutionalized had they not received the intervention. The article also noted whether multivariate analysis was used.

Another review has been provided by Susan Hughes (1985), who identified problems with the definitions of both the treatment and the target population in these studies (the latter was very broadly defined and included those with minimal impairment, the acutely ill, and the chronically ill).

Note: After *The Digest* went into production, we discovered a dissertation with a long literature review describing a number of social experiments among the frail elderly of which we had no prior knowledge. To supplement this chapter, we refer the reader to the dissertation: Kirsi Kinnunen, "Postponing of Institutional Long-Term Care in the Patients at High Risk of Institutionalisation," doctoral dissertation, University of Helsinki Medical School, 2002, available at http://ethesis .helsinki.fi/julkaisut/laa/kliin/vk/kinnunen/postponi.pdf.

References

Hughes, Susan. 1985. "Apples and Oranges? A Review of Evaluations of Community-Based Long-Term Care." *Health Services Research* 20(4): 461–88.

Weissert, William G., Cynthia Matthews Cready, and James E. Pawelak. 1988. "The Past and Future of Home- and Community-Based Long-Term Care." *Millbank Quarterly* 66:309–88.

Continued Care

SUMMARY: This demonstration, conducted from 1963 to 1971, tested the effects of public health nurse home visits on a medium-sized sample of elderly noninstitutionalized individuals. Subjects were followed for two years.

COST: Not available.

TIME FRAME: Demonstration period, 1963–71.

TREATMENTS TESTED: The treatment group received public health nurse home visits. The control group received no demonstration services but could seek out existing long-term care services.

OUTCOMES OF INTEREST: (1) Nursing home use; (2) Hospital use; and (3) Patient functioning.

SAMPLE SIZE: Treatments, 150; controls, 150.

TARGET POPULATION: Elderly patients who had been in a rehabilitation hospital for at least a week before being discharged to a noninstitutional setting.

NUMBER OF TREATMENT GROUPS: Two (with one control group).

NUMBER AND LOCATION OF SITES: One—Cleveland, Ohio.

RESEARCH COMPONENTS:
- Process analysis: No process analysis information is available.
- Impact analysis: Comparison of means.
- Benefit–cost analysis: Not conducted.

MAJOR FINDINGS:
1. Over the two-year period during which each sample member was followed, only 11 percent of the control group ever entered a nursing home, and about one-third entered the hospital. This is indicative of poor targeting.
2. Treatment group members entered nursing homes less than control group members (−1.1 percent) and spent less time there (−7.3 days per capita). Statistical significance was not reported for the total sample, although subgroup analyses showed that significantly fewer treatment group members who had physical disabilities and were socially deprived used nursing homes than did control group counterparts.
3. Significantly more treatment group members were admitted to hospitals during the study period (9.6 percent) than were control group members. There was no difference in the number of total days, per capita, in the hospital.
4. There were no significant differences between groups on measures of physical or mental functioning.

TIME TRENDS IN FINDINGS: None reported.

DESIGN ISSUES: This project was not very effective at targeting those frail elderly individuals who were most likely to be institutionalized.

REPLICABILITY: Replicable.

GENERALIZABILITY: Weissert, Cready, and Pawelak (1988) did not address this issue. However, given the poor targeting and fairly small sample size, generalizations would be speculative.

FUNDING SOURCE: U.S. Department of Health, Education, and Welfare.

TREATMENT ADMINISTRATOR: Case Western Reserve University School of Medicine.

EVALUATOR: S. Katz, Case Western Reserve University.

ENABLING LEGISLATION: None.

INFORMATION SOURCES: Information for this summary came from William G. Weissert, Cynthia

Matthews Cready, and James E. Pawelak, "The Past and Future of Home- and Community-Based Long-Term Care," *Millbank Quarterly* 66(1988): 309–88; the source document cited is S. Katz, A. B. Ford, T. D. Downs, M. Adams, and D. I. Rusby, *Effects of Continued Care: A Study of Chronic Illness in the Home,* DHEW Pub. No. (HSM) 73-3010, Case Western Reserve University School of Medicine, 1972.

PUBLIC-USE ACCESS TO DATA: Not available.

BRI Protective Services

SUMMARY: This demonstration, conducted from 1964 to 1966, tested the effects of case management and ancillary services on a small sample of elderly individuals with mental disabilities. Subjects were followed for one year.

COST: Not available.

TIME FRAME: Demonstration period, 1964–66.

TREATMENTS TESTED: Case management plus ancillary services including home aide services and legal, medical, and psychiatric consultation and evaluation. Control group members received nothing from the demonstration, but could seek out existing long-term care services from the community.

OUTCOMES OF INTEREST: (1) Nursing home use and (2) Measures of patient functioning.

SAMPLE SIZE: Treatments, 76; controls, 88.

TARGET POPULATION: Elderly individuals mentally incapable of adequately caring for themselves, living in the community without the support of an informal caregiver.

NUMBER OF TREATMENT GROUPS: Two (with one control group).

NUMBER AND LOCATION OF SITES: One—Cleveland, Ohio.

RESEARCH COMPONENTS:
- Process analysis: Preliminary surveys were used to assist in targeting the population and in sample selection. Other interviews were conducted with participants and referring agencies.
- Impact analysis: Comparison of means.
- Benefit–cost analysis: Not conducted.

MAJOR FINDINGS:
1. Twenty percent of control group members entered a nursing home during the study period.
2. The treatment led to a 14 percent *increase* in nursing home use (treatment versus control). The statistical significance of this finding was not reported.
3. There were no significant impacts on physical or mental functioning between groups. However, significantly more treatment group members reported satisfaction with their care services.

TIME TRENDS IN FINDINGS: None reported.

DESIGN ISSUES:
1. Only 50 percent of the treatment group ever received any home health aide service, and no utilization data are reported on the volume of service provided.
2. The sample consisted only of elderly people with mental impairment. The study did not address the possible effect of services on those with physical impairment.

REPLICABILITY: Replicable.

GENERALIZABILITY: Generalizing from this small sample would be speculative. The sample did represent the target population at the time in Cleveland—generally poor white females over 75 years of age. Men, nonwhites, and married persons are underrepresented compared to the general population of frail elderly.

FUNDING SOURCES: U.S. Social Security Administration; Ohio Welfare Administration, Social and Rehabilitative Services; and A. M. McGregor Home of Cleveland.

TREATMENT ADMINISTRATOR: Benjamin Rose Institute, Cleveland, Ohio.

EVALUATORS: M. Blenkner and M. Bloom, Benjamin Rose Institute.

ENABLING LEGISLATION: None.

INFORMATION SOURCES: M. Blenkner, M. Bloom, and M. Nielson, "A Research and Demonstration Project of Protective Services," *Social Casework* 52(1971): 483–89; William G. Weissert, Cynthia Matthews Cready, and James E. Pawelak, "The Past and Future of Home- and Community-Based Long-Term Care," *Millbank Quarterly* 66(1988): 309–88.

PUBLIC-USE ACCESS TO DATA: Not available.

BRH Home Aide

SUMMARY: This demonstration, conducted from 1966 to 1969, tested the effects of home aide visits on a small sample of recently hospitalized elderly people. Subjects were followed for one year.

COST: Not available.

TIME FRAME: Demonstration period, 1966–69.

TREATMENTS TESTED: Home aide visits (escort, health care, housekeeping, leisure and personal care services). The control group did not receive these services.

OUTCOMES OF INTEREST: (1) Hospital use; (2) Nursing home use; and (3) Measures of client functioning.

SAMPLE SIZE: Treatments, 50; controls, 50.

TARGET POPULATION: Elderly patients about to be discharged from a geriatric rehabilitation hospital to a noninstitutional setting and not already receiving organized home aide services from a community agency. These patients were not economically disadvantaged.

NUMBER OF TREATMENT GROUPS: Two (with one control group).

NUMBER AND LOCATION OF SITES: One—Benjamin Rose Hospital, Cleveland, Ohio.

RESEARCH COMPONENTS:
- Process analysis: Services performed by aides were tracked with daily reports.
- Impact analysis: Comparison of means.
- Benefit–cost analysis: Not conducted.

MAJOR FINDINGS:
1. Control group members spent an average of 53.1 days in a nursing home and 11.4 days in a hospital during the study period.
2. Significantly fewer (20 percent) treatment group members entered a hospital than did control group members. Treatment group members spent an average of 4.6 fewer days in the hospital than did control group members. The statistical significance of this finding is not reported.
3. The treatment had no significant impact on physical or mental functioning. However, significantly more treatment group members reported satisfaction with care than did control group members.

TIME TRENDS IN FINDINGS: None.

DESIGN ISSUES:
1. The evaluators claim to have had no prior experience with a more advantaged population and probably provided more services than were necessary. Most clients opted to cancel services at the end of the study period rather than pay fees that were "within their economic capacity."
2. Information regarding cost and level of aide use is not reported, making it difficult to estimate potential policy implications.

REPLICABILITY: Replicable.

GENERALIZABILITY: Generalizing from this small sample would be speculative.

FUNDING SOURCES: A. M. McGregor Home of Cleveland and the U.S. Department of Health, Education, and Welfare.

TREATMENT ADMINISTRATOR: Benjamin Rose Hospital, Cleveland, Ohio.

EVALUATORS: M. Nielson and M. Blenkner were the likely principal investigators, but they could not be reached to confirm.

ENABLING LEGISLATION: None.

INFORMATION SOURCES: M. Nielson, M. Blenkner, M. Bloom, T. Downs, and H. Beggs, "Older Persons after Hospitalization: A Controlled Study of Home Aide Service," *American Journal of Public Health* 62(1972): 1094–1101; William G. Weissert, Cynthia Matthews Cready, and James E. Pawelak, "The Past and Future of Home- and Community-Based Long-Term Care," *Millbank Quarterly* 66(1988): 309–88.

PUBLIC-USE TO ACCESS TO DATA: Not available.

Chronic Disease

SUMMARY: This demonstration, conducted from 1971 to 1976, tested the effects of in-home health care services on a medium-sized sample of elderly subjects. Subjects were followed for one year.

COST: Not available.

TIME FRAME: Demonstration period, 1971–76.

TREATMENTS TESTED: In-home services by an interdisciplinary team (a half-time nurse or social worker, a part-time physician, and two full-time health assistants who provided the bulk of in-home care). The control group received nothing from the demonstration but could seek existing long-term care services.

OUTCOMES OF INTEREST: (1) Hospital use; (2) Nursing home use; and (3) Health care costs.

SAMPLE SIZE: Treatments, 438; controls, 436.

TARGET POPULATION: Elderly patients in an ambulatory care facility or about to be discharged from a hospital, living in a noninstitu-

tional setting, and needing assistance for at least three months.

NUMBER OF TREATMENT GROUPS: Two (with one control group).

NUMBER AND LOCATION OF SITES: Five—two urban and three rural communities in Michigan.

RESEARCH COMPONENTS:
- Process analysis: Information was collected that would allow description and comparison of the participants, description of the use of services, and descriptions of community settings in which services were offered.
- Impact analysis: Conducted using multivariate techniques.
- Benefit–cost analysis: Not conducted.

MAJOR FINDINGS:
1. The control group members spent an average of 14.5 days each in a nursing home and 11.6 days in a hospital. Targeting of at-risk individuals was fairly ineffective.
2. Treatment group members spent fewer days, on average, than control group members in both nursing homes (−5.9 days) and hospitals (−0.6 days). These differences were not statistically significant.
3. Overall average annual per capita cost savings from the treatment was $84 (1988 dollars). This reflects a savings of $630 for inpatient services, −$54 for outpatient services, and −$492 for treatment services.

TIME TRENDS IN FINDINGS: Savings occurred only when treatment was short, and were present only after six months. By 12 months, continued treatment without additional benefits in terms of reduced institutionalization had turned the savings into losses.

DESIGN ISSUES: Only 43 percent of the treatment group used services, thereby making per capita treatment costs appear artificially low. The low intensity of service may suggest the presence of subjects with fewer or less serious health problems in the sample.

REPLICABILITY: Replicable.

GENERALIZABILITY: Targeting difficulties discourage attempts at generalization.

FUNDING SOURCE: U.S. Department of Health, Education, and Welfare (now HHS), National Center for Health Services Research.

TREATMENT ADMINISTRATORS: Different for each site. Included a hospital, a county health department, two ambulatory clinics, and a clinic in a housing unit for the elderly.

EVALUATOR: Margaret Blenkner was the project director until her death in August 1973. The cited text does not identify her successor.

ENABLING LEGISLATION: None.

INFORMATION SOURCES: Joseph A. Papsidero, Sidney Katz Sr., Mary H. Kroger, and C. Amechi Akpom, eds., *Chance for Change: Implications of a Chronic Disease Module,* Michigan State University Press, 1979; additional information came from William G. Weissert, Cynthia Matthews Cready, and James E. Pawelak, "The Past and Future of Home- and Community-Based Long-Term Care," *Millbank Quarterly* 66(1988): 309–88.

PUBLIC-USE ACCESS TO DATA: Not available.

Worcester Home Care

SUMMARY: This demonstration, conducted from 1973 to 1975, tested the effects of case management on a medium-sized sample of the elderly. Subjects were followed for one year.

COST: Cost figures are not available.

TIME FRAME: Demonstration period, 1973–75.

TREATMENTS TESTED: Case management and other services not normally covered by Medicaid (escort, linen, special therapies, transportation). The control group received no services from the demonstration but could seek out existing long-term care services.

OUTCOMES OF INTEREST: Nursing home and hospital use and measures of client functioning.

SAMPLE SIZE: Treatments, 280; controls, 205.

TARGET POPULATION: Either (1) elderly individuals living in the community with some level of service need who primarily receive services from informal sources or (2) institutionalized individuals with the potential to return to the community.

NUMBER OF TREATMENT GROUPS: Two (with one control group).

NUMBER AND LOCATION OF SITES: One—Worcester, Massachusetts.

RESEARCH COMPONENTS:
- Process analysis: No information available.
- Impact analysis: Comparison of means.
- Benefit–cost analysis: Not conducted.

MAJOR FINDINGS:
1. Control group members spent an average of 49.6 days in a nursing home and 4 days in a hospital over the 12-month period.
2. The treatment had no impact on time spent in either nursing homes or hospitals. However, a subgroup analysis found that those in the treatment group members who were "in danger of institutionalization" used nursing homes significantly less often than their control group counterparts. A specific definition of "in danger" was not provided.
3. Impact on client functioning was mixed. There was a positive, though not significant, impact on activities of daily living, a significantly negative impact on mobility, and a negative, but not significant, impact on mental functioning. Treatment group members more often reported satisfaction than did control group members, although this finding was not statistically significant.

TIME TRENDS IN FINDINGS: None.

DESIGN ISSUES: Insufficient information on this study was available to address design issues.

REPLICABILITY: Replicable.

GENERALIZABILITY: Weissert et al. (1988) did not address this issue.

FUNDING SOURCE: Department of Elder Affairs, Commonwealth of Massachusetts.

TREATMENT ADMINISTRATOR: Elder Home Care of Worcester.

EVALUATOR: Unknown.

ENABLING LEGISLATION: None.

INFORMATION SOURCES: Information for this summary came from William G. Weissert, Cynthia Matthews Cready, and James E. Pawelak, "The Past and Future of Home- and Community-Based Long-Term Care," *Millbank Quarterly* 66(1988): 309–88; source document cited is Commonwealth of Massachusetts, *Home Care: An Alternative to Institutionalization: Final Report,* Commonwealth of Massachusetts, Department of Elder Affairs, 1975.

PUBLIC-USE ACCESS TO DATA: Not available.

NCHSR Day Care/Homemaker Demonstration

SUMMARY: This demonstration, conducted from 1974 to 1977, tested the effects of adult day care and homemaker services on a medium-sized sample of the elderly. Subjects were followed for one year.

COST: Not available.

TIME FRAME: Demonstration period, 1974–77; data collected, same period.

TREATMENTS TESTED: Three treatments were tested: (1) an adult day care program with services including meals, nursing, social services, therapies, and transportation; (2) homemaker services including chores, personal care, shopping, and escort; and (3) a combined treatment group. Each treatment had a control group that received neither adult day care nor homemaker services from the demonstration.

OUTCOMES OF INTEREST: (1) Nursing home use; (2) Hospital use; (3) Health care costs; and (4) Client functioning and satisfaction.

SAMPLE SIZE: Day care: Treatments, 194; controls, 190. Homemaker services: Treatments, 307; controls, 323. Combined services: Treatments, 59; controls, 80.

TARGET POPULATION: Elderly individuals needing health care services to restore or maintain functional ability but not 24-hour-a-day supervision. Individuals receiving homemaker services were also required to be post-hospital patients.

NUMBER OF TREATMENT GROUPS: Six (with three control groups).

NUMBER AND LOCATION OF SITES: Six—day care sites: White Plains and Syracuse, New York; homemaker sites: Providence, Rhode Island, and Los Angeles, California; combined services sites: Lexington, Kentucky, and San Francisco, California.

RESEARCH COMPONENTS:
- Process analysis: Evaluators paid special attention to services and activities offered by the program, to subject characteristics, and to the possibility of bias in the analysis.
- Impact analysis: Comparison of adjusted means using multivariate methods.
- Benefit–cost analysis: Costs were calculated, but a formal benefit–cost analysis was not done.

MAJOR FINDINGS:
1. Only 21 percent of the control group was institutionalized (hospital or nursing home) during the observation period. This indicates that few patients who used day care and homemaker services were potential beneficiaries.
2. Day care treatment group members were significantly less likely to enter a nursing home or hospital than were their control group counterparts. Homemaker treatment group members were also less likely to use nursing homes and hospitals than their control group counterparts, although this finding was not statistically significant. This information

is not presented for the combined service groups.

3. Both day care and homemaker services cost substantially more than their respective control group health care costs, because treatment costs were added to existing Medicare-covered services rather than substituting for them. Day care services cost 71 percent more than services for the control group, and homemaker services cost 60 percent more.

4. Treatment group members in all three service groups had significantly lower mortality rates than their control group counterparts. Other measures of physical functioning yielded mostly nonsignificant results, and there were no significant differences in mental functioning between treatment and control group members (although the homemaker treatment produced higher levels of client contentment).

TIME TRENDS IN FINDINGS: None.

DESIGN ISSUES: There was a fairly high level of contamination in the study. A large number (229) of treatment group members never used the services, and some control group members found they were eligible to receive the same or similar services free from a non-study source such as Medicaid-covered day care services in New York. Still other patients dropped out of the study before its completion. For some patients, the assessment teams did not fill in a crucial data item related to activities of daily living, and the patients were classified as missing data. Finally, some patients were accepted without following the randomization procedures. Careful steps were taken in the analysis to compensate for these departures, but conclusions should be drawn cautiously.

REPLICABILITY: Replicable.

GENERALIZABILITY: Generalizability may be hampered because of the heterogeneity of the sample. Better efforts at targeting the elderly who are truly at risk for institutionalization are needed.

FUNDING SOURCE: National Center for Health Services Research (NCHSR), U.S. Department of Health and Human Services.

TREATMENT ADMINISTRATORS: Health care providers at each of the six treatment sites.

EVALUATORS: Thomas Wan, University of Maryland–Baltimore County, Department of Sociology; and William Weissert and Barbara Livieratos, NCHSR.

ENABLING LEGISLATION: Commissioned by Congress under Section 222 of the 1974 amendments to the Social Security Act.

INFORMATION SOURCES: Thomas T. H. Wan, William G. Weissert, and Barbara B. Livieratos, "Geriatric Day Care and Homemaker Services: An Experimental Study," *Journal of Gerontology* 35(1980): 256–74.

William Weissert, Thomas Wan, Barbara Livieratos, and Sidney Katz, "Effects and Costs of Day-Care Services for the Chronically Ill: A Randomized Experiment," *Medical Care* 18(1980): 567–84.

William G. Weissert, Thomas T. H. Wan, Barbara B. Livieratos, and Julius Pelegrino, "Cost-Effectiveness of Homemaker Services for the Chronically Ill," *Inquiry* 17(1980): 230–43.

PUBLIC-USE ACCESS TO DATA: Available through National Technical Information Service, Springfield, Virginia.

Wisconsin Community Care Organization (CCO)—Milwaukee

SUMMARY: This demonstration, conducted from 1975 to 1979, tested the effects of case management and home health services on a medium-sized sample of the elderly. Subjects were followed for up to 16 months.

COST: Not available.

TIME FRAME: Demonstration period, 1975–79.

TREATMENTS TESTED: Case management and other services not normally covered by Medicaid (including adult day health care, home-health aide, housing search, personal care, skilled nursing, and transportation). The control group received nothing from the demonstration but could seek existing long-term health services.

OUTCOMES OF INTEREST: (1) Nursing home use; (2) Hospital use; (3) Health care costs; and (4) Client functioning.

SAMPLE SIZE: Milwaukee only: Treatments, 283; controls, 134.

TARGET POPULATION: Elderly persons at risk of institutionalization, as determined by the project administrators.

NUMBER OF TREATMENT GROUPS: Two (with one control group).

NUMBER AND LOCATION OF SITES: One experimental site—Milwaukee County, Wisconsin. Two other counties, La Crosse and Barron, used a matched comparison design.

RESEARCH COMPONENTS:
▪ Process analysis: A panel study and interviews at the state and federal level were conducted to assist in the project design. Special care was taken in defining and targeting the at-risk population.
▪ Impact analysis: Comparison of adjusted and unadjusted means.
▪ Benefit–cost analysis: Not conducted.

MAJOR FINDINGS:
1. Of the control group, 13.6 percent entered a nursing home and 14.9 percent were hospitalized. This suggests that the demonstration was fairly ineffective at targeting at-risk individuals.
2. Slightly fewer treatment group members used a nursing home during the observation period (approximately 14 months) than did control group members, although the finding was not statistically significant. On average, treatment group members spent significantly fewer days hospitalized (−8.7) than did control group members.
3. Average annual per capita costs were slightly higher for the treatment group than the control group. Inpatient services were $2,027 less for the treatment group and outpatient services were $1,156 less, but treatment services were $3,288 more (total cost savings, −$105).
4. There was a positive, but not significant, impact on client physical functioning.

TIME TRENDS IN FINDINGS: None.

DESIGN ISSUES:
1. The project was initially designed to be at one site and of short duration. It expanded beyond this design at the same time that resources for the evaluation were shrinking. This reduced the "tightness of the design and the data collection." Data had to be collected by Community Care Organization staff rather than evaluators, and service providers carried out randomization. Also, distance costs and staff turnover made training difficult and reliability was less assured.
2. A large portion of the experimental group (71 of the 283) never received services. Some were found ineligible after the initial intake, some were subsequently screened out for having "special needs" (controls were not subsequently screened), some refused services, and some went directly into a nursing home. These 71 were still considered part of the treatment group.

REPLICABILITY: Replicable, though better care needs to be taken in randomization to avoid uneven attrition.

GENERALIZABILITY: Generalizable only to the narrow group of "needy but not too needy" that was eventually provided services in this project. Further, the mean age of the study sample was at least 10 years younger than the average age at admission of nursing homes residents nationally.

FUNDING SOURCE: The Kellogg Foundation. Project officer: Barbara Lee.

TREATMENT ADMINISTRATOR: Wisconsin Community Care Organization, Madison.

EVALUATORS: Fredrick Seidl, University of Wisconsin–Madison; Robert Applebaum, Mathematica Policy Research; Carol Austin, University of Minnesota; and Kevin Mahoney, Connecticut Department on Aging.

ENABLING LEGISLATION: None.

INFORMATION SOURCE: Fredrick W. Seidl, Robert Applebaum, Carol Austin, and Kevin Mahoney, *Delivering In-Home Services to the Aged and Disabled: The Wisconsin Experiment,* D.C. Health and Company, 1983.

PUBLIC-USE ACCESS TO DATA: Not available.

Georgia Alternative Health Services (AHS)

SUMMARY: This demonstration, conducted from 1976 to 1980, tested the effects of case management and home care services on a medium-sized sample of the elderly. Subjects were followed for one year.

COST: Not available.

TIME FRAME: Demonstration period, 1976–80.

TREATMENTS TESTED: Case management and other services not normally covered by Medicaid (adult day health care, adult foster care, home health aide, skilled nursing, medical transportation and social services). The control group received nothing from the demonstration, but could seek existing long-term care services.

OUTCOMES OF INTEREST: (1) Nursing home use; (2) Hospital use; (3) Health care costs; and (4) Measures of client functioning.

SAMPLE SIZE: Treatments, 819; controls, 257.

TARGET POPULATION: Previously institutionalized elderly individuals, eligible for Medicaid-sponsored nursing home care.

NUMBER OF TREATMENT GROUPS: Two (with one control group).

NUMBER AND LOCATION OF SITES: Seventeen—ten rural and seven urban counties in Georgia.

RESEARCH COMPONENTS:
- Process analysis: Social and health information was collected by caseworkers and reviewed by a project team. A service provider verified team records and recommendations.
- Impact analysis: Comparison of means.
- Benefit–cost analysis: Not conducted.

MAJOR FINDINGS:
1. Of the control group, 15.6 percent entered a nursing home and spent an average of four days in a hospital during the 12-month period.
2. The treatment produced a slight decrease in nursing home use (−1.1 percent less use among the treatment group and an average of seven fewer days compared to the control group). There was a slight increase in hospital use (an average of two more days). The statistical significance of these findings was not reported.
3. Average annual per capita costs were 35 percent higher for the treatment group than for the control group, for all categories of service: in-patient services, +$315; outpatient services, +$38; and treatment services, +$2,632. On average, combined services cost $2,985 more for the treatment group than for the control group.
4. Treatment group members experienced a statistically significant reduction in mortality.

TIME TRENDS IN FINDINGS: None.

DESIGN ISSUES: None.

REPLICABILITY: Replicable.

GENERALIZABILITY: The typical AHS client served was a 75-year-old woman with less than nine years of education. This is similar to those who were being admitted to nursing homes nationally.

FUNDING SOURCE: Georgia Department of Medical Assistance.

TREATMENT ADMINISTRATOR: Georgia Department of Medical Assistance.

EVALUATOR: Medicus Systems Corporation.

ENABLING LEGISLATION: None.

INFORMATION SOURCES: Information for this summary came from William G. Weissert, Cynthia Matthews Cready, and James E. Pawelak, "The Past and Future of Home- and Community-Based Long-Term Care," *Millbank Quarterly* 66(1988): 309–88; source document cited is A. Skellie, F. Favor, C. Tudor, and R. Strauss, *Alternative Health Services Project: Final Report,* Georgia Department of Medical Assistance, 1982.

PUBLIC-USE ACCESS TO DATA: Not available.

Home Health Care Team

SUMMARY: This experiment, conducted between 1978 and 1981, tested the effects of a team approach to long-term home care on a small sample of homebound chronically or terminally ill patients. Subjects were followed for up to six months.

COST: The evaluators were unable to provide estimates of evaluation costs due to substantial donated time and resources. Further, much of the analysis was completed after the grant had expired.

TIME FRAME: Demonstration period, 1978–81; data collected, same period.

TREATMENTS TESTED: A team approach to home care. The team included a physician, nurse practitioner, and a social worker. The team delivered primary health care in the patients' homes, and were available for 24-hour and weekend care. The team physician attended to the patient during any necessary hospitalization. The control group received existing health and home care services available in the community (i.e., not a team approach; limited availability for home visits).

OUTCOMES OF INTEREST: (1) Health care system usage and cost; (2) Patient health status; and (3) Satisfaction with health care.

SAMPLE SIZE: Total, 167; treatments, 85; controls, 82.

TARGET POPULATION: Homebound, chronically or terminally ill elderly.

NUMBER OF TREATMENT GROUPS: Two (with one control group).

NUMBER AND LOCATION OF SITES: One—Rochester, New York.

RESEARCH COMPONENTS:
- Process analysis: Focused on health care team activities, patient characteristics, intake processes, and attrition.
- Impact analysis: Comparison of unadjusted means, as well as multiple regression approaches.
- Benefit–cost analysis: Not conducted.

MAJOR FINDINGS:
1. The average cost per day for all services (in-home and out-of-home) recorded for the treatment group patients was $47.83, or 8.6 percent less than the $52.33 for the control group patients. For treatment group patients, out-of-home services were 61.1 percent of what they were for controls, whereas in-home services were 60.9 percent more.
2. The trend toward reduced hospitalization usage seen among the treatment group is largely related to the considerably higher proportion of treatment patients dying at home.
3. Findings fail to demonstrate any program effects on patient status or morale. There were trends toward higher caregiver and patient satisfaction among the treatment group participants.

TIME TRENDS IN FINDINGS: None reported.

DESIGN ISSUES: The control group was not truly without intervention. They kept health usage diaries and were visited at home by interviewers who sometimes offered advice and support. This may account for an increase in satisfaction among the control group.

REPLICABILITY: Replicable.

GENERALIZABILITY: The sample size was fairly small and the program was voluntary. Roughly 80 percent of those deemed eligible agreed to participate in the study and were subsequently assigned to either the treatment or control group. Thus, these participants (in both groups) were interested in receiving this type of care.

FUNDING SOURCE: National Center for Health Services Research. Key personnel: Julius Pelegrino.

TREATMENT ADMINISTRATOR: Home Health Care Team, an outreach program of the University of Rochester Medical Center's Ambulatory Care Unit. Key personnel: Annemarie Groth-Juncker.

EVALUATORS: James G. Zimmer, research director; Annemarie Groth-Juncker, principal investigator; and Jane McCusker.

ENABLING LEGISLATION: None.

INFORMATION SOURCES: James G. Zimmer, Annemarie Groth-Juncker, and Jane McCusker, "A Randomized Controlled Study of a Home Health Care Team," *American Journal of Public Health* 75(1985): 134–41; James G. Zimmer, Annemarie Groth-Juncker, and Jane McCusker, "Effects of a Physician-Led Home Care Team on Terminal Care," *Journal of the American Geriatrics Society* 32(1984): 288–92.

PUBLIC-USE ACCESS TO DATA: Available through National Technical Information Service, Springfield, Virginia.

Project OPEN

SUMMARY: This demonstration, conducted from 1978 to 1983, tested the effects of case management and home health services on a medium-sized sample of the elderly. Subjects were followed for up to three years.

COST: The Health Care Financing Administration grant for the administrative/research components totaled roughly $1.7 million.

TIME FRAME: Demonstration period, 1978–83.

TREATMENTS TESTED: Case management and other services not normally covered by Medicare (including adaptive/assistive equipment, day health care, drugs, transportation, homemaker, home-delivered meals, therapies, and social day care). The control group received existing long-term care services.

OUTCOMES OF INTEREST: (1) Nursing home use; (2) Hospital use; (3) Health care costs; and (4) Measures of client functioning.

SAMPLE SIZE: Treatments, 220; controls, 115.

TARGET POPULATION: Cognitively aware elderly individuals with medical problems and needing assistance to function independently.

NUMBER OF TREATMENT GROUPS: Two (with one control group).

NUMBER AND LOCATION OF SITES: One—San Francisco, California.

RESEARCH COMPONENTS:
- Process analysis: Not conducted.
- Impact analysis: Comparison of means.
- Benefit–cost analysis: Not conducted.

MAJOR FINDINGS:

1. Only 5.6 percent of control group members entered a nursing home (Medicare-covered skilled nursing facility), and 30.3 percent entered a hospital during the project period (up to three years). This provides a measure of the study's effectiveness in targeting at-risk individuals.

2. The treatment had a slight, though not statistically significant, impact on nursing home use (1.7 percent fewer users in the treatment group than in the control group and an average of 3.6 fewer days). The same can be said for the

treatment's impact on hospital use (−4.1 percent and an average of 1.9 fewer days).

3. The treatment produced average annual per capita cost savings of $1,464. This reflects savings in inpatient services ($3,040) and outpatient services ($1,146) and losses in treatment services (−$2,722).

4. Impacts on client functioning were mixed and not statistically significant.

TIME TRENDS IN FINDINGS: The greatest impact on the participants' health status, usage patterns, and costs occurred during the first six months of participation.

DESIGN ISSUES: Cost reductions in hospital and nursing care were based on nonsignificant differences in nursing home and hospital use between treatment and control groups. Inadequate attention may have been paid to pretest differences between the groups as well as to attrition. Since multivariate analytic techniques were not used to adjust for possible pretest of attrition-induced differences, the results should be interpreted cautiously.

REPLICABILITY: Replicable.

GENERALIZABILITY: The evaluation does not specifically address this issue. The typical client of Project OPEN, whether treatment or control, was a 79-year-old, nonemployed, white widow living alone in her own home or apartment, subsisting on an income of less than $7,000 a year.

FUNDING SOURCE: U.S. Department of Health and Human Services, HCFA.

TREATMENT ADMINISTRATOR: Mount Zion Hospital and Medical Center, San Francisco. Key personnel: Barbara Sklar.

EVALUATOR: Lawrence Weiss, Mount Zion Hospital and Medical Center.

ENABLING LEGISLATION: None.

INFORMATION SOURCES: B. W. Sklar and L. J. Weiss, *Project OPEN (Organization Providing for Elderly Needs): Final Report,* Mount Zion Hospital and Medical Center, 1983; additional information came from William G. Weissert, Cynthia Matthews Cready, and James E. Pawelak, "The Past and Future of Home- and Community-Based Long-Term Care," *Millbank Quarterly* 66(1988): 309–88.

PUBLIC-USE ACCESS TO DATA: Not available.

San Diego Long-Term Care

SUMMARY: This demonstration, conducted from 1979 to 1984, tested the effects of case management and home health services on a medium-sized sample of the frail elderly. Subjects were followed for 18 months.

COST: Not available.

TIME FRAME: Demonstration period, 1979–84.

TREATMENTS TESTED: Case management and other services not normally covered by Medicare (including adult day health care, client/family health education, homemaker/personal care, and transportation). The control group received nothing from the study but could seek out existing long-term care services.

OUTCOMES: (1) Nursing home use; (2) Hospital use; and (3) Measures of client functioning.

SAMPLE SIZE: Treatments, 549; controls, 270.

TARGET POPULATION: Elderly individuals unable to maintain themselves at home without assistance, at risk of long-term institutional placement or frequent acute hospital admissions.

NUMBER OF TREATMENT GROUPS: Two (with one control group).

NUMBER AND LOCATION OF SITES: One—San Diego, California.

RESEARCH COMPONENTS:
▪ Process analysis: No process analysis information was available.

■ Impact analysis: Comparison of adjusted means.

■ Benefit–cost analysis: Not conducted.

MAJOR FINDINGS:

1. For control group members, 46.3 percent entered a hospital, but only 7 percent entered a nursing home during the observation period (18 months on average). This indicates that the study was better at targeting those at risk of acute placement than those likely to seek a long-term institutional placement.

2. Slightly fewer treatment group members entered nursing homes (−1.8 percent) or hospitals (−0.4 percent) than did control group members. However, this finding was not statistically significant.

3. Impacts on physical and mental functioning were mixed and mostly nonsignificant.

TIME TRENDS IN FINDINGS: None.

DESIGN ISSUES:

1. The study was unable to effectively target those most at risk for long-term institutional placement.

2. Aliece Pinkerton feels that this project was terminated before valid outcomes could be obtained.

REPLICABILITY: Replicable.

GENERALIZABILITY: Neither Pinkerton and Hill (1984) nor Weissert et al. (1988) addressed this issue. Given the targeting problem, findings may not generalize to a population at risk for nursing home placement.

FUNDING SOURCE: Health Care Financing Administration.

TREATMENT ADMINISTRATOR: Allied Home Health Association. Key personnel: Aliece Pinkerton, and Deborah Hill.

EVALUATOR: Pinkerton believes the principal investigator was Carl Beatty (affiliation unknown).

ENABLING LEGISLATION: None.

INFORMATION SOURCES: Information for this summary came from a conversation with Aliece Pinkerton, and William G. Weissert, Cynthia Matthews Cready, and James E. Pawelak, "The Past and Future of Home- and Community-Based Long-Term Care," *Millbank Quarterly* 66(1988): 309–88; the source document cited is Aliece Pinkerton and Deborah Hill, *Long-Term Care Demonstration Project of North San Diego County: Final Report,* NTIS no. PB85-10391, Allied Home Health Association, 1984.

PUBLIC-USE ACCESS TO DATA: Not available.

Florida Pentastar

SUMMARY: This demonstration, conducted from 1980 to 1983, tested the effects of case management and home health services on a medium-sized sample of the at-risk elderly. Subjects were followed for 18 months.

COST: Evaluation costs, approximately $100,000.

TIME FRAME: Demonstration period, 1980–83.

TREATMENTS TESTED: Case management and other services not normally provided by Medicare (including adult day health care, homemaker, skilled nursing, therapies, and transportation). The control group received existing long-term care services.

OUTCOMES OF INTEREST: (1) Nursing home use and (2) Measures of client functioning.

SAMPLE SIZE: Total, 935; treatments, 723; controls, 212.

TARGET POPULATION: Elderly individuals at risk for institutional placement within a year and in need of project services. The sample was further limited to those eligible for Medicaid.

NUMBER OF TREATMENT GROUPS: Two (with one control group).

NUMBER AND LOCATION OF SITES: Five sites in Florida.

RESEARCH COMPONENTS:

- Process analysis: There was a fairly extensive process evaluation involving site visits—a survey of service providers and a survey of a non-randomly assigned comparison group. It focused on where the participants were drawn from, staff turnover, and participation patterns.
- Impact analysis: Comparison of means, simple and adjusted.
- Benefit–cost analysis: Not conducted.

MAJOR FINDINGS:

1. Of the control group, 5.7 percent entered a nursing home during the 18-month observation period. This provides a measure of the study's effectiveness in targeting at-risk individuals.
2. A slightly smaller percentage of treatment group members entered a nursing home compared with members of the control group (−0.6 percent). However, this finding is not statistically significant.
3. On average, the treatment group members scored significantly lower on several measures of physical functioning. There was no significant impact on mental functioning.

TIME TRENDS IN FINDINGS: None.

DESIGN ISSUES: None.

REPLICABILITY: Replicable, though quality of case management will vary.

GENERALIZABILITY: Designed to generalize to the population of Medicaid-eligible elderly in the state of Florida. The Medicaid-eligible population, as a whole, is less impaired than participants in most of the long-term care studies that have been conducted.

FUNDING SOURCE: Florida Department of Health and Rehabilitative Services, under a federal waiver.

TREATMENT ADMINISTRATOR: Florida Department of Health and Rehabilitative Services, Department of Adult Services.

EVALUATOR: Nancy Ross, Department of Health and Rehabilitative Services, Office of Evaluation.

INFORMATION SOURCES: Information for this summary came from a conversation with the evaluator and William G. Weissert, Cynthia Matthews Cready, and James E. Pawelak, "The Past and Future of Home- and Community-Based Long-Term Care," *Millbank Quarterly* 66(1988): 309–88; the source document cited is J. M. Maurer, N. L. Ross, Y. M. Bigos, M. Papagiannis, and T. Springfield, *Final Report and Evaluation of the Florida Pentastar Project,* Florida Department of Health and Rehabilitative Services, 1984.

PUBLIC-USE ACCESS TO DATA: Not available.

South Carolina Community Long-Term Care

SUMMARY: This demonstration, conducted from 1980 to 1984, tested the effects of case management and home health services on a large sample of nursing home applicants. Subjects were followed for one year.

COST: Not available.

TIME FRAME: Demonstration period, 1980–84.

TREATMENTS TESTED: Case management and other services not normally covered by Medicaid (including adult day health care, home-delivered meals, medical social services, personal care, and therapies). The control group received nothing from the demonstration, but could seek out existing long-term care services.

OUTCOMES OF INTEREST: (1) Nursing home use; (2) Hospital use; (3) Health care costs; and (4) Measures of client functioning.

SAMPLE SIZE: Treatments, 802; controls, 789.

TARGET POPULATION: Nursing home applicants certified as eligible for Medicaid-sponsored nursing home care.

NUMBER OF TREATMENT GROUPS: Two (with one control group).

NUMBER AND LOCATION OF SITES: Three—Spartanburg, Cherokee, and Union counties.

RESEARCH COMPONENTS:
- Process analysis: Internal peer review, development of care planning guidelines, and external review by representatives from nursing homes and home health agencies.
- Impact analysis: Conducted using multivariate techniques.
- Benefit–cost analysis: Costs were analyzed, but a formal benefit–cost analysis was not conducted.

MAJOR FINDINGS:
1. South Carolina was quite effective at targeting at-risk individuals, as shown by the high percentage of control group members entering nursing homes (58.6 percent) and hospitals (38.8 percent) during the observation year.
2. A significantly smaller percentage of treatment group members entered nursing homes than did control group members (–16.1 percent) and they spent significantly fewer days there (on average, 40 fewer days for the treatment group). The impact on hospital use was in the same direction but was not significant (–5.5 percent and two fewer days for the treatment group).
3. Average annual per capita costs were higher for the treatment group. On average, combined services cost $744 (1988 dollars) more for the treatment group (inpatient services cost $1,175 less; outpatient services cost $413 more; and treatment services cost $1,506 more).
4. There were no significant impacts on client physical or mental functioning.

TIME TRENDS IN FINDINGS: None.

DESIGN ISSUES: Because randomization took place prior to screening for eligibility and appropriateness of treatment services, many of those assigned to the treatment group were never real candidates to use the services. Only 42 percent of the treatment group used treatment services.

REPLICABILITY: Replicable.

GENERALIZABILITY: Designed to generalize to the entire state of South Carolina.

FUNDING SOURCE: South Carolina Department of Social Services with federal matching grants.

TREATMENT ADMINISTRATOR: South Carolina Department of Social Services. Key personnel: Tom Brown, project director; and Geraldine Nantz, site supervisor.

EVALUATOR: Berkeley Planning Associates. Key personnel: John Kapitman, Brandeis University.

ENABLING LEGISLATION: None.

INFORMATION SOURCES: Information for this summary came from William G. Weissert, Cynthia Matthews Cready, and James E. Pawelak, "The Past and Future of Home- and Community-Based Long-Term Care," *Millbank Quarterly* 66(1988): 309–88; source document cited is T. E. Brown Jr., D. K. Blackman, R. M. Learner, M. B. Witherspoon, and L. Saber, *South Carolina Long-Term Care Project: Report of Findings,* South Carolina State Health and Human Services Finance Commission, 1985.

PUBLIC-USE ACCESS TO DATA: Not available.

National Long-Term Care (Channeling) Demonstration

SUMMARY: This demonstration, conducted from 1982 to 1985, tested the effects of two case management models on a large sample of older people with severe impairments. Subjects were followed for up to 18 months.

COST: Evaluation costs, approximately $13 million.

TIME FRAME: Demonstration period, February 1982–March 1985; data collected, same period; final report, 1986.

TREATMENTS TESTED: Two models of comprehensive case management were tested. The basic case management model included screening, assessment, case planning, service initiation, monitoring, and reassessment. A limited amount of funding was provided to fill gaps and purchase community services. The financial control model added several elements to the basic model, including expanded service coverage, a funds pool, and case manager authorization power in order to provide more financial support for community services. There were expenditure limits and cost sharing by clients. The control group participants received existing community services without the channeling case management.

OUTCOMES OF INTEREST: (1) Use of community care services; (2) Nursing home admissions; (3) Hospitalizations; (4) Client quality of life; and (5) Health care costs.

SAMPLE SIZE: Total, 6,326. For basic model sites: Treatments, 1,779; controls, 1,345. For financial control model sites: Treatments, 1,923; controls, 1,279.

TARGET POPULATION: Older people (minimum age, 65) with severe impairments who require long-term care and are considered at high risk for institutionalization. Several specific criteria relating to disability and unmet needs were applied. Participants resided in the community or were soon to be discharged from a nursing home. Participants needed to be covered by Medicare Part A to be eligible for the financial control model sites.

NUMBER OF TREATMENT GROUPS: Four (with two control groups).

NUMBER AND LOCATION OF SITES: The basic model operated in five sites: Eastern Kentucky; Southern Maine; Baltimore, Maryland; Middlesex County, New Jersey; and Houston, Texas. The financial control model operated in five sites: Miami, Florida; Greater Lynn, Massachusetts; Rensselaer County, New York; Cleveland, Ohio; and Philadelphia, Pennsylvania.

RESEARCH COMPONENTS:
  ▪ Process analysis: All procedures were reviewed and pretested. Efforts were made to minimize the control group's contact with channeling services. Interviews were conducted with staff to measure success of implementation.
  ▪ Impact analysis: Conducted using multiple regression.
  ▪ Benefit–cost analysis: Conducted.

MAJOR FINDINGS:
1. The increased costs of case management and expanded community services were not offset by reduced nursing home costs. During the evaluation period, total costs under the basic model increased by 6 percent over the control group costs. Total costs under the financial control model increased by 18 percent over control group costs.
2. Nursing home use was lower among the treatment group than among the control group under both models, but the difference was small and not statistically significant.
3. Channeling did not affect longevity, hospital use, or use of physicians and other medical services. It also had no effect on measures of client functioning.
4. Channeling significantly reduced the unmet needs for care reported by clients. Treatment group clients (both models) also reported an increase in confidence and satisfaction with life. Informal caregivers of treatment group clients also reported significantly higher satisfaction with arrangements for care.

TIME TRENDS IN FINDINGS: None reported.

DESIGN ISSUES:
1. Caseload buildup was slower than planned, and it took roughly one year for all projects to reach their planned caseload levels.

2. The baseline interviews for treatment and control participants were conducted by separate staff. Whereas this served to insulate the control group members from the channeling project, there was some noncomparability of baseline data. Some variables were replaced with screening interview data or were dropped.

3. Proxy respondents were used for 40–45 percent of the follow-up interviews owing to the frailty of some sample members. When treatment and control groups are compared, the percentages of proxy respondents are quite similar. Because of this, it is less likely that there was a major distortion of impacts. However, there was an indication that the use of proxies artificially inflated the impact on client satisfaction with life, even after controlling for disability and cognitive impairment. Proxy respondents may have indicated their own satisfaction rather than that of the sample members.

4. Existing services in some areas and for some clients provided comprehensive case management similar to that offered by the channeling treatments. It is estimated that 10–20 percent of the control group members received comprehensive case management.

REPLICABILITY: Replicable.

GENERALIZABILITY: Designed to generalize to the entire nation with the following caveats: (1) Site selection was not a probability sample. Sites were selected based on interest, commitment, capacity to perform the case management functions, and the quality of their proposals; and (2) Channeling clients were younger, slightly less disabled, and more likely to be married than a national sample of nursing home residents. Also, a higher proportion of the channeling sample was nonwhite (27 percent versus 7 percent nationally).

FUNDING SOURCE: Funding was through a consortium at the U.S. Department of Health and Human Services (HHS) including the Health Care Financing Administration (HCFA), Office of the Assistant Secretary for Planning and Evaluation (ASPE), and the Administration on Aging (AOA). Key personnel: Mary Harahan and Robert Clark.

TREATMENT ADMINISTRATOR: HHS had overall responsibility for the demonstration. Within the department, the three agencies above were responsible for design and conduct of the demonstration. Key personnel: Linda Hamm for HCFA; Mary F. Harahan for ASPE, and Barbara Fallon for AOA. Temple University Institute on Aging provided technical assistance (key personnel: Barbara Schneider). Frontline administration was handled by the agencies at the state level.

EVALUATOR: Mathematica Policy Research. Key personnel: Peter Kemper, Randall Brown, principal investigators; and George Carcagno.

ENABLING LEGISLATION: None.

INFORMATION SOURCES: Peter Kemper, Randall S. Brown, George J. Carcagno, Robert A. Applebaum, Jon B. Christianson, Walter Corson, Shari Miller Dunstan, Thomas Grannemann, Margaret Harrigan, Nancy Holden, Barbara R. Phillips, Jennifer Schore, Craig Thornton, Judith Wooldridge and Felicity Skidmore, *The Evaluation of the National Long-Term Care Demonstration: Final Report,* Mathematica Policy Research, 1986. Also, the April 1988 issue of *Health Services Research* is devoted to this demonstration.

PUBLIC-USE ACCESS TO DATA: Available through National Technical Information Service, Springfield, Virginia.

Neighborhood Team Experiment

SUMMARY: This experiment, conducted from 1983 to 1985, tested the effects of a neighborhood team model of case management on a medium-sized sample of elderly and chronically ill patients. Subjects were followed for up to two years.

COST: Evaluators were unable to provide estimates of evaluation costs owing to substantial donated time and resources.

TIME FRAME: Demonstration period, April 1983–July 1985; data collected, same period.

TREATMENTS TESTED: This experiment compared the neighborhood team model of case management (treatment) with the centralized individual model (control), which was the status quo in Monroe County. In the team model, team case managers had smaller caseloads and were assigned specific geographic regions. They performed client assessments, case planning, some direct services, and reassessment. In the centralized individual model, case management functions were delegated to hospitals and certified home health agencies.

OUTCOMES OF INTEREST: (1) Health care usage and expenditures; (2) Participant satisfaction; and (3) Health status.

SAMPLE SIZE: Total, 476; treatments, 273; controls, 203.

TARGET POPULATION: Elderly and other chronically ill patients who required long-term care. DMS-1 scores (a measure of the level of disability) of 180 or higher were required for eligibility.

NUMBER OF TREATMENT GROUPS: Two (with one control group).

NUMBER AND LOCATION OF SITES: One—Rochester, New York.

RESEARCH COMPONENTS:

▪ Process analysis: Attrition (due to refusal to participate and mortality) was closely monitored. Patient characteristics and case histories were documented. Health care usage diaries were kept for each patient. The evaluators also paid close attention to the randomization process.
▪ Impact analysis: Comparison of means.
▪ Benefit–cost analysis: Not conducted.

MAJOR FINDINGS: "Old cases"—patients who were receiving services when the project began—and "new cases"—patients who entered the program after its initiation—were analyzed separately and in the aggregate.

1. Among old cases, the treatment group experienced both less hospital usage (27 percent less, or $6.04 less per patient per day) and less home care usage (28 percent less, or $12.08 less per day) and expenditures. These findings are significant at the .10 level.
2. Among new cases, the treatment group experienced less hospital usage (30 percent less, or $9.78 less per day). However, home care usage was greater for the treatment group (15 percent more, or $2.29 more per day). The latter finding was not statistically significant.
3. When old and new cases were aggregated, the average day cost was $62.27 for treatment cases and $72.08 for controls. Both hospital and home care estimated expenditures were lower for the treatment cases, but they used more nursing home care and slightly more ambulatory care. Overall, treatment cases averaged 14 percent lower ($9.81 lower) estimated costs than controls, significant at the .084 level.
4. There were no significant differences between groups on a measure of patient and caregiver satisfaction.
5. Patients with either a diagnosis of dementia or high initial assessment ratings on psychobehavioral problems showed the greatest reduction in use and estimated cost for the treatment group as opposed to controls (41 percent lower costs).

TIME TRENDS IN FINDINGS: Treatment group savings were not significant during the first six-month period, were greatest during the second six-month period (29 percent), and continued at roughly half that percentage for the remaining two six-month periods.

DESIGN ISSUES: The fraction of the sample assigned to treatment status changed during the final six months to increase the team caseload, but the assignment procedure remained random.

REPLICABILITY: Replicable.

GENERALIZABILITY: Designed to generalize to a population of frail, elderly patients needing long-term care. The sample had a median age of 76, half were Medicaid eligible, and they were slightly more impaired than the overall U.S. impaired noninstitutionalized population.

FUNDING SOURCES: The Robert Wood Johnson Foundation and U.S. Department of Health and Human Services, Health Care Financing Association.

TREATMENT ADMINISTRATOR: Monroe County Long-Term Care Program/ACCESS, Rochester, New York. Key personnel: Gerald Eggert, director.

EVALUATORS: Gerald M. Eggert, James G. Zimmer, W. Jackson Hall, Bruce Friedman, and Patricia Chiverton.

ENABLING LEGISLATION: None.

INFORMATION SOURCES: Gerald M. Eggert, James G. Zimmer, W. Jackson Hall, and Bruce Friedman, "Case Management: A Randomized Controlled Study Comparing a Neighborhood Team and a Centralized Individual Model," *Health Services Research* 26(1991): 471–507; James G. Zimmer, Gerald M. Eggert, and Patricia Chiverton, "Individual versus Team Case Management in Optimizing Community Care for Chronically Ill Patients with Dementia," *Journal of Aging and Health* 2(1990): 357–72.

PUBLIC-USE ACCESS TO DATA: Not available.

Team Approach to Outpatient Geriatric Evaluation Experiment

SUMMARY: This experiment, conducted from May 1983 to October 1985, tested the effects of a team approach to geriatric evaluation on a small sample of frail older persons. Subjects were followed for one year.

COST: Evaluators were unable to provide estimates of evaluation costs due to substantial donated time and resources.

TIME FRAME: Enrollment period, May 1983–October 1984; data collected for one year after enrollment.

TREATMENTS TESTED: An outpatient geriatric consultative service that included a team approach to evaluation. The team could include internists, psychiatrists, nurses, social workers, and nutritionists. Aside from evaluation, the team also provided counseling and family support services. The control group received a geriatric evaluation by a qualified internist from the community who was paid his or her usual and customary fee.

OUTCOMES OF INTEREST: (1) Costs of medical care and social services; (2) General health and functioning; (3) Hospitalizations and nursing home placements; and (4) Participant satisfaction.

SAMPLE SIZE: Total, 117; treatments, 58; controls, 59.

TARGET POPULATION: The program targeted noninstitutionalized frail older people age 65 or older who had changing medical and social needs.

NUMBER OF TREATMENT GROUPS: Two (with one control group).

NUMBER AND LOCATION OF SITES: One—Monroe County (Rochester), New York.

RESEARCH COMPONENTS:
- Process analysis: Health care diaries and intake interviews were used to monitor service delivery and participant characteristics.
- Impact analysis: Comparison of adjusted means.
- Benefit–cost analysis: Cost-effectiveness figures are computed.

MAJOR FINDINGS:
1. At eight months, there was an indication that the treatment group experienced less deterioration in general health and functioning than the control group, although the finding was not statistically significant. Total scores on the functional scales of the Patient Assessment Forms (PAF) increased by 26.3 percent for control subjects and by 5.1 percent for treat-

ment subjects. An increase in PAF scores indicates a decline in functioning.

2. At eight months, usage diaries collected over a two-week period showed substantial savings in hospital costs for the treatment group compared with the control (average cost per subject: treatment, $4,297; control, $7,018), but an increase in nursing home costs (average cost per subject: treatment, $2,288; control, $1,756). The estimated savings in total costs for the treatment group over this two-week interval was 63 percent ($p = .06$). Over the full 12 months, total institutional costs for the treatment group were roughly 25 percent lower than those of the control group.

3. There were no significant treatment–control differences on measures of institutional placement or satisfaction with care.

TIME TRENDS IN FINDINGS: With time, control subjects spent progressively more days in the hospital, whereas treatment subjects experienced a decline in hospital days.

DESIGN ISSUES:

1. The control group received high-quality care from excellent general internists who were paid their customary fee. It was felt that the randomization process should not jeopardize vulnerable older people by leaving medical care for the control group to chance. Thus, findings may underestimate the benefits that might accrue if compared with usual medical practices (i.e., what would occur if patients chose general internists from those available, some of whom might provide less-than-excellent service at a lower price).

2. The usage levels were highly variable and very skewed. Fifteen percent of the clients accounted for 75 percent of the costs. One-half incurred costs averaging less than $5 daily, whereas 7 percent incurred costs averaging over $100 daily. This skewed distribution makes any treatment effects difficult to identify.

REPLICABILITY: Replicable.

GENERALIZABILITY: The sample was representative of the frail, older, noninstitutionalized population, but the small sample size and implementation issues discourage attempts at generalization.

FUNDING SOURCES: Robert Wood Johnson Foundation and National Institute on Aging.

TREATMENT ADMINISTRATOR: Geriatric Ambulatory Consultative Service of Monroe Community Hospital.

EVALUATORS: Mark Williams, University of North Carolina School of Medicine; T. Franklin Williams, James Zimmer, W. Jackson Hall, and Carol Podgorski.

ENABLING LEGISLATION: None.

INFORMATION SOURCE: Mark E. Williams, T. Franklin Williams, James G. Zimmer, W. Jackson Hall, and Carol A. Podgorski, "How Does the Team Approach to Outpatient Geriatric Evaluation Compare with Traditional Care? A Report of a Randomized Controlled Trial," *Journal of the American Geriatric Society* 35(1987): 1071–78.

PUBLIC-USE ACCESS TO DATA: Not available.

15

Nonelderly People with Disabilities

Training in Community Living

SUMMARY: This demonstration, conducted from 1972 to 1976, tested the effects of on-call care and case management by trained staff members on a small sample of adults with mental disabilities. Subjects were followed for up to three years.

COST: Unknown.

TIME FRAME: Demonstration period, 1972–75; data collected, 1972–76; final report, April 1980.

TREATMENTS TESTED:
1. Controls were treated in hospital as long as necessary, and referrals were made on release to community agencies. Outpatient follow-up was available.
2. Experimentals were seldom hospitalized initially and received 24-hour, on-call care from specially trained staff members focusing on coping skills (laundry, shopping, grooming, finding work, problem solving on the job, constructive use of leisure) over a 14-month period. Staff assertively sought out patients when they missed appointments or failed to show up for work, monitored use of medication, and counseled family members and employers.

OUTCOMES OF INTEREST: (1) Reductions in institutionalization; (2) Reductions in unemployment; and (3) Increases in earnings.

SAMPLE SIZE: Experimentals, 62; controls, 60.

TARGET POPULATION: Residents of Dane County, Wisconsin, age 18–62, voluntarily seeking admission to a mental hospital, with any diagnosis other than severe organic brain syndrome or primary alcoholism.

Note: After *The Digest* went into production, we discovered an article that described a number of social experiments among persons with mental illness of which we had no prior knowledge. To supplement this chapter, we refer the reader to the article: Susan D. Phillips. Barbara J. Burns, Elizabeth R. Edgar, Kim T. Mueser, Karen W. Linkins, Robert A. Rosenheck, Robert E. Drake, and Elizabeth D. McDonel Herr, "Moving Assertive Community Treatment into Standard Practice," *Psychiatric Services* 52(6): 771–79.

NUMBER OF TREATMENT GROUPS: Two (with one control group).

NUMBER AND LOCATION OF SITES: One—Madison, Wisconsin.

RESEARCH COMPONENTS:
▪ Process analysis: Not conducted. Researchers could not say to what extent the effects observed were primarily due to increased compliance with prescribed medications.
▪ Impact analysis: Comparison of means.
▪ Benefit–cost analysis: Formal social benefit–cost analysis conducted.

MAJOR FINDINGS:
1. Significant reduction in time spent in psychiatric institutions. Significant differences extending over the first 16 months.
2. No significant differences in time spent in penal or general medical institutions.
3. Significant increase (through 20 months) in time spent in unsupervised living situations.
4. Significant reduction (through 28 months) in time spent unemployed, mostly achieved through substantial increase in time spent in sheltered employment.
5. Significant increases (through end of observation period) in nonsheltered earned income.
6. Net social benefits of $399 per patient. (Valued costs exceeded valued benefits by $6,128 for controls, $5,729 for experimentals.) However, the reduction in transfer payments of $564 per patient is essentially treated as a social benefit, which is not customary.

TIME TRENDS IN FINDINGS: All differences except in nonsheltered earnings tended to erode after treatment ended.

DESIGN ISSUES: The main employment effect comes from increasing use of sheltered employment. Where sheltered employment opportunity is less available than in the treatment community, this result may not generalize. Also, the use of sheltered placements raises questions about (1) possible displacement of other people who might have found work in the sheltering agencies and (2) whether increased subsidies were needed by these sheltering agencies, which are not included as costs. If they were, the analysis did not include them.

REPLICABILITY: Requires specially trained, "assertive," around-the-clock staff.

GENERALIZABILITY: Investigators could not extrapolate the findings to larger or smaller communities, or to different labor-market conditions. See also comments on sheltered employment in "Design Issues."

FUNDING SOURCE: National Institute of Mental Health.

TREATMENT ADMINISTRATOR: Mendota Mental Health Institute. Key personnel: Leonard Stein and Mary Ann Test.

EVALUATORS: Mendota Mental Health Institute and Institute for Research on Poverty. Key personnel: Burton Weisbrod.

ENABLING LEGISLATION: None.

INFORMATION SOURCES: Leonard Stein, Mary Ann Test, and Burton Weisbrod, "Alternative to Mental Hospital Treatment," *Archives of General Psychiatry,* 37(April 1980): 392–412; Burton Weisbrod, *Benefit–Cost Analysis of a Controlled Experiment: Treating the Mentally Ill,* Institute for Research on Poverty Reprint 444, University of Wisconsin–Madison, 1981.

PUBLIC-USE ACCESS TO DATA: We have no information about a public-use file for this information.

Job Path

SUMMARY: This demonstration, conducted from 1978 to 1980, tested the effects of subsidized and supervised work assignments on a small sample of adults with mental retardation. Subjects were followed for 18 months.

COST: Not available.

TIME FRAME: Demonstration period, 1978–79; data collected through 1980; final report, 1983.

TREATMENTS TESTED: The experimental treatment placed subjects in supported work assignments, initially in the public sector, for 35 hours a week. They were paid a subsidized minimum wage while learning skills related to food service, clerical work, mailroom work, maintenance work, housekeeping, and messenger work. Supervisors were assisted by Job Path counselors. Expectations were gradually increased over time, with transfers to more demanding job sites, sometimes going from the public to the private sector. Counseling and supervision were structured to give subjects feedback on how well they were doing, and weekly group meetings for trainees provided mutual support. Controls were returned to the referral agencies from which they had come; six of the controls subsequently were allowed to enter the experimental treatment after the research intake was completed, which complicated the interpretation of some research findings.

OUTCOME OF INTEREST: Employment.

SAMPLE SIZE: Experimentals, 60; controls, 60.

TARGET POPULATION: Adults with mental retardation who did not hold unsubsidized employment (many of them worked in sheltered workshops).

NUMBER OF TREATMENT GROUPS: Two (with one control group).

NUMBER AND LOCATION OF SITES: One—New York City.

RESEARCH COMPONENTS:

Process analysis: Not conducted in the usual sense; this was more like a pilot program. The project report authors stated that extensive job development work had to be performed (2,020 telephone contacts, etc.) to prepare 71 training sites and 34 unsubsidized jobs. They also reported the subjective responses of experimental subjects to the changes in their lives resulting from working in nonsheltered employment.

Impact analysis: Conducted as a difference in means.

Benefit–cost analysis: Not conducted.

MAJOR FINDINGS: In general, the authors did not report whether differences were statistically significant.

1. Employment: Six months after intake, 44 percent (24 out of 54) of experimentals had full-time, unsubsidized jobs (usually this was their last Job Path job, and the employer had hired them without subsidy). Twenty percent (13 out of 54) of controls had full-time jobs without subsidies; another 24 percent of controls had part-time, unsubsidized jobs.

   Twelve months after intake, 61 percent of experimentals held full-time, unsubsidized positions, 24 percent of controls held such jobs, and another 12 percent had part-time jobs without subsidy.

   Fifteen months after intake, 61 percent of experimentals held unsubsidized jobs (hours unspecified), whereas 30 percent of controls did.

   Eighteen months after intake, 72 percent of experimentals and 42 percent of controls had unsubsidized employment, a statistically significant difference.
2. Wages: Fifteen months after intake, the average weekly earnings of employed experimentals was $146; of employed controls, $117.
3. Benefits: Most employed experimentals had private health and dental insurance, paid sick days and vacations, and workers' compensation coverage. Most employed controls did not. Sample sizes declined over time.

TIME TRENDS IN FINDINGS: Given above.

DESIGN ISSUES: The labor market deteriorated over the course of the experiment.

REPLICABILITY: Replicable, but pilot project staff were frequently more able or more enthusiastic than staff in regular projects.

GENERALIZABILITY: Not generalizable, because of small sample size and site. New York City is a more difficult environment for independent adults with mental retardation than some other areas; on the other hand, there is a larger variety of employers. However, see the Structured Training and Employment Transitional Services Demonstration and Transitional Employment Training Demonstration summaries (pages 379 and 381).

FUNDING SOURCE: A private foundation. Hillsman does not recall which one.

TREATMENT ADMINISTRATOR: Vera Institute of Justice. Key personnel: Arlene Silberman.

EVALUATOR: Vera Institute of Justice. Key personnel: Sally T. Hillsman and Janet Weinglass.

POLICY EFFECTS: Sally Hillsman has stated that this study's treatment and findings have helped change the nature of support services to individuals with developmental disabilities in New York and across the country.

INFORMATION SOURCE: Sally T. Hillsman, Janet Weinglass, and Arlene Silberman, "Fostering Independence in Developmentally Disabled Adults: Supported Work as a Rehabilitative Mechanism," paper presented at the annual meeting of the American Orthopsychiatric Association, Boston, April 1983.

PUBLIC-USE ACCESS TO DATA: We have no information about a public-use file for this demonstration.

Harbinger Mental Health Project

SUMMARY: This demonstration, conducted from 1979 to 1982, contrasted the effects of intensive community-based therapy on a small sample of mentally ill patients presenting for hospital admission. Subjects were followed for 66 months.

COST: Not available.

TIME FRAME: Demonstration period, 1979–82; data collected, same period.

TREATMENTS TESTED: Intensive community support, instead of hospitalization, during periods of crisis, and continued access to community treatment programs.

Control group members were admitted to hospitals and at discharge were provided with aftercare case management.

OUTCOMES OF INTEREST: (1) Hospitalizations; (2) Employment; and (3) Social functioning.

SAMPLE SIZE: Total, 121; experimentals, 59; controls, 62.

TARGET POPULATION: Clients who presented for admission to psychiatric hospital.

NUMBER OF TREATMENT GROUPS: Two (with one control group).

NUMBER AND LOCATION OF SITES: One—Grand Rapids, Kent County, Michigan.

RESEARCH COMPONENTS:
  Process analysis: Conducted.
  Impact analysis: Descriptive statistics.
  Benefit–cost analysis: Not conducted.

MAJOR FINDINGS:
1. At 30-month follow-up, compared with the control group, a significantly larger percentage of Harbinger clients lived alone, with family, and with friends: 85 percent versus 77 percent. A significantly larger percentage (23 percent) of control group clients than Harbinger clients were living in supervised care (15 percent).
2. Twenty-one percent of Harbinger clients were employed, compared with 7 percent of control group clients.
3. Harbinger clients scored higher on a self-rated scale of social functioning than controls (6.62 versus 5.45).

4. At 66-month follow-up, there was no significant difference between treatment and control groups on outcomes of interest.

TIME TRENDS IN FINDINGS: Differences in outcomes between treatment and control groups dissipated over time.

DESIGN ISSUES:

1. Treatment and control group clients came from among clients who approached the hospital for treatment. A smaller group, long-term residents of the state psychiatric hospital, were discharged to either the treatment group (*N* = 10) or usual aftercare (*N* = 11) on a nonrandom basis. This group was included in the impact analysis.
2. At 30-month follow-up, 12 percent of the treatment group could not be located for interview, compared with 41 percent of the control group. However, hospitalization data were available on all participants.

REPLICABILITY: Replicable.

GENERALIZABILITY: Given the small sample size, the commingling of randomly and nonrandomly assigned subjects, and the differential attrition rate, the general applicability of the findings is unclear.

FUNDING SOURCE: Michigan Department of Community Health. Key personnel: Thomas Plum.

TREATMENT ADMINISTRATOR: Harbinger, Inc., Grand Rapids, Michigan. Key personnel: Ted Masterton.

EVALUATORS: Carol Mowbray, School of Social Work, University of Michigan, and Mary Collins, School of Social Work, Boston University.

ENABLING LEGISLATION: None.

INFORMATION SOURCE: Carol Mowbray and Mary Collins, "Harbinger I: The Development and Evaluation of the First Pact Replication," *Admin-istration and Policy in Mental Health* 25(1997, 2): 105–23.

PUBLIC-USE ACCESS TO DATA: Available on request. Contact Carol Mowbray, The University of Michigan, School of Social Work, 1080 South University, Ann Arbor, MI 48109-1106.

Structured Training and Employment Transitional Services (STETS) Demonstration

SUMMARY: This demonstration, conducted from 1981 to 1984, tested the effects of training, work placement, and follow-up services on a medium-sized sample of young adults with low IQs. Subjects were followed for up to three years.

COST: $2.5 million for service delivery; research cost, $1.2 million.

TIME FRAME: Demonstration period, November 1981–June 1984; data collected through October 1984; final report, 1985.

TREATMENTS TESTED: Experimentals received a three-phase treatment of up to 18 months. Phase 1 consisted of initial training and support services in a low-stress work environment, with paid employment of up to 500 hours. Phase 2 was a period of on-the-job training (subsidized or unsubsidized) in local firms and agencies, emphasizing job performance and work stress resembling the demands faced by nondisabled workers in the same types of jobs. Phase 2 jobs were intended as potentially permanent jobs in which participants would continue after the withdrawal of program support. Phase 3 consisted of up to six months of follow-up services to workers who had made the transition into unsubsidized, competitive employment. Controls received no STETS services.

OUTCOMES OF INTEREST: (1) Employment; (2) Earnings; (3) Transfer recipiency; and (4) Payments.

SAMPLE SIZE: Experimentals, 236; controls, 231.

TARGET POPULATION: Young adults age 18–24 with IQ scores between 40 and 80, limited prior work experience, and no severe secondary handicaps.

NUMBER OF TREATMENT GROUPS: Two (with one control group).

NUMBER AND LOCATION OF SITES: Five— Cincinnati, Ohio; Los Angeles, California; New York City; St. Paul, Minnesota; and Tucson, Arizona.

RESEARCH COMPONENTS:
- Process analysis: Conducted. The project report authors believed the evidence suggests that ongoing programs would have an impact greater than that found in the full sample; the employment behavior of experimentals and controls was found to differ most, and the administrative cost per participant was lowest, during the "steady-state period," defined as the five months during which client intake reached its maximum monthly rate and during which operations were relatively smooth.
- Impact analysis: Conducted with ordinary least squares (OLS). Probit and tobit were also used where appropriate and did not yield substantively different results.
- Benefit–cost analysis: Conducted from participant, taxpayer, and social perspectives.

MAJOR FINDINGS: See table. Subgroup analysis found that the greater the retardation of the subject (the lower the IQ), the greater the impact, with essentially no impact on those with slight retardation.

Major Findings

	Month 6	Month 15	Month 22
Employment in regular (unsubsidized) job:			
Experimentals (%)	11.8	26.2*	31.0*
Controls (%)	10.7	16.8	19.1
Average weekly earnings from regular job (includes zeros):			
Experimentals ($)	11.81	26.90*	36.36*
Controls ($)	9.81	16.31	20.55
Average weekly earnings from any job (includes zeros):			
Experimentals ($)	52.39*	37.91*	40.79*
Controls ($)	25.93	26.48	28.41
Percentage in any training (including STETS):			
Experimentals	61.7*	20.6*	16.6*
Controls	40.6	28.4	29.1
Percentage in any schooling:			
Experimentals	7.5*	6.2	8.0
Controls	15.7	10.1	11.4
Percentage receiving any cash transfers (most commonly SSI, SSDI):			
Experimentals	31.7*	44.5*	49.6
Controls	43.1	51.5	52.0
Average monthly income from transfers (includes zeros):			
Experimentals ($)	80.23	114.78	126.53
Controls ($)	99.98	138.72	136.08
Average weekly personal income (including earnings, transfers, and other regular sources):			
Experimentals ($)	71.72*	67.22	71.59
Controls ($)	50.94	59.67	62.39

* Experimental/control difference is statistically significant at the 5 percent level.

From a social perspective, total benefits were predicted to outweigh the costs. The taxpayer investment would be repaid within four and one-half years in lower outlays; from the social perspective, the investment would pay for itself after two and one-half years.

TIME TRENDS IN FINDINGS: Shown in table.

DESIGN ISSUES: None apparent.

REPLICABILITY: Replicable.

GENERALIZABILITY: The study findings "are based on only five judgmentally selected urban sites, whose programs were specially designed and implemented for this demonstration. We cannot be certain whether other program operators in other sites who operate ongoing programs under different social, political, and economic conditions would have similar experiences. . . . It is also problematic whether similar programs could be efficiently and effectively operated in rural areas or even in more dispersed labor markets." Findings may be compared with the previous Job Path and the subsequent Transitional Employment Training Demonstration (TETD) experiments (pages 376 and 381).

The subgroup analysis finding (that the greater the retardation of the subject, the greater the impact) is the opposite of the finding in the TETD. Thornton has explained this as a difference in the sample: IQs in STETS ranged from about 40 to about 80, whereas IQs in TETD were, at worst, too low to test and, at best, somewhat over 70. He noted that higher-IQ individuals who get into this type of program tend to have severe secondary problems inhibiting employment, whereas those with severe retardation are probably unemployable. He contended the intervention is most likely to succeed with those between the extremes.

FUNDING SOURCE: U.S. Department of Labor, Employment and Training Administration.

TREATMENT ADMINISTRATOR: Manpower Demonstration Research Corporation. Key personnel: Judith M. Gueron.

EVALUATOR: Mathematica Policy Research. Key personnel: Stuart Kerachsky and Craig Thornton.

INFORMATION SOURCE: Stuart Kerachsky and Craig Thornton, "Findings from the STETS Transitional Employment Demonstration," *Exceptional Children* 6(April 1987): 515–21.

PUBLIC-USE ACCESS TO DATA: Public-use file does not exist.

Transitional Employment Training Demonstration (TETD)

SUMMARY: This demonstration, conducted from 1985 to 1988, tested the effects of job placement, on-the-job training, and follow-up services on a medium-sized sample of adults with mental retardation. Subjects were followed for up to three years.

COST: Research only, $1,271,307.

TIME FRAME: Demonstration period, June 1985–June 1987; data collected through December 1988; final report, July 1989.

TREATMENTS TESTED:

1. Experimentals were placed in unsubsidized, potentially permanent jobs; they were provided specialized on-the-job training that was phased out over time; and they received postplacement support and follow-up as necessary. These "core services" were to be provided within one year of intake into the experiment; subsequent services were to be arranged as necessary but had to be funded from a source other than the demonstration.

2. Controls received none of these services but were free to seek other services in the community.

One goal of the experiment was to test various approaches to service delivery. Providers were competitively selected to represent different methods and philosophies of service delivery.

OUTCOMES OF INTEREST: (1) Employment; (2) Earnings; (3) Wage rates; and (4) SSI payments.

SAMPLE SIZE: Experimentals, 375; controls, 370.

TARGET POPULATION: SSI recipients with mental retardation. Participants had to apply to enter the experiment, and had to be between 18 and 40 years old. The average IQ score was 57. Prior to random assignment, intake workers excluded people who had severe emotional problems or who would otherwise not benefit from the treatment.

NUMBER OF TREATMENT GROUPS: Two (with one control group).

NUMBER AND LOCATION OF SITES: Eleven—Dover, Delaware; Harrisburg, Lancaster, Philadelphia, and York, Pennsylvania (Lancaster and York served by the same agency); Monmouth County, New Jersey; Chicago, Illinois; Boston, Massachusetts; Los Angeles, California; Milwaukee, Wisconsin; Portland, Oregon; and Chippewa, Dunn, Eau Claire, and Pepin Counties, Wisconsin (all four counties served by a common agency).

RESEARCH COMPONENTS:
  Process analysis: Conducted. It showed that the treatment was substantially implemented as planned and (among other things) that transportation barriers were often as serious or more serious than the lack of job skills.
  Impact analysis: Conducted with raw means and ordinary least squares (OLS).
  Benefit–cost analysis: Conducted.

MAJOR FINDINGS:
1. Two-thirds of experimentals were placed on jobs. One half of those placed (one-third of experimentals) were "successfully stabilized" on a potentially permanent job. These results were consistent with the initial expectations of the program designers.
2. By the third year after enrollment, 45 percent of experimentals were in unsubsidized jobs, compared with 30 percent of controls. (Experimentals spent 32 percent less time than controls in sheltered workshops.)

3. Estimated treatment effects on earnings over three years ("amount of change" represents the increase over the raw mean of the controls):

Year	Impact (%)	Amount of change ($)
1	66.5	108
2	90.9	96
3	74.2	63

4. Effects on SSI payments were small, on the order of $240, or 2 percent, over three years. Earnings increased but generally remained below the income disregards in SSI regulations.
5. Earnings impacts varied considerably across sites. The New Jersey project raised earnings by $2,000 a year over three years; it tried to place experimentals in light manufacturing and assembly jobs. Projects in Portland and Los Angeles were exceptions to the general rule of treatment impacts declining over time.
6. Treatment impacts rose with IQ scores. People with IQs over 70 had an earnings gain of over 200 percent, whereas those with IQs under 40 had a gain that was not statistically significant.
7. Average treatment costs per person enrolled were $5,600.
8. The treatment raised the net income of experimentals, but SSI savings did not offset the costs from an SSI-budget perspective. From a government-budget perspective, the costs and benefits were about equal, because the program costs were offset by reductions in the use of sheltered (and subsidized) workshops. Targeting services to currently sheltered workers would mean that the program would have a neutral effect on budgets. From a social perspective, the benefits exceeded the costs.

TIME TRENDS IN FINDINGS: Note the impact reductions in item 3 under "Major Findings"; most projects showed impacts declining over time.

DESIGN ISSUES:

1. The training organizations were competitively selected from 80 providers who applied. These agencies were chosen to reflect different treatment approaches; generally, the less rigid treatment approaches appeared to have the most success. The findings are from a mix of successful and unsuccessful programs, all conducted by the agencies that were judged to offer the best versions of alternative approaches; findings from a mix of agencies offering the same, relatively successful, approach, but with different degrees of competence, might not be the same.

2. In determining benefits and costs, whether the alternative was sheltered employment or no employment turned out to be important. Budgetary savings were possible if the alternative was sheltered employment but otherwise did not occur.

REPLICABILITY: The eight treatment providers had different methods and philosophies, each of which could be replicated.

GENERALIZABILITY: The experiment represents a reasonably large-scale national test; the only region excluded was the South. Those enrolled in the experiment represent about 5 percent of those who were sent initial invitation letters; two-thirds of those responding were screened out at intake. Enrollees therefore do not represent the population of SSI recipients with retardation but the part that volunteered for these services and were thought to have some probability of benefiting from them. In addition, transitional employment (and some of the agencies) were unfamiliar; only the more adventuresome members of the population would have left the well-established, sheltered work sites. As agencies become more established, this would be less true. Findings from the experiment will not necessarily reflect the impacts of the treatment on a less adventuresome population.

FUNDING SOURCE: U.S. Department of Health and Human Services, Social Security Administration. Key personnel: Aaron Prero.

TREATMENT ADMINISTRATORS: Eight training organizations. Key personnel: Too many to list.

EVALUATOR: Mathematica Policy Research. Key personnel: Craig Thornton.

ENABLING LEGISLATION: Social Security Disability Amendments of 1980.

INFORMATION SOURCE: Craig Thornton and Paul T. Decker, *The Transitional Employment Training Demonstration: Analysis of Program Impacts,* Mathematica Policy Research, July 1989.

PUBLIC-USE ACCESS TO DATA: We have no information about a public-use file for this demonstration.

Project NetWork

SUMMARY: This demonstration, conducted from June 1992 to March 1995, tested the effectiveness of providing case- and referral-management services to a large sample of Social Security Disability Insurance (SSDI) recipients and disabled Supplemental Security Income (SSI) beneficiaries and applicants. Subjects were followed for two or three years. In a follow-up study earnings impacts were updated for six postenrollment years, and SSDI benefit receipt information was updated for seven postenrollment years for SSDI beneficiaries based on administrative records.

COST: Benefit–cost analysis indicates an operating cost on the order of $8 million. The research cost was $4.3 million.

TIME FRAME: Demonstration periods: Model 1, June 1992–June 1994; Model 2, January 1993–January 1995; Model 3, February 1993–February 1995 in New Hampshire and March 1993–March 1995 in Virginia; Model 4, January 1993–January 1995; data collected, January 1990–December 1997 (administrative records update in 2002); final report, March 1999.

TREATMENTS TESTED: Treatment group members received case- or referral-management services sponsored by the Social Security Administration (SSA). These services included assessing the individual, developing an employment plan, and identifying and arranging for services necessary for achieving the individual's employment plan. These services were provided to treatment group members by one of four different models, each of which operated for 24 months.

Control group members were eligible for all non-NetWork services that were already available to them. Some of these services were quite similar to Project NetWork services.

Members of both treatment and control groups were also offered waivers of the SSDI and SSI rules that were viewed as disincentives to work.

In Model 1, case management services were provided by SSA staff.

In Model 2, case management services were provided by private rehabilitation organizations, which operated under contract to SSA.

In Model 3, case management services were provided in SSA offices by state vocational rehabilitation agencies, which operated under contract to SSA.

Model 4 featured the provision of referral management services by SSA staff. The referral managers found services for clients that were already being provided in the community, including case management services. Each model was tested in 2 sites.

OUTCOMES OF INTEREST: (1) Employment; (2) Earnings; (3) SSI and SSDI receipts; and (4) Health and well-being.

SAMPLE SIZE: Total, 8,248; treatments, 4,160; controls, 4,088. Total Model 1, 1,899; treatments, 956; controls, 943. Total Model 2, 2,112; treatments, 1,088; controls, 1,024. Total Model 3, 2,214; treatments, 1,087; controls, 1,127. Total Model 4, 2,023; treatments, 1,029; controls, 994.

TARGET POPULATION: Beneficiaries of SSDI and disabled applicants for and recipients of SSI. Participants were all volunteers and were eligible for Project NetWork regardless of their age or the nature of their disabilities.

NUMBER OF TREATMENT GROUPS: Five (with one control group).

NUMBER AND LOCATION OF SITES: Eight—Dallas and Fort Worth, Texas (Model 1); Phoenix, Arizona/Las Vegas, Nevada and Minneapolis, Minnesota (Model 2); New Hampshire and Richmond, Virginia (Model 3); and Tampa, Florida/Carrollwood, Florida and Spokane, Washington/Coeur d'Alene, Idaho (Model 4).

RESEARCH COMPONENTS:
- Process analysis: Conducted from interviews with demonstration staff, sampling of the case folders of participants, and from an automated client tracking system. The process study focused on operational issues at the different demonstration sites and on the similarities and the differences among the four models.
- Impact analysis: Conducted as a difference in regression-adjusted means.
- Benefit–cost analysis: Conducted from the perspectives of federal and state governments, recipients, and society.

MAJOR FINDINGS:
1. All four models were able to enroll large numbers of participants and to provide them with rehabilitation and employment services "on a substantial scale."
2. Treatment group members experienced a statistically significant 6 percentage point increase in the receipt of rehabilitation, employment, and training services.
3. Treatment group members experienced a statistically significant $220 (11 percent) increase in their annual earnings for the first two years of the experiment. For SSDI beneficiaries, earnings were subsequently followed up for six postenrollment years, and persisted throughout this longer follow-up period, with an annual average of $239 for the six-year period (2002 dollars). Treatment group members did not experience a statistically significant reduction in SSI or SSDI receipt during the follow-up period for the initial evaluation. For SSDI beneficiaries 84-month follow-up data also

did not indicate a statistically significant reduction in SSDI receipt.

4. The evaluation did not detect statistically significant improvements in the health or well-being of treatment group members relative to control group members.

5. Project NetWork increased the average number of months employed by a statistically significant 3 weeks (21 percent) during the first two follow-up years.

6. A nonexperimental comparison indicated that the referral model had an estimated impact on earnings statistically significantly smaller than impacts in the other three models.

7. When asked if they would participate in Project NetWork if they had to make the choice over again, 77 percent of treatment group members said they would.

8. Project NetWork generated a net cost to taxpayers of $2,019 per experimental.

TIME TREND IN FINDINGS: See items 2 and 3 under "Major Findings."

DESIGN ISSUES:

1. There were "substantial delays" between the assessment of individuals and the development of the employment plans for the individuals. This delay caused some members of the treatment group to lose interest in the demonstration.

2. Managers in the case management models stated that they wished they had more training in the development of individual employment plans for clients. Managers in the referral management model stated that they would have liked more training in the development of individual referral plans.

3. Both treatment and control group members were offered various waivers to facilitate implementation, and therefore the estimated net impacts are conditional on the presence of the waivers. A nonexperimental evaluation of "waiver effects" was inconclusive. However, the process analysis showed that the waivers were not implemented as planned, suggesting that "waiver effects" were probably negligible during the evaluation period.

REPLICABILITY: Replicable. See Wood et al. (1996) and Leiter et al. (1997).

GENERALIZABILITY: Generalizable. However, prior to the demonstration, the employment rates of people with disabilities were slightly higher than the national average in all sites. This may reflect a greater willingness by local employers to hire people with disabilities, which would bias the results upward.

FUNDING SOURCE: SSA.

TREATMENT ADMINISTRATOR: SSA. Key personnel: Leo McManus and Kalman Rupp.

EVALUATOR: Abt Associates Inc. Key personnel: Robert J. Kornfeld, Michelle L. Wood, Larry L. Orr, and David A. Long.

POLICY EFFECTS: Under the new "Ticket to Work" program, SSA has moved toward a system of payments to service providers contingent on participant outcomes. The limited success of the cost reimbursement–based Project NetWork case management demonstration contributed to the impetus for initiating this radical change.

INFORMATION SOURCES: Leo McManus, Kalman Rupp, and Stephen H. Bell, "Project NetWork: A Return-to Work Project for Social Security Disability Applicants and Beneficiaries." In *Partners for Independence: Models that Work, Conference Proceedings. The Fifth North American Regional Conference of Rehabilitation International*, 1993.

Kalman Rupp, Stephen H. Bell, and Leo McManus, "Design of the Project NetWork Return-to-Work Experiment for Persons with Disabilities." *Social Security Bulletin* 57(2, 1994).

Michelle Wood, Valerie Leiter, Debbie M. McInnis, and Stephen H. Bell, *Case Management at Work for SSA Disability Beneficiaries: Process and In-Program Results of the Project NetWork Return-to-Work Demonstration*, Abt Associates, September 1996.

Kalman Rupp, Michelle Wood, and Stephen H. Bell, "Targeting People with Severe Disabilities for Return-to-Work: The Project NetWork Demonstration Experience," *Journal of Vocational Rehabilitation* 12(1, 1996).

Valerie Leiter, Michelle L. Wood, and Stephen H. Bell, "Case Management at Work for SSA Disability Beneficiaries: Process Results of the Project NetWork Return-to-Work Demonstration," *Social Security Bulletin* 60(3, 1997).

Kalman Rupp, Dianne Driessen, Robert Kornfeld, and Michelle Wood, "The Development of the Project NetWork Administrative Records Data Base for Policy Evaluation," *Social Security Bulletin* 62(2, 1999).

Robert J. Kornfeld, Michelle L. Wood, Larry L. Orr, and David A. Long, *Impacts of the Project NetWork Demonstration: Final Report*, Abt Associates, March 1999.

Robert Kornfeld and Kalman Rupp, "The Net Effects of the Project NetWork Case Management Experiment on Participant Earnings, Benefit Receipt, and Other Outcomes," *Social Security Bulletin* 63(1, 2000).

Kalman Rupp and Stephen H. Bell, "Provider Incentives and Access in the Ticket to Work Program: Implications of Simulations Based on the Project NetWork Field Experiment." In *Paying for Results in Vocational Rehabilitation,* edited by Kalman Rupp and Stephen H. Bell, The Urban Institute, 2003.

PUBLIC-USE ACCESS TO DATA: Not available.

EXPERIMENTS ONGOING AT PUBLICATION

Consumer-Operated Services Program

STARTING YEAR/YEAR FINAL REPORT EXPECTED: 2001/2003.

INFORMATION SOURCE: Material posted on the web, http://www.cstprogram.org. This multisite study involving seven sites is funded by the Center for Mental Health Services of the Substance Abuse and Mental Health Services Administration. The principal investigator is Jean Campbell, University of Missouri-Columbia School of Medicine. Data analysis will be conducted by R.O.W. Sciences, Inc. in Rockville, Maryland.

EXPECTED COST: $20 million.

PRINCIPAL INTERVENTION: The consumer-operated services are vocational and housing programs, drop-in centers, peer counseling, case management services, crisis alternatives to hospitalization, advocacy training, and business ventures.

TARGET POPULATION: Individuals with mental illness.

OUTCOMES OF INTEREST: Housing, employment, and institutionalization.

Employment Intervention Demonstration Program

Employment Intervention Demonstration Program is a set of eight related demonstrations, testing the effects of combined vocational rehabilitation with clinical services and supports on mental health consumers, funded by the Center for Mental Health Services of the Substance Abuse and Mental Health Services Administration.

STARTING YEAR/YEAR FINAL REPORT EXPECTED: 1995/2003.

INFORMATION SOURCE: Judith A. Cook, "Employment Intervention Demonstration Program," Coordinating Center, University of Illinois at Chicago, Department of Psychiatry.

TARGET POPULATION: Mental health consumers.

OUTCOMES OF INTEREST: Finding and retaining employment.

Principal investigators are as follows: Judith Cook (Coordinating Center), Michael Shafer (Arizona), Kim Mueser (Connecticut), Bill McFarlane (Maine), Anthony Lehman (Maryland), Cathaleene Marcias (Massachusetts), Laura Blankertz (Pennsylvania), Neil Meisler (South Carolina), Marcia Toprac (Texas).

Arizona

PRINCIPAL INTERVENTIONS: Full array of case management and supported services from an integrated treatment team (integrated employment program), and traditional referral and purchase of service arrangements.

Connecticut

PRINCIPAL INTERVENTIONS: Individual placement and support, transitional employment, and standard services.

Maine

PRINCIPAL INTERVENTIONS: Family-aided assertive community treatment and participation of potential employers—the Mental Health Employers Consortium.

Maryland

PRINCIPAL INTERVENTIONS: Individual placement and support, and transitional and supported employment services.

Massachusetts

PRINCIPAL INTERVENTIONS: Assertive community treatment and clubhouse program—a planned community of staff and consumers who work together on a daily basis.

Pennsylvania

PRINCIPAL INTERVENTIONS: Long-term employment training and support, and nonvocational peer support.

South Carolina

PRINCIPAL INTERVENTIONS: Assertive community treatment, individual placement and support, and transitional supported employment services.

Texas

PRINCIPAL INTERVENTIONS: Employment Assistance through Reciprocity in Natural Supports and standard supported employment services.

State Partnership Initiatives

State Partnership Initiatives is a set of four related demonstrations, testing the effects of benefits counseling and other work support services on certain populations of Supplemental Security Income (SSI) and Social Security Disability Income (SSDI) recipients.

STARTING YEAR/YEAR FINAL REPORT EXPECTED: 1998/2003.

INFORMATION SOURCE: Craig Thornton, Roberto Agodini, and Vinita Jethwani, "Design for Evaluating the Net Outcomes for the State Partnership Initiative," Mathematica Policy Research, October 2000.

Principal investigators are as follows: Deb Russell (Illinois), JoAnne Malloy (New Hampshire), Valerie Melburg (New York), Dan O'Brien (Oklahoma).

Illinois

PRINCIPAL INTERVENTIONS: Benefits counseling, service coordination assistance to promote transition from school to adult activities.

TARGET POPULATION: High school students who receive SSI or SSDI benefits and receive services from the Illinois Office of Rehabilitation Services.

OUTCOMES OF INTEREST: Use of SSA work incentives, employment, earnings, SSI/SSDI benefits, total income, and Medicaid expenditures.

New Hampshire

PRINCIPAL INTERVENTIONS: Benefits counseling, integrating employment services using one-stop centers, and employment assistance and support.

TARGET POPULATION: SSI/SSDI beneficiaries with a diagnosis of severe mental illness or physical developmental disability.

OUTCOMES OF INTEREST: Receipt of SSI or SSDI benefits, benefit amounts, employment, hours worked, earnings, duration of employment, and health insurance coverage.

New York

PRINCIPAL INTERVENTIONS: The intervention includes the following components: (1) benefits counseling, (2) an employment support team that assesses service needs and then helps to arrange and coordinate those services, and (3) special waivers to the SSI program that will enable participants to participate in employment and keep more of their earnings without risking their eligibility.

TARGET POPULATION: SSI beneficiaries with mental illness.

OUTCOMES OF INTEREST: Receipt of SSI or SSDI benefits, benefit amounts, employment, earnings, and duration of employment.

Oklahoma

PRINCIPAL INTERVENTIONS: Provision of vouchers giving participants choices among alternative employment support service providers. Supports include benefits counseling.

TARGET POPULATION: SSI beneficiaries with mental illness.

OUTCOMES OF INTEREST: Receipt of SSI or SSDI benefits, benefit amounts, employment, earnings, and health insurance coverage.

16

Multiple Groups

National Supported Work Demonstration (NSWD)

SUMMARY: This demonstration, conducted from 1975 to 1980, tested the effects of supported work experience on a large sample of Aid to Families with Dependent Children (AFDC) recipients, ex-offenders, substance abusers, and high school dropouts. Subjects were followed for two years.

COST: $82.4 million administration (but this includes $10.6 million in sales of goods and services produced); research, $11.1 million.

TIME FRAME: Demonstration period, March 1975–December 1978; data collected, April 1975–mid-1980; final report, 1981.

TREATMENTS TESTED: Experimentals were offered employment in a structured work experience program involving peer group support, a graduated increase in work standards, and close sympathetic supervision, for 12 to 18 months. Local agencies contracted with Manpower Demonstration Research Corporation (MDRC) to employ the experimentals in a broad range of activities, with pay starting at the minimum wage (or slightly higher, depending on local market conditions), and bonuses and merit increases for workers who met increasing work standards. Agencies maintained a high ratio of supervisors to participants (1:8 to 1:12), and implemented different on-site methods for crew interaction and shared responsibility. Typical work activities were construction, building maintenance, and child day care. Controls received no treatment.

OUTCOMES OF INTEREST: (1) Increases in post-treatment earnings; (2) Reductions in criminal activity; (3) Reductions in transfer payments; (4) Reductions in drug abuse.

SAMPLE SIZE: Experimentals, 3,214; controls, 3,402.

TARGET POPULATION: (1) Long-term recipients of AFDC (30 of last 36 months, no children under age six); (2) Ex-addicts following drug rehabilitation treatment (within past six months); (3) Ex-offenders, age 18 or over, incarcerated within past six months; (4) Young school dropouts, age 17–20, not in school past six months, at least 50 percent having delinquent or criminal records.

NUMBER OF TREATMENT GROUPS: Two (with one control group).

NUMBER AND LOCATION OF SITES: Twelve— Atlanta, Georgia; Chicago, Illinois; Hartford, Connecticut; Jersey City and Newark, New Jersey; New York City; Oakland and San Francisco, California; Philadelphia, Pennsylvania; and three sites in Wisconsin.

RESEARCH COMPONENTS:
- Process analysis: Conducted.
- Impact analysis: Comparison of means; regressions performed in earlier work produced similar results.
- Benefit–cost analysis: Conducted from taxpayer, subject, and social perspectives. Results very sensitive to assumptions about the social costs of criminal activity, somewhat sensitive to extrapolation of earnings effects.

MAJOR FINDINGS:
1. Major positive effect on earnings of AFDC-recipient group.
2. Minor increase in earnings of ex-addicts, and major reduction in criminal activity.
3. No discernible effects on young dropouts.
4. No clear effects on ex-offenders.
5. Benefits exceeded costs for AFDC recipient and ex-addict groups by $8,000 and $4,000 per person, respectively. Costs exceeded benefits for young dropouts. For ex-offenders, the bulk of findings show costs substantially exceeding benefits (experimentals were arrested more frequently), but a small-sample, three-month follow-up shows the reverse tendency.

TIME TRENDS IN FINDINGS: Earnings differences showed little decay over time among AFDC recipients; criminal activity differences fell over time among ex-addicts.

DESIGN ISSUES:
1. Displacement effects could occur, as the agencies competed for local government contracts; they had to set up small businesses and win service contracts that other businesses might have obtained.
2. Both controls and experimentals underreported arrests. A research finding that underreporting seemed to be of the same magnitude between controls and experimentals is critical to results.

REPLICABILITY: Treatment seems to require development of entrepreneurial local project management.

GENERALIZABILITY: The large number of sites and subjects adds power to the findings. However, site and contractor self-selection are certainly present.

FUNDING SOURCES: U.S. Department of Labor (DOL), Employment and Training Administration; U.S. Department of Justice, Law Enforcement Assistance Administration; U.S. Department of Health and Human Services (HHS), National Institute on Drug Abuse (NIDA); U.S. Department of Housing and Urban Development, Office of Policy Development and Research; U.S. Department of Commerce, Economic Development Administration; and the Ford Foundation. Key personnel: Howard Rosen and Fritz Kramer for DOL, Mike Barth and Bill Barnes for HHS, Stan Breznoff for Ford Foundation, and Deborah Hastings Black for NIDA.

TREATMENT ADMINISTRATOR: MDRC. Key personnel: Judith M. Gueron.

EVALUATORS: Mathematica Policy Research and Institute for Research on Poverty, University of Wisconsin–Madison. Key personnel: Peter

Kemper, David A. Long, and Craig Thornton for Mathematica, and Robinson G. Hollister Jr. for Wisconsin.

ENABLING LEGISLATION: AFDC sample required waivers to Social Security Act.

INFORMATION SOURCES: *Summary and Findings of the National Supported Work Demonstration,* MDRC, 1980; Peter Kemper, David A. Long, and Craig Thornton, *The Supported Work Evaluation: Final Benefit–Cost Analysis,* MDRC, 1981.

PUBLIC-USE ACCESS TO DATA: Public-use access file exists; contact MDRC.

AFDC Homemaker–Home Health Aide Demonstrations

SUMMARY: This demonstration, conducted from 1983 to 1986, tested the effects of having Aid to Families with Dependent Children (AFDC) clients work as aides in the homes of the elderly/impaired on large samples of both the elderly/impaired and AFDC recipients. Subjects were followed for two years.

COST: Research only, $8 million.

TIME FRAME: Demonstration period, January 1983–June 1986; data collected, same period; final report, 1987.

TREATMENTS TESTED: Experimental elderly/impaired subjects (clients) could receive up to 100 hours per month of homemaker and home health aide services as needed for the duration of the demonstration. These services were free if subjects' incomes were less than two times the AFDC standard of need in their state; people with incomes above that level were charged on a sliding scale.

Control elderly/impaired subjects could not receive these services.

Experimental AFDC subjects (trainees) received a four- to eight-week training course to become a homemaker–home health aide, followed by a year of subsidized employment. Wages averaged $3.84 per hour, and hours averaged 75 per month.

Control AFDC subjects did not receive this training, nor did they receive subsidized employment.

OUTCOMES OF INTEREST:
For clients: (1) Changes in other informal or paid in-home care; (2) Changes in survival; (3) Changes in hospital and nursing home usage; (4) Changes in Medicare and Medicaid reimbursements; and (5) Changes in health outcomes. For trainees: (1) Employment; (2) Earnings; and (3) AFDC and food stamp payments and receipt.

SAMPLE SIZE: Elderly/impaired: Experimentals, roughly 9,500; controls, roughly 9,500. AFDC: Experimentals, roughly 4,750; controls, roughly 4,750.

TARGET POPULATION: Elderly/impaired subjects had to be elderly or disabled and at risk of institutionalization, and home health aide services could not "reasonably or actually" be available to them. AFDC subjects had to be currently eligible for AFDC and had to have received it for the past 90 days. They could not have been employed as a homemaker–home health aide during that period, and they had to have applied to enter the program.

NUMBER OF TREATMENT GROUPS: This was a two-component experiment. There were two AFDC-recipient groups (with one control) and two elderly/impaired groups (with one control).

NUMBER AND LOCATION OF SITES: Seven—Arkansas, Kentucky, New Jersey, New York, Ohio, South Carolina, and Texas.

RESEARCH COMPONENTS:
Process analysis: The process analysis was generally limited to observing that the treatments were delivered as planned to the groups for whom they were designed. One salient finding, however, was that intake workers' ratings of AFDC subjects' potential had little value in selecting applicants who would most benefit from the demonstration.

- Impact analysis: Conducted with ordinary least squares (OLS).
- Benefit–cost analysis: Conducted from social, taxpayer, client, and trainee perspectives.

MAJOR FINDINGS:

Note: In the tables following, asterisks denote results that are statistically significant at the .05 percent level.

1. Clients
   a. Experimental effect on hours per week of care ("total" is not the sum of formal and informal; effects are estimated from three different regressions):

	Formal	Informal	Total
Arkansas	4.92*	−0.62	4.20*
Kentucky	1.20*	−0.47	0.72
New Jersey	3.47*	−0.55	3.26*
New York	4.21*	0.34	4.83*
Ohio	1.58*	−0.63	1.09*
South Carolina	8.29*	−1.42*	7.05*
Texas	4.02*	−0.19	4.26*

Survival: There was no significant impact on mortality.

Percentage of period spent in hospitals: The only statistically significant effect was in New York and in the wrong direction (clients spent an additional 4.5 percent of their time in hospitals).

Percentage of period spent in nursing homes: There was no significant impact on institutionalization.

   b. Experimental effect on Medicare/Medicaid reimbursement:

	Medicare	Medicaid
Arkansas	−$39	−$40*
Kentucky	+32	+1
New Jersey	−240*	−30
New York	−30	Data not collected
Ohio	−66	+13
South Carolina	+25	−59*
Texas	+26	0

Health and functioning: Clients were slightly less likely than controls to be completely dependent, they communicated somewhat better, and their medical conditions were less likely to have worsened during the demonstration period.

2. Trainees

   In the following tables, effects are computed per participant, by dividing the effect per experimental by the fraction of assigned experimentals who actually entered training.
   a. Experimental effect on average monthly earnings over 30-month follow-up period:

Arkansas	$122*
Kentucky	148*
New Jersey	216*
New York	39
Ohio	210*
South Carolina	140*
Texas	141*

In the following tables, year 1 is the 12 months following the time when the typical trainee left subsidized employment. Year 2 is the next 12 months.
   b. Experimental effect on percentage employed:

	Year 1 (%)	Year 2 (%)
Arkansas	3	31*
Kentucky	0	2
New Jersey	9*	12*
New York	−2	−13
Ohio	6*	13*
South Carolina	3	3
Texas	−3	28*

   c. Experimental effect on hours worked per month:

	Year 1	Year 2
Arkansas	3	24*
Kentucky	3	11
New Jersey	15*	22*
New York	–9	–10
Ohio	14*	25*
South Carolina	4	–2
Texas	1	48*

d. Experimental effect on earnings per month:

	Year 1 ($)	Year 2 ($)
Arkansas	10	101*
Kentucky	28*	161*
New Jersey	81*	126*
New York	–36	12
Ohio	68*	105*
South Carolina	26*	22
Texas	8	215*

e. Experimental effect on percentage receiving AFDC or food stamps (during a typical follow-up period month):

	AFDC (%)	Food Stamps (%)
Arkansas	–13*	–1
Kentucky	–28*	–3*
New Jersey	–26*	–11*
New York	–3*	5*
Ohio	–27*	–15*
South Carolina	–39*	–8*
Texas	–11*	–1

f. Experimental effect on dollars received monthly per participant:

	AFDC (%)	Food Stamps (%)
Arkansas	–31*	–16*
Kentucky	–52*	–17*
New Jersey	–106*	12*
New York	–2	6*
Ohio	–84*	–28*
South Carolina	–68*	–42*
Texas	–18*	–8*

TIME TRENDS IN FINDINGS: Shown above for trainee earnings. Savings in AFDC and food stamps drop sharply over time.

Benefit–cost analysis: The unit of analysis chosen is dollars per hour of service. The analysis is dominated by the failure of the treatment to reduce the usage of hospitals and nursing homes. Trainees and clients are net gainers by the treatment, but taxpayers are worse off.

Net social benefit in dollars per hour of service:

Arkansas	–$9.67
Kentucky	–4.47
New Jersey	+15.75
New York	–40.00
Ohio	+13.47
South Carolina	–0.39
Texas	–3.68

DESIGN ISSUES: Orr has stated that there are several reasons why New York was an extreme outlier. The first is turnover at the upper management level, with half a dozen people holding the project director position at one time or another. The second is that contract negotiations with local providers took too long, and implementation was too slow; in some respects, the demonstration never properly got off the ground. The third is that New York has a heavy turnover in its AFDC population; controls would catch up to experimentals more quickly there than elsewhere for other interventions as well.

REPLICABILITY: Replicable.

GENERALIZABILITY: This demonstration is massive, but the sites are not a representative sample of the United States. States were selected for their strong interest in home care. In some ways, this makes the negative results on the client side more striking.

FUNDING SOURCE: Health Care Financing Administration. Key personnel: Kathy Ellingson-Otto.

TREATMENT ADMINISTRATORS: Social service agencies in seven states. Key personnel: Joann Barham for Arkansas; Darlene Goodrich for Kentucky; Sybil Stokes for New Jersey; Joe Capobianco for New York; Ruth Ann Sieber for Ohio; Mary Frances Payton for South Carolina; and David Chavez for Texas.

EVALUATOR: Abt Associates. Key personnel: Larry L. Orr, Stephen H. Bell, and Nancy R. Burstein.

ENABLING LEGISLATION: Omnibus Budget Reconciliation Act of 1980.

POLICY EFFECTS: Orr has stated that this is one of several studies that dampened enthusiasm for home care as a substitute for institutionalization. Although the findings suggest positive effects from the component that trained and employed AFDC recipients, the findings have not been used at the federal level, perhaps because the funding agency for the experiment is not the agency with responsibility for AFDC.

INFORMATION SOURCE: Stephen H. Bell, Nancy R. Burstein, and Larry L. Orr, *Overview of Evaluation Results,* Abt Associates, December 1987.

PUBLIC-USE ACCESS TO DATA: Public-use file exists; contact Abt Associates.

PART 3

EXPERIMENTS OUTSIDE THE UNITED STATES

1

Africa

Teacher Incentives—Kenya

SUMMARY: This quasi experiment, conducted from 1998 to 1999, tested the effects of bonuses for teachers on students in a small sample of primary schools in Kenya. Subjects were followed for three years.

COST: One of four demonstrations whose total cost was $450,000 (covering the interventions and some but not all research costs).

TIME FRAME: Demonstration period, 1998–99; data collected, 1998–2000.

TREATMENTS TESTED: In schools randomly assigned to treatment, all teachers in grades 4 through 8 would receive bonuses if students at the school did well on district-wide examinations. The bonuses ranged in value from 21 to 43 percent of typical monthly pay (2 to 4 percent of annual pay). Prizes were awarded to both "top-scoring" and "most-improved" schools and were distributed to 24 of the 50 treatment schools in both 1998 and 1999. Teachers in control schools received no performance bonuses. (To discourage gaming behavior by teachers, students who failed to show up for testing received very low scores.)

OUTCOMES OF INTEREST: (1) Student test scores and dropout and (2) Teacher attendance and other behavior.

SAMPLE SIZE: Total, 100 schools; treatments, 50; controls, 50.

TARGET POPULATION: Pupils and teachers in schools in Busia and Teso districts, Western Kenya. The Kenyan Ministry of Education deemed these 100 schools had particular need for assistance. These schools had not participated in earlier demonstrations and had somewhat lower scores than the area averages.

NUMBER OF TREATMENT GROUPS: Two (with one control group).

RESEARCH COMPONENTS:
- Process analysis: Conducted through random visits to schools; surveys of students and faculty.
- Impact analysis: OLS and difference-in-differences regression analyses.
- Benefit–cost analysis: Not conducted.

MAJOR FINDINGS: Relative to control schools:

1. Students in treatment schools were more likely to take the district-wide exams and score higher on at least some of them. However, on other exams (including the school-leaving exam, which determines which secondary school, if any, the student can attend) there was no difference.[1]

2. Dropout rates did not fall.

3. Teacher attendance did not improve. Teachers are relatively well paid in Kenya, but their salaries depend on education and experience, not performance.[2] Process analysis indicated 20 percent teacher absence rates in both treatment and control schools. High teacher absenteeism rates were widespread. Moreover, while teachers were absent from their *schools* for 20 percent of the random visits, they were absent from their *classrooms* during 45 percent of these visits.

4. Homework assignment in treatment schools did not increase; treatment teachers did not change instructional methods, and evinced no increase in caring or energy.

5. Teachers in treatment schools were more likely to conduct test preparation sessions outside of normal class time. Teacher time in the classroom was not significantly related to student test scores, but the relation between test prep sessions and student test scores was highly significant.

6. Treatment school students retained none of their gains after the end of the demonstration.

TIME TRENDS IN FINDINGS: Impacts rose from year one to year two, an effect ascribed to learning by teachers—particularly learning about the negative effect of students not taking the test.

DESIGN ISSUES: Like nearly all quasi experiments, this one has a relatively small number of sites, and accordingly has low power.

REPLICABILITY: Replicable.

GENERALIZABILITY: Substantial. Evaluators note that test-based bonuses to U.S. teachers are often of comparable relative size. Low teacher attendance is common in many less-developed countries.

FUNDING SOURCES: International Christelijk Steunfonds, a Dutch nonprofit organization, funded the treatment; the World Bank and the MacArthur Foundation funded the evaluation.

TREATMENT ADMINISTRATOR: International Christelijk Steunfonds.

EVALUATORS: Paul Glewwe, University of Minnesota; Nauman Ilias, Competition Economics; Michael Kremer, Harvard University.

ENABLING LEGISLATION: None.

INFORMATION SOURCE: Paul Glewwe, Nauman Ilias, and Michael Kremer, "Teacher Incentives," working paper 9671, National Bureau of Economic Research, April 2003.

PUBLIC-USE ACCESS TO DATA: Contact the authors.

Notes

1. This paragraph summarizes the evaluators' conclusions. However, the treatment-control difference is statistically significant on just one exam (Geography-History-Christian Religion) out of seven in just one year of two at the 95 percent level, and the difference for the sum of all test scores is significant at the 90 percent level in just one year of two. The GHCR exam "is arguably the subject that involves the most memorization," the authors note. They detect more impacts using "difference in differences" estimation.

2. Sometimes local school committees raise money for bonuses for very good teaching, and very bad performance might result in a transfer to a school in an undesirable location.

School Meals—Kenya

SUMMARY: This quasi experiment, conducted from January 2000 to December 2001, tested the effects of school meals on children in a small sample of preschools in Kenya. Subjects were followed for two years.

COST: One of four demonstrations whose total cost was $450,000 (covering the interventions and some but not all research costs).

TIME FRAME: Demonstration period, January 2000–December 2001; data collected, same period.

TREATMENTS TESTED: Children in 25 randomly chosen private preschools in a pool of 50 were provided subsidized meals. Control schools did not participate in the meals program. (The government does not fund preschools in most districts in Kenya.)

OUTCOMES OF INTEREST: (1) School attendance; (2) Educational achievement; and (3) Price effects of school meals.

SAMPLE SIZE: Total, 50 schools; treatments, 25; controls, 25.

TARGET POPULATION: Pupils and teachers in preschools in Busia and Teso districts, western Kenya.

NUMBER OF TREATMENT GROUPS: Two (with one control group).

NUMBER AND LOCATION OF SITES: Fifty—selected preschools in Busia and Teso districts, Western Kenya.

RESEARCH COMPONENTS:
- Process analysis: Conducted.
- Impact analysis: Regression.
- Benefit–cost analysis: Not conducted.

MAJOR FINDINGS:
1. The average school attendance of children in the treatment schools was 30 percent, compared with 22 percent for control schools.
2. The increased attendance rates in treated schools created crowding in the classroom, and the pupil-teacher ratio increased substantially.
3. After the start of treatment, the schools reacted to the experiment by raising the price; a day in preschool cost parents approximately 60 percent more in treated schools than in control schools.
4. Total test scores in treated schools increased significantly, but only when the teacher was well trained. An interaction term of teacher training with treatment yielded an increase of 0.42 standard deviations in test scores.
5. There is no evidence that the treatment affected pupils' height or weight.

TIME TREND IN FINDINGS: The overall effect of the program was smaller in 2001 than in 2000.

DESIGN ISSUES:
1. During program implementation, over half of the control schools started feeding programs of their own funded by parents. By September 2001, 14 control schools out of 25 were organizing their own meal program. This may have reduced the magnitude of the impact estimates.
2. Some children who had a choice of school transferred out of control schools into treated schools. (The estimation process accounted for these transfers.)
3. Matching of pupil school attendance to the schools' baselines was imperfect for a variety of reasons. But the difficulties occurred at both treatment and control schools, so the problem was unlikely to affect the impact estimation.

REPLICABILITY: Replicable.

GENERALIZABILITY: The author states that the context in which school meals are implemented is very important. "A program that increases school participation in an environment of low teaching quality is likely to fail to translate into better educational achievement."

FUNDING SOURCE: International Christelijk Steunfonds, a Dutch nonprofit organization.

TREATMENT ADMINISTRATOR: International Christelijk Steunfonds.

EVALUATOR: Christel Vermeersch, Harvard University.

ENABLING LEGISLATION: None.

INFORMATION SOURCE: Christel Vermeersch, *School Meals, Educational Achievement and School Competition: Evidence from a Randomized Evaluation,* Harvard University, November 2002.

PUBLIC-USE ACCESS TO DATA: Contact the author.

Deworming Drug Take-Up—Kenya

SUMMARY: This quasi experiment, conducted from January to December 2001, tested the effects of a drug price increase on children in a small sample of elementary schools in Kenya. Subjects were followed for one year.

COST: Not available.

TIME FRAME: Demonstration period, January 2001–December 2001; data collected, same period.

TREATMENTS TESTED: Common parasitic intestinal worms in the area of the demonstration include hookworm, roundworm, and whipworm. For between one and three years, schools in the experiment had previously participated in a demonstration involving health education about avoiding infection by intestinal worms and free medication for infected children. Twenty-five schools from a sample of 50 were randomly selected to pay user fees (approximately $0.30 per child—a partially subsidized price, since the average per child treatment cost of the program was approximately $1.49) for deworming treatment, while students

at the remaining 25 continued to receive the medication free of charge.

OUTCOME OF INTEREST: Drug take-up.

SAMPLE SIZE: Total, 50 schools; treatments, 25; controls, 25.

TARGET POPULATION: Primary school pupils in Busia district, western Kenya.

NUMBER OF TREATMENT GROUPS: Two (with one control group).

NUMBER AND LOCATION OF SITES: Fifty primary schools in Busia, western Kenya.

RESEARCH COMPONENTS:
- Process analysis: Conducted.
- Impact analysis: Regression.
- Benefit–cost analysis: Not conducted.

MAJOR FINDINGS:
1. Cost-sharing significantly reduced drug take-up: seventy-five percent of the households in free treatment schools received deworming drugs in 2001, while only 18 percent in cost-sharing schools did. Children in cost-sharing schools were 62 percentage points less likely to receive deworming drugs in 2001 than children in free treatment schools, a statistically significant finding at the 99 percent confidence level.
2. Cost-sharing had roughly the same effect on drug treatment rates regardless of the actual price per child. Variation in the deworming price per child was generated by the fact that cost-sharing was in the form of a fee per family, so parents with more children in primary school faced a lower price per child.

TIME TRENDS IN FINDINGS: None.

DESIGN ISSUES: None apparent.

REPLICABILITY: Replicable.

GENERALIZABILITY: Process analysis indicates that families considered worms uncomfortable but not dangerous or debilitating. Results are probably not generalizable to life-threatening ailments in similar communities.

FUNDING SOURCES: International Christelijk Steunfonds (a Dutch nonprofit organization), The World Bank, the National Institutes of Health, Forgaty International Center, and the University of California, Berkeley, Center for Health Research.

TREATMENT ADMINISTRATOR: International Christelijk Steunfonds.

EVALUATORS: Edward Miguel, University of California, and Michael Kremer, Harvard University.

ENABLING LEGISLATION: None.

INFORMATION SOURCE: Edward Miguel and Michael Kremer, *Why Don't People Take Their Medicine? Experimental Evidence from Kenya,* Harvard University, November 2002.

PUBLIC-USE ACCESS TO DATA: Not yet available.

2

Asia-Pacific

Women as Policy Makers—India

SUMMARY: This demonstration, conducted from 1998 to 2002, tested the effects of mandated representation of women on village councils in two districts in two different states of India on a medium-sized sample of villages. Subjects were followed for two years.

COST: Evaluation only, $9,000.

TIME FRAME: Demonstration period, 1998–2000; data collected, same period.

TREATMENTS TESTED: In the treatment villages, headship in one-third of village councils and one-third of membership in village councils in West Bengal and Rajasthan were reserved for women. In the control villages, seats were not reserved for women, and in all but 6.5 percent of these villages, men headed the councils.

OUTCOMES OF INTEREST: (1) Investment in public goods and (2) Women's participation in policymaking.

SAMPLE SIZE: Total, 265 villages; experimentals, 104; controls, 161.

TARGET POPULATION: Villages.

NUMBER OF TREATMENT GROUPS: Two (with one control group).

NUMBER AND LOCATION OF SITES: Two—Birbhum district, West Bengal, and Udaipur district, Rajasthan.

RESEARCH COMPONENTS:
  Process analysis: Conducted.

▪ Impact analysis: Regression-adjusted.
▪ Benefit–cost analysis: Not conducted.

MAJOR FINDINGS:

1. At public meetings of the village councils in West Bengal, women complained about drinking water and roads; men complained about roads, irrigation, drinking water, and education. In Rajasthan, women complained about drinking water, welfare programs, and roads; men complained about roads, irrigation, drinking water, and education. (Within each group, the complaints are listed in order of importance the group places on the topic.)

2. Treatment village councils were significantly more likely than control councils to invest in drinking water infrastructure and road construction in West Bengal, and drinking water in Rajasthan. Treatment councils in West Bengal were nearly twice as likely to invest in drinking water equipment and were 20 percent more likely than control councils to repair major roads.

3. Treatment councils invested less than control councils in public goods more closely linked to men's concerns: education in West Bengal, and roads in Rajasthan. However, treatment councils were more likely to invest in buildings used for adult education than were control councils.

TIME TRENDS IN FINDINGS: None.

DESIGN ISSUES: Treatment councils presided over smaller and poorer villages, and the women heads were more likely to be classified as poor. The authors state that these discrepancies are not large enough to affect the findings.

REPLICABILITY: Replicable.

GENERALIZABILITY: The key result that "the identity of a decision maker influences policy decisions" does not seem limited to the particular circumstances of these districts in India.

FUNDING SOURCES: National Institutes of Health and the John D. and Catherine T. MacArthur Foundation.

TREATMENT ADMINISTRATOR: The States of West Bengal and Rajasthan, India.

EVALUATORS: Raghabendra Chattopadhyay (Indian Institute of Management, Calcutta) and Esther Duflo (Economics Department, MIT).

ENABLING LEGISLATION: None.

INFORMATION SOURCE: Raghabendra Chattopadhyay and Esther Duflo, *Women as Policy Makers: Evidence from an India-Wide Randomized Policy Experiment,* working paper 8615, National Bureau of Economic Research, December 2001.

PUBLIC-USE ACCESS TO DATA: Not available.

Matriculation Awards Pilot—Israel

SUMMARY: This demonstration, conducted from 1999 to 2000, tested the effects of cash incentives for learning on a medium-sized sample of low-achieving high school seniors with a low probability of matriculation. Subjects were followed for one year.

COST: The combined cost of this experiment and the quasi experiment on the same topic is as follows: Bonuses paid to students, $650,000; evaluation, $25,000.

TIME FRAME: Demonstration period, 1999–2000.

TREATMENTS TESTED: Experimental students were provided an opportunity to earn a bonus (a choice of $800 in cash, a $1,000 voucher to be used toward a trip of educational value, or a $1,200 voucher to be used toward the cost of higher education) conditional on success on the Israeli high-school matriculation tests. Only students projected to have either moderate (neither very low nor very high) probability of matriculation were randomized. Control students were not provided the incentive.

OUTCOMES OF INTEREST: (1) Matriculation and (2) Further education.

SAMPLE SIZE: Total, 252; treatments, 125; controls, 127.

TARGET POPULATION: Low-achieving high school seniors.

NUMBER OF TREATMENT GROUPS: Two (with one control group).

NUMBER AND LOCATION OF SITES: High schools in Israel.

RESEARCH COMPONENTS:
▪ Process analysis: Conducted.
▪ Impact analysis: Regression.
▪ Benefit–cost analysis: Not conducted.

MAJOR FINDINGS: The treatment had no effect on achievement, though a null hypothesis of modest effects cannot be rejected either.

TIME TRENDS IN FINDINGS: None.

DESIGN ISSUES:
1. Treated students were notified of the incentive later than originally planned, reducing the scope for changes in behavior that could have increased the likelihood of matriculation.
2. Simple random assignment within schools was seen as inequitable; therefore a hybrid within-school experimental design was used. Using school-specific quintiles, about half of eligible students within each school were offered an incentive.
3. School administrators objected to simple within-school randomization as difficult to justify to participants and outside observers.

REPLICABILITY: Replicable.

GENERALIZABILITY: Because of the design issues, the results of the demonstration are not generalizable. Indeed, a modified demonstration, which used schools as the unit of analysis, obtained statistically significant findings (see page 406).

FUNDING SOURCES: Ministry of Education, Israel, and Sacta-Rashi Foundation.

TREATMENT ADMINISTRATOR: Ministry of Education, Israel.

EVALUATORS: Joshua D. Angrist, MIT Department of Economics, and Victor Lavy, Hebrew University, Department of Economics.

ENABLING LEGISLATION: None.

INFORMATION SOURCE: Joshua D. Angrist and Victor Lavy, "The Effect of High School Matriculation Awards: Evidence from Randomized Trials," working paper 9389, National Bureau of Economic Research, December 2002.

PUBLIC-USE ACCESS TO DATA: No public-use data yet. Contact Joshua D. Angrist, MIT Department of Economics, angrist@mit.edu.

Assisting the Long-Term Unemployed—Australia

INFORMATION SOURCE: Robert Breuning, Deborah Cobb-Clark (Australian National University), Yvonne Dunlop (Victoria University of Technology), and Marion Terril (Department of Family and Community Services), "Assisting the Long-Term Unemployed: Results from a Randomized Trial," Institute for the Study of Labor, Germany (IZA) Discussion Paper No. 628, November 2002.

SUMMARY FROM ABOVE SOURCE: A large sample of long-term unemployed workers on income support for over five years in Australia was divided into treatment and control groups. Individuals in the treatment group were invited to participate in an intensive interview process focusing on backgrounds and situations. The goal of the evaluation was to determine whether expanded counseling and monitoring resulted in increased economic and social participation of the long-term unemployed on income support, leading to decreased dependence on social welfare.

Participants totaling 4,740 were to be randomly allocated to control and treatment groups. A letter was sent to each individual in the treatment group, asking him or her to attend an interview. Interviews were conducted in September/October 2000 and in November/December 2000 by employment support staff. A final 20-minute interview was conducted in March/April 2001 by a market research firm. Comparison data from the first face-to-face interview and the follow–up telephone interview formed the basis for analysis of the impact of full participation in the trial. Full treatment was defined as consisting of receipt of letter and participation in both in-depth interviews conducted by employment support staff.

In September/October 2000, control group members were sent letters informing them of the interview process. Those who agreed were interviewed at the same three points in time as the treatment group by the same market research firm that conducted the final intervention among the treatment group. However, controls did not meet with employment support staff.

According to the study, randomization was achieved through the use of administrative longitudinal data set (LDS), which provided fortnightly observations on benefits and limited demographic data. The evaluators used administrative data to test random assignment and to assess the factors related to an individual's decision to fully participate in the treatment (or, in the case of the control group, to agree to be interviewed in all three waves).

The findings were that individuals who participated in the full intervention were more likely to engage in study and training and, as a consequence, they were more likely to stay longer on income support. For both treatment and control groups, there was no change in either average earnings or in proportion of individuals engaged in paid work.

However, randomization was seriously flawed. Using administrative data, the evaluators found that the statistics for key demographic variables for treatment and control groups were not consistent with randomization. For instance, no individuals over the age of 50 were assigned to the control group, although about 10 percent of the individuals in the treatment group were over the age of 50.

In addition, there were problems with data collection and retention. Individuals in the control group who did not have telephones were dropped. This accounted for 50 percent of the control group. Different data-gathering techniques, face-to-face versus telephone, were used for the treatment and the control group. Large numbers in both the treatment and control groups dropped out of the experiment, and no data were collected on the dropouts.

The evaluators further state that the intervention was modest and the analysis time frame short.

NUMBER AND LOCATION OF SITES: Twenty sites across Australia.

TREATMENT ADMINISTRATOR: Department of Family and Community Services, Australia.

EVALUATORS: Robert Breuning, Deborah Cobb-Clark (Australian National University), Yvonne Dunlop (Victoria University of Technology), and Marion Terril (Department of Family and Community Services).

Matriculation Awards—Israel

SUMMARY: This quasi experiment, conducted from October 2000 to October 2001, tested the effects of cash incentives for learning on students at a small sample of low-achieving Israeli high schools. There was no follow-up after matriculation tests were administered.

COST: The combined cost of this quasi experiment and the true "pilot" experiment on the same topic is as follows: Bonuses paid to students, $650,000; evaluation, $25,000.

TIME FRAME: Demonstration period, October 2000–October 2001; data collected, same period.

TREATMENTS TESTED: Students in treatment schools were provided an opportunity for a cash bonus conditional on success in the Israeli high school matriculation tests. The total amount at stake for a student who passed all the achievement tests was nearly $2,400. Students in control schools were not provided the incentive.

OUTCOME OF INTEREST: Matriculation.

SAMPLE SIZE: Total, 39 schools; treatments, 20; controls, 19. There were about 2,000 students in each group (only seniors received bonuses).

TARGET POPULATION: Students in their senior year at low-achieving high schools.

NUMBER OF TREATMENT GROUPS: Two (with one control group).

NUMBER AND LOCATION OF SITES: Thirty-nine high schools throughout Israel, including Jewish religious and Arab schools.

RESEARCH COMPONENTS:
- Process analysis: Conducted.
- Impact analysis: Regression.
- Benefit–cost analysis: Conducted.

MAJOR FINDINGS:
1. Using matched pairs methodology, evaluators conclude that the achievement awards program increased matriculation rates on the order of 6–8 percentage points. Effects were concentrated among students in the highest quartile of performance on predemonstration testing. There was no systematic difference between treatment and control schools in the year prior to the demonstration.
2. Students in treated schools reported studying 2.7 hours per week, 11 percent more than the 2.4 average hours of study in control schools.

TIME TRENDS IN FINDINGS: Not applicable.

DESIGN ISSUES: Due to adverse publicity the demonstration was suspended after one year. It was planned to last three years. As a consequence awards were given for only one year.

REPLICABILITY: Replicable.

GENERALIZABILITY: Low-achieving students were probably overrepresented in the sample because a majority of schools that participated in the demonstration were low-achieving. Findings are probably generalizable to other countries, although low-achieving Israeli high schools are characterized by special issues, notably enrollment that fluctuates because of high levels of external and internal immigration.

FUNDING SOURCES: Ministry of Education, Israel, and Sacta-Rashi Foundation.

TREATMENT ADMINISTRATOR: Ministry of Education, Israel.

EVALUATORS: Joshua D. Angrist, MIT Department of Economics, and Victor Lavy, Hebrew University Department of Economics.

ENABLING LEGISLATION: None.

INFORMATION SOURCE: Joshua D. Angrist and Victor Lavy, "The Effect of High School Matriculation Awards: Evidence from Randomized Trials," working paper 9389, National Bureau of Economic Research, December 2002.

PUBLIC-USE ACCESS TO DATA: No public-use data as yet. Contact Joshua D. Angrist, MIT Department of Economics, angrist@mit.edu.

3

Canada

Manitoba Basic Annual Income Experiment

SUMMARY: This demonstration, conducted from 1975 to 1979, tested the effects of experimental tax rates and guaranteed income levels on a medium-sized sample of low-income households. Subjects were followed for three years.

COST: The original project grant for both the experimental and saturation sites was approximately Can$17 million. However, the government contribution in terms of services is not counted in this figure.

TIME FRAME: The Manitoba Basic Annual Income Experiment (Mincome) began in 1975 and officially ended in 1979. The original research design was not fully implemented. The data were archived and made available again in 1983. Some analysis of the data has occurred since 1983.

TREATMENTS TESTED: The eight experimental treatments were varying combinations of tax rates and guaranteed cash benefits. See table on page 410.

The control group received existing Income Assistance (Canada's primary welfare program) benefits. Saturation site families (see below) received treatment 3.

OUTCOMES OF INTEREST: (1) Labor supply response for primary and secondary earners: hours worked, resources devoted to job search; (2) Family income; (3) Job satisfaction; and (4) Measures of family behavior—formation and disintegration.

SAMPLE SIZE: Total, 1,187; treatments, 575; controls, 612.

TARGET POPULATION: Low-income households—families with able-bodied heads under 58 years of age and incomes below Can$13,000 for a family of four.

Treatments Tested

Treatment	Maximum annual cash benefit ($, based on family of four in 1975)	Tax rate
1	3,800	0.35
2	4,800	0.35
3	3,800	0.50
4	4,800	0.50
5	5,800	0.50
6	3,800	0.75
7	4,800	0.75
8	5,800	0.75

NUMBER OF TREATMENT GROUPS: Nine (with one control group).

NUMBER AND LOCATION OF SITES: One—Winnipeg, Manitoba. In addition, there was one saturation site—Dauphin, Manitoba.

RESEARCH COMPONENTS:
- Process analysis: Not conducted.
- Impact analysis: Conducted using regression models.
- Benefit–cost analysis: Not conducted.

MAJOR FINDINGS:
1. In general, there is no conclusive evidence regarding treatment–control group differences in relation to labor supply outcomes. The data show declining hours worked from the first (preexperimental) year to the other three (experimental) years for most treatment groups, as well as for the control group.
2. However, for one of the regression models, there were some significant differences. For males, on average, the experimental groups worked significantly fewer annual hours than did the control group (−92 hours). For female heads of household, the effect is also negative and significant. The experimental group, on average, worked 100 hours less than did controls.

TIME TRENDS IN FINDINGS: None reported.

DESIGN ISSUES:
1. The overarching problem may be that the funding and interest for this project waned prior to its completion. This limited the experiment's implementation and analysis.
2. The experiment limited payments to three years. This poses a problem for the prediction of effects of permanent programs because it implicitly assumes that the experimental families will make the same adjustment within three years that they would to an indefinite-length national program.
3. For some families, regular reporting and periodic interviews may influence behavior in addition to the effect of receiving payments. The reporting requirements alone may lead families to have more accurate views of their financial situation than they otherwise would. Only a portion of the control group had these requirements.

REPLICABILITY: Replicable.

GENERALIZABILITY: Designed to generalize to, at least, the entire province of Manitoba. The experiment's sample was narrower than the population that would be covered by a universal guaranteed income program. The aged, institutionalized, and disabled were excluded.

FUNDING SOURCES: Health and Welfare Canada and Manitoba Ministry for Health and Social Development.

TREATMENT ADMINISTRATOR: Manitoba Ministry for Health and Social Development.

EVALUATORS: Department of National Health, Welfare Canada, and Manitoba's provincial counterpart. Key personnel: Derek Hum.

ENABLING LEGISLATION: None.

INFORMATION SOURCES: Derek Hum and Wayne Simpson, *Income Maintenance, Work Effort, and the Canadian Mincome Experiment,* Minister of Supply and Services Canada, 1991.

Derek Hum and Wayne Simpson, "Economic Response to a Guaranteed Annual Income: Experience from Canada and the United States," *Journal of Labor Economics* 11(1993): 5263–96.

Derek P. Hum, "Social Security Reform during the 1970s," in *Canadian Social Welfare Policy: Federal and Provincial Dimensions,* edited by J. Ismael Institute for Public Administration in Canada, McGill–Queen's University Press, 1985.

PUBLIC-USE ACCESS TO DATA: Data are lodged with the Canadian and Manitoba governments. Derek Hum believes the Canadian government deposited its set of data in the National Archives. He is unsure about its accessibility.

Self-Sufficiency Project (SSP)

SUMMARY: This demonstration, conducted from November 1992 to December 1999 in Canada tested the effects of a substantial cash incentive to find and keep full-time work on a large sample of long-term welfare recipients. Subjects were followed for up to four years.

COST: Estimated gross transfers and administrative cost Can$249 million.

TIME FRAME: Demonstration period, November 1992–December 1999; data collected, same period.

TREATMENTS TESTED: SSP offered a temporary monthly cash supplement equaling half the difference between a participant's earnings and an annual earnings benchmark (Can$30,000 in New Brunswick and Can$37,000 in British Columbia) to single parents on Income Assistance (IA) for at least one year if they left income assistance for full-time work (at least 30 hours per week). The control group was not offered the supplement.

OUTCOMES OF INTEREST: (1) Employment; (2) Earnings and income; (3) Welfare dependence; and (4) Children's welfare.

SAMPLE SIZE: Total, 5,729; treatments, 2,880; controls 2,849.

TARGET POPULATION: Long-term single-parent welfare recipients in the Canadian provinces of British Columbia and New Brunswick.

NUMBER OF TREATMENT GROUPS: Two (with one control group).

NUMBER AND LOCATION OF SITES: Two—British Columbia and New Brunswick, Canada.

RESEARCH COMPONENTS:
 Process analysis: Conducted through surveys, administrative records, focus groups, and ethnographic interviews.
 Impact analysis: Regression.
 Benefit–cost analysis: Conducted.

MAJOR FINDINGS:
1. The Self-Sufficiency Project (SSP) had a statistically significant 15 percentage point impact on full-time employment at the beginning of the second year of the demonstration. During the first year of the demonstration, the proportion of the treatment group working full time peaked at 30 percent at the beginning of the second year. During the same period, full-time employment for the control group peaked at about 15 percent.
2. SSP had a significant effect on earnings. Earnings effects peaked in the second year, when the treatment group earned $370 per month, on average, compared with $269 for the control group; thus, the impact was $101 per worker per month. Employment and income effects declined thereafter, but in the fourth year of the demonstration the treatment group still earned significantly more—on average, $52 per month—than the control group.
3. SSP significantly raised family income. After a year, the average treatment group after-tax income was $165 per month higher than for the control group. After three years, the average treatment group income was $102 more than the control group average. The differences were statistically significant.
4. At the end of the four-year follow-up period, treatment and control group members were

equally likely to work and to receive income assistance.

5. SSP did not significantly affect the functioning of very young children. There were no statistically significant effects on children in any of the age cohorts.

6. In theory, the incentive might have resulted in extended stays on welfare among recipients who would otherwise have exited earlier. The incentive did produce a delayed exit effect from Income Assistance, but it was very small.

7. SSP provided more than $5,200 in extra income and other benefits to the average family in the treatment group. The cost to the federal and provincial governments was about $2,700 per treatment group member beyond what was spent on the control group. These net costs to the government are for the short run; the long-run effects are not clear. Thus, SSP increased the financial well-being of and reduced poverty for many families; it provides an efficient mechanism for income transfer.

TIME TRENDS IN FINDINGS: Effects on employment, earnings, and welfare receipt declined with time as the control group "caught up." By around the fifth year after random assignment, differences between the treatment and control groups had disappeared.

DESIGN ISSUES:

1. In Canada, disabled people who were unable to work were included in the general category of welfare recipients. Thus, the sample of long-term welfare recipients in SSP may be more disadvantaged than a similar sample in the United States would have been.

2. Study constraints did not permit an examination of entry effects onto IA to qualify a year later for SSP. Only delayed exit effects from IA among those already on IA could be examined.

REPLICABILITY: Replicable.

GENERALIZABILITY: Because British Columbia and New Brunswick are very different in their economics, demography, and environment, these

results ought to be reasonably representative of Canada as a whole.

FUNDING SOURCE: Human Resources Development Canada: Key personnel: Jean-Pierre Voyer and Allen Zeesman.

TREATMENT ADMINISTRATORS: Family Services Saint John Inc., New Brunswick, and Bernard C. Vinge and Associates Ltd., British Columbia. Key personnel: Shelly Price and Linda Nelson for Families Services and Betty Tully and Elizabeth Dunn for Bernard C. Vinge.

EVALUATORS: Manpower Demonstration Research Cooperation (MDRC) and Social Research and Demonstration Corporation (SRDC). Key personnel: Charles Michalopoulos for MDRC and Reuben Ford for SRDC.

ENABLING LEGISLATION: None.

INFORMATION SOURCE: Charles Michalopoulos, Doug Tattrie, Cynthia Miller, Philip K. Robins, Pamela Morris, David Gyarmati, Cindy Redcross, Kelly Foley, and Reuben Ford, *Making Work Pay: Final Report on the Self-Sufficiency Project for Long-Term Welfare Recipients,* SRDC, July 2002.

PUBLIC-USE ACCESS TO DATA: No routine public-use file available; access for specific projects may be permitted; contact SRDC.

SSP Entry Effects

SUMMARY: This demonstration, conducted in Canada from January 1994 to March 1995, tested the effects of the future availability of an earnings supplement on a large sample of newly enrolled Income Assistance (IA) recipients. Subjects were followed for 13 months.

COST: See summary for Self-Sufficiency Project, page 411.

TIME FRAME: Demonstration period, January 1994–March 1995; data collected, same period.

TREATMENTS TESTED: Experimentals were informed that if they remained on income assistance for the next 12 months, they would thereafter be eligible for a temporary monthly cash supplement to their earnings, provided that they worked full-time (see Self-Sufficiency Project). The offer was not made to controls.

OUTCOMES OF INTEREST: (1) Duration of welfare recipiency and (2) Employment.

SAMPLE SIZE: Total 3,315; treatments, 1,648; controls, 1,667.

TARGET POPULATION: Single parents recently starting a new spell of IA in the Canadian provinces of British Columbia and New Brunswick.

NUMBER OF TREATMENT GROUPS: Two (with one control group).

NUMBER AND LOCATION OF SITES: Two—lower mainland British Columbia and Vancouver.

RESEARCH COMPONENTS:
- Process analysis: Conducted.
- Impact analysis: Regression.
- Benefit–cost analysis: Not conducted.

MAJOR FINDINGS:
1. There was a modest delayed exit from welfare among the experimental group relative to the control group. After a year, about 2.5 percent more of the experimental group were still on IA, and thus potentially eligible for SSP, than the control group. This impact estimate is statistically significant.
2. At 12 months, the probability of working while receiving welfare did not increase significantly, relative to the control group.

TIME TRENDS IN FINDINGS: There was limited evidence of widening gaps between the experimental and control groups in the last months of the experiment. In the 12th month after entering Income Assistance, an extra 2.7 percent of the experimental group was still on IA relative to the control group. The regression-adjusted estimate of the gap is 3.0 percent, and is just significant at the 10 percent level.

DESIGN ISSUES: None apparent.

REPLICABILITY: Replicable.

GENERALIZABILITY: These results should be reasonably representative of Canada as a whole (see Self-Sufficiency Project).

FUNDING SOURCE: Human Resources Development Canada. Key personnel: Jean Pierre Voyer and Allen Zeesman.

TREATMENT ADMINISTRATORS: Social Research and Demonstration Corporation and Manpower Demonstration Research Corporation. Key personnel: Gordon Berlin.

EVALUATOR: Social Research and Demonstration Corporation and Manpower Demonstration Research Corporation. Key personnel: David Card and Philip Robins.

ENABLING LEGISLATION: None.

INFORMATION SOURCES: Gordon Berlin, Wendy Bancroft, David Card, Winston Lin, and Philip K. Robins, *Do Work Incentives Have Unintended Consequences? Measuring "Entry Effects" in the Self-Sufficiency Project*, SRDC, March 1998; David Card, Winston Lin, and Philip Robins, *How Important Are "Entry Effects" in Financial Incentive Programs for Welfare Recipients? Experimental Evidence from the Self-Sufficiency Project*, SRDC, August 1997.

PUBLIC-USE ACCESS TO DATA: No routine public-use file is available; access to data for specific projects may be permitted; contact SRDC.

SSP Plus

SUMMARY: This demonstration, conducted in Canada from November 1994 to December 1999, tested the effects of adding an offer of employment-related services to the financial component of SSP on a medium-sized sample of long-term welfare recipients. Subjects were followed for five years.

COST: Demonstration was a component of the larger Self-Sufficiency Project, page 411.

TIME FRAME: Demonstration period, November 1994–December 1999; data collected, same period.

TREATMENTS TESTED: Participants in the SSP demonstration were randomly assigned to a SSP Plus group, a regular SSP group, or a control group. The SSP Plus group was eligible for the SSP financial incentive for full-time employment (see Canada Self-Sufficiency Program summary). In addition, they were offered employment-related services: an employment plan, résumé service, job club, job coaching, job leads, and self-esteem workshops.

Members of the SSP Regular group were offered the financial incentive only. The control group did not receive either component.

OUTCOMES OF INTEREST: (1) Supplement receipt; (2) Employment; (3) Wages; and (4) Earnings.

SAMPLE SIZE: Total, 892; SSP Plus, 293; SSP Regular, 296; controls, 303.

TARGET POPULATION: Long-term single-parent welfare recipients in New Brunswick.

NUMBER OF TREATMENT GROUPS: Three (with one control group).

NUMBER AND LOCATION OF SITES: One—New Brunswick, Canada.

RESEARCH COMPONENTS:
- Process analysis: Conducted.
- Impact analysis: Regression.
- Benefit–cost analysis: Conducted.

MAJOR FINDINGS:
The impacts of the combination of financial incentives and services tended to last longer than the impacts of financial incentives alone. See tables below and on next page.

SSP Plus services significantly increased the earnings supplement take-up rate. Welfare recipients who were offered the services were 16 percentage points more likely than regular SSP group members to have received at least one supplement over the course of the follow-up period.

SSP and SSP Plus Impacts on Employment and Earnings

Outcome	Average Outcome Levels			SSP Plus vs. Control	Regular SSP vs. Control	SSP Plus vs. Regular SSP
	SSP Plus	SSP-R	Control	Impacts of FI & S	Impacts of FI	Added impact of services
Monthly full-time employment rate (%)						
Year 1	22.4	21.1	12.1	10.3***	9.0***	1.3
Year 2	33.6	35.9	16.5	17.1***	19.5***	−2.4
Year 3	36.6	34.1	19.5	17.1***	14.6***	2.5
Year 4	40.1	32.8	25.7	14.4***	7.0**	7.4**
Year 5, Q1	38.0	33.2	30.9	7.1*	2.3	4.8
Year 5, Q2	39.7	33.4	31.3	8.4**	2.1	6.3
Average earnings ($)						
Year 1	2,945	2,490	1,897	1,048***	593***	455*
Year 2	4,507	4,528	2,966	1,541***	1,562***	−21
Year 3	5,330	4,731	3,743	1,587***	989**	599
Year 4	6,886	5,300	4,878	2,008***	422**	1,586**
Year 5, Q1	6,956	5,770	5,808	1,148	−38	1,186
Year 5, Q2	7,118	5,784	6,178	940	−395	1,334

SSP and SSP Plus Impacts on IA and Total Cash Transfers

	Average Outcome Levels			SSP Plus vs. Control	Regular SSP vs. Control	SSP Plus vs. Regular SSP
Outcome	SSP Plus	SSP-R	Control	Impacts of FI & S	Impacts of FI	Added impact of services
Monthly rate of IA receipt (%)						
Year 1	81.9	82.5	90.9	−9.1***	−8.4***	−0.6
Year 2	57.1	59.3	75.5	−18.4***	−16.2***	−2.3
Year 3	50.4	55.7	69.2	−18.8***	−13.5***	−5.3
Year 4	44.3	55.3	61.5	−17.3***	−6.2*	−11.00***
Year 5, Q1	42.9	51.7	54.5	−11.6**	−2.8	−8.8**
Year 5, Q2	39.7	46.2	46.0	−6.4	0.2	−6.6
Average payments from IA & SSP ($)						
Year 1	8,542	8,425	7,731	811***	694***	117
Year 2	7,895	7,641	6,489	1,406***	1,152***	254
Year 3	7,229	7,272	6,044	1,186***	1,228	−42
Year 4	5,863	6,026	5,445	418	581*	−163
Year 5, Q1	3,808	4,458	4,596	−788**	−138	−650*
Year 5, Q2	3,492	3,969	3,913	−421	56	−477

* Statistically significant at the .10 level.
** Statistically significant at the .05 level.
*** Statistically significant at the .01 level.

TIME TRENDS IN FINDINGS: The impacts of SSP Plus relative to Regular SSP increased with time:

1. Peak full-time employment rate: Regular SSP peaked at 39 percent at month 18 of the demonstration; the peak occurred at 42 percent at month 45 with SSP Plus.
2. During the fourth year of the demonstration (the first post-treatment year), the SSP Plus group had a higher monthly full-time employment rate—by 7.4 percentage points—than the regular SSP group. SSP Plus group members were also less likely to receive income assistance (11 percentage points less) than regular SSP group members. Net income of the SSP Plus group averaged $1,586 more than that of SSP-Regular in the fourth year of the demonstration.

DESIGN ISSUES: Because there were fewer than 300 members in each research group, the differences between the groups were not statistically significant unless they were quite large.

REPLICABILITY: Replicable.

GENERALIZABILITY: The demonstration was conducted at one site in New Brunswick, an economically depressed province. Findings from this one site might not generalize to the rest of Canada.

FUNDING SOURCE: Human Resources Development Canada. Key personnel: Jean-Pierre Voyer and Allen Zeesman.

TREATMENT ADMINISTRATOR: Family Services Saint John Inc., New Brunswick. Key personnel: Shelly Price and Linda Nelson.

EVALUATORS: Manpower Demonstration Research Cooperation (MDRC) and Social Research and Demonstration Corporation (SRDC). Key personnel: Charles Michalopoulos for MDRC and Reuben Ford for SRDC.

ENABLING LEGISLATION: None.

INFORMATION SOURCES: Charles Michalopoulos, Doug Tattrie, Cynthia Miller, Philip K. Robins,

Pamela Morris, David Gyarmati, Cindy Redcross, Kelly Foley, and Reuben Ford, *Making Work Pay: Final Report on the Self-Sufficiency Project for Long-Term Welfare Recipients,* SRDC, July 2002; Gail Quets, Philip K. Robins, Elsie C. Pan, Charles Michalopoulos, and David Card, *Does SSP Plus Increase Employment? The Effect of Adding Services to the Self-Sufficiency Project's Financial Incentives,* SRDC, May 1999.

PUBLIC-USE ACCESS TO DATA: No routine public-use file available; access for specific projects may be permitted. Contact SRDC or Statistics Canada.

Earnings Supplement Project

SUMMARY: This demonstration, conducted in Canada between 1995 and 1996, tested the effect of a reemployment earnings supplement on two large samples of the unemployed. Subjects were followed for up to three years.

COST: Can$14 million.

TIME FRAME: Enrollment period, March–June 1995; data collected for 15 months following random assignment, data collected on subsamples for up to two additional years.

TREATMENTS TESTED: Eligible claimants could volunteer to participate in the demonstration. Those volunteers assigned to the treatment group were offered an earnings supplement as an incentive to quickly take new jobs. To receive supplements, experimentals had to begin working at new full-time jobs within 12 weeks (for repeat UI users) or 26 weeks (for displaced workers). Experimentals who accepted jobs that paid less than their previous jobs could receive supplements equal to 75 percent of the difference. Payments were capped at $250 per week and could continue for up to two years. Treatment group members who did not find jobs within the time limit could continue to receive regular

unemployment benefits. The remaining volunteers formed the control group and were not offered supplements.

OUTCOME OF INTEREST: Program participation and employment.

SAMPLE SIZE: Displaced workers total, 8,144; treatments, 4,081; controls, 4,063. Repeat UI users total, 3,414; treatments, 1,707; controls, 1,707.

TARGET POPULATION: Displaced workers (workers who suffered job loss after at least three years of continuous employment) and repeat users of unemployment insurance (UI—workers receiving UI benefits for the fourth consecutive year).

NUMBER OF TREATMENT GROUPS: Two (with one control group).

NUMBER AND LOCATION OF SITES: Displaced workers were tested in five sites—Granby, Quebec; Oshawa, Ontario; Toronto, Ontario; Saskatoon, Saskatchewan; and Winnipeg, Manitoba. Repeat UI users were tested in four sites—Halifax, Nova Scotia; Lévis, Quebec; Moncton, New Brunswick; and St. John's, Newfoundland.

RESEARCH COMPONENTS:
- Process analysis: Information collected from site visit reports, a staff survey of the Human Resource Centres of Canada (HRCC), and a telephone log. A "mini-survey" was also conducted on a combined supplement group sample of displaced workers and repeat UI users.
- Impact analysis: OLS regression.
- Benefit–cost analysis: Conducted.

MAJOR FINDINGS:
1. Participation rates were substantially higher among displaced workers than repeat UI users. Almost all displaced workers (97 percent) who were asked to volunteer for the experiment agreed to do so, but only 41 percent of repeat UI users who were asked agreed to participate. Among the repeat UI users who were randomly

assigned to the supplement group, only 4.7 percent actually received supplement payments. Because few displaced workers who expected to be recalled to their former employer actually received a supplement, much of the analysis focused on the 5,912 displaced workers who did not expect a recall.

2. The program had no observable effect on full-time employment rates until follow-up month 6, when the supplement group rate began to exceed that of the control group. However, the part-time employment rate in months 1 through 7 was lower for the supplement group than for the control group, ranging from −0.8 to −2.1 percentage points, all statistically significant.

3. The program reduced unemployment benefits received by displaced workers by less than the cost of the supplement.

4. Among the repeat UI users in the supplement group who received at least one payment, only 20 percent (amounting to 16 people) received a supplement in each of the follow-up months.

5. The program did not reduce the number of weeks of unemployment or the amount of unemployment benefits.

TIME TRENDS IN FINDINGS: The full-time employment rate for the supplement group only significantly exceeded those of the control group in months 5, 6, 7, and 10 following random assignment. There were no differences thereafter.

DESIGN ISSUES: None noted.

REPLICABILITY: Replicable.

GENERALIZABILITY: Apparently generalizable. The program sites were chosen to represent a variety of geographic locations, communities, and local economic conditions.

FUNDING SOURCE: Human Resources Development Canada (HRDC). Key personnel: Jean-Pierre Voyer and Russ Jackson.

TREATMENT ADMINISTRATOR: Local HRCC staff.

EVALUATOR: Social Research and Demonstration Corporation (SRDC). Key personnel: Doug Tattrie, Howard Bloom, and Saul Schwartz.

ENABLING LEGISLATION: The Employment Insurance Act of 1996 authorized funds for active reemployment programs, such as the supplement program tested by ESP.

INFORMATION SOURCES: Howard Bloom, Barbara Fink, Susanna Lui-Gurr, Wendy Bancroft, and Doug Tattrie, *Implementing the Earning Supplement Project: A Test of a Re-employment Incentive*, SRDC, October 1997.

Howard Bloom, Saul Schwartz, Susanna Lui-Gurr, and Suk-Won Lee, *Testing a Re-employment Incentive for Displaced Workers: The Earnings Supplement Project*, SRDC, May 1999.

Doug Tattrie, *A Financial Incentive to Encourage Employment among Repeat Users of Employment Insurance: The Earnings Supplement Project*, SRDC, May 1999.

PUBLIC-USE ACCESS TO DATA: No public-use file at this writing. Contact Statistics Canada regarding policy on research use.

EXPERIMENTS ONGOING AT PUBLICATION

Community Employment Innovation Project

STARTING YEAR/YEAR FINAL REPORT EXPECTED: 2000/2008.

INFORMATION SOURCE: "The Community Employment Intervention Project," http://srdc.org/english/projects/ceip.htm, viewed May 7, 2003.

PRINCIPAL INTERVENTIONS: As an alternative to transfer payments, subjects are offered 35 hours per week of employment at a "community wage"—Can$300—in community-organized projects in high-unemployment areas.

TARGET POPULATION: Unemployed Employment Insurance and Income Assistance recipients on Cape Breton.

OUTCOMES OF INTEREST: Education, training, poverty, total household income, family formation, migration.

Learn$ave

STARTING YEAR/YEAR FINAL REPORT EXPECTED: 2001/2009.

INFORMATION SOURCE: "Learn$ave: A national demonstration project of individual development accounts for learning," http://srdc.org/english/projects/learnsave.htm, viewed May 7, 2003.

PRINCIPAL INTERVENTIONS: Treatment group members have up to three years to save up to Can$1,500 in an individual development account. The project contributes $3 for every $1 saved. Allowable uses of the account are for training, education, and small business start-up.

TARGET POPULATION: Low-income, low-wealth families in Vancouver, Toronto, and Halifax that are not currently enrolled in school full-time.

OUTCOMES OF INTEREST: Savings, education, and training activity.

4

Continental Europe

Intensified Employment Services—Sweden

SUMMARY: This demonstration, conducted between March 10 and June 6, 1975, tested the effectiveness of providing intensified employment services on a medium-sized sample of unemployed workers in Sweden. Subjects were followed for approximately nine months.

COST: SKr54,000, primarily for three additional personnel.

TIME FRAME: Demonstration period, March–June 1975; data collected, March–December 1975; final report, 1978.

TREATMENTS TESTED: The employment office in Eskilstuna received additional personnel for the period of time over which the experiment took place. Due to the personnel reinforcement, members of the experimental group received an average of 7.5 hours of employment assistance, compared with an average of 1.5 hours for the control group. The experimental group received more personalized service. The normal service received by members of the control group consisted of the provision of general labor market information.

OUTCOMES OF INTEREST: (1) Employment and (2) Earnings.

SAMPLE SIZE: Experimentals, 216; controls, 194.

TARGET POPULATION: Unemployed job seekers who had been registered at the Eskilstuna employment office for at least three months.

NUMBER OF TREATMENT GROUPS: Two (with one control group).

NUMBER AND LOCATION OF SITES: One—Eskilstuna.

RESEARCH COMPONENTS:

▪ Process analysis: Not conducted formally. The personnel at the employment office had a great deal of enthusiasm for the project. Their eagerness to have the demonstration yield positive outcomes may have biased the results of the experiment upward.

▪ Impact analysis: Comparison of means.

▪ Benefit–cost analysis: Conducted.

MAJOR FINDINGS:

1. At the end of the experimental period, 48 percent of the experimental group and 34 percent of the control group were employed.

2. The experimental group had an average of 11 weeks of unemployment from the start of the experiment until the follow-up nine months later. The control group had an average of 18 weeks of unemployment over the same period.

3. According to a nonexperimental comparison, employed members of the experimental group had average earnings of SKr3,588 over the data collection period, while employed members of the control group had average earnings of SKr3,386 over the same period.

All the findings above are statistically significant.

4. A personal communication from the evaluator to the authors of the *Digest* states that a cost-benefit analysis was conducted "in terms of the net increase of the amount of goods and services produced, valued by market prices, from the start of the experiment until the follow-up. The net gain was estimated at about SKr6,000 per participant in the experiment group."

TIME TRENDS IN FINDINGS: None.

DESIGN ISSUES: No major issues.

REPLICABILITY: Information on the exact nature of the services provided the treatment group is not available in English.

GENERALIZABILITY: Eskilstuna is a manufacturing city of about 89,000 people located about 100 miles from Stockholm. The site was chosen because its labor market in the 1970s was considered to have features similar to the labor markets of other Swedish industrial regions. However, the sample is not large, and relevance may fade with time and distance from Sweden.

FUNDING SOURCE: The Expert Group for Labour Market Research at the Swedish Ministry of Labour.

TREATMENT ADMINISTRATOR: County Employment Board, Eskilstuna.

EVALUATOR: Lennart Delander, School of Management and Economics, Vaxjo University.

INFORMATION SOURCES: L. Delander, "Studier kring den arbetsförmedlande versamheten," *Statens Offentliga Utredningar,* Vol 60, 1978 (in Swedish); A. Björklund and H. Regnér, "Experimental Evaluation of European Labour Market Policy," in G. Schmid, J. O'Reilly, and K. Schömann, ed. *International Handbook of Labour Market Policy and Evaluation,* Edward Elgar, 1996.

PUBLIC-USE ACCESS TO DATA: Data were deposited with the Department of Statistics, University of Stockholm, but their accessibility is unknown.

Counseling and Monitoring I—Netherlands

SUMMARY: This demonstration, conducted between 1989 and 1990, tested the effects of intensive job search assistance on a medium-sized sample of the unemployed. Subjects were followed for one year.

COST: Total evaluation costs, approximately f.200,000. Total project costs (excluding evaluation), f.1,200,000–1,400,000.

TIME FRAME: Intake period, November 1989–January 1990. Data were collected and subjects were followed for up to one year after intake.

TREATMENTS TESTED: The treatment was an intensive job search assistance program provided by the staff at the Joint Administrations Office (JAO).

More time was spent with each unemployed person to discuss job applications, direct the job search, offer suggestions, and provide information regarding vacancies that might be suitable. More time was also spent in checking information given by the unemployed to detect falsification and administer penalties. The control group received the traditional, less intensive service.

OUTCOMES OF INTEREST: (1) Period of unemployment and (2) Cost savings.

SAMPLE SIZE: The original sample was 1,631 but fell to the 722 used for analysis because a full "search history" was not available for all of the original sample members. Roughly half were assigned to each group.

TARGET POPULATION: Unemployed people making application for benefits at a JAO in the Netherlands. To be eligible, applicants had to be younger than 57.5 years old and willing to apply for permanent employment.

NUMBER OF TREATMENT GROUPS: Two (with one control group).

NUMBER AND LOCATION OF SITES: Seven— Apeldoorn, Arnhem, Haarlem, Maastricht, Rijswijk, Venlo, and Vlaardingen.

RESEARCH COMPONENTS:
■ Process analysis: Conducted through interviews with subjects. Search activities and labor market events of the sample were recorded.
■ Impact analysis: Effects were estimated by means of a job search model in which the job finding rate was analyzed as the product of application intensity and the conditional matching probability.
■ Benefit–cost analysis: Conducted.

MAJOR FINDINGS:
1. The treatment group participants made significantly more job applications than the control group participants. However, the matching (or success) probability was not significantly different for the two groups. In fact, the treatment group had a slightly lower matching probability. Overall, the estimated program effects on the job-finding rate were not statistically significant, although they did favor the treatment group.
2. For the full sample, there was a weakly statistically significant reduction of unemployment for the treatment group of 8–14 percent. This translates to a reduction in unemployment duration of two to four days. The associated cost savings to the JAO, based on this reduction in unemployment, were estimated at between f.8 million and f.9.6 million. This greatly exceeded the costs of the Counseling and Monitoring program.

TIME TRENDS IN FINDINGS: None.

DESIGN ISSUES:
1. It appears that cost savings reported in finding 2 above are based on statistically insignificant group differences regarding the job-finding rate. Gorter and Kalb (1996) did not provide the statistical significance of the unemployment duration reduction separately, although Gorter mentioned an unpublished JAO analysis that did find "(very) weakly significant values" for this finding.
2. It is noted that despite the large sample loss (from 1,631 to 722) due to the addition of other selection criteria, the random assignment remained valid. The randomness was confirmed by a test showing no difference between groups on labor market history variables.

REPLICABILITY: Replicable.

GENERALIZABILITY: Designed to generalize to the entire nation (the Netherlands).

FUNDING SOURCE: Department of Statistics and Research, Joint Administration Office, the Netherlands.

TREATMENT ADMINISTRATOR: Joint Administration Office.

EVALUATORS: Guyonne R. J. Kalb, Department of Statistics and Research, JAO, Amsterdam; and Cees Gorter, Department of Regional Economics, Free University, Amsterdam.

ENABLING LEGISLATION: None.

INFORMATION SOURCE: Cees Gorter and Guyonne R. J. Kalb, "Estimating the Effect of Counseling and Monitoring the Unemployed Using a Job Search Model," *Journal of Human Resources* 31(1996): 590–610.

PUBLIC-USE ACCESS TO DATA: Available through October 1999 from Cees Gorter, Department of Regional Economics, Free University, Amsterdam.

Labour Market Training (LMT)—Norway

SUMMARY: This demonstration, conducted in 1991, tested the effects of Norway's publicly funded Labour Market Training (LMT), which provides short-term vocational preparation, on a medium-sized sample of unemployed workers. Subjects were followed for six years, 1989–94.

COST: Treatment costs cannot be broken out from the ordinary budget of the Public Employment Service, which organizes such programs on a regular basis. The research costs, covering collection of survey data, data processing and analyses, as well as presentations and reports, run to a total of $339.

TIME FRAME: Demonstration period, 1991. Impacts were measured in 1992, 1993, and 1994. The data cover 1989 to 1994. Data from surveys conducted in 1991 and twice in 1992 were combined with register data on the unemployed.

TREATMENTS TESTED: Subjects in the treatment group applied for LMT, were offered the opportunity to participate, and accepted this offer. LMT courses typically last for 5–20 weeks, although they can last up to 40 weeks. These basic and vocational education courses are intended to maintain and improve the skills of the unemployed. The control group also applied for LMT but did not get an offer.

OUTCOME OF INTEREST: Effects on post-training earnings.

SAMPLE SIZE: Total 770; treatments, 511; controls, 259.

TARGET POPULATION: Unemployed applicants for LMT.

NUMBER OF TREATMENT GROUPS: Two (with one control group).

NUMBER AND LOCATION OF SITES: Three— Hedmark, Østfold, and Sør-Trøndelag counties.

RESEARCH COMPONENTS:
- Process analysis: Implementation was monitored through collection of staff reactions. Withdrawals from the program prior to assignment to training were also examined.
- Impact analysis: Ordinary least squares, fixed effects models, random growth (RG) and modified random growth (MRG) models. Pre- and post-training tests and model restriction tests (for the RG and MRG models) were also used.
- Benefit–cost analysis: None conducted.

MAJOR FINDINGS:
1. The estimated training effect of LMT on annual earnings was positive and statistically significant at the 5 percent level in 1994 and just missed statistical significance at the 5 percent level in 1993. The overall OLS-impact estimate for 1993 is NKr10,000—a 12 percent increase in annual earnings. The overall OLS-impact estimate for 1994 is NKr14,000—a 15 percent increase in annual earnings.
2. The impact on earnings was statistically significant for women in both 1993 and 1994, but insignificant for men.

TIME TRENDS IN FINDINGS: The second-year impact (1994) was as large as—or larger than— the first-year impact (1993).

DESIGN ISSUES:
1. Many administrators of LMT agencies were strongly opposed to randomly assigning LMT participants to courses, and LMT administrators could circumvent the random selection process by withdrawing eligible applications for LMT.

2. Subjects who applied to participate in LMT in one county but were rejected may have applied in another county or at a later time. This may have contaminated the control group; however, very few controls took part in training during the treatment period.

REPLICABILITY: Treatment and control conditions appear to be replicable.

GENERALIZABILITY: The evaluators believe these three counties are reasonably representative of Norway as a whole.

FUNDING SOURCES: Norwegian Ministry of Local Government and Labour, Department of Labour.

TREATMENT ADMINISTRATOR: The Directorate of Labour, and the local branches of the Public Employment Services

EVALUATORS: Oddbjørn Raaum and Ragnar Frisch, Centre for Economic Research, University of Oslo; and Hege Torp, Institute for Social Research, Oslo.

ENABLING LEGISLATION: None.

INFORMATION SOURCE: Oddbjørn Raaum and Hege Torp, "Labour Market Training in Norway–Effects on Earnings," *Labour Economics* 9(2, 2002): 207–47.

PUBLIC-USE ACCESS TO DATA: The data are confidential and are being stored for only a limited period. A license from the Norwegian Data Inspectorate is necessary to obtain the data for research purposes.

Job Training—Denmark

SUMMARY: This demonstration, conducted in 1994, tested the effects of job training on a medium-sized sample of unemployed workers in Denmark. Subjects were followed for six to eight months.

COST: Total evaluation costs, DKr1,313,000.

TIME FRAME: Demonstration period, April–December 1994.

TREATMENTS TESTED: Study participants consisted of unemployed individuals who applied for participation in classroom training courses in April 1994. The experimental group was offered classroom training in the areas of land transportation, the metal industry, and computers. The control group was not offered training.

OUTCOME OF INTEREST: Unemployment.

SAMPLE SIZE: Total, 812; experimentals, 425; controls, 387.

TARGET POPULATION: Unemployed Danish applicants for job training courses.

NUMBER OF TREATMENT GROUPS: Two (with one control group).

NUMBER AND LOCATION OF SITES: Five training sites across the country.

RESEARCH COMPONENTS:
  Process analysis: Not conducted.
  Impact analysis: Variety of increasingly sophisticated tools, including tobit analysis.
  Benefit–cost analysis: Not conducted.

MAJOR FINDINGS: Job training significantly increased unemployment rates by 5–15 percent.

TIME TRENDS IN FINDINGS: None.

DESIGN ISSUES:
1. The job training program for this study is a national program in Denmark designed primarily for skills enhancement of the employed. Therefore, it appears possible that the treatment for this study may not have matched the needs of experimental group participants, who were unemployed.
2. The job training programs used are a weak treatment: an average job training course is two weeks long.
3. Almost one-quarter of the control group, who were supposed to be denied job training, received training anyway. This result may

have biased the estimate of the effects of job training on the experimental group.

4. Over half of the participants in the experimental group chose not to receive training.

REPLICABILITY: Appears replicable (in Denmark, or other countries with active labor market policies).

GENERALIZABILITY: This study was designed to generalize to the unemployed population in Denmark. It is likely that this study could only be generalized to other countries with similar labor market policies.

FUNDING SOURCE: Danish Ministry of Labour, Danish National Institute of Social Research.

TREATMENT ADMINISTRATOR: Danish Ministry of Labour, Danish National Institute of Social Research.

EVALUATOR: Klaus Langager, Socialforsknings-institututtet (Danish National Institute of Social Research).

ENABLING LEGISLATION: None.

INFORMATION SOURCES: Michael Rosholm, "Is Labour Market Training a Curse for the Unemployed? More Evidence from a Social Experiment," working paper, Socialforsknings-institututtet, April 2001; Klaus Langager, "Unemployed in Classroom Training," Report, Socialforskningsinstituttet, 1996.

PUBLIC-USE ACCESS TO DATA: Not available.

Bergen Worker Sickness—Norway

SUMMARY: This demonstration, conducted from April 1995 to December 1997, tested the effects of rehabilitation on a medium-sized sample of Norwegian workers on extended sick leave. Subjects were followed for two years and eight months.

COST: We have no information on costs.

TIME FRAME: Demonstration period, April 1995– December 1997; data collected, same period.

TREATMENTS TESTED: A group of workers on sick leave for eight weeks or more with diagnosis given by a general medical practitioner were enrolled in a rehabilitation program lasting four weeks. The experimentals were given individual advice by medical personnel at three, six, and 10 months after they received treatment. The control group was not provided this service. After 12 months both the treatment and control groups underwent a new examination.

OUTCOMES OF INTEREST: (1) Rehabilitation; (2) Return to work; and (3) Earnings.

SAMPLE SIZE: Total, 560; treatments, 358; controls, 202.

TARGET POPULATION: Private-sector Norwegian employees on sick leave.

NUMBER OF TREATMENT GROUPS: Two (with one control group).

NUMBER AND LOCATION OF SITES: One—Bergen and the surrounding five municipalities.

RESEARCH COMPONENTS:
- Process analysis: Conducted.
- Impact analysis: Regression
- Benefit–cost analysis: Not conducted.

MAJOR FINDINGS:
1. There was no difference in the incidence of returning to work between the treatment group and the controls.
2. Relative to controls, the treatment group had a 6 percent reduction ($1,300) from pre-program earnings. However, the difference was not statistically significant.

TIME TREND IN FINDINGS: None.

DESIGN ISSUES: The evaluators state that there might have been a "randomization bias" in the experiment. Rehabilitation services may have been offered to the controls by competing rehabilitation clinics. However, the evaluators conclude that in the Bergen experiment, nonexperimental evaluation based on sample selection estimators is highly unreliable.

REPLICABILITY: Replicable.

GENERALIZABILITY: Probably generalizable to countries with welfare systems similar to Norway's.

FUNDING SOURCES: Ministry of Social Affairs, Norway and the Norwegian Research Council.

TREATMENT ADMINISTRATOR: Ministry of Social Affairs, Norway.

EVALUATORS: Espen Brathberg and Alf Erling Risa (University of Bergen, Norway, Department of Economics), and Astrid Grasdal (Center for Social Science Research, Bergen, Norway).

INFORMATION SOURCE: Espen Brathberg, Astrid Grasdal, and Alf Erling Risa, "Evaluating social policy by experimental and nonexperimental methods," *Scandinavian Journal of Economics* 104(2002): 147–71.

PUBLIC-USE ACCESS TO DATA: We have no information about a public-use file for this demonstration.

Bergen Pain—Norway

SUMMARY: This demonstration, conducted between January 1996 and March 1997, tested the effects of alternative psychosocial treatments on a medium-sized sample of long-term sick-listed employees disabled by musculoskeletal pain. Subjects were followed for 14 months.

COST: Unknown.

TIME FRAME: Demonstration period, January 1996–March 1997; data collected, same period.

TREATMENTS TESTED: Three treatment groups differing in a prognosis score

(good, medium, poor) for return to work were randomly assigned to three outpatient treatments, each with a different level of intensity (ordinary treatment, light multidisciplinary treatment, and extensive multidisciplinary treatment).

Patients in ordinary treatment were referred back to their general practitioner. General practitioners usually prescribed pain medication and referred patients to physiotherapists or chiropractors.

Multidisciplinary regimes taught that pain was normal in the recovery process and that fear of pain would delay recovery. Light multidisciplinary regimen consisted of individual and group therapy, physiotherapy, and psychological treatment. The extensive multidisciplinary program included cognitive-behavior modification, education in coping with pain and stress, physiotherapy exercises, and occasional workplace intervention.

OUTCOME OF INTEREST: Return to work.

SAMPLE SIZE: Total, 654; ordinary treatment, 263; light multidisciplinary treatment, 222; extensive multidisciplinary treatment, 169.

NUMBER OF TREATMENT GROUPS: Three (with one control group).

TARGET POPULATION: Long-term sick-listed employees with musculoskeletal pain. Due to missing data, government-employed patients were excluded from the evaluation.

NUMBER AND LOCATION OF SITES: One—Bergen and five surrounding municipalities.

Participants According to Prognosis

Screening prognosis	Treatment			
	Ordinary	Light M	Extensive M	N
Good	70	46	26	142
Medium	120	116	92	328
Poor	73	60	51	184
Total	**263**	**222**	**169**	**654**

M = multidisciplinary.

RESEARCH COMPONENTS:

- Process analysis: Not conducted.
- Impact analysis: Regression.
- Benefit–cost analysis: Conducted.

MAJOR FINDINGS:

1. Good prognosis: Neither of the multidisciplinary treatments had an impact on the rate of return to work for patients with good prognosis compared with the ordinary treatment.

2. Medium prognosis: Those undergoing light multidisciplinary and extensive multidisciplinary treatments were more likely to return to work—63 percent and 62 percent, respectively, compared with 48 percent for those undergoing ordinary treatment. These differences are statistically significant.

3. Poor prognosis: Extensive multidisciplinary treatment had a statistically significant impact, compared with ordinary treatment.

4. Most patients returned to work if the treatment they were given corresponded with the screening category hypothesized to be correct for their status—i.e., ordinary treatment for good prognosis, light multidisciplinary treatment for medium prognosis, and extensive multidisciplinary treatment for poor prognosis. Between 55 and 64 percent of subjects had returned to work after 14 months in each prognostic group when given the "right" treatment.

5. Gender and age influenced the prognosis score and return to work. Women were more often classified as having a medium or poor prognosis than men. Older patients with poor prognosis were less likely to return to work than younger patients with poor prognosis.

6. A subgroup analysis of 195 patients with chronic low back pain was carried out for 24 months. The light multidisciplinary treatment was found to be cost-effective for male patients among this subgroup.

TIME TRENDS IN FINDINGS: None apparent.

DESIGN ISSUES: None apparent.

REPLICABILITY: Replicable.

GENERALIZABILITY: Generalizable with caution. Pregnant women, foreigners with insufficient knowledge of Norwegian, and those with a variety of medical conditions were excluded. Only 33 percent of those invited agreed to participate in the study.

FUNDING SOURCES: The Royal Norwegian Department of Health and Social Affairs and City of Bergen Department of Health and Social Welfare. Key personnel: Jan Utkilen.

TREATMENT ADMINISTRATORS: University of Bergen, Office for External Projects, National Insurance Services, and Outpatient Spine Clinic.

EVALUATORS: Ellen M. Halland Haldorsen and Jan Sture Skouen (the Outpatient Spine Clinic, Haukeland University Hospital, Bergen, Norway), Astrid L. Grasdal and Alf Erling Risa (Department of Economics, University of Bergen, Bergen, Norway), Kartsen Kronholm (Department of Health and Social Services, County of Sogn and Fjordane, Leikanger, Norway), and Holger Ursin (Department of Biological and Medical Psychology, University of Bergen, Bergen, Norway).

ENABLING LEGISLATION: None.

INFORMATION SOURCES: Ellen M. H. Haldorsen, Jan S. Skouen, Astrid L. Grasdal, Alf E. Risa, Kartsen Kronholm, and Holger Ursin, "Is There a Right Treatment for a Particular Group? Comparison of Ordinary Treatment, Light Multidisciplinary Treatment, and Extensive Multidisciplinary Treatment for Long-Term Sick Listed Employees with Musculoskeletal Pain," *Pain* 95 (2002): 49–63; Jan S. Skouen, Astrid L. Grasdal, Ellen M. H. Haldorsen, and Holger Ursin, "Relative Cost-Effectiveness of Extensive and Light Multidisciplinary Treatment Programs versus Treatment as Usual for Patients with Chronic Low Back Pain on Long-Term Sick Leave: Randomized Controlled Study," *Spine* 27(9, 2002): 901–09.

PUBLIC-USE ACCESS TO DATA: Not available.

Counseling and Monitoring II—Netherlands

SUMMARY: This demonstration, conducted between 1998 and 1999, tested the effect of job search assistance on a medium-sized sample of the unemployed. Subjects were followed until they left the unemployment insurance (UI) system or until February 1999, whichever occurred first.

COST: Not available.

TIME FRAME: Demonstration period, August 1998–February 1999; data collected, same period.

TREATMENTS TESTED: Individuals assigned to Counseling and Monitoring (C&M) were required to attend monthly meetings for six months, during which previous job search activities were evaluated and a plan for the next period was made. Both the control group and the experimental group members were required to submit a status report every four weeks. For the treatment group, these reports were discussed during the C&M meetings; the control group members had only to submit their reports. There were no other requirements for the control group.

OUTCOME OF INTEREST: UI benefit receipt and duration.

SAMPLE SIZE: Total, 394; treatments, 205; controls, 189.

TARGET POPULATION: Unemployed individuals who have sufficient marketable skills and therefore have the highest probability of reemployment (Type I on a scale of I to IV).

NUMBER OF TREATMENT GROUPS: Two (with one control group).

NUMBER AND LOCATION OF SITES: Two—one in each of two of the largest cities in The Netherlands, referred to as City 1 and City 2.

RESEARCH COMPONENTS:
- Process analysis: Administrative records and follow-up survey.
- Impact analysis: Bivariate and multivariate analysis.
- Benefit–cost analysis: Conducted from the perspective of the Dutch National Institute for Social Security (unemployment agency).

MAJOR FINDINGS:
1. None of the estimated program effects was statistically significant.
2. There were no differences between the two cities in the probability of exit to work.
3. The monitoring (of work search activities) component encouraged formal job search methods at the expense of informal job search methods.

TIME TRENDS IN FINDINGS: The initial cost-effectiveness was estimated to rapidly diminish over time.

DESIGN ISSUES:
1. More individuals received the follow-up questionnaire than there were in the final database. Attempts at matching the individuals who responded to the questionnaire with the individuals in the database were only successful for 104 individuals (49 experimentals and 55 controls).
2. The experiment was not performed as planned in City 2. Type II workers (i.e., insufficient skills) entered the experiment. Type II workers who were selected into the treatment group were identified at the intake meeting of C&M and excluded from the experiment. However, some Type II workers may have remained in the control group. Since Type II individuals are expected to require intensive job search assistance, the estimated effect of C&M could be slightly upward biased.

REPLICABILITY: Replicable.

GENERALIZABILITY: According to the evaluators, the sample was intended to be representative for the cities from which they were drawn, but the sample is unlikely to be representative for the Dutch population of unemployed workers with similar characteristics.

FUNDING SOURCE: Dutch National Institute for Social Security.

TREATMENT ADMINISTRATORS: Local unemployment agencies.

EVALUATORS: Gerard J. van den Berg, Free University Amsterdam, Tinbergen Institute, IFAU-Uppsala and CEPR; and Bas van der Klaauw, Free University Amsterdam.

ENABLING LEGISLATION: None.

INFORMATION SOURCE: Gerard J. van den Berg and Bas van der Klaauw, *Counseling and Monitoring of Unemployed Workers: Theory and Evidence from a Controlled Social Experiment,* September 2001.

PUBLIC-USE ACCESS TO DATA: Not available.

Targeted Negative Income Tax—Germany

SUMMARY: This demonstration, conducted from 1999 to 2002, tested the effects of targeted and time-limited negative income tax plans in seven small and medium-sized samples of unemployed public assistance recipients in the German states of Baden-Wuerttemberg and Hesse. Subjects were followed for about two years.

COST: Research costs, approximately €750,000.

TIME FRAME: Demonstration period, 1999–2002.

TREATMENTS TESTED: Targeted and time-limited negative income tax (TNIT) plans. The specifics of the tested program varied from site to site. Benefit-reduction rates were around 50 percent, but the exact formula varied considerably among sites. Earnings had to be below the public assistance break-even level to qualify for TNIT payments. Time limits were around one year in most sites but were somewhat longer in a few sites. Controls were eligible for the regular public assistance program, which after a disregard typically

taxed earnings at around 100 percent. Thus, the TNIT provided stronger work incentives.

OUTCOMES OF INTEREST: (1) Employment; (2) Net income; and (3) Receipt of public assistance.

SAMPLE SIZE (for sites with random assignment only): City of Freiburg: treatments, 754; controls, 754. County of Tubingen: treatments, 44; controls, 29. County of Fulda: treatments, 120; controls, 120. County of Kassel: treatment group I, 230; treatment group II, 181; controls, 186. City of Kassel: treatments, 206; controls, 206. County of Odenwald: treatments, 45; controls, 45. City of Offenbach: treatments, 260; controls, 240.

TARGET POPULATION: Long-term unemployed people on public assistance. The exact nature of the target group varied from site to site.

NUMBER OF TREATMENT GROUPS: Two (with one control group) in all but one site; the County of Kassel had three groups with one control group.

NUMBER AND LOCATION OF SITES: Seven—In the State of Baden-Wuerttemberg: City of Freiburg and County of Tubingen; in the State of Hesse: County of Fulda, County of Kassel, City of Kassel, County of Odenwald, and City of Offenbach.

RESEARCH COMPONENTS:
- Process analysis: Conducted using a checklist on implementation issues (e.g., letters sent to recipients, press information, oral interviews, etc.).
- Impact analysis: Conducted using comparison of means and probit analysis.
- Benefit–cost analysis: Not conducted.

MAJOR FINDINGS: Small positive and statistically significant effects on employment were found in Fulda, Hesse. Implementation problems were not important in this site (see "Design Issues"). In the remaining sites, implementation was sufficiently flawed that no conclusions about impacts are possible.

TIME TRENDS IN FINDINGS: Not analyzed.

DESIGN ISSUES: The planned test of the TNIT experienced considerable implementation problems at many sites. For example, in most (but not all) sites, those eligible for the TNIT, which involved a complex change from their current situation, were simply notified of the change by letter, without any further attempts at follow-up.

REPLICABILITY: The demonstration could be replicated. However, more control would have to be exercised at the demonstration sites to avoid implementation problems.

GENERALIZABILITY: Uncertain.

FUNDING SOURCES: Ministries of Social Affairs in Baden-Wuerttemberg and Hesse.

TREATMENT ADMINISTRATORS: County or city governments in each location.

EVALUATOR: Institute for Applied Economic Research (IAW). Key personnel: Alexander Spermann and Andrea Kirchmann, IAW and University of Freiburg.

ENABLING LEGISLATION: §18 Abs. 5 BSHG, the Federal Public Assistance Act.

INFORMATION SOURCES: Sabine Dann, Andrea Kirchmann, Alexander Spermann, and Jurgen Volkert, *Targeted Negative Income Tax: Idea, Transposition and a Provisional Result after 15 Months in Baden-Wuerttemberg*, 2002.

Sabine Dann, Andrea Kirchmann, Alexander Spermann, and Jurgen Volkert, *Einstiegsgeld in Baden-Wurttemberg: Wissenschaftliche Begleitforschung des Hessischen Modellversuchs* ("Entry Earnings in Baden-Wurttemberg: Accompanying Scientific Study of the Hessian Trials"), Sozialministerium, 2002.

Sabine Dann, Andrea Kirchmann, Alexander Spermann, and Jurgen Volkert, *Modelversuch "Hessischer Kombilohn"* ("Piloting the TNIT in Hesse"), Institut fur Angewandte Wirtschaftsforschung, 2002.

Note: Most of the material in this summary was obtained through correspondence with Alexander Spermann, the project director. The two final reports are written in German and were not translated into English prior to publication of the *Digest*.

Zurich Bike Messengers— Switzerland

SUMMARY: This demonstration, conducted in 2000, tested the effects of a pre-announced temporary increase in piece-rate wages on a small sample of bike messengers. Subjects were followed for four months.

COST: Unknown.

TIME FRAME: Demonstration period, August–November 2000; data collected, January–November 2000.

TREATMENTS TESTED: Bike messengers are paid a fixed percentage of the revenue from each delivery. They can sign up for more or fewer shifts and can increase or decrease the number of deliveries they choose to handle per shift. This demonstration randomly assigned messengers to two groups. Group A received an increase in the fixed percentage from 39 percent for males (44 percent for females) to 49 percent (54 percent for females) between September 11 and October 6, 2000, while group B members worked at their usual rates. Group B received the increase between October 30 and November 24, 2000, while group A worked at their usual rates. The experiment was announced in August 2000.

OUTCOMES OF INTEREST: (1) Shifts worked and (2) Deliveries per shift.

SAMPLE SIZE: Group A, 22; group B, 22.

TARGET POPULATION: Bicycle messengers of the Veloblitz Delivery Service.

NUMBER OF TREATMENT GROUPS: Two (with one control group).

NUMBER AND LOCATION OF SITES: One—Zurich.

RESEARCH COMPONENTS:

- Process analysis: Conducted through administration of questionnaires and "lotteries" (see "Major Findings").
- Impact analysis: Conducted through OLS, survivor functions, and Cox regressions.
- Benefit–cost analysis: Not conducted.

MAJOR FINDINGS:

1. Shifts worked:

	When Group A had higher piece rate	When Group B had higher piece rate
Group A	13.3	8.7
Group B	8.7	11.4

Taking into account duration effects (the probability of working today is an increasing function of having worked yesterday) and personal characteristics, the evaluators estimated a conditional probability of working that is 18 percent higher given a 25 percent increase in the piece rate. They also estimated an intertemporal elasticity of substitution in this sample of 0.8.

2. Revenues per shift (effort) (in Swiss francs):

	When Group A had higher piece rate	When Group B had higher piece rate
Group A	297	314
Group B	304	293

Taking into account personal characteristics and other factors, the evaluators estimated that a 25 percent increase in the piece rate induces a 6 to 8 percent reduction in effort per shift, implying an intertemporal elasticity of substitution of about –0.3. Similar results are obtained when effort is measured in number of deliveries rather than in revenues.

3. The authors interpret the effort result as evidence that some messengers have a target income per shift: that is, they are averse to earning less than the target but not highly motivated to earn much more than the target. To test this interpretation, they invited the subjects to participate in a second round experiment involving choice under uncertainty, eight months after the initial experiment. Subjects could accept or reject participation in certain lotteries, all of which had positive expected payoffs but involved the possibility of loss. From subject choices over these lotteries, they derived a measure of loss aversion. They report that reductions in effort during the main experiment are confined to those who rejected participation in the follow-up lotteries. Loss aversion had no impact on choice of shifts.

TIME TRENDS IN FINDINGS: Not applicable.

DESIGN ISSUES: To guard against Hawthorne effects, messengers were not informed that the purpose of the study was to study labor supply behavior, or that their shift and delivery records were to be analyzed. They were instead told that the purpose was to study wages and job satisfaction.

REPLICABILITY: Replicable.

GENERALIZABILITY: The sample size is very small.

FUNDING SOURCE: Swiss National Science Foundation.

EVALUATORS: Ernest Fehr and Lorenz Götte, University of Zurich.

TREATMENT ADMINISTRATORS: Veloblitz Delivery Service and the evaluators.

ENABLING LEGISLATION: None.

INFORMATION SOURCE: Ernest Fehr and Lorenz Götte, "Do Workers Work More If Wages Are High? Evidence from a Randomized Field Experiment," working paper no. 125, Institute for Empirical Research in Economics, University of Zurich, October 2002.

PUBLIC-USE ACCESS TO DATA: We have no information about a public-use file for this demonstration.

Undergraduate Student Achievement—Netherlands

SUMMARY: This experiment, conducted during the 2001–02 academic year and the following summer, tested the effects of financial rewards on the academic achievement of a small sample of first-year undergraduate economic and business students at the University of Amsterdam. Subjects were followed for one year.

COST: Approximately €28,000 for financial bonuses and payments to students for completing two questionnaires. There were no additional costs other than the evaluators' time, which was donated.

TIME FRAME: Random assignment, October 2001; demonstration period, October 2001–August 2002; data analyzed, 2002–03.

TREATMENTS TESTED: To obtain a university degree in economics or business at a Dutch university, students must pass *all* their first-year economics exams at some point. It is in the interest of the economics department that they pass them earlier rather than later.

Students in two different treatment groups were given financial rewards if they passed *all* their first-year requirements before the start of their second academic year. These requirements consisted of passing a series of (mostly) multiple-choice tests. Although students could do this by passing makeup exams after their second academic year began, they could qualify for a financial bonus only by passing all the exams when they were first given or by passing makeup exams given before September 2003. The bonuses for those randomly assigned to the high and low bonus groups were €681 and €227, respectively.

The control group was not eligible for financial rewards.

OUTCOMES OF INTEREST: (1) Student study effort; (2) First-year passing rates; and (3) Academic credit points.

SAMPLE SIZE: Total, 249; high bonus group, 83; low bonus group, 84; control group, 82.

TARGET POPULATION: First-year undergraduate economic and business students at the University of Amsterdam. Ninety-eight percent of all eligible students volunteered to participate in the experiment.

NUMBER OF TREATMENT GROUPS: Three (with one control group).

NUMBER AND LOCATION OF SITES: One—the University of Amsterdam.

RESEARCH COMPONENTS:
- Process analysis: Questionnaire sent to students at the end of the experiment.
- Impact analysis: Comparisons of means.
- Benefit–cost analysis: Not conducted.

MAJOR FINDINGS:
1. The first-year passing rate for the high bonus group was 23 percent versus 20 percent for the low bonus group and 20 percent for the control group. These differences are not statistically significant.
2. Among those students whose fathers have a higher education degree (133 of the 249 students in the sample), the passing rate for the high bonus group was 27 percent versus 18 percent for the low bonus group and 20 percent for the control group. These differences are not statistically significant, probably because of the small sample size.
3. Among those students classified as having good math skills on the basis of their secondary school grades in math (107 of the 249 students in the sample), the passing rate for the high bonus group was 45 percent versus 39 percent for the low bonus group and 33 percent for the control group. These differences are not statistically significant, probably because of the small sample size.
4. Eligibility for the financial bonuses did not increase student (self-reported) study time. However, in the questionnaire given at the end of the experiment, 37 percent of the students assigned to the high bonus group and 21 percent of the students assigned to the low

bonus group reported that they studied harder in response to the financial incentives.

5. The evaluators conclude that "financial incentives can only have an impact if [meeting] the requirements are feasible" and, given the very low passing rate, meeting the requirement to receive a financial bonus was not very feasible for average or below-average students.

TIME TRENDS IN FINDINGS: Time-trend analysis is not relevant to this experiment.

DESIGN ISSUES: Other than low statistical power resulting from the small sample size, no design issues are apparent.

REPLICABILITY: Replicable.

GENERALIZABILITY: Generalizable to programs at other universities that have similar degree requirements—for example, the undergraduate programs in economics and business offered by five other Dutch universities.

FUNDING SOURCE: Self-funded from the research funds of the evaluators.

TREATMENT ADMINISTRATOR: Department of Economics, the University of Amsterdam. Permission to conduct the experiment was given by the Dean of the Department of Economics, Jacques van der Gaag.

EVALUATORS: Edwin Leuven, Department of Economics, the University of Amsterdam; Hessel Oosterbeek, Department of Economics, the University of Amsterdam; and Bas van der Klaauw, Department of Economics, the Free University in Amsterdam.

ENABLING LEGISLATION: None.

INFORMATION SOURCES: Edwin Leuven, Hessel Oosterbeek, and Bas van der Klaauw, "The Effect of Financial Rewards on Students' Achievement: Evidence from a Randomized Experiment," unpublished manuscript, May 2003.

PUBLIC-USE ACCESS TO DATA: Not available.

5

Latin America

PACES (Programa de Ampliación de Cobertura de la Educación Secundaria)—Colombia

SUMMARY: This demonstration, conducted from 1993 to 1997, tested the effects of school vouchers on a large sample of children from low-income families in two large Colombian cities. Subjects were followed for up to five years.

COST: Evaluation, $60,000; experiment, roughly $1,000,000.

TIME FRAME: The Colombian government established the Programa de Ampliación de Cobertura de la Educación Secundaria (PACES) in 1991. This demonstration focused on the 1993 and 1997 vouchers' applicant cohorts from Bogotá and the 1993 applicants from Cali. Survey was conducted in 1998–99. Final report, June 2001.

TREATMENTS TESTED: A lottery was conducted among 125,000 pupils from low-income families in Colombia. Experimentals received school vouchers that covered approximately half the tuition cost of private secondary school. The controls did not receive private school subsidies from the government.

OUTCOMES OF INTEREST: (1) School attendance and completion; (2) Families' educational expenditure; (3) Hours worked and age of marriage; and (4) Government educational expenditure.

SAMPLE SIZE: Total, 6,156; experimentals, 4,050; controls, 2,106. Completed interviews: Total, 1,618; experimentals, 830; controls, 788.

TARGET POPULATION: Pupils from low-income families residing in poor neighborhoods in two large cities in Colombia.

NUMBER OF TREATMENT GROUPS: Two (with one control group).

NUMBER AND LOCATION OF SITES: Two—Bogotá and Cali.

RESEARCH COMPONENTS:
- Process analysis: Not conducted.
- Impact analysis: Conducted using regression and probit.
- Benefit–cost analysis: Conducted.

MAJOR FINDINGS:
1. Lottery winners (experimentals) completed an additional year of schooling compared with controls.
2. Lottery winners worked 1.2 fewer hours per week than the controls.
3. Winning the lottery induced households to devote more net resources to education.
4. The program increased public educational expenditure by approximately $24 per lottery winner.
5. Lottery winners' net resource contribution to education was $19, on average; PACES will most likely raise lottery winners' wages by $36 per year.

TIME TRENDS IN FINDINGS: None.

DESIGN ISSUES:
1. The applicant survey was conducted over the telephone, but almost none of the applicants in one city, Cali, had phones. The survey was done in only one suburb of Cali where applicants had access to phones.
2. An attempt was made to interview almost 3,000 applicants. The overall applicants' interview response rate was only 54 percent.
3. The completed interviews were only about a quarter of the original sample size, 6,156 applicants.
4. Response rates for lottery winners and lottery losers were almost equal; this reduces the probability of sample selection bias.

REPLICABILITY: Replicable.

GENERALIZABILITY: The authors say that the findings are generalizable to countries with weak public school systems and well-developed private education sectors.

FUNDING SOURCES: World Bank and the Colombian Institute for Education, Credit and Training Abroad (ICETEX). Key personnel: None.

TREATMENT ADMINISTRATORS: World Bank and ICETEX.

EVALUATORS: Joshua D. Angrist and Eric Bettinger.

ENABLING LEGISLATION: None.

INFORMATION SOURCE: Joshua D. Angrist, Eric Bettinger, Erik Bloom, Elizabeth King, and Michael Kremer, *Vouchers for Private Schooling in Colombia: Evidence from a Randomized Natural Experiment,* working paper 8343, National Bureau of Economic Research, June 2001.

PUBLIC-USE ACCESS TO DATA: Contact the National Bureau of Economic Research.

School Facility Improvements—Bolivia

SUMMARY: This quasi-experimental study, conducted from 1993 to 1997, tested the effects of investment in physical facilities through a Social Investment Fund on a small sample of schools in Bolivia. Subjects were followed for five years.

COST: Cost of two education projects, this one and another with no randomization component, was $82 million. The total cost of the evaluation of the Social Investment Fund, which also comprised projects in health, water, and sanitation, was $880,000.

TIME FRAME: Demonstration period, 1993–97; baseline data collected, 1993, and follow-up data collected in 1997.

TREATMENTS TESTED: Treatment schools were made eligible to receive funding under this demand-driven program. Actual investment depended on approved proposals, and comprised infrastructure improvements and learning materials. Control schools were left as they were and were not provided additional inputs.

OUTCOMES OF INTEREST: (1) School-level outcomes (such as availability of blackboards and teacher-student ratios) and (2) Student-level outcomes (such as enrollment, school attendance, and academic achievement).

SAMPLE SIZE: Total schools, 200; treatments, 86; controls, 114.

TARGET POPULATION: Elementary school children in Bolivia.

NUMBER OF TREATMENT GROUPS: Two (with one control group).

NUMBER AND LOCATION OF SITES: One—Chaco region in Bolivia.

RESEARCH COMPONENTS:
- Process analysis: Not conducted.
- Impact analysis: Regression-adjusted.
- Benefit–cost analysis: Not conducted.

MAJOR FINDINGS:
1. The treatment resulted in statistically significant improvements in the infrastructure of schools and additional inputs such as desks and textbooks.
2. No statistically significant effects were found on enrollment, attendance, or academic achievement. Among student-level outcomes, only the dropout rate displayed a statistically significant impact. Because of control noncompliance (see "Design Issues"), a point estimate of the impact is not provided, only a range of between −4 and −6 percentage points (the dropout rate for all Chaco schools was 9 percent). The upper bound limit on the estimate (−4 percent) is significantly different from what the upper bound would be if the intervention had no effect, with a p-value of .08, but the lower bound limit is not significantly

different from the corresponding lower bound statistic.

TIME TRENDS IN FINDINGS: None.

DESIGN ISSUES: The intention was to exclude control schools from the benefits of the intervention by failure to promote it to them. Some schools, however, learned of the treatment by word of mouth, applied for funds, and received them. The evaluators' use of "Manski bounds" to estimate impact is motivated by the fact that some control schools "crossed over."

REPLICABILITY: Replicable.

GENERALIZABILITY: Because the worst-off and best-off schools were excluded from the sample, the study's findings cannot be generalized to all schools even in the Chaco region. These findings tend to confirm nonrandomized studies suggesting that absent teacher upgrades, other education investments tend not to result in significant impacts on students' education outcomes. However, the combination of small sample size and control noncompliance results in a test of such low power that impacts might not be reliably measured.

FUNDING SOURCES: The World Bank and the German Institute for Reconstruction and Development.

TREATMENT ADMINISTRATOR: Bolivian Social Investment Fund.

EVALUATORS: John Newman (World Bank), Menno Pradham (World Bank), Laura B. Rawlings (World Bank), and Geert Ridder (University of Southern California).

ENABLING LEGISLATION: None.

INFORMATION SOURCE: John Newman, Menno Pradham, and Laura B. Rawlings, "An Impact Evaluation of Education, Health, and Water Supply Investments by the Bolivian Social Investment Fund," *The World Bank Economic Review* 16(2, 2002): 241–71.

PUBLIC-USE ACCESS TO DATA: Contact the evaluators. The data have not been stored in a public-use file, but might be available to interested researchers.

PROGRESA (Programa de Educación, Salud, y Alimentación)—Mexico

SUMMARY: This quasi experiment, conducted from October 1997 to October 1999, tested the effects of transfer payments tied to school attendance on poor families in a medium-sized sample of localities in Mexico. Subjects were followed for three years.

COST: The cost of the demonstration cannot be separated from the larger overall program cost.

TIME FRAME: Demonstration period, October 1997–October 1999; data gathered from baseline household surveys administered in October 1997 and March 1998 and from two follow-up surveys administered at approximately one-year intervals.

TREATMENTS TESTED: Experimentals received the PROGRESA subsidy package, consisting of a cash subsidy for school attendance averaging $55 per month (depending on sex and grade level of the child), health clinic services, and nutritional supplements. The supplements were available if the household had children less than 2 years of age, a pregnant or lactating mother, or malnourished children up to 5 years of age.

Households in control localities received no treatment.

OUTCOMES OF INTEREST: (1) Ages of school matriculation; (2) Number of grades completed; (3) Grade repetition; (4) Dropout rates; and (5) School reentry rates among dropouts.

SAMPLE SIZE: Total randomly assigned localities, 506; treatments, 320; controls, 186. 30,000 children participated in the quasi experiment.

TARGET POPULATION: The poorest families in rural Mexico, as determined by a discriminant analysis.

Key variables used in the analysis were measures of household assets, dependency rations, and number of children.

NUMBER OF TREATMENT GROUPS: Two (with one control group).

NUMBER AND LOCATION OF SITES: 506 localities, 31 states in Mexico.

RESEARCH COMPONENTS:
- Process analysis: Not conducted.
- Impact analysis: Regression.
- Benefit–cost analysis: Not conducted.

MAJOR FINDINGS:
1. There were statistically significant impacts on school enrollment—on average, about 0.4 grades over three years for poor children due to the program, about 0.5 for girls and 0.3 for boys.
2. For children age 6 to 10 years, program participation was associated with less grade repetition and better grade progression. For children age 11 to 14, the program decreased the dropout rate.

TIME TRENDS IN FINDINGS: Results based on a simulation evaluating the effects of longer terms of exposure to the program indicate that if children were to participate in the program between ages 6 and 14, they would experience a significant increase in average educational attainment levels and a significant increase in junior secondary school attendance.

DESIGN ISSUES:
1. The program was expanded into many of the control localities toward the end of the demonstration period, potentially influencing the behavior of the control households that probably anticipated receiving the benefits.
2. Because the treatment was limited to a community's poorest families, there may have been negative spillover effects on the education of children from ineligible families, which were relatively better off. This was not taken into account by the impact analysis. For

instance, at ages 8, 9, and 12, ineligible children residing in the treatment communities had a lower grade retention rate in the most prevalent grade levels than children in the control communities. Overall, however, the differences were not statistically significant.

REPLICABILITY: Replicable.

GENERALIZABILITY: Learnfare demonstrations in the U.S. appear to have had much lower impacts than those reported here, but there is no obvious reason that similarly generous tied transfer programs would not have similar impacts in other developing countries.

TREATMENT ADMINISTRATORS: Government of Mexico and International Food Policy Research Institute (IFPRI).

EVALUATORS: Jere Behrman and Piyali Sengupta, University of Pennsylvania, and Peter Todd, University of Pennsylvania and National Bureau of Economic Research.

ENABLING LEGISLATION: None.

INFORMATION SOURCE: Jere Behrman, Piyali Sengupta, and Petra Todd, *Progressing through Progresa: An Impact Assessment of a School Subsidy Experiment,* University of Pennsylvania and IFPRI, April 2001.

PUBLIC-USE ACCESS TO DATA: The Mexican government owns the data sets. They are not publicly available.

Proempleo—Argentina

SUMMARY: This demonstration, conducted from 1998 to 2000, tested the effects of wage subsidy and specialized training for private-sector jobs on a medium-sized sample of Argentinean workers in workfare employment. Subjects were followed for 18 months.

COST: Approximately $150,000.

TIME FRAME: Demonstration period, January 1999–June 2000; data collected in December 1998 (baseline) and during the demonstration period.

TREATMENTS TESTED: Two treatments were tested: a wage subsidy and training.

One group of experimental workers received a wage subsidy voucher; a second group of workers was provided skills training as well as a wage subsidy voucher. The voucher entitled a hiring employer to a wage subsidy of $150 per month for workers more than 45 years old and $100 per month for younger workers. The subsidy was paid directly to the worker as part of his/her salary. The employer would then discount the amount of the subsidy from the gross wages paid to the worker. The employer was compensated for the subsidy conditional on formally registering the worker. For example, an employer hiring a voucher recipient at the minimum wage of $200 and registering this fact would incur a Social Security charge of $60, but receive a subsidy of $150, and thus would only pay a net wage of $110.

Controls received neither benefit.

OUTCOMES OF INTEREST: (1) Employment and (2) Income.

SAMPLE SIZE: Total, 848; vouchers, 354; vouchers and training, 213; controls, 281.

TARGET POPULATION: Argentinean workers temporarily employed under workfare employment programs.

NUMBER OF TREATMENT GROUPS: Three (with one control group).

NUMBER AND LOCATION OF SITES: Two—Cutral Co and Plaza Huincul, towns in the department of Confluencia in the province of Nuequen.

RESEARCH COMPONENTS:
- Process analysis: Not conducted.
- Impact analysis: Regression.
- Benefit–cost analysis: Cost-effectiveness calculation performed.

MAJOR FINDINGS:

1. The proportion of the sample of workfare participants getting a private-sector job was 14 percent for randomly selected voucher recipients versus 9 percent for the control group, a statistically significant difference.
2. Both the voucher-only and the voucher-plus-training treatments increased the probability of employment in the private sector to the same degree, by approximately 6 percentage points—that is, no additional impact resulted from skills training.
3. The treatment did not have a significant effect on self-employment or wage earnings.
4. Take-up of the wage subsidy by private firms was low; the subsidy was conditional on the employer registering the worker and thereby incurring non-wage costs.

TIME TRENDS IN FINDINGS: A statistically significant impact on employment was found after six months and 18 months, but not after 12 months.

DESIGN ISSUES:

1. The last six months of the study saw a contraction of the workfare program nationally and in the study towns, and a reduction in workfare benefits from $200 to $160 per month.
2. The Ministry of Labor did not announce the experiment publicly, nor were subjects told that they were part of an experiment.
3. Unregistered employers in the informal sector, which employs half of the Argentinean workforce, were not eligible for subsidy.

4. The evaluators corrected for selective take-up of the training component.

REPLICABILITY: Replicable.

GENERALIZABILITY: Generalizable to countries with labor laws similar to Argentina's. Labor laws in Argentina require formal sector employers to bear worker monthly Social Security costs and administrative costs, as well as severance payments when the worker is let go.

FUNDING SOURCES: Ministry of Labor, Government of Argentina, and the World Bank. Key personnel: Polly Jones and Martin Ravallion for the Ministry and Agustin Salvia for the World Bank.

TREATMENT ADMINISTRATOR: Ministry of Labor, Government of Argentina.

EVALUATORS: Emanuela Galasso and Martin Ravallion, Development Research Group, the World Bank.

ENABLING LEGISLATION: None.

INFORMATION SOURCE: Emanuela Galasso, Martin Ravallion, and Agustin Salvia, *Assisting the Transition from Workfare to Work: A Randomized Experiment,* Policy Research Working Paper 2738, World Bank, December 2001.

PUBLIC-USE ACCESS TO DATA: Scheduled for public access from the World Bank by January 1, 2003, pending agreement with the Ministry of Labor, Government of Argentina.

6

United Kingdom

Electricity Pricing

SUMMARY: This demonstration, conducted from 1966 to 1972 in Great Britain, tested three different pricing schemes for electricity on a large sample of residential consumers. Subjects were followed for five years.

COST: Not available.

TIME FRAME: Demonstration period, 1966–72; data collected, same period.

TREATMENTS TESTED:

A. Subjects in this treatment group received a seasonal tariff. This rate was approximately 150 percent of the normal tariff rate, 24 hours a day for the months of December, January, and February. During the remaining months, the price was approximately 70 percent of the normal tariff. Restricted-hour tariffs were available to consumers at the standard rates.

B. Subjects in this treatment group received a seasonal time-of-day (STD) rate. This rate was approximately 300 percent of the normal tariff on working days, during the hours of 8:00 AM to 1:00 PM, and again from 4:30 PM until 7:30 PM during the months of December, January, and February. The rate for the remaining hours was approximately 40 percent of the normal tariff. Restricted-hour rates were not available to these consumers.

C. Subjects in this group received the load rate. These subjects set a target amount of electricity that they would consume yearly, with the setting priced at £4–£5 per kilowatt yearly. When consumption was above the target amount, the price per kilowatt was 100 to 200 percent of the £4–£5 standard. When consumption was below the setting, the price was roughly 60 percent of the £4–£5 standard. For a fee of £1 per year, the "overload" register could be disabled at night. Restricted-hour tariffs were not available to these subjects.

D. Controls received block rates. The price per kilowatt fell with increased consumption to a final rate. Restricted-hour rates were available to consumers upon request, but these only applied to certain applications, such as space and water heating. One Area Board used day/night rates for all applications in 1965, with night rates lower than day rates. This pricing was later made available throughout England and Wales.

OUTCOMES OF INTEREST: (1) Effects of differential pricing on electricity consumption and (2) Cost-effectiveness of differential pricing.

SAMPLE SIZE: Total 3,420; Group A (seasonal), 840; Group B (STD), 840; Group C (load rate), 840; controls, 900.

TARGET POPULATION: Consumers purchasing 3,000 or more kilowatt-hours (kWh) yearly.

NUMBER OF TREATMENT GROUPS: Four (with one control group).

NUMBER AND LOCATION OF SITES: Six Area Boards—South Eastern, South Western, Eastern, East Midlands, South Wales, and Merseyside and North Wales.

RESEARCH COMPONENTS:
▪ Process analysis: None conducted.
▪ Impact analysis: Comparison of means.
▪ Benefit–cost analysis: Conducted from consumer perspective.

MAJOR FINDINGS:
1. All three pricing schemes increased the load factor, or the annual energy sold as a percentage of the energy which would have been sold if average daytime demand during winter had persisted for a year. The seasonal scheme, together with restricted-hour rates, was the most effective in increasing the daytime load factor, doing so by 10 percentage points.
2. The STD rate was the most effective at diverting consumption away from peak times, doing

so by 116 kWh on average. This was linked to the disincentive of a tripled price.
3. The load rate was the least effective in increasing the daytime load factor. Electric consumption by group C was not statistically different from that of the controls.
4. There was no evidence that differential pricing affected the acquisition of electric appliances. STD pricing resulted in a 38 percent increase in the average installed load of storage heating or space heating used in off-peak hours. The result with seasonal pricing was 15 percent, and the load rate exhibited no impact.
5. "In general, all the consumers taking part in the experiment—even those on the more punitive high rates of the split samples for pricing—thought their tariffs worth continuing and would recommend them to friends."
6. Broad estimates indicate that, on average, differential pricing results in a net loss to the community of £0.8/kWh each for the seasonal and load rate tariffs and £1.7/kWh for the STD rate.

TIME TRENDS IN FINDINGS: None reported.

DESIGN ISSUES:
1. The lengthy duration of the experiment made it difficult to keep all original houses in the sample as owners changed. Approximately 25 percent of households originally enrolled in the study dropped out as they moved out of the area.
2. Incentives, in monetary form and in the form of suppression of meter rentals, affected consumers' willingness to participate in the experiment and suffer peak pricing and unusual metering.
3. The authors note that the experiment was costly. "Smaller scale and shorter experiments could be mounted at reduced cost though the credibility of the findings would suffer."

REPLICABILITY: New technology may have lowered the cost of the complex metering used when the study was first conducted. This could facilitate replication.

GENERALIZABILITY: The study was designed to generalize nationally to the United Kingdom and to consumers of even larger amounts of energy, perhaps as much as 5,000 kWh or more.

FUNDING SOURCE: The Electricity Council.

TREATMENT ADMINISTRATORS: Local Area Electricity Boards.

EVALUATOR: J. G. Boggis, Assistant Commercial Advisor, Load and Market Research, The Electricity Council.

ENABLING LEGISLATION: None.

INFORMATION SOURCE: J. G. Boggis, *Domestic Tariff Experiment,* Load and Market Research Report No. 121, The Electricity Council, 1974.

PUBLIC-USE ACCESS TO DATA: We have no information about a public-use file.

Restart

SUMMARY: This evaluation of an ongoing program in Great Britain, conducted from 1989 to 1991, examined the effects of mandatory interviews with a counselor on a large sample of unemployment benefit claimants. Subjects were followed for one year after the interview was scheduled.

COST: Evaluation, approximately £750,000.

TIME FRAME: Demonstration period: Restart became a national program in 1987–88. Random assignment took place between September and December 1988, just prior to the date of the Restart interviews. Data collected: summer 1989–spring 1990.

TREATMENTS TESTED: Mandatory interviews of 15 to 20 minutes with a counselor six months after becoming a claimant, and every six months thereafter, with a possible follow-up interview at the counselor's discretion. In principle, failure to attend a scheduled interview could lead to reconsideration of benefit eligibility. The counselor attempted to link the unemployed person with appropriate services and, hence, would schedule

appointments with service providers (e.g., job clubs, training providers, and Employment Service job placement staff) if appropriate.

Members of the control group did not see the counselors six months after becoming a claimant unless they requested an interview but were eligible for the same services as members of the treatment group. After 12 months, members of the control group were included in the full Restart process.

OUTCOMES OF INTEREST: (1) Time as an unemployment benefit claimant; (2) Time to exit unemployment; (3) Time to enter employment; (4) Time in employment; (5) Whether entered training; (6) Time in training; (7) Time in nonactivity (i.e., as a nonclaimant without a job or in training); (8) Job search efforts; and (9) Wage rates.

SAMPLE SIZE: Total, 8,189 cases (of these, 4,807 were interviewed in the first survey and 3,419 in both surveys); treatments, 7,661; controls 528 (of these 323 were interviewed in the first survey and 246 in the second survey).

TARGET POPULATION: People on the unemployed benefit claimant rolls for five and one-half months.

NUMBER OF TREATMENT GROUPS: Two (with one control group).

NUMBER AND LOCATION OF SITES: Every Employment Service local office in Britain.

RESEARCH COMPONENTS:
- Process analysis: Conducted. Included visits to local employment service offices and descriptive statistical analyses of the extent to which clients attended scheduled interviews with counselors, client reactions to interviews, topics covered in interviews, and services received by clients.
- Impact analysis: Conducted using highly sophisticated econometric techniques including multivariate survivor models.
- Benefit–cost analysis: Not conducted. However, Restart was found to cost around £20–£25 per interview with a counselor.

MAJOR FINDINGS:

1. Over 80 percent of those people for whom an interview with a counselor was scheduled attended. About two-thirds of the remainder were formally excused and most of the others already had found employment. Thus, sanctions were rarely imposed.

2. Restart reduced unemployment claims by around 5 percent. People in Restart spent less time as an unemployed claimant during the study period and took less time to leave the unemployed claimant register and find employment or enter a training program. Restart had an effect on time in a training program, but not on the use of job search or on wage levels, job stability, or job quality. The analysis of whether Restart affected time in employment was inconclusive. Restart tended to move participants into a nonclaimant, nonemployment status for a short period immediately after the counselor interviews, but over the longer run this effect was reversed. Most of the effects of Restart were similar for men and women. Particular efforts were made in Restart to help claimants who appeared to be at a disadvantage in the labor market (e.g., those with little work experience or disabilities).

TIME TRENDS IN FINDINGS: The effect of Restart on movement into nonclaimant status mainly occurred about one month after the interviews with counselors. Effects on movements into employment and training did not emerge until around six months after the interviews.

DESIGN ISSUES:

1. A large fraction of the sample was not interviewed in the surveys. However, administrative data, which were not potentially subject to attrition bias, were used as a check on findings based on the survey data. Findings based on these two types of data were broadly consistent with one another.

2. The control group was too small to permit analysis of subgroups.

3. About one-quarter of the control group had Restart interviews with counselors. However, several analyses indicated that this did not seriously bias the evaluation findings. For example, the conclusions from the analysis were similar regardless of whether those who had Restart interviews were included in or excluded from the analysis sample.

REPLICABILITY: Replicable.

GENERALIZABILITY: Because the evaluation was national and based on a random sample of unemployment benefit claimants, it can be generalized to all parts of Great Britain and to all claimants. The evaluation pertains to a period of low unemployment. Program effects could differ in periods of high unemployment.

FUNDING SOURCE: Employment Service.

TREATMENT ADMINISTRATOR: Employment Service.

EVALUATOR: Policy Studies Institute. Key personnel: Michael White and Jane Lakey. Surveys were conducted by Social and Community Planning Research.

POLICY EFFECTS: Michael White indicates that the study contributed to strengthening the government's view that mandatory interviews with counselors are worth doing. Restart still exists, and other British programs have adopted similar policies. The evaluation may have also contributed to increased emphasis on employment counseling in other OECD countries.

INFORMATION SOURCE: Michael White and Jane Lakey, *The Restart Effect: Evaluation of a Labour Market Programme for Unemployed People,* Policy Studies Institute, 1992.

PUBLIC-USE ACCESS TO DATA: Available from the British Employment Service.

13-Week Review

SUMMARY: This demonstration, conducted from November 1991 to December 1991 in the United

Kingdom, tested a new unemployment insurance program on a large sample of individuals collecting unemployment benefits. Subjects were followed for six months.

COST: The evaluation costs, including data collection, were probably less than $30,000.

TIME FRAME: Demonstration period, November–December 1991; data collected, November 1991–May 1992.

TREATMENTS TESTED:

A. These claimants were the control subjects and were not exposed to any part of the new review process.

B. Upon their 11th week of unemployment, claimants in this group were issued a letter explaining the conditional nature of their benefits, asking them what actions they had been taking to find work, and offering further help in finding employment. At their 13th week of unemployment, a signing clerk reviewed claimants to determine if they were available for work and actively seeking employment. Interviews with claimant advisers occurred only upon client request or if there was serious doubt about whether a claimant was available for work and was actively seeking work.

C. Like the claimants in group B, claimants in group C received the letter at the 11th week of unemployment and the review at the 13th week. In addition, they were required to participate in interviews with claimant advisers, unless there were good reasons for exemption.

OUTCOMES OF INTEREST: (1) Number of claimants on the unemployment register; (2) Length of benefit collection; and (3) Amount of benefits collected.

SAMPLE SIZE: Total 2,469; group A, 821; group B, 832; group C, 816.

TARGET POPULATION: Unemployed workers who had received at least 10 weeks of benefits.

NUMBER OF TREATMENT GROUPS: Three (with one control group).

NUMBER AND LOCATION OF SITES: Twenty-six—local Employment Service offices in Battersea, Bootle, Coatbridge, Colne, Diss, Dunstable, Falmouth, Gorseinon, Hartlepool, Hounslow, Ilford, Ilkeston, Kirkaldy, Leeds, Llangollen, Maltby, Mexborough, Mold, Newcastle, Redditch, Sandbach, Sheffield, Stretford, Sutton Coldfield, Trowbridge, and Washington.

RESEARCH COMPONENTS:
▓ Process analysis: None conducted.
▓ Impact analysis: OLS and log-rank tests.
▓ Benefit–cost analysis: Not conducted, but unpublished cost-effectiveness ratios were computed.

MAJOR FINDINGS:

1. Over the six-month tracking period, 45 percent of the claimants in group B and 47 percent of the claimants in group C left the unemployment register, thereby terminating their receipt of unemployment benefits; only 41 percent of the claimants in group A, the control group, left the register. Fifteen percent of the control claimants who left the register later signed on again, compared with 19 percent in both groups B and C.

2. Clients in groups B and C left the register more rapidly than controls, a statistically significant result. There was no meaningful difference between claimants in groups B and C.

3. On average, over the six-month tracking period, claimants from group C spent five days less time on the register than claimants in group B, and claimants in group B spent four days less time on the register than controls. Thus, the evidence suggests that the interview, notification letter, and review by the signing clerk reduce the amount of time claimants stay on the register and, hence, collect unemployment benefits.

TIME TRENDS IN FINDINGS: None reported.

DESIGN ISSUES: Of the original sample enrolled in the study, missing information meant that 156 clients could not be tracked.

REPLICABILITY: Replicable.

GENERALIZABILITY: The study was conducted on a nationwide scale.

FUNDING SOURCE: Employment Service.

TREATMENT ADMINISTRATORS: Employment Service local offices.

EVALUATORS: Employment Service, Research and Evaluation Branch. Key personnel: Andrew Birtwhistle, Janet Gawn, Sue Jones, and Jayne Harrison.

ENABLING LEGISLATION: None.

INFORMATION SOURCE: Andrew Birtwhistle, Janet Gawn, Sue Jones, and Jayne Harrison, *Evaluation of 13-Week Review,* Research and Evaluation Branch, Employment Service Report No. 87, September 1993.

PUBLIC-USE ACCESS TO DATA: Not available.

30-Month-Plus Restart

SUMMARY: This demonstration, conducted from May 1992 to December 1992 in the United Kingdom, tested the effects of using more experienced advisers in conducting Restart interviews on a large sample of unemployment benefit claimants. Subjects were followed for six months.

COST: The evaluation costs, including data collection, were probably less than $30,000.

TIME FRAME: Demonstration period, May–June 1992; data collected, May–December 1992.

TREATMENTS TESTED: Use of a more experienced, rather than a less experienced, adviser in interviews with unemployment benefit claimants. Treatment subjects were interviewed by an experienced client adviser (EO), who recorded their activities over the past six months, offered advice, and then confirmed an agreed upon back-to-work plan.

Subjects in the control group met with a less experienced client adviser (AO), who explained their benefit eligibility and referred them to either a program or a more experienced adviser (EO). In addition, the AO checked the client's back-to-work plan and then summarized the agreed upon plan.

OUTCOME OF INTEREST: Exit from the unemployment compensation register.

SAMPLE SIZE: Total 1,422; treatments, 716; controls, 706.

TARGET POPULATION: Individuals who had been unemployed for 30 months or more and were currently collecting unemployment benefits.

NUMBER OF TREATMENT GROUPS: Two (with one control group).

NUMBER AND LOCATION OF SITES: Thirty-six—local Employment Service offices in Abertillery, Airdrie, Bishopsworth, Blackpool, Blayden, Bridgend, Brighton, Chelmsley Wood, Dudley, Edinburgh, Enfield, Gloucester, Hanley, Harion, Hessle, Houghton-Le-Spring, Inverness, Ipswich, Leeds, Leicester, Leigh, Llandudno, Lowestoft, Manchester, North Shields, Park Court, Redruth, Saltcoats, Sheffield, South Kirby, Stavely, Stockton, Stratford, Wallasey, Weymouth, and Wrexham.

RESEARCH COMPONENTS:
- Process analysis: None conducted.
- Impact analysis: Comparison of means.
- Benefit–cost analysis: None conducted.

MAJOR FINDINGS:
1. EO interviewers were more effective in getting clients to agree to a course of future action than controls.
2. The data suggest that more EO clients than AO clients moved on to other benefits as a result of the referrals, but this result is not statistically significant.
3. There was no statistically significant difference between EO and AO clients in movements on and off the register, nor were there any significant differences in why clients terminated their benefits.
4. There was no significant difference between EO and AO clients in time over which they collected benefits.

TIME TRENDS IN FINDINGS: None reported.

DESIGN ISSUES: Because local offices had different operational systems, each was allowed to adapt its own office system, instead of all offices receiving a comprehensive set of instructions. This may have led to differences in the treatment of clients.

REPLICABILITY: Apart from changes in the environment since the study was completed, this study appears replicable.

GENERALIZABILITY: Study was conducted on a national scale, suggesting that the results are generalizable nationwide.

FUNDING SOURCE: Employment Service.

TREATMENT ADMINISTRATOR: Employment Service local offices.

EVALUATOR: Employment Service Research and Evaluation Branch. Key personnel: Janet Gawn and Sue Jones.

ENABLING LEGISLATION: None.

INFORMATION SOURCE: Janet Gawn and Sue Jones, *Evaluation of 30 Month + Restart Interviews,* Research and Evaluation Branch, Employment Service Report No. 84, August 1993.

PUBLIC-USE ACCESS TO DATA: Not available.

Supportive Caseloading

SUMMARY: This demonstration, conducted in 1993, tested the effects of mandatory consultation sessions on a medium-sized sample of the unemployed in the United Kingdom. Subjects were followed for up to 26 weeks.

COST: Estimated internal staff costs, £30,000.

TIME FRAME: Demonstration period began April 1993, end date unclear; data collected through 26 weeks.

TREATMENTS TESTED: Supportive caseloading services consisted of a series of interview sessions, each lasting about 20 minutes. During the ses-

sions, trained advisers assisted clients in developing strategies to overcome factors that the clients believed were barriers to employment.

OUTCOMES OF INTEREST: (1) Unemployment register off-flow; (2) Unemployment benefit receipts; and (3) Employment.

SAMPLE SIZE: Total, 643; treatments, 489; controls, 154.

TARGET POPULATION: Unemployed individuals who were not participating in other Employment Service programs.

NUMBER OF TREATMENT GROUPS: Two (with one control group).

NUMBER AND LOCATION OF SITES: Two offices in North Norfolk—Cromer and North Walsham.

RESEARCH COMPONENTS:
- Process analysis: Examined sample characteristics, the random assignment process, unemployment register off-flows, and status after leaving the register.
- Impact analysis: Comparison of means.
- Benefit–cost analysis: None conducted.

MAJOR FINDINGS:
1. The largest impact was observed at the 13-week tracking period. However, only 450 of the 643 clients had been in the study long enough to be included in the 26-week tracking period.
2. At 13 weeks, 40 percent of the treatment group was no longer receiving unemployment benefits, compared with 23 percent of the control group.
3. At 26 weeks, 22 percent of the treatment group had found employment compared with 8 percent of the control group, a 2 percentage point increase over the impact observed at 13 weeks.

TIME TRENDS IN FINDINGS: The effects at 26 weeks were similar to those observed at 13 weeks.

DESIGN ISSUES: Random assignment at the Cromer office was seriously compromised. A large number of clients who were ineligible for treatment were assigned by error to the treatment group but not the control group. The Cromer piece of the evaluation appears to be essentially nonexperimental.

REPLICABILITY: The treatment should be replicable.

GENERALIZABILITY: The evaluators were cautious about generalizability. Because this study was conducted on a rather small number of clients, and the part of the evaluation that focused on the Cromer office is essentially nonexperimental, findings might not generalize.

FUNDING SOURCE: U.K. Employment Service.

TREATMENT ADMINISTRATORS: Local Jobcentre Employment Services staff. Four advisers (two in each of the site offices) conducted the majority of the interview sessions.

EVALUATOR: Employment Service Research and Evaluation Branch. Key personnel: Andrew Birtwhistle.

ENABLING LEGISLATION: None.

INFORMATION SOURCE: Andrew Birtwhistle, Diane Barnes, and Colleen Looby, *Evaluation of Supportive Caseloading (1-2-1) in North Norfolk: Tracking Study,* Research and Evaluation Branch, Employment Service, November 1994.

PUBLIC-USE ACCESS TO DATA: Not available.

Jobplan

SUMMARY: This demonstration, conducted in 1993, tested the effects of an intensive goal-setting workshop on a large sample of unemployed workers. Subjects were followed for three months.

COST: Estimated internal staff costs were £30,000. These costs pertain to only the random assignment component of the evaluation.

TIME FRAME: Demonstration period, September–December 1993; data collected three months after random assignment.

TREATMENTS TESTED: A mandatory five-day workshop, intended to help clients who have been unemployed for 12 months set achievable goals to compete successfully for jobs. Failure to attend could result in sanctions of up to 40 percent of income support for one week. Members of the control group were not required to attend a workshop.

OUTCOME OF INTEREST: Effect on employment register.

SAMPLE SIZE: Total, 1,785; treatments, 1,052; controls, 733.

TARGET POPULATION: Long-term unemployed workers.

NUMBER OF TREATMENT GROUPS: Two (with one control group).

NUMBER AND LOCATION OF SITES: Ninety-one regional offices throughout the United Kingdom.

RESEARCH COMPONENTS:
- Process analysis: Administrative records.
- Impact analysis: Bivariate analysis.
- Benefit–cost analysis: Conducted.

MAJOR FINDINGS: Compared with the control group, 5.2 percent more of the Jobplan members were off the unemployment register 16 weeks after random assignment. Of this, 2.1 percentage points are attributed to those who found work and the remainder is equally divided between those who enrolled in work training and other reasons. Only the combined effect is statistically significant. It was not possible to separate the effect of the assistance Jobplan provided from the deterrent effect of Jobplan on individuals who were, in fact, not available for work.

TIME TRENDS IN FINDINGS: None.

DESIGN ISSUES: The study was designed to measure the effect of requiring clients to attend a Jobplan workshop, rather than the effect of attending a workshop. Control group members who asked to attend Jobplan were allowed to do so. In addition, 20 percent of the control group was required to attend Jobplan, perhaps because their adviser forgot about the study. In part because of this problem, nonexperimental analysis was also conducted. The analysts made a best judgment as to the true value of the impact by combining the results of these analyses.

REPLICABILITY: The concept is replicable.

GENERALIZABILITY: The study was designed to be generalizable to the United Kingdom, but, given the compromised control group, the impact measured by the experimental analysis may be understated.

FUNDING SOURCE: U.K. Employment Service.

TREATMENT ADMINISTRATORS: Local Employment Service offices.

EVALUATOR: Employment Service Research and Evaluation Branch. Key personnel: J. Kay.

INFORMATION SOURCES: J. Kay, *Jobplan Evaluation: Tracking Study,* Research Management, Employment Service, December 1994; A. Birtwhistle, *Jobplan Evaluation: Summary of Findings,* Research and Evaluation Branch Employment Service, December 1994.

PUBLIC-USE ACCESS TO DATA: Not available.

1–2–1/Workwise

SUMMARY: This demonstration, conducted in the United Kingdom from April 1994 to April 1996, tested the effects of mandatory interviews, assessment, and guidance and job search on a large sample of long-term unemployed youths. Subjects were followed for two years.

COST: The evaluation costs, including data collection, were probably less than $30,000.

TIME FRAME: Demonstration period, April 1994–April 1996; data collected, same period.

TREATMENTS TESTED: 1–2–1 required clients to attend up to six mandatory caseload interviews with

an Employment Service adviser; Workwise was a mandatory four-week program that combined assessment, guidance, and practical job search assistance (i.e., completing application forms, compiling a CV, help in contacting employers, and advice on where to look for a job and how to prepare for interviews). The two programs were designed to work as a package to meet the particular needs of clients. The control group did not receive any of the services.

OUTCOMES OF INTEREST: (1) Employment; (2) Education; and (3) Training.

SAMPLE SIZE: Total, 1,960; treatments, 998; controls, 962.

TARGET POPULATION: Young people between 18 and 24 years old on Jobseeker's Allowance who had been unemployed for at least a year.

NUMBER OF TREATMENT GROUPS: Two (with one control group).

NUMBER AND LOCATION OF SITES: Nine—East Midlands & Eastern, London & South East, Northern, Northwest, Office for Wales, Office for Scotland, South West, West Midlands, and Yorkshire & Humberside employment offices.

RESEARCH COMPONENTS:
- Process analysis: Conducted.
- Impact analysis: Regression.
- Benefit–cost analysis: Not conducted.

MAJOR FINDINGS:
1. In the period between 13 and 24 weeks after random assignments, 35 percent of clients in the treatment group either found work or enrolled in training and education; 22 percent of the controls achieved these objectives. This 13 percentage point difference is statistically significant.
2. Clients with better educational qualifications were more likely to find employment or to take up training and education opportunities more quickly.

TIME TRENDS IN FINDINGS: None.

DESIGN ISSUES: Employment Service advisers had some flexibility in deciding who was referred to which treatment among the five different combinations of 1–2–1 and Workwise, and the order in which they should be referred. The original concept of the combined program was to move subjects through 1–2–1 and then, if no intended results were achieved, to Workwise.

REPLICABILITY: Replicable.

GENERALIZABILITY: Intended for nationwide generalizability, but some regions, notably Northern and Wales, were overrepresented in the study, while others, especially London and the South East and South West regions, were underrepresented. Movement of clients off the unemployment register was strongly correlated with region, but the report states, "there are no serious implications for the evaluation."

FUNDING SOURCE: Employment Service.

TREATMENT ADMINISTRATOR: Employment Service.

EVALUATOR: Employment Service: Key personnel: J. Kay and J. Fletcher.

ENABLING LEGISLATION: None.

INFORMATION SOURCE: J. Kay and J. Fletcher, *Evaluation of 1–2–1/Workwise for 18–24 Year-Olds: Tracking Study,* Employment Service, London, October 1996.

PUBLIC-USE ACCESS TO DATA: Not available.

Lone Parent Caseworker Pilots

SUMMARY: This demonstration, conducted from 1994 to 1995 in England, tested a pilot unemployment assistance program on a medium-sized sample of single-parent welfare recipients. Subjects were followed for eight months.

COST: Evaluation, £141,922.

TIME FRAME: Demonstration period, November 1994–June 1995; data collected, same period.

TREATMENTS TESTED: Subjects in the treatment group were contacted and invited to attend an interview, which was mainly about in-work benefits and local child care provision, with a caseworker within the (then-) Benefits Agency (welfare). They might then have an interview with an adviser from the (then-) Employment Services Jobcentre about entering paid work.

Controls were not contacted or invited to participate in a caseworker interview.

OUTCOMES OF INTEREST: (1) Employment and (2) Welfare benefits.

SAMPLE SIZE: Administrative data: total, 3,123; treatments, 1,507; controls, 1,616. Survey data: total, 915; treatments, 543; controls, 372.

TARGET POPULATION: Single parents with children five years of age or older.

NUMBER OF TREATMENT GROUPS: Two (with one control group).

NUMBER AND LOCATION OF SITES: Four—nationwide. The sites are unnamed and designated as Areas 1–4 to protect the confidentiality of the participants.

RESEARCH COMPONENTS:
- Process analysis: Interviews were conducted with Benefit Agency and Employment Services staff, and administrative records were monitored. The speed with which the pilot was implemented and a shift in objectives during the study created difficulties for the evaluation (see "Design Issues").
- Impact analysis: Comparison of means.
- Benefit–cost analysis: Conducted from single parent and government perspectives.

MAJOR FINDINGS:
1. Participation in the program was low at first, but picked up during the demonstration's six-month lifespan.
2. Virtually the same proportion of treatment subjects and control subjects did not change their job status and, thus, did not change their

benefit receipt. Of those who did change their circumstances, there was no significant difference between treatment and control group members concerning why they changed their official status. No employment effects could be attributed to the intervention.

3. Seven percent of treatment group members started education or training during the first six months, compared with 5 percent of controls.

4. There was no statistically significant difference between treatment and control groups in movement off Income Support (social assistance paid to lone parents and other groups).

5. Twenty-eight percent of the treatment group reported looking for paid work, compared with 23 percent of controls.

6. Net overall cost of the program per treatment subject per week was approximately as follows:

Area 1	Area 2	Area 3	Area 4	Overall
£3.12	£1.57	£1.99	£12.75	£5.17

TIME TRENDS IN FINDINGS: None reported.

DESIGN ISSUES:
1. Different economic and labor market conditions in Area 4 appear to have skewed some data in that area upward. This particularly affected the benefit–cost analysis.
2. The short time period of the pilot did not allow for sufficient examination of certain changes made in the objectives of the treatment.

REPLICABILITY: An entirely altered policy environment, in which work-focused interviews for lone parent welfare recipients is now universal, suggests this study would not be replicable in England.

GENERALIZABILITY: This study was conducted nationally. The four areas examined are economically and socially very different, which skewed some of the data.

FUNDING SOURCE: The former Department of Social Security.

TREATMENT ADMINISTRATORS: Offices of the former Benefits Agency and Employment Service.

EVALUATOR: Centre for Research in Social Policy, Loughborough University. Key personnel: Jill Vincent, Robert Walker, Barbara Dobson, Bruce Stafford, Matt Barnes, and David Bottomley.

ENABLING LEGISLATION: None.

INFORMATION SOURCE: Jill Vincent, Robert Walker, Barbara Dobson, Bruce Stafford, Matt Barnes, and David Bottomley, *Lone Parent Caseworker Pilots Evaluation: Summary Report*, CRSP263, Centre for Research in Social Policy, Loughborough University, September 1998.

PUBLIC-USE ACCESS TO DATA: Not available.

1–2–1 for the Very Long Term Unemployed

SUMMARY: This demonstration, conducted in the United Kingdom from June 1996 to April 1997, tested the effects of voluntary interviews, assessment, and guidance and job search on a large sample of long-term unemployed (30 months or more) workers. Subjects were followed for six months.

COST: The evaluation costs, including data collection, were probably less than $30,000.

TIME FRAME: Demonstration period, June 1996–April 1997; data collected, same period.

TREATMENTS TESTED: Unemployment services such as interviews, assessment, and guidance were provided on a voluntary basis to the treatment group. Controls were not provided the services.

OUTCOMES OF INTEREST: (1) Exits from unemployment register; (2) Employment; (3) Education; and (4) Training.

SAMPLE SIZE: Total, 1,628; treatments, 883; controls, 745.

TARGET POPULATION: Long-term unemployed between 18 and 50 years old.

NUMBER OF TREATMENT GROUPS: Two (with one control group).

NUMBER AND LOCATION OF SITES: Fourteen— Bridgend & Glamorgan Valleys, Derby St. Peters, Durham South, East Durham, East London (5 offices), Gateshead & South Tyneside, Greater Nottinghamshire, Heads of the Valley & Caerphilly, Newcastle West, and South Glamorgan unemployment offices.

RESEARCH COMPONENTS:
▪ Process analysis: Conducted.
▪ Impact analysis: Regression-adjusted.
▪ Benefit–cost analysis: Not conducted.

MAJOR FINDINGS: Six months into the treatment, the likelihood of exit from the unemployment register increased by 13 percentage points; 34 percent of the treatment group exited the unemployment register versus 21 percent of the controls. This impact estimate is statistically significant. Most of the exits were into training and education rather than employment.

TIME TRENDS IN FINDINGS: None.

DESIGN ISSUES: In a few sites there was incorrect nonrandom allocation into treatment and control groups. The evaluation reports states, "Although this is unlikely to affect the analysis, follow up work is being carried out to confirm that there is no bias." It was not possible to find any information about the results of this follow-up work.

GENERALIZABILITY: Nationally generalizable, given the broad sample of British unemployment offices.

FUNDING SOURCE: Employment Service.

TREATMENT ADMINISTRATOR: Employment Service.

EVALUATOR: Employment Service. Key personnel: S. Boutall and M. A. Knight.

ENABLING LEGISLATION: None.

INFORMATION SOURCE: S. Boutall and M. A. Knight, *Evaluation of the 1–2–1 for the Very Long Term Unemployed: Tracking Study,* Employment Service, London, April 1998.

PUBLIC-USE ACCESS TO DATA: Not available.

Benefits Agency Visiting Officer/NDLP

INFORMATION SOURCE: Jill Whitehead of the Martin Hamblin Group, *A Report on the New Deal for Lone Parents: BA Visiting Officer Pilots Evaluation,* The Employment and Benefits Agency, London, December 2000.

SUMMARY FROM ABOVE SOURCE: This pilot test began in the United Kingdom in spring 2000. Sample follow-up varied between three and six months. Benefits Agency visiting officers made and maintained direct contact with lone parents receiving Income Support (welfare) through a series of face-to-face interviews. The objective was to encourage participation in the New Deal for Lone Parents (NDLP), a voluntary program designed to assist unemployed lone parents in returning to work or obtaining training. The pilot test was to be evaluated by random assignment. Of the 406 individuals who agreed to participate in the demonstration, 189 were randomly assigned to the treatment group and 217 to the control group. In the event, only fractions of these groups were actually surveyed by the evaluators: 101 (53 percent) from the treatment group and 140 (65 percent) from the control group. The evaluators attributed the low response rate to a number of contact problems, including the use of box addresses, rather than residential addresses; the boarding up of homes; contact information becoming obsolete; and refusal to answer the door. Moreover, although both the treatment and control groups were surveyed between April and June 2000, those in the treatment group were mainly contacted toward the beginning of this period, while controls were mainly contacted toward the end of the period. Because of the small sample available for the evaluation, only a few treatment group–control group comparisons were made, and tests of statistical significance were not conducted. The evaluation mainly relied on a qualitative analysis. Only 14 people (14 percent) actually joined the NDLP program, and, of these, only 9 said they found the program useful. Six of the 14 joined an NDLP training course in computers.

A separate qualitative analysis appended to the evaluation report states that the research "missed the mark by not meeting its objectives in comparing the rates of participation in NDLP and the outcomes of treatment and control groups."

NUMBER AND LOCATION OF SITES: Random assignment took place in Salford and Grimsby in the United Kingdom.

COST: £50,000 for work performed by the Martin Hamblin Group.

TREATMENT ADMINISTRATOR: Employment Service. Key personnel: Alison Herrington.

EVALUATOR: Martin Hamblin Group. Key personnel: Sue Quinn and Neil Bellamey.

PUBLIC-USE ACCESS TO DATA: Not available.

New Deal 25 Plus

INFORMATION SOURCE: David Wilkinson (Policy Studies Institute), *New Deal for the Long-Term Unemployed: Random Assignment Pilots Evaluation Survey Data Analysis,* U.K. Department of Work and Pensions, April 2003.

SUMMARY FROM ABOVE SOURCE: The British New Deal 25 Plus program was originally largely voluntary but has been mandatory since April 2001 for Jobseeker Allowance (unemployment insurance) beneficiaries who have been unemployed for 18 months or 18 out of 21 months and are between 25 and 50 years old. Clients are required to participate in Gateway, during which they have weekly meetings with a New Deal Personal Adviser, who helps them with techniques to find

work and in developing an Action Plan. This phase of the program can last for up to 16 weeks, though it is often shorter. Short-term work preparation training and brief temporary jobs are made available during this time. Those who do not find work during the Gateway phase are referred to a mandatory Intensive Activity Period, which lasts between 13 and 26 weeks, for training courses, subsidized employment, work experience placements, or help with self-employment. An education and training opportunity of up to 52 weeks may also be available. If clients do not find work during this stage, they must participate in a "Follow Through" period in which they return to regular meetings with an adviser, who helps them capitalize on the training or work experience they have received and during which they have access to further training.

Until they had been unemployed for 24 months, the comparison group (a control group was intended) could volunteer to receive the kinds of services normally offered by the Employment Service to the long-term unemployed. Otherwise, they were only required to show that they were actively seeking work. At 24 months, the Gateway component of New Deal 25 Plus became mandatory for the comparison group, but the Intensive Activity and the Follow Through stages were not mandatory.

Random assignment was conducted at two different sites for unemployed people who became eligible for the program between November 1998 and March 2001. At one site, the intervention occurred after 12 months of unemployment, and at the other site, after 18 months of unemployment. Eligibility for the standard New Deal 25 Plus program at that time did not occur until after 24 months of unemployment.

The process analysis indicated that the assignment of individuals into treatment and control groups was executed without major problems. However, the information systems used to collect data for the control group failed, partly because caseworkers were not made aware of the importance of these data and partly because of technical problems with the systems. As a result, only limited information was consistently available for the control group.

This meant that while it was possible to identify precisely when members of the treatment group were assigned *to* the treatment, it was not possible to identify when members of the control group were assigned *out of* the treatment, or to be wholly certain when the observation period for control group members began. Because of this, the evaluators matched members of the treatment group to individuals randomly assigned to the control group on the basis of claim start dates and other available data, and conducted the analysis for matched comparison groups, rather than for randomly assigned groups. Thus, although the evaluators felt the assignment worked well, they could not fully exploit random assignment.

The analysis included a limited number of variables available from administrative data, plus analysis of survey data, which allowed some identification of what treatment each group received. Unfortunately, response rates to the surveys were only around 38 percent. At each site, the sample size was roughly 170 respondents for the treatment group and 170 respondents for the comparison group.

Both data sources indicated that at both sites, between 6 and 10 percent fewer members of the treatment group were unemployed 15 months after becoming random assignment than members of the comparison group. However, it was not clear whether the program had a positive effect on being in work. For participants who were employed at the time of the survey, hourly pay was lower for the treatment group than the comparison group at both sites. At one site, however, there were more full-time jobs, fewer temporary jobs, and more training for members of the treatment group; but at the other site, there were fewer full-time jobs, more temporary jobs, and less training.

NUMBER AND LOCATION OF SITES: Two in the vicinity of London—the Bexley and Greenwich areas; and the Ealing, Hillingdon, Hounslow, and Richmond areas.

TREATMENT ADMINISTRATOR: Jobcentre Plus, United Kingdom. Key personnel: Maureen Moroney and Jane Hall.

EVALUATOR: David Wilkinson, Policy Studies Institute.

Intensive Gateway Trailblazers (IGT)/NDYP

SUMMARY: This demonstration, conducted in 1999, tested the New Deal for Young People's new job placement program on a large sample of young adults. Subjects were followed for nine months.

COST: Evaluation work was done in-house by the British Employment Service, at small cost.

TIME FRAME: Demonstration period, October 1999–March 2000.

TREATMENTS TESTED: The U.K. Gateway of New Deal for Young People is a four-month program in which unemployed youths develop an "action plan" with the help of a personal adviser. The treatment group was to be provided a more intensive training and counseling program, with a mandatory course and more time with personal advisers. Controls remained in the original Gateway program with no mandatory course and less contact with their personal advisers.

OUTCOMES OF INTEREST: (1) Speed and effectiveness with which participants found work; (2) Attempts by participants to enhance their employability; (3) Development of "soft skills," early identification of clients' special needs, and prompt and appropriate referrals; and (4) Intensiveness of IGT's gateway.

SAMPLE SIZE: Total 4,700; about half assigned to the treatment and control groups.

TARGET POPULATION: Young adults, 18–24, who have been unemployed for six months or more. Such individuals must participate in the United Kingdom's New Deal for Young People program to continue receiving unemployment benefits.

NUMBER OF TREATMENT GROUPS: Two (with one control group).

NUMBER AND LOCATION OF SITES: Twelve—Bedfordshire, Forth Valley, Glasgow, Hackney, Lincolnshire, Liverpool, Luton (Sheffield), North Devon, North East Wales, Shropshire, Sunderland, and West Dunbartonshire.

RESEARCH COMPONENTS:
- Process analysis: Interviews with personal advisers and clients were conducted throughout the demonstration period to monitor the structure and effectiveness of meetings and classes.
- Impact analysis: A "quick" in-house statistical impact analysis was conducted. No written information on this analysis is available.
- Benefit–cost analysis: None conducted.

MAJOR FINDINGS:
1. As previously indicated, there is no available written report on the impact analysis. However, the evaluators indicate that there was "some" indication that Intensive Gateway Trailblazers (IGT) increased at the margin the proportion of young adults entering jobs and reduced length of stay on Gateway.
2. The IGT provision is more intensive than the original Gateway, but the degree of intensity varies across locales and programs.
3. Initially, the IGT program did not sufficiently address special client needs, yet was more effective in doing this than the original Gateway program. This is in part due to disorganization within the original program.
4. Client interviews indicate that IGT improved "soft skills," as well as clients' confidence. However, there was no mechanism to fully assess the effectiveness with which such skills were developed.

5. The reluctance of personal advisers to request or clients to disclose pertinent personal information reduced the effectiveness with which special needs were identified and administered to.

TIME TRENDS IN FINDINGS: None reported.

DESIGN ISSUES: In practice, the services received by clients enrolled in the treatment group did not differ very much from those received by control clients. For example, there was difficulty in securing attendance at the mandatory courses. As a result, program impacts were expected to be small.

REPLICABILITY: Replicable.

GENERALIZABILITY: Gateway program is a national program, and IGT was tested nationally.

FUNDING SOURCE: Employment Service.

TREATMENT ADMINISTRATORS: Gateway regional offices.

EVALUATOR: ECOTEC Research and Consulting Limited. Key personnel: Vicky Davies and Pat Irving.

ENABLING LEGISLATION: None.

INFORMATION SOURCE: Vicky Davies and Pat Irving, *New Deal for Young People: Intensive Gateway Trailblazers. A Final Report to the Employment Services,* ECOTEC Research and Consulting Limited, May 2000.

PUBLIC-USE ACCESS TO DATA: Available if a written application is made to the United Kingdom's Job Centre Plus.

In-Work Training Grant (IWTG)

INFORMATION SOURCE: Jane Lakey, Jane Parry, Helen Barnes, and Rebecca Taylor, *New Deal for Lone Parents: A Qualitative Evaluation of the In-Work Training Grant Pilot,* Department for Work and Pensions, London, July 2002.

SUMMARY FROM ABOVE SOURCE: This pilot test, which began in the United Kingdom in June 2000 and continued for 12 months, offered grants for training of up to £750 to lone parents participating in the New Deal for Lone Parents program at the time they moved from unemployment into jobs. The pilot test was to be evaluated by random assignment. Of 2,542 eligible lone parents who expressed an interest in the IWTG when they were informed of it, 1,273 were randomly assigned to the treatment group and 1,269 to the control group. However, only 15.6 percent of the treatment group (199 lone parents) actually went on to take training and, of those who did, almost half used it to take driving lessons. Because of this low take-up, it appeared likely that any experimentally measured impact of IWTG on such outcomes as employment retention, which was based on comparing the entire treatment group with the entire control group, would be negligible.

The Employment Service therefore abandoned the impact analysis and instead commissioned a qualitative analysis, which was based largely on in-depth interviews with 72 lone parents from 13 of the 40 pilot districts. The qualitative analysis highlighted the value of the grant to those lone parents with clear training goals. Participants welcomed the flexibility of training grants that could be used for training of their own choice. The study particularly highlighted the popularity of driving lessons.

The analysis suggested that the lower-than-expected take-up of the grant was due at least in part to constraints in program design. For example, the training plan had to be completed within 12 weeks of beginning employment and required employer approval. Some employers held up approval past the 12-week deadline, either purposefully (some of the training would have required time off from work) or because they simply did not get around to completing the necessary paperwork. Some newly employed lone parents had little time for training and had difficulty arranging for the necessary child care. Some members of the treatment group did not understand the process required to get a training plan approved or felt uncomfortable about approaching their new employers for training plan approval, and some did not keep their jobs long enough to complete a training plan. The evaluators suggest that more research should have been conducted prior to initiating the pilot program to determine the likely program take-up rate.

NUMBER AND LOCATION OF SITES: Random assignment took place in 40 Employment Service districts located throughout the United Kingdom.

EVALUATION COSTS: £88,864 for the qualitative analysis performed by the Policy Studies Institute.

TREATMENT ADMINISTRATOR: The Employment Service. Key personnel: Kate Collins, Laura Twomey, and David Betteley.

EVALUATOR: Policy Studies Institute. Key personnel: Jane Lakey, Jane Parry, Helen Barnes, and Rebecca Taylor.

PUBLIC-USE ACCESS TO DATA: Not available.

EXPERIMENT ONGOING AT PUBLICATION
Employment Zones

STARTING YEAR/YEAR FINAL REPORT EXPECTED: 2000/?

INFORMATION SOURCE: An analysis of individuals who were randomly assigned has been conducted by the British Department of Work and Pensions, but the government has not yet released a report describing the findings.

PRINCIPAL INTERVENTIONS: Employment Zones operate on a pilot basis in 15 high-unemployment areas in Great Britain. Random assignment was conducted in four of these areas. Employment Zones are mandatory for long-term Jobseekers

Allowance (unemployment compensation) recipients and operated by private sector contractors. In the Employment Zones, clients and a personal adviser first develop an action plan and then the client undertakes the prescribed actions. Employment Zone contractors receive incentive payments for each client placed in employment within 39 weeks and for each placed client who retains employment for at least 13 weeks.

TARGET POPULATIONS: Unemployed people who have been receiving Jobseekers Allowance for 12 or 18 months (depending on the area).

OUTCOMES OF INTEREST: Employment and the receipt of Jobseekers Allowance.

PART 4

TRENDS

1

The Social Experiment Market

David Greenberg, Mark Shroder and Matthew Onstott
Reprinted from the *Journal of Economic Perspectives*

Social experiments are field studies of social programs in which individuals, households or (in rare instances) firms or organizations are randomly assigned to two or more alternative policy interventions, or "treatments." Treatments tested by social experiments have included negative income taxes, low-income housing assistance, co-insurance rates, re-employment bonuses, welfare-to-work initiatives, job training, time-of-day electric rates, and "case management" models of human service delivery. The results of such experiments not only supply the public with policy-relevant information, but also provide employment and insight to economists. This article examines the social experiments market and the characteristics of the rather complex product exchanged in this market.

We investigate the social experiment industry with data extracted from *The Digest of Social Experiments* (Greenberg and Shroder, 1997), augmented by interviews with buyers and sellers in the market. To qualify for a 2–3 page entry in the *Digest,* the human subjects had to be randomly assigned among the treatments, each of which could involve different incentives, opportunities, or constraints. Data were then collected on market and/or fiscal outcomes, and subjected to professional evaluation. The definition of experiment used for the *Digest* and this article is deliberately narrow: we do not cover the numerous evaluations of social programs that did not use random assignment, randomized trials that did not seek to measure market or fiscal outcomes (like clinical tests of health care or teaching techniques), or trials that did not test policy interventions (like fair housing audits).

The *Digest* provides summaries of 143 social experiments that were completed by the end of 1996 and fit these criteria. Public-use files exist for slightly over one-third of the 143 completed experiments in our sample, including many of the larger and more recent experiments; the *Digest* describes how to find these data. The *Digest* also contains abstracts for 74 additional experiments initiated by

459

the end of 1996, but not yet complete. Sources where additional information on each experiment can be obtained are noted. We made exhaustive efforts to uncover as many experiments as possible, through literature search and contacts with evaluators and agency staff. We know we missed a few; we intend to describe both subsequent discoveries and more recent experiments in a supplement to the *Digest,* but we do not expect the new material to change our conclusions.

The beginning of social experimentation is often attributed to Heather Ross, an MIT graduate student in economics who wanted to conduct a negative income tax experiment as her dissertation research and wrote a funding proposal to the federal government. Ross's idea directly resulted in the New Jersey Income Maintenance Experiment. Although there were a few earlier social experiments, they tended to be very small relative to the New Jersey demonstration. Of the earlier experiments, only the Perry Preschool Project, which began in 1962, captured the attention of policymakers and other social scientists, and much of this attention occurred only after adult earnings were available for the preschool children in the study sample, many years after initiation. The New Jersey experiment is therefore generally regarded as the beginning of social experimentation.

Figure 1 indicates the number of social experiments initiated each year between 1962 and 1996. Greenberg and Robins (1986) suggest dividing the time period into three eras. From 1962–74, a relatively modest number of elaborate, lengthy, costly social experiments were used to test fundamental changes in social policies. From 1975–82, while the number of experiments increased substantially, the goals of the new experiments were modest, often testing modifications in existing programs. Finally, from 1983 to the present, the number of social experiments has again increased. Experiments in the most recent wave have typically been less costly than those in the first period, but often much larger than those of the second time period.

The next section of this article describes the products of the social experiments industry, examining trends in design and policy objectives. For example, most experiments test policy interventions narrowly targeted on a disadvantaged subgroup, rather than the general population. The following section discusses the two sides of the market: agencies that fund social experiments and the institutions that design, implement and evaluate them. It is intriguing that while many institutions would seem to have the skilled labor and other specialized factors for conducting experiments, three suppliers dominate the market. A concluding section suggests explanations for our major findings and makes some projections about the future of the industry.

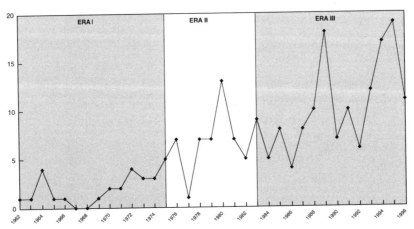

Figure 1 Number of Experiments Begun by Year (n = 217)

THE PRODUCTS

Policy Objectives

Most social experiments test programs targeted at persons or families who are somehow disadvantaged. Of the 143 social experiments completed by 1996, 35 percent targeted public assistance recipients, another 14 percent looked at low-income families, and yet another 13 percent looked at the unemployed. About 12 percent of the experiments were focused on youth, and almost all of those targeted young people from low-income families. Clearly, without a strong policy interest in the poor, far fewer social experiments would be conducted.

The scarcity of experiments involving the middle and upper class is extraordinary. Dozens of experiments have tested transfer policy, but only one has focused on tax policy. There have been a few Medicaid experiments, but none for Medicare. There have been a few tests for Supplemental Security Income recipients, but none for Social Security retirement recipients. The government has tested innovations in food stamps, but not farm subsidies. Although some experiments have tested middle-class sensitivity to time-varying electricity pricing and to co-payments and deductibles for health insurance and others have been conducted on such non-impoverished parties as employers and health care agencies, there is clearly a much stronger tendency to evaluate programs aimed at the disadvantaged than programs affecting the rest of society.

Given the tendency to focus on the poor, it is not surprising that the great bulk of interventions have focused on labor markets. Most of these interventions were intended to increase the potential earnings or income of persons in treatment groups through education and training or job placement. Table 1 shows the different interventions that have been tested by social experiments. The 143 completed social experiments on which we have data included 293 separate interventions, because many experiments have tested several different treatments. For example, tests of programs that combine training, work experience, job counseling, and/or assistance in finding a job have been common. Of the 293 treatments, 92 involved some form of education and training, 94 involved various forms of job placement and job search assistance, and 57 treatments looked at information and counseling, which was typically job related. Still another 24 treatments involved income transfers, often changes in welfare, food stamps, or housing assistance. This leaves only 26 treatments focusing on areas outside of employment and work; these were mainly in health care, with a few involving electricity rate structures and tax compliance. Testing of treatments that provide education, training, and work experience appear to have grown rapidly in the 1980s and 1990s.

The outcomes measured by social experiments also demonstrate their concentration on labor markets. The effects of the experimental treatment on employment status or earnings or both were used as impact measures in 60 percent of the studies in the 1962–74 time period and 81 percent in the period from 1983 to the present. The next most prominently used impact measure has been the effect of the experimental treatment on welfare payments, but this impact has rarely been measured when impacts on employment or earnings were not also measured.

Beyond direct outcome measurement, social experiments also often feature two other types of analysis: process analysis and benefit-cost analysis. Process or implementation analysis entails learning about how a program actually operates and the environment in which it operates. Most experiments now have some process analysis, but the nature of that analysis varies from extensive study of whether the experimental treatments were available to, used and understood by the population under study to a few interviews with responsible administrators. Benefit-cost analyses have been made in just under half the completed experiments on which we have data and have become increasingly common.

Table 1 Type of Intervention by Era (number of interventions in each category)

Intervention	Era I 1962–1974 (n = 21)	Era II 1975–1982 (n = 52)	Era III 1983–1996 (n = 70)	Total (n = 143)
Education and Training				
Preschool	2	0	0	2
Basic Education/ABE/GED	2	1	14	17
Prevocational/Vocational	2	2	11	15
Life Skills/Social and Emotional/Family Skills	0	0	6	6
Post-secondary	0	0	2	2
Work Experience/OJT	1	12	19	32
Education Subsidy	0	1	1	2
Incentive Bonus to Participate	0	0	5	5
Other/Unspecified Education and Training	0	0	11	11
Obtaining Employment				
Job Placement	1	5	1	7
Job Search Assistance	2	13	18	33
Job Clubs	2	8	2	12
Other Services	0	3	10	13
Wage Subsidy	0	10	4	14
Employer Tax Credit	0	1	0	1
Bonus for Employment	1	4	5	10
Child Care	1	0	3	4
Income Transfers				
Guaranteed Income	4	2	0	6
Housing Assistance	1	1	4	6
AFDC Monthly Reporting	0	3	0	3
Changes in AFDC Benefit Rules	0	0	5	5
Food Stamp Cash Out	0	0	4	4
Tax System				
Tax Compliance	0	0	1	1
Health				
Home Health Care	6	8	3	17
Health Insurance Cost-sharing Rates	1	0	1	2
Nursing Home Incentive Payments	0	1	0	1
Incentive to Immunize Children	0	1	0	1
Electricity				
Electricity Rate Structure[a]	0	3	1	4
Information and Counseling				
Case Management	4	9	19	32
Counseling	1	12	9	22
Mentoring	0	0	3	3
TOTAL	31	100	162	293

a. There were, perhaps, as many as eight additional experiments that tested changes in electricity rates that were not summarized by Greenberg and Shroder (1997).

Participation in social experiments can be usefully categorized as either voluntary or mandatory. In voluntary experiments, individuals first apply to participate in the experiments and then are randomly assigned to either a treatment or control group. Mandatory experiments impose obligations on public assistance or unemployment compensation recipients in exchange for benefits. For example, welfare recipients assigned to a treatment group might be required to work off their grants in a community service job. The distinction between voluntary and mandatory programs is often critical to interpreting findings from evaluations of these programs (Friedlander, Greenberg and Robins, 1997). Moreover, the chief ethical issues differ. The ethical issue in conducting voluntary experiments is the denial of the treatment to members of the control group, as individuals are only likely to volunteer if they hope to be better off under the experimental treatment. The ethical issue in conducting mandatory experiments is that members of the control group are able to escape the obligation imposed by the tested program, but members of the treatment group are not. None of the early experiments was mandatory, but almost 40 percent of those begun after 1982 are.

One final direction of product evolution is that experiments have increasingly been used to test incremental changes to existing programs, rather than new programs. From 1962–74, over 80 percent of all initiated social experiments tested new programs, including guaranteed incomes, low-income housing allowances, and supported work programs. However, since 1983, only about one-quarter of the completed social experiments have looked at new programs. A more conservative political climate and reduced availability of public funds to invest in potentially expensive new social programs are at least partly responsible for this trend. It is also consistent with the view that political support can usually be more readily mustered for incremental changes in existing programs than for new programs (Baumgartner and Jones, 1993, for example).

Interestingly, of the 143 completed social experiments in our sample, only three assessed the effectiveness of an already existing program; all three were conducted fairly recently. The reluctance to use random assignment to evaluate existing programs may arise because members of control groups must be denied services to which they previously had access, or because an experimental evaluation might seem to threaten a program in which some group has a stake.

Product Design

Information on the costs of social experiments is often difficult to gather. For older experiments, cost records are sometimes inaccessible and institutional memories have often faded. An experiment may have been part of a larger research project, and costs may not have been separately allocated to the experimental and nonexperimental parts of the research. Even when some cost data are available, the relevant costs may be hard to ascertain. For example, should the cost of the treatment be counted or just the cost of the research? Sometimes only one of these two types of costs is available; in other cases, the two types of costs cannot be easily separated.

Those warnings noted, it appears that the designs of the largest social experiments have become simpler over time and that the experiments themselves less costly to run. One reason, as suggested above, is that the treatments themselves have become less expensive. The most important cost-cutting design innovation has been the use of existing automated administrative databases, which contain welfare records and employer-reported earnings information, rather than special surveys; this development has also reduced sample attrition. In addition, programs tested in social experiments have been increasingly administered by agencies already established to serve the target populations of these programs—for example, welfare and unemployment compensation agencies. This tends to lower costs of administration and data collection. In the 1960s and early 1970s, about two-thirds of all experiments were administered by organizations established especially for the experiment; from 1983 to 1996, only about 8 percent of the completed experiments were run in this way.

Costs have also been reduced because the time period over which participants are tracked is shrinking. From 1962–74, the median experiment collected data on participants for nearly 5 years after random assignment began; since then, the median experiment completed data collection about 2 1/2 to 3 years after the first intake.[1] The philosophy behind this trend seems to be that long-term effects from certain interventions, such as training and work experience, are likely only if short-term effects also occur.

Experimental designs themselves have become somewhat simpler. For example, about four-fifths of the experiments since 1983 use only two groups (one treatment, one control); in the earlier time periods, only half used two groups, while most of the rest had either three or four groups. But funding agencies have been increasingly interested in straightforward comparisons of existing programs to incremental changes in those programs. Complex designs are more difficult to run through existing administrative agencies and harder to explain to cabinet-level officials and members of Congress.

Greater simplicity can have its drawbacks. Most social experiments have tested services or combinations of services that can only be varied in discrete lumps; that is, subjects receive either package A or package B. Such experiments provide only limited information on how moderate variations in the designated schemes tested would affect their impacts. The analytical problem becomes even harder when experiments combine a package of services and incentives— for example, job training *and* child care assistance *and* job search assistance—as only the combined impact of these components can usually be measured.

However, twelve of the 143 completed social experiments were designed to estimate effects of an intervention with continuous variables. In such experiments, each experimental subject is assigned to one cell in a large multidimensional table of treatment parameters that vary moderately from cell to cell. For example, in a negative income tax experiment, the household might be assigned to an income guarantee somewhere between 50 and 125 percent of the poverty line, with a tax rate on earnings somewhere between 30 and 50 percent. In a health insurance study, the subject might confront a maximum deductible somewhere between zero and $1,000 and a coinsurance rate somewhere between 0 and 95 percent. Such a design is difficult to administer. Moreover, the variation in treatment is still discrete, rather than continuous. However, this type of design does permit estimation of point elasticities over a wide range of values. These elasticities can then be used to project the effects of any program with the same basic features as the one tested. Of the twelve experiments which took this approach, six were initiated from 1962 to 1974, four from 1975–1982, and only two from 1983–1996.[2]

A final reason for the falling cost of experiments is that considerable effort has also gone into analyzing experimental data more quickly, not only to reduce costs but also to make findings available while they are still policy relevant.

With simpler designs, less expensive treatment, and lower administration costs, funding agencies have been able to afford larger samples. The increasing reliance on administrative data is particularly important in this regard. As shown in Table 2, the samples used in social experiments have varied enormously in size, ranging from under 100 to over 10,000, where sample size includes both the control and the treatment groups, and typically refers to the number of individuals or households involved.[3] Table 2 reports the distribution, means, and medians for the samples used in social experiments in each of the three eras. The increase in sample size over time, especially the percentage of experiments with samples of over 10,000, is notable. Two

Table 2 Sample Size by Era (percentage in each category)

	Era I 1962–1974 (n = 21)	Era II 1975–1982 (n = 50)	Era III 1983–1996 (n = 69)	Total (n = 140)
< 200	42.0%	10.0%	17.4%	18.6%
200–499	19.0	24.0	10.1	16.4
500–999	9.5	22.0	11.6	15.0
1,000–1,999	14.3	18.0	7.2	12.1
2,000–4,999	9.5	12.0	21.7	16.4
5,000–9,999	4.8	6.0	8.7	7.1
10,000 & up	0.0	8.0	23.1	14.3
Median	401	870	2,312 (2,259[a])	1,010
Mean	1,093	2,741	10,226 (6,054[a])	6,183

a. Excludes two Wisconsin experiments that each had samples of 150,000.

recently completed experiments in Wisconsin changed the methods for computing AFDC benefits for 90 percent of the state's caseload, with the remainder randomly assigned to the control group; the analyses relied entirely on automated administrative records and used the entire caseload, about 150,000 families.

BUYERS AND SELLERS

The buyers of social experiments are the agencies that fund them. The sellers are the persons or institutions that design, implement and evaluate them. On rare occasions, state government agencies have circumvented the market entirely by funding, operating and evaluating a social experiment in-house.

Funding Sources

The major funding source for social experiments has been the federal government. It was the sole source for 57 percent of the 143 social experiments completed by 1996 and helped to fund another 16 percent of the experiments in combination with other levels of government or nongovernmental organizations. State governments—often partially reimbursed by the federal government—

have also been an important source of funding. They were the sole source of funding for 18 percent of the experiments completed by 1996 and contributed to the funding of an additional 11 percent. Nongovernmental organizations, mainly nonprofit foundations, most notably the Ford Foundation, also have had a significant role in funding social experiments, having contributed to 20 percent of the 143 experiments. Local governments have so far played a negligible role in the funding of social experiments, and we discovered only two experiments funded by for-profit corporations—both of them electric utilities.

The federal role in funding social experiments, although still dominant, has diminished over time, while that of state governments has grown. The federal government funded all or part of 80 percent of the completed social experiments initiated from 1962–82, but just 64 percent of those initiated from 1983–96. Meanwhile, states funded all or part of 18 percent of the completed experiments begun from 1962–82, but have supported 40 percent of those initiated from 1983–96. One reason for the increase in state funding is that after 1981, states were increasingly encouraged to make changes in their welfare systems. Before 1996, however, if a state wanted a federal waiver allowing it to change its welfare system, it was typically required by the federal government to evaluate its alternative policy with a social experiment.

Table 3 Market Share by Era (percentage of experiments evaluated)

	Era I 1962–1974 (n = 21)	Era II 1975–1982 (n = 52)	Era III 1983–1996 (n = 70)	Ongoing (1989–1997) (n = 65[a])
Big Three	11.9%	28.8%	47.1%	44.6%
Abt	4.8	4.8	17.1	18.5
MDRC	0.0	11.5	15.8	12.3
MPR	7.1	12.5	14.3	13.8
Vera Institute	4.8	5.8	0.0	0.0
IRP	11.9	1.0	0.0	0.0
RAND	4.8	1.9	1.4	0.0
SRI International	4.8	0.0	1.4	0.0
Government agencies	4.8	8.6	10.0	4.6
Academic	16.7	23.1	18.6	29.2
Others	40.5	30.8	21.4	21.5

a. Excludes nine experiments for which the evaluator had not yet been determined.

Suppliers of Experimental Evaluations

Social experiments are increasingly evaluated by three organizations: Abt Associates, the Manpower Demonstration Research Corporation (MDRC), and Mathematica Policy Research (MPR), denoted hereafter as "the Big Three." As indicated in Table 3, the Big Three served as primary evaluators for nearly half the completed experiments that have started since 1983, and as of late 1996, had contracted for 45 percent of the ongoing experiments. Moreover, the experiments these firms evaluate tend to be among the more costly and prominent ones.[4] Of the other half of the experiments started after 1983 and completed by 1996, about 19 percent were primarily evaluated by academics, especially some of the smaller experiments; 10 percent were primarily evaluated by government agencies, usually the employees of state employment or welfare departments that ran the experiments being evaluated; and the rest mainly by a variety of think tanks and private sector firms—such as SRI International, the RAND Institution, Batelle Memorial Institute, Deloitte and Touche, Public/Private Ventures, Berkeley Planning Associates, and Maximus. These organizations have typically been the primary evaluators

on only one or two social experiments, although some have served as subcontractors on others.

Back in the 1960s and 1970s, there were two other significant players in the social experiment industry, the Vera Institute of Justice and the Institute for Research on Poverty (IRP) at the University of Wisconsin, which apparently exited the industry by the 1980s. Indeed, the IRP was responsible for designing and evaluating the New Jersey Income Maintenance Experiment, which is usually viewed as the first social experiment, while Mathematica Policy Research administered the experiment and collected the evaluation data. Thus, together, IRP and MPR may be considered the industry founders. However, IRP's interest in designing and evaluating social experiments diminished once the basic methodology was developed and social experimentation became less novel.

REMAINING QUESTIONS

Will the Big Three firms continue to dominate the market for social experiments? Will the market for social experiments be applied to new policy areas and target groups, or will interest in this methodology recede? Will this methodology expand beyond North America? Is this a promising field for young economists and social scientists? What skills are needed by this industry? To gather insights and opinions about these and other questions, we carried out a series of informal telephone interviews in early 1998 with 16 individuals, including employees of all the Big Three firms, non-Big Three research organizations, and state and federal government agencies.

Market Concentration

It seems broadly agreed that the Big Three dominate the provision of social experiments because of their ability to deliver good products, their reputations, and their highly skilled employees. As one respondent put it, "accumulated skill and reputation has created a rather high barrier to entry, affording [the Big Three] effective oligopoly power in this market." By hiring a Big Three firm that has previously conducted successful evaluations and has known expertise in the specific program area, a funding agency is, as one respondent suggested, "buying credentials" from a firm with a "track record." Further enhancing their market position, Mathematica Policy Research and Abt can field large-scale surveys in-house when they are needed and Manpower Demonstration Research Corporation can run the experimental program itself if asked to do so. Other firms know that they have a low probability of winning a competition against the Big Three for evaluating a social experiment and become reluctant to invest the substantial resources often required to write a good proposal.

To maintain their domination of the social experiment market, the Big Three firms must maintain a standing capacity to conduct complex experiments. For most experiments, the research team must more or less remain intact for three to five years. Team members specialize, rarely devoting themselves exclusively to a single experiment over this time period. As they will not be needed

on a continuous basis, the firm must have work for them on several different projects. To maintain a research team for social experiments, therefore, a firm must continually try to win new large evaluation projects.[5]

Will the current level of market concentration continue into the future? Because the number of large projects is limited, only a few firms can maintain the teams needed to staff social experiments. One interviewee at a large non-Big Three research firm told us, the Big Three firms can deliver "the whole package—they can commit 30 people, we can commit three." Another interviewee at a large non-Big Three firm stated simply that "[we] are not staffed up for experiments." Moreover, the teams at the Big Three firms have a considerable advantage over teams elsewhere because of their involvement in previous experiments. Funders would have to pay for a new team to learn what the teams at the Big Three already know. Furthermore, the Big Three firms have centralized organizational structures that can mobilize this experience to carry out experiments. High-powered social science research organizations such as RAND, the Urban Institute, and universities, in contrast, tend to have decentralized structures in which individual researchers have considerable latitude to develop their own research projects. A decentralized structure allows individuals and small groups to run and evaluate modest experiments, but may not support competing to become the primary evaluator for expensive, complex experiments.

Several factors may reduce the longer-run level of market concentration. To the extent states carry out social experiments to evaluate their recent welfare reforms, they might conduct more evaluations of them in-house or contract with in-state universities. According to our respondents who work for state governments, using in-state universities instead of the Big Three would be less expensive, would require less complicated procurement procedures, and would be more politically attractive. Also, to develop the capability of non-Big Three firms to compete in the social experimentation industry, the U.S. Department of Labor is currently funding experiments that require the primary contractor to employ a small research firm as a subcontractor. It remains to be seen whether these small firms will ever do more than compete for small experiments.

The Scope of Future Experimentation

Important information could be obtained by widening the scope of social experimentation. Policy is changing constantly in many areas, but without the sophisticated knowledge base experiments provide. The structure of taxes, disability programs, retirement policy including Social Security, the link between school and work, and health policy including Medicare and Medicaid are all important areas where social experimentation has not been extensively utilized, but could be. Taboos against experiments targeted on the middle class have not been absolute in the past, and recent conflict concerning Social Security and health policy could encourage experimentation. However, no evidence that the scope of social experimentation is widening has yet emerged.

The next few years may see fewer social experiments targeted at the disadvantaged, the population of traditional focus. One reason is that some interventions have already been the subjects of several experiments—for example, cashing out food stamps—and there is little more to be learned from additional experiments. Moreover, many recent tests of state-administered welfare programs were conducted because the federal government made random assignment evaluation a condition for giving states waivers to modify these programs. Welfare reform legislation (the Personal Responsibility and Work Opportunity Reconciliation Act of 1996), which turned the federal contribution to welfare into a state-run block grant, led to some of these evaluations being canceled. Indeed, social experiments are often unpopular with state officials, for several reasons. Experiments usually require that two or more distinct programs be run out of the same office, which makes them difficult to administer. Some officials are uncomfortable with the ethics of using a random process to select the benefits or services for which individuals qualify. Finally, some officials may want to avoid having their programs subjected to the rigors of an experimental evaluation. There seems to be a consensus that at least in the near term, as welfare policy shifts to the states, the number of state-run social experiments will decline, giving way to nonexperimental, descriptive, and process studies. This shift away from social experiments in the near term makes some analytical sense; state welfare policy is still in flux and the environment facing members of control groups is highly unstable—making the results of experiments more difficult to assess. However, a welfare program official from one state thought that while social experimentation "initially will decline," in the longer term "there will be a return to random assignment because people will see how difficult it is to do good nonexperimental [evaluations]."

Our respondents had little trouble in suggesting policies aimed at the economically disadvantaged for which new experiments might be especially useful: financial incentives to the disadvantaged to work or to employers to hire them; changes in the Earned Income Tax Credit; welfare payment family caps; welfare payment time limits; programs for noncustodial parents; policies directed at prisons and prisoners; and interventions to aid at-risk children. Important future topics for social experimentation clearly exist in the social welfare area, but the extent to which they will be funded is not yet evident.

Geographic Concentration

All but two states—Alaska and Idaho—have either previously served or are currently serving as the site of an experiment. Indeed, New York has provided sites for 27 different completed experiments; California for 26; Illinois and Pennsylvania for 19 each; Ohio for 16; and Florida, Massachusetts, Texas, and Washington for 13 experiments each. We are also aware of one completed experiment and two ongoing experiments in Canada. Also, the Canadian government has recently expended considerable sums to establish an independent research organization in Canada modeled after the Manpower Demonstration Research Corporation. However, we found only one social experiment outside of North America, an unemployment counseling program in the Netherlands. Of course, we were more likely to have missed experiments conducted abroad than in the United States. Still, the U.S. hegemony in social experimentation is clear.

The reasons for the U.S. domination of social experiments are partially rooted in our federalist system of government. The United States is the only developed country with both strong subnational governments and a strong separation of powers between the federal legislative and executive branches. One result of this pattern is that a sponsor of a proposed reform in, say, the U.S. Senate, may have to deal with opposition in the House of Representatives, in the executive branch, and at the state level. Reformers often find themselves in a situation where they don't have the power or the votes to enact nationwide change, but they can enact funding for demonstrations. Moreover, federal funds for particular programs may be used with considerable discretion by the states, encouraging the view that the states should literally be the laboratories of democracy. Social experimentation in the United States is sometimes also encouraged by private foundations. No other country has a nonprofit, nongovernmental, nonreligious sector with comparable resources and social policy interests.

Yet the separation of powers and the participation of foundations do not seem enough to explain fully the striking difference in social experimentation between the United States and the rest of the world. The differing history and social philosophies of other countries must also be responsible for their apparent lack of interest in experimental methods. For example, western Europe has more of a commitment to universal access to government-provided benefits or services than does the United States. As a result, the United States may be more willing to deny services to some potential program participants through randomization.

Social Experiments and Economists

Economists have played a major role in designing, operating, and evaluating social experiments.[6] Economic research has also provided much of the analytical justification for such experiments. Economists have led the way in pointing out how nonexperimental program evaluations may be subject to selection bias. Several studies by economists have compared estimates of program impacts obtained from experiments with estimates obtained by matching the same treatment groups with carefully drawn nonexperimental comparison groups—and found considerable differences in the results (LaLonde, 1986; Fraker and Maynard, 1987; LaLonde and Maynard, 1987). These findings have encouraged government agencies to fund experiments, and, perhaps, have also prompted Congress and state legislatures increasingly to mandate evaluations. As mentioned earlier, before the 1996 welfare reform act, experimental evaluations were usually required by the U.S. Department of Health and Human Services as part of granting waivers to states permitting them to vary elements of their welfare systems. Also based on these findings, the U.S. Department of Labor decided that a proposed national evaluation of the Jobs Training Partnership Act, until recently the nation's major government-funded training program, would be based on experimental, rather than nonexperimental, methods; the department has subsequently continued to use random assignment in conducting important program evaluations.

Relative to the 21,000 members of the American Economic Association, the number of economists who actually work on social experiments directly is not large, but is not trivial either. Our respondents at the Big Three firms indicated that together these firms employ approximately 65 Ph.D. economists who work on social experiments—and most of these persons work on nonexperimental projects as well. The number of economists at non-Big Three firms or in academia or government who have worked on social experiments at one time or another is surely substantially larger. Non-economists play a large role as well. At Abt, for example, economists account for only about one-fifth of the professional staff members who have worked on social experiments. At the Big Three firms, non-economists who work on social experiments include data processing experts; senior analysts with administrative experience in the program area (such as welfare, health, unemployment compensation); interviewers who conduct process analyses and sometimes also lead focus groups; and a field staff that oversees the carrying out of the experiment itself.

If the market for randomized social experiments is to grow, it will be in part from intellectual pressure by economists. Our sense is that in the past, few economists have made use of data available from social experiments. However, economists are likely to be prominent among those who will be proposing hypotheses and policy reforms that can be tested by social experiments—perhaps even experiments aimed at the middle class.

A final note: the federal government has never established a central depository for final reports of social experiments conducted with federal funds, nor have state legislatures or foundations. Until it does, we would be grateful to anyone sending us reports on any experiments that we have overlooked, so we could add them to our ongoing digest.

David Greenberg is Professor of Economics, University of Maryland at Baltimore County, Baltimore, Maryland. Mark Shroder is an economist at the U.S. Department of Housing and Urban Development, Washington, D.C. Matthew Onstott is a program analyst at the U.S. Department of Education, Washington, D.C. Their e-mail addresses are dhgreenb@umbc.edu, Mark_D._Shroder@HUD.gov and Matthew_Onstott@ed.gov, respectively.

The authors are indebted to Kathleen Carroll, Larry Orr, and Philip Robins for many helpful comments and suggestions on earlier drafts of this article and to numerous individuals for providing the information discussed in this article. Alan Krueger, Brad De Long, and Timothy Taylor contributed substantially to making this paper JEP-worthy. The findings and conclusions presented in this article do not represent the official position or policies of the organizations with which the authors are affiliated. We gratefully acknowledge funding from the Institute for Research on Poverty at the University of Wisconsin-Madison and from the graduate school of the University of Maryland, Baltimore County.

Notes

1. This conclusion is not materially affected by right-censoring of the sample; we know the planned follow-up periods of ongoing experiments.
2. We were unable to find information on what may have been as many as eight experiments that tested variations in electricity pricing structures. Several of these experiments, which were conducted before 1983, probably attempted to estimate how different combinations of pricing would affect usage.
3. The table is based on the 140 completed social experiments for which we have the necessary data. In all but six of these experiments, sample observations consisted of either individuals or families. One experiment had a sample that consisted of 36 nursing homes and a second had a sample of 47 health care agencies. In the four remaining social experiments, the sample observations were individual firms. These four experiments were not necessarily small; the largest had a sample of 1,089 firms.
4. A firm or agency is given credit for each experiment on which it served as the primary evaluator. There were a few experiments in which two evaluation firms were more or less equally important. In such cases, each firm

is given half credit. In measuring market share, we would have liked to use net sales—rather than raw number of experiments conducted—but, as previous discussed, revenues per experiment are not always available.

5. Of course, not all the new evaluation projects need to be social experiments, as opposed to other kinds of analyses. Representatives of the Big Three firms told us that, in general, the skills needed for experiments and for other research projects do not greatly differ, although a few individuals do specialize in experimental design issues involving social experiments. For example, econometricians can deal with design issues in the case of social experiments and treat selectivity problems in the case of non-experimental evaluations.

6. Previous articles in this journal have reported findings from social experiments (Gueron, 1990; Burtless, 1990) and debated the efficacy of experimental methodology relative to other research methods (Burtless, 1995; Heckman and Smith, 1995). Elsewhere, Boruch (1997) and Orr (1998) have provided practical guidance for conducting social experiments.

References

Baumgartner, Frank R. and Bryan D. Jones. 1993. *Agendas and Instability in American Politics.* Chicago: University of Chicago Press.

Boruch, Robert F. 1997. *Randomized Experiments for Planning and Evaluation.* Thousand Oaks, CA: Sage Publications.

Burtless, Gary. 1990. "The Economist's Lament: Public Assistance in America." *Journal of Economic Perspectives.* Winter, 4, pp. 57–78.

Burtless, Gary. 1995. "The Case for Randomized Field Trail in Economic and Policy Research." *Journal of Economic Perspectives.* Spring, 9, pp. 63–84.

Fraker, Thomas and Rebecca Maynard. 1987. "Evaluating Comparison Group Designs with Employment-Related Programs." *Journal of Human Resources.* Spring, 22, pp. 194–227.

Friedlander, Daniel, David H. Greenberg, and Philip K. Robins. 1997. "Evaluating Government Training Programs for the Economically Disadvantaged." *Journal of Economic Literature.* December, 35, pp. 1809–1855.

Greenberg, David and Mark Shroder. 1997. *The Digest of Social Experiments,* 2nd edition. Washington, D.C.: The Urban Institute Press.

Greenberg, David and Philip K. Robins. 1986. "The Changing Role of Social Experiments in Policy Analysis." *Journal of Policy Analysis and Management.* Winter, 21, pp. 340–62.

Gueron, Judith M. 1990. "Work and Welfare: Lessons on Employment Programs." *Journal of Economic Perspectives.* Winter, 4, pp. 78–98.

Heckman, James J. and Jeffrey A. Smith. 1995. "Assessing the Cases for Social Experiments." *Journal of Economic Perspectives.* Spring, 9, pp. 85–110.

LaLonde, Robert J. 1986. "Evaluating the Econometric Evaluations of Employment and Training Programs with Experimental Data," *American Economic Review,* September, 76, 604–620.

LaLonde, Robert J. and Rebecca Maynard. 1987. "How Precise are Evaluations of Employment and Training Programs? Evidence from a Field Experiment," *Evaluation Review,* August, 11, 428–451.

Orr, Larry L. 1998. *Social Experiments: Evaluating Public Programs with Experimental Methods.* Thousand Oaks: Sage Publications.

2

A Postscript

The preceding reprinted article is based, in part, on a detailed analysis of data extracted from the experiments summarized in the previous edition of the *Digest*. With a few exceptions, the additional social experiments that have been summarized in this edition provide little reason to modify our earlier conclusions. In this postscript to the article, we briefly discuss the exceptions.

One thing that has changed considerably is the pace at which experiments are being initiated. For example, in the six years from 1991 to 1996, 104 social experiments were initiated,[1] while in the six years and four months from 1997 to April 2003, only 52 experiments were initiated. Probably the key reason for the drop-off was passage of the Personal Responsibility and Work Opportunity Reconciliation Act in 1996. Prior to passage of this legislation, states had usually been required to conduct experimental tests of proposed welfare reform provisions in exchange for receiving federal waivers. This had resulted in a large number of random assignment evaluations of initiatives targeted at the welfare population. But the 1996 legislation removed the need for states to obtain waivers in most instances.

Although the reprinted article predicted that there would be fewer social experiments targeting welfare recipients, at least in the short run, it missed another emerging trend, an increase in the proportion of the social experiments that have taken place or are taking place outside the United States—about 15 percent of the 1991–96 experiments versus 29 percent of the 1997–2002 total. As we are more likely to miss ongoing experiments conducted outside the United States than inside, this second figure is probably an undercount.[2] We are also particularly likely to have missed early non-U.S. experiments. However, only 3 percent of all the social experiments listed in the *Digest* as beginning prior to 1991 were conducted outside the United States.

Although the vast majority of social experiments continue to be initiated in the United States, it does appear that other countries are increasingly adopting the methodology. Ultimately, if this trend continues, it will reduce the extent to which the Big Three dominate the market for social experiments. This domination is discussed in some detail in the reprinted article.

Interestingly, Americans have often played major roles in foreign experiments initiated in recent years. For example, MDRC helped implement and evaluate two recent Canadian experiments and, connected with this effort, established an MDRC-like independent evaluation firm in Canada. MDRC was also involved in designing a social experiment in the United Kingdom that, when initiated in late 2003, became the largest ever conducted there. Working closely in a consortium with several British research firms, MDRC will also be involved in the evaluation of this experiment. Also working in a consortium with British firms, Abt is involved in a large-scale evaluation in the United Kingdom that was initially to be based on random assignment, although a decision was later made to conduct the evaluation nonexperimentally. In anticipation of a random assignment evaluation, representatives from Abt gave a course in the United Kingdom on conducting social experiments. The information transfer resulting from these efforts is noteworthy, as quite a few (although far from all) foreign experiments that have not involved Americans knowledgeable about social experimentation have suffered from serious flaws. Finally, and importantly, several economists at American universities have been involved in implementing and evaluating social experiments and quasi experiments in developing countries.[3] The World Bank has funded a number of these efforts.

Another important recent trend is the increased involvement of academics in social experimentation, a trend that should also tend to erode the domination of the Big Three. Academics have, of course, always played a role in social experimentation. For example, as indicated in the reprinted article, the Institute for Research on Poverty at the University of Wisconsin was heavily involved in several of the earliest social experiments, including the New Jersey Income Maintenance Experiment. Since then, academics have frequently been used as consultants by research firms that have won government contracts to evaluate social experiments. Increasingly, however, these evaluation contracts have been won by universities, rather than by independent research firms. Thus, university involvement in social experimentation is becoming more direct. Moreover, since the previous edition of the *Digest* was published, a number of ideas for social experiments have been generated by academics, who have then successfully designed, implemented, and evaluated randomized field tests based on these ideas, sometimes seeking government funding to do this work.[4] Doing this provides an opportunity for academics to publish empirical articles based on an especially rigorous research design. It will be interesting to see how much academics use this approach in their future research.

Notes

1. This number includes the 75 experiments that figure 1 indicates were begun during this period plus 29 newly discovered experiments that were begun during the same period. As mentioned in Part I, 23 of the 75 experiments counted in figure 1 as initiated between 1991 and 1996 were subsequently terminated (mainly as a result of passage of the Personal Responsibility and Work Opportunity Reconciliation Act of 1996), and in two additional cases, the random assignment evaluation design was dropped.

2. In making these calculations, as well as those in the previous paragraph, we ignored quasi experiments. Of the eleven quasi experiments summarized in the *Digest*, seven were initiated outside the United States, six of which began between 1997 and April 2003, while only four were conducted in the United States, only one of which began after 1996.

3. Interestingly, most of the experiments and quasi experiments in Asia, Latin America, and Africa have focused on the effectiveness of educational institutions.

4. Several recent experiments listed in this edition of the *Digest* have followed this model, including the Undergraduate Student Achievement experiment in the Netherlands, the Targeted Negative Income Tax experiment in Germany, the two matriculation reward experiments in Israel, and the Seed Money and Retirement Plan Decisions experiments in the United States.

About the Authors

David Greenberg is Professor Emeritus of Economics at the University of Maryland, Baltimore County (UMBC). His research focuses on the evaluation of government programs targeted at the low-income population, especially in public assistance, employment, and training. Before coming to UMBC in 1982, he worked as a senior economist in several private and public research and policymaking institutions. Since 1989 he has been a visiting professor at the University of Wisconsin–Madison, the Budapest University of Economic Science, and the Centre for Research in Social Policy at Loughborough University in the United Kingdom. In 2002 he worked with others on the design of a large-scale British social experiment at the Prime Minister's Strategy Unit, and he is presently responsible for cost-benefit analyses of three United Kingdom labor market programs. With others, he is currently conducting meta-analyses of random-assignment evaluations of United States voluntary training and mandatory welfare-to-work programs. David Greenberg has published widely on social experimentation, cost-benefit analysis, and employment and training program, including a recent review of government-funded programs for the disadvantaged in the *Journal of Economic Literature.* His meta-analyses of training programs have appeared in *Industrial and Labor Relations Review, Journal of Human Resources, Evaluation Review, Evaluation,* and *Fiscal Studies.* He is the coauthor of *Social Experimentation and Public Policymaking* (Urban Institute Press, 2003), and is currently working with his coauthors on the third edition of his widely used textbook on cost-benefit analysis (Prentice Hall).

Mark Shroder is an economist with the Office of Policy Development and Research at the U.S. Department of Housing and Urban Development. His publications in the *Review of Economics and Statistics,* the *National Tax Journal,* and *Economic Design* test and extend the theory of public assistance provision in a federal system of government. His articles in *Cityscape,* the *Journal of Housing*

Economics, the *Journal of Housing Research*, and the *Journal of Urban Economics* explore the nature and effects of housing assistance in the United States, while his work on landlords in *Urban Studies* examines the supply side of the rental market. At HUD he has contributed to the design and evaluation of the Moving to Opportunity for Fair Housing and Welfare to Work Housing Voucher experiments and other major research programs.

Index